Sexualia

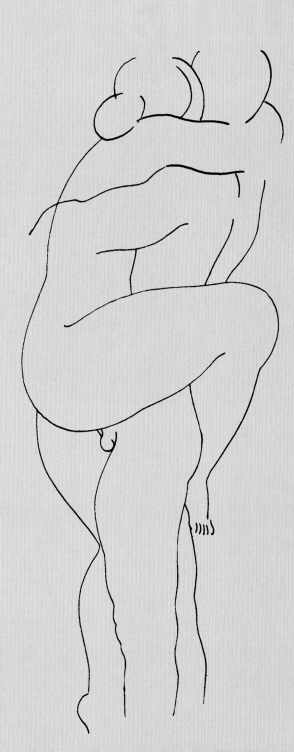

Clifford Bishop • Xenia Osthelder

Sexualia

From Prehistory
to Cyberspace

KÖNEMANN

Preface

It is possible that some of the first images ever made by human beings were of vaginas and penises – during the Palaeolithic, natural fissures in cave walls were daubed with ocher and surrounded with phallic lines. It seems that no sooner had man learned to make a mark than he was making erotica. Furthermore, there is a chance that men were painting their bodies, or making other, degradable, art that has not survived, for thousands of years before they began painting in caves. Then again, the fissures and their decorations may have had no sexual connotations at all. In the modern world, even the reference to "man" is contentious - we have to acknowledge that the earliest artists could have been women, and realize all the implications that this would have for how we view the development of culture.

It is not only stone-age gender-relations that remain a puzzle. Almost any statement about sex plunges us into a labyrinth of qualifications, equivocations and second guesses. This shouldn't be surprising – if genetics and evolutionary theory have taught us anything, it is that sex is all about hedging your bets. It came into existence some 2000 million years ago, when cells stopped reproducing by cloning exact replicas of themselves, and began combining with other cells to produce something new. The result – so far – is a planet that is home to millions of different species. Sex has proved to be the most successful reproductive method because it shuffles the genetic material available to generate a potentially infinite series of permutations. Many are flawed, or redundant, but ultimately, in a changing world, there is no way of knowing what attributes – or attitudes – are going to prove valuable for survival. Variety is not just the spice of life, it is also the best guarantee there is that life of some kind will continue, whatever natural or man-made disasters may occur.

And in the same way that sex stirs the genetic pool, it also, among people, acts as an agent that blends cultures, prejudices, pieties and ideas. This may occur through intermarriage or simply through sexual curiosity, or even envy, and it produces often astonishing results. Some of the most inventive and sensual erotic paintings

ever made arose when the Islamic Moghuls – coming from a background that discouraged any kind of representational art – conquered northern India, and found themselves seduced by what they had taken. Would-be ascetic Buddhists, settling among the peoples of the Himalayas and their virile local demons, evolved a complementary pantheon of gods and Bodhisattvas who derived much of their power from copulating with female consorts.

But sex is not just an engine of social change – it is often the arena in which a society defines itself, through its choice of taboos, customs, moral codes; its rules governing whom it may, or may not, be permissible to marry, and even its visions of religious transcendence. Yet no matter how complex these socio-sexual constructions become, they are inevitably defined in relation to "nature", and to what may be considered "natural". Vastly differing cultures have justified their practices in this way, and throughout history sex has been the force that mediates between the social and the natural worlds. For repressive medieval Christians, the world came into being antiseptically, as an act of will. For taboo-breaking Tantric Hindus, it exists only as vibrations emanating from the copulating bodies of a god and goddess. Some authoritarian powers manage to catch their followers in an ascetic circular argument: they condemn acts such as homosexuality or bestiality because they are unnatural, while nevertheless claiming that to be natural is to be ungodly, and therefore damned anyway.

If sex provides a philosophical link between nature and society, it provides a political link between society and the individual. In the never-ending war between social needs and private freedoms, human sexuality is one of the fiercest battlegrounds. Is it a given? Or can it be shaped? And if so, who has the right to shape it, and how much force have they the right to apply?

For thousands of years, people have rushed to provide answers, with a certitude which indicates that they never thought there was a question in the first place. The serious students of sexuality have often been silenced or ignored, where possible. If they were too eminent for this, their works fell victim to posthumous censorship or communal acts of selective amnesia. Plato's analysis of the merits of homosexuality was an open secret among scholars for centuries; the works on reproduction and contraception of physicians such as the Greek physician, Soranus disappeared from the Western canon, and were only preserved by Islamic doctors. The conscientious, comparative investigation of sexuality, across cultures, classes and academic disciplines, is a recent phenomenon, little more than two to three centuries old. Our understanding of ourselves has been revolutionized by people such as Antonie van Leuwenhoek, who discovered spermatozoa in the 18th century, Richard von Krafft-Ebing, who classified all the known sexual "deviances" of the late 19th century, Sigmund Freud, who explored the relationship between sex and the unconscious, Bronislaw Malinowski and Margaret

Mead who, in the 1920s and 1930s, helped make sexual anthropology into a scientifically respectable field, and Alfred Kinsey, who in the 1940s and 1950s provided the first in-depth survey of American sexual behavior.

Where sexuality was once a monolithic secret, it is now revealed as multifarious, adaptable and constantly mutating. Yesterday's perversions have become today's alternative lifestyles. Yesterday's myths are our commonplaces, and vice-versa. There are now more descriptions of human sexuality available than ever before; more blueprints for what it is to lead a sexually fulfilling life; more vocabularies in which intimacy – or its imitations – can be traded; and more technologies that serve the age-old process of turning power into sex, and sex into power. This book has yet barely managed to scratch the surface of its subject. However, it provides at least a survey of the many ways that we, as human beings, have tried and are trying to define what is "natural", for ourselves and for others.

Clifford Bishop

Still from the pornographic film *Diamond Baby,* 1984. The more easily an image or an idea can be disseminated, the harder it is to suppress. New forms of technology, such as the internet, are breaking down the boundaries between the public and the private. In the world of pornographic videos, one of the most popular genres is the "gonzo" film, which is made by, or created to look as if it has made been by, amateurs filming their own unscripted sex lives.

Opposite: **Attr. to Charles Antoine Coypel, *Leda and the Swan*, 18th cent. British Libary, London.** One of the ways in which society tries to control its members is in deciding what they can or cannot see. However, there have always been strategies for escaping the censors. For centuries, mythological themes provided an excuse for painters to depict naked bodies engaged in acts of seduction, rape or lovemaking.

Contents

MIND AND BODY   Clifford Bishop, Jane Hobden

MAKING LOVE   Clifford Bishop, Jane Hobden, Shahrukh Husain

MATRIMONY AND PARTNERSHIP   Clifford Bishop, Jane Hobden, Shahrukh Husain, Angelika Tramitz

ORIGINS – THE EVOLUTION OF SEXUAL CULTURE   Clifford Bishop, Shahrukh Husain, Piers Vitebsky

THE CLASSICAL WORLD   Clifford Bishop, Piers Vitebsky

WHEN DESIRE TURNS TO SIN   Clifford Bishop, Angelika Tramitz

PROSTITUTION IN THE WESTERN WORLD   Angelika Tramitz

THE EROTIC MUSE – ART AND ARTIFICE   Clifford Bishop, Cristina Moles Kaupp

A CULTURE STEEPED IN SEX – EUROPE AND THE USA   Angelika Tramitz, Igor Kon

THE ART AND SCIENCE OF SEX – INDIA AND THE HIMALAYAS   Clifford Bishop

FORBIDDEN ZONES – CHINA AND JAPAN   Sabine Hesemann, Ken Watanabe

SEXUAL CRUCIBLES   Clifford Bishop, Piers Vitebsky

Mind
and
Body

Mechanisms of Desire

A combination of ignorance, gullibility and inventiveness has led human beings to tell many amazing stories about sex. In different places and at different times, it has been believed that sexual intercourse is not necessary for reproduction, that men have wombs and that children can have multiple fathers. Or at least, these beliefs have been reported. Modern anthropologists disagree as to whether these views were ever genuinely held, or were merely the result of early researchers' misunderstanding what they had been told. Some of these misconceptions may appear fanciful, but anyone who reads the advice column in a modern magazine will be aware of how many sexual delusions still survive in the West, in an age of mass communication and sex education. The beliefs that may exist in traditional societies, and the controversies surrounding them, will be examined in detail in later chapters. This chapter concentrates on the physical aspects of sex and desire which appear to be universal, and considers broadly how the attitudes to them may vary between cultures.

The basic reason for sex is reproduction, and however much human ingenuity has obscured this fact – by devising contraceptives, exploring different sexual techniques or finding different love objects, whether artificial, same-sex or other-species – the possibility of successful reproduction still often dictates what is looked for in a partner. Whether hetero- or homosexual, whether searching for a mate or just a casual encounter, we tend to be attracted to signs of fertility, such as youth, and lustrous hair.

Although in the modern, multi-cultural world the factors that govern what shade of skin is attractive are many and complex, in isolated communities (and historically) beauty is almost always equated with pallor. Those whose skins are slightly lighter than the average for their region are considered more alluring than those who are slightly darker. This is especially true of women, and occurs because skin lightens at puberty, and then begins to darken again with age. A woman's skin also darkens slightly with each pregnancy, so that relative pallor is a sign that she is at her most nubile, with all her childbearing years ahead of her.

Tastes appear to vary throughout history. The richly fleshed nudes glorified by Rubens appear to have little in common with modern pin-ups such as Cindy Crawford. Similarly, many different body shapes are considered attractive across the world, but once again there is a common factor, related to fertility. Even in cultures where heavy women are considered the most beautiful, the loveliest of all are those with low waist-to-hip ratios, because they are thought to look younger and more fertile. It seems there is a good deal of truth in this ancient, universal folk wisdom. A Dutch study of women who were undergoing *in vitro* fertilization revealed that those with the lowest waist-to-hip ratios had the best chance of conceiving, and that for every 10 percent increase in the ratio, the chance of conceiving dropped by 30 percent. A fertile, and therefore attractive, male is generally perceived as being taller than average, with a waist-to-hip ratio of about 80 to 90

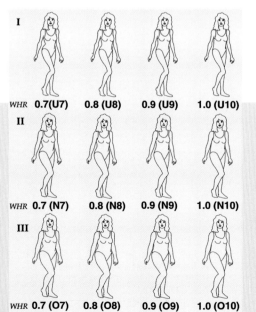

WHR	0.7(U7)	0.8 (U8)	0.9 (U9)	1.0 (U10)
WHR	0.7 (N7)	0.8 (N8)	0.9 (N9)	1.0 (N10)
WHR	0.7 (O7)	0.8 (O8)	0.9 (O9)	1.0 (O10)

Psychologist Devendra Singh, from the University of Texas, noticed in the early 1990s that *Playboy* models and Miss America contestants gradually became thinner between 1960 and 1980, but the ratio between their waists and hips stayed constant, with the waist measurement always lying between 68 and 72 percent of the hip size. Singh then made outline drawings of twelve women, four thin, four average and four heavily built, and manipulated their waist-to-hip ratios (WHRs). He asked 580 men of different ages, races, and backgrounds to rate the drawings according to attractiveness, and found that WHR was more important than body shape – men who preferred averagely built women, for example, picked N7 (0.7 = waist being 7/10 of hip measure) and N8 first, but moved on to some combination of U7, U8, O7 and O8 before returning to the average women with higher ratios. These results were duplicated worldwide. Women who bind themselves into corsets are deliberately exploiting – to the point of parody – the attractiveness of a low WHR.

Young men watching a woman, 1956. When groups of men subject a passing woman to wolf-whistles, innuendo and other forms of unwelcome attention, most of them will be responding to peer-pressure rather than to any genuine sexual stimuli.

percent. However, indications of wealth, power and status traditionally play a far larger role in a man's perceived attractiveness, compared to that of a woman.

Not all stimuli are visual, and research done at the University of Bern in 1995 suggests that we partly choose our ideal partners through incredibly subtle distinctions in odor, once again with the subconscious idea of successful reproduction. A group of men were told to wear T-shirts for two days, without using aftershave or perfumed soap, or eating odoriferous foods such as garlic. In this Swiss survey a group of women was then invited to sniff the T-shirts and say which they found most attractive. At the same time, both groups gave a sample of blood, which was tested for its genetic make-up. There are three small groups of genes, called the major histo-compatibility complex, or MHC, which govern our immunity to disease. Parents whose MHCs differed as much as possible would be likely to have the healthiest children, immune to the greatest variety of diseases, and, remarkably, nearly all the women in the test were most attracted to the odors of the men whose MHCs were dif-

ferent from their own. They claimed that the smells they found sexiest reminded them of boyfriends or ex-boyfriends. In other words, these women were subliminally choosing partners who smelled as if they would father the healthiest children.

All over the world, across various cultures and periods, different beliefs about procreation, menstruation and conception exist. Some date back to prehistoric times.

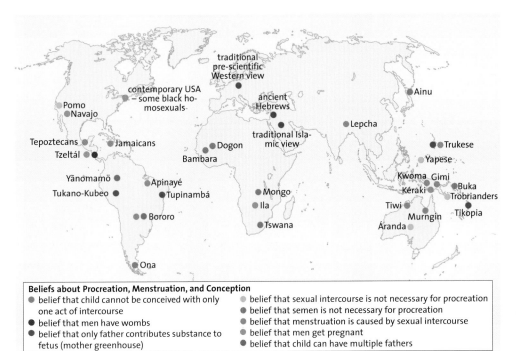

Beliefs about Procreation, Menstruation, and Conception

- belief that child cannot be conceived with only one act of intercourse
- belief that men have wombs
- belief that only father contributes substance to fetus (mother greenhouse)
- belief that sexual intercourse is not necessary for procreation
- belief that semen is not necessary for procreation
- belief that menstruation is caused by sexual intercourse
- belief that men get pregnant
- belief that child can have multiple fathers

Differences Between Men and Women

The differences between the two genders are both physiological and psychological, and are the result of biological programming in the womb and the environment in which we are brought up. Whether we are male or female is determined when sperm from the father fertilizes an egg from the mother. While an egg always contains an X sex chromosome, a sperm carries either an X or Y sex chromosome. If an X chromosome sperm fertilizes the egg, the child will develop as a female with combined XX chromosomes. If a Y chromosome sperm fertilizes the egg, the child will develop as a male with XY chromosomes. Within weeks of conception, the primary sexual characteristics or gonads – the testes in males and ovaries in females – have formed.

The brain also undergoes sexual differentiation in the womb. In male fetuses, testosterone causes the hypothalamus in the brain to become insensitive to the female hormone estrogen, while in female fetuses the absence of testosterone causes the hypothalamus to become sensitive to estrogen. These differences may account for variations in how male and female brains develop and in differing types of behav-ior. The right-hand side of the brain is needed for visual-spatial tasks while the left-hand side is needed for verbal function. Testosterone in the male fetus causes the right-hand side of the brain to grow more than the left, resulting in men's greater ability to undertake spatial awareness tasks such as reading maps, argue some pediatricians. Equally, female sex hormones developing the left side of the brain may result in girls showing superior verbal skills in early childhood.

Differences between male and female behaviors are also apparent from an early age, with

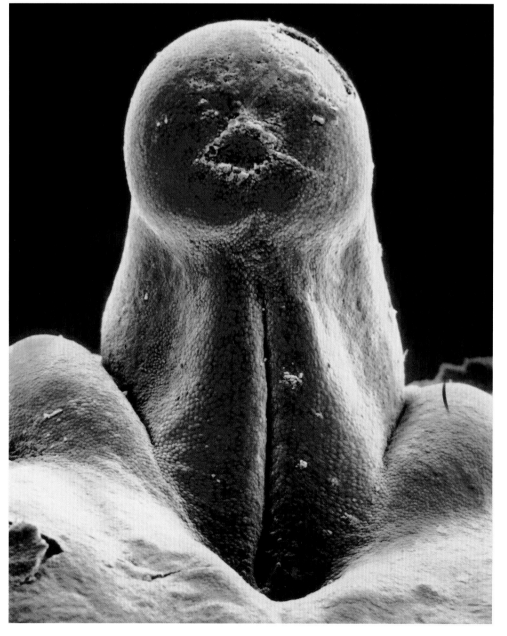

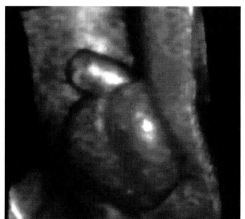

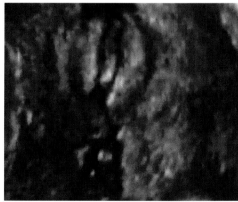

Above: These photos show two fetuses, one male (above) and one female (below), which are 24 weeks old. During the last months of pregnancy important developments occur like the development of the brain. At the same time the testicles of the male fetus move to the scrotum.

Left: The photo shows the fetal genital system of a human embryo between the 9th to the 10th week of its development. It is only after the second month that the undifferentiated stages of the embryonic genital system become visible.

boys often predisposed to aggressiveness and rough-and-tumble play and girls more likely to show gentler, more nurturing qualities. Whether these differences are caused by nature or the environment is constantly being debated. While some experts argue that our brains are programmed during fetal development, others believe that upbringing and social learning plays a greater role in shaping how we behave as male or female.

Social and cultural expectations of differences between the genders can profoundly affect our sense of what it means to be a man or woman. Traditionally, in many societies, men are viewed as sexually aggressive and women as sexually passive. Men are expected to make sexual advances and initiate sexual "moves" whilst women are the sexual gatekeepers, waiting to be asked out and determining how far the advances should go. Men in the "dominant" role are expected to know instinctively what a woman wants, while women in the "submissive" role may not feel that it is appropriate to express their sexual preferences. It is also accepted in many cultures that men are naturally obsessed with sexual activity and want to "sow as many wild oats" as possible, whilst women are believed to have fewer sexual needs and are looking for the special partner. Some theorists argue that it is primitive biological instincts that drive the male desire to impregnate as many women as possible, and the female desire to find an appropriate man to father her children.

All these stereotypes are clearly limiting and do not take into account an individual's needs and feelings, or that women and men have both "masculine" and "feminine" traits. Fortunately, in many Western cultures, attitudes are changing and women are becoming more sexually confident while men are more comfortable expressing feelings of vulnerability and tenderness.

The character of male and female sexual desire also varies, although whether this relates to nature or nurture is unclear. Research into male and female sexual fantasies by writer Nancy Friday (*My Secret Garden*, 1973; *Men in*

Love, 1980; *Women on Top*, 1991) and others, has found that men's fantasies tend to focus on explicit detail and impersonal sex whereas women's fantasies often revolve around emotional involvement and the general mood of the sexual encounter. During sex with a partner, there are also differences between men and women. Driven by high testosterone levels, men are aroused quickly and are keen to proceed to sexual intercourse, whereas women become aroused more slowly, often preferring extended caressing and foreplay before moving on to intercourse.

Women and men also differ in relation to the qualities that they look for in a partner. Research in Europe and the United States shows that men place more importance on physical attractiveness than women, but also look for emotional warmth, faithfulness, kindness, honesty and sensitivity in a long-term partner. Men are also often attracted to women younger than themselves, which may be a subconscious awareness of childbearing potential. Women are less interested in physical attractiveness, although they tend to prefer men slightly taller than themselves. Qualities which show a man's potential as a father appear to be important, including kindness, honesty, warmth, faithfulness and attentiveness. Women can be attracted to men of any age: older men may be attractive through wealth and status and younger men for their sexual energy.

M. Butterfly, still from the film by David Cronenberg, 1993, John Lone as Shi Bei Pu and Jeremy Irons as René Gallimard.

M. Butterfly

The boundaries between male and female and the way that these boundaries can be subverted are illustrated by the true story of a French diplomat. In the 1980s, Bernard Boursicot was arrested in Paris for espionage. He had been passing sensitive information to his Chinese lover Shi Pei Pu, a Beijing opera singer, whom he had met while stationed as a diplomat in Beijing in 1964. Unknown to Boursicot his "little Butterfly" was a spy. At the trial, it was revealed that Shi Pei Pu was a man, a fact of which Boursicot insisted that he was completely ignorant, in spite of their sexual relationship lasting 20 years. The story was turned into a Broadway play by David Henry Hwang. Its title, *M. Butterfly*, is an ironic reference to the tragic story of Puccini's opera *Madame Butterfly*. The play later became a film directed by David Cronenberg.

Changing Sex

Occasionally a person feels that he or she was born with the wrong gender identity and wishes to live as a member of the opposite sex. The condition, known as transsexualism, results in the person wanting to be rid of their own primary sexual characteristics and to have characteristics of the opposite sex. In a process known as sex change or gender reassignment, they may undergo hormonal treatment and surgery to achieve this.

Transsexualism is rare, affecting about one in 100,000 men and one in 130,000 women. It has a huge psychological impact on the individual, resulting in feelings of isolation within society and of alienation from their true selves.

The sense of being trapped in the wrong body often begins in childhood. Many transsexuals recall that as children they showed distinct cross-gender preferences in play and dress, although of course, such preferences do not necessarily denote transsexualism. Male transsexuals often report that they preferred wearing pretty dresses and playing with dolls, while female transsexuals often say that they preferred playing rough-and-tumble games with boys. Adolescence is a particularly distressing time for transsexuals because their bodies begin to develop sexually. Boys may be disgusted by puberty changes including the growth of hair on their bodies and their voices breaking, while girls may be repelled by the onset of menstruation, and the growth of breasts, which they may try to disguise.

Sexual orientation is not of central importance to transsexuals. Some are attracted to people of their own anatomical gender and others to the opposite gender. Many transsexuals appear to have a low sex drive.

There is no clear understanding of what causes transsexualism. One theory suggests it may be triggered by a disturbed parent-child relationship where the child is drawn to the parent of the opposite gender and wants to emulate them. Another theory focuses on hormonal imbalances during prenatal development, causing the brain to develop masculine or feminine characteristics while the reproductive system develops the opposite way.

Some transsexuals undergo gender reassignment in order to attain the physical appearance that they believe coincides with their psychological identity. Because the process requires drastic medical intervention, the person undergoes a thorough psychiatric evaluation

To Wong Foo, Thanks for Everything! Julie Newmar, **still from the film by Beeban Kidron, 1995, with John Leguizamo, Wesley Snipes, and Patrick Swayze.** Playing drag queens was in sharp contrast with these actors' usual roles as action figures or womanizers but didn't seem to damage their image.

Transvestism

The desire of a man to dress as a woman is known as transvestism or cross-dressing. This may range from occasionally wearing female underwear in private to constantly wearing women's clothes in public. Unlike transsexuals, transvestites do not believe themselves to be trapped in a body of the opposite sex. Most see cross-dressing as a way of expressing another side of their personality. By wearing clothes and make up which are normally denied to men, they are, as British comedian and transvestite Eddie Izzard (1926–1989) puts it, claiming "total clothing rights". For some individuals, cross-dressing helps relieve anxiety and for others it provides sexual excitement. Transvestites may be heterosexual or homosexual.

Christine Jorgensen was one of the first men to become a woman. Here she holds a press reception at the London Pavilion cinema, September 1970 .

before treatment is given. The person may be required to live openly as a person of the other gender for at least a year before surgery. Treatment with sex hormones is also given. Female-to-male transsexuals receive androgens causing the voice to deepen, the face to become hairier, the body to become more muscular, and the clitoris to enlarge. Male-to-female transsexuals receive estrogen causing the skin to soften and become less hairy, and fatty deposits to develop in the breasts and hips. The male-to-female sex change operation is more common and is generally more successful. The penis and testicles are first removed. Skin from the penis is then used to make the lining for an artificial vagina. A penis-shaped form is inserted into the vagina to keep it open during healing. The skin of the scrotum is used to make labia and prosthetic breasts may be inserted. In the female-to-male sex change, mastectomy is performed to remove the breasts. This is followed by an operation to remove the ovaries, fallopian tubes and uterus. A penis and scrotum are sometimes constructed with tissue from the abdomen, labia and perineum. The urethra is rerouted through the penis, allowing the person to urinate standing up.

Although the artificial penis cannot become erect naturally, injections and implants can be used to create an erection. Both operations are mainly cosmetic, affecting the appearance of the external sex organs. The internal reproductive organs of the other gender cannot be implanted. As a result, the person looks like someone of the opposite sex, and can be sexually active, but they cannot produce children. Cultural responses to transsexualism differ. In many Western cultures there is widespread curiosity, but there are still some who feel revulsion towards people who are transsexuals. Transsexual people are therefore left feeling isolated and alienated. However, in other cultures such as Brazil and the Philippines, transsexualism – particularly male to female – is much more accepted and even celebrated as part of the diversity of human sexuality. In Brazil, transsexuals regularly take part in exuberant transsexual revues where they dress up in magnificent costumes, provide entertainment to onlookers and celebrate carnival in the streets.

***Orlando*, still from the film by Sally Potter, 1992. Tilda Swinton in the role of Orlando.** Swinton became a gay and lesbian icon after this film.

Androgynous Hero

In Virginia Woolf's (1882–1941) novel *Orlando,* the main character Orlando is androgynous, switching from male to female during a brilliantly imagined pageant of English history and society spanning four centuries. By depicting Orlando as both male and female, Woolf liberates herself from the restraints of time and gender in order to reappraise the nature of the sexes. The book, published in 1928, explores the boundaries of gender and sexuality, implying that there may be more than one person in each body, and that each individual has many selves. It also captures the universality of human experience. For Woolf, the book was also a tribute to Vita Sackville-West with whom she had a passionate affair in the 1920s.

In 1993, British filmmaker Sally Potter adapted *Orlando* for the screen. Potter also blurred the boundaries of gender in her film. At the beginning of the film, the young man Orlando, played by British actress Tilda Swinton, is a court favorite of Queen Elizabeth I, played by Quentin Crisp. Hence a queen being played by a gay man is flirting with a woman playing a man who will turn into a woman.

A transsexual prostitute touts for business at the roadside. The clientele will be, almost exclusively, men who describe themselves as "straight".

Homosexuality

Sexual attraction to members of one's own gender has always been with us, although people did not use the term "homosexual" to describe themselves until the late 19th century. In Egypt, the Old Kingdom tomb of male lovers Niankhkhnum and Khnumhotep, overseer of the manicurists to King Niuserre of the Fifth Dynasty (2498–2345 B.C.), was discovered in 1964, decorated with a scene of the two men in an intimate embrace. In the 6th century B.C., the poet Sappho was writing exquisite love poems to her female lovers on the Greek island of Lesbos. In Ancient Greece, it was common for older men, who were often married with children, to have homosexual relationships with younger men.

Yet within Judeo-Christian traditions and Islam, homosexual activity has always been censured. In the Bible, God destroyed the cities of Sodom and Gomorrah as a punishment for the homosexuality of their citizens (Genesis 19). Hence the term sodomy is sometimes used to describe anal intercourse. The Book of Leviticus also condemns homoerotic sex, saying that where it takes place, both men "have committed an abomination; they shall be put to death, their blood is upon them" (Leviticus 20:13). These early religious perspectives came to shape secular law within Europe. By the late Middle Ages, there were penalties for homosexual activity as well as for other non-procreative forms of sex such as masturbation, oral sex and bestiality.

It was not until 1861 that the death penalty for male homosexual acts was dropped in England, to be replaced by life-long imprisonment. Two years later, in 1863, the German lawyer Karl Heinrich Ulrichs (1825–1895) became the first person in modern times to publicly declare himself homosexual, using the then-common German term *Urning* for a homosexual man. During the early part of the 20th century, homosexual activity was still a criminal offence forcing many people to deny their sexuality or to live secret lives. It was not until the latter half of the 20th century that many countries legalized homosexual acts between men. However, legislation did not sweep people's prejudice away, so homosexuals were often still subjected to it as well as discrimination. Homophobia took many forms including the use of derogatory names, physical and verbal abuse, the rejection of people known to be gay by family and friends, and their exclusion from social, employment and housing opportunities.

At the beginning of the third millennium in Western Europe and in other countries, there is broader acceptance of homosexuality, with many gay men and lesbians, including public figures like the English pop singer Elton John, the comedienne Ellen DeGeneres and her partner actress Anne Heche, singer Melissa Etheridge and former tennis champion Martina Navratilova, being open about their sexual orientation.

Constitutio Criminalis Carolina by **Emperor Charles V, Frankfurt, 1577, title page, Staatsbibliothek, Berlin.** The *Constitutio Criminalis* was the first general criminal code to be established by the Holy Roman empire. The notorious article 116 says that all those who are unchaste, man with beast, man with man, and woman with woman, are to be burned at the stake. In the 17th century the punishment was made less severe by beheading the culprits before the burning.

Oscar Wilde and the Culture of Hypocrisy

The Irish playwright Oscar Wilde's homosexuality proved to be his downfall. In February 1895, *The Importance of Being Earnest* was premiered in London and Wilde was at the peak of his success, with London society at his feet. But within one hundred days, he was subjected to extreme public humiliation and was facing a two-year prison term for "indecent acts" with young men. Wilde's trial followed an earlier trial for libel, which he had brought against the Marquess of Queensberry, the father of his lover, Lord Alfred "Bosie" Douglas. Queensberry, who had sent a note to Wilde's club addressing him as "Oscar Wilde posing Sodomite [sic]", was exonerated. Two days later Wilde was arrested and jailed. At his trial in May 1895, he was found guilty of homosexual acts and sentenced to two years' hard labor in prison. The press almost universally praised the jury's verdict. Wilde's reputation was destroyed. After his release from Reading Prison in May 1897, he was suffering from poor health and facing bankruptcy. For the remaining three years of his life, Wilde settled in Paris where he lived a desolate, lonely existence, ostracized by almost all who knew him. On 30 November 1900, Oscar Wilde died in French exile, aged only 46.

Oscar Wilde (1854–1900) with his lover, "Bosie" (Lord Alfred Douglas). Bosie spent his later years denigrating the relationship, and maligning Wilde's talent and reputation.

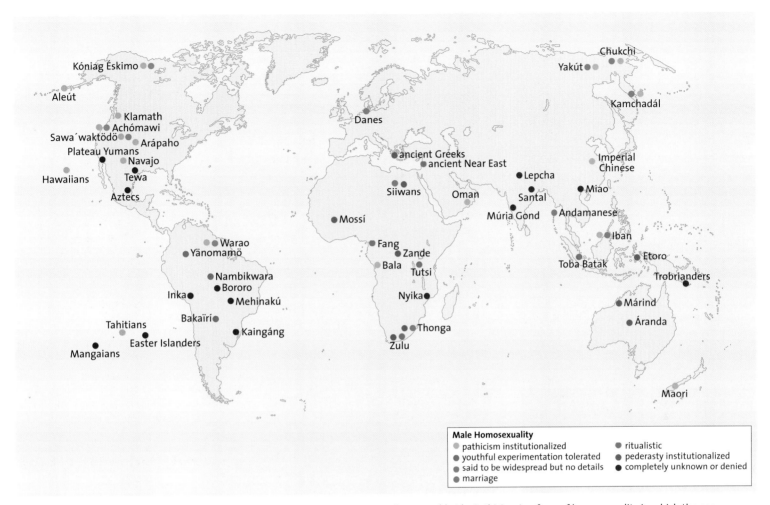

Male Homosexuality	
● pathicism institutionalized	● ritualistic
● youthful experimentation tolerated	● pederasty institutionalized
● said to be widespread but no details	● completely unknown or denied
● marriage	

The historical map indicates the responses to male homosexuality across various cultures worldwide. Pathicism is a form of homosexuality in which the passive partner undergoes a role change and becomes de-masculinized both socially and sexually. Ritualistic homosexual acts are committed during the course of some religious ceremony.

Research has also shown how common homosexuality is. Sexologist Alfred Kinsey's surveys in the 1940s suggest that 13 percent of men and seven percent of women are either mainly or exclusively sexually active with people of their own gender. Yet prejudice is still widespread.

The gay movement was born in New York on the night of 17 June 1969 when police officers raided the Stonewall bar, a popular homosexual haunt in Greenwich Village. Instead of going home, angered patrons flooded onto the streets and for the first time openly challenged the police. They threw bricks and bottles and scrawled signs on the bar such as "Legalize gay bars" and "Support gay power". It was the beginning of the gay liberation movement that spread through the United States, Canada and Europe. Since then, gay and lesbian movements have campaigned extensively for equality in all areas of life such as bringing the age of sexual consent into line with that of heterosexuals, enabling gay couples to get married or adopt a child, and for equal rights in the workplace, including military settings.

Cultural studies show that in many non-Western cultures, male-to-male sexual behavior is considered normal. In a 1950s study, American researchers Clellan Stearms Ford and Frank Ambrose Beach found that in 49 out of 76 preliterate societies, sexual interactions between men were deemed socially acceptable for some members of the group. Male-to-male activity is more likely in societies where female virginity is highly valued before marriage. In some cultures, such as among the Sambian people of New Guinea, male sex is part of the rite marking a young man's initiation into adulthood. Female-to-female sexual behavior in non-Western societies appears to be less common, being identified by Ford and Beach in only 17 of the 76 societies that they studied. However, this may be due to there being less openness about female sexual behavior in general, or the fact that female-to-female activity is less acceptable within these societies.

Axel and Eigil Axgil on their "wedding day". Copenhagen, 1 October 1989. Axel and Eigil Axgil were the first gay couple in the world to get "married" in the town hall of Copenhagen.

Jean Broc, *Death of Hyacinth* (detail), 1804. Oil on canvas, 100 x 70 cm, Musée Sainte-Croix, Poitiers, France. Hyacinthus was the youth beloved and accidentally killed by the Greek god Apollo.

Christopher Street Day Parade, New York. This is one of many annual gay parades throughout the world, including the Gay Pride march in London and Mardi Gras in Sydney.

Gay Culture

Over the last 100 years there have been many important gay artists, writers and musicians. Many painters such as Keith Vaughan (1912–1977), Francis Bacon (1909–1992), and David Hockney (b. 1937) have shown their appreciation for the male form and have depicted homoerotic scenes. Gay writers such as Jean Cocteau (1889–1963) and the American poet Walt Whitman (1819–1892) have explored the nature of homosexual identity in their work. Lesbian artists include the Argentine-born Leonor Fini (1908–1996) and Jeanne Mammen (1910–1976) whose paintings captured the diverse lesbian subculture in Berlin of the 1920s. The English writer Radclyffe

Hall (1886–1943) wrote one of the earliest lesbian novels *The Well of Loneliness*, 1928. The visibility of lesbian art has grown significantly over the past 30 years with a rich diversity of painters, photographers and sculptors including Swedish-born artist Monica Sjoo (b. 1938) who powerfully depicts lesbian sexuality, and American sculptor Nancy Freid (b. 1945) who fashioned domestic scenes in the life of two lesbian women out of bread dough. British artist Sadie Lee (b. 1967) has focused on her own relationship with her partner in some of her paintings.

Many cities within Western societies have a booming gay culture consisting of bars, clubs, restaurants, and other venues where gay people

and lesbians can meet and socialize. Gay rights organizations, helplines, and newspapers are often available to offer support and information. Gay Pride festivals are held every year in numerous cities across the world including San Francisco, Sydney, London, Cologne, and Rome, while the Gay Games, an international sports festival, take place every four years, and have so far been held in San Francisco, Vancouver, and New York City. In the 1993 Gay and Lesbian March, hundreds of thousands of people marched on Washington to campaign for equal rights for gay people in the military. Such events provide a means of reinforcing people's sense of belonging to a wider gay community and of supporting each other against

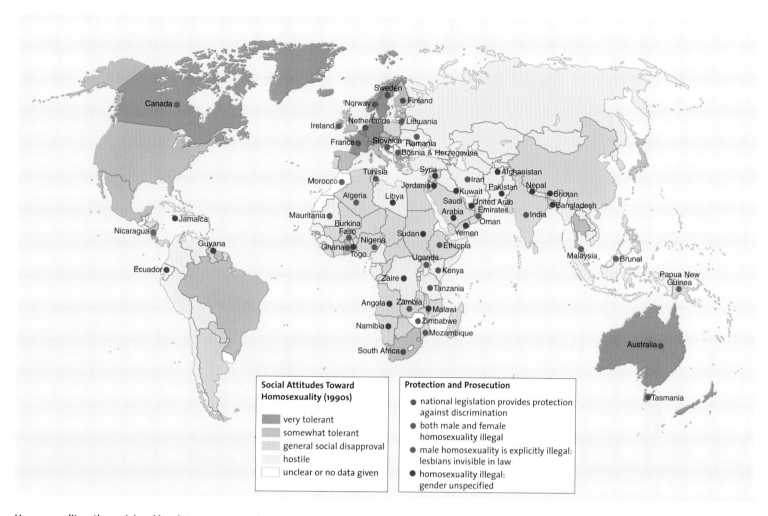

Social Attitudes Toward Homosexuality (1990s)

- very tolerant
- somewhat tolerant
- general social disapproval
- hostile
- unclear or no data given

Protection and Prosecution

- national legislation provides protection against discrimination
- both male and female homosexuality illegal
- male homosexuality is explicitly illegal: lesbians invisible in law
- homosexuality illegal: gender unspecified

Homosexuality – the social and legal status. Despite the advances made in this century, prejudice against homosexuality is still widespread. While countries including Germany, Britain, France, Spain, Holland and Mexico have decriminalized gay sexual activity, in some US states "sodomy laws" still exist which prohibit "unnatural" acts between consenting adults.

the backdrop of an often-hostile mainstream society. Gay culture has also created its own erotica in the form of magazines, art, photography, films, music and literature. While gay male erotica has had the higher profile, lesbian erotica is quickly catching up with the production of films such as *I've Heard the Mermaids Singing*, 1987, directed by Canadian-born Patricia Rozema (b. 1958) and photographers such as Della Grace (b. 1968). Women writing from the lesbian perspective include Pat Califia (b. 1954), Jeannette Winterson (b. 1959), and Carol Duffy (b. 1955).

The internet also plays a central role in gay culture. *Planet Out*, a popular American website for gay people, supplies information about news, arts, entertainment, and lifestyle issues as well as hosting chat rooms where people can make contact with other gay men and lesbians. There are even homosexual dating agencies on the internet.

Gustave Courbet, *Sleep*, 1866. Oil on canvas, 135 x 200 cm, Musée du Petit Palais, Paris. *Sleep* was a private commission, painted for the Turkish ambassador in Paris, and it was from about this time that lesbianism became a common theme in erotica aimed at a heterosexual male audience.

The Face of Sex

Although men and women look for the obvious signs of fertility in a prospective mate, such as good health, clear skin and a well-proportioned body, there are many other, more subtle factors that govern just how attractive we find each other. One of the most important is symmetry. Researchers at the University of New Mexico in the 1980s measured several hundred students to find out just how symmetrical their faces and bodies were, then asked them a number of questions about their sex-lives, such as when they lost their virginity, and how many partners had they been involved with since. Hands, feet and ear-size were among the features measured, and discrepancies between the left and right sides were often barely noticeable. Nevertheless, the researchers found that the more symmetrical members of either sex were much more active sexually, and in the case of the men, they had, on average, lost their virginity three to four years earlier than less well-balanced individuals.

Later research suggested that symmetrical people are healthier and less prone to emotional extremes. Most controversially, the New Mexico scientists even proposed that symmetrical men were more likely to stimulate an orgasm in their female partners. Another intriguing discovery, made at the University of Liverpool, is that when women are ovulating their faces become more symmetrical because of a slight swelling of the soft tissue, meaning that they are, marginally, at their most alluring just when they are likeliest to conceive.

Marilyn Monroe and Cary Grant still represent the current ideals of beauty in Hollywood. Their faces are to a large degree symmetrical, as is made clear by the superimposed lines which measure asymmetry. The lines are drawn in horizontally between noticeable points of the face, such as the corners of the eyes and mouth. Their respective mid-points are then joined with a perpendicular line. The more jagged this is, the more asymmetrical the face.

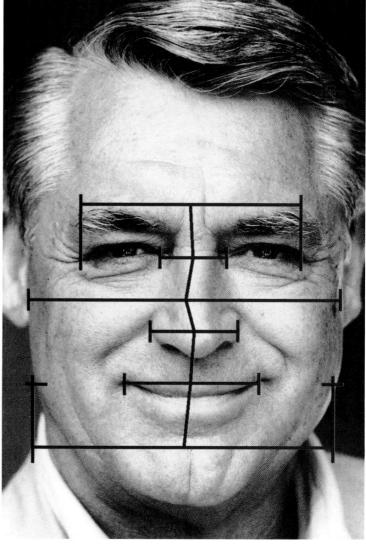

The people we find most attractive are not always the most striking. At the University of Texas, Judith Langlois fed a number of faces into a computer and programmed it to merge them together into a perfect average. When included in a selection of photographs of real people, this averaged face was almost always chosen as more appealing by observers, whatever their cultural background. Moreover, even babies spent more time looking at them, leading Langlois to suggest that we are born able to recognize beauty, and that some kind of "idealized averageness" is the template we use.

There are other researchers, though, who disagree. They claim that the perfect face is indeed based on averageness, but is improved by slightly adjusting one or two of the features. The ideal man has a larger jaw and a stronger chin. To make an ideal woman, the average face is given a smaller jaw, prominent cheekbones and large eyes. The face as a whole is also lengthened and flattened slightly.

These changes probably reflect the way that the sex hormones, testosterone and estrogen, alter the body during puberty. In men, a surge of testosterone broadens the jaw, and a man with signs of a high testosterone level is attractive because he promises to be a strong, protective mate, as well as having greater immunity to disease. In women, an increase in estrogen leads to a small chin and high forehead, and since estrogen levels are tied to fertility, these physical characteristics are signs that a woman is capable of producing many children. The large eyes are an indication of youth, which also holds out the possibility of many productive childbearing years.

When psychologist David Perret, at the University of Edinburgh, repeated these experiments he discovered an extra, surprising, ingredient in the ideal face. He showed a test subject the normal array of real faces, a computer-averaged image and an improved average, and asked him or her to give attractiveness ratings. But he also included a picture of the subject's own face, which had been computer-morphed into the opposite sex, so that men were looking at female versions of themselves,

This face was constructed from the portraits of over 100 American women and therefore represents the classic average face. It is felt to be more attractive than any individual woman's face, and irregular features, such as small, large or pointed noses, are balanced out. This average face is relatively symmetrical and, to current tastes, considered beautiful. Perhaps more interesting still is an experiment conducted by the American photographic artist Nancy Burson in 1982, in her work *Androgyny*. Using a computer, she fused the faces of six men and six women. The resulting countenance had clearly feminine characteristics – evidence, for the artist of the primacy of the female.

and vice versa. Very often, without realizing it, people would choose their own sex-changed face as the most attractive of all. Opposites may attract, but twins, it seems, attract even more. This effect has been described as sexual self-censoring. Although most of us admire physical perfection, we recognize on a deep subconscious level that we are more likely to interest – and make a good match with – someone whose attractiveness is on a par with our own. This is borne out by many experiments. For example, if ten randomly chosen married couples are all photographed separately, and their pictures mixed together, a complete stranger will often be able to match them up into the correct pairs, based purely on their looks.

Cartoons as Sex Symbols

From Betty Boop to Jessica Rabbit and the Manga stories of Japan, cartoonists have produced an array of female characters which are not meant simply to amuse, but also to represent a believable object of desire. Whether they knew it or not, they always did this by exaggerating those features which, in an ordinary woman, represented youth and/or high estrogen levels. The eyes became impossibly large, the forehead high, the chin and especially the nose small to the point of vanishing altogether. These caricatures of sexual attractiveness can have a powerful erotic effect. Pinup artists, who in theory painted real women for men's magazines and calendars, invariably exaggerated the length of the model's legs, sometimes by as much as 50 percent. This technique exploits and overemphasizes the natural leg-lengthening that a girl experiences as she reaches sexual maturity. The singer Mariah Carey took advantage of this same erotic effect when she had her legs lengthened by computer graphics on the cover of one of her albums.

Max Fleischer created the American cartoon character Betty Boop in 1915. She was based on the real "boop-a-doop" singer Helen Kane. The popularity of the Betty Boop cartoon increased after they attracted the attention of US censors; careful examination of surviving cartoons reveals the occasional lifted skirt or dropped shoulder strap that the censors missed.

Shaping Beauty

Two African Ndebele women – with marriage rings. Stretching the neck with brass rings typically weakens it to the point where the rings themselves are not merely decorative, but necessary in order to support the head.

When Charles Darwin asked himself, in 1871, why different cultures had such varied standards of beauty, and often modified their bodies dramatically to conform to them, one of his conclusions was that a people prized exaggerated forms of the traits it already possessed. For example, a naturally hirsute people would glorify men with luxurious beards, and might even go to the lengths of the Japanese Ainu, whose women tattoo moustaches onto their upper lips. A people that had very little hair would be more likely to admire depilated bodies. Although this opinion is open to debate, it is generally true that what people consider beautiful, they also regard as natural. In fact, our notion of beauty expresses our ideal of what we consider to be natural. The Ndebele people of Zimbabwe as well as the Padaung women of Burma stretch their necks with the help of brass rings, but do not consider this a form of muti-

The men of various tribes in Africa and central South America make a hole in their lower lips at a young age and work at enlarging it until it can take a wooden plug, even though this interferes with eating and talking.

lation, or deformation. The rings simply help them to attain their proper shape.

Achieving the physical ideals of one's society may involve being scarred, stained, stretched or compressed; having foreign objects inserted or parts of the body amputated. It is clear that body modification in a traditional culture is a powerful sign of social commitment – the individual undergoes pain, or at least discomfort, to conform to the society's idea of what is right. Western plastic surgery is often much more drastic than anything practiced

in traditional cultures. The most popular operations among women are facelifts (where the skin of the face is stretched to remove wrinkles), liposuction (in which fat is sucked out from beneath the skin, usually on thighs, buttocks and stomach) and breast enlargements and reductions (the latter are sometimes performed for medical reasons, such as reducing back strain). Men are increasingly having nose jobs and facelifts, and are being offered a growing range of implants to accentuate the shape of calf and pectoral muscles, or increase the length of the penis.

These operations generally reinforce ideals established by Western media, through advertisements, films, celebrities or even toys (several women have had multiple operations to make themselves look more like the doll, Barbie). However, unlike in traditional societies, cosmetic surgery is not seen as a commitment to those ideals, but as the exact opposite – an expression of individual freedom. Some anthropologists find this a dangerous tendency, and think that it contributes to what they perceive as an ongoing erosion of social values in the West. They claim that we should encourage more distinctive, "tribal" forms of physical modification, such as the tattoos and piercings found not only among subgroups such as sadomasochists.

Worldwide, noses, ears and lips are the parts of the body most commonly pierced. Extreme examples include the multiple nose plug (short lengths of bamboo inserted through the nose from side to side) worn by the men of the Awyu, in New Guinea, and the lip plates worn for example by Sara women in the Ubangui-

The Slovakian top-model Adriana Sklenarikova was chosen "Miss Wonderbra 1998" from a group of 1000 contestants. The Wonderbra pioneered a generation of bras that promised a cosmetically enhanced bust without the need for surgery.

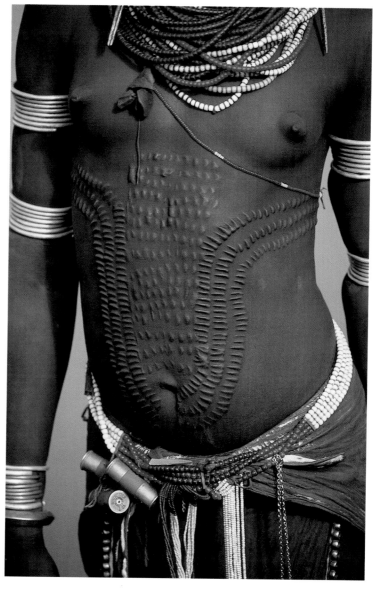

The women of the Karo in the southeast of Ethiopia are adorned with permanent scars indicating age and status.

Chari region of Africa. The Sara are especially interesting, because it is said that they originally adopted the plates to make themselves unattractive to slave traders, but that, over time, the plates and the distended lips associated with them became a mark of beauty. Under Western influence, Sara tastes have changed and the use of lip plates is dying out.

Tattoos are found more extensively, and probably reach their peak among peoples of the South Pacific, such as the Maori, and in the tattoo clubs of Japan, where both men and women may have their whole bodies covered with elaborate designs. Traditionally, the content of tattoos is rarely erotic, and may often be completely abstract, but the tattoos themselves are regarded as highly erotic objects. The same is true of the scarifications found through much of Africa (it has been suggested that scarifica-

tion is more popular among peoples with dark skin, where tattoos would not show up as clearly as on light skin). The Bala women of the Congo are scarred from the breasts down to the groin, and Bala men avoid sex with any woman who lacks scarring. Another common way of treating the skin has been to bleach it, a practice still popular with many African and West Indian women, despite the harmful effects of the chemicals used (the desire for lighter skin, and the associated dangers, have not been restricted to dark-skinned women – in the 17th century, one Signora Toffana allegedly introduced a skin bleach to the Italian court which was so powerful that 600 men were said to have been poisoned to death just by kissing their wives and mistresses).

Body modifications made in the name of beauty are frequently harmful to one's health.

The foot-binding of women, which used to be customary in China, was excruciatingly painful, and made walking any distance almost impossible. Nilotic peoples of Africa frequently remove up to six of the lower teeth from girls when they reach puberty. The teeth are either knocked loose or, even more painfully, dug out with an object like an ice pick. Various southern African Bantu peoples have preferred to file their teeth to points, like the Mindanaoan Phillipinos, although this habit is now dying out. Another defunct practice is that of head-shaping, in which an infant's head (which is quite malleable) used to be molded using boards or tightly tied bands. This used to be popular among North Pacific Coast Native Americans. Under the influence of phrenologists, who believed that head-shape governed character, it survived in rural France into the 20th century.

Clothing and Modesty

In the opinion of many zoologists and students of early humankind, clothes were a form of display long before they were worn for reasons of modesty – and probably even before they were adopted for protection and warmth. They were an artificial counterpart to the peacock's tail, or the proboscis monkey's fleshy nose – a sign of power and sexual potency. If only for this reason it is impossible to equate clothing with modesty, and nakedness with lechery. In fact, many cultures have adopted the opposite position. Among the South African Zulu, for example, it was always thought that licentiousness made the body sag, and a number of ritual dances required unmarried girls to dance bare-breasted so that the firmness of their bodies would demonstrate their purity. Ironically, under the influence of Christianity in modern South Africa, many young women cover their breasts during these dances out of modesty, although in the eyes of their elders this is a sure indication that they have doubtful morals and something to hide. In the West, too, nakedness has frequently been used as a sign of purity. Allegorical paintings of the 15th – 18th centuries invariably show Truth as a naked figure, and modern organized nudism, which began in Germany in the 19th century, deliberately discourages any displays of overt sexuality. In its literature and in practice nudism portrays itself as a form of Arcadian naturism, encouraging families to participate *en masse* and generally showing suspicion toward any single men who want to join.

Among traditionally naked peoples, modesty training is often intense, and begins in childhood. Among the Kwoma of New Guinea, for example, boys are chastised, often violently, for looking at female genitals, and girls are taught always to sit with their legs straight and knees together. When adult males meet women they generally look at the ground, or even turn their backs, and any woman who sees a boy or a man out in public with an erection is expected to beat his penis with a stick.

In societies where clothing is worn, it is often the case that the men wear less than the women, or at most the same amount. This phenomenon can be observed even on modern nudist beaches, where the men may be completely naked while some of the women continue to wear bikini

Penis Sheaths

In many societies throughout the world the men go naked except for a penis-covering, or sheath. This may be enormous – up to two feet long – and tethered to the body to create the impression of an erection. Although it would seem to be a form of decorative display, intended to draw attention to the genitals, the wearer almost always claims that it has only two functions – as protection against thorns, undergrowth or wildlife; and to protect his modesty by covering the glans. Penis sheaths are almost never intended as contraceptive devices, and are usually removed to urinate. A related practice, found in parts of the Amazon, Marquesans and Japan, is tying the foreskin closed, also with the intention of covering the glans.

The sheaths can be made from a variety of materials, even within the same village. Leaves, ivory, horns, gourds, fabric, leather and bamboo are all traditional materials, but as increasing contact has been made with the West, native peoples have learned to improvise. In New Guinea, penis sheaths are now often made of tin cans and film containers, and are regularly worn beneath trousers even by people who have adopted Western clothing.

It has been suggested that, in some cultures, penis sheaths are status symbols, and that the prestige and power of the wearer is reflected by the angle at which they are worn, as shown by these men on West Iriano, Indonesia (here the one on the left is considered higher).

Titian, *Sacred and Profane Love*, 1515. Oil on canvas, 118 x 279 cm, Galleria Borghese, Rome. The ambivalent status of nudity is illustrated in Titian's painting. No indication is given as to which of the figures is which. They could even be aspects of the same woman.

bottoms. Interestingly, this is one of the situations where a man who does cover his genitals can be viewed with great suspicion, as a potential voyeur.

Whenever people living in hot climates wear clothing that does not obscure the genitals, the purpose is decoration or status symbol rather than modesty. Among many Native North Americans of California and the Great Basin, for example, people would wear cloaks that covered only their shoulders. If a culture has no genital taboo, there will be no prohibitions about revealing any other body part. Many older authorities point to the Naaga of India as a counterexample, claiming that the women reveal their pudenda (because these were already visible when they were born) but cover their breasts (which are a mark of adulthood). However, it is now known that the necklaces worn by Naaga women are decorative, and often do not even cover the whole of the breast. Often, covering a body part serves only to eroticize it. In many parts of the South Pacific, women have traditionally gone topless, and the breast has not been considered a particularly sexy body part. Wherever younger women have begun to cover their breasts as a result of Western influence, however, young men have begun to find breasts intensely erotic, while their fathers remain largely indifferent. It is

also true that clothing fetishes become more common, and more intense, the more clothes people are expected to wear. Fetishes for stockings, drawers, petticoats and bodices were especially rife in Victorian England, at a time when prudery was so rife that it was joked that even table-legs had to be covered on grounds of modesty.

Modesty taboos are more intense among peasant communities and the lower classes within a given society. The ruling classes often flout them as a display of their power and their freedom from cultural mores. A law passed in England during the reign of Edward IV is not unusual in declaring that: "No knight under the rank of lord … shall wear any gown, jacket or cloak, that is not long enough, when he stands upright, to cover his privities and his buttocks, under the penalty of 20 shillings." In 1940s America, Alfred Kinsey discovered that working class men would often refuse to go bare-chested even before their own wives.

Clothing often indicates one's sexual, as well as social, status. Studies of European peasant communities reveal that the women expose their hair and wear bright clothing before they are married, to advertise their availability and compete for the attention of men. After marriage they switch to drab clothing and wear scarves or handkerchiefs around their heads.

However, their husbands actually start dressing more colorfully – possibly to display their new status (and thus desirability) as head of a family. The most widespread device by which women are expected to hide their sexuality is the veil, which dates back at least to Mesopotamia in the second millennium B.C. Traditional Muslim women are expected to wear the veil from the beginning of menstruation until old age, removing it only in the company of close relatives, other women, children or husbands. Among the Tuareg of the Sahara, it is the men and not the women who wear veils – or mouth mufflers – as symbols of their social position. The higher up his nose a man wears his veil, the greater is the status gap between himself and his companion. Tuareg men almost never remove their veils in company, and have to use special spoons with long curved handles in order to eat.

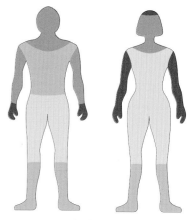

touched by mother

Regions out of bounds. Modesty is not just a matter of what people are prepared to reveal, but also of what parts of their bodies they will allow others to touch. Like visual modesty, this varies from culture to culture, between sexes and from relationship to relationship. In the 1970s in America, researchers asked graduate students to divide their bodies into different zones, and to report how often they were touched on each by their mothers, their fathers, their same-sex friends and their friends of the opposite sex. The diagram indicates what percentage of subjects reported being touched in the different areas by these groups.

There is a predictable link between the strongest taboos and the genital regions, and a more powerful chest taboo for women than for men (even between mothers and daughters). Some of the results are more surprising, however. Mothers touch their sons much less than their daughters on the hair and arms – possibly because this is interpreted as, respectively, grooming or guidance: acts resisted by the son because they return him to an infantile state. Female friends touch each other on the legs less than male friends. Males touch female friends on the knees much more than vice versa, but females tend to touch their male friends on the pelvis much more than might be expected.

Richard Ziegler, *Young Widow*, 1922. Oil on canvas, 102 x 61 cm, The Marvin and Janet Fishman Collection, Milwaukee, Wisconsin, USA. Complex attitudes can often have relatively simple historical origins. In the late Italian Renaissance, the invention of a cheap black dye meant that black clothing became ubiquitous, and the color black became a symbol of modesty, mourning, piety, frugality and – eroticism, worn alike by nuns and prostitutes. Richard Ziegler's painting plays with these ambiguities, revealing the erotic potential of supposedly demure widow's weeds.

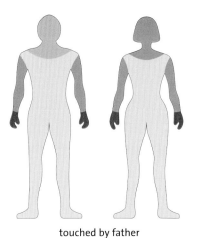
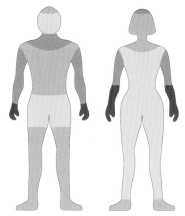
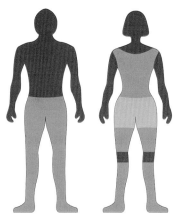

touched by father   touched by same-sex friend   touched by opposite-sex friend

	76-100%
	51-75%
	26-50%
	0-25%

Gay Signals

There is no such thing as exclusively homosexual clothing. Whatever is identified in one place and time as a gay style will have no special significance for another culture, and will inevitably be overtaken by fashion even in its own milieu. Gay styles of dress often influence fashion in general. A typical example is the ear stud. For a while in the 1970s in America, a single stud in the right ear was regarded as a sure sign of homosexuality, until the trend was adopted first by black, and then by white heterosexuals. At the end of the 19th century, heterosexual males in many American cities would not wear red ties, as this was generally taken to be the sign of a male prostitute. Stereotypically macho – or "over-masculine" – clothing has been associated with homosexuality since the 1950s. This includes biker-gear, cowboy hats and leathers and a wide variety of police- or military-influenced uniforms. Even within these broad categories, there are more subtle signs. For example, in the 1960s gay sadomasochistic scene, sadists revealed their inclinations by wearing chains, handcuffs, studs or other piercings on the left hand side. Masochists used to wear theirs on the right, until fashion eventually rewrote this code and masochists also began "dressing to the left", because it was considered more stylish.

This gay couple from Hamburg, Germany are dressed stylishly, though rather conservatively. Perhaps only their crew cats and accessories hint at their sexual orientation.

Puberty – The Journey to Adulthood

Puberty is the stage of development in a young person marking their growth to sexual maturity and the beginning of their reproductive ability. It includes changes to the primary sexual characteristics, such as the sex organs, and the appearance of secondary sexual characteristics – features which differentiate males and females but which are not directly involved in reproduction.

In girls, the first signs are usually at about ten to twelve years, when the follicle-stimulating hormone (FSH) and luteinizing hormone (LH) released by the pituitary gland stimulate the ovaries to secrete estrogen. This causes breasts to begin to grow (known as breast budding), and the uterus, vagina and vulva to enlarge. Another characteristic sign of puberty is the menarche, or first menstruation, although ovulation may not occur until a year or two later. The age of menarche has fallen dramatically in Western societies over the last century. In the mid-1800s, girls tended to start menstruating at about 17 whereas now the average age is 12–13. It is believed that better health and nutrition mean that girls reach a certain weight, of about 42 kg, more quickly, which triggers puberty.

In boys, the first sexual changes are usually at about 12–14 years. The changes are caused by increased production of FSH and LH, which stimulate the testes to boost their testosterone output. The penis grows longer and increases in circumference. By around 13 or 14 years, erections become frequent. Increased testosterone levels stimulate the testes to produce sperm and cause the prostate gland and seminal vesicles, which produce semen, to mature. At this stage boys are likely to have their first ejaculation. About a year later they may also begin to have nocturnal emissions or "wet dreams", when spontaneous ejaculation takes place during sleep. Body growth is rapid during puberty, with shoulders widening and muscle growth increasing. In the year of maximum growth, a gain of up to 10 cm (four inches) is normal.

The physical changes, which take around three to four years to complete in both girls and boys, are accompanied by emotional changes. For many young people this is a time of conflicting emotions as they have to come to terms with the changes going on in their bodies, and the transition from childhood to adulthood. Mood swings, feelings of self-consciousness and worries about body image are all common experiences during puberty.

Young people also often have a strong desire to develop their own identity and be independent of parents. They may start to test the boundaries laid down by their parents by being argumentative and behaving provocatively over issues such as clothing, alcohol and staying out late. Puberty is also the time when young people become increasingly aware of their sexual feelings and may start to have sexual relationships.

Edvard Munch, *Puberty,* **1894. Oil on canvas, 151.5 x 110 cm, National Gallery, Oslo.** The shadow here represents the girl's sexuality, with all its uncertainties and dangers. Like many other artists of his time, Munch viewed female sexuality as a terrible – even mortal – threat.

Table Showing Stages of Puberty Development by Age Range for Males and Females

Males

9 – 14 years
Testicles begin to grow.
Skin of the scrotum becomes redder and coarser.
A few pubic hairs appear at the base of the penis.
Muscle mass develops, the boy quickly grows taller.
The areola grows larger and darker.

11 – 16 years
Penis grows longer.
Pubic hair becomes coarser, more curled, and spreads.
The shoulders broaden and the hips narrow.
The larynx enlarges, resulting in a deepening of the voice.
Facial and underarm hair appears.

11 – 17 years
Penis increases in circumference as well as in length (though more slowly).
The texture of the pubic hair is more like an adult's.
Growth of facial and underarm hair increases.
First ejaculation occurs.
In nearly half of all boys, gynecomastia (breast enlargement) occurs, albeit temporarily
Increased skin oils may produce acne.

14 – 18 years
The body nears final adult height, and the genitals. achieve adult shape and size, with pubic hair spreading to the thighs and upward toward the belly.
Chest hair may appear.

Females

8 – 12 years
Pituitary hormones stimulate ovaries to increase production of estrogen.
Internal reproductive organs begin to grow.

9 – 15 years
First the areola and then the breasts increase in size and become more rounded.
Pubic hair appears.
Body fat continues to round body contours.
A normal vaginal discharge becomes noticeable.
Sweat and oil glands increase in activity, and acne may appear.
Internal and external reproductive organs grow.

10 – 16 years
Areola and nipples grow, often forming a second mound sticking out from the rounded breast mound.
Pubic hair begins to grow in a triangular shape and to cover the center of the mons.
Underarm hair appears.
Menarche occurs.
Internal reproductive organs continue to develop.
Ovaries may begin to release mature eggs capable of being fertilized.
Growth in height slows.

12 – 19 years
Breasts near adult size and shape, pubic hair fully covers the mons and spreads to the top of the thighs.
The voice may deepen slightly (but not as much as in males).
Menstrual cycles gradually become more regular.

Félicien Rops, *Premier Émoi*, c. 1878 –1881. Chalk, pencil and crayon, 25.8 x 18.0 cm, Musée provincial Félicien Rops, Namur, Belgium. Even in his maturity Rops identified with the permanently longing adolescents he portrayed. He described himself as "at the age of 30, as futile as Cherubino ... [the lovestruck youth in Beaumarchais' *Marriage of Figaro*]"

From the age of about twelve years on the male genitalia gradually grow in size and circumference. Secondary sexual characteristics may also begin to appear at about this time.

Neoteny

Much of our social behavior is governed by the fact that we are, uniquely, animals that walk upright. In other words, when naked we are in a state of permanent, involuntary sexual display, exposing the genitals and erogenous zones that other species keep hidden until they are actually ready to mate. This fact lies at the origin of many of our taboos and notions of modesty, and our acute awareness of sex in everyday life. But ironically, we can only walk upright because we are neotenous – we retain infantile or even fetal characteristics into adult life. Other mammals develop in the womb with their heads aligned along the spine, like ours, but theirs rotate backwards before they are born so that the animal does not stare at the ground when it is on all fours. If we did not retain the attributes of a fetus, we would naturally be gazing at the sky. We have many other neotenous features, for example the small teeth and their late development and the absence of brow ridges (compared to other apes), but the most important is the brain, which is only 23 percent of its final size at birth. The brain of a chimp, for example, is fully grown years before it is sexually mature – a human brain does not stop growing until about ten years after sexual maturity.

Erogenous Zones

Our sense of touch plays a powerful role in how we experience sex. Body parts that are especially sensitive to touching during sexual arousal are known as erogenous zones, a phrase derived from linguistic roots meaning "giving birth to erotic sensations." Primary erogenous zones are so called because they are richly supplied with nerve endings. They include the genitals, the inner thighs, breasts (especially nipples), ears (especially the ear lobes), mouth, lips and tongue, neck, lower stomach, buttocks, perineum and anus. Many women and men find that their toes and fingers can be exquisitely sensitive to the touch. However, preferences vary from person to person. For instance some men find having their nipples caressed highly erotic while for others it has little or no effect, or may even make them feel uncomfortable because they associate the action with fondling a woman's breasts. Other areas of the body – known as secondary erogenous zones – take on erotic significance because the person associates them with sexual stimulation.

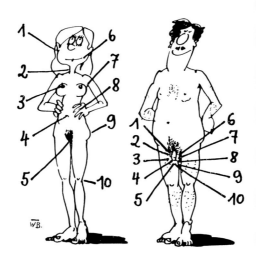

Erich Rauschenbach: _Erogenous Zones ... of Woman ... and Man._ Men are frequently mocked for their habit of ignoring all other body parts in their rush for the genitalia.

For example, if a woman's lover gently caresses the small of her back during intercourse, she will begin to associate this action with sex and so it becomes eroticized. During their research for _Human Sexual Response_, published in 1966, William Masters and Virginia Johnson found that a few women were even able to reach orgasm when the small of their back was rubbed. This example demonstrates the importance of the mind in creating a sexual response within our erogenous zones. Since people are highly responsive to images and fantasies, the brain itself is sometimes referred to as an erogenous zone, although technically it is not, because the brain cannot be stimulated directly by touch. However, by selecting and interpreting the messages received from our erogenous zones, the brain can generate erotic sensations through fantasy and memory.

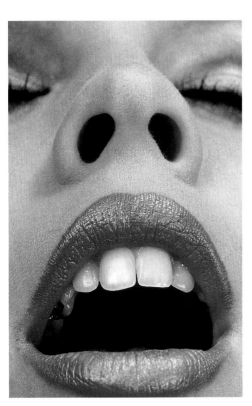

When men and women are sexually aroused their lips typically become swollen with blood, and even more sensitive than usual.

Opposite: **Lucien Clergue, _Nus de la Mer,_ c. 1958.** The body can respond sensually to a wide range of stimuli, both natural and artificial, planned and accidental.

G-spots

The G-spot is named after the German gynecologist Ernst Gräfenberg who, in 1950, claimed to have discovered a specific place inside a woman's vagina that gives intense erotic sensations when stimulated. The G-spot's existence has remained the subject of controversy and is still widely debated by researchers, although many women are convinced of its reality. The area lies about 3–5 cm (1–2 inches) inside the vagina and consists of soft tissue that swells when stimulated. It can be stimulated by the woman's or her partner's finger, or by penile thrusting in certain positions such as woman-on-top and rear-entry.

"The male G-spot" is the term used to reflect the intense erotic sensations that can be produced by stimulating a man's prostate gland during sex. The prostate – which lies a short distance inside the rectum – is a small gland just under 2 cm (1 inch) in diameter that produces the fluid which gives semen its characteristic odor and consistency. Stimulation of the prostate gland by a finger inserted a short way into the rectum, combined with slight downward pressure to the front, can be highly pleasurable for some men and may induce a particularly intense orgasm.

Ear Lobes as Sexual Objects

Ear lobes in human beings are mysteriously enlarged compared with other mammals, serving no apparent purpose. One of the primary erogenous zones, they are rich in nerve endings and highly sensitive to the touch. With their fleshy, pendulous shape, and their often-flushed appearance during intercourse, they can also look highly sexual, echoing female and male sex organs. During lovemaking, many people find having their earlobes kissed, nibbled or caressed a powerfully erotic experience. For both women and men in many different cultures, adorning the ear lobes with rings, jewels, feathers and other accessories has been one of the most popular and enduring means of decorating the human body.

A Woman's Sex Organs

A woman's external sex organs are known collectively as the vulva, a Latin word meaning "wrapper" or "covering". The vulva consists of the two fleshy folds of skin, the labia (Latin for "lips") which surround the clitoris and two openings: the vagina and the urethra. Below the abdomen and just above the genital area is the mons veneris. Consisting of fatty tissue it covers the pubic bones beneath the skin, which also has the advantage of acting as a cushion during sexual intercourse. At puberty, the mons becomes covered in pubic hair which varies greatly in thickness, color and texture.

The labia majora, or outer lips, are large folds of skin. Usually covered in pubic hair on their outer surfaces, their shape and size vary widely. The outer lips are richly endowed with nerve endings and during sexual arousal their inner surfaces secrete mucus which provides lubrication. When closed together they usually hide the other external organs.

Between the labia majora are the labia minora, or inner lips. Hairless and lighter colored than the outer lips, the inner lips are plentifully supplied with blood vessels and nerve endings and are highly sensitive to sexual stimulation when they darken and swell. Varying widely in appearance, they can be large and crinkled or small and neat looking. In some cultures, such as the Hottentots of Africa, labia minora which form protruding flower shapes are valued, and some Hottentot women deliberately elongate theirs by tugging at them.

The top of the inner lips joins to form a hood protecting a small round knob of tissue, the clitoris (Greek for "hill" or "slope"). Many cultures have their own name for the clitoris. In Polynesia, the Tuamotuan people have ten words to describe it. The only known sexual organ whose sole function is sexual pleasure, its mass of nerve endings makes the clitoris highly sensitive to touch. During sexual stimulation it swells and becomes erect. Usually protected by the clitoral hood, known as the prepuce, the clitoris can be exposed by gently pulling back the hood.

Below the clitoris and above the vagina is the urethral opening, through which urine passes from the woman's body. The urine passes down a short tube called the urethra from the bladder. The nearness of the urethral opening to the vagina and rectum means that women are particularly vulnerable to bladder infections. Hygiene is important, for instance always ensuring clean hands are used to touch the vulva and always wiping the vulva before the anus after urinating or emptying the bowels.

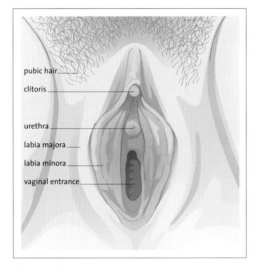

The female's external sexual organs.

The vagina, which is beneath the urethral opening, is a muscular passage connecting the cervix (the lower end of the uterus) with the external sex organs. Only the vaginal opening is visible when the labia minora are parted. About 7–10 cm (3–4 inches) in length, the vaginal walls have three layers: the outer layer is a fibrous covering, the middle layer is muscular and the inner layer is a membrane which feels fleshy, soft and slightly ridged. During sexual activity, the walls become engorged with blood and expand to accommodate the man's penis. During childbirth the vagina stretches considerably to allow the baby to pass through.

The womb or uterus is a hollow muscular organ in which the fertilized egg implants and develops until birth. The uterus is about the same size and shape as an upside-down pear, although when a woman is pregnant it expands significantly to accommodate the fetus. The uterus is lined with endometrium, a special type of tissue which undergoes changes during the menstrual cycle. In most women the uterus tilts forward.

Two ovaries lie at the top on either side of the uterus, to which ligaments attach them. Each ovary contains numerous capsules or follicles in which eggs develop. When a female baby is born, her ovaries contain about 400,000 potential eggcells of which about 400 might be released from her ovaries, at the rate of about

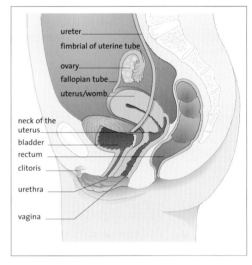

Cross-section through vagina, cervix, and ovaries.

one a month, during her reproductive life. In addition to producing eggs, these almond-shaped glands manufacture the female sex hormones estrogen and progesterone. Estrogen is a term covering several hormones responsible for puberty and for regulating the menstrual cycle, while progesterone also regulates menstruation and prepares the uterus for pregnancy by stimulating the development of the endometrium.

Extending from the upper part of the uterus to each ovary are the two fallopian tubes. Ova, or eggs, pass from the ovaries down the tubes on their way to the uterus. The tubes – each about 10 cm (4 inches) long – are lined with tiny hairs called cilia. Moving back and forth they help to push the eggs along the tubes at a rate of about 2–3 cm (1 inch) a day.

The Symbol of the Vulva in Feminist Art

Feminist art has depicted the vulva, and other parts of the female body, as a means of exploring life and sexuality from a woman's perspective. In her famous flower paintings, American artist Georgia O' Keeffe (1887–1986) endows each flower with the qualities of the vulva with their fleshy petals and dark internal spaces. One of the driving forces behind the art of French sculptor and painter Louise Bourgeois is the celebration of female desire and the eroticism of touch. In many of her works she depicts the vulva and breasts using highly tactile materials such as rubber and fabric. Chicago-born artist Judy Chicago uses female imagery to demonstrate woman's experience throughout history. In her 1972 film *Womanhouse* she used tampon-filled bathrooms as well as continual ironing performances to explore female captivity within the home.

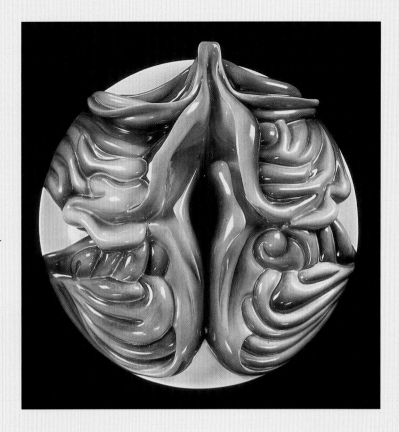

Judy Chicago, *Georgia O'Keeffe Plate* from the *Dinner Party*, 1979. China-paint on porcelain, 35.6 cm in diameter, Winthrop University/Winthrop Gallery, Rock Hill, South Carolina, USA. In her *Dinner Party* installation, Judy Chicago constructed place settings for 39 famous women using a wide range of female imagery, including a vulva-shaped flower to symbolize the poet Sappho.

The Hymen: Proof of Virginity?

At birth, a thin fold of membrane known as the hymen is usually present across a baby girl's vaginal opening. Found only in female humans and horses, its function remains a mystery. It typically has a central perforation, which is sometimes stretched or torn by first sexual contact (although, in fact, there are physical variations: the annular hymen has a single large opening; the septal hymen has two side-by-side semicircular openings; the cribriform hymen has many small openings; and the imperforate hymen has no openings).

Historically, in some cultures, the hymen has been called "the maidenhead" and its presence was used as proof of a girl's virginity and her chastity before marriage. Virginity indicated purity and passivity, which were the most important feminine virtues. Yet it is an unreliable guide. Many girls tear their hymens during normal physical activity such as riding a horse or bicycle, or when using tampons. Sometimes girls are born with incomplete hymens.

Despite popular myth that the tearing of the hymen during sexual intercourse is extremely painful, women's accounts of the first time they had sex show that it usually causes little pain or distress although some bleeding often occurs. In feudal Europe there was an alleged right – possibly mythical – of the lord to deflower a virgin bride on his estate before she became her husband's sexual property. In many Arabian and European cultures, bloody sheets were, in some places still are, ceremoniously displayed in local villages on the wedding night as proof of the bride's virginity. Sometimes, the well-prepared bride would smear the blood of a dead pigeon on her sheets in case she did not bleed.

However, even in the Middle Ages, some texts urge caution about the significance of the ruptured hymen as proof of virginity. The popular 17th-century sex encyclopedia *Aristotle's Masterpiece* (London, 1684) whose author is unknown, states that if a man does not "find the tokens of his wife's virginity on the first copulation ... then he has no reason to think her divirginated if he finds her otherwise sober and modest."

Today, the hymen continues to be perceived as significant in some cultures. In the Middle and Far East, many surgeons offer services repairing and replacing ruptured hymens.

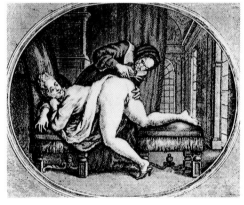

***Anonymous, Restoration of Virginity, c. 1700.* Copperplate engraving.** Women anxious to restore the illusion of their virginity have resorted to many extreme measures, from wearing blood-soaked vaginal sponges to having their labia partially sewn together. In modern times, hymen reconstruction is a more sophisticated procedure, requested comparatively often of cosmetic surgeons in India, Japan, and some Islamic countries.

Menstruation

The word menstruation comes from the Latin "mensis", meaning "month". Menstruation takes place as part of a regular cycle usually lasting about 28 days. During the cycle, the uterus is preparing itself to receive the fertilized egg. If fertilization does not take place, the thickened uterine lining is shed and bleeding takes place over several days. The whole process repeats itself continuously over about 35 years from a girl's first period (menarche) until menopause, which marks the end of her reproductive life.

The first day of a woman's menstrual cycle is the first day of her period. Once the bleeding has stopped, the proliferative phase begins. The hypothalamus in the brain triggers the pituitary gland to release follicle stimulating hormone (FSH), which in turn causes about 20 eggs to grow within their follicles. Normally only one follicle, called the Graafian follicle, develops to full maturity in the days before ovulation. At the same time, the ovaries start producing estrogen, causing the endometrium (uterine lining) to thicken in preparation for a possible fertilization.

When estrogen levels are sufficiently high, they trigger the ovulatory phase: the Graafian follicle ruptures and releases the mature egg. This usually takes place at around the middle

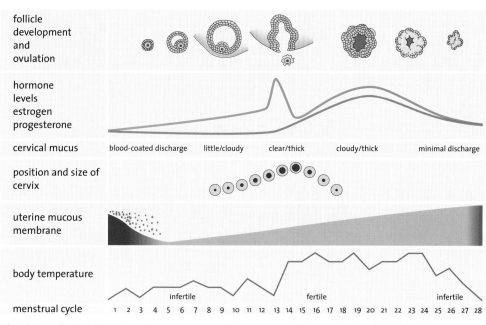

This chart indicates the various changes occuring during the monthly menstrual cycle in female humans: proliferative phase – thickening of the endometrium – ovulation – luteal phase – decomposing of the corpus luteum.

of the cycle. Following ovulation is the secretory or luteal phase – named after the ruptured follicle, which is called the corpus luteum. Under the influence of luteinizing hormone (LH), the corpus luteum begins to produce progesterone as well as estrogen, causing the uterine lining to thicken further to sustain an embryo in case implantation has occurred. Where no implantation has taken place, the egg disintegrates and LH and FSH levels fall, leading the corpus luteum to decompose.

In the final menstrual phase, the uterine lining is shed in the menstrual flow through the cervix and the vagina. Menstruation occurs when estrogen and progesterone levels decline to the point where they can no longer sustain the uterine lining. The low estrogen levels stimulate the pituitary to secrete FSH, which triggers the ovaries to secrete estrogen, and the onset of a new proliferative phase.

Although menstrual flow can last for several days, most women lose only around 20 – 100 milliliters (0.68 – 3.38 fluid ounces) of blood during each cycle. To absorb their menstrual flow, women throughout history have used a variety of methods. In Ancient Egypt, women inserted a tampon made of softened papyrus into their vaginas to absorb the blood. In Ancient Rome, women used greased or waxed wool in a similar way. In England, right up to the Second World War, many women used strips of old sheets or towels during their periods, which were washed and reused. In Germany, women used knitted strips because they absorbed better. Sanitary towels were invented in the 1890s. In 1933, tampons were introduced in Europe and the United States. The plug of cotton, worn in the vagina to absorb the flow, gave women more freedom to wear less cumber-

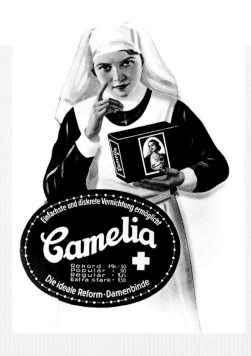

The Success of the Sanitary Towel

In the 1890s sanitary towels were invented, but because they were expensive only wealthier women were able to afford them.

The new "Camelia" brand was sold through clothing retail, since women bought their knit pads from clothing stores and thus didn't have to go out of their way. The company offered Camelia customers an additional service. They delivered white precut paper to the shops for the discrete packing of the blue cartons. For the buyer there was also a small card reading "Please give me a discreetly packed box of Camelia." Thus even the most bashful customers were won over to the new product.

The Moon and the Goddess

Throughout the ages, the moon has been linked with female sexuality and with the so-called "feminine principles" of intuition, emotion, and spiritual wisdom. Religious ceremonies honored the moon goddess who demanded that men should pay women spiritual and sexual homage. The moon is also traditionally seen as a source of spiritual power and insight that inspires female creativity. In ancient times, women identified when they were most fertile by charting their own monthly circles according to the monthly phases of the moon. In the latter part of the 20th century, with the advent of feminism, some women have come to perceive menstruation as a process of renewal linked to the rhythms of nature and to the moon's monthly cycle. In rural areas of the United States, England, and other parts of Europe, people can still be found who plant seeds when the moon is new, which they believe encourages better growth of their plants.

Christopher Wood, Reclining Nude, 1922. Oil on panel, 31.1 x 40.6 cm, private collection. Menstruation is a theme which rarely arises in the depiction of the female nude, but this study perhaps provides an exception. The figure reclines against a dark background, a red strip of cloth draped across her thighs and genitals. Only the angle of her head hints at any possible discomfort she may be experiencing, though this is not revealed in her facial expression.

some clothing, as well as enabling them to swim during menstruation.

Today, in developing countries, women still tend to use old strips of sheeting or cloth to absorb their menstrual blood. In contrast, women in the Western cultures have a wide variety of sanitary products to choose from. While most of these products are disposable and used only once, increased awareness of ecology issues in Western Europe has prompted the revival of a washable sanitary pad, this time made from organic cotton and viscose.

Women have probably always experienced menstrual pains, and because the cause was not known, they were often labeled neurotic. Period pains, (medical name: dysmenorrhea from a Greek word meaning "difficult menstrual flow") are usually caused by the muscles of the uterus contracting. Today they are alleviated by painkillers, or exercise.

Sex During Menstruation

Many couples have sexual intercourse during the woman's menstrual period, but others abstain. The latter may be due to religious beliefs, feelings that menstruation is ritually unclean, or concerns about the "mess" of the menstrual flow. Sex during menstruation has been taboo throughout history in many cultures. The Old Testament explicitly warns against intercourse with menstruating women. In Native North American Navajo villages, women had to live in special huts during their menstrual period to avoid ritually contaminating others.

Even today the fear of contact with menstruating women exists. Orthodox Jews are forbidden to have any type of sexual contact during menstruation and the week that follows. Because the woman's body is considered impure, sexual relations can only resume after the woman's body has undergone a ritual cleansing in the bath known as *mikveh*. Although Muslim men are discouraged from having intercourse with their wives during menstruation, other forms of sexual contact are permitted. According to Al-Chazaalil, writing in the Middle Ages, if a menstruating woman covers her body from navel to knee with a cloth, she may masturbate her husband with her hands. Sexual intercourse is also forbidden to Hindus during menstruation, and once it is over, ritualized bathing must take place. However, historically in a few societies, menstrual blood was considered beneficial. In medieval Europe it was used to treat leprosy and Louis XIV of France believed in its aphrodisiac powers. The Ainu of Japan use menstrual blood as a medicine for relieving aches and pains, and also believe that it brings wealth and success. Menstrual blood also plays an important part in Tantric rituals.

The magical powers – both good and bad – associated with menstruation probably originate from the human tendency to ritualize any act involving the spilling of blood. For many cultures, the ability of a woman to pour blood from her body is awe-inspiring.

While traditional attitudes in many cultures associate menstruation with uncleanness, there is no evidence that sexual intercourse during this time is harmful for either partner, and may actually be beneficial to women as orgasm can help to relieve pelvic cramps that often occur during menstruation.

Cultural Perspectives on Menarche

Menarche is viewed in many societies as an important event signaling a girl's passage to womanhood. In the West, it is sometimes marked with a celebration. In Thailand, menarche is seen as transforming a girl into a complete woman. For the Kurtachi islanders who live off the coast of New Guinea, a girl's menarche is celebrated with an elaborate ceremony. The girl, her mother and other female relatives paint their bodies in seclusion, before dancing and feasting with the other villagers. For Hindus, menarche represents the loss of purity and during menstruation the girl is expected to abstain from cooking for the family or attending religious ceremonies.

A Man's Sex Organs

A man's sex organs consist of the penis and testicles, which hang in a loose sack of skin called the scrotum. Composed of three cylinders of spongy tissue and blood vessels, the penis is an erectile organ, usually measuring about 12–18 cm (4.7–7 inches) long when erect. When the man is sexually aroused, the cylinders become engorged with blood and the penis hardens. At its tip the penis enlarges to become the glans or head of the penis. The main body of the penis is the shaft, which is free swinging. In addition to being used during sexual intercourse, the penis is also used for urination. One of the cylinders of spongy tissue – the corpus spongiosum – contains the urethra, which takes urine through the penis to the urinary opening at the tip.

Like the clitoral glans, the penile glans is highly sensitive to sexual stimulation. Other sensitive areas include the corona, a ridge separating the glans from the shaft of the penis, and the frenulum, a thin strip of tissue on the underside of the penis, connecting the glans to the shaft. The penis itself is hairless with loose skin to allow for expansion during erection. At the tip the skin covers part or all of the glans, and is known as the prepuce or foreskin. However, sebacious gland secretions, or smegma, can build up under the foreskin causing it to stick to the glans. This build-up can cause infection, and

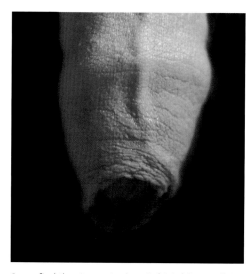
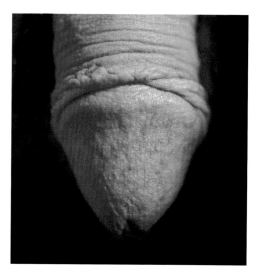

Some find the circumcised penis (right) "neater" than the uncircumcised (left), or may even be repelled by the covered glans as somehow "feminizing".

therefore hygiene is important for both the man and his partner.

Hanging beneath the penis is the scrotum, which holds the testicles or testes. Each testicle is held in place by a spermatic cord containing the vas deferens (the sperm duct), blood vessels and nerves. Also contained within the scrotum are the cremaster muscle and the dartos muscle, which move the testicles closer to or further away from the body in order to regulate the temperature for sperm production and during sexual activity. The optimum temperature is normally lower than normal body temperature, at about 93.02 degrees Fahrenheit (33.9° C) as opposed to 98.6 degrees Fahrenheit (37° C). The dartos muscle also triggers changes to the surface area of the scrotum. Tightening of the scrotum surface conserves heat and gives a wrinkled appearance in cool weather; relaxing of the scrotum surface gives a smooth appearance, which allows a more effective release of heat in hot weather.

The testicles themselves are equivalent to the female ovaries, in that they produce sex cells (in this case, sperm) and produce and release hormones such as testosterone. In most men the left testicle hangs lower than the right. Within each testicle, tiny lobes are packed with tightly coiled structures called seminiferous tubules, which are constantly making and storing sperm. Immature sperm are dispatched to a single tube called the epididymis where they develop a

head, body and tail. Each epididymis empties the sperm into a vas deferens, a cylindrical tube that acts as a container for mature sperm.

Near the point where the two vas deferens come together are two seminal vesicles, small glands that secrete fructose, helping the sperm to swim quickly. At the base of the bladder, each vas deferens joins a seminal vesicle, forming an ejaculatory duct that carries the sperm to the urethra where they are ejaculated from the body through the tip of the penis. The ejaculatory duct runs through the middle of the prostate gland where sperm are mixed with a milky fluid produced by the gland, giving semen its characteristic texture and smell. Lying beneath the prostate are Cowper's glands. During sexual arousal they secrete clear fluid into the urethra, which precedes the ejaculate. Its function is not fully understood but may help the passage of seminal fluid through the urethra.

Only about one percent of the content of semen is sperm. The rest is made up of fluids from the seminal vesicles, prostate gland and Cowper's glands. Containing water, mucus, fructose, acids and other substances, semen nourishes and keeps the sperm healthy while protecting it from vaginal acidity. The average ejaculate, which is about 3–5 milliliters (1–1.7 fluid ounces) in volume, contains between 200 and 400 million sperm.

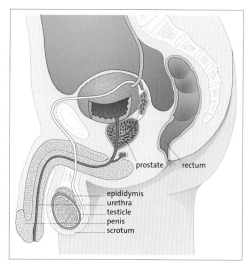

prostate   rectum

epididymis
urethra
testicle
penis
scrotum

Cross-section of penis, testicles, and seminal vesicles.

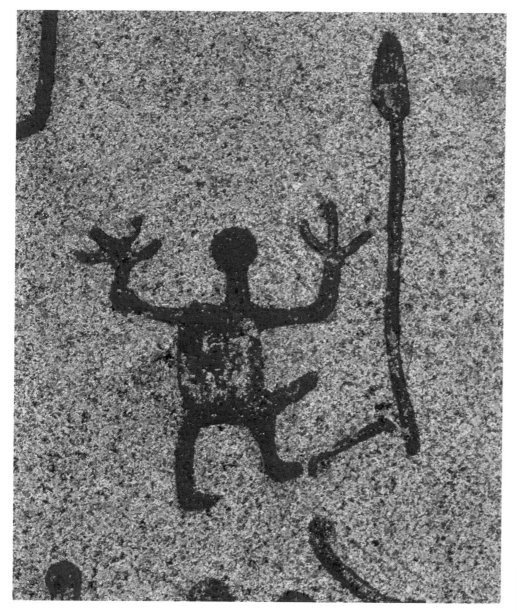

Man with spread fingers and giant phallus, Rock engraving. Vitlycke, Sweden. The association of the erect penis and the spear is a common one in prehistoric art, and has given rise to many different theories. Perhaps it suggests that prehistoric peoples themselves saw sex as an inherently violent activity. On the other hand, it may indicate a deep appreciation of the natural cycle of life and death. Or it may be a form of magic, emphasizing a man's potency in order to guarantee success in the hunt.

The Phallic Symbol

The penis has been glorified as a symbol of generative power since prehistory, but its potency is not limited to reproduction. The erect penis has widely been regarded as a powerful symbolic weapon, and phallic symbols have been used to guard fields and houses as far apart as Japan and Italy. Reflecting this, the phallus has been celebrated in art using metaphorical images as diverse as the plough, sword or axe. During Dionysian processions, the Ancient Greeks carried huge phallic symbols and regularly adorned themselves with phallic rings and necklaces. They also depicted the phallus with wings to emphasize its divine nature, and pay homage to its power. Similarly in Ancient Rome, the goddess of love Venus was honored by parading a large float in the shape of a phallus, while in Ancient Egypt, the penis was also glorified in sacred processions. Even today, veneration of male genitalia is widespread. Phallic gods have survived into most modern religions, whether as the lingam of Hinduism, the terrifying tutelary deities of Tibetan Hinduism or the wax votive penises that were used to promote fertility among the Roman Catholics of Isernia near Naples until the early 20th century. In the secular realm, men who have large genitals are the source of respect and envy, particularly amongst other men. Certain porn stars, such as the late John Holmes (1945–1988), have become legends even outside the confines of their genre. As well as fueling the myth that a man's sexual prowess is related to the size of his penis, this modern type of phallic worship also has the effect of creating anxiety and inadequacy in many boys and men about the size of their own organs.

Stone columns carved as a phallus, from the Avenue of Priapus, Delos, third cent. B.C. Because of their protective function, the Greeks and Romans used phallic symbols as roadside markers and shrines.

Genital Mutilation

The male genitals are much more commonly mutilated than those of the female, and the mutilations are more varied. However, it is female genital mutilation that has aroused most controversy and political debate, because it is more clearly a form of oppression, resulting in removing the possibility of the woman enjoying sex. In fact, there is no clear, simple reason for any form of genital mutilation. Perhaps the first person to speculate about the purpose of the custom was the Greek historian Herodotus, in the 5th century B.C., when he wrote about the Egyptians that they "practice circumcision for the sake of cleanliness, considering it better to be clean than good-looking." Circumcision, or the complete removal of the foreskin, is the most widely practiced form of genital mutilation. Egyptian images of circumcised men date back more than 4000 years, and today it is estimated that up to half the men on earth are circumcised.

Advocates believe that circumcision is more hygienic because it prevents the build-up of secretions, which can result in the growth of bacteria and infection. However opponents believe that with regular cleaning under the foreskin, such drastic steps are unnecessary. The "cleanliness" that is frequently cited as a reason for circumcision often seems to be metaphorical, or spiritual, rather than physical, although there is evidence that circumcised

men are less likely to suffer from cancer of the penis. It is perhaps better interpreted as "purity", because circumcision is mainly a badge of membership, a way of demonstrating that one belongs – whether to a race, a caste, a faith or even to the male sex in general. Among most peoples, circumcision is generally performed at puberty, as a mark of passage into manhood. The pain endured is one of the tests on this journey, and for the first time in his life, the circumcised boy is not allowed to turn to his mother for comfort.

Cross-culturally, Jewish circumcision is also unusual, in that it is practiced on a child who is himself oblivious to the significance of the rite. For Jewish people, circumcision is performed as a sign of the covenant between God and the people of Abraham. According to the commandments of the prophet Mohammed contained in the religious book, the so-called *sunna*, circumcision should also be carried out on all male Muslim babies seven days after birth because it is believed to be more hygienic. In the Western world, circumcision is also sometimes undertaken for hygienic reasons, although many pediatricians do not recommend it. Occasionally the operation is performed for medical reasons, for example phimosis, when the foreskin is too tight or if there is recurrent infection under the foreskin. It has been argued that the exposed glans

Master of the Tucher Altar, Nuremberg School, *Circumcision of Christ*, c. 1450. Oil on pine, 101 x 90 cm, Suermondt-Ludwig-Museum, Aachen, Germany. Dozens of "authentic" foreskins of Jesus exist as holy relics throughout Europe.

makes circumcised men more sensitive to sexual stimulation and therefore more prone to premature ejaculation, whilst conversely, others argue that removing the foreskin results in less sensitivity. However, clinical research indicates that there is no significant difference in sensitivity between the circumcised and uncircumcised penis.

In most cases genital mutilation requires the subject to be fully aware. It is performed without anesthetic. The Dowayo of Cameroon do not

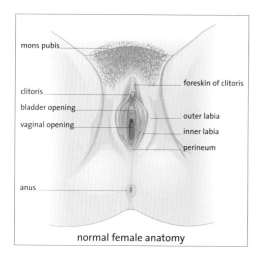

normal female anatomy

mons pubis
clitoris
bladder opening
vaginal opening
foreskin of clitoris
outer labia
inner labia
perineum
anus

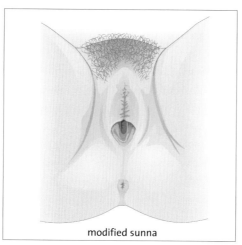

modified sunna

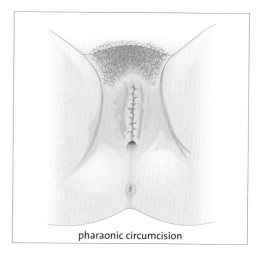

pharaonic circumcision

Female genital mutilation. The example on the left indicates a vulva in its natural state. The one in the middle shows the modified *sunna* genital mutilation which is common among the Sunnites. The one on the right is known as pharaonic circumcision, practiced for example in Somalia or among the Djibouti. Before marriage or births it is reversed, but the women are frequently infibulated again afterwards. They may be at greater risk for HIV/AIDS since intercourse often involves vaginal tearing.

merely remove the foreskin, but peel the entire penis, and in parts of Arabia the penis, scrotum, inner legs and lower belly are all flayed, with the boy's intended bride watching the whole operation. She may refuse to marry him if he flinches. A common variant in the South Pacific islands is superincision, where the foreskin is not actually removed, but split lengthwise.

Aside from circumcision, the men of traditional societies may also be subjected to subincision, where a cut is made through the urethra, along the length of the penis, so that the organ can be flattened out; genital hacking, or the bleeding of the penis, without actually removing any part of it; and hemicastration, or the removal of one testicle. This last has now died out, but was attempted as recently as the Second World War in Micronesia. It was considered a mark of bravery, and loyalty to the chief. Complete castration, which used to be commonly found in

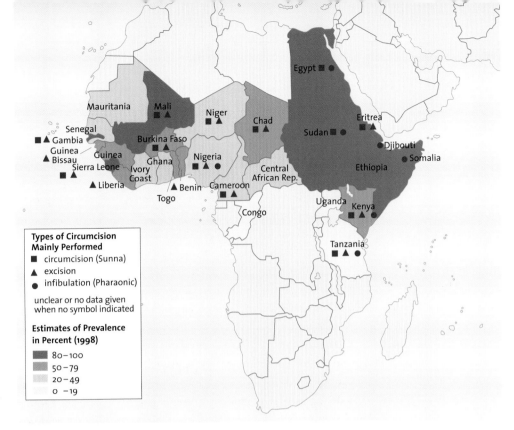

Extent and types of female genital mutilation (fgm). Fgm has traditionally been practised in Sub Saharan Africa and Egypt. Some incidence has also been reported for Australia, Europe and North America due to refugee or immigrant populations from regions where fgm is common. It is performed on young girls to ensure their sexual purity and shape their bodies to conform to the prevailing ideas of femininity. In those cultures where female genitalia are considered unclean, circumcision serves to purify them. Female genital mutilation reduces women's sexual response.

Circumcision of a girl, Ethiopia. Although female circumcision is fiercely condemned by Western and African feminists and women's-rights campaigners, it is often women who have been circumcised themselves who are its most stubborn defenders. In some villages, the custom is no longer practiced due to the influence of local women's rights groups.

certain religious cults, and among slaves, has also more or less disappeared (an exception are the hijras in India). Instead of cutting away parts of the genitals, men have often inserted additional materials, either through the shaft, through loose skin or beneath the foreskin. These range from tiny bronze bells in Burma to bone, bamboo or metal rods in Borneo, to the wide range of studs, rings and other decorations favored by some in the modern West. These are often reported as increasing sexual pleasure.

There are three main forms of genital mutilation practiced on women (aside from decorative piercings). Clitoridectomy – often called female circumcision – is the removal of the clitoris, sometimes along with other parts of the genitalia. It only occurs in areas where male circumcision can also be found, but is much more rare. Almost unbelievably, it has been championed occasionally over the last 200 years in the West, as a cure for frigidity, nymphomania or masturbation. A number of peoples – especially in Islamic countries – practice circumcision, where only the prepuce, rather than the entire clitoris, is cut away.

An extreme form of female genital mutilation is infibulation, also known as pharaonic circumcision, which is largely restricted to east-

ern Africa. There are several varieties of infibulation, but in all them parts of the clitoris and vaginal lips are cut away. Most commonly, whatever is left of the vaginal lips is then sewn together, leaving only a small hole for urination. The woman remains sewn up until she is married. Among the Conibo of Peru – probably the only Native Americans to have developed a form of infibulation – it was said that a clay dildo was inserted into the woman's vagina, which was then sewn around it. The dildo was a replica of her fiancé's penis, so that the couple should fit together perfectly. Introcision, or cutting of the perineum, occurs only in parts of Australia (and sometimes in Western hospitals to aid childbirth).

One unusual, purely decorative form of genital alteration is found among the Marquesans, Trukese and various South Pacific islanders, the African Dahomeans, the Bemba of Zambia, and the Kgatla-Tswana. Among these peoples, long labia minora are found especially exciting (the Kgatla call them "the exciter of the bull"). When they reach puberty, girls pull on their labia to lengthen them, sometimes enlisting the help of friends and using traditional magic ointments if the labia are stubbornly inelastic.

Sexually Transmitted Diseases

Sexually transmitted diseases (STDs) are at epidemic proportions. According to the World Health Organization, the annual incidence of curable STDs (which excludes AIDS) was at least 331 million cases in 1995. STD is the term used for any disease that is transmitted sexually, for instance, through vaginal or anal intercourse, or oral sex. Also known as venereal diseases (VD), after Venus, the Roman goddess of love, STDs are most often caused by microorganisms that thrive in warm, moist places in the human body, such as the genitals, anus and sometimes the mouth and throat. Most of the 30 STDs in existence worldwide are not life-threatening, but some diseases can cause long-term problems such as infertility if left untreated.

Chlamydia Trachomatis

During the 1990s, chlamydia trachomatis became one of the most common STDs, contracted by up to ten percent of sexually active young people. Around 89 million people are infected every year. Transmitted by vaginal or anal intercourse, symptoms may include a discharge from the vagina or penis and pain or burning on passing urine. Women may also have pain in their lower abdomen. However, symptoms, particularly in women, are often unnoticeable, which is why chlamydia is sometimes called "the silent disease". Treatment is with antibiotics. If left untreated, chlamydia can cause pelvic inflammatory disease, which may block the fallopian tubes, resulting in infertility. Chlamydia may also cause eye infection if a person touches his or her eyes after handling the genitals of an infected partner. Newborn babies can also contract eye infections as they pass through the birth canal of an infected mother.

Gonorrhea

Infection rates from gonorrhea fell substantially in Europe and the United States in the 1970s and 1980s but in the mid-1990s began rising again. Around 62 million cases are

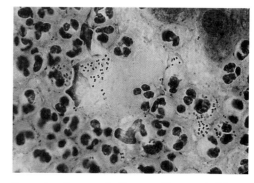

Gonorrhea Gonococci – the causative agent of the so-called "clap" – in a pus sample, scale 1000:1.

reported worldwide every year. Gonorrhea – also known as "the clap" – may be passed on by vaginal, anal or oral sex. Infected men may have a yellowish discharge and a burning sensation when they urinate, while women may have increased discharge, burning on urination and irregular menstrual bleeding. However, in many women there are no early symptoms. The eyes may also become infected after contact with infected genitals. As with chlamydia, treatment is with antibiotics. A penile discharge which was probably gonorrhea is well-documented in ancient texts. It is mentioned in the Old Testament (Leviticus 15) as well as being described in Egyptian and Chinese writings.

Global transmission of STDs. While sexually transmitted diseases are at epidemic proportions, report-based STD surveillance systems tend to underestimate substantially the total number of new cases. More than 30 bacterial, viral and parasitic diseases have now been identified that can be transmitted by the sexual route; the majority, however, are acquired through low hygiene standards or poor living conditions, which explains why the highest percentage of STDs can be found in developing regions of the world.

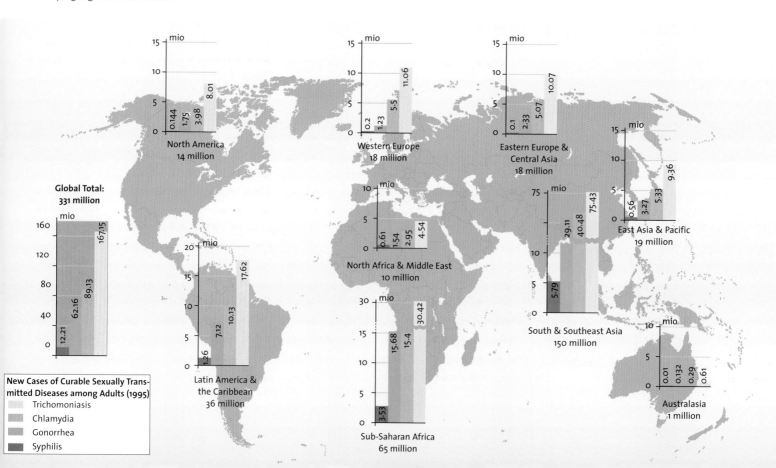

North America
14 million
0.144 / 1.75 / 3.98 / 8.01

Western Europe
18 million
0.2 / 1.23 / 5.5 / 11.06

Eastern Europe & Central Asia
18 million
0.1 / 2.33 / 5.07 / 10.07

East Asia & Pacific
19 million
0.56 / 3.27 / 5.33 / 9.36

Global Total: 331 million
12.21 / 62.16 / 89.13 / 167.15

Latin America & the Caribbean
36 million
1.26 / 7.12 / 10.13 / 17.62

North Africa & Middle East
10 million
0.61 / 1.54 / 2.95 / 4.54

South & Southeast Asia
150 million
5.79 / 29.11 / 40.48 / 75.43

Sub-Saharan Africa
65 million
3.53 / 15.68 / 15.4 / 30.42

Australasia
1 million
0.01 / 0.132 / 0.29 / 0.61

New Cases of Curable Sexually Transmitted Diseases among Adults (1995)
- Trichomoniasis
- Chlamydia
- Gonorrhea
- Syphilis

The Curse of God?

The word "syphilis" was first used in a poem written by the great 16th-century Veronese naturalist, physician and poet Hieronymus Fracastorius. It told how a shepherd called Syphilis, by constantly blaspheming, offended the god Apollo, who cursed him with a revolting new disease. The poem was incredibly popular, and went through a hundred editions by the end of the century.

Fracastorius was only following in a tradition established by the Holy Roman Emperor Maximilian I, who within a year of the disease appearing in Europe, in 1495, proclaimed that it was a punishment for blasphemy. Until Europeans developed some partial tolerance for the illness, its symptoms were considered particularly revolting, and it surpassed leprosy as a symbol of sinful living.

Albrecht Dürer, *Syphilis*, 1496. Woodcut, Staatliche Museen Preussischer Kulturbesitz, Berlin. This woodcut about a 1494 syphilis epidemic is an allegorical presentation of the "French disease".

Trichomoniasis

Caused by the single-celled organism *trichomonas vaginalis*, trichomoniasis often leads to vaginal infection and if left untreated, can cause infertility. According to the World Health Organization, it affected around 167 million people worldwide in the mid-1990s. Symptoms in women include a greenish yellow vaginal discharge accompanied by inflammation of the vulva, but sometimes there are no symptoms. In men the infection is usually symptom-free, although some experience a slight burning or irritation on passing urine. Male partners of an infected woman must also be treated, even if the infection is not found on them, as they can otherwise reinfect the woman.

Syphilis

Syphilis is historically one of the best-known STDs. Since the introduction of penicillin (available from 1940), the incidence of syphilis has fallen dramatically. Caused by a spiral shaped bacterium that penetrates broken skin or mucous membranes in the genitals, rectum

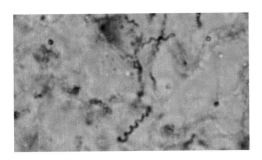

Spirochata pallidus – the causative agent of syphilis, scale 1000:1.

or mouth, it is passed through sexual contact. The risk of infection during one sexual encounter with an infected person is about one in three. The first sign of syphilis is a painless but highly infectious chancre or sore at the site of the infection. After several weeks, headaches and fever may occur, along with a rash or sores appearing elsewhere on the body. The disease may then lie dormant for many years before eventually progressing to the final, potentially fatal stage where ulcers may form on the skin, muscle tissue or any internal organ, and infection attacks the central nervous system or the heart and major blood vessels. All forms of the disease are treated by penicillin, but organ damage caused by the disease cannot be reversed. The dermatologist Iwan Bloch (1872–1922), one of the founders of modern sexology, put forward the opinion in his work *The Cause of Syphilis*, 1901, that the illness was introduced to Europe from North America. The physician Karl Sudhoff first rejected this thesis in 1912. He had already found earlier evidence of syphilis. Prehistoric finds proved him right: in 1927 skeletons were found in a Neolithic cave in the Marne valley which showed typical syphilis damage.

Herpes

The viral infection, herpes, caused wide concern as a result of its rapid spread in the Western world during the 1970s and 1980s, but has received less attention with the advent of AIDS. Herpes occurs in two forms, both of which can be transmitted sexually. Once in the body, the virus stays there permanently. Oral herpes (caused by herpes simplex virus type 1) is characterized by cold sores or blisters on the lips and mouth. As well as being transferred to the genitals by the hands or through oral sex, the virus is able to survive outside the body for several hours, so can be picked up by direct contact with infected objects such as cups or toilet seats. Genital herpes (caused by herpes simplex virus type 2) is passed on through oral, anal, and vaginal sex, resulting in outbreaks of blisters and sores on the genitals that may heal but still leave the person harboring the virus. Because many people do not realize that they are infected and show no symptoms, they may unknowingly transmit the virus to others.

AIDS

Over the last 20 years of the 20th century Acquired Immunodeficiency Syndrome, or AIDS, has probably had a greater impact on human sexual behavior than anything else. The disease is caused by damage to the immune system due to infection with HIV (human immunodeficiency virus). The first cases were reported in 1981 in the United States, when a number of previously healthy young men died from a rare form of pneumonia that had only affected people with suppressed immune systems, such as those being treated for cancer. Young men also began to develop a rare form of skin tumor, Kaposi's sarcoma, and unlike previous cases of older sufferers, they quickly deteriorated and died. Other rare infections, which only affected those with damaged immune systems, were also reported amongst younger men. The only clear link between these men was that all of them were homosexual.

Many people took little notice of the rapidly growing epidemic, which was given the name AIDS in 1982. In 1983, the disease was first discovered amongst the heterosexual population: chiefly intravenous drug users and hemophiliacs, suggesting that transmission was related to blood as well as sexual activity. In May of that year, the virus was isolated in Paris by researcher Luc Montagnier, and was eventually named HIV in 1986.

As a retrovirus, HIV copies its genetic material into the genetic material of the person's own cells. This results in infected cells remaining infected permanently. It is thought that HIV damages the immune system by infecting a group of white blood cells, called CD4 cells or T-helper lymphocytes, which are crucial for regulating the immune system's fight against infection. The infected cell may die or the infection may lie dormant and possibly be reactivated later.

Many people who become infected with HIV do not notice that they have been infected and they may remain asymptomatic for many years. In other cases people develop symptoms including chronically swollen lymph glands, fatigue and unexplained weight loss. To confirm whether a person is infected with HIV, they undergo a blood test to check for the presence of antibodies to the virus. If the result is positive they have been exposed to the virus and are carrying the infection, sometimes known as being "HIV-positive".

Eventually, in most cases, the number of infected cells in the body swells and begins to take over the immune system, eventually destroying the body's ability to defend itself. AIDS is diagnosed with the appearance of one of the AIDS defining disorders, such as Kaposi's sarcoma, PCP (a type of pneumonia), or toxoplasmosis of the brain, all of which are severe, terminal diseases. These are known as opportunistic infections because they only become problematic if a person's immune system has been damaged.

No cure for AIDS has yet been found although improved treatments for both HIV infection and the opportunistic infections have altered the course of the disease for many people. Antiviral drugs such as AZT and Ritonavir, usually taken in combinations, can help to delay progression of the disease while more effective treatment is available for opportunistic infections such as PCP.

The result is that many people, even once diagnosed with AIDS, can continue to lead

AIDS Memorial Quilt

The AIDS Memorial Quilt is perhaps the world's most famous tribute to people who have died from AIDS. Started in San Francisco in 1987 by Cleve Jones, whose best friend Marvin Feldman had died of AIDS. It consists of over 42, 000 panels each of which is dedicated to the life of a person who has died of AIDS. Each panel is designed and sewn by family members, lovers, friends or co-workers. Panels from the quilt are displayed in community centers and office buildings all over the world. The Memorial Quilt draws upon the American tradition of quilting, when family, friends and neighbors would gather in groups to sew old scraps of fabric together, to gossip, share stories and enjoy each other's company, and to give comfort in times of grief.

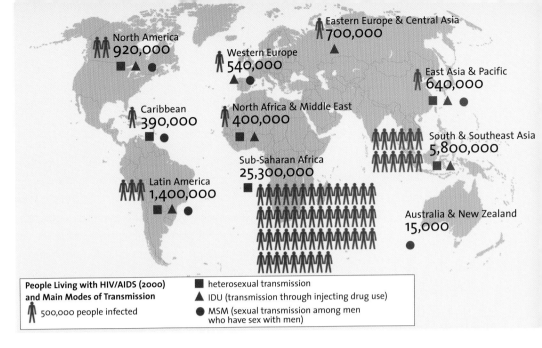

North America
👤 920,000
■ ▲ ●

Eastern Europe & Central Asia
👤 700,000
▲

Western Europe
👤 540,000
▲ ●

East Asia & Pacific
👤 640,000
■ ▲ ●

Caribbean
👤 390,000
■ ●

North Africa & Middle East
👤 400,000
■ ▲

South & Southeast Asia
👥👥👥👥👥 5,800,000
■ ▲

Latin America
👤 1,400,000
■ ▲ ●

Sub-Saharan Africa
25,300,000
■ 👥👥

Australia & New Zealand
15,000
●

People Living with HIV/AIDS (2000) and Main Modes of Transmission
👤 500,000 people infected

■ heterosexual transmission
▲ IDU (transmission through injecting drug use)
● MSM (sexual transmission among men who have sex with men)

healthy lives for long periods. Research is continuing in both Europe and the United States into the development of vaccines and the further development of drugs. But for the foreseeable future, prevention through safer sex practices such as using condoms and non-penetrative sex is a key strategy.

HIV is passed from one person to another when there is contact with infected body fluids, including blood, semen, vaginal secretions and breast milk. Saliva, tears and urine may contain HIV but are unlikely to be important in transmission. Sexual contact is one of the main methods of transmission, through anal or vaginal sex, and possibly through oral sex if the person has bleeding gums or mouth ulcers. It can also be passed through needle-sharing in drug users or through blood transfusions using infected blood. A mother with HIV can transmit the virus to her baby during childbirth or breastfeeding. HIV is not passed on by non-sexual contact such as touching, hugging, coughing, sneezing, sharing cutlery or toilet seats.

Worldwide, the AIDS epidemic is growing. According to the World Health Organization, at the end of 2000, 36.1 million people had HIV or AIDS worldwide, 8 percent more than 1997. More than 90 percent of HIV infected people now live in the developing world, which has also experienced 95 percent of all deaths from AIDS. Over 75 percent of infections are due to male-to-female sexual activity. The rest are made up of homosexual activity, transmission through intravenous drug use and transfusions with infected blood. Sub-Saharan Africa has been most severely affected, accounting for 70 percent of all cases of HIV and AIDS. In the urban areas of some countries, such as Zimbabwe and Zambia, up to a third of all adults are believed to be infected. Most infections are among young adults at the height of their productive and reproductive years. In South and Southeast Asia, the rate is also soaring, with 5.8 million people already infected. Transmission in Thailand and India is often via prostitutes. In cities such as Bangkok, Bombay and Madras, about one third of prostitutes are thought to be infected. But it is also spreading amongst preg-

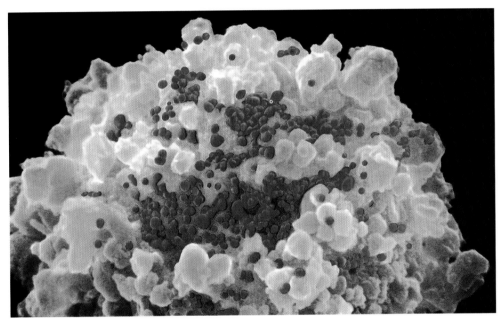

nant women and in rural areas that had appeared relatively spared by the epidemic. HIV is also growing in Eastern Europe, Latin America and the Caribbean, through men who have sex with men, heterosexual sex and drug-users who share needles. Poorly funded health education programs in many areas have done little to change men's reluctance to use condoms. In poorer countries, expensive antiviral drugs are unaffordable, meaning that HIV and AIDS progress faster once a person is infected. Every major outbreak of venereal disease has been greeted, in some quarters, as a punishment from God. Not surprisingly, AIDS, because it seemed to target homosexuals and drug users, was regularly described in this way, especially by some fundamentalist American preachers, who proclaimed that Judeo-Christian morality was the only effective defense.

Top: **AIDS transmission worldwide**. On world average, women represent about 40 to 45 percent of all present HIV/AIDS cases. HIV/AIDS is associated with higher rates of poverty and for many women occasional prostitution is part of their economic survival package. In Africa, female genital mutilation increases transmission rates, especially since women are often not in a sufficiently powerful situation to negotiate safe sex and men often consider it their prerogative to have multiple sex partners. In Russia the rate of infection with HIV almost doubled between 1999 and 2000, mainly due to intravenous drug use.

Above: The colored electron micrograph shows a T-lymphocyt blood cell (green) infected with HIV (red), the causative agent of AIDS. The virus has infected the T-cell and instructed it to reproduce viruses. The surface of the T-cell has a lumpy appearance with irregular protusions. Spherical structures on the cell surface are HIV virus particles budding away from the cell membrane. This viral budding causes the death of the T-cell. The ultimate destruction of the immune system is mainly due to the depletion of the number of T-cells in the human body.

Contraception

Ever since the link was made between sexual intercourse and conception, women and men have practiced contraception in order to prevent pregnancy. The Greek physician Soranos (second century A.D.) recommends making a paste from pomegranate skins or dry figs and oil, which would have created an acid environment for the sperm.

In contrast, other suggestions appeared to be based merely on myth and superstition. For example, the 9th-century Islamic physician Rhazes (c. 850 – c. 932) named 17 substances for women to use, including cabbage, animal ear wax and whitewash. This thinking on spermicides continued also in Europe up to around the 16th century. A more logical approach was reinstated by 16th-century English physician Roger Ascham (1515 – 1568), who suggested using acid to kill the sperm, by mixing oil of spindle (containing acetic acid) with honey and pitch.

From the 1600s, vaginal douches were used after intercourse. In 1885, English pharmacist Walter Rendell developed the first commercial vaginal suppository, using cocoa butter and quinine sulphate. This was eventually replaced by the more powerful spermicides developed in the 1950s.

The First Condoms

Men in Ancient Egypt used decorative penile sheaths, but these were intended to protect

Novelty condoms are rarely trustworthy as forms of birth control. Although amusing, novelty condoms often carry disclaimers that they are not suitable for birth control.

against disease and insects rather than for contraceptive use. As far as we know the first real condom was not invented until 1564, when the Italian physician Gabrielo Fallopia (who also discovered the tubes named after him) recommended a moistened linen sheath as a protection against sexually transmitted diseases. Until the mid-18th century, condoms were made from animal intestines, and in the 1840s rubber condoms were introduced shortly after the vulcanization of rubber, invented by Charles Goodyear in 1843.

Natural Family Planning

Natural family-planning methods have always been popular, and abstinence from intercourse is another ancient method of birth control. However, it was not until the mid-19th century that the female ovum was identified by the German embryologist Karl Ernst von Baer (1792 – 1876), and in the 1930s, Japanese and Austrian studies showed when ovulation and thus conception occurred. As a result a more accurate natural family-planning method could be developed. Introduced in 1934, the calendar method was promoted by the Roman Catholic Church, which denounced all artificial methods of birth control. By the 1940s, the temperature method, which charted changes in a woman's temperature during her menstrual cycle, was being used. Following research into cyclical changes in cervical mucus, the Billings or ovulation method was introduced in 1964. Nowadays, the symptothermal method, combining all indicators of fertility, is most widely used. Various kits are now available to monitor changes in urinary hormones, temperature and saliva during a woman's menstrual cycle.

Vaginal Barriers

From ancient times, devices were also used to create a vaginal barrier to block the sperm's path. Early vaginal barrier methods included leaves, sponges and absorbent materials. In the 1880s the introduction of the diaphragm and cap contributed to the emancipation of women, giving them the opportunity to control their fertility for the first time. Although female condoms (known as "capote anglaise" or "feminine

sheaths") were first introduced in the early 1900s, the most recent female condom, made of polyurethane, was introduced in 1992.

There is some evidence that the idea behind intrauterine devices (IUDs) began with the invention of an intra-womb device to promote fertility. One of Hippocrates' works suggests inserting a lead tube into the womb which could then be filled with mutton fat in order to keep the cervix open to allow the sperm through. By the 17th century the German physician Johann Scultetus (1621 – 1680) was using stem pessaries, where the stem was inserted into the cervix. While these devices were used to treat infertility, many doctors protested that they actually prevented conception. A German physician developed the first specifically designed IUD, a ring of silkworm gut, in 1909. However, for some reason they fell into disrepute, and it was not until the 1950s that the IUD was hailed as a new and effective form of contraception. In the 1960s plastic IUDs were introduced, followed by copper IUDs. In 1996, a hormonal releasing device, known as an intrauterine system (IUS) was introduced. This changes the mucus around the cervix, making it more difficult for the sperm to reach the egg. A year later, in 1997, experts developed a frameless IUD, made of small copper beads threaded on nylon.

Portio cap, c. 1840. German Museum of Medical History, Ingolstadt. Portio caps were long used to keep the cervix closed. They had to be fitted by a doctor.

Oral Contraceptives

Oral contraceptives – or what were believed to be contraceptives – were first taken orally more than two thousand years ago. Different cultures had their own recipes. The Ancient Hebrew method was to eat "a cup of roots" according to Midrash, the rabbinical writings that explain biblical texts. The Ancient Chinese text

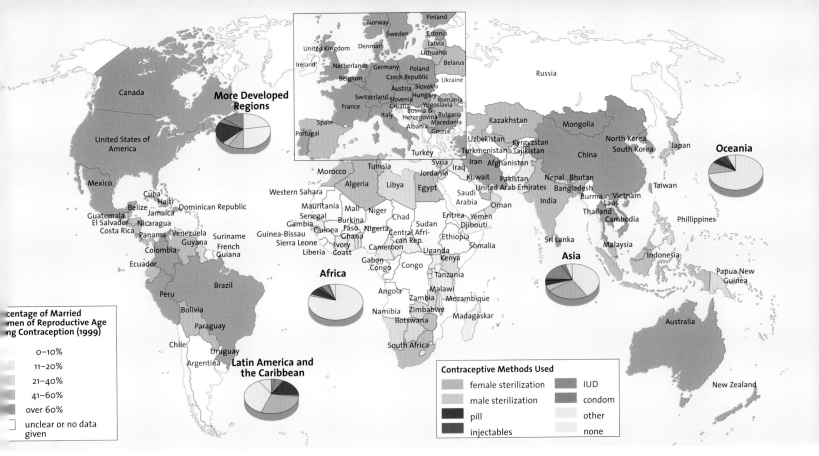

World contraceptive use. More than 60 percent of women in Canada, the USA, the greater part of South America, Europe, China, and Australia use contraception. Oceania, Africa, and Russia are among the areas where almost no contraception is practiced. As with STDs the availability of contraception appears also to be linked to economic factors.

Thousands of Gold Prescriptions suggests the poisonous mixture of oil and quicksilver to which a jujube seed was added. Another recipe involved grinding wheat flour, kidney beans and apricot stones into a paste, adding liquor and drinking it before menstruation. The Indian 12th-century text *Pancasayaka* recommends that the fruits and flowers of the salami tree are mixed with melted butter and swallowed, so that the womb "becomes unfruitful". In his book *On Vegetables and Plants* the Dominican scholar Albertus Magnus (1200–1280) mentions recipes to both inhibit and promote conception. In 1956 the first clinical trials began for a combined oral contraceptive pill. In 1961 a contraceptive pill containing estrogen was approved for use in Great Britain. The combined pill, which brings together synthetic forms of the hormones estrogen and progesterone, works by fooling the brain into acting as though the woman is already pregnant so that ovulation is suppressed.

Injectable Contraception

Injectable contraception was first experimented with in 1953. Trials began using the injectable drug – called Depo-Provera – as a human contraceptive in 1963. Initially it was granted a license for short-term use only, but in 1984, the license was extended for long-term use.

Implants

Hormone-filled implants, which were inserted under the skin and could release hormones gradually, began to be developed in 1967 in the United States. In the 1990s, Norplant, consisting of six progesterone-releasing rods, was introduced into Europe. Several different types of hormonal implant are now being developed with fewer rods and different progesterones. Other hormonal methods currently being researched include hormone-releasing vaginal rings and contraceptive skin patches and gels.

Sterilization

Sterilization for women was first mentioned by Hippocrates (460–377 B.C.). In the 19th and early 20th centuries, the procedure involved major abdominal surgery and weeks of hospitalization. At the beginning of the 21st century, sterilization is performed by sealing or blocking the fallopian tubes. For women who want potentially reversible ligation, the tubes can be pinched closed with clips rather than severed. Techniques for male sterilization, or vasectomy, were first experimented with around 1830. In the 20th century, with better surgical techniques, vasectomy became widely available. The operation involves cutting or blocking the vasa deferentia, the tubes carrying sperm from the testes to the penis.

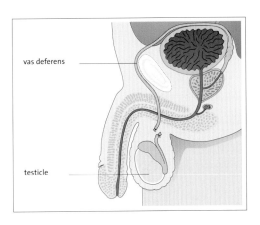

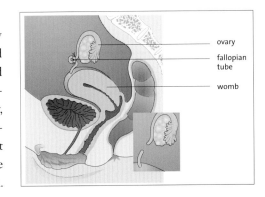

Male and female sterilization techniques. In men (top) a common procedure is the excision of the vas deferens or a portion of it. This is called vasectomy, a term which has been in use since 1895. In women (above) the functions of the fallopian tubes are inhibited by sealing or blocking them, which destroys the ability to reproduce. A variety of surgical methods are employed in order to achieve this.

Conception and Pregnancy

Conception takes place when an egg from a woman and a sperm from a man meet and fuse. This fusion usually takes place in the fallopian tubes, which link a woman's ovaries with her uterus. It is the result of two extraordinary, and very different journeys.

At ovulation, a mature egg is released from the ovary. The egg is carried down the fallopian tube by contractions and by waving cilia, tiny hair-like cell extensions on the walls of the tube. Each egg, which is about the size of a pinhead, survives for about 12–24 hours. Meanwhile, coming in the opposite direction, sperm are deposited by the man during ejaculation. Once in the woman's vagina, the sperm enter the womb through the cervix by swimming through the cervical mucus. At around the time of ovulation the mucus becomes thin and stretchy, helping the sperm to move easily into the uterus. Of the hundreds of millions of sperm released during one ejaculation, only a few – the fastest and most promising – make it to the fallopian tubes. This is where fertilization may take place.

The fertilized egg begins to divide and travels down to the uterus where the lining, which has thickened due to hormonal changes, is ready to receive it. About seven days later the fertilized egg implants in the uterus and pregnancy begins. At this stage the egg has divided many times to form a ball of cells called a blastocyst. This produces a hormone called human chorionic gonadotrophin (HCG), which prevents the endometrium (uterine lining) from being shed and menstruation from taking place. The inner cells of the blastocyst form the embryo and the outer cells will form the placenta. At this stage the woman may have begun to detect changes in her body as the ovaries begin to produce increased progesterone levels. Early pregnancy signs include tender breasts, nausea and feelings of tiredness.

About four to six weeks after fertilization, the embryo is usually less than 0.5 cm (0.2 inches) long, although it is already forming a heart, and developing eyes. A groove appears in the outer layer of the embryo's cells making a hollow tube called a neural tube. This will become the baby's brain and spinal cord. The embryo floats in fluid within the amniotic sac, which provides it with physical protection throughout pregnancy. At this stage, the placenta, which carries oxygen and nutrients from the mother to the embryo via the umbilical cord, is becoming established. At about seventh week, the heart begins to beat and buds appear on either side of the embryo forming arms and legs as the embryo develops.

By the ninth week, the embryo is recognizable as a human baby with a face, limbs, fingers and toes. At this stage, the embryo becomes known as a fetus. All the major parts of the body are now in place including the basis of reproductive organs. During the rest of the pregnancy, the fetus grows quickly, increasing in weight from about 25g (1 ounce) at eight weeks to a weight of around 3 kg (6.5 pounds) when it is born. Its many organs, including the brain, will continue to develop, and its proportions will change dramatically. While the eight-week-old fetus has a gigantic head, a small body and tiny limbs, by 16 weeks its proportions are

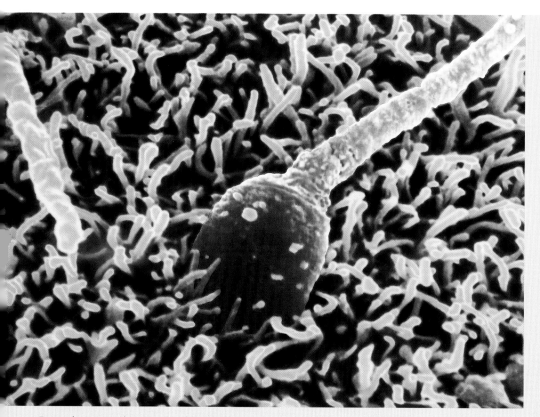

Egg and sperm at the moment of fertilization.

Sperm Races

On average, around 400 million sperm are produced with each ejaculation. In theory, each is capable of swimming the 20-cm (8-inch) journey along the vaginal canal, through the mucus in the cervical canal, up into the uterus and then along the fallopian tube to the egg.

However only a fraction of the original number of sperm will reach the egg, and, in most cases, only one will fertilize it. Of the 400 million ejaculated, around 10, 000 may reach the uterus where perhaps 2000 reach the fallopian tubes. Of these only about half will swim into the fallopian tube containing the egg, and perhaps 100 will reach the egg. While, in most cases, only one sperm fuses with the egg, several other sperm may help to weaken the egg's jelly-like outer coating or zona pellucida. Each sperm attaches itself headfirst to the zona pellucida, releasing enzymes which help to dissolve it. The successful sperm then fuses with the nucleus of the egg to fertilize it.

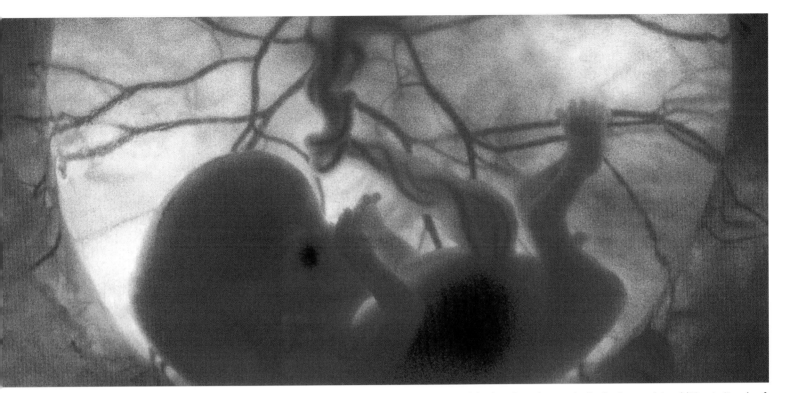

The human fetus at 11 weeks. The blood vessels of the placenta, connected to the fetus via the umbilical cord, can be seen in the background. In addition to its role of transferring gases, nutrients, and waste products, the placenta also synthesizes steroid hormones — similar to those made by the pituitary gland.

nearly those of a baby at the end of pregnancy. At this 16-week stage, the mother should also begin to feel fetal movements.

By the 20th week, hair, eyebrows, and eyelashes are in place, followed by fingernails and toenails. The nervous system continues to develop. Tiny lungs have also formed, although these are filled with fluid and do not have a respiratory function until the baby's birth.

For the rest of the pregnancy up until its birth at around 40 weeks, the fetus continues to grow and to build up fat under the skin. Organ systems continue to develop and mature, with the heart and lungs becoming increasingly capable of working independently. At 28 weeks after fertilization the fetus usually turns upside down in the uterus so that it will be head-first for delivery.

In the last four weeks before the birth, the baby places huge demands on the mother's body. Her ribs have to spread out to give her lungs space due to the increasing size of the uterus. She may also have to stand and walk leaning backwards to counteract the weight of the bulge in the front of her body.

From ovulation to implantation. About one week after conception the fertilized egg implants itself in the uterus lining. This defines the beginning of pregnancy.

Environmental influences have a significant impact on prenatal development. Alcohol and chemicals inhaled during smoking can pass across the placenta into the fetus's bloodstream, which is why health professionals advise women to limit their alcohol intake and stop or cut down on their smoking. The effects of smoking and drinking excess alcohol include low weight of the newborn child, increased risk of miscarriage and birth complications, and defects. Drugs, including non-prescription drugs such as aspirin, are also potentially harmful, so pregnant women need to consult a medical professional before taking any.

Diseases and infections can also affect the developing fetus. Rubella in early pregnancy can lead to serious organic damage to the fetus, in particular, but not only, to the eyes and heart. Toxoplasmosis, which is found in cat feces or infected garden soil, can also damage the developing baby, if caught during pregnancy. A healthy varied diet also plays an important role in ensuring that the embryo and fetus develop properly. During the first 12 weeks of pregnancy, folic acid is often recommended as a supplement (400 mg daily) to help prevent spina bifida (congenital cleft of the vertebral column, a form of neural tube defect).

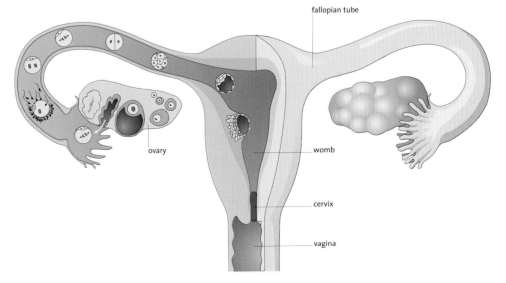

fallopian tube

ovary

womb

cervix

vagina

The Birth of a Child

In the final month before the birth, the baby's head sometimes moves down in the pelvis and is said to be "engaged". As a result the woman may feel lighter with less pressure on her diaphragm. Sometimes women experience mild contractions, which may continue sporadically for days before labor itself begins. A baby's imminent birth is sometimes signaled by blood in vaginal secretions caused by fetal pressure on the pelvis rupturing blood vessels in the vaginal passage or birth canal. Tissue that plugs the cervix, probably to prevent infection from entering the uterus, may also become dislodged, leading to a discharge of bloody mucus. Within a day of labor, the amniotic sac around the baby breaks and the fluid escapes – often described as "the water breaking".

Labor takes place in three stages. During the first stage, contractions of the uterus push the baby down towards the cervix at the bottom of the uterus. At the same time, the cervix gradually widens to about 10 cm (4 inches) in diameter to allow the baby to pass through. Initially mild, short and widely-spaced at around 10–20 minute intervals, as labor continues the contractions become longer, stronger and more frequent. This is part of a process whereby contractions stimulate the mother's pituitary gland to secrete the hormone oxyticin, which produces even stronger contractions. The first stage may last anywhere from a few hours to more than a day. It ends with a process called transition during which the cervix becomes nearly fully dilated and the baby's head moves into the birth canal. Usually lasting about 30 minutes or less, the contractions come very quickly during this period.

The second stage of labor begins when the cervix is fully dilated allowing the baby to enter the birth canal, and culminates with the baby's birth. Contractions push the baby along the canal towards the vaginal opening. Once the baby's head becomes visible – sometimes described as "crowning" – the baby usually emerges within minutes. This stage is quicker than the first, lasting anything from several minutes to about an hour. Once the baby is breathing properly, the umbilical cord is clamped and cut, and the baby becomes, for the first time, a separate human being.

After the baby is delivered, the third stage of labor begins. Usually taking about 20 to 30 minutes, it involves painless contractions causing the uterus to expel the placenta or afterbirth. The uterus then begins the process of contracting to a smaller size.

Pain relief is often used during childbirth to reduce the intense pain caused by contractions and the stretching of the cervix and birth canal. Enonox (gas and air), when inhaled, dulls the brain's perception of the pain and is effective for coping with powerful contractions. An epidural – a spinal injection of anesthetic – is sometimes given early on in labor to relieve pain. Some women use other techniques for relieving pain such as massage, acupuncture, reflexology and hypnosis. Being immersed in water can also help to ease the pain of labor and childbirth.

In the developed world, most births take place in a hospital, where medical staff and equipment are available should there be complications. However, some women choose to have their babies at home attended by a midwife, particularly if they have a history of normal births. In developing countries, childbirth tends to take place within the woman's home. Skilled midwives and doctors are also far less likely to be present and pain relief is usually not available.

Mother goddess from Ur, Babylonia, second millennium B. C. Like the majority of images of Mary, this statue shows the infant Christ held to her left breast.

Nursing the Child

A baby is born with a sucking reflex which allows it to feed from the mother's nipple or a bottle teat. The hormone prolactin, released from the pituitary gland, stimulates the production of breast milk in the gland cells of the breast. When the baby sucks on the nipple, the pituitary gland releases another hormone, oxytocin, which makes the muscles in the breast contract, moving milk towards the nipple as the baby sucks. Breast milk contains all the nutrients needed by the baby in the most easily digestible form. It also reduces the general risk of infections to the baby by transmitting the mother's antibodies to the baby and reducing the incidence of allergy.

In a wide-ranging historical survey of Madonna-and-child paintings, it was discovered that 373 out of the 466 examined showed the Madonna holding Christ to her left breast. This figure accurately reflects the real-life situation, where some 80 percent of mothers spontaneously nurse their babies to the left. Milk of course is produced in both breasts equally, and both have to be emptied if trouble is to be avoided. Baby-care manuals, indeed, stress the need for mothers to start each nursing session with the left and right breast alternately. Attempts have been made to explain the left-side preference by closer proximity to the heart; there is no doubt that babies find heart-beats – to which they have been accustomed in the womb – soothing. But the reality is probably more prosaic: namely that most women, and most artists' models, are right-handed.

There is often no equipment or expertise to handle complications and emergencies. These factors mean that in some of the poorest countries one in ten pregnant women will not survive and 130 babies per 1000 are stillborn or die in the first week of life.

Who Is Present at the Birth?

The midwife plays a crucial role in the birth of the baby, not only in terms of providing medical expertise but also equally importantly, by supporting the woman throughout labor. It is now fashionable in the West for the father to be present at the birth in order to share the experience and to provide his partner with emotional support. His role may include the symbolic cutting of the umbilical cord. Sometimes if a woman does not have a partner, she may choose to be accompanied by a female relative or friend during labor. In Brazil and other non-Western cultures, a woman may choose to have a "doula" present, a birthing companion who is trained and experienced in supporting women in labor. Increasingly this option is becoming available in Western Europe and the United States.

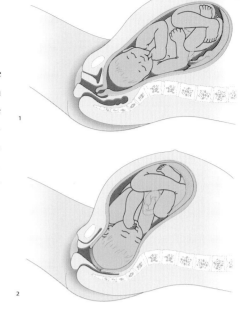

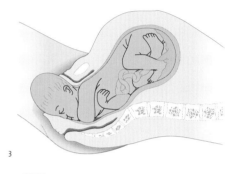

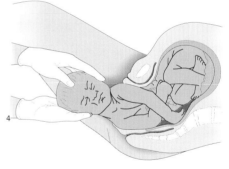

Above:
1 Fetus immediately before birth. Labor pains begin.
2 In the first stage of labor the cervix dilates.
3 + 4 Gradually the head and eventually the entire body emerge. Following the birth the placenta is released.

Left: **Application of Coriander, Woman Attending a Birth, mid-13th cent. Manuscript miniature from the pseudo-Apuleius Herbal.** This page from the medieval herbal shows coriander being applied as an aid to parturition.

Abortion

Heinrich Zille (1858–1929), *Article 218, "Rich Folks Go to Sanitariums – We Go to Jail".* Zille's title of his drawing refers to Article 218 of the German penal code introduced on 15 May 1871.

These abortion tools, which were confiscated by the imperial police of Berlin, Germany, at the turn of the 20ᵗʰ century, are now on display in the Polizeihistorische Sammlung, Berlin.

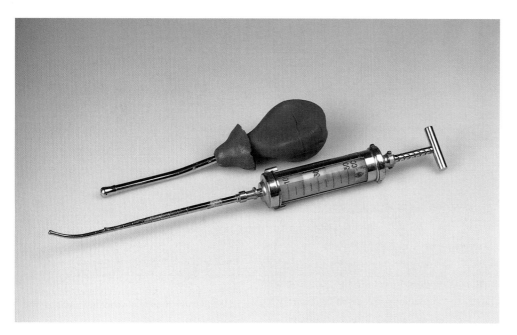

Abortion, or the deliberate termination of a pregnancy, is common throughout the world, although in many places it is highly restricted or sometimes outlawed altogether. Even amongst countries where abortion is legalized, there are wide variations regarding the circumstances in which a woman may have an abortion. This can include a gestational time limit, the types of health professionals licensed to perform abortions, and whether a woman's husband has given permission.

About 90 percent of abortions in Western countries are carried out early, in the first twelve weeks of pregnancy. Women choose to have abortions for many reasons, which may be psychological, physical, or social. Abortions may be carried out where there is a risk of the baby being born handicapped, or where there is physical or psychological risk to the mother or any existing children. The woman may feel that she is too young or old to have the child, or have concerns about the social and economic disadvantages that would be likely to face her and any existing children if she was to continue with the pregnancy.

In Western Europe and the United States, the campaign for legalized abortion began at the turn of the century, when in 1904 Countess Gertrud Bülow von Dennewitz in Germany published her pamphlet *Das Recht zur Beseiti-* *gung des keimenden Lebens* (The right to remove budding life) under the pseudonym Gisela von Streitberg. In the 1930s the English Women's Co-operative Guild advocated legalized abortion. However, it did not become a matter of widespread public debate until the 1960s and 1970s, when the women's liberation movement enabled women to challenge traditional policies, and legalization of abortion was secured. In Eastern European socialist states, such as Russia and East Germany, abortion was made legal in the 1950s, but its availability was regulated according to state population policy as opposed to women's demands for it.

In all countries before abortion became legalized, it was a private matter, surrounded by secrecy. Back-alley or self-administered abortions were common. In Victorian times, the only means of family limitation for most women was abortion. Methods included eating lead tablets or other poisons, drinking gin, falling downstairs, and puncturing the cervix using sharp pointed objects. Back-alley abortions in many developed countries continued right up to the late 1960s and 1970s when abortion was made legal. Women's experiences were invariably traumatic and painful, often resulting in terrible infections, loss of fertility, and sometimes even death. In developing countries, where legal abortion is still not readily available and there are few medical facilities, clandestine abortions are widespread. Each year, according to the World Health Organization, around 70,000 women die from unsafe abortions, the majority of whom are from Asia, Africa and Latin America. Hundreds of thousands more suffer from non-fatal consequences. In Vietnam, for example, where abortion is legal and widely practiced, anesthetic is not routinely used. In addition to this, surgical instruments are not sterilized, leading to widespread infection.

Attitudes towards abortion have varied across cultures throughout history. While abortion was permitted in Ancient Greece and Rome, women in ancient Assyria were impaled on stakes for attempting it. For most of its history, the Roman Catholic Church followed Aristotle's

Abortion policies worldwide. The legal status of abortion does not necessarily reflect the reality of abortion. Legality is not the same as availability. Most states which do allow abortion do so only under various degrees of restriction. In 15 countries abortion is generally illegal; in another 52 countries abortion is allowed only to save the life of the mother. Almost everywhere in the world restrictions on abortions exist: most countries have a gestational time limit, many require that only licenced doctors perform abortions, many others require a waiting period. In many countries women need the consent of their husbands, and minors of their parents.

belief that a male fetus did not gain a soul for 40 days, and a female fetus for 66 days after conception. In 1588 Pope Sixtus V declared all abortions murder, a definition reaffirmed in 1869 by Pope Pius IX. Since then, abortion at any stage of fetal development has been considered murder by the Catholic Church. The impact of this standpoint has been particularly felt in poorer Catholic countries such as Brazil and Mexico where the pressure on women not to have abortions is intense. Today, feelings about abortion continue to run high. In many countries anti-abortion activists – known as "pro-life" groups – argue that abortion is the taking of human life and should be made illegal, while the "pro-choice" groups argue that women have the right to control what happens to their bodies.

Several methods are currently used for abortion. Up until twelve weeks of pregnancy, abortion may be carried out using several surgical methods, where suction is used to remove the contents of the uterus, or by medical abortion, where drugs are given to induce the abortion. Vacuum aspiration is one of the most common methods of surgical abortion. The cervix is dilated and the contents of the uterus are emptied by suction with a device called a vacuum aspirator, through a thin plastic tube. Another method, called dilatation and curettage (D&C),

involves the cervix being dilated and an instrument being used to scrape the contents of the endometrium (uterine lining).

Medical or drug-induced abortion can also be used up to nine weeks into pregnancy. The woman takes RU 486 (Mifegyne), a drug that contains an antiprogesterone called mifepristone. This blocks the production of the progesterone, the hormone which enables the fertilized egg to stay attached to the uterine lining. Tablets or pessaries containing prostaglandin hormones are then given two days later, which make the uterus contract and trigger the abortion. Medical abortion is widely available in Europe but is not available in the United States due to the opposition from anti-abortion groups. In France, nearly half of all women seeking an abortion prefer the medical method to the surgical one.

Later abortions, from 13 to 24 weeks, are more traumatic both physically and emotionally because the woman is aborting a larger, more developed "baby-like" fetus. In addition to looking pregnant, the woman may also be conscious of fetal movements inside the womb, which may result in feelings of intense guilt and distress. In medical induction, drugs are also used to induce labor. Prostaglandins are given by pessary or injected into the uterus. After contractions, the

fetus is expelled. In about half of all cases, a vacuum aspiration or D&C is needed to completely empty the uterus. From 13 to 16 weeks, dilatation and evacuation (D&E) is used.

As in Europe in the 1970s, especially in France, England and Germany, some women in the United States demonstrated against the restrictive abortion legislation practiced by the majority of states and the cuts in governmental funding which meant that abortion was no longer available to poor women.

Making
Love

Taking a Position

The methods people choose to gain sexual satisfaction depend upon their culture, upbringing, age, gender orientation, state of health and a myriad of other factors, including the purpose – ranging from procreation to pleasure to profit. The methods also crucially depend upon the individual's choice of partner, because humans are the only animals known to teach each other about sex, and the only ones that consciously experiment in an effort to improve their love lives. This means that, in addition to coitus (classically defined as the insertion of a penis into a vagina), the human sexual repertoire includes oral and anal sex, interfemoral (between the thighs) and intermammary (between the breasts) sex, interspecies sex and a seemingly limitless menu of fetishes and obsessions. Most of them have been around for thousands of years, and have passed in and out of favor from culture to culture. Even within a society, customs vary enormously with social class and educational level. When the American sexologist Alfred Kinsey began compiling the material for his two groundbreaking reports – *Sexual Behavior in the Human Male*, 1948 and *Sexual Behavior in the Human Female*, 1953 – he found that the less well-educated men were, the more likely they would be to condemn oral sex, masturbation, pornography, breast licking and other forms of petting. When they had sex it was usually over quickly and performed in the "missionary position", with

minimal foreplay. They often kept on some item of clothing. Better-educated men would typically start having sex later in life, but when they did, it was likely to be in the nude, and much more adventurous. Although class structures have changed since those reports, the general findings seem to hold true throughout the world: even in relatively simple societies, status goes hand in hand with sexual sophistication, curiosity and experimentation.

Ever since the very first sex manuals, writers have been obsessed with cataloging and classifying the various possible positions, as if the sheer number of available alternatives would, on its own, be enough to guarantee a satisfying sex life. The *Handbook of the Dark Girl*, written in China before A.D. 200, contented itself with only nine, and gave them all poetic titles such as "cranes with long necks". The 7th-century Chinese physician, Tung-Hsuen, increased this number to 30, but most of them were merely variations on four basic types. The most famous sex book, the *Kamasutra* of Vatsyayana, written between the third and 5th centuries A.D., is the most glaring example of this trend to exaggerate the number of possible positions by labeling every minute, insignificant variation. It lists 529 in total, but most of them are physically indistinguishable. The position known as "congress of a cow", for example (the woman bends over, supporting herself on her hands and feet, and the man enters her from

behind), can be transformed into "the congress of a dog, the congress of a goat, the congress of a deer, the forcible mounting of an ass, the congress of a cat, the jump of a tiger, the pressing of an elephant, the rubbing of a bear, the mounting of a horse" simply by making the appropriate animal noises.

In the man-on-top position, the couple face each other with the man lying between the woman's legs supporting himself on his arms. As the man's penis glides in and out of the woman's vagina, the sexual momentum builds, leading to quicker thrusting, which usually results in orgasm. However, in this position, there is little opportunity for clitoral stimulation for the woman, and the man may tire of supporting himself on his hands. The position's other name, the missionary position, is probably derived from missionaries to the South Pacific islands who disapproved of the wide sexual repertoire adopted by local people. They tried to limit them to this single position and labeled it the only natural way of undertaking sexual intercourse. The man is in the dominant position, as husbands are supposed to be, according to Saint Paul (Colossians 3:18), and the chances of impregnation are relatively high, because sperm is retained in the vagina (and childbirth is, in traditional Christian thought, the only proper goal of sex). In parts of Italy it is so highly regarded that it is known as "the angelic position". The variations mostly

Rosewood toiletry case from China with eleven hidden miniatures. In China, books or collections of erotic paintings were once a common wedding gift, intended to give the new couple a crash-course in lovemaking technique. This 18th- or 19th-century box contains foldout panels, each depicting a different position.

involve the woman changing the position of her legs, for example by wrapping them around the man's waist, or bending them back along her own body. Although the missionary position is not especially efficient for stimulating the woman's genitalia, it is very popular even among the sexually sophisticated of both sexes because of the sensual eye- and full-body-contact it allows.

If the man squats between the woman's legs, rather than lying on top of her, he has adopted what is sometimes known as the oceanic position, because of its popularity in the islands of the South Pacific, although recently, under Western influence, there is evidence that it is falling out of favor even here. It is often recommended because deep penetration is possible, the man is visually stimulated by seeing the woman's naked torso and his own penis entering her, and the penis or a hand can stimulate the woman's clitoris directly. The Tallensi, in Africa, mention another advantage for the woman: if she gets bored, she can kick the man away very easily.

Since the time of the Greeks, rear-entry sex has been recommended as one of the best methods for impregnation. Couples can also use it during the late stages of pregnancy. Rear-entry positions can be highly stimulating for both partners, although some may find that they create emotional distance because the partners cannot see each other's faces. In traditional societies, it appears to be the favorite method

for quick, possibly forbidden couplings that are likely to be interrupted. The same is true of standing positions, which among the Fijians, for example, are reserved for people having affairs. The difficulty of maintaining balance during sex while standing can be solved in many imaginative ways. The Brazilian Mehinaku stand in water up to their chests, while Trukese lovers in the South Pacific each keep one foot supported on a tree stump. It is also common for one partner to lean against a wall. One of the most popular and often-portrayed positions in antiquity – first seen in a relief from the city of Ur, in Mesopotamia – involves the man lying on his back with the woman on top.

Count de Waldeck after Marcantonio Raimondi, *Aretino's Positions*, 1858. Some of the most influential erotic prints ever to be made in Europe were the *Sixteen Positions* engraved by Marcantonio Raimondi in 1524. According to legend, they were copies of drawings made by the artist Giulio Romano – a pupil of Raphael – on the wall of the Sala di Constantino in the Vatican. The papal censor destroyed the original plates, and only fragments of Raimondi's prints still exist, but the images have been preserved in a set of drawings made by the Count de Waldeck in 1858.

Niki de Saint-Phalle, *Lifesaver Fountain*, **1991/1993. Duisburg city center, Königstrasse.** The image of the *Lifesaver Fountain* is reminiscent of Asian temple carvings and of Tibetan sculptures that show Bodhisattvas and gods copulating with their female counterparts.

This has once again become a favorite in the modern West, at least in films. The woman sits astride the man and can control the pace and angle of penile thrusting. It also means that her partner can stimulate her clitoris manually, making her more likely to reach orgasm. For most of the Christian era this position was viewed with great suspicion. It was considered unnatural for the woman to be superior, and any man who preferred this method was suspected of homosexual tendencies.

A related position involves the man sitting – either on the ground or in a chair, while the woman squats over him. Both these postures are widely cited as the most satisfying for the woman, although in one cross-cultural survey it was asserted that no more than five percent of societies use them. They are also fairly restful for the man, and are thus useful during illness or convalescence. On the other hand, they are of limited use for impregnation, because semen is not retained in the vagina.

The positions in which neither partner is on top, but face each other lying side by side, are rarely mentioned in Western surveys, but are favored across much of Africa. Even peoples who do not choose them habitually, such as the Zande, often mention them as a good alterna-

A small Chinese ivory carving of lovers, 19th cent. C. 9 cm high, D. M. Klinger Collection, Nuremberg. Although the Taoists of China placed a great emphasis on sexual proficiency, Chinese artists were also adept at showing the tenderness and emotional bonds that existed between lovers.

tive when the woman is pregnant. Like the woman-on-top postures, they are usually quite restful, although many men find difficulty in penetrating the woman.

Many of the most acrobatic positions that are occasionally described in sex books, manuals and pornographic literature appear to be little more than fantasies. This includes the "flying fox", recorded in Fiji, in which the couple hang from a beam, and the "grand exploit" described

by the 16th-century Tunisian writer, Sheikh Nefzawi, in which the man sits on the woman's chest with his back to her face, and then grips her hips and bends her over until he slots her vagina over his penis. To his credit, Nefzawi notes that: "This position, as you perceive, is very fatiguing and difficult to attain. I even believe that the only realization of it exists in words." Other exotic possibilities require props and a retinue of helpers. One example, apparently found in expensive brothels from Shanghai to New York, incorporates a seat with a hole cut in the bottom, suspended from a pulley in the ceiling. The woman sits cross-legged (or in the lotus position) in the chair and is gently lowered by one or more assistants onto the penis of the man, who lies on his back beneath her. Then another assistant revolves the chair back and forth providing, in the words of one reporter, "a unique experience for the man and the woman".

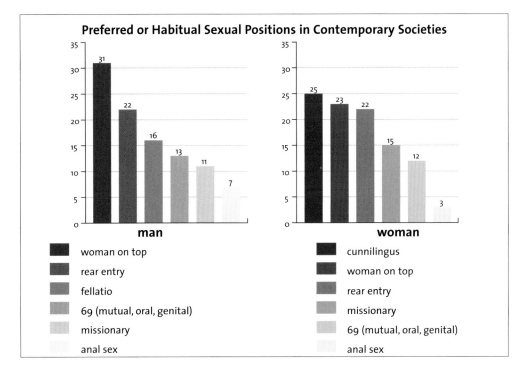

This chart is an average of the results obtained by magazine surveys conducted in Europe between 1995 and 1999. They were popular magazines aimed at a readership in the late-teen to mid-30 age range. The readers were asked what their favorite method of having sex was. The figures have been rounded to the nearest percent.

Arousal

Many factors trigger sexual arousal, and people vary greatly in terms of what turns them on sexually and how often they experience these feelings. Our senses play an important part in influencing what arouses us. Many of us are initially aroused by visual stimulus: by a person's appearance and by other visual cues such as erotic films and magazines. Touch can also be sexually stimulating. A lover's touch both during sex and at other times can be highly erotic. Our sense of hearing can also be a means of becoming sexually aroused, whether it is the voice of a lover during sex, a particular piece of music, or the voice of a particular film star or singer that we find attractive. Equally our sense of smell can lead to arousal. For instance, a waft of someone's perfume may trigger memories of an ex-lover.

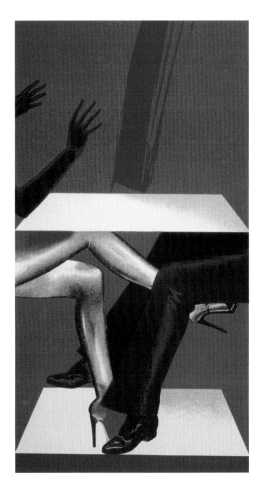

Allen Jones, *Magician Suite IV*, 1976. Screenprint, 10 x 7 cm, Cecil Higgins Art Gallery, Bedford. Playing footsy is the most popular form of secretive petting undertaken in public places.

Sexual arousal brings about changes in the body that prepare it for sexual activity. Describing the various stages of sexual response, American sexologists William Masters and Virginia Johnson called this phase the "excitement phase". In a woman's body, the most noticeable change is vaginal lubrication, which may occur instantaneously but can take up to 30 seconds from when stimulation begins. The secretions that are normally present in the vagina increase, giving a slipperiness which assists penile penetration. In a process called vasocongestion, increased blood flow within the genital tissues causes the clitoris and labia minora to swell, and flattening the labia minora, and spreading them apart. The inner two thirds of the vagina also expand and the vaginal walls turn a deeper purplish color due to the extra blood flow. The breasts swell and the nipples become erect.

In men, vasocongestion causes the penis to engorge with blood resulting in what is commonly known as an erection. The expansion of the arteries boosts blood flow dramatically, so that the penis hardens and becomes erect, increasing in length to about 12–18 cm (5–7 inches). To maintain the erection, the blood is prevented from leaving penis by the compression of veins, which run through the outer sheath of the penis, trapping the blood inside. The internal pressure rises and the blood flow in and out of the penis slows down. The response to stimulation tends to occur much more quickly in men than in women, with an erection often taking place within 5-10 seconds, although it may take longer in older men. The scrotum also tightens and thickens, and the testes swell and become raised.

In both women and men, the heartbeat and breathing rate increase. Muscle tension, known as myotonia, also takes place causing involuntary muscle spasms in the legs, arms and face. A reddening of the skin, or "sex flush", may appear across the chest and shoulders as the blood vessels near the surface of the skin become more prominent.

With increased sexual stimulation, the level of sexual arousal builds steadily to reach an advanced stage before sexual excitement peaks at orgasm. Masters and Johnson called this the "plateau phase". In women, the outer third of the vagina swells, which has the effect of contracting the vaginal opening. As the tissues around the clitoris swell further, the clitoris withdraws inside the hood. About three in four women have a sex flush at this stage. The areolas of the breasts may also become further engorged. A mucus-like fluid is secreted by the Bartholin's glands, which lie just inside the labia minora.

In men, the coronal ridge of the penis swells further and the Cowper's glands secrete a few drops of fluid, which appear at the end of the penis. The testes enlarge and are brought closer to the body to prepare for ejaculation. In both sexes breathing becomes more rapid, and may develop into panting. Blood pressure also begins to rise.

Flirting and Body Language

When people are sexually attracted to each other, a subtle, interactive body language takes place, often without any words being exchanged. They flirt through eye contact and by smiling at each other, often mirroring the other's expressions and gestures as a means of signaling their mutual attraction. The relationship usually builds slowly with each person giving and responding to small gestures of encouragement. Where verbal communication takes place, lighthearted conversation or "small talk" may be used while each assesses their feelings of attraction, determines whether they are mutual, and decides whether to try to develop the relationship. The communication may be further reinforced by moving closer together and by some form of body contact, such as touching the other person's arm. This type of discussion gives the opportunity to exchange information and to find common ground without disclosing intimate information until it is decided that the relationship should become more consolidated. In other instances, the eye contact and other body language used in flirting is an end in itself: an opportunity to behave amorously without there being any serious intention to develop the relationship further.

The Ritual of Getting Intimate

A glance establishes eye contact. Her expression encourages him to approach her.

He comes closer, but her hands – as if protecting her genitalia area – suggest overhastiness on his part.

He takes her hands and holds them in his – a greetings ritual, but also an attempt to establish trust.

He places his arm around her waist to try and establish some intimacy between them.

The center of attention moves from hands to lips and she lets him place his hand on her neck – a sign of trust.

They embrace each other. He has her firmly in his grasp – she holds him tightly.

Now his hand is moving to more private areas: her thigh. He still holds her with his other arm.

A touch on the breast is yet more intimate. A positive response to this would be for her to kiss him.

Aphrodisiacs and Love Spells

There have always been chemicals that have been used to heighten sexual pleasure – or at least increase the likelihood of sex – by reducing inhibitions. They include alcohol and marijuana, which, however have the serious disadvantage of simultaneously inhibiting performance, in the man at least, hence the phenomenon of the so-called "brewer's droop", a problem suffered by the porter in Shakespeare's *Macbeth*. Although there are now effective impotence cures, such as Viagra (which makes erections easier to achieve and sustain by increasing the flow of blood into the penis), most medical experts would contend that there is no such thing as a genuine aphrodisiac – a drug or other substance that, on its own, creates, prolongs or intensifies desire. Nevertheless, sexual lore is full of references to such substances. Some of them work by irritating the genito-urinary tract when they are excreted, which stimulates an artificial sense of arousal in the process, a sensation that some find enjoyable. The mashed-up seeds of the mucca-mucca plant are inserted directly into the penis by some of the natives of the Guianas in order to produce a similar effect, but the most famous of aphrodisiacal irritant is Spanish Fly, made from the dried and powdered bodies of cantharides beetles. These insects are also known as blister beetles because of the effect they have on human skin. Not surprisingly, Spanish Fly is considered extremely dangerous, and has been linked to a number of deaths among overeager lovers.

Another aphrodisiac thought to work in the same way is yohimbine, a crystalline substance made from the bark of the yohimbe tree, which

Lytta vesicatoria or Spanish Fly contains the poisonous substance cantharidine, used as aphrodisiac.

Scene from a comedy: Visit to a Sorceress, c. second cent. B.C. Mosaic from Pompeii, State Museum of Archeology, Naples. A sorceress is preparing a love potion for two young women. On the table there are a vessel, a pan for smoking herbs and a twig of laurel.

comes from the forests of the Cameroon and has apparently been used there by the Yohimbe people for centuries. Medical research suggests that its effects are purely psychosomatic, however, as it has to be taken in toxic amounts to produce any measurable physiological effects. The Fang, who come from the same part of Africa as the Yohimbe, probably use more aphrodisiacs than any other group on earth, but they are all based on magic rather than medicine, and include such objects as the bones of albinos and the teeth of chieftains. Most supposed aphrodisiacs, in fact, are magical in nature. Many are thought to take their power from their phallic shape, which explains why ginseng root is used in China and Southeast Asia, stag horn was once used in Europe and rhino horn is still used in much of the Far East. Less metaphorically, one of the earliest aphrodisiacs, popular in Ancient Egypt, was pow-

A Welsh Love Spell

A Celtic spell, which was still used in the early 20th century in rural Wales, calls for the lover to rise before dawn on a night when the moon is waxing and the Pleiades stars are in the night sky. He digs up a mandrake without damaging its root, while reciting over and over: "Gwyn eu fyd y pridd, y gwreiddyn a'r noson hony," – "Blessed be this earth, this root, this night." Then he carves it into an approximation of the beloved and gives it her name, before taking it to a churchyard or crossroads and reburying it. Any silver object is used to draw a cross in the soil, and then a mixture of one part milk and three parts water, with a few drops of the lover's blood, are sprinkled on the spot, to the chant: "Wrth y bedd y gwaed a'r llaeth/Wnaeth gadw A. i mi'n gaeth." –"Blood and milk upon the grave/Will ever make A. my slave."

dered crocodile penis. The mandrake root, which may resemble a tiny human figure or the genitals of either sex, was thought to be a cure for sterility throughout the ancient Levant. There is a reference to it as such in Genesis 30:14, although the only medical properties it actually appears to possess are as an emetic and an anesthetic. It is occasionally mentioned in medieval herbals as an aphrodisiac, but features more commonly in spells designed to awaken the desire or win the hearts of others. Another widespread belief in the ancient Near East and Mediterranean was that the liver was the seat of all passions, and that the liver of a young person who died while in love made both a powerful aphrodisiac and an irresistible love potion. Perhaps the earliest recorded love spell dates back to Ancient Sumeria, and consists of mixing the milk and fat of holy cows in a green bowl and sprinkling the resulting potion on the breasts of a young girl.

More commonly, love magic involves gaining power over the loved one by acquiring some personal object or body part, such as hair and nails, or alternatively, to bring the beloved into contact with one's own sweat, semen or menstrual blood. A typical spell comes from the Santeria cult, which originated among slaves taken to Cuba from the Yoruba nation of West Africa, and spread from there to Miami and New York. All the would-be lover has to do is make a hamburger, soak it in his or her own sweat (menstrual blood is also sometimes used) and then feed it to the object of desire. A comparable Scottish spell called for the lover to draw a circle on a wafer with blood from his or her ring finger, and then eat half the wafer while somehow getting the beloved to eat (or at least touch) the other half. Some cultures are especially renowned for their love magic, such as the Romanies in Europe, the Cree in North America, the Hausa in West Africa and the Trobriand Islanders in the South Pacific. Strangely, these are often also the people with the most pragmatic or even cynical attitude to desire: the Hausa, for example, have a saying that translates as: "The real charm for getting a woman is money."

Master from the Lower Rhine, *The Love Spell*, mid-15th cent. Oil on panel, 24 x 18 cm, Museum of Fine Arts, Leipzig. A heart made from wax is being melted in a container before the fire – an attempt, through sympathetic magic, to melt the heart of the beloved who, drawn by the spell, appears in the doorway.

***Codex of Dioscurides*, 5th cent. A.D. Austrian State Library, Vienna.** Dioscurides describes the qualities of the mandragora which is given to him by Euresis the goddess of invention. The plant had many magical uses, including love spells and mortal curses. In the foreground a dog is dying having eaten from the root.

The Kiss

It was Darwin's belief that the "drive to caress a beloved is innate." Yet kissing is allegedly unknown among the Somalians, the Thonga of South Africa, the Lepcha of Sikkim and the Siriono of Bolivia. It is fairly common in most other parts of the world and universal in the West. Westerners and Hindus are believed to be the most sophisticated kissers of all. The ancient Hindu manuals, including the *Kamasutra* of Vatsyayana, believed to have been completed between the third and 5th centuries A.D., describe many ways and stages of kissing on the lips, neck, shoulders and breasts. Kisses according to these texts can be used variously to arouse, comfort, express tenderness or form the playful, teasing and child-like qualities of love-making. A 7th-century work by the Chinese physician Tung Hsuen, which discusses the ritual of kissing, disproves the common Western misconception that the Chinese found it abhorrent. In fact it was regarded as a form of intimacy and sexual interchange so intense as to be comparable to coitus. As a result it was practiced only in the total privacy of the Jade Chamber. If a woman was seen kissing in public, her behavior was judged to be no better than that of a common prostitute. Kissing was the prelude to sexual intercourse and the man was advised to act with consideration, care and tenderness, indulging in exploration. Tung Hsuen suggested that even after the man's "jade stalk" was erect and the woman's "cinnabar cleft" moist, he should resist penetration, hovering over her genital area as he planted a

Gone with the Wind, **still from the film by Victor Fleming, 1939.** Clark Gable as Rhett Butler and Vivien Leigh as Scarlett O'Hara share one of the great, iconic screen kisses.

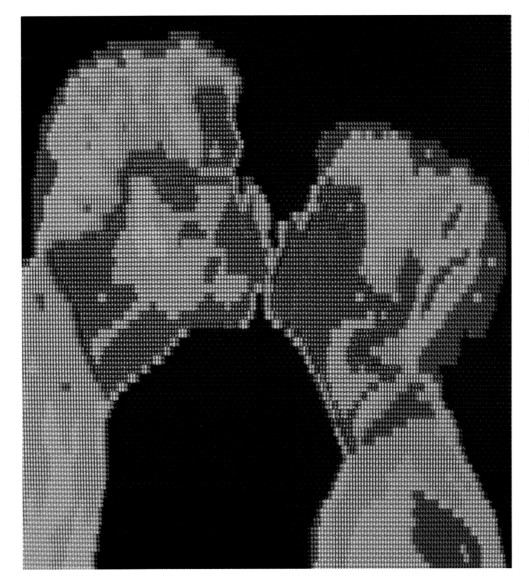

This thermal image of a couple kissing shows areas of increased blood flow due to arousal, as well as the heat shared between the kissers. The color chart runs from yellow, the hottest regions recorded, through to purple, the coolest.

strong kiss on her mouth before proceeding to intercourse. The Taoist Wu-Hsien wrote that the woman's saliva or "jade spring" was beneficial in that it involved the transfer of yin juices to the male.

Kissing publicly is regarded as immoral in some societies such as areas of the Islamic world, where couples may be prosecuted for "indecent behavior", a case in point being the arrest and indictment of a teenage couple in Kuwait in 1974 found kissing in a park. In the West, where mouth-to-mouth kissing in public is entirely normal and widely practiced, mostly by the young or among older people who are in the process of pair-bonding, it may be regarded as a "tie-sign". More established couples tend to kiss only lightly on the mouth in public places unless they have been or are about to be separated for a long period. They might also do so when in the process of rebonding after a profound mutual experience such as bereavement.

Whatever the circumstances of a kiss, it is always an indication of the desire to make a connection, albeit on a temporary or superficial basis. It is perhaps this seizing of license that reflects the well-known resistance of prostitutes to kiss customers on the mouth though they will indulge in all kinds of other sexual acts and practices.

The kiss, it would seem, is not entirely a sexual act but also an expression of tenderness, affection and good faith. This is probably why people embrace and kiss, in a non-sexual way, as part of a standard greeting. In many Mediterranean cultures this involves both men and women kissing on the mouth. In some parts of the Western world, particularly in high society, among the middle classes and the avant-garde, kissing on one or both cheeks is common, though more often than not the actual exchange involves no more than brief cheek to cheek contact popularly ridiculed as "kissing

the air". The gesture has been explained by some as an antidote to marking someone's face with lipstick. Photographs of politicians kissing babies in an attempt to show their human side to the world are much maligned and have taken on the status of a popular joke. The image is almost universally mocked and closer in the public psyche to the treacherous kiss of Judas that betrayed Jesus rather than a demonstration of genuine goodness.

Some anthropologists subscribe to the view that the origins of kissing lie in the old practice among birds, primates, and some humans, of the mother chewing food to soften it before passing it into the mouth of her infant. In response the young one probes inside the mother's mouth to forage for as many scraps as it can get, using the tongue to reach into the crevices beneath the tongue and the inner cheek area. These are precisely the movements replicated in the well-known French kiss.

Moustache Kiss, c. 1890. Even in purely social kissing, facial hair can evoke a wide variety of responses in the person being kissed, from pleasure to disgust. Between lovers, these feelings are magnified. Some enjoy the tickling sensation of a moustache, or even the abrasive qualities of a stubble. Others will not tolerate them.

Here the tongues of the kissers, which penetrate each other's mouths for exploration and stimulation, mirror genital sex. One might question then, why the mother-infant activity does not lead to more instances of incest. In 1971, sociologist Joseph Shepher working in Israel with second-generation adolescents and adult participants in several kibbutzes, suggested that at some stage between the ages of three and six, children develop a spontaneous sexual aversion to those who they see on a daily basis. This includes members of their family. The kiss thus serves its alternative function as a social exchange or greeting.

At its most basic, kissing is simply the act of touching another with one's lips and the area upon which the kiss is planted is significant, often suggesting a hierarchy. As a general rule, kisses to the head signify superiority; to the face, neck and torso, equality; to the hands and below, inferiority. An adult or parent may kiss a child upon the head, the forehead or, in the case of small children, on the tip of the nose, thus establishing an adult-to-child dynamic. In some countries such as Iran and some parts of Pakistan, for example, younger members of the family and social group kiss the hands of elders, an action which involves bowing or at least inclining the head as a mark of subservience. This was also noted as an act of deference among the chimpanzees at the Arnhem Zoo in

the Netherlands in an experiment begun in 1971, where inferior male chimps bowed their heads and stooped their shoulders to kiss the hands, feet, neck and chest of the alpha male. In Europe until the turn of the 20th century it was part of accepted protocol for a man to kiss a woman's hand on meeting. Again, this involved a bow, which many men used with a flourish to emphasize their gallantry and sophistication. However, the more dominant male preferred to raise the lady's hand up to his lips to avoid bowing. This apparently neutral and widespread kiss could be used to convey great admiration and sexual interest by its quality and length as well as by accompanying signs such as extra pressure on the hand or the locking of the gaze.

Such interactions continue to be exchanged among acknowledged lovers. In public the love-glance or "copulatory gaze" is a frank, private statement of sexual interest involving defiance, risk-taking and bonding – a kiss without physical contact, perhaps across a crowded room. In a private, sexual context, hierarchical kissing expresses the many levels of romantic love: gentleness, playfulness, reverence and many other replications and transformations of love from the diverse contexts of human experience: maternal tenderness, protectiveness, child-play, mock battles or play violence.

The first kiss in a relationship has immense significance and has provided much inspiration for both movies and romantic novels. Perhaps the most famous fictional kisses are those that awoke both Sleeping Beauty and Snow White from sleep as deep as death. These life-restoring kisses may be a resonance of the Orphic view, propounded through Plato, that the kiss constitutes the exchange of souls between Lover and Beloved. These kisses give a spiritual dimension also accessible in the lives and works of courtly poets.

In any event, the kiss is a powerful interaction, often the first act of sexual exchange, which awakens deep-seated sexual desires. The physical reactions to kissing in the early stages of a relationship may include a pounding heart, a dry mouth and sweaty palms. Some sense of disorientation may also be experienced. This is understandable since at this stage of a potential relationship, deep and disturbing emotions are also very much part of the romantic equation, bringing to the fore feelings of self-doubt, reciprocation and jealousy. In women's fiction such as that produced by the well-known publishers Mills and Boone, writers are often advised to build tension for several chapters following the instant and recognizable attraction of the central couple, before introducing the first kiss. It may well come as a complete shock to the female character who imagines that her love-object dislikes her. Much feminist controversy has been generated by the often vi-

olent nature of this first kiss, which at times comes almost in the form of an attack or at the very least an act to establish dominance, and may leave the heroine not simply dazed but also with a "bruised" mouth. However, when desire is mutual, the depth and intensity of the first kiss is undeniable whether tender and anticipated or rough and sudden.

In the initial stages of a relationship, kissing in the heat of passion often becomes frenetic and frequently involves some "hurting" activity. Biting, sucking and scratching are quite common and leave visible signs on the relevant part of the body, such as the infamous "love-bite", most common among adolescents and new lovers. Lips, too, become obviously reddened and inflamed, occasioning comparison with the vulva. However, as relationships become more established, the kiss generally loses its initial

intensity, though for most couples it remains an intimate and pleasurable activity and one that continues to express affection, and intimacy, echoing the passion of earlier stages in a relationship.

In 1967, the zoologist Desmond Morris suggested that the human attributes of breasts and "everted" lips are evolutionary replications of the genito-sexual areas in female animals, where the rump and vulva are constantly available as indicators of sexual readiness to the male. They are thus the focal points that trigger the reproductive response in males and arouse their sexual instincts. The reddening of the lips, once regarded as a sign of immorality, employed by prostitutes and "scarlet" women to openly attract men, continues to be discussed in feminist discourse, though no consistent conclusion has yet been reached.

H. Lefler and J. Urban, The Prince Wakes Sleeping Beauty from Her Sleep with a Kiss, from a calendar of fairy-tale motives, 1914. In fairy tales the kiss is a symbol of transformation and redemption – whether waking Sleeping Beauty or Snow White or turning a frog back into a handsome prince, a kiss has a restorative effect.

Erotic Eating

In the Old Testament Song of Songs, the lovers compare each other to aloes, apples, cinnamon, honey, mandrake, milk, nuts, orchard fruits, saffron, unspecified spices, wine, wheat and grapes. The list of exotic foodstuffs is long, but not unusual in declarations of love. Sheikh Nefzawi in the 16th-century erotic manual, *The Perfumed Garden*, describes a woman's flesh as "mellow like fresh butter," and girls have frequently been complimented on their peaches-and-cream complexions or the fruitlike bloom of their youth. But it was probably the novelist Henry Fielding (1707–1754) who was most brutally explicit about the nature of hunger, both sexual and otherwise, when he wrote in *Tom Jones* (1749) about, "what is commonly called love, namely the desire of satisfying a voracious appetite with a certain quantity of delicate white human flesh". The 1963 film of *Tom Jones*, directed by Tony Richardson, contains what is probably the most erotic "eating scene" in cinematic history.

The link between food and desire is hardly surprising. Both eating and sex stimulate a primitive region of the mid-brain called the nucleus acumbens, which floods the brain with dopamines, and in sufficient quantities causes an almost narcotic high. More specifically, some particularly addictive foods such as chocolate are rich in phenylethylamine (PEA), a mood-altering chemical which one researcher describes as providing a "feeling of post-coital bliss". (In its alcoholic form, PEA is the fragrance of rosewater, so the now-outdated habit of turning up on a first date with a bouquet of roses and a box of chocolates may have a sound biochemical basis.) Some foods also duplicate sexual odors – the characteristic pheremonal male scent, for example, can be found in parsley and truffles, although it is rarely identified as such. Innumerable other foods, including oysters, spices, tomatoes, and lampreys, have at different times been touted as aphrodisiacs, although this seems based on their appearance or flavor rather than on any demonstrable effect: the warmth of a spice might be thought to warm the passions, for example, while lampreys are vaguely phallic-shaped fish, and oysters have been compared to a woman's genitalia. Sex often mimics the actions of eating. A number of anthropologists have speculated that the kiss originated as a feeding gesture among our ancient ancestors, and Sigmund Freud described an entire stage of human sexuality as

La Grande Bouffe, **still from the film by Marco Ferreri, 1973.** This film tells the story of four successful middle aged men who decide, one weekend, to eat themselves to death, and of the women who join them – three prostitutes, who do not last long, and a local teacher who stays to the end. The emotions of the characters are revealed between bouts of eating and intercourse.

Billy Boys. Billy Boys are popular Belgian rolls, baked into the shape of genitalia. They continue a tradition that probably dates back to at least the ancient Egyptians.

the "oral phase". He thought that the child sucking at its mother's breasts was fulfilling a sexual urge and did not in fact differentiate between eating and sexual pleasure. Later psychiatrists, such as Melanie Klein, extended this analysis beyond the pleasure of sucking, and considered the fear, denial, anger and loss that might be associated with a mother's refusal to feed, or the withdrawal of her breast from the child. Such theorists point out that, while all children first experience female flesh (the mother's breast) as something to be consumed, boys continue to feel this to be their natural right. Girls learn to repress their feelings and to see themselves as a source of nourishment rather than appetite. It is almost always women who are compared to food in literature. Even such a famous libertine as Lord Byron could not stand watching women eating heartily. It could be said that he believed that their role was to be consumed by him, and any display of reciprocal appetite was not arousing, but a threat to his masculinity.

Be Tender, Penguin, **still from the film by Peter Hajek, 1982.** This German film parodies the conventions of the sex film, including the "decadence" of being fed.

A great deal of chocolate's stimulating effect comes from the presence of the alkaloids caffeine and theobromine.

Eating and Absorbing

The anthropologist Claude Lévi-Strauss referred to cannibalism as "alimentary incest", and the taboos governing both the act of cannibalism and the act of incest often show striking parallels. Australian Aborigines have a complicated set of marriage restrictions, based on clans or totem groups, each of which has a specific sacred animal, which is regarded as the spiritual ancestor of the group. Among other rules, individuals are not allowed to marry within their own clan. Neither are they allowed to hunt or even touch their own totem animal, except on certain ceremonial occasions, when they are obliged to kill and eat it.

This is only metaphorical cannibalism, but the genuine thing can also serve as a symbolic way of claiming fellowship or ownership. The Tupinamba of South America, before they ate the bodies of enemies, adopted them into the tribe, offering them wives, making them welcome and almost treating them as pets. Eating them was simply the final stage in absorbing them and making them wholly Tupinamba. This process of absorption provides the erotic charge that can be detected in many cannibal stories. Eating another human being fuses their flesh with one's own; a dream at the core of so many sexual fantasies and one that, in this case, does not have to end with orgasm. The serial killer, Jeffrey Dahmer (1960 –1994), is one of the most grotesque modern examples of this impulse. Pale and physically unthreatening, he chose male lovers who complemented him – black or Asian men, symbolic to Dahmer of strength, potency and danger – and, unsatisfied with sex, chose to incorporate them into himself by eating them.

In popular culture, this powerfully sexual idea of two people fusing into the same essence is most easily observed in vampire stories and films, from Bram Stoker's original *Dracula* to the more modern, overtly erotic stories of Anne Rice and Poppy Z. Brite. A vampire may simply choose to dine on its victim, but if it wants to turn the victim into a vampire like itself, it must first feed on the victim by sucking his blood, and then break its own skin and allow the victim to feed on it, forming a living circuit of vital fluid.

Interview with the Vampire, **still from the film by Neil Jordan, 1994.** Tom Cruise plays the vampire Lestat, and Brad Pitt is his victim, and later partner, Louis, in a film based on the novel by Anne Rice.

Foreplay

Foreplay, or erotic stimulation before intercourse, plays a major part in arousal and in preparing each partner for the sexual activity that follows. It exists in many forms including kissing, hugging, caressing, mutual masturbation and oral sex. The pattern of foreplay and its duration depends on both individual and cultural factors. Researchers conducting a study found that prolonged foreplay was the norm in about half the societies they looked at, while almost non-existent in a third. In Western countries, women tend to want more foreplay than men. Because arousal in a woman takes longer, extended foreplay may help her to reach orgasm as well as increasing her overall sense of sexual satisfaction. Women, and many men, also find the touching and caressing of foreplay highly enjoyable in its own right and view it as a means of deepening intimacy between partners. Kissing as part of foreplay can be either light and soft or deep and more intense. During light

kissing, the mouth is closed, while in deep kissing, the mouth is open and the tongue is sometimes used. As well as mouth-to-mouth kissing, people often enjoy having other parts of their body kissed during foreplay, such as hands, feet, neck, earlobes, breasts and genitals.

Like kissing, caressing the entire body, paying particular attention to the erogenous zones, is highly arousing for both men and women. The hands, mouth or other parts of the body can all be used for this purpose. A woman may prefer to have other parts of her body stimulated, such as breasts, lower abdomen and inner thighs, before her partner moves on to genital touching. Genital touching may include gently caressing or stroking the clitoral area, the vaginal lips and the mons. Some women enjoy having one or two fingers inserted into their vagina as part of foreplay. In addition to having other parts of their body touched, men may prefer direct stroking of their genitals early during

Opposite: **Louis Léopold Boilly, *Prélude*, c. 1786. Oil on canvas, 33 x 40 cm, Pushkin State Museum, Moscow.** In the socially rigid world of the salon and drawing room, men were expected to perfect the art of the elaborate, theatrical, long-drawn-out seduction, but they rarely brought the same patience and attention to detail to their lovemaking.

Egon Schiele, *The Embrace (Lovers II)*, 1917. Oil on canvas, 100 x 170.2 cm, Österreichische Galerie, Vienna. Schiele's paintings emphasize the desperation and struggle in sex. Although there is often great pathos, there is usually little room for tenderness.

body that are normally hidden become exposed gradually. As a way of building sexual tension, some couples undress each other and engage in other types of foreplay such as kissing and caressing. Staying partially dressed throughout sex is another turn-on for many people, adding to the sense of excitement and urgency. A person's underwear may or may not be sexually arousing to their partner. Some men like women to wear "sexy" underwear, such as fine, lacy brassieres, which leave the breasts and nipples partly exposed. Many women prefer men to wear boxer shorts and a T-shirt rather than briefs and a vest.

Foreplay is often viewed as a prelude to sexual intercourse, but as the sexual excitement builds through genital touching, mutual masturbation or oral sex, it may become an end in itself, leading to orgasm.

foreplay. Typical stimulation includes caressing the shaft and head of the penis, or using fingers to encircle the coronal ridge between the head and shaft of the penis, and moving the fingers up and down. At the same time, men also often enjoy having the skin of their scrotum lightly squeezed. Some, but not all, men, enjoy having their nipples caressed. The partners may also carry out mutual masturbation, when

they stimulate each other's genitals simultaneously. Communication is a vital part of satisfying foreplay, so partners need to make their preferences clear by describing or showing what they like, by listening to each other and by watching body language and facial expressions. Undressing as part of foreplay can be highly arousing. For maximum erotic effect, clothes need to be removed slowly, so that parts of the

The Art of Massage

Many couples find that a sensual massage as part of foreplay is both highly pleasurable and arousing. The act of being touched or stroked slowly and deliberately during massage can be powerfully erotic for both partners. As well as heightening anticipation for sex, massage promotes a relaxed state, allowing a person to focus solely on their partner's touch and their body's response to it. For the masseur too, the act of massaging is also highly erotic, both in terms of discovering – or rediscovering – their partner's body, and in enjoying their response to the massage.

Massage as foreplay should be a completely sensuous experience. Many couples light candles, play soft or sexy music, and ensure that the room they are using is warm and comfortable. Massage oils – often scented – are an important part of the experience, allowing the masseur's hands to glide over their partner's body. Communication should ideally be through touch alone and non-verbal feedback. Sensual massages tend to involve caressing the entire body before focusing on the person's erogenous zones, including their buttocks, inner thighs, breasts and finally their genital area.

The Caress, **Peruvian terra-cotta sculpture, Institute for Sex Research, Bloomington.** Masturbation, whether as a solitary or a shared activity, was a common theme of ancient South American ceramics.

Oral Sex

The use of the mouth and tongue to stimulate a partner's genitals is an important means of giving and receiving sexual pleasure for many people. In some ways it is the most intimate of sexual acts and can be deeply satisfying for both partners.

Stimulation of the male genitals – called fellatio – may include kissing or licking the glans or shaft of the penis, or taking the penis into the mouth and moving the mouth up and down to simulate the motion of the penis during vaginal intercourse. The soft, warm and moist interior of the mouth is highly stimulating for the penis, sharing many qualities with the vagina. The muscles of the mouth and jaw, and the use of tongue can be used to vary pressure and type of oral caress. Licking or nibbling the scrotum can also have a powerfully erotic effect.

Stimulating a woman's genitals orally is known as cunnilingus. Many women find this a more effective means of reaching orgasm than sexual intercourse. They can become highly aroused by their partner's tongue because it is soft, warm and well-lubricated. In performing cunnilingus, a woman's partner may start by kissing and licking her inner thighs or lower abdomen before using the tongue to caress the vulva and vagina, and then eventually moving on to oral stimulation of the clitoris.

Some people do not feel comfortable about engaging in oral sex. This may be due to shyness or embarrassment about having this most intimate part of their bodies in direct view of their partner, or fears that they or their partner will smell or taste bad. Some perceive the genitals as "dirty" because they are close to the urinary and anal openings. However, with proper hygiene there should only be the normal healthy smell of genitals during sexual arousal, which is usually perceived as erotic by sexual partners. Women may dislike the thought of swallowing semen. This can be avoided by a woman asking her partner to let her know when he is nearing ejaculation so that she can remove his penis from her mouth while continuing stimulation with the fingers to bring him to orgasm. Perhaps the most famous oral sex technique is the sixty-nine or *soixante-neuf* position, refer-

The "standing-kneeling" position for oral sex is fairly uncommon among heterosexual lovers, because of the apparently submissive attitude of the kneeling partner.

ring to mutual oral sex. The name is used because the position of the partners resembles the number in written form – the couple face each other's genitals by lying side by side but having their heads in opposite directions. However, many couples find the position unsatisfactory as it does not allow either person to focus completely on either giving or receiving oral sex, and so many prefer to take it in turns. Oral sex has long been an important expression of human sexuality. However, historically it was

often condemned in Western, Christian-based societies because it was about sexual pleasure rather than procreation. In preliterate societies where sexual experimentation was accepted and enjoyed, oral sex was often practiced between men and women, and between men. In the 1880s, a white American doctor working on a reservation of American Crow Indians was horrified to discover the practice was common, noting that of all the many varieties of sexual perversions, this seemed to him the most debased that could be conceived of. In the second half of the 20th century, oral sex has become increasingly widespread in the Western world, due in part to a widespread acceptance that sex is about pleasure rather than just reproduction. In a 1953 study in the United States, sexologist Alfred Kinsey found that 48 percent of women aged 18–36 had performed fellatio while 51 percent of their partners had performed cunnilingus. In 1994, another American researcher, Edward O. Laumann, found that around 74 percent of women and 80 percent of men had experienced oral sex. Sociocultural factors also influence its practice. American research has shown that higher incidence of oral sex correlates with higher levels of education.

In the United States, ethnicity also plays a part in the incidence of oral sex. African Americans, it seems, are less likely to engage in the practice than white Americans. This is perhaps due in part to some cultural groups having more traditional ideas about what is regarded as acceptable sexual behavior.

Hans Baldung Grien, *Young Witch and Dragon*, 1514. Drawing, 29.5 x 20.7 cm, Staatliche Kunsthalle, Karlsruhe. This drawing shows a common fantasy – the tongue as penis-substitute.

Viennese illustrator "AL", *69 Position*, 1989. Charcoal drawing, 23 x 29.5 cm, D. M. Klinger Collection, Nuremberg. Most books and illustrations, when they show the 69 position, have the woman on top, as here. In practice, this often gives the man a crick in the neck. If the couple lie on their sides they can avoid this problem. The cascade position is another variant on *soixante-neuf*, in which the man stands while the woman hangs upside down.

Intercourse and Orgasm

Sexual intercourse, when the penis enters the vagina, is also known as coitus – from the Latin word *coire*, meaning "to go together". Although many other types of sexual activity, such as oral sex and mutual masturbation, can be continued right up to orgasm, vaginal intercourse is usually perceived as the ultimate goal of a sexual encounter.

Intercourse can be undertaken in numerous positions; hundreds are described in the ancient Indian text *Kamasutra*. However as with all sexual activity, communication and sensitivity to each other's needs are more important than technique or athleticism.

As well as using different positions, intercourse can be varied in other ways, such as by altering the depth and rate of thrusting and by introducing additional sexual stimulation, such as simultaneous masturbation.

At the height of sexual excitement, orgasm occurs in both women and men when they experience an explosion of intense physical sensation. In their description of the sexual response cycle, researchers Masters and Johnson refer to this as the "orgasmic phase". In men, this feeling is usually accompanied by ejaculation, which is when semen spurts from the penis. Contractions of the vas deferens, seminal vesicles, ejaculatory duct and the prostate gland cause seminal fluid to collect in the urethra. The internal sphincter in the bladder also contracts, preventing urine from mixing with the semen. The flow of semen in the urethra produces feelings in the man that ejaculation is inevitable. Muscular contractions in

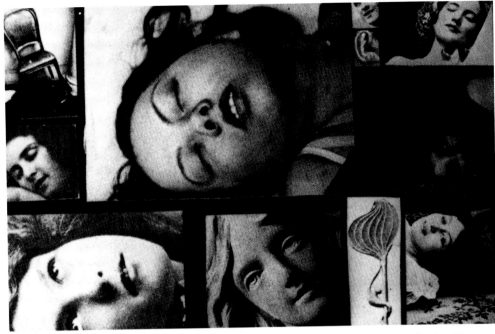

Salvador Dalí, *Le Phénomène de l'Extase* (detail), 1933. Photocollage, 27 x 18.5 cm, private collection. The experience of orgasm has been widely compared, by poets, philosophers, novelists and religious visionaries, to a "little death" – a moment of oblivion in which the ego dissloves and the boundaries that separate the self from the rest of the universe disappear.

the urethra and penis pump the seminal fluid through the urethra and out of the body. These contractions are accompanied by feelings of intense pleasure. The strength of the orgasm varies from man to man depending on age, level of arousal, sexual experience and other factors.

In the aftermath (the "resolution phase" of the sexual response cycle) the body relaxes and heartbeat, breathing and blood pressure return to normal. In what is called a refractory period, the man quickly loses his erection and is incapable of experiencing another ejaculation, for a few minutes or up to a day, depending on age.

In women, the strength of orgasm also varies from individual to individual. It is usually accompanied by rhythmical contractions of the pelvic muscles surrounding the vagina, and of the uterus and anal sphincter. During sexual arousal, the clitoris and other sex organs are engorged with blood, and a sex flush spreads over the upper torso. The nipples also swell and become erect. As in men, there may also be muscular spasms in other parts of the body. The woman feels the orgasm beginning around the clitoris, vagina and uterus often with intensely pleasurable feelings spreading throughout the body. Some women experience a type of ejaculation during orgasm when a clear fluid produced by glands near the opening of the urethra is expelled from the urethra.

During the resolution phase, the sex organs reduce to their pre-aroused state, the nipples return to normal size and breathing rate and blood pressure subside. Unlike men, women do not undergo a refractory period and can quickly become rearoused with continued stimulation. Additionally, they may be able to experience multiple orgasms.

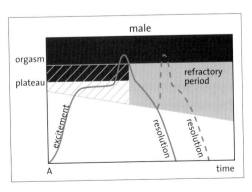

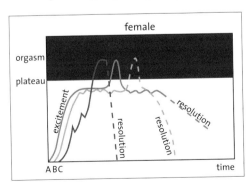

Levels of sexual arousal. The two graphs are showing four phases of sexual response: excitement, plateau, orgasm, and resolution. For men, the refractory period becomes longer after each orgasm. As for women, the course of sexual arousal is different for every woman or even for one and the same woman at different times.

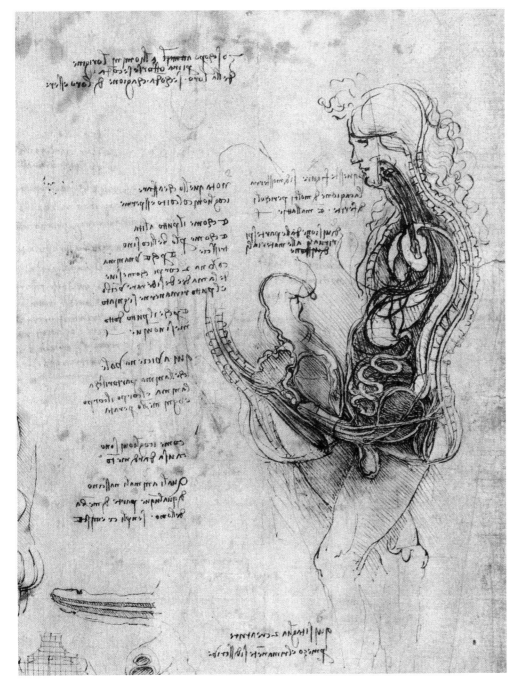

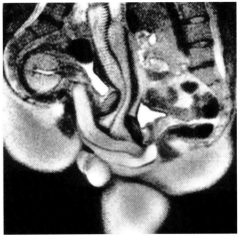

Leonardo da Vinci, Coition of Hemisected Man and Woman, 1501. Pen and ink, 27.3 x 20.2 cm, Anatomical Manuscript c. III. 3, Collection of Her Majesty the Queen, Windsor Castle, Windsor. Despite his reputation as a pioneering anatomist, Leonardo makes a number of mistakes on this sketch. He shows a duct leading from the brain to the testes (it was commonly believed, following the ancient Greek physicians, that semen came from the brain). He also shows the penis as a more-or-less straight structure (in order to achieve the correct proportions, Leonardo bent the woman over backwards).

This magnetic resonance image of the male and female genitals during coitus shows that during "missionary position" coitus, the penis is not straight, but has the shape of a boomerang.

There have been many myths about the female orgasm. Psychoanalyst Sigmund Freud suggested that there were two types of orgasms: clitoral and vaginal. He believed that clitoral orgasm was achieved through direct clitoral stimulation such as masturbation, and was connected with a childhood fixation. In contrast, vaginal orgasms were achieved through deep penile thrusting, and were perceived as more intense and the result of a mature sexuality. However, sexologists Masters and Johnson found during their research that women had the same type of orgasm whether it occurred during sexual intercourse, masturbation or oral sex. They also showed that the clitoris played a central role in enabling women to experience orgasm during intercourse, due to the stimulation of the clitoral hood by the man's penis or pelvic bone rubbing against the clitoris. It is now widely accepted that most orgasms are achieved by clitoral stimulation, and for many women this is most likely to happen with a direct approach such as oral or manual stimulation as opposed to sexual intercourse.

Anal intercourse is also practiced by some male-female couples (sometimes as a contraceptive technique), as well as by male couples. In some countries anal intercourse is illegal, and many people are repelled by it. However, there are others who are attracted by the dominant and submissive roles that it entails and the sensations it triggers. Because the rectum is rich in nerve endings, it is highly sensitive to sexual stimulation. Anal sex can damage the delicate rectal lining and has a higher risk of transferring sexually transmitted diseases especially AIDS. For women, bacteria can also be transferred from rectum to vagina. Using a strong condom and plenty of lubrication can reduce the risk.

Sexual Difficulties

Woman Looking for Man's Potency in His Pants with a Light. It is rare to show a woman as anxious as her husband about his virility, even in cartoons.

Many people experience sexual problems from time to time. They can occur at any stage in a person's life, triggered by stress, boredom, fatigue, childbirth, illness, physiological disorders and many other factors. Often the cause is both physical and emotional. This type of problem can put a heavy strain on sexual relationships, resulting in feelings of guilt, anxiety, frustration and failure for both partners. Many people also feel embarrassed about seeking help. Yet while some problems may need medical treatment or counseling, some difficulties can often be solved or even avoided, with open, honest and sensitive communication between sexual partners.

Impotence, or the inability to maintain or achieve an erection, is common amongst men of all ages. Psychological factors such as stress, fatigue, lack of sexual arousal or anxiety about sexual performance are often the cause. The anxiety of not being able to achieve an erection may create a vicious circle in which every instance of impotence leads to further anxiety. The "sensate focus technique" – playful, non-coital, non-goal-oriented touching and caressing between partners, that grows in intimacy at a pace that both find comfortable – is sometimes recommended to help with the problem. There may also be physical reasons why some men have erection difficulties. These include spinal cord disorders, diabetes, alcohol abuse and the side effects of both prescription and recreational drugs. Additionally, as men get older, altered circulation and lower testosterone levels may make it more difficult for them to achieve or sustain an erection.

Several types of treatment are available to these men. Injections, which are often self-administered just before intercourse, increase blood flow within the penis causing an erection. A second method is the vacuum device. This is fitted over the penis and pumped to remove air, engorging the penis with blood. A constricting rubber band around the base of the penis helps to maintain the erection. Another method involves inserting penile implants or prostheses made from silicon. The modern drug, Viagra, is also sometimes used to overcome erection difficulties by increasing blood flow in the penis, as well as boosting libido.

Premature ejaculation is the most common problem among younger men. Because they are so easily aroused, it may take less than a minute for them to reach ejaculation during intercourse. Techniques to delay ejaculation include the squeeze technique where the erect penis is grasped near the base and squeezed gently to reduce arousal. The stop-start technique, developed by American sexologists Masters and Johnson, is also highly effective. This involves the man learning to recognize the feelings just before ejaculation becomes inevitable, and stopping all forms of sexual stimulation for several seconds so that his arousal levels drop.

Retarded ejaculation is another problem, where the man finds it impossible to ejaculate during intercourse. Causes may be physical, such as spinal cord damage, or psychological, where the problem can often be overcome with sex therapy. Painful intercourse, sometimes called dyspareunia, may have several causes including soreness or chafing of the penis as a result of too much sex, a sexually transmitted disease or infection, or a tight foreskin resulting in a painful erection. In the former case, temporary abstinence or lubrication may help, and in the latter two cases medical help should be sought. Female sexual difficulties also have a complex range of physical and psychological dimensions. One of the most distressing problems is vaginismus, which is when the vaginal muscles contract involuntarily, making penetration by the penis painful or impossible. Caused by a fear of penetration, women with vaginismus may have deep-seated fears about sex and a history of sexual trauma. In mild cases, less focus on penetration during sex may gradually ease the problem. In more serious cases, sexual counseling combined with physical awareness exercises is often effective.

Painful intercourse may be the result of vaginal dryness, vaginismus, a vaginal infection, sexually transmitted disease, or pelvic inflammatory disease. Emotional factors such as a fear of sexual contact may also play a part.

RABE

The development of the anti-impotence drug Viagra was a source of mirth to millions, and secret relief to millions more. It works by relaxing the muscles in the penis and unconstricting the blood vessels so that the penis becomes engorged.

During and after the menopause, many women suffer from vaginal dryness. Hormonal changes mean that a woman produces less lubrication when sexually stimulated. Dryness can also be a problem for younger women, and is usually the result of insufficient stimulation before intercourse. The problem can be solved with longer foreplay to ensure that the woman is fully aroused before penetration is attempted, and the use of lubricants such as KY jelly.

Lack of sexual desire often occurs at specific times in a woman's life. The physical and emotional strain of pregnancy and childbirth may cause a woman to lose interest in sex for several months or even longer. Couples need to take time to relax together and to enjoy each other's bodies, for example through kissing, caressing and massage, before gradually reintroducing intercourse when the woman is ready. Hormonal changes during menstruation or the menopause may also result in loss of libido. As for men, a woman's lowered sex drive can also be specific to a certain partner, or due to stress, fatigue, illness or a lack of self-esteem. Sex therapy and simple exercises such as the sensate focus technique can help to overcome these problems.

Inability to achieve orgasm is relatively common, affecting around one in ten women. Because in most cases women can learn to have orgasms, the term used to describe the condition is "preorgasmic". With sexual counseling a woman discovers, through masturbation, what stimulates her sexually, and then subsequently learns to incorporate this into sexual activity with her partner.

Sex Aids and Sex Toys

The sex toy industry is always ready to exploit the insecurities of women, and, more particularly, men. The vacuum devices that are sometimes used to treat impotence are repackaged as "guaranteed" penis enlargers. For the man who feels that his penis is inadequate but is not prepared to plunge it into a vacuum chamber, there are any number of strap-on-sheaths and extensions, designed to be soft and lubricated on the inside, while allowing the man to feel that he is providing his lover with up to several inches extra in length or girth. Those cursed with premature ejaculation can find sprays and creams that promise to give "total control, for as long as is needed." Most of these are complete scams and do not even contain the mild local anesthetic that their packaging suggests.

"Lifelike" is the promise most often made by the manufacturers of sex toys, and the one least often kept. Inflatable dolls are often advertised as having hair, although this may be little more than a glossy dab of paint. Female dolls usually have three orifices – mouth, vagina and anus. In deluxe models, one or more of these may have battery-powered vibrating action. There are also inflatable male dolls, with erect penis and mouth and anal orifices.

Masturbation – The Imaginary Curse

More than any other aspect of sexual behavior, the subject of masturbation has always been a magnet for pamphleteers, Bible-thumpers and zealots. Although the Bible has nothing concrete to say on the subject, masturbation came to preoccupy generations of Jewish and Christian moralists, so much so that at least one Hebraic text recommends the death sentence for indulging in it. The 13th-century Catholic theologian, Thomas Aquinas, considered it to be even worse than fornication. Aquinas was greatly influenced in his opinions by the Greek philosopher Aristotle, who taught that semen comes originally from the brain and carries the stuff of the soul, or psyche, which is what forms and shapes the fetus in the womb (women providing nothing more than the raw material which is molded by the father's spirit). There-

fore, to Aquinas, spilling the seed carelessly was a crime morally equivalent to wasting the essence of one's sacred being.

The belief that semen and brain-matter are the same substance is an ancient, shamanic idea that has at some time or another permeated most of the world's cultures (before and after Aristotle, the Greeks typically explained the inferiority of women by pointing out that they had thinner semen, and therefore weaker brains and smaller, or non-existent, souls). For thousands of years the Taoists of China have warned about the harmful effects of depleting one's reserves of semen, and traditional Hindu medicine similarly teaches that semen is a precious fluid, coagulating from the blood (one source states that it takes 40 days for 40 drops of blood to make one drop of semen). If it is not wasted it rises in the body to nourish the brain. However, in the West, masturbation was usually condemned on moral rather than medical grounds, a situation that changed in the early 18th century when a clergyman called Dr. Bekkers decided to combine the two approaches. His book, *Onania*, was named after the biblical character of Onan, who was destroyed by God for spilling his seed on the

floor. Strictly speaking, Onan's real sin was his refusal to do as God had commanded him. Nevertheless, since Bekker, onanism has been the prude's favored name for masturbation. Bekker's main innovation, however, was to introduce Oriental ideas of semen depletion. "The blood is made into the seed," he preached, "which is further elaborated and purify'd in the Epidydimides." As a result, emptying the testicles consumes "the finest and most Balsamic part of the blood," leading to infertility, ulcers, insanity and death. Bekker's ideas were elaborated by the Swiss physician, Simon André Tissot, who extended them to women in his 1776 treatise on the *Diseases Produced by Onanism*. Tissot was undeterred by the lack of any semen to deplete. "The symptoms which supervene in females," he wrote, "are explained like those in men. The secretion which they lose, being less valuable and less matured than the semen of the male, its loss does not enfeeble so promptly, but when they indulge in it to excess, as their nervous system is naturally weaker and more disposed to spasms, the symptoms are more violent."

These patently insane theories should have done little harm, but Tissot's book went through multiple reprints, and parents, teach-

Thai godmiché made of wood. Godmichés (an old word for dildo) were made of wood, leather, metal, or rubber.

Dildos

Artificial penis substitutes have been known since at least the days of the Babylonians. Although they have traditionally imitated the shape of the male member, many different forms and materials have been adopted. In parts of Siberia, women masturbate using the calf muscle of a reindeer. Bottles, vegetables, fruit, items of furniture and shoes have all been pressed into service, while modern plastic dildos have been molded to resemble anything from dolphins to saints to outstretched hands. They may be manually operated, or designed to vibrate, oscillate, twist, thrust or rotate. Although they are clearly designed to be inserted into the vagina (or anus), few women actually use them in this way. Most prefer to masturbate by using the dildo outside the vagina, massaging the clitoris. The most popular alternative to dildos are the Oriental *rin-no-tama* – two little balls which are inserted into the vagina and vibrate intensely against each other with every tiny movement. At different times, different countries have held the monopoly on dildo manufacture. In the 17th century it was Italy, and the dildo was widely known in Europe as "signor dildo". By the 18th century the French were masters of dildo manufacture. At the end of the 19th century, British household and ladies' magazines were full of advertisements for vibrating devices that promised the housewife "relaxation and relief". Victorian men – many of whom did not even believe in the existence of the clitoral orgasm – were blithely unaware of the true use for these objects. However rigorously they policed the self-abuse of their daughters, they considered their wives incapable of such an act. By the early 20th century the home of the best dildos was Japan, and it was only after American servicemen brought them back as souvenirs after the war that they again became popular in the West.

ers and doctors enthusiastically embraced his views. They also crossed the Atlantic and gained an even wider audience through the work of 19th-century American health gurus such as Sylvester Graham and John Harvey Kellogg, inventor of the cornflake, who railed against red meat, warm showers and unregulated passions. Kellogg devised "thirty-nine signs" of degeneracy, listed in his book, *Plain Facts for Old and Young* (first published under *Plain Facts about Sexual Life* in 1877) which included sleeplessness, round shoulders, fingernail-biting, swearing and tobacco-use. Since two of his signs are mock-piety and capricious appetite, it is likely that nobody America, including Kellogg himself, could be excluded. To confirm suspected degenerate behavior in children, he recommended that parents spy on them: "If the suspected one becomes very quickly quiet after retiring, the bedclothes should be quickly thrown off under some pretence." For a boy who was discovered with an erection, Kellogg suggested circumcision without anesthetic as a deterrent. If a girl was discovered with a "congested" clitoris, he advised the application of carbolic acid as "an excellent means of allaying the abnormal excitement."

Kellogg's books were read by millions, and affected attitudes well into the 20th century. It was only after the 1960s that masturbation was increasingly reclaimed as a healthy act: a way of exploring one's body and discovering how to give and receive pleasure, both alone and in a partnership. It has been claimed that a man is incapable of truly giving a woman pleasure until he has seen her masturbate, an opinion supported by repeated surveys showing that only 30 percent of women achieve orgasm through intercourse, while 80 percent achieve orgasm through solitary masturbation, or masturbation during intercourse: not only stimulating the clitoris, but also having the option of concentrating on the labia minora and the very receptive perineal area in general.

However, masturbation has still not completely escaped the stigma of shame and misunderstanding. When Shere Hite made her nationwide survey of American female sexuality in

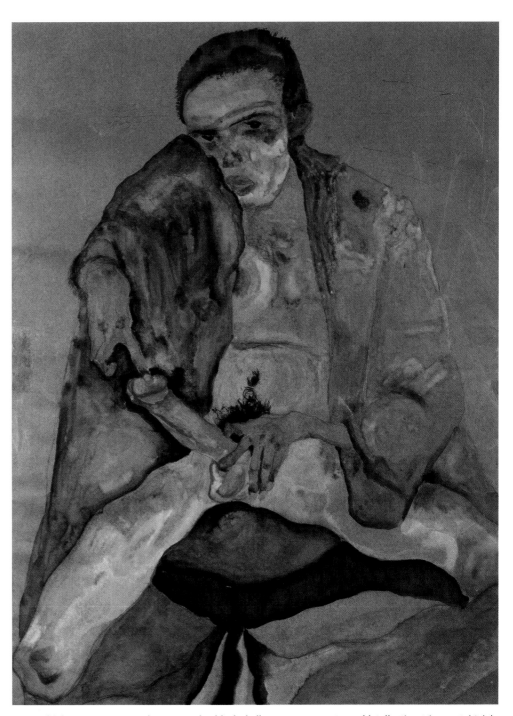

Egon Schiele, *Eros*, 1911. Gouache, watercolor, black chalk, 55.9 x 45.7 cm, Leopold Collection, Vienna. Schiele's portraits of himself and others masturbating were seen as deliberate attempts to outrage contemporary bourgeois morals. Other interpretations see the artist's nude self-portraits as an expression of self-experience and the search for inner energies.

the early 1970s, women reacted with horror to the question: "Do most men masturbate you?" Although the word was being used as a synonym for manual stimulation, the women resented what they saw as a form of intercourse being "demeaned" in this way.

Among the many misconceptions surrounding masturbation is the question of when it begins. Although infants play with their genitals from an early age (boys may grip their penises before they are one year old, children of both sexes fondle themselves from the age of three or four, and begin exploring each other's genitals at the age of five or six), it is only when the sex hormones begin to be produced (at age ten or eleven) that they do so to derive sexual pleasure. Another myth is that "too much" masturbation is unhealthy, especially for the nerves, although invariably in surveys people consider "too much" to be a frequency higher than the one they adopt themselves. There is no evidence that masturbation causes nervousness or mental illness.

Matrimony and Partnership

Master of the Amsterdam Cabinet, *Gotha Couple*,
c. 1484. Tempera on panel, 114 x 80 cm, Schlossmuseum Gotha, Germany. This, often thought to be
a wedding portrait, is in reality a representation of
the Count of Hanau-Münzberg with his mistress in
a liaison that was still illegitimate. Only when the
Count, after the death of his first wife, could find no
other consort of his own class, did he live together
officially with this lady of bourgeois origin.

Types of Marriage

Jan van Eyck, *The Portrait of Giovanni Arnolfini and His Wife Giovanna Cenami (The Arnolfini Marriage)*, **1434. Oil on panel, 84.5 x 62.5 cm, National Gallery, London.** The painting shows the couple, probably at their marriage ceremony. In the 15th century the presence of a priest was not necessary. It was sufficient to promise mutual faithfulness, to join hands and for the groom to give a gift to the bride. The bride's green cloak stands for youth and matrimony, the blue dress underneath for fidelity. In the convex mirror on the wall the witnesses of the marriage can be seen.

When the Weyewa people of Sumba, an island in eastern Indonesia, are told about Western marriage customs, they react with disgust. Weyewan society is based on the elaborate exchange of gifts. They regard this as a cosmic principle, and divide everybody they know into two categories: wife-givers (those who might give them women), and wife-takers (or those to whom they might give their own women.)

Whenever a woman is exchanged between two family groups, so-called female goods, such as pigs and cloth, accompany the bride to her new husband, while the husband's family sends male goods (gold and cows) in return. The gift-swapping is so extravagant that anyone who wants to marry needs the assistance of large numbers of kin, and the various exchanges of goods are a powerful guarantee of the resulting social bonds. Divorce is almost unknown, as it would be impossible to untangle all the different obligations and ensure that property returned to its original owner. The Weyewa regard Westerners who marry for love, without such extreme gift-swapping rituals, as doing little more than copulating like animals. It happens outside the dictates of society, and is simply immoral.

This may seem like an extreme example, but throughout history marriage has been less a personal act than a matter of forging economic or political ties. The ancient Romans distinguished between free marriage, in which a woman and her property did not become a part of her husband's estate, and a marriage with *manus*, in which she literally came under her husband's hand, and took on the legal status of one of his children. The Dahomey of West Africa have a more complex system of 13 different kinds of marriage, distinguished by the various kinds of economic relationships involved. Although there are many regional variations, the French anthropologist Claude Lévi-Strauss pinpointed the mechanism of the economic marriage when he pointed out that "men exchange women; women never exchange men."

There is some archaeological evidence that women were being traded between tribes more than 30,000 years ago. The analysis of prehistoric human bones, at the site of Téviec, on the coast of northwest France, for example, indicates that the men were raised on foods that would be found locally (shellfish in the case of Téviec), whereas the women had often spent their formative years elsewhere. According to Lévi-Strauss, this movement of women from group to group was an important way of forging alliances among our early ancestors, as well as a valuable method of disseminating skills.

There is no way of knowing what rules governed the relationships between men and women in primitive societies, but by 1750 B.C. the laws of marriage had been rigidly codified, at least in Babylon. They are mainly concerned with ownership, and treat women – or more precisely their fertility – as the property of men. The goal of marriage was to provide the man with children who could inherit his power and wealth, and to guarantee their legitimacy by imposing strict penalties on women who had sexual encounters outside the marriage. These laws, drawn up by the Babylonian leader Hammurabi, are still the cornerstones of many marriage contracts made today.

Cross-culturally, there is such a widespread need to guarantee that children are the legitimate offspring of both parents that anthropologists often define this as the main purpose of marriage. The nature of the guarantee, however, can be purely symbolic. A Nayar girl, from the Malabar coast of India, undergoes before her first menstruation a four-day ceremony that links her to a man who becomes her ritual husband. She does not live with him, but rather stays in the communal house occupied by her mother's family, where she is free to receive as many "visiting husbands" as she chooses. The ritual husband's only role is to legitimize, in the eyes of the group, any children that are born, though he has no claims on them, nor they on him. Sometimes biological parents disagree as to what is or is not a legitimate child. Nayar women may become the lovers of men from among the neighboring, high-caste Nambutiri Brahmans. Any children produced are considered to be bastards by the Nambutiri, but are status symbols to the Nayar. In many societies, a bride's virginity provides the best guarantee that a child born to her was fathered by the bridegroom. However, a concern with premarital purity is hardly universal. In a wide-ranging survey of 141 different societies, carried out in 1975/76, it was discovered that, while 36 insisted on brides being virgins and punished any who weren't, 34 took the opposite view, and strongly approved of some premarital sexual experience in women. The rest were less extreme, with a common attitude being that premarital sex would be tolerated as long as it was discreet. In the majority of cultures, males are expected to have some sexual experience before marriage.

There are several explanations for the great variation in attitudes. A popular but discredited idea is that more advanced societies place greater barriers in the way of premarital sex. A more sophisticated theory claims that a powerful concern with bridal virginity occurs in societies where the bride and groom are expected to live with one or other of their families. Wherever the couple makes their own home away from the existing family unit, there tends to be a more permissive attitude. An explanation based on economics is that, among peoples with few inheritable possessions, such as hunter-gatherers, there would be little need to establish the legitimacy of children, and correspondingly little concern about premarital sex.

Marriage Symbols

Traditional wedding celebrations are always, in part, fertility rites. The throwing of confetti or rice outside a Western church dates back to the "sowing" of barley or wheat over the newly-married couple. The wedding cake itself can be traced back to the Roman custom of breaking a cake over the bride's head while she held ears of wheat in her hand. In Hinduism, the fertility spell has entered the ceremony, which occurs when the bride and groom sprinkle water or rice over each other's heads.

The joining together of the couple is also commonly symbolized. The Sikhs, along with various Mesoamerican groups, tie together scarves worn by the bride and groom, while in Theravada Buddhism their wrists are bound together while they eat from the same bowl. In the West, the ring, a symbol dating back at least as far as ancient Egypt, represents the unbroken unity of the married couple.

Wedding in Cuzco, Peru. Grains of wheat, barley, and oat are traditional fertility symbols and used to be thrown over the bride and groom, the wedding procession or arranged in the bride's hair. Sometimes they were placed in her shoes without her knowing. Confetti showers have become a modern substitute in many cultures.

Child marriage in Rajasthan. A popular way to ensure the virginity of a bride has always been child marriage. This was common among the royal families of Europe in the Middle Ages. Children were married to each other when they were barely able to repeat their vows. Although child marriage is mostly banned today, it still survives in Pakistan and India, where children are promised to each other at the age of five, or earlier, and married at puberty. In Rajasthan, in 1985, 50,000 children were betrothed to each other in two days.

Such issues become more important with increasing prosperity. Certainly, in Haiti and other parts of the Caribbean, where up to 70 percent of children may be born outside wedlock, wealthy families contract orthodox marriages while poor couples may not throw a wedding reception (or fete) until after their children are full-grown and some money for a marriage ceremony is available.

In the absence of laws (or traditions) to the contrary, rich, powerful men tend to accumulate as many wives or concubines as they can support. Probably the largest harem ever recorded belonged more than 500 years ago to one of the kings of Monomatapa, in present day Zimbabwe, and contained some 3000 women. It has been estimated that nearly half of the world's societies regard polygyny as the marital ideal, with many others tolerating it alongside monogamy. Only about one-sixth of the world's cultures actually insist on monogamy being the only acceptable form of marriage. Yet by far the majority of married people worldwide live in monogamous relationships — although so-called serial monogamy, or a succession of partners, is becoming common in the West, as it has always been for ethnic groups such as the American Hopi.

It has been argued that monogamy advances hand in hand with democracy, because a situation in which a few men monopolize the marriageable women, leaving many other men sexually frustrated, creates too many social tensions in a culture where the rulers do not wield absolute power. Many societies throughout history have taken great pains to ameliorate such tensions. The Inca (or emperor) of Peru used to circulate the women in his harem; those who reached the age of 30 were passed on to his aides, lords and regional chiefs. Other cultures, including the Zande of Africa and several Australian aboriginal groups, practice "widow inheritance", in which the older, more powerful men take all the women for themselves, and younger men wait to marry until they are in their 30s or 40s, or they inherit their fathers' women (although no son inherits his own mother).

Polyandry, in which one woman marries several men, is exceedingly rare. One example occurs among the Nyinbar of the Himalayas, where several brothers may share one wife, primarily to avoid breaking up the family's property and land. The Paharii, of northern India, have a similar custom, because the bride-price — the gift given by the groom to his bride's family — of a Paharii woman is so high that brothers

The crowns that feature in the wedding ceremonies of many different cultures, as seen in this Russian-Orthodox wedding ceremony, usually signify that the couple enjoy the grace of god, but may also indicate that the couple themselves become godlike in their newly granted procreative rights.

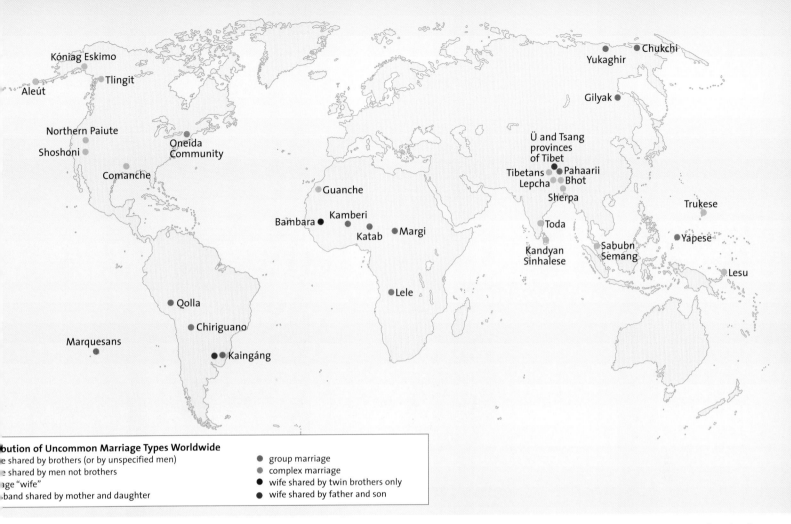

Köniag Eskimo
Aleút
Tlingit
Northern Paiute
Shoshoni
Oneida Community
Comanche
Marquesans
Qolla
Chiriguano
Kaingáng
Guanche
Bambara
Kamberi
Katab
Margi
Lele
Yukaghir
Chukchi
Gilyak
Ü and Tsang provinces of Tibet
Tibetans
Lepcha
Pahaarii
Bhot
Sherpa
Toda
Kandyan Sinhalese
Sabubn Semang
Trukese
Yapese
Lesu

bution of Uncommon Marriage Types Worldwide

- e shared by brothers (or by unspecified men)
- e shared by men not brothers
- age "wife"
- band shared by mother and daughter
- group marriage
- complex marriage
- wife shared by twin brothers only
- wife shared by father and son

True group marriage, in which all the men of the group share all the women, is especially rare. The form of group marriage known as complex marriage – found in the Oneida community – aroused so much local hostility that the community's founder, John Humphrey Noyes, recommended in 1879 that the practice be abandoned.

will usually pool together and acquire one wife between them. As they are able to afford more wives, they continue to share them among the group, and for this reason are said to practice group marriage rather than true polyandry. In parts of Nigeria, a wife may circulate between several husbands, who all live in different houses. Each husband may have several other wives living with him, but a woman never lives with more than one man at a time.

Utopian communities will often invent their own marriage customs. One of the most famous was the so-called complex marriage of the Oneida Community, founded in Vermont / USA in 1841. In this system, every man was considered to be married to every woman, and vice versa. But not all marriages involve a man and a woman. In the West, there is growing pressure for homosexual marriages to be accorded the same status as heterosexual unions, and in 1989 Denmark was the first country to legally recognize such partnerships.

Often a man – or his sperm, acquired from a donor clinic – is required only for biological fatherhood, after which one or more women

Badjao wedding party, Philippines, Lake Sulu. The sea gypsy Badjao are boat dwellers. Despite the Badjao's poverty and their low status in Philippine society their wedding parties are lively and joyful with the bridesmaids dancing on the boats.

fulfill the social and symbolic roles of fatherhood. This is not only true of female single parents and in some modern lesbian relationships. Among African peoples, such as the Nuer, a wealthy but infertile woman may marry another woman, who is usually younger and capable of bearing children. A male friend or family member impregnates the "wife" but plays no further part in raising the child, which grows up referring to the infertile woman as "father".

At various times there have also been so-called "pseudomarriages", fulfilling various ritual, symbolic or spiritual goals. These include the Mormon practice of posthumously marrying unbelievers to members of the church, to improve their chances of getting into heaven, and the Chinese tradition of marrying the ghosts of children who had been promised to each other but had died before reaching adulthood. One of the more unusual symbolic marriages, which illuminates the link between wedlock and the stability of a society, occurred on the northern Pacific coast of America. There, among the Kwakiutl, it was possible for men to marry themselves to the arm or leg of the chief.

Choice of Partner

Rudolf Jordan, *Marriage Proposal on Heligoland*, 1834. Oil on canvas, 62.7 x 70 cm, National Gallery, Berlin. Exploitation or expediency? The suitor in this painting is clearly comparatively wealthy – he can at least afford boots – and although the older man appears to be coaxing the girl into accepting him, in reality she would have very little choice and would be forced into the match by her family.

Anonymous, Dutch school, *Portrait of Lysbeth van Duvenvoorde*, c. 1430. Oil on parchment, 32.5 x 20.5 cm, Rijksmuseum, Amsterdam. This picture could be seen as a forerunner of the modern dating agency video – the words on the banner read: *Mi verdriet lange te hopen – wie is he die sijn hert hout open.* ("I don't want to wait a long time, where is he whose heart is open.")

The contemporary romantic ideal of East and West rests on the notion that a life partner is chosen primarily on the basis of love. The fairytale assumption is that the mere vision of the Other is enough to arouse sufficient passion for the lover to set out in quest of the beloved. Occasionally even the portrait or account of the "hero" or "heroine" is enough to provoke a full-fledged quest. Men are aroused by descriptions of beauty and virtue, women by tales of chivalry and redemption.

Today however, marriage is not the only option. Many couples in Western Europe prefer to be in long-term relationships without the formality of a marriage, one advantage of this being that it reduces the ability of interfering relatives to get involved in the personal affairs of the couple.

In reality, however, throughout history, parents have played a substantial role in choosing partners for their children. Despite the still fairly superficial change in the West, in most countries of the world it remains the norm for parents to be involved in their children's choice of partner. The primary criteria for selection in an arranged marriage are undoubtedly social and economic. In the South Asian subcontinent, perhaps the best known for its continuing tradition of arranged marriages, the method of bringing a couple together can be extremely varied. In some cases neither bride nor groom has any information about a prospective partner while in others, young men and women are introduced to each other at social events and a controlled form of self-selection is facilitated. Arranged marriages work on the principle that the relationship is expected to develop after marriage. This expectation is nurtured from an early stage in life so that boys and girls, particularly the latter, are programmed to work hard towards compromises to make possible a permanent relationship. The man is expected to provide financial support, the woman to fulfill the duties of a wife, mother and caretaker. Thus the concept of duty is paramount. At the most orthodox end, the lower social strata and in the village context, the success of a marriage may be measured in terms of the lowest common denominators: sexual interaction resulting in children and a stable relationship which will allow the smooth running of the household. Among the more educated or wealthier families the attitude is more flexible. Though a failed marriage still carries stigma for the woman, the chances of her being reintegrated into society are much better. Poorer women may well find themselves unwelcome by their own families who feel their obligations to her have been met with the dowry. She thus becomes alienated from her community.

With divorce rates soaring both in India and Pakistan as well as diaspora communities where these groups have settled, it is widely recognized that couples expect more from marriage than was once the case. They may well express resistance to arranged marriages, claim the right to refuse partners selected by others and if forced into marriage, they have a legal right to release themselves from an unsatisfactory match. Thus in recent years more attention has been paid to the choice of partner. The paramount importance of sexual attraction and compatibility are acknowledged and parents attempt to assess the prospective partner in the light of their child's taste.

In the United States and the United Kingdom, South Asian communities in all the major cities have introduced "singles parties" as a forum to find suitable partners. These are organized by young members of the community and have in general been met with the approval of community elders. Though those attending often describe them as "meat markets", it is generally understood that those present are looking for a marriage partner.

Franz von Stuck, *Fighting for a Woman*, **1905. Oil on panel, 90 x 117 cm, State Hermitage Museum, St. Petersburg.** Influenced by the somewhat fanciful anthropological text *The Golden Bough* von Stuck put a classical sheen on this scene of prehistoric conflict, and even used himself as a model for one of the combatants.

Among young, second and third generation South Asians in the West, the popularity of singles parties has superseded the more traditional choices of advertising in community papers or using marriage bureaus of which there are relatively few.

The Asian singles parties are a modified offshoot of the Western "singles-bars", which have existed in the United States and the United Kingdom and other Western countries since the 1980s. The main difference lies in the fact that those who frequent the singles-bars are generally interested in short-term sexual interludes or even one-night stands. Sexual attraction is of primary importance.

Attraction studies conducted within control groups, and among the public at large, over the past three decades, have yielded surprisingly uniform results when judging from photographs. Notions of physical "attractiveness", however, become much more variable where the person is (a) interviewed face to face, when mannerisms, voice and personality become much more significant and (b) assessing the attractiveness of friends when physical attractiveness becomes secondary to the chemistry of the relationship. Culturally, too, there are many variables. An exceptionally tall woman, for example, may be considered attractive in the Western world where supermodels are selected among other qualities for their height. In India or China on the other hand, men and women are generally smaller, so the petite and feminine is more valued. Social scientists have furthermore found that when people meet in cheerful and pleasant surroundings they are more predisposed to be attracted to each other. This is enhanced if they are listening to their favorite music, if admiration is expressed or if the meeting occurs in a celebratory situation. The continuation of the relationship naturally depends on whether this first allure can be maintained and developed into something more mature and lasting.

The vast majority in industrialized Western societies choose several sexual partners during their lifetime, adding to the basic criteria their personal preferences with regard to appearance, morals, financial potential, lifestyle and the ability and willingness to have children. Obviously these standards become far more important when the choice of partner is for life or the longer term. The proliferation of novels spawned by the huge success of Helen Fielding's 1996 novel *Bridget Jones's Diary* reflects the growing preoccupation of professional women

Abducting a Wife

Wife capture was, in all likelihood, once an honored and lauded activity among many warrior tribes, although its popularity in primitive cultures was greatly exaggerated by certain 19th-century neo-Darwinists such as J.F. McLennan and Lord Avebury. Nevertheless, forms of bride-capture appear to have survived into the 20th century in parts of Africa, South America and Oceania, and marriage customs that appear to stem from ancient bride-capture are widespread. "Standing up with the groom" is a vestige of marriages to abductees when a cordon of men surrounded the couple to defend it against a possible counter-attack from the bride's people.

Giambologna (Giovanni da Bologna), *Rape of the Sabines*, 1583. Marble, 410 cm high, Loggia dei Lanzi, Florence. In *The Early History of Rome* (59 B.C.) Livy criticizes the Romans under Romulus for abducting the Sabine women for brides. In order to promote peace, however, the women chose to stay with their captors.

Matchmaking

The services of matchmakers were once nothing short of detective work. It was their responsibility to procure suitable partners for people from a wide social range and also to ascertain the character, quality and financial standing of the prospective couple as well as their families. Though not nearly as demanding today, the job of the matchmaker remains much the same. Whether the professional practices from a corporate base as an introduction agency or marriage bureau or in the traditional manner as a respected member of a community performing a social duty in return for a fee, the matchmaker functions as presenter and counselor.

Internet agencies now offer to introduce subscribers to potential partners from around the world, including countries that are famous for their "mail-order" brides.

Transpacific Marriage Agency

International Marriage & Friendship Agency

in their thirties for a long-term partner because their "biological clock is ticking away", reducing their chances of domestic bliss. These women's despair is connected not only to societal expectation but also to the survival instinct. Seen in this light, it becomes easier to understand why single women and men from a certain age on are willing to compromise on the choice of partner.

For men and women unable to find a suitable partner in their own country, the option exists of package holidays organized with the specific purpose of introducing men to women in developing countries who wish to marry and move to the Western world. Focused on areas of horrendous poverty such as the Philippines, Thailand, Russia and South America, such opportunities are weighted vastly in favor of the Western men who maintain the right to choose. A woman from a poor region may turn down a man from the West, but for her this would mean continued poverty in addition to the emotional burden of letting down her family who might have profited from her marriage to a "rich" man. For such a woman the choice of partner is obviously far more pragmatic and offers a life of relative economic security.

Clubs and networks function likewise in the West, as an alternative to dating agencies, for those with more unusual needs. Magazines which cater to all sexual tastes are widely available on newsstands, and they often include personal columns and advertisements for alternative sex with partners of a more adventurous kind, such as cross-dressers, dominatrixes and sado-masochists. Hotels, clubs and parties cater to a specific clientele providing appropriate partners. The more fetishistic sexual partnership will, in most cases, remain secret and therefore is unencumbered by the social expectations of class, character or job. However, even ordinary homosexual relationships may pose a problem at the outset when a same-sex partner has to be introduced to the family.

Parents and society remain involved in partnerships even today. One symbol of approval is the celebration of marriages, though the tensions during preparation often reflect the anxieties of parents and relatives about the suitability of the match, generally based on notions of a social and personal nature. Though it is unacceptable, even legally impossible, to prevent a marriage in contemporary society where the choice of an individual in marriage or sexual partnership is sovereign, personal approval is another matter. In order to avoid these pressures many couples prefer simply to cohabit. It is not unheard of for parents to show disapproval by "disowning" an errant child or by withdrawing their time and affection.

Psychoanalytic studies demonstrate that the relationship with parents can be a seminal influence in the child's choice of partner. According to one line of thought, the adult "child" selects a partner who mirrors the parental qualities with which the child had issue. Transactional analysis would sum this up as an attempt of the adult-child to "rewrite a life-script" based on past experience in order to achieve a more fulfilling ending. According to another line of thought, partners are chosen for their ability to fill a void in the individual or to take over the servicing of an unfulfilled need. This may create a problem in the relationship since the Other is only seen as a reflection of one's own need – the missing half – rather than an individual in their own right. Whatever the theory, physiological, conscious and unconscious factors all play such a vital part in the choice of a partner – one may even say, in falling in love – that there is in reality very little actual freedom of choice.

Exchange of Goods

The institution of marriage was not always a romantic one exclusively based on mutual love and compatibility. Rather it was, and in many countries still remains, a contractual matter predicated by economic, political, social and physical considerations. Consistently, important attributes which are considered in arranging a marriage include those indicating sound "stock", since good health, fertility and virtue are liable to influence the future of the family. These qualities not only raise the value of the prospective bride but also affect notions of attractiveness. Financial substance also boosts eligibility, since the literal exchange of material goods is a second vital factor, either from the husband in the form of a bride-price or from a wife in the form of her dowry.

Often goods will be exchanged both ways between the bride's and the groom's families. When this occurs, the payments will typically carry a weight of sexual symbolism. For example, the man or his family pay for the bride with spears or other weapons, while the woman's family may reciprocate with payments of cotton or kitchenware.

At some time or other the concept of a wife as property existed in all societies. The bride-price, also known as bride-wealth, generally consists of a verbal or written contract whereby the man, in return for a bride, provided a certain sum of money or occasionally a quantity of land or goods and, less commonly, a specific service for the family of the bride. Among many tribes of Africa where this system was

most efficiently in use, the husband had no physical, financial or sexual rights over his wife until the bride-price was paid in full. The return of such effects would indicate divorce. A similar contract exists to this day in Islam where the family elders of a couple agree on a sum of money, or *mihr*, to be paid to the bride on the wedding night, prior to consummation. If the new bride chooses, however, she can forgo the gift as a sign of her faith in her husband. In any instance involving bride-wealth, the gift from groom to bride is recognized as a transfer of rights from father to husband, which is meant to compensate the woman for her loss of autonomy over her body, her property and her finances. Paradoxically, however, the bride-price enhances a woman's value and is intended in part to ensure that she is properly treated. The custom of the bride bringing a dowry into the marriage is a different version of this power dynamic. Among the pre-Islamic Bedouin, a woman brought as her dowry a tent and a sword and after a minimum agreed period, was allowed to withdraw from the marriage if she had cause for complaint.

Inevitably, a bride with a substantial dowry generally has greater self-assurance and status than her less wealthy sisters. This is particularly the case in cities or when she lives close to her own relatives. Women not considered to have brought enough dowry or whose kin are unlikely to be able to provide gifts in the future have often been subjected to appalling treatment. The "dowry-deaths" of India, a savage example of this, still occur to this day.

The marriage gift from the bride to the groom came in the form of a dowry in exchange for the assurance that the daughter would be well looked after. In the 17th century, middle class women in England were married off with a large sum of money, known as a "portion". This was paid to the bridegroom's father on the understanding that in the event of his son's death, the widow would be entitled to an annual income commensurate with her lifestyle during the marriage. It was quite common for the father-in-law to use the "portion" for his own daughter's dowry.

Elsewhere too, the dowry tradition continued to thrive. As late as the early 20th century, many

Crispyn de Passel, Symbolic Representation of a Marriage for Money, 17th cent. Copperplate engraving, Staatliche Museen, Preussischer Kulturbesitz, Berlin. Cupid's arrows stem from the bride's dowry, not from her charm or beauty.

wealthy traditional Jewish families in Eastern Europe looked among the scholarly and other respectable professions for promising young men to marry their daughters in exchange for a better lifestyle and greater opportunities.

In the case of women, whilst financial status far outweighed the importance of appearance or education, chastity was also of great value as a bargaining counter in all societies. An unmarried woman was infinitely more valuable if she was a virgin and known to be morally pure. If tainted in any way by carnal knowledge she was regarded as "used" or "damaged" goods and could be an enormous expense to her family who might have to pay large amounts of money to marry her off. In such cases her husband was often below her in financial or social status.

The emphasis placed on chastity resulted in the widespread restraint of female sexuality before marriage. No doubt this was partially a reflection of the attitude to women which had its roots in ancient times in literary demonesses

Ambrogio Lorenzetti, *Saint Nicholas and the Three Poor Girls*, c. 1340. Oil on panel, 29 x 20 cm, Musée du Louvre, Paris. According to a 14ᵗʰ-century legend Saint Nicholas threw three lumps of gold through the window to the three impoverished daughters of a nobleman as a dowry to save them from prostitution. This story throws light on the fate of women who could bring no worldly goods into a marriage.

like the biblical Lilith and the blood-sucking Meroe of Apulleius's *Golden Ass.* A remarkable culmination of this widespread terror of female lust can be found in the malicious 15ᵗʰ-century work on witchcraft, known as the *Malleus Malleficarum*, 1487, written by the Dominican friars Jakob Sprenger and Heinrich Kramer, which depicts women as lascivious creatures with destructive, insatiable sexual appetites. Early marriage was therefore advocated in most cultures as an antidote to the inappropriate gratification of sexual cravings. Thus the material and moral value of the woman were closely linked and early marriage provided the perfect answer.

Palma Veccio (Jacopo de Negretti), *Jacob and Rahel*, c. 1520. Oil on canvas, 146.5 x 250.5 cm, Gemäldegalerie Alte Meister, Dresden. Working for a man in order to "pay" for the hand of a woman is still fairly common, especially in Africa. In the Bible, Jacob had to serve Laban for 14 years before he earned Laban's daughter, Rahel.

Marriage à la Mode

William Hogarth, *The Marriage Settlement* (detail). **Oil on canvas, 69.9 x 90.8 cm, National Gallery, London.** The English painter and engraver William Hogarth (1697–1764) invented his series of "moral subjects" in order to revive the medieval tradition of "pictured morality". Hogarth's first modern moral subject was *A Harlot's Progress* (1730–31), but the *Marriage à la Mode* series (1743–45) was his masterpiece. The first plate shows a nobleman – glorying in his family tree – and a wealthy alderman arranging the marriage of the former's son to the latter's daughter, oblivious to the fact that the young man is in love with his own reflection, and the young woman views her suitor with contempt. The real marriage is here between wealth and social standing.

William Hogarth, *The Tête à Tête* (detail). **Oil on canvas, 69.9 x 90.8 cm, National Gallery, London.** The loveless couple at breakfast, after a riotous night. The young lord has a lady's cap in his pocket, and carries a sword, indicating that he has been involved in fighting and debauchery. The book on the floor is by Hoyle, the expert on card games, the candles are lit in daytime, and the servant holds a clutch of unpaid bills, all indicating the wasteful mess and untrustworthiness of the aristocracy.

William Hogarth, *The Inspection* (detail). **Oil on canvas, 69.9 x 90.8 cm, National Gallery, London.** Because of his dissipations, the young lord's health begins to fail, and along with his mistress he visits a doctor. However, the pewter basin and broken comb, along with a unicorn's horn placed to suggest a bar- ber's pole, all indicate that the man is a charlatan, with no real medical expertise. The arrangement of skulls and mummies are nothing more than props, designed to intimidate and fool the credulous.

William Hogarth, *Toilette Scene* (detail).
Oil on canvas, 70.5 x 90.8 cm,
National Gallery, London.
The old nobleman has died, and so the young couple are now Earl and Countess. She has tired of his
indifference, and has taken a lover (the lawyer who
appeared in the first plate, helping to negotiate the
marriage settlement). He lounges on a sofa beside
her, showing off the tickets he has bought for a
masquerade that evening, and arranging a tryst.
An Italian singer entertains the salon, to the fascination of some of the women, and the contempt of
the black servant.

William Hogarth, *The Death of the Earl* (detail).
Oil on canvas, 70.5 x 90.8 cm,
National Gallery, London.
The suspicious Earl has followed his wife and her
lover and surprised them together in a brothel's
hired bedroom, but in charging at the adulterous
couple has suffered a mortal sword wound. The
Countess's lover escapes through a window, while
she crouches at her husband's feet and begs his forgiveness. The brothel's other customers, alarmed by
the noise, are pouring into the room, illuminated by
the lantern of a cautious watchman, nervous of
interfering in the affairs of his betters.

William Hogarth, *The Death of the Countess* (detail).
Oil on canvas, 69.9 x 90.8 cm,
National Gallery, London.
The grief-stricken Countess has returned to her
father's home and, having bribed a servant to bring
her laudanum, has taken her own life. Her child, who
appears already to share the symptoms of his father's
venereal diseases – note the "beauty patch" covering
the syphilitic sore – grieves for her, along with a
nurse. Nobody seems to care. The apothecary who
was treating her for her nerves appears angry that he
has lost the opportunity to peddle more of his
potions. Her father is already pulling her wedding
ring from her finger, and calculating how much he
can sell it for.

Breaking the Maidenhead

Medieval records make occasional reference to *droit de seigneur* or *ius primae noctis*, the right of the feudal lord to sleep with the virgin brides of his vassals. In *The History of Human Marriage*, 1889, Edward Westermarck (1862–1939), the Finnish philosopher and anthropologist, mentions that the bishops of the French city of Amiens continued the practice despite opposition from both Philippe VI (1328–1350) and Charles VI (1380–1422). Further afield there is some indication of its practice in Russia as late as the 18th and 19th centuries.

However, surviving registers in the rest of Europe only record instances when the lord forfeited that right in lieu of payment or receipt of gifts or services. The feudal rights of many lords included the right to select wives for vassals, which provided a convenient means of disposing of women, through marriage, who might have been violated by himself or a member of his family.

Discussion about the origin and purpose of the custom of *droit de seigneur* has not as yet yielded a valid explanation. Some scholars trace its source to the primitive tribes of Europe where an initiation rite required the defloration of virgins by a senior member of the tribe. A man not eligible to be the young woman's husband carried this out. Its spiritual significance lay variously in purification of the woman and the infusion into her of the tribal spirit, which she then passed on to her male progeny. Later the act of defloration, performed by a priest or elder, came to be understood as an offering to the tribal divinity in return for continued beneficence.

On a practical plane a bride, often still a child, was exposed to considerable danger at the hands of an inexperienced and sexually aroused husband. Therefore, the breaking of her maidenhead by a sometimes closely related elder may have originated as a means to protect her.

Paying off the *Ius Primae Noctis*, after a colored woodcut from the 15th cent. *Ius primae noctis* appears to have been just another means for making vassals pay tithes. The drawing illustrates one of these tithes. The bride had to give the feudal lord money or a frying pan of a size to fit her buttocks.

Wild Woman with Unicorn (detail), 15th cent. Strasbourg Tapestry, 75 x 63 cm, Historisches Museum, Basel. This tapestry depicts a scene from one of the bestiaries, the unicorn being tamed by a "wild woman", a mythical creature, who became popular particularly in the Alpine regions of central Europe. She was covered from head to foot with a thick coat of hair, only the face, hands, feet and breasts were left bare.

The Virgin and the Unicorn

Nobody knows where the unicorn came from, but we have a small sculpture dating from the second millennium B.C., discovered in Persia. It was the ancient Greeks and the Bible (Job 39, 9-11) which brought the concept of the unicorn to Europe. Its horn was reputed to be a strong antidote to various poisons and heal numerous diseases as well as being an effective aphrodisiac. Its manifold contradictory symbolic and mystic meanings – among other things it stands for chastity as well as voluptuousness – were attributed to it by the Christian faith. The *Physiologus*, written in Alexandria and Syria at the end of the second century A.D. and translated from Greek into many languages, describes the unicorn as a small animal notable for its courage. Hunters could not get near it, because it was so strong. Only a virgin could catch it. The unicorn would leap into her lap, she would tame the animal and take it to the king's palace. From the *Physiologus* the bestiaries developed collections of moralized fables, popular in the Middle Ages. They emphasized the erotic aspect of the unicorn. When dwelling in the lap of the virgin, not only did the unicorn take the place of the child she was going to give birth to, but the horn stood for the male organ penetrating her. The virgin attracted the unicorn by her scent, she bared her breasts and received it like a lover. She offered the unicorn her milk which made it fall asleep in her lap. Should the unicorn find that she was not truly a virgin, it stabbed her with its horn.

From Plutarch we know of the marriage customs of the ancient Greeks and the Romans of his time: Lycurgus, the Spartan lawgiver of the 9th century B.C., decreed that girls were to be made brides "only when they were fully ripe and eager for it, in order that intercourse with a husband, coming at a time when nature craved it, might produce a kindly love, instead of the timorous hate that follows unnatural compulsion." First-century Romans on the other hand gave their maidens in marriage when they were twelve years old, or even younger. This was considered the best way to ensure that both their bodies and their dispositions would be pure and undefiled when their husbands took control of them. Such social control of female virginity was not shared in other parts of the ancient world. In Egypt, women had autonomy over preservation or disposal of their own virginity. At the festivals of the naked Hathor and Bastet, goddesses of sexuality and fertility, girls ritually offered their virginity to the goddesses during the feast, returning to their normal lives after the celebration was over. Similarly in Baalbek, Lebanon, girls dedicated their hymen to the goddess Attar. Hierodules and divine prostitutes in all cultures underwent rituals involving the sacrifice of the hymen as part of their consecration to a particular divinity. The Indian *devadasis* (handmaiden of the gods) entered a symbolic marriage with the king as representative of God. It is possible that *ius primae noctis* is a remnant of a profanization of that right as local lords and clan heads appropriated the privilege of kings and divinities. In fact there is no evidence that the *droit de seigneur* – if it really existed – was ever exercised. Still the existence of the idea is intriguing.

According to Strabo, the Greek geographer born c. 63 B.C., young women in Egypt were selected carefully from noble families to serve as divine prostitutes. Their rigorous training included an initiation ceremony in which the high priest inducted them into the mysteries of sexual union. In the Far East the intervention of priests had quite a different function. The Tchin-chan ceremony of 13th-century Cambodia involved the obligatory defloration of girls before marriage. Similar duties were also expected from the

Jean-Baptiste Greuze, *The Broken Pitcher*, 1785. Oil on canvas, 108 x 86 cm, Musée du Louvre, Paris. Greuze was a heavy-handed symbolist and a furtive pornographer. The broken pitcher represents the girl's lost virtue, but it has been pointed out that she is extremely young, and must surely have been raped, thus providing the audience with a titillating subtext to a stolidly moralistic work.

clergy of 15th-century Thailand and in Chinese Turkestan as recently as the 20th century. The involvement of holy men was probably the result of superstitions relating to the evil inherent in female bleeding. In the Veda, the oldest Indian religious literature, the blood of the broken hymen is denounced as "the root of all evil" and numerous tribal beliefs across India hold that the blood contains an evil spirit who wishes to possess the virgin and will consequently attempt to destroy her groom.

Lovesickness

Scientific studies of romantic love and love-sickness have generated controversy in the world of psychology. Scientific study demands consistent results in each experiment, while human nature is rarely consistent, given that the interplay of nature (genetic) and nurture (social) is deep-seated and unique in each individual. Nevertheless it is possible to garner some similarities in the type of romantic love described as "lovesickness". Clinicians may see this state as sickness or pathology while social psychologists consider it part of a developmental process in individuals as they work through filial attachments to move into adult friendships and sexual relationships. A more or less accurate description of lovesickness would include an addictive or obsessional quality that persists in the face of all difficulties even when unreciprocated. Since the love-object is often either forbidden or unattainable, this kind of love is marked by dysphoria. A fleeting glance at any of the important love tragedies in literature will confirm this.

Many of the literary tales have their origins in folk material and legend, which may be grouped under the theme of "bridal-death". In the Islamic world, Sufi mystic poets appropriated many stories of this category. Here the verse descriptions of the grand passion of the lover became analogous with the mystic quest – the search of the devotee for the divine. Separation, unattainability, sustained opposition, as well as hardship, characterize this quest. The only possible way in which proper union may be envisaged in this context is by mutual death. The most famous of these tales are those of Leila and Majnun (Arab), Shireen and Farhad (Irani) and Hir and Ranjha (Pakistani). All exact the ultimate sacrifice of life and Self.

Limerence

This was the name given to "unhealthy" love by the psychologist Dorothy Tennov following a survey in 1979 of over five hundred teenagers classed as "passionate lovers". All interviewees agreed that love was a "bitter-sweet" experience. Tennov concluded that "the limerent fantasy, intricate as it may be, is satisfying only when it retains fidelity to the possible." Thus, though the object of limerent love may not reciprocate, the lover's expectation remains fixed. According to M. R. Liebowitz, in *Chemistry of Love*, 1983, the sufferer alternates between extremes of euphoria and dysphoria depending on gratification or withdrawal of love by the object. This creates "emotional turmoil" as the lover is flung between hope and despair. Both clinicians attribute the condition to physical stimuli. According to Tennov, it is an inbred, biochemical deficiency, particular to women, whereas Liebowitz puts it down to "inadequate regulation of neurotransmitters" treatable by anti-depressants. In psychodynamic theory a greater emphasis is placed on environmental rather than biological factors. Sufferers from regular, prolonged limerence are thought to have suffered disturbances in their infantile attachment processes. Some psychoanalysts would argue that what the sufferer specifically craves is the feeling of desire, and that the best way to ensure the continuation of this state is to ensure that the desire is never satisfied. Therefore, subconsciously, the limerent man or woman will choose a love object that they know will never reciprocate their feelings, in order to prolong the sensation of desire.

Opposite: **Jan Steen, *The Lovesick Woman* (detail), c. 1660. Oil on canvas, 61 x 52.1 cm, Alte Pinakothek, Munich.** Steen, one of the most folk-oriented painters of 17th- century Holland, often presented scenes from simple peoples' lives in a slightly ironic light. This work is a good example. The quack, given the signs surrounding him, should have found it easy to make a clear diagnosis. The figure of Cupid over the entrance, the matchmaker, and the glowing thread from the brazier (whose stink supposedly illicited a strong reaction if a woman was pregnant) – all of these signs point to an ailment which is summarized by the paper in the patient's hand. It reads: "No medicine will help when it is love-pain."

Right: **Morange after S. Amand, *Lotte and Werther at the Piano*, c. 1780. Colored engraving, 33.2 x 26.4 cm, Goethe-Museum, Düsseldorf.** When Johann Wolfgang von Goethe's love story *The Sufferings of Young Werther* appeared in 1774 numerous young people all over Europe followed the hero's example and committed suicide out of unrequited love.

Karl Pavlovich Bryulov, *Narcissus*, 1819. Oil on canvas, 16.2 x 20.95 cm, State Russian Museum, St. Petersburg. The Greek myth tells the tale of the beautiful son of the river god Kephissos who scorned the love of the nymph Echo. As a punishment, the goddess of love, Aphrodite, made him fall in love with his own reflection.

Narcissism

Sigmund Freud attributes the origin of the term "narcissism" to Havelock Ellis (1859–1939) who described cases in which individuals treated their own body like that of a lover. Psychoanalytically, narcissism includes autoeroticism, or masturbation, but Freud's understanding of the condition was considerably expanded: it defined a state in which libidinal energy is invested in oneself rather than someone else. The ego thus becomes its own love-object. In terms of development, this state can belong to a growth stage. However, if it continues into adulthood it becomes a fixation and is used to describe self-obsession of many kinds. A narcissistic object-choice may extend to an object similar to oneself.

A narcissistic personality disorder is characterized by an exaggerated sense of self-importance, a conviction in one's own uniqueness and an insatiable need for admiration. People suffering from such a disorder lack empathy – or indeed any awareness that others might have feelings at all – and tend to be extremely manipulative in their personal relationships.

Famous Lovers

Right: ***The Taming of the Shrew,* still from the film by Franco Zeffirelli, 1967, Elizabeth Taylor and Richard Burton as Katharina and Petruchio.** The fiery Burton-Taylor relationship was always more compelling and dramatic than anything they managed to produce on-screen, and constantly made headline news. The couple's arguments were held to media scrutiny as were their reunions, which were marked by ever-larger gifts of diamonds as Burton achieved greater success.

The former King Edward VIII of Great Britain and his wife Wallis, née Warfield, formerly Simpson, formerly Spencer. It was said, probably maliciously, that her sexual techniques held him in thrall.

"All the world loves a lover" as the saying goes. But even the most cursory examination reveals that the love affairs which most caught the popular imagination and survived over centuries, were marked by intense parental or societal opposition, sacrifice and tragedy. Many occurred in the "forbidden zone" violating social or ethical barriers such as an existing marriage, a privileged relationship like that between doctor and patient or tutor and pupil, difference of race or status, even exceptional disparity in age. Such affairs have become the stuff of literature. In the 20th century, they have been extensively reconstructed on television and in the cinema.

One prominent affair, though it lasted only a thousand days, is that of Henry VIII (1509–1547) with Ann Boleyn. Repeatedly dramatized, it contains all the elements of romantic melodrama. The flouting of the aristocratic liaison between Henry and his first wife, Catherine of Aragon, was in itself a politically questionable move. Added to this was the violation of religious principles, the corruption of the clergy, the creation of divorce and the birth of a new Church – all, apparently, for the love of a woman. In spite of its ardor the king's love withered quickly. Within three years, he had discredited Ann Boleyn and sent her to the Tower to be decapitated.

Just as Henry's short-lived passion is enshrined in the Church of England, so the lifelong devotion of the 18th-century Indian Emperor Shah Jehan is manifest in the magnificent mausoleum known as the Taj Mahal in Agra. The powerful Empress Nur Jehan, having earmarked her husband's third son Shah Jehan as a suitable husband for her daughter, secured his position as heir to the throne. But Shah Jehan fell instantly and deeply in love with the Empress's niece and, despite serious opposition, married her. The enraged Empress sent him on increasingly dangerous battles until eventually he was forced to mutiny. Throughout their marriage, Shah Jehan's wife Mumtaz accompanied her husband on his many war expeditions and was closely involved in matters of state because her husband could not endure the thought of life without his beloved. On her death in 1630 during childbirth he locked himself up in his bedchamber, refusing entry to his attendants for several days. When he emerged his hair and beard had turned completely white. For the remainder of his reign, his only pleasure came from the planning and construction of his dead wife's mausoleum, the Taj Mahal, now one of the wonders of the world. Shah Jehan was dethroned and spent the rest of his life imprisoned. At his own request, he was kept in the Agra Fort. He kept a shard of mirror in his cell which allowed him to see the full reflection of the Taj Mahal each day. Perhaps the most powerful media image of the Taj Mahal at the end of the 20th century is that of Princess Diana, sitting in solitude, watching the sunset over perhaps the most magnificent monument to love.

Another royal courtship involving considerable sacrifice was that of Edward VIII, King of Great Britain from January to December 1936. The Church of England would not countenance the King's marriage to a divorcee, despite having itself been founded with the express purpose of acquiescing in a royal divorce. Consequently Edward was forced to choose between the monarchy and the love of his life, Wallis Simpson. He abdicated. Edward and Wallis married and remained in love for the rest of their lives. The liaison of Cleopatra and Mark Antony cannot go unmentioned in any tale of famous lovers. Trusted, and deeply loved by Julius Caesar, Antony (81–30 B.C.) later became involved in an affair with Caesar's former lover, Cleopatra, Queen of Egypt (69–30 B.C.). He declared Egypt independent and the partnership ended in tragedy when Octavian (later the Emperor Augustus) invaded Egypt. Antony fell on his sword, and Cleopatra followed him by clasping a poisonous asp to her breast. They were buried together.

One of the most publicized on-off celebrity romances of the 20th century was that of actors Elizabeth Taylor and Richard Burton, who played the parts of Cleopatra and Antony in one of the most lavish Hollywood productions of all time. Great emphasis was laid on the relative newcomer, Burton (1925–1984), who abandoned his wife and children in the United Kingdom to succumb to his passion for the actress. Like the many-times married Cleopa-

To Have and Have Not, still from the film by Howard Hanks, 1944, Humphrey Bogart and Lauren Bacall as Harry Morgan and Slim (Mary Browning). This May-December relationship appealed to the public imagination as a reflection of the romance between the characters of the movie in which the young female character challenged and provoked the formidable older man and effectively tamed him. This remains a popular motif of love stories in movies and in real life to this day.

tra, Taylor (b. 1932) was also held responsible for other broken marriages; her previous husband Eddie Fisher had left his singer-actress wife Debbie Reynolds in a blaze of notoriety not many years before.

Less troubled was the earlier but no less talked-about Hollywood romance of the veteran star Humphrey Bogart and the model/actress Lauren Bacall whom he met on the set of the film *To Have and Have Not*, 1943. At 19, she was roughly half his age. Bogart, or "Bogey" as he was affectionately called, a well-known "hell-raiser", nevertheless had an idyllic marriage. Two other film-star marriages to become pub-

licly mythologized were those of Rex Harrison and Kay Kendall (1957) as well as Laurence Olivier and Vivien Leigh (1940). Both actresses died relatively young of leukemia casting their husbands in the archetypal role of grieving Orpheus.

Pierre Abélard's scandalous seduction of his student Héloise began in 1118 and is another relationship to survive the passage of centuries. This is because of the exquisitely expressed passion recorded in their letters. The philosopher and teacher Abelard had heard of Héloise's brilliance and was fascinated by her even before he was appointed as her tutor.

Left: **Everard d'Espinques, *The Death of Tristan*, c. 1480. Miniature, Bibliothèque du Musée Condé, Chantilly, France.** In this version of the *Roman de Tristan*, the lovers decide to live far apart for the sake of honor and duty, but when Isolde learns that Tristan is dying, she hurries to his side, only to arrive too late.

Opposite: **Ford Madox Brown, *Romeo and Juliet*, 1870. Oil on canvas, 135.7 x 94.8 cm, Delaware Art Museum, Wilmington, USA.** This story, as retold by Shakespeare in *Romeo and Juliet,* is perhaps the most famous of all doomed love affairs. The playwright describes his lovers as "star-crossed", but it was the enmity between their families that truly decided their fate.

It was after the birth of their son that their passionate affair came to light. This runs contrary to the popular conception of an affair between two people of the cloth, which fuels prurient fantasies around the sexual transgressions of those pledged to chastity, and the love of God. Abelard paid the greatest price, being castrated on the orders of Héloise's uncle Canon Fulbert of Notre Dame cathedral; he then persuaded Héloise to take the veil and found a convent. The two continued to exchange letters and when Abelard died, Héloise, by then widely recognized as a scholar, gained permission to bury his body in the grounds of her convent. Myth and legend, too, yield rich romantic traditions. The superhuman love of Orpheus moved the gods to bend the laws of nature and allow him into the Underworld to retrieve his dead wife. Another enthralling story of devotion tells of Tristan and Isolde. King Mark sent his nephew, Sir Tristan, to Ireland to effect a peace treaty

and win him the hand of the beautiful Isolde. On the journey back, the pair drank a love potion thinking it was wine. Though Tristan's loyalty forced him to hand over Isolde to Mark, the lovers never managed to separate. Various endings exist for the tale, including one of a suicide pact in which they both drink from a poisoned chalice. In others, Mark stabs Tristan in the back. Yet others have Tristan dying of despair because he believed that the black sails of Isolde's approaching ship showed she no longer loved him. When she saw him dead, she too died of a broken heart. A rose grew from her grave, a vine from his and they intertwined in perpetuity.

Other tales from the Celtic canon include the Irish tale of Deirdre and Naoise with a similar tragic ending. Also of Irish origin is the tale of the bold, determined Grainne, who achieved a somewhat happier fate with her beloved, Diarmuid. After she and Diarmuid eloped from

her engagement feast to hunter-god Finn McCumhail, they spent many years as fugitives from him and his revenge. They were unusual in surviving the wrath of the betrayed betrothed to live a happy and fruitful life together. But in an addendum to the tale from Lady Wilde, the famous playwright's mother and celebrated collector of Irish folktales, Finn tracked down and killed Diarmuid in their middle years and eventually won Grainne's hand.

The appeal of most love stories, real or fictional, no doubt lies in the universality of love and the capacity of most people to identify with passion at a very profound level.

Fairy-tale Weddings

Right: **Peter Paul Rubens,*The Marriage by Proxy of Princess Maria de Medici and King Henry IV of France in the Cathedral, Florence, 5 October 1600.* Oil on canvas, 394 x 295 cm, Musée du Louvre, Paris.**
In 1600 Henri IV of France married the Italian Maria Medici. Rubens recorded the event with a cycle of 21 paintings. One depicts the formal, legally binding marriage ceremony, during which Maria was married to a representative of the king. The wedding with Henri took place when the bride arrived in her new country. The sumptuous gold and white wedding dress which Maria was wearing set a trend for wealthy fashionable brides throughout Europe. However, at various times there have been vogues for other colors – during the 19th century (and at other times among some Protestant groups) even black became fashionable.

Above: **Wedding clothes from Nuremberg in 1577. Germanisches Nationalmuseum, Nuremberg.**
Bridal dresses of the 16th, 17th and 18th centuries reflect society's strict division into classes. The white wedding dress became popular only with the beginning of the 20th century.

Fairy tales generally end happily in a fabulous wedding ceremony. The one that best epitomizes this is the story of Cinderella, found under a variety of names all over the world, in several thousand versions. In Europe, one of the most famous is in *Contes de ma Mère l'Oye* by Charles Perrault (1628–1703). Cinderella's magnificent horse-drawn carriage, her elegant slippers and her splendid gowns all provide the prototype for the perfect wedding. In some versions of the tale, the heroine's dresses, inherited from her mother or ordered for her by her father, are described in glorious detail. Often three gowns are mentioned, one of gold, one silver and another light blue, respectively representing the sun, the moon and the sky. Mostly, though, they are magical garments provided by a fairy godmother. Thus the tradition of exquisitely embroidered, ornate white dresses in a combination of rich, rustling silks with frothy gossamer, net accessories, and long trains, undoubtedly evoke a magical atmosphere.

The British princess Diana's wedding dress instantly comes to mind as the archetypal fairy-tale gown. The famous images of her walking up the aisle of St. Paul's Cathedral with a sweeping train supported by several cherub-like youngsters and leaving in a horse-drawn carriage, complete the fairy-tale ensemble.

An early source of the wedding-day idyll may well be the mythical concept of *hieros gamos*, the holy wedding of a God and a Goddess celebrated in Babylonian and Greek fertility cults. The celebration was believed to be of great significance to the universe since it enhanced the well-being and fertility of the earth.

It is popularly thought that the whiteness of the wedding dress signifies virginity, but this has not been true at all times and in all places. In some Oriental cultures white is the color of mourning, and in Japan, for example, the traditional white wedding dress symbolizes the ancient belief that, when she marries, the bride is dead to her old family.

Self-written Vows

With the advent of the 1960s sexual revolution and the rapidly improving status of women in the West, traditional marriage vows came into question. Some women and men rejected the reference to women as "goods and chattels". One way forward was to omit sections from the vows. Another, more innovative idea, was for the couple to write their own vows reflecting their own aspirations. This idea gained popularity in California and is now fairly common. The practice has also been adopted in Western Europe but in general it is neither as frequent nor as elaborate as in the United States.

Princess Diana's dress, designed by the husband-and-wife team, the Emanuels, had a 5.5m long train to accentuate an air of fantasy and fairy-tale.

A History of the Bed

The bed has always been more than a place to sleep. At various times, it has also served as an altar: the ancient Mesopotamians appear to have made special beds, carved with erotic scenes, on which priestesses would sleep, awaiting the visit of a god who would couple with them to assure the prosperity of the land. In 18th Dynasty Egypt, it was common to plant a bed with seeds, arranged in the shape of the fertility god Osiris. When the bed was watered, the deity sprang forth in all his tangled greenery. The beds of the poor have usually been little more than sacks filled with straw, possibly laid on a shelf or pallet – an arrangement that has probably not altered since prehistoric times. But for the wealthy, the bed has always been a stage from which to display their status and power. The biblical Book of Esther describes the great iron bed of Og, the King of Bashan, which was approximately 5 m (16.5 feet) wide, although this did not prevent it being carried off as a prized war trophy. In Roman times, Petronius noted the famous silver bed of the millionaire, Trimalchus, and Martial tells the story of a man who feigned illness so his friends would have to visit him in bed and admire the rich coverings he had bought from Alexandria. In medieval Europe, many of the royal beds were so large that some historians believe they must have been used by a number of people simultaneously, and the beds of the 15th- century French kings became so enormous that a special courtier was employed whose only job was to beat the mattress with a staff, both to smooth it down and to check for intruders hiding underneath. Among royalty, the bed has often been a substitute throne. At meals and parties the nobles of Mesopotamia habitually reclined on couches surrounded by their wives and concubines, who sat, and entertainers or servants, who either stood or knelt, waiting to be called upon. This was the origin of court protocol for the next 3000 years. As late as the 18th century in Europe, it was still common for the king to hold court lying in bed – the *lit de justice*, or later the *lit de parade* – with any princes present sitting around him, while the high officials stood and the lesser ones knelt. Even when empty, the royal bed was an object of reverence. Visitors would genuflect to it in passing, and it would have a permanent guard, to prevent anyone from hiding weapons in it, or sprinkling it with poisons or spells. European royals chose the bed as the stage on which to display themselves on many formal occasions, both before and after death. Some of their

Rogering Stool or *siège d'amour* from a Paris bordello, c. 1890. Brothels frequently had custom-built beds and rogering chairs, designed to support their clients in unusual or athletic positions.

marriages were even accompanied by official beddings: when the 15-year-old princess Mary Stuart (1662–1694) married the 14-year-old Prince of Orange, they appeared in bed before the whole court for three-quarters of an hour. The ceremony was also done by proxy – when Emperor Maximilian did not appear for his own bedding, his ambassador stripped off a shoe and stocking and placed his leg, naked from the knee down, in the bed with the bride. This custom was not restricted to royalty. Seeing the bride in bed was a regular part of wedding celebrations well into the 19th century at all social levels. It was also customary, the day after the wedding, for the bride to receive guests while sitting in bed. The marriage bed was displayed publicly in churches and processions as a symbol of plenty, bearing fruit, flowers, dowry and gifts, in cultures as far afield as Hungary, the Philippines, Iceland, Cyprus and India.

The birth of a noble baby meant that a room had to be specially decorated for the lying-in of the lady of the house. Edward III of England (1312–1377) spent a fortune preparing the natal chamber of his expectant wife, Philippa.

Anonymous, *Bed of Muhammad Khan Abbasi IV*, 1882. Watercolor, Musée Christofle, Paris. This clockwork bed was built in Paris, and had four life-size, mechanical nude statues as the posts. When the Khan lay on it, his body weight set off a musical box, and activated the statues, two of which fanned his face while two whisked flies away from his feet.

William Hogarth, *The Idle Prentice Return'd from Sea and in a Garret with a Common Prostitute* (detail), published according to Act of Parliament 30 Sept. 1747. Engraving, 25.7 x 34 cm, Victoria and Albert Museum, London. The stuffed-straw bed of a common prostitute in 18th-century London would have had an entire ecosystem of its own, crawling fleas, lice, mites and possibly even rodents, as well as the parasites imported by her many customers.

The room had two beds, the bed of state, where Philippa received visitors for a period of a month, and the *lit de misère* at the other side of the room, to which she was transferred for the actual birth. Throughout the lying-in of Isabella of Bourbon, five large green beds lay empty in the room with her, waiting for the christening ceremony of her child, when they held all the assembled guests.

Attendants and ladies-in-waiting used to sleep in the royal bedroom on mats or wheeled truckle (or trundle) beds that could be hidden under the main bed by day, although high-ranking courtiers or ladies sometimes slept with the king or queen. The idea that bed-sharing inevitably leads to sex is a fairly recent one, and sharing a bed was once a common practice even among sometime enemies: Charles VIII (1470–1498) invited the Duke of Orleans to share his bed as a gesture of reconciliation, and after the battle of Moncontour, the Prince de Condé (1538–1569) shared a bed with his captive, the Duc de Guise. When the deceased Henry IV of France (1553–1610) lay in state at the Louvre, many visitors sat on the queen's bed to console her, and some even sat alongside the corpse. It was only in the 17th century that it became unacceptable to sit on someone else's bed.

For some people, the orientation of a bed is more important than its luxury or comfort. In China, the bed is aligned according to principles of Feng Shui, which attempt to ensure a harmonious flow of energy through the rooms of the house. In the West, it is often thought desirable to lie facing north, and to this end Charles Dickens used to carry a compass with him whenever he traveled. Dr. Marie Stopes (1880–1958), the birth control pioneer, believed that her body was naturally magnetized, and that a part of her spine could detect the north pole. If, while traveling, her bed was too heavy to move, she would lie on a diagonal.

Jealousy

Lucas Cranach the Elder, *The Age of Silver*, 1527. **Oil on red beech, 52.5 x 36 cm, Schlossmuseum Weimar**. *The Age of Silver* is a theme that Cranach returned to several times. The silver age of human existence was supposed to have ended with the introduction of jealousy, leading men to acts of extreme violence.

Researchers are at a loss to define the pathology of jealousy. The emotion itself could be described as a combination of possessiveness, passion and suspicion. It may strike at any time from the early, passionate throes of romance, through an apparently stable stage of cohabitation and even continue after divorce or separation. Its only constant quality is that it is associated with excessive dependency on a partner. Beyond this its causes and processes are impossible to define in a general way. It may be triggered by a single, specific event or manifest itself gradually over a period of time. One theory, posited by evolutionary biologists, explains it as the urge of the male to guard his mate and ensure survival of his genes and of the female to secure supplies and resources for her young. It is possible that over the centuries these basic survival stimuli developed into moral norms. Men were ridiculed as "cuckolds" if their wives were discovered to be unfaithful, and women were expected to be demure and preserve an unsullied reputation for the sake of their husband's bloodlines and their joint social standing.

Psychological surveys conducted in the Western world, particularly in the US, indicate that jealousy occurs equally in both sexes though the genders react differently. Women tend to forgive transgressions more easily, particularly if they are merely sexual, and do not involve a commitment to another partner. Men on the other hand find sexual infidelity hardest to forgive and research undertaken in the US reveals that a high number of suicides committed there are the result of male jealousy.

The phenomenon is not confined to the Western world by any means. Middle Eastern cultures have traditionally demanded high standards of duty and commitment from women, particularly among rural cultures where immense importance is placed on the possession of land. In addition, the importance of traditional status given to old and respected families in a highly community-oriented context elevates the concept of "family honor", thus transforming sexual transgression into a serious social crime. Here, the faithfulness of a woman becomes a matter of the highest importance. Even a one-off extramarital sexual liaison, or the mere possibility of it, can cast doubt on the parentage of her child and haunt the family for generations. In such instances, the only redemption for the dishonored man may lie in the murder of his wife and his rival. Though few legal systems would offer justification for murder, it is not unknown in the

Robert Alexander Hillingford, *Othello Relating His Adventures to Desdemona*, 1869. **Oil on canvas, 50 x 72 cm, Christopher Wood Gallery, London.** The Moor of Shakespeare's play claimed to have loved "not too wisely, but too well". The critic Ruskin even claimed that Othello's name meant "the careful", deriving from the Greek *othomai*, meaning "to have a care for".

more far-flung areas of both Mediterranean Europe and the Middle East for such events to be effectively covered up by the local population and for the relevant authorities to turn a blind eye.

Without doubt the subject of jealousy has a great fascination for writers. The most famous literary work on sexual jealousy is Shakespeare's *Othello*, where a Moor, in predominantly white Venice, is married to Desdemona, a beautiful, white, younger woman. Increasingly deluded by his supposed friend, who cunningly preys on his own feelings of inadequacy, he succumbs to the "green-eyed monster who mocks the flesh", eventually murdering his innocent wife.

In myth, jealousy finds a more archetypal place. Like many other qualities, it is the prerogative of the immortals but needs to be acknowledged and quelled among humans. The deity most famously associated with jealousy is perhaps the goddess Hera, sister-wife of Zeus. Her attacks on the women with whom Zeus coupled were legion. This infernal side of Hera, however, is said to be activated in the interest of other women: Hera is patroness of married women and the sanctity of marriage itself. Her acts of revenge are therefore a formidable warning both to men and to women who act against their own kind.

In modern times, the law has been uncertain on the status of jealousy as a mitigating factor. In a 1955 *cause célèbre* in England, Ruth Ellis was hanged for shooting her boyfriend in a jealous rage. In 1960 Ernest Fanthe was sentenced to two years in prison for killing his wife's lover. He successfully pleaded "diminished responsibility".

It is widely acknowledged that the powerful grip of jealousy is hard to break. Women's refuges in the West are proof that even in progressive society, jealousy and its effects persist. Maltreated women, often beaten and confined to the home over the course of several years for imagined infidelities, are stalked by their husbands during their marriages and pursued even after divorce or separation. In these situations, jealousy is prompted by the need for control and domination. The obsessional nature of the condition may be caused by a large number of variables depending on the childhood, social background and personal experience of the individual. It has little to do with logic or genuine justification.

Noël Hallé, *The Transformation of the Nymph Io into a Heifer*, 18th cent. Oil on canvas, Christie's, London. Io was a priestess of Hera, who caught the eye of Hera's husband Zeus. In order to deflect the suspicions of his wife, Zeus turned Io into a white heifer, but the cunning Hera asked for the animal as a gift, and placed it under the guard of the hundred-eyed giant Argus. Zeus sent Hermes to free her, but the jealous Hera then dispatched a gad-fly to torment her. The maddened Io fled across land and sea to Egypt, where she was finally returned to human shape by the touch of Zeus's hand.

Guarding the Woman

Evolutionary biology identifies "guarding" as an essential instinct that stems from the male's need for genetic survival and the female's need for immediate survival. Exclusivity thus becomes necessary both for the assurance of paternity and the preservation of resources. Ways of holding female affection involve "love acts" such as the giving of gifts, guarding behavior and displays of virility while females are expected to show a greater degree of physical affection and readiness to forgive.

The mutual need for exclusive pair bonding is reflected in the cultural institution of marriage. Scientists believe that prehistoric man and woman would have exhibited strong guarding behavior. However we are then left with a contradiction: if exclusivity among couples does indeed cater to a basic need common to most living creatures in which the genetic survival of the male is paramount, then how can the wide-spread popularity of the ancient fertility cults of women be explained?

The ancient tablets of Sumer (c. 3000 B.C.) indicate that sexual sophistication among women was one of the divine ordinations given to the Goddess Inanna. The texts of the hymns and epics constitute evidence of the dominance of female deities. The Mesopotamian kingdoms, Egypt and various parts of Greece and Rome doubtless worshipped powerful goddesses who were adopted and adapted to the religion of subsequent conquerors.

Paternity under the goddess was less important than female fecundity, which was analogous with the growth of grain and the prosperity of both farmer and field. As the patriarchal religions swept the European continent attitudes changed. Gender became associated with value. Body and spirit were polarized into profane and pure, good and evil, male and female.

Anonymous, Husband Receiving the Key to the Chastity Belt, 17th cent. Oil on canvas, Staatliche Museen Preussischer Kulturbesitz, Berlin. It has been suggested that originally chastity belts were developed to protect women from being raped. They were only later, opportunistically, seized upon by jealous husbands. According to medieval satirists, however, resourceful wives would always make a duplicate key.

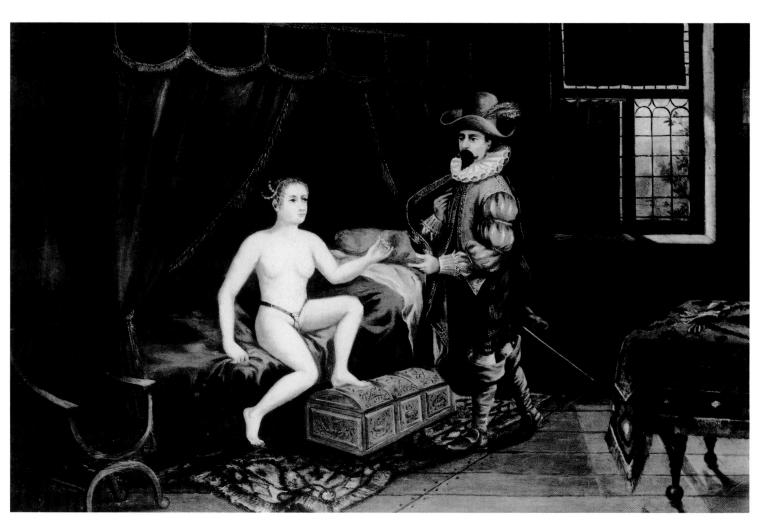

Judaism, the first of the Abrahamic religions, worked assiduously towards the banishment of fertility cults such as that of Asherah. Temples, once devoted to the exaltation of the human body as a living instrument for the glorification of divinity, now rejected the body in favor of a soul, split from its earthly container.

Women paid the highest price for the rupture that followed. Female chastity became synonymous with family honor, the purity of family pedigrees and protection of property. The guarding instinct was strongly reflected in the patriarchal attitude to marriage and the family. For centuries men remained polygamous to some extent and even after monogamy became the norm extramarital sex was not a serious matter. It was the opposite for women, particularly after marriage when the hymen no longer remained as proof of chastity.

One particularly barbaric antidote to female philandering was the chastity belt, which was probably developed in Italy in the 14th century. The medieval version consisted of a lockable metal hoop that ran from front to back through the crotch of the woman, possessing small holes for the elimination of waste, but effectively preventing sexual intercourse. A more humane method of protection was the constant presence of a moral guardian in the person of a decent, older woman. Often, as in Shakespeare's *Romeo and Juliet*, these were nurses or governesses. Other social sentinels were the gossips, lethal in societies where exposure of sexual activity was almost greater than the misdemeanor itself and often led to ostracization. All these factors served as powerful deterrents for potential wayward impulses past puberty. Even when women did flirt, they were wary of excessive touch in case it led to "carnal sin" and, the worst fate of all, illegitimate conception.

Above: **Illustration from *Fortune's Remedy* by Guillaume de Machaut, c. 1350. Bibliothèque Nationale, Paris.** The artist claims by the title of his picture that a woman's favors are a medicine for the pains of love, although the barred entrance and the ladies-in-waiting conspire to prevent any dispensation.

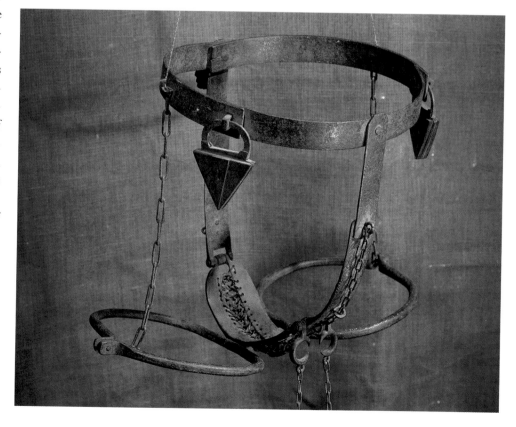

The chastity belt survived for centuries – examples can be found in catalogs of surgical instruments in the 1930s, although they were intended to stop masturbation rather than infidelity.

Infidelity

Infidelity describes a breach of loyalty to a long-term partner, applicable, arguably, even in the absence of copulation. Though frowned upon by religion and society the world over, extramarital sex has always found legitimacy in certain cliques. Romantic liaisons were always most common among the aristocracy where marriages marked coalitions of power leaving each partner to look elsewhere for romance. The Queen or Lady was accorded the full benefit of her position but romance with her husband was not a necessary part of the contract. One solution to this problem was the "courtly love" of the 12th century. First mentioned in the songs of court minstrels, it swiftly spread throughout Europe, forming the basis of some of the most enduring works of literature dedicated by the poet-lover to his beloved lady. *Amor cortois* followed strictly codified rules of conduct. Faithfulness was of the highest importance and infidelity to the beloved was no less a sin than sacrilege. The honor of the lady was paramount, so consequently corporeal relations were excluded. Lancelot and Guinivere's famous breach of the code ruptured the sanctity of the royal marriage, believed to be a vital influence on the well-being of the land. Chrétien de Troyes (1160–1190) among the most illustrious of troubadours, produced some of the first Arthurian romances in dedication to Marie de Champagne. Marie's mother, Eleanor of

Pierre-Antoine Baudouin, *The Indiscreet Wife*, c. 1760. Gouache, 30.5 x 27.5 cm, Musée des Arts décoratifs, Paris. In the playful and frivolous Rococo period "infidelity" was seen as gallantry. Baudouin, the favorite painter of the Marquise de Pompadour, presented the theme of "infidelity" twice in both form and content: it's not the husband grabbing the maid who is portrayed as indiscreet, but the wife who secretly observes the scene. She is in turn observed by the beholder. Without being seen, the viewer has two perspectives on this couple who think that no one is watching.

Aquitaine, wife of Louis VII of France and later of Henry II of England, was the inspiration behind the best works of Bernard de Ventadour in the 12th century. In the early 13th century Gottfried of Strasbourg produced the tragedy of Tristan and Isolde. Such texts reached their apogee with the *Divine Comedy* (begun in 1303), where Dante Alighieri synthesized courtly love with mysticism, elevating his earthly beloved Beatrice to divine guide in Paradise in the manner of Middle-Eastern mystics encountered during the Crusades. The poet-lover's devotion to his lady as a bridge to the divine was typical.

"Distant love", as described by the various minnesingers, caused the lover to remain constantly swinging between ecstasy and despair because true union with the beloved was impossible.

By 1660 the English aristocracy was indulging almost indiscriminately in extramarital liaisons; promiscuity had become a la mode at court; "adultery" was renamed "gallantry". The indulgence of sexual experimentation trickled down from the nobility to the lower middle classes. It became acceptable, even for women, to make love for pleasure and not simply for procreation. The sexual revolution of the Enlightenment had its critics and after a century of rampant excesses, society began to respond to the efforts of reformers.

However, for some, an entirely chaste lifestyle had become impossible after such enormous levels of freedom. The nobility continued their liaisons. Men often had mistresses, generally drawn from the educated, refined professional or merchant classes, whose families had lost their fortunes. These young women – rarely more than girls – were generally given a house to live in. Their children were not socially stigmatized, particularly the males, and frequently the father's household included children of the illicit liaisons of both husband and wife. In addition to keeping mistresses, men visited the salons of professional entertainers, not only for the gratification of their "baser desires" but also for social and sexual initiation. The courtesans of India, highly trained in the classical arts of

dance, music and literature, routinely received young men of wealthy and noble families for cultural and sexual instruction.

Institutionalized forms of infidelity rarely caused distress to the families concerned unless there was a breach of the code and a man was tempted to flout social convention by attempting to marry again. As far as society was concerned, as long as he put his wife and family first and gave his wife the respect and support to which she was entitled, she was considered to have no cause for complaint.

Philip Hermogenes Calderon, *Broken Vows*, 1857. Oil on board, 29 x 22 cm, Ashmolean Museum, Oxford. This painting represents the Victorian moral backlash to the excesses of the Enlightenment. Infidelity was no longer regarded as a romp, but as a life-destroying betrayal.

Womanizers

Thomas Phillips, *Portrait of George Gordon*, **6ᵗʰ Lord Byron (1788–1824)**, **19ᵗʰ cent. Oil on canvas, 90 x 70 cm, private collection.** Lord Byron and, below, a selection of his lovers in chronological order.

The legend of Don Juan is that of a depraved aristocrat who invites the statue of a former murder victim to join him for dinner. The statue or "Stone Guest" accepts the invitation but at the conclusion of dinner delivers his host into the fires of hell. Tirso de Molina's *El Burador de Sevilla* (1630) was the first work to introduce the character of this womanizer to literature. He caught the imagination of many a European writer. In France Molière found him an appropriate subject for the current preoccupations of French society. Mozart's opera *Don Giovanni* is the work which is considered to have earned the character the greatest fame.

The two most famous works in English to deal with Don Juan are Lord Byron's incomplete, eponymous, epic satire (1819–1824) and Bernard Shaw's *Man and Superman* (1905): a comedy and a philosophy. Act III is given over to Don Juan's assertion to Satan that man's life is given meaning because God depends upon him to execute His will. Here too, Don Juan ends up facing the infernal flames of hell. Interestingly, however, both works reflect an alteration in the character of Don Juan who changes from a debauched and exploitative character to one who becomes the sex object of lustful women. Thus Lord Byron's Don

Juan romps and performs on demand through 15 cantos pursued by mostly oriental sexually insatiable women and, in between, frequently manages clandestine liaisons of his own choice. Molière's character, on the other hand, is forced to abduct his wife (Elvira), suggesting a flaw in his allegedly irresistible attraction. It is quite conceivable that Byron with his innumerable *affaires de cœur* with married and unmarried women, including his half-sister Augusta Leigh and the obsessive Caroline Lamb, was himself the model for his mostly pleasant and at times amusingly helpless Don Juan.

The original legend, though its source is unknown, paints a picture of a different kind. Originally, Don Juan's profoundly unpleasant character is immediately apparent both in his taunting invitation to the statue (or ghost) of his own victim and in the moralistic conclusion of the tale where he finds himself bound for eternal damnation. The modern association with the term "Don Juan" falls somewhere between the two character types: it suggests a man devoted to the pursuit of women but also one who possesses superhuman sexual charisma. The label is simultaneously complementary and censorious. Any exploration of the Don Juan character inevitably raises the question

Anonymous, *Augusta Leigh*, **Lord Byron's sister, Christie's, London.** According to Byron the one woman whom he most loved.

Sir Thomas Lawrence, *Portrait of Lady Caroline Lamb*, **1809. Oil on canvas, Bristol City Museum and Art Gallery, Bristol.** She pursued Byron hysterically.

Sir George Hayter, *Miss Millbank*, **1812. Christie's Images, London.** She married Byron and bore him a child before leaving him in 1816.

Casanova

The last name of Giacomo Girolamo Casanova (1725–1798), like that of Don Juan, has long been a synonym for a sexually immoral man who exerts enormous power over women. He was expelled from a seminary in Venice after his involvement in a sexual scandal and became an adventurer, indulging in his carnal lusts everywhere he went and making a living through gambling and magic. He became the director of the French state lottery, a position that enabled him to meet King Louis XV and Madame Pompadour. His 12-volume *Memoirs*, which he began to write in 1790, contain fantastical accounts of his sexual exploits and turned him into a legendary lover whose reputation flourishes to this day.

Johann Berka, *Giacomo Girolamo Casanova Aged 63*, 1788. Copperplate engraving. The myth of Casanova as a consummate womanizer was strengthened by the French poet Jean Laforgue, who edited *Memoirs* for publication in the 19th century, and inadvertently added to their suggestive nature while attempting to censor them.

of insecurity so deep-rooted that it propels the subject forward as if his demons may be kept at bay only by persistent, frenetic activity – in this case sexual. The flamboyance, the glamor, the libertinism is merely a smoke-screen for inner emptiness, and the character seeks to fill the void through relentless intercourse with women. To this extent the typical womanizing personality is similar to that of any other kind of addict: the search continues because any external solution can only be immediate and temporary.

Womanizers are often given to flagrant exaggeration. The envy and admiration generated by their sexual braggadocio supply instant ego gratification. The illusion of sexual success that they paint ensures their popularity with other men who may wish to emulate them or by basking in their reflected glory become entitled to their rejects. For women on the other hand their allure lies in the challenge of conquest, of snaring and taming the wildness and laying claim to the trophy through marriage or fidelity – generally an unattainable goal.

Pathological womanizers, though on the surface colorful and convivial, are sadly damaged people. Their need for serial sexual relationships constitutes a continual search for security and love to compensate for their intolerable self-loathing.

Sex Addicts

The growing field of addiction studies in psychology includes sex addiction, which became well-known following the treatment of some Hollywood stars and celebrity socialites. The basic theory defined as addiction or dependency is created in early childhood through poor parenting. Children suffering from poor self-image, or narcissistic disturbance, aim their actions so substantially to please others that praise and approval become their mode of survival. Thus the need arises to control and manipulate the positive response of others. In sex-addicts, where inadequacy may be an issue, the mind-altering effect, or "buzz", comes from serial sexual conquest and intercourse. The male sex addict tends to split women into madonnas and whores: the former to be wed but excluded from lascivious fantasies, the latter lecherous, insatiable and unworthy. The unconscious aim is to acquire unconditional love but the sex-addict's fear of intimacy rules this out. Treatment involves the decision to break the cycle of shame and gratification, to acknowledge the problem and accept individual limitations.

English School, *Portrait of Countess Guiccioli*. Lithograph, The Illustrated London News Picture Library, London. She found Byron "a celestial apparition".

English School, *Portrait of Mary Chaworth*. Lithograph, The Illustrated London News Picture Library, London. With her Byron might have lived happily.

La Femme Fatale

It has been claimed that the femme fatale – the irresistibly attractive woman who brings disaster upon any man who loves her – is a peculiarly late 19th-century invention, but in fact she is more timeless than that. John Keats's celebrated 1814 poem *La Belle Dame sans Merci*, which anticipated the late Romantic fascination with deadly women, tapped into existing Celtic notions about fairies, which were seen as mysterious, merciless beings, immortal, ungodly and illusory, for their beauty was not always genuine, but the result of a spell or "glamor". A typical effect of La Belle Dame's enchantment was to produce a life-sapping obsession with the object of love.

The "Loathly Lady", another aspect of the same kind of creature, is found in many folk tales where a beautiful young woman metamorphoses into an ugly hag (Edmund Spenser's *Faerie Queene*, 1590) or indeed, a hag becomes a beautiful woman. Each year in the Land of Faerie or "Tuatha de Danaan" is the equivalent of a hundred earthly years and those who are transported there, in thrall to a fairy, return to find themselves aged beyond mortal existence. The most famous example is the Irish Oisian, son of Finn MacCumhail, who fell

in love with the fairy Naevhe and returned three hundred years later to his earthly home. Another deadly female from folklore was Loreley, an exquisite water nymph sometimes thought to be a German girl who drowned herself in the Rhine after her lover jilted her. In this otherworldly form she uses her seductive powers to avenge the wrongs done to her by striking blind or dead those who look at her. An alternative tale is that the water nymphs left their home when activity increased on the river and its banks. Only one nymph stayed behind, singing in the moonlight while combing her golden tresses. Sailors, entranced by her song and her beauty, became oblivious to the dangers of a powerful whirlpool at the bottom of the cliff she sat on and drowned. Whatever her origins, she is clearly linked to the deadly sirens, gifted with heavenly song, of Greek myth.

However, it was only in the late 19th century that the femme fatale became an almost universal cliché among playwrights, authors, composers and artists, as part of the Romantic obsession with death and the dark, destructive side of human nature. As such, she was a sex-changed version of the earlier, Byronic hero, destined, as one commentator described him, to wreck his own life and those of everyone near to him. The femme fatale was, as the Byronic hero had been, pale, distant, cold, impassive, mysterious and with an irresistible magnetism – in other words, the personification of death itself.

Some have suggested that the reason women were suddenly given this role in the 19th

Eduard Jakob von Steinle, *Loreley*, 1864. Oil on canvas, 213.5 x 135.4 cm, Schack-Galerie, Munich. Steinle captures the demonic, Nordic aspect of the vengeful water sprite.

century was to do with an outbreak of male anxiety, based on unacknowledged guilt at having kept women oppressed for so long, and in response to their growing demands for emancipation. The playwright Johan August Strindberg (1849–1912) said of his character, Miss Julie, that she was an example of the "man-hating half-woman" who had existed throughout history, and was modern only to the extent that she had been discovered, and "begun to make a noise". Others point out that the vogue of the femme fatale coincided with a

Born in the Netherlands, Margaretha Geertruida MacLeod (1876–1917), née Zelle, also known as Mata Hari, became the prototype for the insatiable female spy who sent thousands of French soldiers to their deaths by using her enormous sexual panache to entice secrets from high-ranking German and French intelligence officers. A French military court deemed her to be that rare creature, a "genuine femme fatale". She was executed by firing squad in 1917 at the age of 39 despite enormous contradictions in the evidence against her. Her lovers included prominent European personalities after she burst upon the Paris scene with her highly erotic but ersatz temple dances, capturing the imagination of the *Belle Époque*.

Mata Hari's theatrical image is undoubtedly more interesting than the substance of her life. She has been described as a minor figure in the world of espionage. Her sexual skills were also, apparently, exaggerated. Her fame is above all a tribute to the world's insatiable appetite for femmes fatales.

John William Waterhouse, *La Belle Dame sans Merci*, 1893. Oil on canvas, 111 x 81 cm, Hessisches Landesmuseum, Darmstadt. The fairy traps the knight with her long hair – a common symbol of unbridled sexuality since at least the Middle Ages, and therefore, to the artists of the 19th century, a palpable threat.

Aubrey Beardsley, Illustration for Oscar Wilde's *Salome*, 1891. Private collection. For many artists, decapitation was clearly a metaphor for castration, and characters such as Salome and Judith were archetypes of the emasculating female.

period of especial fear about the dangers of syphilis – so that sex and death were inevitably conjoined in the male imagination.

Whatever the reason, artists became obsessed with knowing, seductive, deadly women, whom they approached with a mixture of desire and revulsion. The exploits – real or imagined – of Cleopatra, Helen of Troy, Salome, Judith and others began to be recycled endlessly in fiction and paintings. If there was no convenient biblical or historical character, one could be invented, as Gustave Flaubert did with his cold, murderous Carthaginian queen, Salammbo. Meanwhile painters such as Edvard Munch and Gustav Klimt were filling their canvases with images of vampiric temptresses. It was not long before life imitated art, and society ladies

began to ask their portraitists to depict them as femmes fatales. Actresses, dancers and writers, too, including Sarah Bernhardt, Ida Rubinstein and Colette, reveled in this image. It became fashionable for a man to be ruined by a notorious courtesan - such as Cora Pearl, La Paiva or Lillie Langtry - and the courtesans in turn measured their success and built their reputations upon how many lovers they had driven to despair or destitution. Notoriety was their goal and their fatal, aphrodisiacal attraction. Cora Pearl famously treated her horses better than her men, but this only increased her desirability.

The world has not lost its appetite for the femme fatale. Although she ceased to be a major subject for serious painters after the

death of Klimt in 1918, she migrated successfully to the cinema, and was embodied over the years by actresses such as Louise Brooks in *Pandora's Box* (1929), Mary Astor in *The Maltese Falcon* (1941) and Sharon Stone in *Basic Instinct* (1992). In the real world, too, the femme fatale remains a potent symbol. Wallis Simpson (1896–1986) was – absurdly but sincerely – reputed to have enormous sexual skills, learned in an Oriental whorehouse, which enabled her to lure Edward VIII from the throne. Even the patently unremarkable Camilla Parker Bowles (b. 1947) was portrayed as a femme fatale when the British public could find no other reason why the Prince of Wales might prefer her to their beloved "fairy-tale" Princess Diana.

Too Close for Comfort

Cuzco School, Detail from *Genealogy*, 18th cent. Pedro de Osma Museum, Lima. Mama Ocllo, an Inca princess, dressed as the moon, from an 18th-century illustrated Peruvian genealogy. She holds a mask, in the form of the sun, which bears the features of her husband-brother.

The prohibition against incest may be the oldest and most widespread of all human taboos. In one of his more far-fetched theories, Sigmund Freud suggested that it stemmed from a primordial sense of guilt about prehistoric acts of patricide and cannibalism, surviving from a time when the only way that young men could gain sexual access to women was by killing and eating the dominant male (their father) and taking his wives (who were their mothers). There are a number of more plausible explanations. Repeated inbreeding tends to produce weak or deformed children. It has been pointed out that ancient peoples had no knowledge of genetics, and would have blamed such events on witchcraft or the gods. Nevertheless, it is telling that the most common cross-cultural argument against incest is that kinfolk share the same blood, and that mixing it would be harmful. Ignorant or not, cultures that allowed incest would have died out, and those that banned it (for whatever reason) would have survived and, by breeding outside the group, spread their ideas with them. Outbreeding peoples would also be more likely to thrive because of the new bonds and alliances they were constantly making through marriage. Their incest taboos would have also prospered with them. According to the anthropologist Bronislaw Malinowski (1884–1942), incest was banned because it confused peoples' roles within the family, causing instability and conflicting duties and passions. Sexologist Henry Havelock Ellis (1859–1939) simply thought that children who were reared together became sexually uninterested in each other, a claim supported by experience in some of the kibbutzes of Israel between 1950 and 1990, where children were brought up in large communal nurseries and encouraged to form intense emotional bonds with each other. Although many lifelong friendships were forged, nobody ever married another person from the same nursery. Ellis's theory, while plausible, only attempts to explain the incest prohibition between siblings (and fails to explain why a taboo should be necessary at all). However, this is the form of incest that has most often been institutionalized, especially among kings and nobility. The Peruvian Inca, the Egyptian pharaohs and the kings and queens of Hawaii all practiced brother-sister marriage. In all cases, however, this was to lay claim to a form of divinity – to emphasize that they were gods, and not subject to the laws of men. The Roman emperor Caligula, who also considered himself a god, had sex with all three of his sisters and married one of them, Drusilla, although this was not permitted under Roman law, even for emperors. Brother-sister relations are more generally permitted by some cultures that have a sociological, rather than biological, definition of kinship. The Lamet of southeastern Asia allow brother-sister marriage if the pair were raised in different households. The Swedish courts also accepted this viewpoint in a case in the 1980s, when a government official accidentally discovered that a married couple were brother and sister. They were unaware of this themselves, having been separated as children, and successfully argued that, having been raised apart, their marriage should be allowed to stand. Malinowski's theory seems more relevant to parent-child incest, which is the most common

Jan Pieterszoon Saenredam after Hendrik Goltzins, *Lot and His Daughters*, 1597. Copperplate engraving, 18.9 x 24.3 cm, Rijksprentenkabinett, Amsterdam. After the destruction of Sodom and Gomorrah, Lot's daughters decided that they had to get their father drunk with wine and "lie with him, that we may preserve the seed..." and perpetuate the human race. Their actions are not condemned in the Bible.

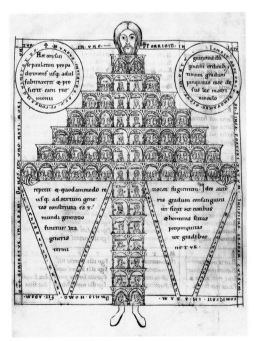

Isidor of Seville's *Etymologiae*, c. 1150. Cod. Lat. 13031, folio 102 v. 34 x 23.5 cm, Bayerische Staatsbibliothek, Munich. A consanguinity tree showing the range of prohibited marriages, from mother and father at the center to distant cousins on the periphery.

form in the modern Western world. A survey in the United States in the mid-1980s concluded that 10–14 percent of under-18-year-olds had been sexually abused by a parent or step-parent. The overwhelming majority of such cases involved a father and daughter. Mother-son incest, by contrast, is the rarest form of all, although it is said to be compulsory as a rite of passage among the Kubeo of South America, and has been reported occasionally among the Tutsi of Kenya and the Kóniag of Alaska.

Most cultures legislate for incest far beyond the immediate family. An ancient custom still found among Eastern Orthodox Christians and Muslims is milk incest, where people who have been breast-fed by the same woman may not marry. A law against name incest forbids a person from marrying anyone who has the same given name as a parent or sibling. It occurs among the Orthodox Jews, as well as the Bushmen of southern Africa. Various other customs forbid people from marrying their godparents (Eastern Orthodox Christians and Catholics), the midwives who assisted at their birth (the Sémang of southwest Asia and the Zande of central Africa), and their teacher's daughter (Balinese).

Some of the most complex incest taboos relate to cousin-marriage, which is proscribed in some form by more than two-thirds of the world's cultures. The problem lies in defining what degree of cousin one can or cannot marry. For example, the Bible does not forbid cousin-marriage at all, but in the 6th century Pope Gregory the Great banned marriage between third cousins, an edict that was extended to sixth cousins by Pope Gregory III in 731. Because it was almost impossible for many people to get married under these rules, the conditions were once more relaxed to third cousin by Pope Innocent III in 1215, and to second cousin by the Council of Trent in 1563. This is currently the position of the Roman Catholic Church on cousin-incest, although sometimes special permission is given for marriage between first cousins as well.

Monogamy

Una cum uno (one woman with one man) is the state-recognized, ideally life-long form of cohabitation of one woman with just one man. This particular form of marriage results not so much from sexual inclination as from the social necessities that predominate in Western Christian social structures, regardless of the lifestyle of the populace. It means the willing or imposed limitation of sexual life – an institution of reason, not of emotion. Precisely because the Church held that sinful lust should be kept to a minimum, there are no polygamous or polyandrous ways of life in Christian areas. The critics of monogamy play with the connection with monotony: fidelity is boring, and it makes one boring. In the end, the partner will be reproached for this boredom.

Those not opposed to eroticism and sexuality but still in favor of closed marriage follow the argumentation of many sexual reformers. They start from the position that sex fulfills a noble purpose in marriage; if not that of producing children, then that of cementing the bond between husband and wife. New erotic variations have to be tried – not out of curiosity, but out of a sense of duty. Thus it's especially the defenders of monogamy who support erotic variety in marriage and consider mastery of various sexual techniques necessary.

The French couple Armand (99) and Jeanne (98) Giraud celebrate their 80th wedding anniversary. The couple got married in 1918. Historically, a marriage "till death us do part" was in most cases significantly shorter than it would be today. While women have statistically always outlived men, nevertheless they ran a great risk of dying in childbirth. Until the mid-19th century, when the Viennese obstetrician Dr Ignaz Semmelweiss (1818–1865) promoted rigorous hygiene, many women giving birth died of infections caught from their doctor. Because of longer life-expectancy, in many parts of Europe marriages are on average lasting longer than they ever have, despite rising divorce rates and serial monogamy.

Honoré Daumier, *Six Months of Marriage*, 1839. Lithograph, 23.1 x 18.7 cm, Bruno and Sadie Adriani Collection. Daumier parodies the tedium of monogamy but many are grateful for what the actress, Mrs Patrick Cambell, called "the deep calm of the marriage bed after the hurly-burly of the chaise longue".

Some proponents of free love claim that the true beneficiary of infidelity is not the philanderer, but the "betrayed" spouse. The faithful partner – not as often the woman as used to be assumed – could enjoy the attention of the unfaithful partner, who, conscious of his or her guilt, would be much more attentive and friendlier than one forced to live monogamously.

Serial Monogamy

The "life-stage partner" is not a modern invention. Serial monogamy – mainly the remarriage of widowed people – has actually been quite widespread and, although frowned upon in Christendom, was considered a religious duty among Mosaic Jews. The life of a long-lived person was defined by a series of marriages, but each marriage came to an abrupt and complete end in death. A new mother was needed for the surviving children and the man usually couldn't manage the household on his own. Society was arranged in familiar communities that could only survive as groups. If a member disappeared, he or she had to be replaced, regardless of how much he or she was loved.

The intact family was never considered more important than it was in the 19th century, as the old institution underwent a significant change. In the previous centuries, the monogamous couple didn't have to love each other; first and foremost they had to work together to cope with daily life. What the children had to learn was taught to them by those they lived with. Workplace and living space weren't divided; not for craftsmen, not for farmers. But as a result of the Industrial Revolution, the daily lives of men and women diverged. Instead of staying with his family, the head of the household was busy with his work outside of the house. The marital union needed support from something other than economic necessity.

At the end of the 20th century, serial monogamy has once again become widespread, although more as a result of internal rather than external pressures. It's no longer the partner who dies, but one's feelings for him or her. At the beginning of the third millennium, one can marry a new, more "love-worthy" partner while the first is still alive. The change in values is also apparent in a different assessment of the survivor. Widowed

partners who don't cope in timely fashion with the loss of their loved one and show no interest in new relationships aren't considered especially faithful or virtuous, but instead ready for therapy. They haven't managed their "mourning assignment" – like dilatory students who haven't done their homework.

Who has the greatest interest in monogamy? It is believed by some that as soon as an abandoned woman can demand monthly financial support from her wage-earning husband, women lose interest in maintaining monogamy. Sexologist Ernest Bornemann was convinced that every form of contractual monogamy was a consequence of *pater semper incertus*, men can never be entirely certain of their paternity.

Peter Parler, Emperor Charles IV and His Four Wives, from 1374. Stone sculptures, Triforium of the St. Vitus Cathedral, Prague. *From left to right, above:* **Emperor Charles IV, Blanche of Valois, Anna of Pfalz,** *below:* **Anna von Schweidnitz, Elisabeth of Pomerania.** The four-times married Emperor Charles IV (1316–1378) was a master of making royal connections through marriage. Through his first wife Blanche, he was closely linked to the French royal family. She died in childbirth at the age of 22. In 1349 he wedded Anna of Pfalz who died at 24. Her successor, Anna von Schweidnitz, brought Charles rule over Silesia and bore him an heir, Wenceslas, in 1361. In 1363, again a widower, Charles married Elisabeth of Pomerania. Charles had portraits of all of his wives carved in stone, perhaps as a sign that he treasured or loved them.

Last of the Summer Wine

The old and lustful have been ridiculed for centuries. Very often, such people were publicly humiliated. In the 17th century one would sing mock serenades and caterwauls known as "charivari" under the windows of old men who had married young women. Toothless ecstasy was mercilessly made fun of. It has long been believed that the older partners failed to recognize that the young ones were after material advantages when they seemingly reciprocated the elders' desires. Material interests are always implied in old portraits of May-December couples.

Up to a few decades ago, society encouraged the aging to believe that the waning of sexual desires was natural. This attitude has since

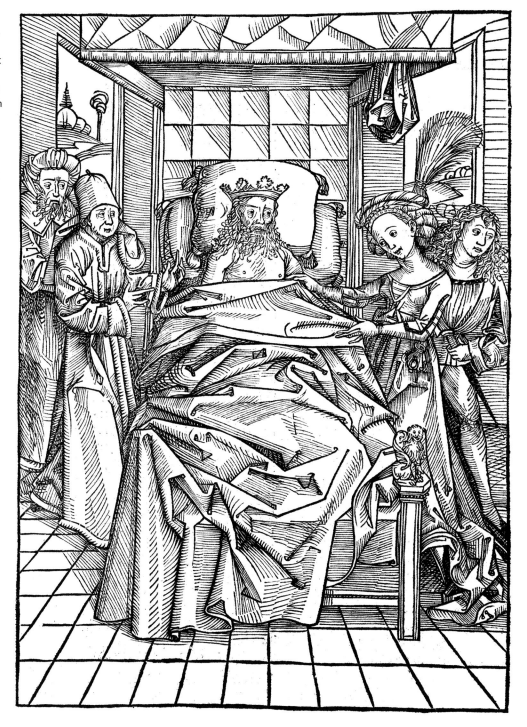

Anonymous, *King David and Abishag the Shunammite*, 1491. Woodcut from the Treasury, Nuremberg. The concept of Shunammitism alleges that youth has a generally invigorating and rejuvenating effect on the aged. The word "Shunammitism" has its origin in the Bible (Kings, 1:1–4): "Now King David was old and stricken in years; and they covered him with clothes, but he gat no heat. Wherefore his servants said unto him, Let there be sought for my lord the king a young virgin: and let her stand before the king, and cherish him; and let her lie in thy bosom, that my lord the king may get heat. So they sought for a fair damsel throughout all the borders of Israel, and found Abishag the Shunammite, and brought her to the king. And the damsel was very fair; and she cherished the king, and ministered to him; but the king knew her not."

Lucas Cranach the Elder, *The Unequal Couple*, c. 1535. 51 x 36 cm, The Picture Gallery of the Academy of Fine Arts, Vienna. Wisdom and dignity are qualities which distinguish the older man from the younger and therefore he is met with respect. Passion and being in love are considered feelings overcome by an old man. When he runs after a woman or even submits himself to her rule he is seen as a fool making himself ridiculous. In this picture the purse clearly indicates why the young woman accepts him.

A fully gratifying sexual relationship can be possible at any age, although in older people it generally requires more attentiveness, understanding and patience.

changed entirely. Since sexuality and reproduction have been de-coupled, erotic desires have become a sign of vitality and thus of youth. In 1998, nearly a fifth of the American men over 75 who were surveyed had sexual intercourse at least once a week. Among women it was about one in ten. In the 60–74-year-old group it was still a quarter of the women and a third of the men. With increasing age it's not lust that dies, but the partner.

Although the desire for a sexual relationship may still exist, available older women in particular have problems finding partners. If a never-married, divorced or widowed woman doesn't happen to bump into an old male friend her own age who also lives alone, she remains alone. Older single men seldom look for partners their own age. For 75-year-old men who place personal ads, 60-year-old women are often already too old.

The women's rights activist Betty Friedan, herself born in 1921, described the dilemma of older single women: Men of the same age are "either dead or married". But she at least can imagine alternatives. Older women could live with each other in lesbian relationships, look for younger partners, or they could share a man.

The remark of a 100-year-old woman who had a crush on her young attendant sends a ray of hope: "It's only platonic!" she emphasized, thereby making it clear that she can imagine the situation otherwise. In fact, the simple proximity of attractive young people is naturally invigorating for the aged. The belief in so-called Shunammitism is as old as the Bible; the "vapors" of virginal women have as revitalizing an effect on older men as that of male youths on older women.

New Forms of Cohabitation

The construct of monogamous marriage suffers from the fact that shared life and economic interdependence do not necessarily lead to reciprocal, partner-directed erotic desires. An emotionally-defined and thereby delicate situation is supposed to be written down formally in a marriage contract. Mutual love, respect, and faithfulness are ideal states whose lifelong continuity seldom corresponds to real married life.

For as long as monogamous marriage has represented the only form of adult cohabitation tolerated by church and state in the Christian West, singles, couples and entire groups have tried to come up with means of escaping its obligations. Privileged couples, who either don't care, or don't have to care what others think of them, have always had some freedom, whether openly or secretly. In order to maintain respect and mutual love in the long term, they often abandon fidelity in the narrower sense. Except among the petite bourgeoisie, where the married partners had neither the space nor the time to get away from one another, these couples kept a distance from each other, which sometimes fostered erotic desires. In addition, at least one member of the couple had sexual freedom, more often by verbal than written agreement and most often simply through the silent consent of the financially dependent partner.

The discrepancy between the monogamous pretensions and polygamous reality has become all the clearer since life expectancies have risen and married couples have been able to – or have had to – live together for decades. The possibility of divorce and remarriage, which arose in the meantime in Protestant Northern Europe, led to *de facto* serial monogamy. Children often determined the duration of a couple's life together.

Today couples try to reinterpret the marriage contract even for this period, redefining "fidelity". Many consider themselves faithful to their spouse if the partner can rely on them even when they are having affairs and starting other liaisons. An interesting and often-tried compromise is the *ménage à trois*: a relationship between two women and one man or vice versa,

Will McBride, *The House Is Full,* **Munich, 1970.** Silver emulsion, 26.7 x 40.5 cm, Uwe Scheid Collection. "Our house, in fact, for my taste, was overpopulated. There was at least one relationship too many (actually there were even more). Since then I learned how thin everyone's wall around himself is. If you disrespect another person's body space, then you quickly make him uneasy, even fearful and angry." (Will McBride)

lived in so-called "uncle-marriages" or "wild marriages" because they would have lost their pensions had they remarried. It must be noted that in those cases, sexual freedom was not the highest priority.

In fact, at the beginning of the 21st century, new unofficial forms of marriage, "living together", which look rather traditional, had established themselves. Especially in large cities, many unmarried professional couples share an apartment (and a bed) and have children together. Same-sex households are also becoming more and more common.

At the same time, more and more couples are living in "weekend marriages" because the two partners can't find work in the same city. This situation strongly affects the definition of fidelity. Mobility indirectly lightens the burden on those couples who used to suffer from too little time and space for themselves; even families in which toleration of outside lovers was unthinkable are now openly trying such alternatives.

Since the sexual revolution of the 1960s, marriage has more and more often been described as a state- and church-prescribed institution that only leads to the limitation of erotic freedom. Those who were questioned the bourgeois worldview was especially against sexual possessiveness. The alternative meant "everyone with everyone", although most such "communes" were more like old-fashioned harems.

Left: **Jean-Paul Sartre and Simone de Beauvoir, 1950.** The couple shared an open relationship, although he found it less emotionally taxing than she did.

Below: Jules and Jim, **still from the film by François Truffaut, 1961.** This seminal French New Wave Film tells the story of the volatile *ménage à trois* between the willful Catherine (Jeanne Moreau) and the two men who grow to love her (Oskar Werner and Henri Serre).

like the one François Truffaut portrayed in his 1961 film *Jules and Jim.*

The liberalization of sexuality is leading to a desexualization of marriage. People who are allowed by society to be sexually active prior to marriage – as are most of today's youth in the industrialized West – and similarly, people who are allowed to fulfill their sexual desires in widowhood, will no longer see marriage as "permission given by society to two people for reciprocal sexual satisfaction", as Immanuel Kant once put it.

The assumption that every marriage implies a sexual union in no way corresponds to reality. After being married for some time, many spouses no longer have sex with each other. They either have none at all (or only with themselves) or they have it with other people. In Germany until 1970, cohabitation without a marriage certificate was just about impossible as long as landlords were threatened by a section in the penal code, which was actually aimed at brothel-keepers, if they rented to unmarried couples. However especially after the Second World War, many German widows

La Vie en Rose

History has unquestionably been unfair to lesbians with few historical records available prior to the last few hundred years, with the exception of Sappho's writing in the 6th century B.C. Certainly, intimate relationships were common among women prior to and during the Victorian era, as can be gleaned from the passionate and intimate, though largely sanitized, accounts of friendships between women. In some societies where women and men are segregated, such as on the Asian sub-continent where virginity is highly prized, secret, erotic liaisons between women have always passed without comment. Lesbian relationships were also tacitly acknowledged in past times as a "passing phase" in the development of female sexuality. In the West there is some evidence that they may even have been encouraged as a means through which women learned to experience their own sexuality in preparation for a heterosexual marriage. This became a threat to society only if a woman decided to remain single. The women who adhered steadfastly to their sexual preferences by refusing marriage and sexual relations with men tended to be those who were educated, strong-willed and individualistic.

Novelist Charlotte Brontë's correspondence with her friend Ellen Nussey may contain clues to sexual passion, though the physical aspect of the relationship can no longer be established. The argument that the language of the letters was simply part of normal contemporary discourse is considerably reduced when it is noted that not only did the Brontës make every attempt to limit relations between the women, both personally and by post, they also burned her letters after her death and demanded that Ellen burn Charlotte's letters, too. When writing Charlotte's biography, Elizabeth Gaskell edited significant phrases out of her letters as in this example dated 20 January 1842 where

Djuna Barnes and Thelma Wood, 1920s. Barnes and Wood appear to have fallen into traditional "couple" roles in this picture where the former is dressed as the "femme" and the latter as "butch". Their relationship was characterized by Wood's wildness and dominance and Barnes' loyalty and endurance.

Role-play

It is not entirely certain if role-play in a lesbian relationship simply imitates dominant gender constructions or if it is, as described by some writers, an "authentic" aspect of lesbian sexuality. Certainly, it symbolizes power-relations and eroticizes dominance and submission. In the eight-year-long relationship between Djuna Barnes and Thelma Wood, the latter, a "tall, handsome, hard-drinking woman from St. Louis" played the polygamous male. The two cut a dashing picture in Parisian café society, with their black cloaks and hats and smart canes. Barnes claimed to have remained monogamous and constantly pleaded for the same from her errant lover. Though she was the bread-winner, Barnes wrote to friends that she was frightened of Wood: at a reading of her novel *Nightwood* in which she savaged Wood following their break-up, the latter punched her in public. Barnes broke off the relationship when Wood fell in love with Henriette Metcalfe, a wealthy widow. The three discussed the terms of separation, as in a heterosexual marriage, and the new couple left for New York. Wood's last lover was Margaret Behrens with whom she lived in Monroe, "where in all seasons [Wood] wore a navy-blue tam and mannish clothes" and drove in a jeep alongside Margaret "in a beret, dangling a long, booted leg on the side". Barnes and Wood each claimed that the other was the love of her life.

Joseph Granie, *The Kiss*, 1900. Oil on canvas, private collection.

the final phrase was censored. "You tantalize me to death with talking of conversations by the fireside and between the sheets." Brontë, who married her father's curate in her late thirties, wrote she did so only to secure his old age. She often found it onerous to contend with marriage and her husband's authority.

Some half-century later, the lesbians of Parisian café society, made up largely of expatriates from North America and England, displayed similar characteristics. They were independent and individualistic: novelists, poets, sculptors and painters. Their tastes varied hugely from the salon of Djuna Barnes' patroness Natalie Barney, devoted to the delights of the *Belle Époque* to Gertrude Stein's exclusive soirees, which reflected her commitment to cubist art and modernism. While Stein kept company with the leading artists and writers of the time, generously promoting them and patronizing their work, her live-in lover Alice B. Toklas kept house, produced elegant meals and entertained their wives. Though Stein's infidelity caused Alice considerable unhappiness, she remained

Tamara de Lempicka, *Les Deux Amies*, 1923. Oil on canvas, 60 x 130 cm, Musée du Petit Palais, Geneva. Although married twice, Lempicka was bisexual. Her tastes appear to run to more voluptuous figures than were fashionable among the "garçonne", or tomboy, lesbians of the time.

Gertrude Stein and Alice B. Toklas, 1944. The manuscript of Gertrude Stein's famous poem *A / rose is a / rose is a / rose ...* ends with the verse "She is my rose" referring to her lifelong lover, muse and secretary Alice B. Toklas whom she met in 1907 in Paris. Among the many avant-garde painters they received in their famous salon were Matisse, Picasso and Braque. After the First World War their home became a meeting point for young American writers for whom Stein coined the famous phrase "the lost generation".

devoted to her all her life and, after her lover's death, embraced Catholicism so that she might be reunited with her in Paradise. They share the same gravestone in Paris. The same panache and daring characterized other famous lesbians of the time. Vita Sackville-West, an English aristocrat and member of the Bloomsbury inner circle, recognized her sexual "duality"early in life, as did Thelma Wood in St. Louis, USA. Both before and after her marriage Vita indulged in the odd sexual escapade with a number of women, including Virginia Woolf. Though these women undoubtedly lived full sexual lives with their female partners on and off the Parisian "scene", it does not follow that genital sex must always be a part of lesbian relationships. The "stone butch" lesbians, while demanding absolute submission from their partners, never allowed their lovers to reciprocate the lovemaking. The controversy on this issue continues among radical feminists such as Anne Koedt, who insist that any kind of sexual commitment imposes limitations on individual development.

Lesbian Marriage

One of the most publicized lesbian "marriages" in the early 20th century was the on-off passion between Vita Sackville-West and her girlhood friend Violet Keppel, later Trefusis. Though Vita had always partly recognized her "dual" nature in her sexual attraction to women, she successfully remained monogamous in her marriage. But when her husband Harold Nicolson was forced to reveal his homosexual encounters to her following a possible diagnosis of venereal disease, Vita was shattered and reassessed her life. She temporarily set up home with the still-unmarried Violet, which extended to years. Harold, deeply ashamed of his actions, tolerated the relationship but nursed a profound resentment for Violet whom he described as "evil" and accused of wanting to break up his marriage. The two women continued for many years in a double triangle, eloping together often but always returning to full sexual relationships with their husbands. At the same time, they demanded "chastity" from one another. The relationship of Djuna Barnes and Thelma Wood, was similarly referred to as a marriage. The women in both cases saw themselves as couples in which their partnership with each other was paramount.

Untying the Knot

Commentators saw the high divorce rate in societies around the world at the start of the third millennium as the decline of marriage or a change in attitude in the continuing popularity of marriage as an institution. Attitudes to divorce differ dramatically, for example, between conventional rural societies and industrial ones, where a modern, global worldview allows greater freedom. Occasionally, the authorities have seen quick divorce as a lucrative source of income. In around 1927, some states of the US started to compete for ever-quicker divorces. Across the Atlantic, meanwhile, France advertised private divorces, having banned reportage of divorce cases in the press. Out-of-state divorce became an attractive option.

In nations where religious beliefs are enshrined in the law, divorce is generally harder than in secular or democratic state systems. Even at the beginning of the 21st century, Catholic countries still look unfavorably on divorce, as do scattered Catholic communities where individuals may prefer to apply for papal dispensation for annulment. In Hindu societies, particularly within some of the more orthodox Brahminic groups, divorce is considered sinful. Thus the dissolution of marriage is effected in covert ways. These informal means of dissolving a marriage make divorce statistics almost impossible.

Recent figures in the Western world show that in the years 1960–1997 the divorce rate had more than doubled, but researchers believe this is a limited picture. Unofficial partings and trial separations account for many more marriage breakups which remain unofficial because of the feelings of failure and shame which still accompany the breakdown of a solemnized relationship.

One of the most obvious causes of divorce is the increasing financial independence of women since the 19th century. In England, for example, in 1857, the law was changed to allow women rights over their own property and by 1893, women had legal control over it. By the end of the 19th century they were entitled to their own income and to have savings. English women had a right to their own wages from 1907. During the 20th century, the lifestyle of

Henry Nelson O'Neill, *The Trial of Catherine of Aragon* (detail), 19th cent. Oil on canvas, 42.5 x 64.8 cm, Birmingham Museum and Art Gallery, Birmingham. Henry VIII married Catherine of Aragon, his brother's widow, in 1510. Disappointed by her inability to produce a male heir and infatuated by the 20-year-old Anne Boleyn, he persuaded himself that he was living in mortal sin with Catherine and appealed to the Pope for an annulment of his marriage. When this was not granted he broke with Rome, declaring himself head of the Church of England. In May 1533, the new archbishop, Thomas Cranmer, presided over a trial that declared Henry's first marriage annulled.

women was further revolutionized. Being better educated and able to go out to work, women were capable of supporting themselves and the foundation on which marriage had so far rested was destabilized. The division of domestic labor altered as women chose to find themselves jobs outside the home rather than fulfill the traditional role of homemaker and child-rearer. Equally, the husband was no longer obliged to support the family entirely on his own and the power balance was drastically altered. The economics of the situation had an effect on the sexual life of individuals. With the sexual revolution of the 1960s, women, more willing to acknowledge their sexual needs, began citing sexual dis-

satisfaction as a legitimate reason for divorce. The improved financial and sexual status of women had a direct impact on moving divorce further up the social agenda of most nations.

Divorce research has revealed that high on the list of women's reasons for seeking divorce are "lack of love", financial problems, violence, abuse, alcoholism, and the husband's neglect of family and home. For men sexual disagreement is the commonest complaint, alongside the rather startling complaints against the in-laws. Failure to consummate a marriage has always been acceptable grounds for annulment or divorce even in the most conservative societies, though here it is arguable whether a woman would confess to the situation. Most modern legal systems regard infidelity of either partner as a sufficient cause for divorce.

Unofficially, parents and the family group continue to have a say in the breakup of marriages but on the whole, today, divorce is a matter for the individual couple to decide. In traditional socities stigma remains attached to divorce and often serves to deter couples from considering it as the solution to marital problems.

The details of the divorce procedures vary from country to country but on the whole, in the industrialized world, divorce could not be easier: mutual consent and the catch-all phrase "irreconcilable differences" help dispatch the marriage conveniently and quickly. Should the partners disagree and the relationship becomes abusive, injunctions may be brought by one or other partner to stop the other entering the shared home. Refusal by one partner to sign the documents is an effective way for the vengeful spouse to force the process into delays and complications. In recent years divorce therapy has become available to help couples work through their feelings of resentment during and after the breakup of their marriage to ensure an amicable relationship particularly where children are involved.

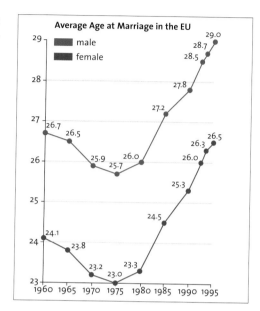

Average Age at Marriage in the EU

Left: **Average marriage age in the EU.** From the mid-1970s onward the average age of getting married has constantly risen for men and women, at more or less the same pace. Men have always married later than women, but this age gap appears to be narrowing gradually.

Below: **Comparative divorce rates (per 1000 population).** On average the divorce rate has markedly increased over the last few decades. Already by 1990, the divorce rate in the USA had achieved a higher percentage than in any other country in 1997. The predominantly Catholic countries like Spain and Italy are exceptions: here the divorce rate is still relatively low.

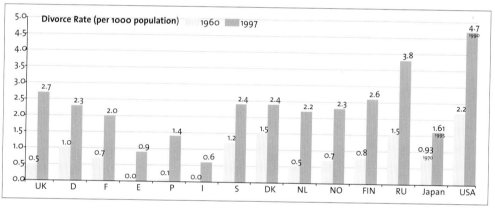

Divorce Rate (per 1000 population) 1960 1997

Kramer vs. Kramer, still from the film by Robert Benton, 1979, Meryl Streep as Joanna Kramer and Dustin Hoffmann as Ted Kramer. Traditionally, in a divorce, the mother was given custody of a child and the father had to pay money for the child's upkeep. The film is remarkable in that it shows a new trend developing over the last three decades of the 20th century: men fighting in court for the custody of their own children.

Origins
The Evolution of
Sexual Culture

Nut is lifted by the air god Shu above the earth god Geb, detail from the painted sarcophagus of Butehamun, scribe of the necropolis at Thebes, 1069 – 945 B.C. (21st Dyn.). Museo Egiziano, Turin.
The god Shu lifts the Egyptian goddess of the sky, Nut, over the recumbent earth god Geb, a symbol of the creation of heaven and earth, and just one example of the large number of sexual connotations involved in representations of creation myths.

Human and Prehuman

Chimpanzee mother and baby. In contrast to human beings, the breasts of the female chimpanzee are purely functional, and appear to serve no purpose in attracting males or providing pleasure for the female.

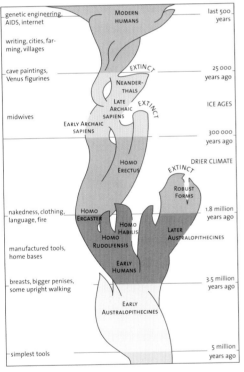

The Hominid Family Tree, with Landmarks in the Evolution of Sexual Features and Culture. Human evolution proceeded in waves, with much interspecies competition. About 1.8 million years ago there were at least six species of hominids – within a million years there were only varieties of homo erectus. There may also have been interspecies breeding. Some experts claim that the Neanderthals did not become completely extinct, but were absorbed into the homo sapiens gene pool.

The most comprehensive and far-reaching claims have been made about the sexual behavior of prehistoric human beings, but these are based on very little concrete evidence. For some, it was men, in their role as hunters and providers, who made all the great evolutionary and cultural gains – growing bigger, more powerful brains, losing body hair and inventing weapons, all to help them kill other animals. As a consequence, sex among the early hominids was brutal, with dominant males fighting for ownership of females who had little or no say in their choice of mate. Others claim that early human societies were peaceful matriarchies, ruled by wise, benevolent women, who were revered as magical givers of life by men completely ignorant of their own role in the process of reproduction. All such theories are little more than fantasy and conjecture – which is not, of course, to say that they are necessarily untrue, just that there is no particular reason for believing any one of them.

Some of the most important evidence in the fossil record consists of nothing more than a set of footprints, preserved in volcanic ash, which were discovered by Mary Leakey in 1979 in Laetolil, Tanzania. These demonstrate that, between 3,800,000 and 3,600,000 years ago, early hominids were already walking upright. This development alone would have had profound effects on their sexual behavior. To begin with, the genitals of the female became less visible, while the genitals of the male were more prominently displayed. To enhance this new form of display, human males developed a penis that, in its flaccid state, is enormous in comparison with those of other primates (the penis of a full-grown silver-back gorilla, for example, is less than an inch long when non-erect).

Walking upright modified the gluteus maximus in both sexes, leading to the growth of rounded buttocks. In the case of the females these became a prominent form of sexual advertisement, taking over from the exposed, engorged vaginal lips that were displayed by ovulating apes. Among other things, the buttocks are a convenient place to store fat, and a woman's body-fat level indicates how likely she is to ovulate regularly, and how likely it is that a fertilized egg will be successfully implanted in the womb lining. The growth of sexually stimulating buttocks led to other physical changes. The females of some species, such as gelada baboons, have bright patches of skin around their nipples which seem to mimic their vaginal displays, allowing them to attract sexual attention while sitting down, and it has been suggested that the fleshy breasts of human females evolved in the same way, as a form of buttock-mimicry. Well-defined, rounded breasts are not necessary for lactation, and humans are the only primates to have them.

The appearance of features such as breasts and an ostentatious penis cannot be put down to straightforward natural selection (defined as the survival of the fittest in the face of envi-

Proboscis monkeys derive their name from the large, pendulous nose of the male which helps to increase the resonance of its honking. A loud noise helps establish its dominance in comparison to other males. However, the proboscis also appears to mimic the male's genitalia, acting as a secondary penile display.

ronmental challenges). In fact, in most situations, they could only have been a handicap. However, Charles Darwin (1809–1882) recognized that, alongside natural selection, another process must operate in order to explain the diversity of life, which he called sexual selection. Whereas the former depended on "the success of both sexes ... in relation to the general conditions of life", the latter was based on "the success of certain individuals over others of the same sex, in relation to the propagation of the species". The two processes could work at cross purposes – Darwin cited the case of the peacock's tail, which has grown so big that the bird is easy meat for predators. But despite being a liability in survival terms, a big tail has the advantage that it excites peahens, and in the absence of too many peacock-predators it is this factor that governed the course of the bird's evolution.

The Naked Hunter

In the same way, many aspects of human biology can probably best be explained in terms of sexual selection. Among them are our relative hairlessness and our large brains. There are numerous theories as to how we became, in the famous phrase, "naked apes". One of the most popular is the man-the-hunter hypothesis, which contends that we lost our body hair so that we would not become overheated by the exertions of the chase. The arguments against this, though, are that the ancestors of other savannah predators, including cheetahs, retained their fur, and the early hominids were likely to use hunting techniques such as stalking and ambush, which would not have involved an enormous investment of energy. Another suggestion is that humans had an ocean-dwelling evolutionary phase, some time between ten and five million years ago, when we evolved naked bodies like those of whales and dolphins. However, there is no fossil evidence for this theory whatsoever, and it ignores the fact that our body fat is much less efficient an insulator than that of the cetaceans, so that if we did live in the sea the human race could have become extinct through hypothermia.

The sexual selection explanation, by contrast, is that the patterns of body hair in the early hominids changed to emphasize certain sexual features, which were then selected not because they helped the individuals survive, but simply because other hominids found them sexy. Losing hair on the buttocks and breasts would make them more visible, and therefore more exciting. Similarly, what body hair remained became centered on the genitals, as a way of drawing the eye. Darwin thought that hairlessness was, initially, only attractive in females. However, in mammals (more than in birds and other creatures) evolutionary changes that occur in one sex are mirrored, closely but more weakly, in the other. So if a deer stag evolves large antlers (which are not for defense but to fight other males in the rutting season) then the hind of the species will also have antlers, albeit smaller ones, even though she does not fight. Similarly, if hairlessness among women were

sexually selected, men would lose hair also, but to a lesser degree, and this is exactly what has happened (this is another argument against the man-the-hunter theory – if hairlessness were primarily being selected for in men, we would expect women to be the hairier sex).

Such a scenario implies that men did all the sexual selecting. There was certainly a greater difference between the size of males and females among the early hominids than there is among modern humans, and this suggests a system of apelike polygyny, in which dominant males would compete among themselves for access to, and control of, harems of smaller females. On the other hand, unlike in apes, the canine teeth of early men and women were comparable in size. Dominant, competitive

males fighting to control harems might be expected to have larger canines, which has led some researchers to propose a "monogamy theory" of hominid sexual behavior. This holds that each female and her offspring would have been the responsibility of a single, hunter-provider mate. Such a relationship would depend on a powerful emotional bond, which suggests at least some reciprocity in the choice of partner. The monogamy theory, however, has been attacked on several fronts, mainly on the basis that the early hominids probably fought with weapons and would not need large canine teeth.

However, even among the great apes, females have a degree of choice over their mates. When a female is subjected to forced copulation – or

Adult male mandrill. The sexual displays of male apes are often on the face, because male apes use their facial expressions to establish dominance over each other. It has been suggested that, primordially, human beards served the same functions as the mandrill's nose flash.

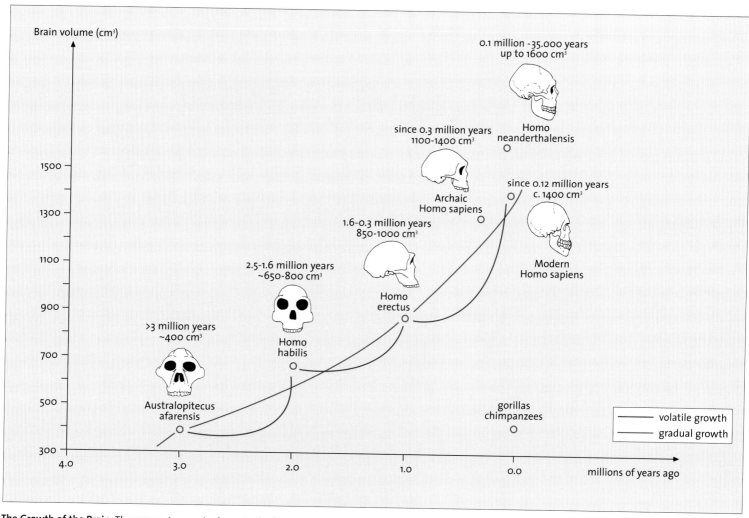

Brain volume (cm³)

0.1 million -35.000 years
up to 1600 cm³

Homo
neanderthalensis

since 0.3 million years
1100-1400 cm³

Archaic
Homo sapiens

since 0.12 million years
c. 1400 cm³

1.6-0.3 million years
850-1000 cm³

Homo
erectus

Modern
Homo sapiens

2.5-1.6 million years
~650-800 cm³

Homo
habilis

>3 million years
~400 cm³

Australopitecus
afarensis

gorillas
chimpanzees

— volatile growth
— gradual growth

1500
1300
1100
900
700
500
300

4.0   3.0   2.0   1.0   0.0   millions of years ago

The Growth of the Brain. There were two major leaps in the brain size of prehistoric humans, 2–1.5 million years ago, perhaps associated with the birth of toolmaking, and a smaller one some 500,000–200,000 years ago, which is connected to no obvious changes in behavior.

"raped" in human terms – she has several strategies to avoid bearing the offspring of her attacker. She may, for example, arrange to copulate frequently with her preferred partner, giving his sperm a greater likelihood of making her pregnant. Female orangutans – among which forced copulation is a regular occurrence – have even been observed deliberately eating the toxic leaves and bark of trees such as Melanochyla, possibly as abortifacients (although of course there is no way of knowing this for sure).

It is likely that sexual selection by females was the driving force behind one of the most important evolutionary changes in human beings – the growth of the brain. For the early hominids there was little or no natural advantage to an increase in brain size. In fact, for a bipedal creature, a large head is a potentially disastrous adaptation, because walking upright causes the pelvic girdle to narrow, making childbirth more difficult and hazardous even without the extra burden of squeezing out a

massive skull. Yet in the period between three million and 100,000 years ago, when anatomically recognizable modern humans first appeared, the hominid brain tripled in volume. To overcome the problems involved in giving birth, babies were born comparatively undeveloped – the head of a newborn chimp is already more than 40 percent of its adult weight, whereas the head of a newborn human is less than 30 percent. The consequence for this is that the human infant needs to be looked after for much longer while it grows and develops its physical and mental capabilities. Even with this adaptation, human birth is much more difficult than that of an ape. A chimp's pelvis has a large, almost uniform cross section, while the pelvis of a human has different cross-sections at its inlet, mid-point and outlet. As a result an infant chimp is born without having to move its head in relation to its body, while a human baby's head has to rotate as it passes down the birth canal. By about 200,000 years

ago, hominid heads were large enough for mothers probably to need help with childbirth, and it is likely that the first midwives appeared around this time.

Despite all the disadvantages of having a large brain, it seems that our ancestors found individuals with large brains sexually attractive, and bred with them. It is worth pointing out that, once the australopithecines developed stone weapons and rudimentary social cooperation, more than two million years ago, there was very little practical advantage to an increase in intelligence until the development of language, more than half a million years later. Yet brains continued to grow. Darwin suggested that the human mind was comparable to the peacock's tail, and that females simply found clever males more attractive, as demonstrated by their social skills, or their ability at making tools, or possibly their talent for adorning or decorating themselves with skins, vegetable materials and pigments.

Venus of Willendorf, c. 30,000–25,000 B.C. Limestone, 9.3 cm high, Naturhistorisches Museum, Vienna. The *Venus of Willendorf*, a Paleolithic limestone figurine, was discovered in 1908 in Austria. Traces of red (probably ocher) survive in the deepest folds, and it is thought to have been completely red at one time.

There is a limit to how much can be inferred about hominid behavior by observing the activity of apes. We may share more than 98 percent of our DNA with the bonobo chimps that are our nearest relatives, but even this discrepancy is enough to suggest that our most recent common ancestor lived more than six million years ago. If there are any lessons to be drawn from the bonobos, it is that sex could have been a much more carefree process for hominids than it is in most modern human societies. Bonobo chimps enjoy frequent, casual, recreational sex with each other, only some of it having any potential for reproduction. Females rub their genitals together, males "penis fence" and infants are usually introduced to sex by their mothers, as part of their normal development. The only recognizable taboo is sex between females and any of their sons that are over six years old.

A jealous bonobo male persistently disturbs a mating couple. Among bonobos such behaviour is not based on the biological need to reproduce, but on sexual frustration.

Modesty or Display?

Because soft materials decay, there is no fossil evidence about when hominids began clothing themselves, but it could have occurred at a very early stage, coinciding with the first loss of body hair. Females might have wanted to cover their buttocks, so that they could flash them selectively at desired males. For their part, males – especially subordinate ones, such as adolescents – would probably have wanted to hide an erection on some occasions, in order to feign indifference and avoid conflict with a larger, more powerful rival. This is much harder to do with an upright posture. Certainly, by about 300,000 years ago, red ocher begins to appear at human settlements, which may have been used for curing hides, or directly on the skin as a form of cosmetic.

Another way of displaying intelligence is through linguistic ability, and although archaeologists disagree about exactly when language first appeared, it may have been as long ago as 1.6 million years. The skull of the Nariokotome boy, a young homo erectus discovered in Kenya, indicates that he possessed a Broca's area – the structure in the brain that is responsible for making language. If he actually was capable of speech (although his rib cage suggests that he would have had poor breath control), then suddenly hominids would have a new way of choosing mates, and thereby selecting for particular qualities in the next generation. Suddenly the females could pick males who would ply them with the prehistoric equivalent of love songs and poetry (and, as one cynical observer has it, the males could pick women who would laugh at their jokes and fake an orgasm).

Art is another sign of intelligence, and although we cannot know when the first words were uttered, the earliest known artwork is a tiny, 230,000-year-old sculpture found in the Golan Heights in Syria. It appears to be a crude representation of the female form, a forerunner to the so-called Venus figurines of Ice Age Europe. These sculptures, created between 30,000 and 24,000 years ago, have been the subject of furious debate since they were first discovered early in the 20th century. The earliest commentators – pointing to the exaggeration of the breasts and buttocks at the expense of the feet and faces – claimed that the Venuses were prehistoric pornography, carved by men for their own titillation. Among themselves, they disagreed as to whether the Venuses were meant to be more-or-less realistic images of living women, or some kind of Paleolithic ideal. In 1996, Le Roy McDermott of Missouri State University used the same features cited by the pornography proponents to argue in a completely opposite direction. According to McDermott the Venuses are self-portraits carved by women – the exaggerations being the

natural result of the foreshortening that would occur when a woman looked down along her own body. This would also explain why the figurines are faceless, as the artists could not see their own features. Critics of this theory point out that the figurines have buttocks, and hair on the back of the head, neither of which a self-portraitist could observe.

The best-known theory is that the sculptures represent a universal "Great Mother Goddess", the chief or only deity of a matriarchal age. In feminist literature this has become an unquestioned orthodoxy, although there is no supporting evidence. It is not clear that the figurines even depict mothers – many of them are fleshy and steatopygous, but they are not obviously pregnant. Some archaeologists have even suggested that they are too stocky to be fertility symbols, and perhaps represent post-menopausal women. In opposition to the matriarchy-model, some theorists argue that the Venus figurines are the product of male-dominated societies in which women were exchanged between groups, either in return for other women, for goodwill or for a "bride-price" of goods, food or services, in much the same way that marriage is contracted in large parts of the world today. They point out that the figurines are smooth, indicating that they were regularly handled, and suggest that, like flesh-and-blood women, they were passed from group to group. Even if this idea is correct, it is impossible to know whether the figurines served as a form of IOU, a token of ownership, or a keepsake.

Whatever the sculptures reveal, the cave paintings of the Paleolithic cast at least some doubt on the theory of a prehistoric matriarchy. The paintings are generally found in caves so inaccessible that their existence was forgotten for thousands of years, until they began to be rediscovered in the 19th century. Soot on the walls reveals that they were made by the light of tallow candles. The images include large game animals, such as bison and mammoths, and strange man-animal hybrids, which are sometimes identified as shamans. It is telling that these active human-like beings are male, and often ithyphallic. There are also many abstract images, and vulva-like symbols carved into the rock and decorated with red pigment to suggest the genital labia. Natural fissures and openings into other chambers are also similarly decorated, turning parts of the cave systems into what appear to be symbolic wombs, from which the next generation of animals, or their spirits, would be born. In many primitive cultures, tallow has been equated with semen, so it is possible that the very act of painting an animal by candlelight was seen as a way of impregnating the cave. The inaccessibility of the caves has also led some to suggest that they

Stylized woman or phallus from Dolní Vestonice, Slovakia, Gravettian culture. Carved mammoth tusk, Archaeological Institute for the Czech Academy of Sciences, Prague. This find highlights the contentious nature of the interpretations surrounding Paleolithic figurines. It is usually described as a minimalist Venus, comprising only breasts and a sticklike torso bearing scratches that are taken to be a menstrual or gestation calendar. However, the "breasts" could be testicles, making this a phallic symbol, or even a dildo.

A scene from a shaft in the Paleolithic caves at Lascaux, France, c. 14,500 B.C. A bison bull, pierced through the groin with a spear, confronts the erect penis of a prostrate man in a birdlike mask (who is sometimes described as a shaman in a trance).

are secret chambers, painted by men, hidden from the eyes of women and meant for the initiation of boys into manhood (in existing tribal cultures, this is seen as a form of rebirth). Whatever the truth, there is little in them to suggest that men were in thrall to women, or that they were ignorant of their role in the cycle of life and death.

The last Ice Age ended about 11,000 years ago, and within a few thousand years human beings were creating the first farming communities. The transition from hunting to farming, known as the Neolithic Revolution, was marked by a huge increase in population. At the end of the Ice Age there were no more than three million human beings on the planet, but within 7000 years the figure had risen to 100 million. The increase was not exclusively due to better nutrition – indeed, in many ways, the Neolithic was a disaster for human life expectancy, introducing many new dietary and animal-related diseases to the species, including tuberculosis, which crossed over from cows. The reason more babies were being born is because existing babies were being weaned more quickly. A sucking baby, especially if it is fed on demand, rather than to a prearranged schedule, is an exceptionally good contraceptive, because it causes the production of high levels of prolactin in the body, which inhibits ovulation. It is not the amount of milk taken that determines the prolactin levels, but the frequency with which it is taken. In hunter-gatherer societies, frequent feeding and late weaning are the norm. The teeth of infants reveal that, by 5500 B.C., they were being weaned early onto a diet of porridge (the very first pottery seems to have been made for this purpose). By 3500 B.C., at the latest, animals were being reared to provide milk for humans, including babies. This change alone would have subjected women to the tyranny of regular pregnancy. It is probably true to say that farming, as much as any other social or cultural revolution, contributed to the inequality of women, by turning them into child-bearing chattels, prisoners more than ever before of their own biology and of the men who used them to make clans and dynasties.

The Grave of the Golden Penis, Varna cemetery, Bulgaria, 4000 B.C. The skeleton in this photograph is not the original, but a plastic replica.

The Golden Penis

The cemetery discovered at Varna, in Bulgaria, in 1968, can demonstrate the difficulties of interpreting archaeological finds. The 250 graves date to about 4000 B.C., and the richest of them contains a skeleton elaborately clothed and decorated with gold. One of the artifacts, found between the skeleton's legs, is a sheet of gold hammered into a shape resembling the end of a penis, about 5 cm (2 inches) long and 3.5 cm (1.5 inches) in diameter. It was obviously meant as an ornament, and is usually described as a penis sheath, like those worn by tribesmen today from Africa to New Guinea. There is a hole in the end, so it would not have to be removed for urinating or ejaculating. However, it is possible that the object is part of a funerary ritual, and was never worn in life. In addition, a row of perforations indicates that it was once sewn onto a fabric of some kind. In this case, it may have served in fertility rites, by being filled with water or meal-porridge and then made to "ejaculate" on the fields. Such acts of ritual masturbation, intended to guarantee a supply of game or a plentiful harvest, can be found among a number of primitive agrarian peoples. In this case, the skeleton may not even be male – it has never been DNA tested – but could be that of a transvestite priestess. It is remarkable how many skeletons – confidently described as male or female by virtue of their size, or the artifacts surrounding them – have never had their sex definitively established.

Sexuality in Mesopotamian Myth

The first written evidence about human sexuality comes from ancient Mesopotamia (now Iraq), some 5000 years ago. However, it is contained in myths, songs, allegories and religious fragments that sometimes call for almost as much interpretation as the most fragmentary prehistoric artifacts and skeletons. As far as we can tell from the surviving texts, the Mesopotamians seem to have considered sexuality as fundamental to a good human life. One of the most characteristic features of demons, which underlay their pitiless nature, was their lack of need for sexual intercourse or for the pleasure of holding children on their knees.

Sexual intercourse and prostitution were among the hundred or so primordial and unchangeable laws of the universe, which the ancient Mesopotamians called *me*. The *me* were considered to be the basic components of action and states of mind that make up human life. They can be interpreted as the powers and properties of the gods, or as principles by which each aspect of society and the cosmos continued to function. The *me* also included other important human actions, qualities of character, moral values and emotions, as well as offices, roles and professions.

For both the Sumerians of the south and the later Akkadians who inhabited the Mesopotamian desert, sexuality was primarily linked with moisture. This is expressed in a series of enigmatic myths. In one Sumerian text the god Enki is addressed as the power of amniotic fluid: "Go forth out of my good ewe, and may she give birth to a good lamb! Go forth out of my pregnant cow, and may she give birth to a good calf!" The Sumerian language used the same word for semen and for the fresh water used for irrigation, over which cities frequently went to war. When Enki had finished organizing the sea, rivers, clouds and rain, he then created the Tigris and Euphrates by filling up the riverbeds and irrigation canals with a stream of his own semen. As he was ejaculating, he begged the goddess Ninhursag to allow him to lie down with her. She agreed, and conceived the goddess Ninsar. Enki's stream of fecundating power was seemingly endless. When his daughter Ninsar had grown up she went out onto the riverbank. Enki looked up at her from down in the water and said, "Why should I not kiss this beautiful young girl Ninsar?" Then he made love to her, and Ninsar in turn gave birth to a daughter whom Enki similarly impregnated.

Enki participates in a New Year ritual, c. 2400–2200 B.C. Akkadian cylinder seal impression, British Museum, London. The god Enki (center right) is participating in a regenerative New Year ritual.

This pattern continued for several generations, with Enki impregnating each of his female descendants. Then the myth moves on from his begetting of women to his creation of medicinal plants. The latest of his descendants refused to yield to Enki's advances unless he brought her the fruits of irrigated gardening in the form of cucumbers, apples and grapes. Enki found a gardener who was suffering from drought and did him the favor of filling up his irrigation canals with more semen. In gratitude the gardener gave him the fruit, which Enki then presented to his beloved. This time, when he made love to her his semen somehow fell on the ground. Now instead of creating a daughter it sprouted into eight different species of plant. When Enki looked up from the river he saw not a beautiful girl, but these plants. He picked them and ate them.

For reasons that are not clear, the eating of these plants made him so sick that he was on the point of death. But his original partner Ninhursag placed the sick Enki in her vagina to heal him, as if giving him a new birth. As he named each part of his body that was in pain, Ninhursag gave birth to a corresponding healing deity that was linked to one of the healing plants.

Babylonian boundary stone (detail), c. 1120 B.C.
Nergal (on the left) and the god Marduk. Negal was often represented, as here, by a lion-headed staff.

Eroticism was not confined to the generative power of water or semen between an upper world of the sky and the underworld beneath. The story in which Ereshkigal, queen of the underworld, is visited by the god Nergal contains a powerful mixture of eroticism and violence, which survived in two versions. In the earlier one, from the 15th or 14th century B.C., Nergal visits the underworld, seizes Ereshkigal's throne, and remains there as king. In the version from the 7th century B.C., Nergal escapes back to the upper world before returning once more to Ereshkigal of his own volition, unable to resist his erotic fascination with death. In fact, in the earlier Mesopotamian script there seems to be a pun between the words for husband and death.

The Law

Although fragments of legal codes survive dating back to the Sumerians, Ur-Nammu and Lipit-Ishtar (c. 2100–1900 B.C.), the most complete surviving set of laws from ancient Mesopotamia is the 282-article code of the Babylonian king, Hammurabi. This was compiled around 1750 B.C., towards the end of his reign. Despite its length, like most Babylonian codes it is incomplete because many laws were considered to be a part of custom or common religious practice, and not worth writing down. Among other matters, it deals with marriage and slavery (which are often difficult to tell apart), and has a special section on "female publicans" – possibly prostitutes or brothel-keepers. Certainly, any priestess or holy woman who stepped into the establishment of a female publican was to be put to death. The Babylonian codes were remarkable for the severity of their sentences, although punishments varied according to whether the accused was a slave, a tenant or a landowner. The laws governing family life do not recognize marriage by capture, but otherwise protect the rights of the husband. An adulterous wife may be put to death, or have her nose cut off (while her lover was either executed or castrated). It was, however, in the husband's power to pardon his wife.

Hamurabi's Code of Law, c. 1792–1750 B.C. Diorite, 2.25 m high, Musée du Louvre, Paris. The top of the stela, discovered in Susa in 1901, bears the Code of Hammurabi. It shows the god Shamash dictating laws to the king.

Inanna and the "Sacred Marriage"

Inanna, called Ishtar in Akkadian, was a goddess of sexual love associated with the planet Venus. Through Mesopotamian myth there emerges a character who is headstrong, ruthless, and dangerously seductive to men.

Whether she appears as a virgin or as sexually promiscuous, she always plays the roles of a young woman and it is significant that the myths never portray her as an older matron or mother. Inanna was also the protectress of prostitutes.

This combination of roles was reflected in a "sacred marriage" or "coupling" between Inanna and a deified king. The sacred marriage was the fundamental rite of kingship in many societies of the ancient Near East. Such early city-states were, so far as we know, the first in human history to be founded upon the wealth of agriculture as opposed to hunting. The sacred marriage may have been acted out historically through an act of ritual sexual intercourse between the real king and Inanna's priestess or temple prostitute. Their physical union replicates a union on the divine level. In Babylon, this rite was performed in particular at the New Year festival called *Akitu*. In one case it is known that a new temple was inaugurated with a performance lasting seven days representing a sacred wedding ceremony between the god and his consort.

Texts deciphered from clay tablets of the third millennium B.C. give a fairly clear picture of the rituals of the sacred marriage. The king played the role of Tammuz (in Akkadian, Dumuzi) while the priestess played the role of Inanna (Ishtar). The format of the ritual consisted of an introduction, a ritual bath, love songs, the sacred marriage itself, and the fixing of the destiny of the king and the land for the coming year to ensure its fertility. One text of the love song includes the words: "For the King, For the Lord, when I shall have adorned my body, when I shall have put mascara on my eyes, when the Lord who sleeps with the pure Inanna will have made love to me on the bed, then I shall fix for him a good destiny." The goddess's ornaments are listed as including numerous beads, rings and breast ornaments of gold, as well as a golden vulva. These objects may have been used for dressing a statue or the priestess playing the part of the goddess may have worn them. Another surviving text from a sacred marriage includes the lines: "You have captivated me, let me stand tremblingly before you, my bridegroom, I would be taken by you to the bedchamber, my lion, let me caress you, my precious caress is more delicious than honey."

Loves of Inanna

On one occasion Inanna descended to the underworld in order to take it over from her

Ishtar as goddess of love squeezing her breasts, second mill. B.C. Clay model for votive statuettes, recently recast, 11 cm high, British Museum, London. The role of Inanna as a guarantor of plenty is revealed in this votive statue, in which she squeezes milk from her breasts.

Man praying before the Great Goddess Ishtar, who is sitting on a griffin, 8th cent. B.C. Bronze, 4.2 cm high, Musée du Louvre, Paris. The goddess Ishtar, seated on a sparrow hawk and surmounted by two of her symbols – the moon and a star – receives a supplicant. It is possible that a priestess would enact the role of the goddess on such occasions.

There appear to have been several grades of prostitute associated with the temples of Mesopotamia. The *ishtaritu* were virginal servants of Inanna (Ishtar), reserved for the pleasure of the gods (probably in the person of the king). The *qadishtu*, who were usually well educated, could sell themselves to worshippers visiting the temple. The *harimtu* seem to have worked mainly in the streets and taverns, but were called upon occasionally when demand at the temples became too great, for example during festivals.

Curly-horned ram, pulling himself up with the aid of a stalk, first half of the third mill. B.C. Gold, lapis lazuli, sea shells, and silver, c. 50 cm high, British Museum, London. A ram trapped in a thicket, from the royal graves at Ur. This is often described as symbolizing the shepherd Dumuzi, caught in the underworld. Dumuzi was the son of Ninghishzida, "Lord of the Wood of Life".

of ground water and moist winds, fertility in herding depends explicitly on the act of mating. The cult of Dumuzi contained strong sexual imagery and his liaison with Inanna served as the model for the sacred marriage among mortal kings. Nevertheless Dumuzi's own priests were transvestites or eunuchs, who are thought to have engaged in ritual homosexual activity. These priests may have castrated themselves in the course of their duties just as, in some versions, the god is thought to have castrated himself. This self-castration is probably a symbol of the god's death and his sojourn in the barren underworld.

Inanna's relationship with Dumuzi is one in a succession of passionate love affairs, in all of which a young man is destroyed. In the Epic of Gilgamesh – the most complete examples of which date from the first millennium B.C. – the hero Gilgamesh was returning to the city of Uruk, after killing the monster, Huwawa, when the goddess invited him to be her lover. But Gilgamesh rejected her advances out of hand with a stream of insults, listing her many lovers, chosen from all walks of life, and the awful fates that she eventually visited upon them. The power of sexuality is also recognized in the story of how Inanna complained to the creator god Enki that he had given domains to all the other deities, but not her. When she asked him what her domain was, Enki replied, "Inanna, you have the power to destroy what cannot be destroyed, and to set up what cannot be set up."

sister Ereshkigal. But she was instead captured and only released on condition that she would find a substitute to die in her place. But when Inanna returned to earth, accompanied under close arrest by demons, she found all her own servants and associates in mourning for her and could not bring herself to hand them over to the demons. Suddenly she came upon her own lover, the shepherd-god Dumuzi, sitting comfortably under a huge apple tree on a splendid throne and not mourning in the least. Inanna was furious and allowed the demons to take him. Later a compromise was negotiated under which Dumuzi would spend only half of each year in the underworld. As the god who died and was resurrected in a seasonal cycle, Dumuzi was sometimes associated with the growth and withering of corn and fruit. But the strongest symbolism links him with the herding of animals. While crops encourage symbolism

Sexuality in Egyptian Myth

The blueprint for Egyptian monarchy is contained in the cosmogony of ancient Egypt and the saga of its Ennead (the nine principal deities of the creation myth). The cosmogony relates how Re, the supreme sun god (also addressed as Atum) was conceived by Nun, the primeval waters. Atum carried within him the sum total of all creation, and in the words of several ancient accounts, when he decided to procreate he took his "fist for a spouse", and masturbated. From his ejaculation came Shu and Tefnut, air and moisture, the first divine couple. They in turn became the parents of the male Geb (earth) and the female Nut (sky). Nut, overarching her partner, was so sexually obsessed with him that she was unable to bring herself to detach her body from his until Atum decreed that Shu separate Nut from her spouse

Geb. From their union came two further paired couples; Isis and Osiris and Nephthys and Seth. These gods form the basis of the primal myth of Heliopolis, the City of the Sun (now Cairo). Osiris represented fertility, rebirth and order, Seth chaos, barrenness and destruction. All the basic ideas relating to life after death, the seasonal cycle, drought and fertility are incorporated in their tale, alongside the reasons for the worldly order with its complex of rules and regulations regarding sovereignty.

In the myth, Isis and Osiris are inseparable but the envious Seth tricks his brother into a jeweled sarcophagus, which he sets adrift at sea until at last it comes to rest in Byblos. Isis goes in search of her other half, finally rescuing him from the trunk of a scented tree that has grown around the sarcophagus and forms a column in

Bottom left: **Egyptian god Min, 4ᵗʰ mill. B.C. Limestone, 1.55 m high, Ashmolean Museum, Oxford.** The fertility god Min shared many of the characteristics of Atum. In statues he is often shown "taking his fist for a spouse".

Bottom right: **God Atum (right) in a sectional view of the Nefertari tomb in the west of Thebes, c. 1250 B.C. (19ᵗʰ Dyn.).** Atum was worshipped as the ancestor of mankind, and the Old Kingdom Pharaohs referred to themselves as "the sons of Re". Each time a new Pharaoh was conceived, it was believed, Re had returned to earth to impregnate the queen.

Papyrus (detail), c. 900 B.C. (21ˢᵗ – 22ⁿᵈ Dyn.). Papyrus illustration, British Museum, London. Here Shu, the god of the air, is separating the bodies of Nut and Geb. Nut is respresented as the sky, her hands and feet touch the earth.

the king's palace. As she brings him back to Egypt on a boat, she succeeds in reviving him long enough to masturbate him to ejaculation, which impregnates her (in an echo of the primal creative act of Atum). As a result she gives birth to Horus, the earthly essence of kingship who inherits the mantle of his father and goes on to recover the throne of Egypt. It is from this traditional, mythic paradigm that the first Egyptian kings claimed their immanence and unchallenged power over ordinary mortals. This composite cycle probably evolved over a long period beginning in the Prehistoric or Gerzean period, when the worship of a dying and returning god reflected an increasingly agrarian culture and the discovery of new plant-forms and their diverse uses. The second phase of the myth, describing the struggle for the throne of Egypt, reflects the rise of the Dynastic rulers – worshippers of Horus and his falcon totem, which superseded the crocodile and the hippopotamus of Seth and the pre-Dynastic kings.

When Horus grew up, he staked his claim to the kingship before a tribunal of the elder gods. Thanks to the eloquent intercession of Isis – who established the principle of succession, by getting Seth to admit that the inheritance rights of a son were greater than those of a brother – Horus was established as king. After a series of challenges that lasted several generations, Seth almost succeeded in reinstating himself but was again defeated by the guile and magic of Isis. His final assault on Horus came in the form of a violent, sexual battle in which each man brutally sodomized the other in an attempt to establish his superiority. But Isis intervened and magically cleared Horus's anus. Thus when Seth demanded an examination in the presence of the gods, he was humiliated when it was his anus and not Horus's that contained semen. In one version of the tale, Seth extended the hand of truce; Horus accepted an invitation to his uncle's house and at night the two men bedded down together. Seth waited for Horus to fall asleep, and then attempted to sodomize him.

Isis with Horus Child, c. 600 – 400 B.C. (26th – 27th Dyn.) Bronze statuette, 44.5 cm high, Egyptian Museum, Berlin. Isis feeding the infant Horus and acting as his throne.

Ever alert, Horus brushed away his uncle's penis but in the process his hand was contaminated by semen. Isis, who is aware that this had the potency of poison, immediately severed Horus's hand and flung it in the river. She then smeared the vegetables in Seth's garden with Horus's semen, thus ensuring that after he ate, Seth's blood was tainted forever. Soon afterwards Seth boasted of how he had defiled his nephew and, as proof, challenged the court of gods to call out to his semen. But it responded to them from the river. When Horus returned the challenge, his own semen responded from his uncle's bloodstream. Seth was thus made a laughing stock before all the gods, and Horus was declared the undisputed king.

The cults of Isis, Osiris and Horus are inextricably entwined and each one can be interpreted to have the ultimate right to rule. In principle, it was the daughter who inherited the mantle of the most prominent divinity, Isis, who was known as the Throne. The king ruled as an extension of the queen. The safest measure for a would-be king was therefore to follow the divine system of sibling marriage, not only emulating divine practice but also ensuring an earthly safeguard that the right to kingship could never be in dispute.

The cult of Isis and Osiris cut across all social and geographical boundaries in Egypt. With it came the concept of sacral kingship: that divinity is embodied in the ruler, whose person symbolizes the prosperity, or otherwise, of his kingdom. Though divine, the king was not immortal, so his physical deterioration through illness, accident or the decay of old age would result in similar disaster for the land. It thus became necessary to end the monarchy at a preordained time by means of a ritual killing. In early Egypt, most rulers were therefore allocated a specific period for rulership followed by a ceremonial sacrifice. This took one of three forms according to the current requirement of the land. If Egypt was dry, then bloodshed took place; if sacred relics were needed all over the land, the king was smothered, hanged or drowned before his dismembered parts were buried along the length and breadth of the country; if lack of fertility was feared, he was burned and his ashes were scattered over fields or running water. In later years there is evidence that an alternative victim was prepared for sacrifice by being appointed ruler for several weeks before suffering the fate otherwise reserved for the king.

Inner room of the western Osiris roof chapel, 30 B.C.–14 A.D. Stone relief, Dendara, Hathor temple. This scene depicts the resurrection of Osiris. It is symbolized by his erect penis above which Isis is hovering in the shape of a kite (in some accounts a sparrow hawk). She will receive his semen and give birth to Horus.

Hathor

Patron of bodily pleasures, Hathor survived well into historical times and was particularly revered at Dendera, the wine festival, an occasion which not only echoed her hedonistic character but also commemorated the occasion when she was pacified with quantities of red wine to assuage her bloodlust against mortals who criticized the gods. Cognate with the creator-goddess Nut, as well as Isis, she was a fertility divinity and presided over promiscuity and activities resulting in fertility. She was the goddess of joy, laughter and ecstasy, and also patronized perfumes, flower gardens and garlands. The handmaidens at her various temples were highly trained dancers and musicians as well as being skilled in the carnal arts, which they practiced with worshippers much like the sacred prostitutes of ancient Greece or India.

Late Period (664–332 B.C.) rituals that enacted the divine marriage of two gods usually centered on Horus and Hathor. One of the most important was the 14-day Festival of the Beautiful Embrace, when a statue of Hathor was taken from her temple in Dendera to the great temple of Horus at Edfu, to the south, in a boat called *Mistress of Love*.

Thebes, Valley of the Queens, c. 1250 B.C. (19th Dyn.). A seated Hathor receiving tribute from the principal wife of Ramses II, depicted on the wall of a tomb. As mistress of dance, music and song, Hathor often chose to embody herself in the sistrum, a musical instrument that was used to drive away evil spirits (the columns of her temple in Dendera were modeled after sistrums). She also enjoyed watching over women while they were making themselves up or applying perfume.

The Phallic Rites of Isis and Osiris

Some versions of the conception of Horus place great emphasis on the role of the phallus as a symbolic generator of life. After Isis had returned to Buto in Egypt with the corpse of Osiris, she placed it for safety among the rushes where Seth happened upon it during a hunting trip. Determined to dispose of the threat to his kingship, he dismembered his brother's corpse and scattered its fourteen parts about the kingdom. Isis went searching for the lost pieces, accompanied by her sister (and Seth's wife), Nephthys, and occasionally her nephew, Anubis. At every location where a piece of the body was found, they constructed a temple to the worship of Osiris. The most celebrated such temples are at Abydos in the south and Busiris in the north. At every spot, Isis gave the local priest a wax effigy of Osiris and explained how it would be imbued with his eternal spirit every time prayers and hymns were dedicated to him. In due course all the body parts were gathered except for the penis, which had been cast into the river and eaten by a fish, or, in some accounts, a crocodile. Isis now fashioned a phallus of gold, which she affixed to the corpse of Osiris. This symbolized the god's powers of regeneration and fertility. Then, transforming herself into a sparrowhawk, she rubbed together her wings, producing the "breeze of life" and bringing Osiris back to life to perform his last act of creation on earth. He grasped his magical phallus with his hand and stimulated it to the point of ejaculation. His seed resulted in the conception of Horus. In the fifth century B.C., the historian Herodotus described groups of women that moved from village to village in rites honoring Osiris, carrying puppets each of which had a "moving male member nearly as big as the rest of the body".

Men and Women in the Time of the Pharaohs

The pharaohs of Egypt are famous for marrying their own sisters, in imitation of the gods. Some of them did not stop there, and indulged in a whole glut of serial incestuous matches – the records of Ramses II (1279–1213 B.C.) reveal that he possibly married his sister, who was first in succession, and certainly her daughter (who may have been his). In the process of fathering about 100 children, he also married all others in the line of succession. Nevertheless, the practice was not universal, and some pharaohs not only married outside their bloodline, but also even took their principal wives from outside the nobility.

Careful distinction was drawn between the activities of the rulers and the ruled. The pharaohs were thought to be descended from the gods, so incestuous marriages were permitted in continuation of divine tradition. For ordinary mortals they were strictly taboo, but there is evidence of high officials marrying their mothers, sisters and daughters in imitation of

Isis embraces Osiris, 13th cent. B.C. (19th Dyn.). Relief from the temple of Seti Abydos I. Isis and Osiris were both brother and sister and husband and wife, and provided the role model for incestuous pharaonic marriage.

An unknown goddess offers her breast to King Unas (detail), c. 2371–2350 B.C. (5th Dyn.). Relief from the temple of Unas, Sakkara (Egypt), Egyptian Museum, Cairo. This image shows the king imbibing divinity, along with kingship, as a right of birth.

Banquet Scene from the Tomb Chapel of Nebamun at Thebes, c. 1400 B.C. (18ᵗʰ Dyn.). Painted plaster, British Museum, London. Wealthy couples enjoyed being entertained by female musicians and dancers. Music and dance accompanied most public events, even funerals.

Medical Manuscripts

The management of sexual and related conditions such as pregnancy forms a substantial part of the surviving ancient Egyptian medical treatises. Of the numerous manuscripts, several concentrate on aphrodisiacs. Others deal with the care of pregnant women and newborn infants, while the Petrie collection, from about the 12ᵗʰ century B.C., includes a manuscript on the treatment of gynecological conditions. The Kahun Papyrus, the earliest surviving Egyptian medical text (1825 B.C.), recommends as a contraceptive a plug of crocodile dung inserted in the vagina, while the Ebers Papyrus, written 300 years later, prefers a piece of lint soaked in acacia tips and honey and maneuvered over the opening to the uterus to create an environment hostile to sperm. Apotropaic spells actually comprised a larger portion of the treatises than medical cures because it was widely believed that demons and malign magic were the source of ill-health and accidents. The spells were often chanted as medication was given.

the pharaoh. In addition, it seems that in Greco-Roman times incestuous marriage became popular among ethnic Greeks who did not wish to mix their bloodlines with the native Egyptians. Although the pharaohs and high officials would typically have a number of wives, it appears that monogamy was the rule for the majority of the population. Parents probably arranged marriages, but there appears to have been no formalizing legal or religious ceremony. A marriage was established when a couple set up house together, and divorce, which was quite common, occurred when they separated. Adultery was frowned upon, especially when committed by women. Several early texts mention death by burning as a punishment, although in later periods adulterous women were simply divorced and their property confiscated. Adulterous men did not escape without consequences, and risked being beaten up by the family and friends of the aggrieved wife. In addition to normal marriage, there seem to have been temporary marriage contracts that lasted only five months.

Women enjoyed great privileges in comparison with other ancient societies. Although they could not become government officials, and were therefore excluded from the higher echelons of wealth and power, they were entitled to appear in court on their own behalf, and could own slaves and property, which they were free to dispose of as they wished. In addition, any property that a woman held jointly with her husband was held to be one-third under her control. With regard to inheritance, the sexes were treated equally: if a parent died without leaving a will, the property was divided equally amongst all the children, regardless of whether they were male or female.

Several of the "triumph-songs" of ancient Egypt extol the freedom of women to wander about without fear of being molested by men. Socially, women and men often enjoyed entertainment in mixed groups. In matters of administration of the family estate and household affairs, the women of the privileged classes maintained considerable authority.

Beautification

The women of ancient Egypt were expert at beautification and the preparation of cosmetics and lotions. They colored their lips with a preparation of red ocher, which was applied with a make-up brush. For the eyes, concoctions of malachite and later antimone (kohl) were carefully prepared. These were not for the women alone. The famous masks and paintings of male monarchs show their faces splendidly decorated as well. Women cut their hair short beneath their wigs, whether they were the short ones of the Old Kingdom or the long and heavy ones of the New. Judging from the recipes that survive, women took pains to encourage their hair to grow vigorously and remain black into maturity. One recipe from Queen Sesh, mother of Teti (2347–2337 B.C.), King of the North and South, prescribes equal portions of paw of dog, hoof of ass and kernels of date to be mixed with oil and cooked in a clay pot to preserve beautiful hair.

Perfume vessel from the tomb of Tutankhamun with statues of the Nile god Hapi, c. 1330 B.C. (18ᵗʰ Dyn.). Alabaster, gold and ivory, Egyptian Museum, Cairo. Cedar was one of the Egyptians' favorite fragrances, but they also used oils, gums and resins of sesame, and many other substances. They were especially fond of perfuming their hair and scalps, and even wore wax wigs that gradually melted, unleashing a powerful fragrance.

Cosmetic spoon with a figure of a lutenist, c. 1300 B.C. (18ᵗʰ–19ᵗʰ Dyn.). Wood, 13 cm high, Musée du Louvre, Paris. An ointment spoon used for holding scented unguents. It is decorated with a girl playing a musical instrument, who would most likely have been a slave.

They shared in overseeing everything from the work of artisans to the harvesting of the fields and the tally of cattle. Often too, they accompanied the men on sporting expeditions such as hunting, and tours of duty such as revenue inspection. It is less clear how the sexes related to each other among the peasant classes.

Outside the aristocracy or the state of marriage, women could find work as high priestesses, midwives, mourners or dancers. Judging from paintings, dancers began training as little girls, accompanying the adults, who presumably tutored them to dance and play musical instruments. They were also adept acrobats, turning somersaults and performing acrobatics in solo acts or as part of a troop that entertained at court and on various stately occasions. Serving the monarch constituted a sacred duty but they were often gifted as slaves to shrines and temples by visiting monarchs, noblemen and high officials. The Egyptians were regarded as a sexually sophisticated people by their neighbors. In the 6ᵗʰ century B.C., Kambyses, the King of Persia, started a war against Egypt because he had apparently heard that "Egyptian women excel all others in passionate embraces" and was aggrieved that the pharaoh would not give him one of his daughters. Egyptian dancing girls were especially prized in Rome for the eroticism of their dances and songs. There is little surviving information about homosexuality,

Portrait of Cleopatra VII, c. 50 B.C. Marble, 35 cm high, Musei Vaticani, Rome. According to the first–second-century Greek biographer, Plutarch, Cleopatra was striking rather than beautiful, with a long nose, a generous mouth and a slim figure which she preserved by careful dieting. It was her wit and charm that most ensnared men, with whom she could converse in a multitude of languages.

although the *Book of the Dead*, a collection of texts and illustrations concerning Egyptian beliefs on death and intended to secure a continued life in the hereafter, does advise (male) souls facing judgment to testify: "I have not copulated with a man." However, as in other ancient cultures, including Greek and Roman, it appears that the shame did not lie in homosexuality as such, but in the act of submission to another man. This is borne out by the myth of Horus and Seth, who each attempted to rape the other in their battle for the throne.

Cleopatra, the Great Seductress

Cleopatra VII is one of the best-known queens of myth and history. Though practically synonymous in the popular mind with the spirit of Egypt, she was in fact descended from the first Ptolemy, a Greek of Macedonian descent who came to Egypt in 323 B.C. She was born in 69 B.C. and died in 30 B.C. She is remembered as a ruthless manipulator and a "black-widow" character who married relentlessly to keep control of the throne of Egypt. Her nickname among the Greeks was Meriochane – "she who parts for a thousand men" – and she was said to have fellated a hundred Roman noblemen in a single evening. Cleopatra first married her eldest brother and then, after his death, a younger one. When Caesar conquered Egypt, he was captured by her charms, and she later claimed an ensuing child to be his. But he never married her, and his assassination set her ambitions back. When Mark Antony arrived in Egypt, she

captivated him too; he did marry her. This set Roman society against him, and eventually she fixed her eyes on the new strong man, Octavian, managing to engineer Antony's suicide. However, she was to follow him to his death after failing to seduce the dour Octavian, who rounded matters off by killing her sons by Caesar and Antony. He also had her daughter by Antony married off to a minor ruler on the outskirts of the empire. Popular fantasy attributed to Cleopatra the accoutrements of wit, cunning, beauty, splendor and sexual sophistication, and she has found resurrection again and again in a succession of biographies, novels and movies, time after time being reconstructed as a powerful seductress who used her astounding sexual charisma and skill to manipulate men and women.

Kneeling figure of Queen Hatshepsut, c. 1460 B.C. (18th Dyn.). Red granite, 75 cm high, Egyptian Museum, Cairo. This statue of Queen Hatshepsut is from Deir el-Bahari, western Thebes. Hatshepsut was at first merely the regent to Thutmose III, one of her husband's sons by a secondary wife, but by the seventh year of his reign she had assumed the titles of the king.

The Beard of Wisdom

The pharaoh would never appear before his public without a crown on his head. Kings were clean-shaven but on state occasions they wore a short, stout artificial beard of plaited hair to represent divine wisdom, which was held in place on the chin by straps affixed to the crown. Very few women became pharaohs, and when Queen Hatshepsut ascended the throne in 1479 B.C., after the death of her husband, Thutmose II, she not only had to concoct for herself a special pedigree showing she was the daughter of Amun the Sun God, but also adopted the false beard to symbolize her strength and wisdom. At first she was depicted in female attire, but soon began to have herself represented in the full costume of a king. Her funeral masks, like those of the other pharaohs, depicted her as the male god, Osiris. After her death, Thutmose III started a campaign to mutilate her statues, apparently in an attempt to eradicate her kingship from Egyptian history. Those monuments that depicted her simply as queen-consort of Thutmose II were left unharmed.

Eroticism in Judaic Scriptures

The carnal love between man and woman and the divine love between man and God are conceived in closely parallel terms in the ancient Hebrew tradition, both using the same verb *aheb*. To fall in love was not to be caught by an uncontrollable passion so much as it was a case of directing one's will and intentionality.

The only book of overt love poetry in the Bible is the Song of Solomon, also known as the Song of Songs or the Canticles, supposedly written by King Solomon. Its place in the Judaic canon was a subject of great debate until the rabbinical synod of Jamnia (70 A.D.), which established the view that the text was about the love of God for his bride, Israel. This has become the accepted interpretation in later Jewish tradition. One rabbi declared, "The whole world is not worth the day in which the Song of Songs was given to Israel, for all the Scriptures are holy, but the Song of Songs is the Holy of Holies." Christian tradition likewise has seen the text as an allegory of the love of Christ for his Church, as a dialogue between the soul and the body, or as a guide for the soul in its quest for union with God.

Some modern interpretations also see it as a collection of poems about human love included in the Bible to sanction such love, perhaps as a form of redemption for the loss of Eden. Recent discoveries of strikingly similar literature in other ancient Near Eastern languages also suggest that the Song may have been adapted for Jewish theological purposes from poems belonging to older Canaanite, Mesopotamian and Egyptian fertility cults.

Interpreting the Song is particularly difficult since it comes without any context. Other books of the Old Testament, even when they seem to invite a heavy allegorical interpretation, do so in the context of a basic narrative or clearly defined piece of storytelling. But the Song has no narrative as such. Moreover, on the surface at least, it seems to make no theological point and does not even mention God. Still, it was included in the canon of the Bible by early editors of great theological seriousness.

The text is highly and unmistakably erotic. Sexuality drives almost every line of the text,

making emotion and desire indistinguishable. But this pervasive sexuality is not expressed in references to intercourse and genitals. The sensuality runs broader, lavishing praise on the beauty of a girl's navel in 7:3 or of her nose in 7:9, references that despite the over-interpretation in some modern commentaries need not be interpreted instead as references to her vulva or clitoris. Indeed, smell, taste, voice and even the outside world around the two lovers are eroticized through their appreciation of each other. Through all these sensuous metaphors and allusions, coitus is not mentioned directly. It is something which always remains just offstage, as on the three occasions when the girl asks her friends, the daughters of Jerusalem, not to disturb their lovemaking which is clearly just about to begin. The characters involved are a man, a woman and the daughters of Jerusalem. Where the rest of the Bible speaks overwhelmingly with a male voice, here the woman is heard loud and clear expressing her own feelings, initiating action and reflecting on her emotions. Some scholars have even seen the entire text as being conceived and written from the woman's viewpoint. Certainly she speaks more than he does and has a clearer personality. She is present in every scene, even those that are not presented in her voice. Thus in verse 2:8, where her lover

The Prophet and the Whore

The prophet Hosea married a whore at God's command (Hosea 1:2). Hosea hoped that he could redeem his wife from her life of harlotry, but she continued to behave like a harlot. In desperation Hosea sold her into slavery but was so in love with her that he ended up buying her back. This time he decided to take her into the wilderness where other prospective lovers would not tempt her. The relationship between Hosea and his wife symbolizes that between God and Israel. While Israel flirts with the pagan deities of her Canaanite neighbors, the Baals, so God seeks to bring them back to the true path. Thus God says about his chosen people: "I will allure her, and bring her into the wilderness, and speak tenderly to her" (Hosea 2:14).

Conrad Kyeser, *The Queen of Sheba from Bellifortis*, c. 1405, Bohemia. Manuscript, Niedersächsische Staats- und Universitätsbibliothek, Göttingen, Germany. The Queen of Sheba – who came to Solomon from Ethiopia (or sometimes Arabia) – was widely assumed to be the female voice in the Song of Songs. At one point she describes herself as "black but comely", although in this illustration Kyeser cannot resist making her a blonde, despite her dark skin.

Pulaki, after Theodore, *King David Plays the Harp while the Shulamite Women Bathe in his Garden*, 17th cent. Oil on panel (decorative panel), 42 x 51 cm Museo Correr, Venice.
In the Old Testament (2 Samuel, 1 Kings), Bathsheba is a beautiful woman seduced by David, who, in order to win her, arranges the death of her husband, Uriah. The Shulamites are best known in Judaic erotic lore as women imported by Solomon (the son of David and Bathsheba) as wives and concubines, and Shulamite is one of the descriptions given to the female voice in the Song of Songs.

bounds over the hill like a gazelle towards her, the reader waits with her as he approaches rather than accompanying him on his journey. However, the man's voice is also authentic. They often use identical phrasing when addressing each other and both desire each other with the same intensity. There is a striking balance and equality between them, a non-

hierarchical mutuality with no anxiety about the commitment of each other's love. There are also no contrasting gender stereotypes such as the pleading or aggressive male, or the unyielding or manipulative female.

However, the girl's freedom of movement is more restricted by outside circumstances and she sometimes worries about what other peo-

ple will say. An additional reason why her voice seems richer and fuller is that, unlike her lover, she has a social context. We hear about her mother and her house, and she talks to her brothers as well as with the daughters of Jerusalem. She has confidantes, and pressures from family and society force her to be more resolute, and almost defiant, in her love.

Old Testament Sins

The Old Testament recognizes from the outset that sexuality is deeply problematic among human beings. When Adam and Eve taste the forbidden fruit of the tree of knowledge, they feel shame and cover their genitals with fig leaves sewn together to make aprons. When God asks who it was that told them they were naked, he asks because he realizes immediately that they have disobeyed the order not to eat the forbidden fruit. They have sinned through the actions of their hands and mouths, and yet their reaction is to cover the genitals. One doctrinal interpretation of this is that man's disobedience to God had resulted in the disobedience of his own body to his own volition or control, thereby emphasizing the uncontrollability of the human sexual urge. The breakdown of trust between man and God is paralleled in a breakdown of trust in the relations between Adam and Eve. Having done what was wrong, they hide from each other and from God the symbols of their own identity as man and woman. The idea of nakedness remains throughout the Old Testament as a metaphor for all forms of sexual sin. "Uncovering someone's nakedness" is the phrase used for having illicit sexual relations, especially of an incestuous sort with close relatives. There may also be an echo here of a Hebrew desire to distance themselves as far as possible from the sexual religious cults of their nearest neighbors such as the Canaanites. Leviticus (18:6–18) gives a long list of forbidden incestuous relationships, all cast in terms of not "uncovering" someone's nakedness. The many incidents of rape that are described in the Old Testament are all met with severe condemnation. The violation which occurs is not only to the purity of the woman, but also to the rights of the man to whom she is married or betrothed. Thus Deuteronomy (22:23–27) explains the difference between a woman raped in the city and one raped in the countryside in terms of her own volition or collusion. If a man rapes a betrothed woman in the open countryside then it is only the man who should die because the young woman was helpless and had no one to whom she could cry for help. But if a man rapes a betrothed woman inside the city walls, then both of them are to be taken out of the city and stoned to death, the young woman because she did not cry for help even though she was surrounded by people who were able to hear. The obligation for a man to harness his sexuality to the requirements of kinship is nowhere clearer than in the story of Onan. Onan's brother Er displeased Yahweh and was slain. Er's father, Judah, then said to his remaining son, "Go into your brother's wife and perform the duty of a brother-in-law, raising up offspring in your brother's name." Onan was reluctant to do this, so when he had intercourse with his brother's wife he withdrew at the last moment and spilled his semen on the ground. This displeased Yahweh who slew Onan as well. The implacable hostility in the Old Testament to male homosexuality may be due not only to the desire to beget offspring, but also to the desire to distinguish Judaism from the religion of neighboring tribes who practiced male temple prostitution. Throughout the period of the kings, male cult prostitution is frequently mentioned as being supported by some kings and suppressed by others. Leviticus (18:22 and 20:13) prescribes the penalty of death for homosexuality. However, it has often been suggested that the love between David and Jonathan was sexual. In the books of Samuel we are told that the soul of Jonathan was "knit" to the soul of David, and that Jonathan loved him as his own soul. When Jonathan is killed along with his father Saul, David laments him saying, "Very pleasant hast thou been to me: thy love was wonderful, passing the love of women" (2 Samuel 1:26). But most commentators argue that this was a passionate friendship rather than a sexual relationship.

A leading message of the story of Sodom and Gomorrah is that sexual transgression is not a private matter, but leads to the punishment and destruction of an entire community. Similar motifs recur with other characters in Genesis 34 and Judges 19–21.

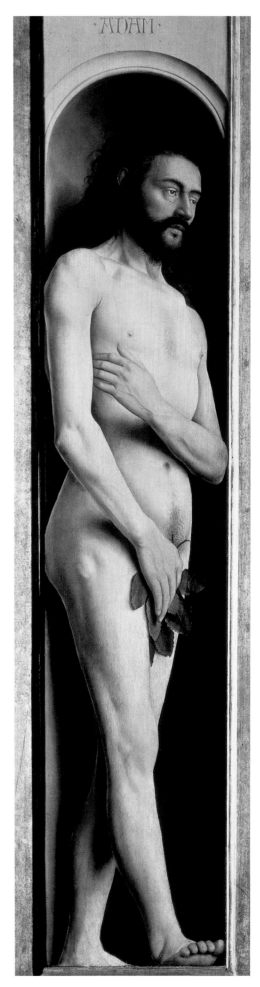

Jan van Eyck, *Adam and Eve* (details), 1432. Oil on panel, 350 x 122 cm each, Sint Baafskathedraal, Ghent, Belgium. Adam and Eve at the far extremities of the altarpiece are the only naked figures, isolated and alone.

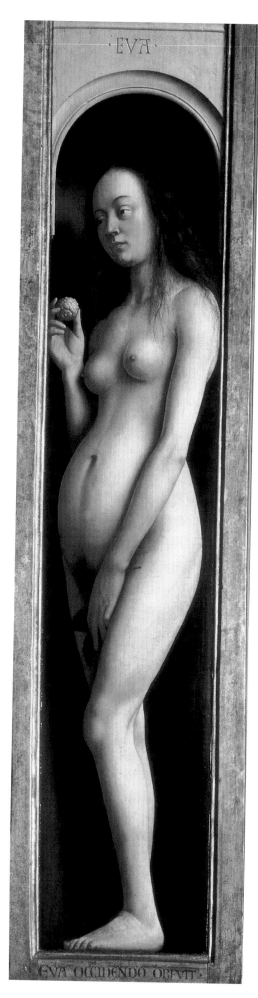

The story of Sodom appears to cover three different forms of sexual impropriety. First there is the threat of homosexual rape, when all the men of Sodom surround Lot's home and demand to "know" the strangers he is sheltering. There is, however, an alternative interpretation of this incident – the men accuse Lot of being a "sojourner": a *ger* or resident alien. They may simply be suspicious of why he is harboring strangers. This view is reinforced by the word used for "know", which is rarely employed in a conjugal sense elsewhere in the Bible, and then only ever in a heterosexual sense. Also, in other parts of the Old Testament (and the Apocrypha), the sin of Sodom is referred to as pride and idolatry. Nevertheless, the widespread reading – that this refers to homosexual rape – is a real possibility.

A second theme is the danger of the rape of Lot's daughters, whom he offers, despite their virgin condition, to the townspeople as a sub-stitute for the visitors he is protecting (or, in the alternative interpretation, simply as a bribe to stop the people from assaulting him). Lot's daughters are expendable for the sake of protecting Lot and/or the male visitors.

The third sexual aberration is the later incest between Lot and his daughters. When Lot's daughters tricked him into impregnating them, they were also, incidentally, serving as the agents of divine punishment for his decision to offer them to the Sodomites. Various forms of incest are listed among the twelve curses in Deuteronomy 27:15–26. The incest between Lot and his daughters has negative long-term consequences, giving rise to the children Moab and Ammon who cause great conflict among the Israelites on their trek from Egypt to Canaan. Strikingly, other rapes in the Old Testament such as those of Tamar (Genesis 38 and 2 Samuel 13) and of the concubine at Gibeah (Judges 19) also lead to civil war.

Jan Brueghel the Elder, *Sodom and Gomorrah* (detail), c. 1595. Copper, 26 x 35.2 cm, Alte Pinakothek, Munich.
As divine punishment for their sins, the biblical Cities of the Plains were destroyed by fire and brimstone. Lot and his family were spared, but Lot's wife was turned to a pillar of salt for turning back to look at the carnage.

Sex and Marriage in Judaism

Wedding ring, 19th cent. Gold-plated silver, Joods Historisch Museum, Amsterdam. Gold rings were used as symbols of Jewish marriage as far back as Moses. In eastern Europe, the ring had to be of a certain minimum value as a guarantee of the groom's financial stability.

Jewish tradition regards marriage as a moral, religious and social ideal. The relationship between God and Israel is generally depicted by the prophets and even in poetry less in the language of erotic love as in the image of marriage between husband and wife. Rabbinical commentaries on the Bible state that the man without a wife remains without joy and happiness. The purpose of marriage was the procreation of children and the commandment to "be fruitful and multiply", given in Genesis (1:28, and 9:1), was placed at the top of the list of the 613 precepts of Judaism. As Rachel cries in Genesis 30:1 "Give me children, or else I die." Ten years of childlessness was regarded as a sufficient reason for divorce. This emphasis on fertility extended to animals too, so that Judaism disapproved of the castration both of men and of animals. In Leviticus (22:24) castrated animals cannot be used at the altar for sacrifice. Other texts prohibit men who have been castrated from marrying within the Jewish community.

Although the story of Adam and Eve in Genesis clearly presupposes monogamy, as does the hymn in praise of the perfect wife (Proverbs 31), polygyny is not forbidden in the Bible and is frequently encountered, as for example with Solomon. Polygyny survived until recent times among Sephardic and Oriental Jews, especially those who lived in Islamic countries where this was approved and accepted by the state. However, state law in Israel prescribes monogamy, and among Ashkenazi Jews in Europe, polygyny was forbidden from the 11th century, though this prohibition probably does little more than reflect existing custom in accordance with surrounding European society.

In the traditional Jewish wedding, the bridegroom gives a ring to the bride in the presence of two witnesses, saying, "Behold, you are consecrated to me by this ring according to the law of Moses and Israel." Traditionally there were two stages of marriage, although in modern times these two stages are usually gone through in a combined ceremony. Prayers and benedictions are recited thanking God for having created humanity in his image and emphasizing the sanctity of marriage. Both parties must consent to the marriage and the husband is normally supposed to give a written document guaranteeing the maintenance of his wife in the event of her becoming widowed, or even of his divorcing her.

Two couples in bed in their tents, c. 1400. Parchment, British Library, London. The Talmud established a minimum frequency for married couples to have sex, depending on the man's occupation: donkey drivers (and scholars) were told to copulate at least once a week, while camel drivers were only obligated once a month. Sailors had the lowest minimum frequency, once every six months, while men of leisure were expected to have sex every night.

Ritual bath, c. 1427. Hebrew manuscript, University Library, Hamburg.

Ritual Immersion

Ritual immersion is used after a thorough washing of the body in order to rid oneself of impurity. Many of these rules of impurity concerned ritual procedure in the Temple in Jerusalem, and since the destruction of the Temple they have applied mostly to the monthly menstrual periods of women. Among some strict Orthodox Jews, men also take a ritual immersion before festivals or even before daily morning prayer. The water used for the immersion is supposed to come from rain or a natural spring, or even from melting ice. So important was ritual immersion that it was even said that the building of the bath, the *mikveh*, was more important than the building of a synagogue.

The rules of cleanliness that applied to ordinary Jews were even more severe for priests, the *cohanim*, and helped to emphasize their hereditary separateness within the community. Priests were expected to wash their hands and feet before Temple services, and were the only people allowed to touch offerings.

At the end of the ceremony a glass is broken to symbolize the destruction of the Temple in Jerusalem, which was demolished by the Babylonians in 586 B.C. Its replacement, begun by King Herod in 20 B.C. was destroyed by the Romans in 70 A.D. Only the "Wailing Wall" remains. This action also shows that the marriage takes place within the community of Jews who were in a state of perpetual exile following that event.

If a Jewish man is married but dies childless there is traditionally an obligation on his brother to marry the widow, a custom known as levirate marriage. If either the widow or the dead husband's brother refuses to make this marriage, elaborate rituals are prescribed to break the obligation. However, modern Reform Judaism no longer requires the dead man's brother to perform his levirate duty.

Jewish tradition strongly condemns adultery, which is forbidden in the Ten Commandments (Exodus 200:13). In the book of Leviticus (20:10) both the adulterer and the adulteress were to be put to death, and the Book of Numbers (5:11–31) gives details of a ritual by which a husband could test the faithfulness of his wife. If the husband suspected her of adultery in a situation where there were no witnesses, he was to bring his wife to a priest along with a small amount of barley meal. This meal was to be presented without any frankincense or oil because it was not a normal holy offering but an "offering of jealousy". The priest would hold a container of

water called "the water of bitterness" and would make the woman swear before Yahweh that she had not committed adultery. Then she had to drink the water, and if she had sworn falsely "the water that causeth the Curse shall enter into her, and become bitter, and her belly shall swell, and her thigh shall rot: and the woman shall be a curse among her people. And if the woman be not defiled, but be clean; then she shall be free, and shall conceive seed" (5:27–28).

Jewish wedding in France. The Jewish wedding contains many ancient elements whose original purpose has been lost. For example, the ceremony used to include a short period for consummation, so that the bride's virginity could be checked on the spot. In modern times, the couple just retires for a while.

Passion in Ancient and Medieval Persia

Most of the body of Persian myth owes its survival to the religious text known as the *Avesta* (1400–1200 B.C.), attributed to the prophet Zoroaster (Zarathustra). The linguistic style of the hymns points to a connection with the Indian *Rigveda*, which is dated around 1700 B.C. The content of the *Avesta* was memorized and passed down orally by Zoroastrian priests and it was recompiled under the Sassanian dynasty in the 6th century A.D. Little of its original content survived and the extant copy of the *Avesta*, translated only as late as 1771 by a French scholar, Auquetil Du Perron, contains just a small fragment of the Sassanian text. The *Avesta* consists of the *Gatha*, or hymns of Zoroaster, the *Visparad*, containing homages to a number of Zoroastrian spiritual leaders, the *Vendidad* or law against demons, the *Khurdeh*, or small avesta, and the *Yasht* or hymns that catalog pagan myths.

Zoroastrianism introduced something new to human sexual culture – the idea that limiting sexual activity was in itself a good thing, and a necessary ingredient in personal salvation. Any sex that was not aimed at reproduction was evil, a notion that was to have a profound effect on the Hebrews. However, Zoroastrians often practiced the opposite of what they preached. Many of them were polygynists, though polygyny was doctrinally condemned. They also appear to have married close relatives – brother-sister, father-daughter and even mother-son marriages occurred.

Possibly as a continuing result of Indian influence, even after Zoroastrianism was superseded, the discourse of love in Persian literature (and that of other Muslim countries) blends the spiritual and the physical. Thus the love of a religious initiate for a male god may be interpreted metaphorically, as it would be today, or as an actual sexual passion. Emotions and actions were clearly differentiated. Homoerotic feeling tended to be accepted as normal within Islamic societies although homosexual activity was proscribed. It was perhaps this tolerance of such emotions which accounted for the widespread incidence of homosexuality between older men and pubescent boys in Iran and other Muslim countries. In many of these

Youth Declaring His Love to a Lady, c. 1547, illustration from Jami, *Tuhfat al-ahrar*, Bukhara. Chester Beatty Library, Dublin. The reign of Safavid ruler Tahmasp (1524–1576) was a time of enormous social change, when, under the influence of the Shi'ites, a well organized ecclesiastical system was replacing the old, loose affiliation of spiritual leaders. This new clergy gradually helped to stamp out such gracefully sensual images.

cases the boys grew to manhood and led a heterosexual life. Jim Wafer of Indiana University points out that a homoerotic element has often appeared in Islamic literature because Islamic cultures in the Arab world, as well as in Iran and Turkey, tended to tolerate and adopt pre-Islamic homosexual customs. Various Persian treatises refer to love of girls and love of "beardless" boys in much the same way. Older men who desired them wrote poems to these boys, who though post-pubescent were still pre-virile. The masculinity of the penetrator was not in any sense impugned because of his sexual liaison with a boy nor indeed was the boy's maleness compromised. Nevertheless in many cases the families of such a boy would consider themselves disgraced. Although it was normal for a boy to receive sexual attention, a passive adult male was considered to be "third-gendered".

An interesting phenomenon was the adoption of Persian love poetry by various Islamic mystical orders, predominantly the Sufis who migrated to Persia in the 8th century A.D., following persecution in their countries of origin. To avoid further prejudice, in their writings the Sufi poets tended to disguise the male Islamic God as a female Beloved, a formulation that was possibly inspired by the *Avesta*. The poet (or religious initiate) was the Lover of the verse, whose goal was to meet and be united with the Beloved. Thus much of the verse decries her faithlessness and laments the torments that result from it. The prevalent images of wine (suggesting recklessness and passion), madness (or divine fervor), the moth expiring in the candle flame which lures it (representing the death-wish) and gardens with their paired inhabitants, such as the nightingale and the rose, were used liberally to describe an undying and ardent love which was easy to interpret literally, and was used frequently by dancing women in their secular performances. The language of divine love was therefore used quite directly in an environment of profanity.

Most Sufi poets were themselves initiates of one or other mystical order and as such affiliated to a *murshid* or "guide" who was also the Sheikh of the order. It was often the case that this Sheikh became eulogized in the verse instead of or along with God. The well-known

Anonymous, Two Adolescents, late 16th cent. Miniature, Musée du Louvre, Paris. In Persian culture, the process of becoming an adult male was synonymous with putting aside the passivity – social and sexual – associated with being a boy.

passion of Jalaleddin Rumi for his initiator, the ecstatic Shams Tabriz, found expression in literally thousands of verses in his dedicatory volume, the *Divan of Shams Tabriz*. After the latter had been brutally murdered and dismembered, in 1247, Rumi's grief was eventually assuaged when he was able to analogize his love with that of the Lover for the Divine Beloved. In 13th-century India, the Persian émigré mystic, poet and musician, Amir Khusro, entertained a similar passion for his Sheikh, Nizamuddin Auliya of Delhi. Writing in Persian and the vernacular Hindi, of which he is sometimes said to be the founder, Khusro often identified in his verse with the bride preparing for union with the groom on his wedding bed. It is alleged that, when in a state of ecstasy, Khusro dressed himself in the garments of a bride, dyed his hands red in the Indian tradition, decked himself in female jewelry, including green glass wedding bangles, and danced to please the absent Nizamuddin.

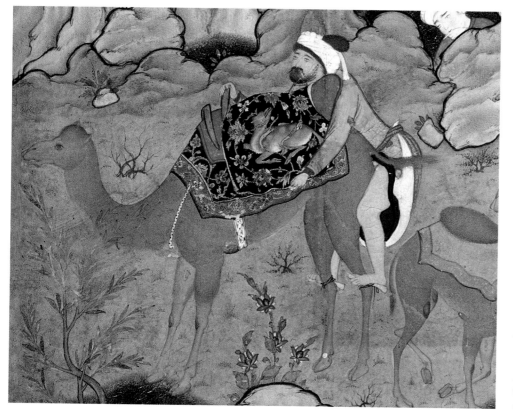

Illustration (detail) from the manuscript *Haft Awrang of Jami* (Seven Thrones), Mashad, 1556. Freer Gallery of Art, Washington D.C. This miniature is an illustration for the Persian tale *Sselsselat us-Sabad* (The Golden Chain), 1485. The steps tied to the camel's rear legs allow the man to climb high enough to penetrate his steed.

Teachings of Islam

The complex language of the Koran led very early in the development of Islam to a proliferation of supportive, interpretative and exegetic literature. In addition to the Koran itself, which is believed to be the revealed word from Allah brought by the angel Gabriel, there are other sources that mediate life in Islam. The *Hadith* is the collected sayings of the Prophet Muhammad as remembered and authenticated by those present or their descendants. Some collections are considered more reliable than others. The *Shari'ah* (Way of the Prophet) is further interpreted by four scholars whose writings form the four schools of Islamic thought.

Some of the most controversial interpretations of Koranic law this century have centered on gender issues, the imbalance between the rights of the sexes and male/female relations. Perhaps the best known of all is the adultery law which was highlighted in 1979–1980 when a Saudi princess was condemned to death for having committed adultery. The law demands the execution of an adulterous woman while a man is subjected to flogging. In Pakistan, too, the Zina Ordinance put in place by General Zia in his period of radical Islamization during the mid to late 1970s, caused controversy when female rape victims were continually given the death sentence under a heinously misused law. In most cases the male turned out to be wealthier and more influential than the victim. Little attention was paid to the actual words of the Koranic injunction that the death sentence may only be imposed in a situation where the couple is consenting and seen *in flagrante delicto* by four incidental witnesses.

The Koranic laws concerning marriage and divorce are also open to abuse. Many Muslims take the Koranic sanction of polygyny as a license to marry repeatedly and with impunity, despite the fact that the conditions for remarrying are relatively well known and fairly stringent. A man may take a second wife if the existing one is either insane or infertile or if he wishes to extend his protection and support to a widow or an orphan. Having met these criteria, he still has to obtain permission from his wife or wives – without coercion – before remarrying. Once remarried, he must ensure that he treats each wife with absolute equality – a condition that even the Prophet himself is said to have considered next to impossible. The relevant verse of the Koran (4, 3), often interpreted as limiting a man to four wives, says: "Marry such of the women as seems good to you; two or three or four … If you fear that you may not be fair, then take only one."

The Birth of the Prophet Muhammad (detail), illustration from Rashid al-Din, *Jámi' al-tawárîkh*, Tabiz, c. 1315. 10 cm high, University Library, Edinburgh. An evolution of Islamic attitudes to the Prophet, childbirth and women in general can be seen to have occurred in the 300 years between these paintings. The first is a comparatively naturalistic scene, the second shows the Prophet born from a golden cloud, with his face obscured out of respect, and his mother kneeling alongside, veiled.

The Birth of the Prophet (detail), illustration from Mustafa Dabir, *Kitab siyar-i Nabi*. 18.5 x 18 cm, Topkapi Palace Library, Istanbul.

The Wedding of Yusuf and Zulaykha, **illustration from the manuscript** *Haft Awrang of Jami,* **(Seven Thrones), Mashad 1556. Freer Gallery of Art, Washington D.C.** This illustration probably alludes to the marriage of Ibrahim Mirza and Gawhar Sultan Khanum, nephew and daughter of the Safavid ruler Tahmasp.

Mut'a

The controversial institution of *mut'a* is practiced among several Shi'a Muslim communities around the world. It is particularly popular among the Isna'Ashari communities of Indian origin settled in East Africa. Translated variably as a marriage of "convenience" or "pleasure", it is essentially a ritual of mercantile origins, in which a man and woman agreed to marry for a limited period of time. The Koran says : "You are permitted to seek out wives with your wealth in decorous conduct but not in fornication; but give them reward [compensation] for what you have enjoyed with them in keeping with your promise" (4, 24). Intended to provide a man with home comforts while on a journey lasting many months or even a few years, it also provides economic and social security to the wife for the duration of the contract. Afterwards she has no claim for maintenance, and the partners do not inherit from another. Any children from a *mut'a* go with their father.

There are many restrictions on who may marry. Unsuitable matches include those between stepsiblings, or people who have shared a wet-nurse; between a stepfather and stepdaughter, or if the man has ever been *in loco parentis* to the woman. A woman may not marry her father-in-law or a man his mother-in-law. Furthermore, a man is forbidden to carry on a relationship with two sisters. If however his wife dies, he may marry her sister.

The assent of a woman in marriage matters has always been vital. The institution of marriage, though important to the Prophet Muhammad and incumbent upon parents of post-pubescent children, was nevertheless not to be forced on a young woman. The bride's approval was necessary and to ensure this, the *nikah* (or marriage ritual) requires the bride to be asked three times in the presence of witnesses to give her agreement to the marriage before signing relevant documents. A virgin forced into marriage can demand divorce on coming of age. The care of the bride is much emphasized in any marriage agreement and the bride-price, known as *mihr*, is agreed with the family of the groom. Rather than being paid to the guardian, it was given to the bride herself on the wedding night and notionally at least was intended to give her a degree of independence. In practice this is generally ignored and most women only receive their *mihr* as part of a divorce settlement – and even this may not occur if, on the wedding night, the groom asked the bride to release him from the debt of *mihr* and she agreed.

Divorce is a permissible option for both men and women. The relatively easy and much-criticized divorce ritual which simply requires a man to repeat three times the word *talaq* (or divorce) is frequently used in Muslim countries even where the country has imposed laws more in line with international norms. There are various categories of conditional divorce, such as *talaq-ul-ehsan*, where divorce conditions are agreed before marriage to achieve an amicable separation. In general, the dissolution of a marriage involves an attempt by a *mullah* or *kadhi* (teacher or judge who interprets the religious laws) to resolve differences. Failing this he lists the debts of each partner before pronouncing the breakdown of the partnership. There is a period of approximately one hundred days during which the couple may reunite without requiring a second ceremony, after which the marriage is considered dissolved.

The Harem and the Great Seraglio

The word "harem" derives from the Arabic *haram* – "that which is not lawful" – a place where certain things, allowed elsewhere, are forbidden. When applied to women, it suggests sanctuary and seclusion. The early Islamic armies adopted many of their customs from those they conquered and those they wished to conquer, and the segregation of women was probably inspired by pre-Islamic Egypt and Persia, but especially by the Greco-Roman culture of Byzantium, where girls were regularly locked away so securely that even servants were not permitted to see them, and most married women had no role outside the home. Within Islam, most poor men could afford to support no more than one wife, although the words of the Prophet Muhammad were usually interpreted as permitting them four. It was only the fairly well-off who could consider taking up their full quota. The financial difficulties of keeping more than one spouse were compounded by the Prophet's command that all wives be treated equally. When combined with the practice of seclusion, this meant that each wife would often have her own room, or occasionally her own house within a larger compound.

The extremely wealthy or powerful, on the other hand, felt no need to restrict themselves to four partners. The harems belonging to the Caliphs of Baghdad, the Emirs of Cairo and

Eugène Delacroix, *Algerian Women in their Chamber*, 1834. Oil on canvas, 180 x 229 cm, Musée du Louvre, Paris.

innumerable Saracen princes were famous in the West from about the time of the first crusades, and became a staple element of Romance tales and other medieval literature. They gained even greater notoriety in the West in the 18th century, when the book *The Thousand and One Nights* was first translated into European languages. The harems were said to contain hundreds of languorous, scantily-clad, sexually-available women, but the lords and princes got around the injunctions of the Koran by rarely bothering to marry any of them. In the early Middle Ages, the Islamic world was ruled by a succession of 38 Abbasid Caliphs, 35 of whom were born illegitimately to foreign slave girls.

The harem system attained its most splendid, ornate and complicated form in the Great Seraglio of the Grand Turk, sultan of the Ottoman Empire. *Seraglio* is an Italian word whose original meaning is "a cage for wild beasts". Strictly speaking it refers not just to the women's quarters (the *haremlik*), but also to the entire royal enclosure, including the *selamlik* (or male domain). Both Europeans and Turks adopted it because it happened to sound like *sarai*, the Persian word for palace or building. Muhammad II built the first seraglio in 1454, after he conquered Byzantium. It was superseded in 1465 by the Topkapi Palace, but continued to play a role in the domestic life of the ruling family, as the *Eski Sarai*, "Old Seraglio", where the harem of the previous sultan was sent on his death.

The secrecy surrounding the *haremlik* was so intense that there are only a handful of reliable eyewitness accounts. The first authoritative description is found in the *Relatione della gran citta di Constantinopoli*, written by Domenico Hierosolimitano, who was court physician to Murad III at the end of the 16th century. It appears that the *haremlik* was a bustling community within the palace, containing up to 1200 courtesans as well as their guards and attendants, who included the Mistress of the Robes, the Reader of the Koran as well as the Keeper of the Baths and the Manageress of the Table.

Top: Jean-Auguste-Dominique Ingres, *The Turkish Bath*, 1863. Oil on panel, 110 cm in diameter, Musée du Louvre, Paris. The contents of the harem inspired the fantasies of writers and artists in the West. Delacroix's painting (opposite) was apparently inspired by a visit to a real harem while on a trip to Morocco. It is clearly much earthier than the Ingres, which was based on nothing more than the artist's daydreams.

Eunuchs

The most suitable harem guards were thought to be eunuchs, who were men who had been emasculated in some way, whose name derives from the Greek word *eunouchos* meaning "he who has charge of the bed". There were several different categories of eunuchs. In some cases the testicles were simply crushed or twisted, causing sterility. Others had their testicles cut off, while others, the "fully-shaved", had penis and testicles removed. In some cases only the penis was removed, leaving the eunuch theoretically, but not practically, capable of fatherhood. Some were castrated voluntarily, as a career move, while others were subjected to castration as prisoners of war. The process was extremely hazardous: in the 17th century along the upper Nile, which produced most of the world's fully-shaved eunuchs at the time, only one in four was expected to survive the operation. Being made a eunuch did not remove a man's capacity for sexual desire, and one of the eunuch's roles in the harem was to satisfy women who had been ignored too long by the sultan. Their great advantage to the ruling classes was not that they could not have sex, but rather that they could not produce heirs.

Anonymous, *The Kislar Agha, or Chief Black Eunuch of the Great Seraglio* (detail), 1670. Copperplate engraving. The black eunuchs (as many as 800 of them) worked in the women's quarters, while the men were attended by white eunuchs.

New girls, who may have been bought at a slave market or presented as gifts, were taught a trade, such as embroidery, coffee-making or musicianship. Most of them could never expect to get near the sultan's bed. Those who were singled out, by the sultan or his advisers, were given separate apartments and their own private servants. Before they were taken to the sultan – which was always done in secrecy – they would be bathed, perfumed, depilated and dressed in fine clothes and jewels. Arriving at the royal bed, a concubine was supposed to show deference by entering at its foot and crawling up until she was level with the sultan. There was a complicated hierarchy in the women's quarters, which were nominally ruled over by the sultan *valideh* – the sultan's mother. However, any concubines who bore male children were promoted to the rank of *kadin* (or sultana), and the favorite *kadin* was usually embroiled in a fierce power struggle with the sultan *valideh*, as well as any other *kadins*. Political skill was an important asset if a *kadin* wanted her children to survive, because the male children of the harem who did not succeed to the throne were likely to be killed or imprisoned by their successful half-brother. From the end of the 15th century this custom entered the statute book, when the Law of Fratricide, passed by Muhammad II, made it compulsory for a new sultan to execute all his brothers. The law was only repealed at the beginning of the 17th century by Achmed I, who preferred to lock his brothers in a small building called "the Cage", with just a few attendants and concubines for company. The Great Seraglio was finally broken up in 1909 with the deposition of Abd ul-Hamid II, who was nevertheless allowed to take three wives and four concubines with him when he was sent into exile at Salonica.

Court Levni, Girl Dancing, 17th cent. Topkapi Museum, Istanbul. Levni was the Court painter to Achmed III. The courtesans of the Islamic world were usually foreigners, either taken in war or sent as a tribute. Many of them were erudite, talented and much more highly educated than was common for Arab or Turkish women. Some, especially those from Persia or India, had a profound effect on Arab and Ottoman culture, by introducing the songs, dances and stories of their native lands. The slave singer was a much sought-after creature – the object of romantic fantasy – and was often showered with gifts and cash. If she became wealthy enough, she could, under Muslim law, buy her freedom.

Above: **Woman in a** *hamman* **(Turkish bath),**
18th cent. Topkapi Museum, Istanbul.
Left: **A Prince in a** *Harem* **Seated under a Canopy and**
Being Offered Wine by a Woman, Persian. British
Library, London. The Ottoman sultans rarely married
their concubines. When Roxelana wedded Suleyman
the Magnificent (1520–1566), it was the first royal
marriage in more than a century. Some sultans only
used concubines to continue the royal line, preferring boys for pleasure. Others, such as the mentally
unstable Ibrahim (1640–1648), had a taste for mass
orgies. Ibrahim once had all his 280 concubines tied
into sacks and thrown in the Bosporus.

The Perfumed Garden of Sheikh Nefzawi

Sheikh al-Nefzawi wrote *The Perfumed Garden* in the 16th century, probably in Tunis. It incorporates material from earlier Arabic and Indian works of a similar nature and is illustrated with anecdotes, amusing episodes, and stories of deceit of a sort similar to those found in *The Thousand and One Nights*. The author presents sexuality as a part of God's design of the world, as an art, a sacrament, even a form of healing – and also as an aid to long-lived marriage. The book opens with the words, "Praise be given to God, who has placed man's greatest pleasure in the natural parts of woman, and has destined the natural parts of man to afford the greatest enjoyment to women." *The Perfumed Garden* is a textbook describing numerous coital positions to suit every type of physique as well as conditions such as obesity and pregnancy, and special needs such as how to enable a tall man and a short woman, or vice versa, to join both their sexual organs and their mouths simultaneously. Readers are earnestly recommended to try out these positions in order to find the ones most suitable for them. The Sheikh adds that the Indians have brought coitus to the level of the greatest art, but considers some of the positions mentioned in their texts physically impossible.

He also discusses the numerous shapes and sizes of sexual organs as well as types of women and men, their desirable characteristics and the relationship between their sexuality and their physical and psychological temperaments. Entire chapters catalog types of men and women who deserve to be held in esteem or in contempt, such as the man who enters a woman with a minimum of foreplay and who ejaculates quickly with no thought for her pleasure. Kissing and nibbling is especially rec-ommended for the satisfaction of the woman; no position is fully satisfactory if it does not allow mouth-to-mouth contact, itself the subject of much technical discus-sion. The reader is given clues about watching for a woman's sighing and for the languid look in her eyes, with great emphasis given to attaining simultaneous orgasm, often expressed as the womb grasping the head of the penis.

Women in the Modern Islamic World

In general, it is the urban elite of a country who tend to represent their nation to the world, despite being the minority culture. In the case of most Islamic countries, this elite group has been heavily influenced by Western culture, usually as the result of colonization leading to a tradition of Western education. The elite often tends to regard itself as being above the rules and norms that are generally applicable. Therefore, at least until the fundamentalist backlashes of the 1970s, certain Muslim countries were thought of in the West as modern or westernized, including Iran, Lebanon, Syria and Egypt. Men and women from the larger cities and towns dressed in Western clothes and often spoke a European language as the result of frequent traveling and interaction with Europeans and Americans or because of a Western education.

Although very often state laws were liberalized to accommodate such issues as human and women's rights, the rural population followed traditions that went back many years. Whereas to the liberal citizen infidelity or adultery were issues to be decided in the civil courts, to the rural population they were a question of tradition and family standing, linked in their collective minds to "honor". To this day, the only solution to such loss of honor continues to be death in provincial villages and towns, and occasionally even the cities. The murder in

Panjab, Pakistan of an allegedly adulterous woman at the dawn of the third millennium is simply one example of many. Because the local judges are part of the tradition the system is open to exploitation, and frequently women are murdered simply as a cover-up following the killing of a local man for other reasons. If a sexual relationship can be alleged, whether adulterous or not, the killer is rarely convicted. The abuse of Islamic law also extends to women with property – ironically, as it is only a progressive attitude towards women that permits them to inherit. The males in the family of a woman owning real property often collude in bringing an accusation of adultery or fornication by providing false witnesses and securing a prison sentence to get her out of the way. According to Islamic law, where a charge of adultery or fornication (*zina*) is brought against a woman, the onus is on her husband or any other accuser to provide rigorous and unassailable evidence in support of his charge (*li'an*), but such evidence is rarely investigated or ratified in practice. Such women can languish forgotten in Pakistani prisons for years and would remain there for life were it not for the unremitting dedication of local human rights activists.

It was probably to avoid precisely the kind of abuse that arises from confusion or false interpretation of religious law that a number of governments in the 20th century attempted to

Benazir Bhutto, c. 1989. After being educated at Harvard and Oxford, Benazir Bhutto became the first female leader of a Muslim nation in modern history when she was elected prime minister of Pakistan in 1988.

secularize their countries, choosing a national identity that harked back to pre-colonial, even pre-Islamic times. Mohammed Reza Shah Pahlavi (1919–1980), last emperor of Iran, referred to Islam as an "interlude" in the vast tradition of Iran which went back to Archaemenid times. The Egyptians focused on a culture going back to the pharaohs, with Hasan al-Banna (1906–1949) and other reformers attempting to emphasize the enlightened spirit of Islam. In Turkey, Kemal Atatürk (1881–1938) instituted radical changes such as banning the veil, insisting on Western dress codes and changing the script from Arabic to Roman while once again pointing to pre-Ottoman cultures as a model for national identity. Such reforms are always under threat from fundamentalist Islam.

Young veiled woman doctor on her way to a patient, Yemen, 1976. The conflicting demands of Islamic codes and practical everyday problems often produce situations that appear incongruous to Western eyes.

Demonstration in Teheran on the occasion of "Women's Day", mid-1980s. Traditionally, Muslim women wear veils from the onset of menstruation until old age, and may only uncover their faces in the company of their husbands, close relatives, other women or children.

One highly visible effect of radical Islamization has been the enforcement of the veil. An icon symbolizing the warring values of Islam and the Western world, it is a distinguishing factor which openly dissociates Islam from the perceived corrupt values of the West: the drinking of alcohol, the eating of pork and perhaps most significantly promiscuity, all of which lead the transgressor away from faith and the righteous path. To the West and to those Muslim women who have been forced to observe the rule that involves the seclusion of women from public observation (*purdah*), the veil (*hijab*) represents abuse of human rights as well as gender-based oppression. Paradoxically, too, the *yashmak*, which covers the nose and mouth of the wearer, contributes to an undeniable mystique and a sexual frisson. It was also frequently associated with prostitutes and belly dancers – the precise reverse of the intended effect, which was to facilitate safe and effective public interaction between men and women.

The fact that women in the Western world are opting for conversion to fundamental Islam, or if Muslim-born opting to take the veil, is rarely analyzed. The widely-posited stereotype of Muslim woman as subservient and passive leads to the assumption that the veil is always enforced. The truth, however, is often that those women who make a free choice take the veil and use it as a form of "power-dressing", to seize the independence offered to them by Islam. It is also a self-conscious way of distinguishing themselves politically from other cultures that may be considered invasive. They are able to disabuse themselves (and others) of the taught traditions dealing with honor, which all too often have little to do with Islam but rather conform to preexistent tribal customs.

Muslim women are no more homogeneous than their sisters in the Western world and elsewhere and it is a nonsense to attempt to classify them as either submissive or progressive. Their attitude and those of others around them varies according to the individual, the environment and its culture. Folklore, often a reliable point from which to take the cultural pulse of a people, attests to the strength, daring and resourcefulness of women from the Arab countries as well as those of Iran, Turkey, India and Pak-istan. Thus there are women who tend the home and children either from choice or lack of it, and those who go to work out of necessity or preference.

Islam espouses the education of a woman and places the responsibility of primary and cultural education of the children on her. She is their first teacher and as such she is required to be literate, the reading of the Koran being a compulsory part of the education of all Muslims. It is entirely inappropriate to assume that the majority of women from Islamic countries are either oppressed, illiterate or submissive. Often, despite a secular manifesto, the reform and modernization that takes place in Muslim countries has its source in Islamic thought. A woman may be educated and choose any career even in Saudi Arabia, perhaps one of the more restrictive of the Islamic countries. However, her education will take place in a segregated environment – for example in an all-female university. It is worth noting that Iran included women in its Foreign Service long before the European states, and Pakistan's first constituent assembly in 1947 included women.

Marriage in Africa

Sex in Africa is closely linked with religion. It is the ancestors who guarantee the fertility of human beings and of the land. They give life by opening or closing the womb and thereby ensure the continued flow of life from the past into the future. The ancestors enable humans to harness this creativity of the cosmos and to control it through systems of kinship and marriage. The emphasis is not so much on the control of sexual activity as such, but on procreation. Therefore ideas like virginity and sexual abstinence are generally not strongly stressed. In many African societies conception before marriage is not nearly as much of a problem as is conception before the puberty ceremony.

Fertility is more important than the sexual exclusiveness of a partnership. So in some communities a new bride will bring with her a younger sister as well, in case the bride herself should prove infertile. Or alternatively, an impotent man may bring in a proxy father to a marriage to beget children on his behalf so that he will have legal heirs. It is also common for a widow to marry the brother of her dead husband and to produce offspring who continue to be thought of as her first husband's children. Similarly, if a young man dies unmarried, a woman may be married to his name so that she will continue to bear children who will be considered his heirs. This practice is commonly known as "ghost marriage".

A distinctive feature of traditional marriage in many parts of Africa is polygyny. The ideal family structure therefore consists of a man, his wives and their children. But it would be impossible demographically for many men to achieve this ideal and it is most commonly found among chiefs and men of high status. This is part of a broader system in which herding cattle or tilling the land is done by a large group of people who cooperate and who are bound together by kinship ties rather than by the relationship of employee to employer.

The relationship between co-wives could be friendly or hostile. The Fon of Cameroon acknowledged the tension between co-wives, who would sing against each other while working in the women's courtyard of a chief's compound: "Woman, your soul is misshapen and was made in haste, your soul was formed without care, the ancestral clay that went into making you was molded in haste, you are a thing of no beauty, your face is not like a face, your feet are not like feet."

Both polygyny and communal labor decrease in the context of the cities and among the new middle class, who tend towards a European kind of nuclear family. There are many potential

Above: **Spirit-lover, Sculpture of a *blolo-bla*, Baule people, Ivory Coast. Wood, 73 cm high.** The Baule believe in a close link between this world and the next. Marriage problems such as sterility or impotence are a clue that the man or woman has a discontented spouse in the spirit realm. The cure is to make the spirit-lover visible in a wooden carving, which is wed in a formal ceremony. Thursday nights are then devoted to the satisfaction of the spirit-lover, with the earthly spouse banished from the marriage bed.

Right: **A Songhai bride from Mali displays her dowry**.

areas for conflict between the old and the new in Africa. In much of south-central Africa and among the Akan-speaking peoples of Ghana, for example, descent is traditionally reckoned through the mother's line, and there are many conflicts between the father's desire to have his wife and children living with him under his own authority and the claims of his wife's kin to keep their women and children with them. Missionary faiths have to acknowledge the various tensions and traditions. Islam coincides closely with traditional African practices of polygyny, whereas Christianity is militantly opposed to them. In areas where both Islam and Christianity are competing for converts the Christian church sometimes turns a blind eye to traditional practices, and sometimes opposes them openly.

Cost of a Bride

A common way of sealing a marriage is for the husband to pay a bride-price, in which he hands over some property to his wife's kin. Among the pastoral peoples of southern and eastern Africa, as well as the Fulani of West Africa, this takes the form of cattle. The cattle are given by the bridegroom's family to the bride's family and are widely distributed among the relatives. All these people now acquire a strong interest in maintaining the stability of the marriage since if it should break down all the cattle have to be returned. In areas where cattle are not important, payment is made in cloth, cowrie shells, spears, beer and meat for feasts, and agricultural implements such as hoes. These kinds of payments are particularly common in parts of East and West Africa and in Rwanda. In the Nuba hills and in parts of Nigeria, the groom will also work for some time for the girl's father before marriage, in a custom known as "bride service". Among the matrilineal peoples of Zambia, such as the Bemba, the groom may work in his father-in-law's village both before marriage and permanently after marriage as well. Bride-price should not be thought of as a form of purchase or enslavement of the bride. It is part of a wider pattern of gift giving which unites the participants in any kind of social

This Surma woman from Ethiopia is wearing a large clay plate in her lip. The size of the plate indicates to potential suitors, and their families, just how many cattle are required for the young woman's bride-price. The larger the plate, the more cattle are needed.

relationship, such as chiefs and commoners, parents and children, and lovers. Each of these patterns of gift giving serves as a way of establishing and expressing a kind of interpersonal behavior. Thus the payment of bride wealth often continues over many years, indeed for the full length of the marriage. This is because it links not only the two partners to the marriage but also two entire kin-groups in an ongoing relationship which is at the same time social, political and economic. Among the Azande of the southern Sudan, people may refer to the institution of marriage as if it were a function of the bride-price. A girl may say, "Someone has paid spears to my father," meaning, "I am married," or else a person may say,

"I am a child of spears," meaning, "I was born to parents who are formally married." Thus the continued movement of cattle and other gifts is a way of reinforcing and sustaining the marriage, which also becomes stronger and more established with the birth of children.

Attitudes towards adultery vary but it is widely believed that a woman's adultery will cause her difficulties during childbirth, or even bring about the death of her child. Among the Bemba, a woman experiencing difficult childbirth is surrounded by midwives and female friends who interrogate her and urge her to confess the list of all her adulterous partners. In many areas a man who committed adultery would traditionally be challenged to a duel by the wronged husband or else ambushed and speared by him. Arrangements for dissolving conjugal unions are also very varied. If a couple are unable to live happily together, divorce is often considered preferable because quarrels lead to violence and bad feeling, which can lead in turn to accusations of witchcraft.

There is much variation in gender relations across Africa. Women often have separate budgets from their husbands and engage in many forms of productive labor on their own behalf. This tendency is perhaps most highly developed in some areas of West Africa, where the married woman is often a forceful, independent market trader and keeper of the family purse. In many kinship systems, mothers and sisters of men have a lot of influence. There is a Swazi riddle: "If your mother and your wife were drowning whom would you save first?" The correct answer is: "My mother, since I can get another wife but I can't get another mother." Among the Lozi of Zimbabwe, men remain very close to their mothers and sisters rather than to their wives with whom their ties are very ephemeral. A man who wants to divorce can just send his wife home without any reason. Similarly, if he pushes her or treats her badly in any way his wife can also walk out on him. By contrast, among the Zulu, marriage is generally very stable and highly valued, and both divorce and adultery are rare. The bond between a Zulu man and his wife is strong and

A young Masai bride, from Kenya, walking away from her family home. She is wearing beaded necklaces and an elaborate headdress as part of the wedding celebrations, and as she walks away it is forbidden to look back. The Masai are one of several East African peoples among whom sex hospitality is reported – men will leave their own huts so that a male guest can be entertained, in solitude, by their wives. Married women are permitted to have sex with any man belonging to her husband's age group.

The Cowrie Shell

Perhaps because of their suggestively sexual shape, cowrie shells play a significant part in the sexual customs of many African peoples, serving a rich variety of symbolic purposes. Among the Fon of Cameroon, there are many forms of marriage with elaborate ceremonies and exchanges of gifts. The key point of the ceremony is when the groom brings gifts to the head of the bride's family. In one form of marriage he brings 720 cowrie shells, a woman's cloth, a man's cloth, a sack of salt and a castrated goat. When the head of the girl's family sacrifices the goat he informs the ancestral spirits that one of the lineage's daughters is to be married. He throws the cowrie shells into the ancestral shrines so that the ancestors can use them to purchase goods in the markets of the dead. The man's cloth is given to the girl's father and is said to replace the one on which the bride's parents lay the night when they conceived the girl who is now to be married. The woman's cloth is given to the girl's mother and is said to replace the one she used to carry her daughter as a baby on her back. If the couple later divorces, these gifts have to be returned. Sometimes, instead of the bride's family receiving a bride-price, it is the bride herself who receives a dowry from her old family to take to her new home. Such gifts can be highly decorative as well as having a symbolic significance, such as the heavy copper bands worn on the legs by the Boende women from Congo.

These Dinka girls of Sudan are each wearing a loose bodice of beads to show that they are at a marriageable age. The cowrie shells on the front are to promote fertility.

if a Zulu man also marries his wife's sister the two wives will often cooperate.

Among the Luo of Kenya, the traditional form of marriage was for the bride to be abducted by the groom and his friends. This still continues in a playful way. The men arrive at night and shout to the old woman in charge of the girls' dormitory to open the door and release her. They rush in and drag the girl away despite her screaming and protesting. A mock fight then takes place before the young men bear the woman away. Very often the girl and the young man have been lovers for a long time and the struggle is only a mock protest – if she was genuinely unwilling, the marriage would not go forward.

Traditionally, the Luo marriage by abduction was consummated when the bride's sister laid an ox hide on the floor of the hut and told the naked bride and groom to lie on it. She extinguished the fire and in the darkness the marriage would be consummated. When the fire was rekindled the man's penis would be examined for traces of the girl's hymen. A party of girls who had been singing outside would enter the hut and beat the bridegroom, saying, "You have killed our sister." The girls would return

home singing all the way and taking the hymen with them. After this ceremonial deflowering the bride would be given a small tail made of fibrous material to wear at the back of her belt. This tail would be worn constantly as a sign of her married status and if a woman heard of her husband's death the first thing she would do would be to remove her tail and to throw it onto the roof of her hut.

Tuareg women building a nuptial tent or *ehan*. This structure, symbolizing the Tuareg marriage, will be dismantled and enlarged daily during the wedding festivities.

The Sex Life of an African Chief

Pre-colonial Africa contained a large number of chiefs and kings whose powers were gradually curtailed and restrained under colonial administration. However, many chiefs remain the spiritual and symbolic leaders of their peoples. An African chief is often considered to embody the fertility of his land and of his people. In addition, it was often politically important for him to take a large number of wives from a wide range of clans in order to draw them into an in-law relationship with the royal family. In the early 20th century the king of Swaziland had more than 40 wives. A large number of wives and their offspring also provide a chief with labor and sustained his position as a wealthy and powerful figure.

The Fon, who are the supreme chiefs in the feudal villages of Dahomey (today Benin), are traditionally said to have a 100 wives and in the past many prominent men were keen for their daughters to marry the Fon in order to have a close political association with the royal family. However, the women themselves often did not find such marriages attractive because women's interests centered on the contacts of the market place, trade and gossip. A king's wife was not even allowed to be seen in the market place and very rarely left the king's compound, least of all unaccompanied.

In parts of East Africa stretching from southern Sudan down to northern Zambia, chiefs were regarded as divine embodiments of the land, and their strength and potency was directly linked to that of their realm. Until the early 20th century they were not allowed to die naturally. Instead, as their strength waned they would give the signal to have themselves ritually killed, thereby forestalling the process of physical decay and the collapse and sterility of the land and people, which would ensue.

The chief of the Bemba of Zambia did not take this initiative himself but would be throttled in the night by special hereditary stranglers. He would then be embalmed in a special bean sauce, symbolizing agricultural fertility, and carried in procession around his entire territory on the way to a sacred burial grove. At various stopping points human sacrifices would be made, but the most important human sacrifice was his head wife, who would be kept until the moment of his burial and then buried alive with him. Even while the chief was still alive,

Royal Zulus, South Africa. King Mswati III of the Zulus leads his royal warriors to appraise the maidens at the traditional swazi reed dance celebrations (left) and two young girls prepare for the dance (right). At the height of Zulu power, in the 19th century, the king exercised enormous power over the marriage rights of his warriors.

The Queen Mothers

A chief's head wife often had particular importance and power. Among the Zulu, at the marriage of a chief to his head wife, the heads of all the social groups under him had to contribute to the cattle for the marriage payment as if she was their own daughter or kin. In this way, a son born to the head wife would also, symbolically, become a son of the whole group, and thus their rightful heir.

Among the Ashanti of Ghana, descent is reckoned in the female line. Thus the King of Ashanti cannot pass his office to his own son. The most powerful figure is the head wife or Queen Mother, who alone can transmit royal blood. This is tied in with the Ashanti belief that only a woman can transmit blood to her descendants, who contain no blood whatsoever from their fathers. Instead men transmit *ntoro*, which means "spirit" or "soul" and is sometimes also used to mean "semen". The blood transmitted through the female is the blood that is observed during childbirth and menstruation. These female functions are considered fully equivalent to the hunting and warfare of the men, and may contribute to the authority and power that women have in Ashanti life in general, and Queen Mothers in particular have in the affairs of royalty.

Dance for a chief at the 25th jubilee of the Ashantehene (King of all Ashanti) Kumasi, Ghana. A head wife's power does not disappear with her husband's death. Even retired Queen Mothers retain great ceremonial importance, performing a range of tasks such as helping dancers prepare for funeral rites.

his head wife would have played an important role in his household. She was the only person who could purify him from the contamination that was thought to occur after sexual intercourse with any of his other wives. So powerful and perilous was the act of sex to a Bemba chief's well-being that before he could have intercourse for the first time with a new wife, a category of special official called "eater of the *chisungu*" (meaning the girl's puberty rite) had to sleep with her first. In this way the official would take upon himself the magical dangers associated with her newfound state of reproductive sexuality. The *chisungu* eaters were killed at the same time as the chief. In contrast to the chief's own body, which was preserved as a source of fertility, the bodies of the *chisungu* eaters were treated as reservoirs of ill-omen, and thrown into the bush for vultures to eat.

The acts of strangling and embalming the Bemba chief's body preserved his spiritual force for transmission to his successor. When a new chief was installed, he and a large number of other hereditary officials would light a fire and perform an act of ritual sexual intercourse with their respective head wives in order to warm the land from its state of coldness following the death of the previous ruler.

Chief's chair from the Pende of Congo. Museum Rietberg, Zurich. This chair decorated with copulating figures depicts the magical link between the chief and fertility.

Initiation Ceremonies

Throughout the African continent there is the idea that it is only through initiation ceremonies that a young boy or girl becomes a fully mature man or woman, capable of sexual relations and parenthood. Initiation is a progressive course of instruction, which makes the novices familiar with their own body as well as the world around them.

The Bantu peoples of southeast Africa initiate their young people in three distinct stages, each giving an increased level of knowledge and of mastery of the social environment. The first stage of the initiation involves only young girls and takes place within their own home villages. Here they learn to understand and to master their own bodies, and to see them as the seat of both social and reproductive functions. They learn the laws of fire, in particular those concerning the hearth, which represents the union of male and female, and those concerning cooking, which also represents the process of gestation of new human life. The location of this ritual within their own village and its focus on their own bodies gives them a small horizon of conceptual space, a microcosm of the wider concerns which will be addressed in later stages of the initiation process.

The second stage of initiation involves girls as well as boys and focuses on domestic matters. This time the young novices are taught the laws of the house in order to understand the role of the family residence and the kinship grouping it represents. For girls, this knowledge is related to their previous instruction in the role of their body in procreation. The house thus appears as a macrocosm of the body. At this stage they are also taught the logic of the categories through which the Bantu peoples classify and understand the world.

In the third phase of initiation young men and women learn the laws of the court and the nation. Here they come to understand how the court is the counterpart to the mythical space of creation. The sequence of initiations thus progressively enlarges its horizon from the village through the region to the capital.

The Bantu peoples of southwest Africa have a similar sequence of three phases of initiation.

A Masai youth has his foreskin cut. The initiate watches impassively as his foreskin is cut. There is minimal loss of flesh and surprisingly little loss of blood in the traditional method used. Among many African peoples, the blood that is spilled as a result of male circumcision is carefully collected and disposed of, to stop it getting into the hands of sorcerers or evil spirits.

In the second stage, where both boys and girls participate, they live together for a month, though strictly without sexual contact. During this time they play at being married, imitating the chores of married people. For example, boys play at taking care of cattle and hunting animals while girls play at preparing meals. Again, the process combines the mastery of the body with the mastery of ever-increasing horizons of social space.

The matrilineal peoples of these regions place the emphasis on the initiation of girls rather than boys. Instruction in the role of wife and mother is reinforced through songs and the display of sacred objects, which carry a message to be learned. For example, Bemba girls are shown a little clay figurine called the "man without arms". This man has no appendages at all except for an enormous penis. The girls learn about this kind of man: he lies around the house all day and finds fault with his wife without doing any work himself. The older women explain to the young girls that they should avoid having such a useless husband themselves. Such songs and figurines teach girls about the correct behavior to expect from their husband and how to behave in return towards the husband and his kin, as well as about routine tasks such as washing themselves and looking after their babies. The Bemba word for their girls' puberty rites, *chisungu*, describes a process of "growing a woman". The *chisungu* changes girls into women, not merely by instructing them but by actually transforming them through the ritual itself, although in the case of the Bemba without any form of circumcision. Initiation rituals throughout Africa tend to have a strong genital focus and various forms of circumcision for young men and women are widespread throughout most of the continent. It is widely said that uncircumcised young men and women either cannot beget children or, if they do, then the children will be sickly or may die. Circumcision makes both men and women more distinct and unlike each other by emphasizing the physical difference between their bodies. Male circumcision removes the foreskin, the part that most resembles the labia on a woman. Female circumcision, or clitoridectomy, removes the feature that most resembles the penis. The Dogon of Niger express this polarization of the sexes clearly when they say that each human being is endowed with two souls, one male and one female. The creator deity Nonno, who was both male and female, drew two outlines on the ground. One outline was of a woman, the other of a man. But since these outlines were drawn on top of each other, the distinction between men and women was blurred. For a woman, the male soul is contained in her clitoris and for a man, his female soul is contained in his foreskin. Until their initiation a child is considered to be androgynous. A boy's foreskin is like his female twin, and needs to be removed before he can become a single, fully male person. Similarly, a girl's clitoris is her male twin, which unless removed would compete with the penis of any man making love to her.

Among the Gisu of Uganda male initiation is seen as analogous to childbirth in women. Young Gisu men ask their fathers to prepare them for initiation when they feel old enough to set up an independent household. Prepara-

tions are made for a great feast. The ancestral groves are cleaned, women brew beer and animals are selected for slaughter. Meanwhile, the young men start wearing distinctive costumes and dancing around the village. A small group of boys stands together and the circumciser appears as if from nowhere. The boys have to stand absolutely motionless and all eyes are on them for any sign of flinching. As each cut is made the assembled women ululate. The foreskin is then disposed of very carefully so that it cannot be used in witchcraft.

Odo-Kuta Masks, Senegal. Many initiation ceremonies incorporate elements that are designed to terrify the young initiates. This may involve men dressing up as ancestral spirits, or monsters, and impresses the initiates with the seriousness of the ceremony.

Sex Instruction and Sex Play

In many areas girls undergo seclusion in separate huts either after their first menstruation or after their puberty rites or clitoridectomy. As well as lessons in being a wife and mother, lessons in sexual techniques are also taught by older women. In Dahomey (Benin), young girls would traditionally assemble before puberty so that an older woman could teach them to pull and stretch their vaginas, rubbing in soot around the entrance to create scar tissue, which was considered to give greater pleasure in later life. Bemba girls would be taught exercises to lengthen their labia as this was considered more attractive.

A *kandjani* (circumcisor) wearing the traditional kalelwa mask from Sandoa, Katanga, Congo. The boy is expected to face the terrifying figure with fortitude.

A Pokot girl of Kenya recovering from her circumcision. During her recuperation, which takes several weeks, the girl is known as *chemerion* ("neither man nor woman") and covers her body with white chalk and a leather cloak to make herself invisible to men.

The message of the circumcision ceremony is that one should be a strong self-controlled man but also at the same time someone supported by a wide range of kin. There is thus more to the process than the physical operation alone and men who have been circumcised in local mission hospitals are often treated as uninitiated and immature and chased away from important rituals. Among the Ndembu of Zambia an uncircumcised boy was traditionally described as someone who lacks whiteness or purity, the same phrase as is applied to a menstruating woman, with the difference that the woman's condition is only temporary. It was believed that dirt is lodged under the foreskin. During

their initiation Ndembu boys were considered to die as children and be reborn again as adults at the place of circumcision, called the place of dying. Masked dancers would appear representing the spirits of deceased ancestors and the boys themselves would believe that these dancers were really the ancestors in person. The dancing ancestors would terrify the boys while at the same time giving them a blessing for their future offspring. In Dahomey the boys who have passed through circumcision together are known as "brothers by the same knife". The young men to be circumcised sit on the ground naked, each with his penis resting above a hole in the ground. The circumcisor severs

the foreskin with a knife and drops it into the hole. Before he does this he looks very carefully into the eyes of his subject to see if he shows fear. He then applies medicine to the penis to prevent scars from forming or an excessive flow of blood. When all the wounds on an entire batch of boys have healed, widows or older women past menopause have the first sexual intercourse with them after their recovery. This act is believed to be extremely dangerous for the women because of the unbridled sexual power in the newly circumcised men, and so the women are given substantial gifts to persuade them to undertake this dangerous role. The mystical danger which an older woman takes onto herself in this way is called the "heat of the razor": in having intercourse with the youth she is cooling his heat.

Forms of female circumcision are widespread in a solid belt from West Africa to the Horn of Africa at Somalia. It is hardly found at all in the northern Sahara or in southern Africa. Female circumcision has provoked outrage among feminists and others both in Africa and in the West, on the grounds that it violates a woman's rights and can lead to medical and sexual problems, robbing the woman of the possibility of clitoral orgasm. There are also indications that the operation continues to be performed even where the accompanying rites of initiation are being abandoned, including the urban middle classes, and that it is increasingly common for it to be performed on very young children. Among the Kikuyu of Kenya, girls who have abandoned the circumcision rites and have became Christians are taunted with the song, "Smell, smell, smell, I have smelled uncircumcised girls passing nearby/ Uncircumcised girls piss in their bed and say the bed has become cold." Western pressure to abandon female circumcision led Jomo Kenyatta (1891–1978), the leader of the independence struggle in Kenya and the country's first president, to support circumcision as a key symbol of anti-colonialism.

Transvestites and Hermaphrodites

Where circumcision rites strive so hard to distinguish male and female, transvestites and hermaphrodites sometimes have a special power. Among the Kuanyama of southwest Africa, male transvestites dress and walk like women, keep the company of women, and have intercourse with other men. They also initiate traditional doctors and are themselves able to cure forms of madness caused by ancestral ghosts, by the use of special rattles made from a calabash. Hermaphrodites can cure male patients of various illnesses by sleeping with them, and it is believed that hermaphrodites are a gift from the god Kalunga.

Young girls of the Ghanaian Krobo carry calabashes to the river to wash themselves as part of the purification ceremony that precedes their initiation.

Ways of the Warriors

Masai warriors wearing olowaru, or lion's mane headdresses. The lion's mane is a mark of bravery, indicating that the young man has killed a lion. It is more highly prized than the feathered headdresses worn by other warriors.

In many parts of Africa, being a warrior has always been closely linked to the stages of a young man's initiation into adult life, generally as a stage separating childhood from marriage and parenthood.

In the early stages of initiation a youth among the Masai of Kenya is called an *olaibartani*. He is subject to numerous restrictions and must be inside his enclosure before the cattle come home at dusk. He is prohibited from sexual contact and is also forbidden to drink blood or to handle meat with his hands. He therefore has to be fed his meat on a stick. When this period of seclusion is over, he finally discards all the trappings of his immature status: his mother shaves his head and eyebrows, helps him discard his headdress of feathers, and she retrieves his coiled metal earrings. She then uses the cowrie shells from his belt to decorate her gourds. The boy has then become a *moran*. The women build a camp for the *morans* who can number up to several hundred, often attended by their mothers and other women. The *morans* help with herding but traditionally they also serve as warriors and, in the not so distant past, went raiding other groups for cattle.

Each set of men, as they were initiated, would become the active army of the nation, forming a regiment of up to several thousand men. After a number of years as a *moran* there is a retirement ceremony and the outgoing warriors become elders. In this state they take on the responsibilities of owning and managing herds and of government functions, as well as looking after the religious life of the community.

The neighboring Samburu have a similar age grade system which is likewise associated with a militaristic society. The young men who serve as warriors stand midway between the category of uninitiated boys and elders. Initiation into the status of warrior or *moran* does not give full manhood, in that it acknowledges sexual maturity but not full social maturity, which is reserved only for elders. A *moran* may take mistresses from among the unmarried girls but he is not allowed to marry or to father children. The *morans* wear a dramatic hairstyle with their hair long and smeared with red ocher. Their behavior is wild and uncontrolled and contrasts strikingly with the reserved restraint and dignity of the elders. The *moran* show off to girls who egg them on to greater acts of daring, including cattle theft and fighting with each other. They also endure formalized harangues from the elders in which they are scolded for

A Masai mother shaves the head of her son to mark his transition out of warriorhood. Head-shaving often marks a transition from one stage in the life of a Masai male to the next. He is often so overcome by the experience that he weeps and trembles openly. It is comparatively rare among African peoples for a mother to have such a prominent role in the rite of passage of a mature man.

A young Samburu warrior from East Africa. Samburu means butterfly, and the warriors spend much of their time decorating their bodies, discussing their looks and admiring themselves in mirrors.

their irresponsibility. However, their irresponsible behavior and the scolding are an expected part of the formal proceedings, which highlight the contrast between young warriorhood and the responsible behavior of parents and elders. The rituals celebrating a recently circumcised boy's transition to moranhood, include the slaughtering of oxen for large feasts. During one feast, the young man must break the hip-bone of his ox with one blow of his club. The young man presents one half of the bone to his mother as a pledge that he will keep the *morans'* most important food taboo, which is not to eat any meat that has so much as been glanced at by a married woman.

Boys who serve as warriors together develop intense friendships. Sub-chiefs and other prominent men among the Bangwa of Cameroon would send their sons to serve as pages in the palace of the chief, where they would learn dancing and the ways of a warrior. The friendships that formed were reinforced by sending the boys on headhunting expeditions or raids against neighboring tribes and would last a lifetime. Whatever their origins, friends regarded each other as complete social equals and would spend a great deal of time in each other's company, holding hands as they walked together. The warrior stage was sometimes integrated into a powerful military machine, as among the Zulu, where warriors were organized into regiments according to age groups. These were under the command of the king and the warriors would remain bachelors until quite late into their lives. At last the king would give them permission to marry the girls from a younger age group, who would be in their twenties. This warrior ethos was accompanied by a high evaluation of chastity. If a young warrior made a girl pregnant it was quite likely the two lovers and even their families would be killed. One way of avoiding this was for the girl to be married off quickly to a man whose regiment had already been given permission to marry. Under this code of chastity, adultery by either men or women was very severely punished.

Boy Wives and Lesbian Wild Cats

In pre-colonial times it was common for the warrior bachelors of the Azande of southern Sudan to take boy-wives, who might be as young as twelve. They would pay a bride-price to the boy's parents and perform services for them, just as they might for a woman. The union was regarded as a legal marriage, but was not expected to last into the warrior's maturity. The practice was usually attributed to a shortage of women, and if a son-in-law impressed his new family, he might be given one of their daughters to replace his boy-wife when the latter went on to become a warrior in his turn.

By contrast, lesbianism was a source of horror to the Zande, because a lesbian was thought to be related to the *adandara* – legendary evil wild cats that sometimes copulated with women. In the past, a prince who discovered that his wife was having a lesbian affair would have her executed. At the beginning of the 21st century, lesbians are usually expelled from the household.

Written on the Skin

Like circumcision, the marking of the skin with patterns of scars or tattoos signifies an irreversible transition from a state of immaturity to a state of maturity and sexual power. Different groups tattoo or scar different parts of the body, and the emphasis of the marking may also vary from place to place. In some areas they are primarily thought of as a tribal marking, with only incidental erotic overtones. Elsewhere they are almost entirely erogenous. In Dahomey such cuts are directly associated with a girl's sexuality. While boys undergo circumcision, girls undergo scar marking which is considered to enhance their erotic zones. Since the cuts are thought to be sexually stimulating in themselves there is much joking and singing of ribald songs. A plant-derived irritant is rubbed into the wounds to help the development of prominent scars. Cuts on the forehead pulsate when a woman is speaking to a man she finds attractive and the man is able to read her mood by watching the behavior of these scars. Other cuts made towards the base of the spine are called "the ones you see when you turn to look back" because when a woman leaves her lover and he turns around to say goodbye to her, he sees these marks on her back as she retreats from him. Another cut on the woman's cheek is called "kiss me". Finally a girl receives 81 small cuts on the inside of each thigh. These are known as "push me" and are considered essential if a girl is to capture and keep the love of the man she wants.

The men who become the lovers of these girls also "share the fire of the knife" with them by receiving a small number of cuts themselves on their face or arm or body. A man who has had a large number of girlfriends will thus gather a large number of cuts and will parade them as a matter of pride.

Kareo people, Ethiopia. During ceremonial functions and other celebrations, it is common for tribal African peoples to impersonate animals. Here, the white spots are intended to copy the plumage of guinea fowl.

Wodaabe woman from the western Sahara. Sometimes a tattoo can have a hidden meaning. Among the Wodaabe, tattoos are mostly decorative, but those at the corners of this woman's mouth are intended to ward off evil influences.

Bottom left: **Yoruba woman with a pail on her head, Ibadan, Nigeria.** The Yoruba are a group for whom the traditional component of scarification, on the whole, outweighs the erotic element, although many men profess to find women unattractive without some form of marking.

Bottom right: **Bumi warrior from Ethiopia.** The scarified design on the face, and the clay hair bun, are symbols of his bravery.

In many parts of Africa cuts are also made on the skin to establish a relationship of blood brotherhood between two men. Such a relationship may be made out of affection or for political alliances. Blood brothers are usually not related, but the relationship of loyalty and mutual protection is said to be even more binding than any bonds of kinship. Among the Azande in Central Africa, the two men make cuts on each other's chest and arms. They then smear their blood on little chips of wood, which they exchange and swallow. Azande blood brothers can joke together, insult each other and take advantage of each other in ways that would be completely unacceptable from anyone else.

The Mating Display

The Wodaabe of Niger are nomads who keep camels, cattle and goats. They acknowledge the tension between the need for stability in marriage and family life on the one hand, and the needs of romantic love and sexual passion on the other, by having two quite different kinds of marriage. The first is made at birth and remains for life, the second is made for love and can change as fleetingly as the emotions themselves. The strong emphasis on personal relationships in the second kind of marriage leads women to move frequently from one man's house to another. But the first kind of marriage ensures that children always remain in their father's lineage and home, thus giving stability to the family and to the clan. The wife of this first sort always takes precedence over other women who come along as the result of love marriages – while they come and go, she stays near the hearth and the children.

Each year after the rains when the desert blooms, the Wodaabe stage the *geerewol* celebration, which includes the *yakke* dance. The dancing lasts for a week and there may be a thousand or more young men all competing for the prize of being declared the most beautiful. The judges are three unmarried girls. The Wodaabe themselves compare this dance competition to the mating dances of birds in which the female chooses the most ornate, energetic and colorful male. In such a competitive climate the use of love magic is crucial and the Wodaabe are famous throughout much of West Africa for their love potions. Such medicines may be rubbed on the body, eaten or drunk in order to enhance a man's charm to women. Magically seductive herbs and powders are also worn in leather pouches around the neck or in the hair.

The atmosphere at the dances is feverish, with both men and women on the lookout for liaisons. There is a subtle code of signs. The woman contrives to indicate her interest in a particular dancer. He will give her a wink, and she will look downwards towards the ground, but not all the way. He will then give a slight twitch with his mouth to indicate where they should meet. This is usually behind a bush where they lie under a blanket, supposedly invisible to everyone around them. There they make love, still wearing their clothes and with the woman covering her face with a shawl so that they do not even see each other's faces. The women lie passively during the lovemaking, and claim to take no physical pleasure from the act.

Young Wodaabe men and women, flirting with each other. The men are cousins, but nevertheless may both be lovers of the same girl, before and after her marriage. In general, the Wodaabe appear to relish emotional dramas.

Wodaabe men. Wodaabe males will cheerfully appropriate almost any bright object to draw attention to themselves. In addition to traditional decorations and weapons, the man on the right adorns himself with a plastic toy rifle.

Earth, Fire, Sex, and Fertility

Heat is connected with excitement and the creation of new life, but at the same time it is also dangerous and can be a cause of disease. Among the Shona of Zimbabwe there are two kinds of heat. One sort can be cooled down by water, as in rain ceremonies that are directed against drought. Other kinds of heat need yet more heat to neutralize them, for example witchcraft, which can be neutralized only by fire. It is considered very dangerous to bring certain kinds of heat into contact with each other. Sexual intercourse itself is a source of great heat, and it is believed that if a sick person is brought into contact with it they are in danger of death.

The Shona of Zimbabwe regard the moment of orgasm as one of intense heat in which a person is smelted in a furnace. This experience is equivalent to a death and can be undone only by the application of cooling water. The association between sexuality and heat also appears in traditional African iron smelting, where the furnace is considered to be a womb in which the ore brought up from underground is brought to birth. Miners and smelters live in a state of strict sexual purity and some do not allow any women near the furnace. Even a workman who has had a nocturnal emission has to be purified before he can approach the forge. One smelters' song goes, "The clitoris and the labia fill me with horror. Keep far away from me. Keep far away from me." It is sometimes said that male and female ores are fused together in the furnace and this clearly resembles male and female sexual fluids mixing in the womb to create a fetus.

Among the Ndembu of Zambia, boys who have been circumcised but whose wounds have not yet healed are not allowed to touch fire or even to gather firewood, since this will prevent their wounds from healing. Among the Bemba, with their *chisungu* rite for girls, the sacredness of fire is expressed in another way. At one point in the ceremony, the fire is extinguished and relit from "new fire". Older women conduct the initiation dance with sticks before laboriously rubbing them together to start a new fire from scratch. The ritual is known as "begging for parenthood". The Bemba believe that sexual relations make a couple hot and it is dangerous for them to approach ancestral spirits, to make any sacrifice or to come into contact with babies and young children. They may even accidentally kill a baby by touching the fire on

Rhythm pounder (*deble*) of the *Poro*, Senufo. Wood, seeds, cowrie shells, c. 91 x 21 cm, Schindler Collection, Museum of Art, Dallas, Texas. The *deble* is used to pound the earth into a state of fertility, possibly in imitation of the act of copulation among animals and humans.

Dogon funeral ceremony. Dogon funeral dances are displays of vitality in the face of death. The masked dancers come into the village from the bush, which is thought to be the home of the Dogon's ritual language and the source of power for their shamans and blacksmiths. The masks are a link between the untamed wilderness and the social life of the Dogon.

Restrictions and Preferences

Numerous sexual practices are considered harmful or dangerous by different peoples. Sex outdoors, for example, is widely condemned. If the spot where the outdoor copulation occurred is discovered, the Nilotic Lango of Uganda, among others, cover the location and every passerby is required to throw leaves or branches on it. The Bini of Nigeria would charge a man caught having sex outdoors with manslaughter, and imprison him for several months. By contrast, most pygmy and bushman peoples prefer sex in the open air.

Sex during daylight is also widely thought to have serious consequences. The Kikuyu and Masai of Kenya believe that, except in certain ritual situations, it brings a risk of sickness among people and cattle. For the Zulu of South Africa, sex during the daytime is a bestial act. Oral sex (including, in some cases, kissing) is also considered unusual in much of Africa, and among the Fang and Ila of Zambia oral-genital contact is considered a crime, and grounds for divorce. The most widely reported sexual position in tribal Africa has the couple lying side by side, facing each other. Traditionally, the man lies on his right, leaving his left hand free, because this is the appropriate hand for touching his own or another's genitals.

Details from the chair of a chief of the Pende of Congo. Museum Rietberg, Zürich. The copulating figures decorating a Pende chief's chair emphasize his spiritual and magical role as a guarantor of fertility.

The Oluwedoku fertility fetish of the Dangme of Ghana. The statue of Oluwedoku will, it is hoped, bring fertility for the next planting: note the oversized genitalia. Decorated with green leaves, it is carried by an initiate, to whom the power of the statue is transferred. The white marks on his lips are a sign that he is under a vow of silence: he must keep his knowledge to himself.

which the baby's food is cooked, thereby contaminating it. After every act of intercourse, a wife must purify herself and her husband from a special small pot of water. Only a husband and wife can carry out the rite together. Adulterers are therefore particularly dangerous since they cannot be purified properly. The Yao, another eastern Bantu people, also have a complex set of beliefs about purity and nourishment. A boy can only eat salt after he loses his virginity, and a man can be killed by salt placed in his food by his adulterous wife.

The pot that a Bemba woman must use is one given to her at the time of her marriage. This pot must be guarded and looked after in great secrecy. After purifying herself and her husband, the wife has to extinguish the fire and light a new one. This removes the condition of heat associated with sex and makes it possible for the couple to carry out normal activities again. This is a particularly striking case of the close interdependence of a husband and wife, since in carrying out the dangerous act of having sex together they put themselves in each other's power and depend on each other for the rite of purification, which they cannot perform for themselves.

Whether among commoners or chiefs, Bemba can only approach their ancestors safely if they have behaved correctly in their treatment of sex and fire. At key moments of the harvest or the founding of a new village, all categories of chiefs and other officials have to engage in an act of ritual sex with their head wife in order to warm the site which otherwise would be cold. They then also light a new fire to complete the process of warming. While the chief is alive his sacred fire, which is the fire of the land, must be kept in a separate hut and watched over by his head wife.

Symbolic Architecture

Sex and gender are closely reflected in architectural forms and customs, which arise out of human use of space. The tent of the nomadic Tuareg of the western Sahara is regarded as a female domain. The woman is completely at home here, just as she is in her mother's tent. The Tuareg have a saying: "A woman's own tent is her mother's", and indeed her tent is composed in part of materials which were given to her by her mother.

Men, on the other hand, are always a guest in a tent, moving as they go into adulthood from their mother's tent to their wife's. On marriage, the new couple's tent is put up near that of the bride's family, and the groom and his best man have to enter by a side entrance, crawling on their hands and knees under a horizontal pole. He must then wait for three nights before consummating the marriage. On the first night, he must behave like the bride's mother and on the second night like her little sister. Only on the third night may he behave like a man, and even then only like her cousin, with whom sexual relations are not possible. This is reminiscent of the custom by which a traveler visiting a camp spends three days outside it before he can come into the camp and share the food of the other men.

The gendering of architectural forms can sometimes be very elaborate. The ground-plan of the traditional Dogon house in Mali, viewed from above, represents a man lying on his side. His stomach is the central room, the kitchen is his head and the grinding stone represents his penis. The Dogon also build thatched granaries. These represent the belly of a fertile woman but are also seen on a cosmic scale as the "belly of the world". The granary contains eight divisions, which are used for storing eight different kinds of seed, which were given to the eight ancestors of the Dogon people. These divisions also correspond to the eight vital organs of the body and reproduce the form of the granary of the "Master of Pure Earth" who came down from the sky on the fourth day of creation.

Granaries, symbolizing the fecundity of the breast, in a Kirdi village in the Mandara Mountains, North Cameroon. Each man has two granaries, each of his wives has one.

Mofu farm, North Cameroon (left) and cross section (right). The design of the structures built by the Mofu is symbolic, and the skills and knowledge necessary for their construction are handed down from generation to generation. The significance of the shapes and forms of the buildings is often only fully understood by the oldest members of the group. The silos of the Mofu are phallic in appearance, and strict rules govern their use. Among the Matakam, for example, only men are allowed to climb into the millet-silos; the others are accessible to women too.

A miniature cotton tent is erected on the back of a camel and used as a canopy to hide a Tuareg bride as she is transported to her new home. It is considered important that no onlookers see her during this journey.

Below: **Dogon house for men, Mali.** The Dogon build close to the cliff face so that as much land as possible can be used for crops. The houses have flat roofs, while those of the granaries are conical. The symbolism of Dogon architecture is mirrored and expanded in the decorations on doors, walls and windows, as well as by complex stories and rituals.

Changing Sexual Attitudes in Sub-Saharan Africa

The growth of towns and cities has led to widespread urban living, independent womanhood and uncontrolled female sexuality. Many people move back and forth between the city and the village and these are still seen as two very different worlds, which call for very different kinds of behavior.

Cosmetics, and especially Western styles, are seen as ranging from the personal advertisement of the prostitute to the elegant statement of the modern woman asserting her independence from men. One consequence is that physical ideals are changing across the continent, influenced by Western media – in many societies, lighter skin and thinner, firmer bodies are increasingly preferred.

Traditional values, even where they are disappearing, are still held up as an ideal, even in the courts of law. For example, in Botswana, where teenage pregnancy rates are rapidly increasing and many women now remain single, women now head about half of all households. It may even be that fewer children are born in marriage than out of it. However, marriage remains an ideal towards which many people strive. A woman who bears a child may seek support or compensation from the father and today this is often done through the courts. The form of this compensation depends on how the relationship compares to the ideal of marriage. If the relationship seems likely to lead to marriage the man will be encouraged or made to pay child support. If the relationship does not look likely to turn into marriage, the woman's parents may demand payment on the grounds that her prospects of marriage are reduced. If an unmarried woman continues to bear children she is unlikely to be compensated as she will be regarded as having a loose character. Civil and common law are not entirely separate domains but influence each other strongly. Ironically, educated middle-class women are more likely to secure a satisfactory settlement from the courts than uneducated rural women, who in most ways conform more closely to tradition. African writers explore the tensions and dilemmas of modern life in many novels. *The Polygamist*, 1972, by Zimbabwean author, freedom

A poster advertising Colgate toothpaste, in Dakar, Senegal. Western products are regularly sold in Africa through advertisements that promise an affluent Western lifestyle. Thus buying a product as simple as toothpaste becomes a rebellion against tradition.

A modern prostitute in Zanzibar. Prostitution represents the best chance many country girls get to make their way to the cities and escape a traditional farmer's life. In the 1950s, the independence of such a life was so highly prized that prostitutes routinely turned down marriage offers.

AIDS

By the beginning of the year 2000, approximately eleven million people were estimated to have died of AIDS-related illnesses in Africa, out of a world total of thirteen million. At this time, AIDS in Africa was claiming 5000 lives a day. Unlike the high-risk groups identified in the West, the early onset of AIDS in Africa was closely associated with heterosexual intercourse. The ritual use of sex in the region makes the propagation of ideas of safe sex extremely difficult. In many areas intercourse is required with additional partners outside the marriage, in order to fulfill the obligation to procreate. Condoms are often considered unacceptable precisely because they act as a barrier against the mixing of sexual fluids. They not only block the creation of children, they also obstruct the healing effects of ritual sex. The spread of the virus is exacerbated by the presence of other diseases, including other venereal diseases that are now less common in the West. Genitalia that are already ulcerated by some other sickness make it easier for the virus to pass from person to person.

fighter and politician Ndabaningi Sithole tells the story of a traditional man whose son commits adultery with one of his father's younger wives. The author makes it clear that the real reason for this is that the old man cannot satisfy the sexual needs of all his wives. As the clan sets up a court to try the case, "Great silence fell upon the court. Every man began to wonder if their sons were doing the same thing with their younger wives."

In a short story by the Kenyan writer Ngugi, a woman falls passionately in love with a shiftless man who has no job or prospects. When the man eventually becomes respectable and converts to Christianity, they decide to arrange a church wedding to formalize their relationship. But in the process of modernizing himself he has lost his virility and at the last moment at the altar the girl says, "I cannot marry this man because I am already married to the man he was before and is no longer".

In a play called *The Dilemma of a Ghost*, 1965 by Christina Ama Ata Aidoo a young man comes home from his studies in America with a black American wife. She shocks his family by her liberated Western behavior, by her chain-smoking and by the fact that she is the descendant of slaves who were captured and taken to America centuries earlier. But the young man's mother is able to forget all of this because she accepts that the girl will have children and will increase the size of the family. In the modern harsh urban environment, women may spread their economic risk by having several part-time partners. The tie which will bind a man to them is to bear his child. The focus on children makes condoms unattractive, as it implies that the relationship is uncommitted and undermines the woman's claim on the man's support. Sex education programs thus often fail because foreign workers do not understand African attitudes toward sex.

The Destabilizing Effect of Christianity

In addition to their hatred of polygyny, Christian missionaries also struck at the heart of circumcision rituals. For example, among the Kikuyu of Kenya, clitoridectomy was considered the culmination of a long process of socialization into Kikuyu culture. The final act of surgery was regarded as a physical confirmation of the transformation of immature girls into mature women. In the early 20th century the refusal by missionaries to allow supporters of female circumcision into their schools led to a massive turning away by the population from Christianity. Traditional ideas about the promiscuity and lack of self-control of uncircumcised girls were reinforced by the way in which the churches would provide refuge to women who wished to break the contract of traditional marriages. The churches thus transferred the mediating role in family disputes from the family to an outside institution, to the intense resentment of the population.

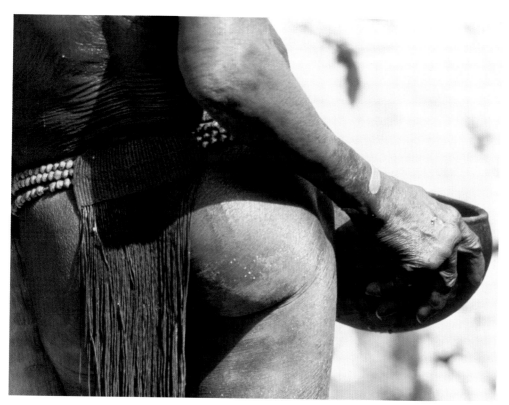

Tasselled belts are traditionally worn instead of clothing in parts of Cameroon. In the 1960s, the government passed a law that all women had to wear cotton skirts in public, and tasselled belts are now only found in remote villages.

The *pikuran* is a piece of phallus shaped pubic jewelry once worn by women in Cameroon, but now found only in extremely rural areas.

The Classical World

The Three Graces. **Mosaic, National Museum, Naples.**
The three Graces are goddesses of beauty, who
present people with loving gifts. In Olympus, the
three daughters of Zeus are part of the retinue of
the love-deities Aphrodite and Eros or the god of
the Muses, Apollo. The Humanists of the Renaissance gave the Graces additional significance by
interpreting them as the threefold form of love –
beauty, desire, fulfillment.

Systems of Dominance

The Trojan War, in which a fleet of Greek ships besieged and finally destroyed the non-Greek city of Troy in the 12th century B.C., was the key mythical event in Greek historical consciousness. But archaeology has shown that a sophisticated Greek world existed in the eastern Mediterranean for centuries or even millennia before this, in the Minoan civilization in Crete. It is also clear that much of what we call Greek culture was strongly influenced by a constant interaction with the cultures of ancient Persia, Babylon, the Levant and Egypt.

It has been claimed by some archaeologists and feminists that early Greek society in the Bronze Age was matriarchal, or dedicated to the worship of a supreme goddess. Certainly, there is a tradition of making statuettes and other figures in which women are prominently portrayed, as in the Cycladic figurines or the so-called Minoan Snake Goddess. But though many of these images clearly refer to women's generative powers, it is extremely difficult to interpret the political or gender relations in the societies in which they were made. In particular, it is hard to explain the supposed dramatic reversal from a matriarchal society to an extremely patriarchal one, even when looking at written historical accounts.

Though forms of writing were used for palace accounts from at least the 15th century B.C., the earliest surviving literary works are the *Iliad* and the *Odyssey*. These long epic poems which tell the story of the Trojan War were sung by bards throughout the Greek world and were finally written down around the 7th century B.C. and ascribed to an author called Homer. They portray a world of heroic kings and warriors in which sexuality is focused on male-female relations, often with considerable tenderness. By the 6th and 5th centuries, in what is now considered the height of Greek civilization, literary evidence as well as the iconography of painted pottery suggests a tighter, harsher tone in male-female relations, with elaborate and socially institutionalized forms of male homosexuality. This largely corresponds to an expansive militarism among competing city-states. In the Hellenistic period from the 4th century onwards, as the city-states became absorbed into the empires, first of Alexander the Great and then of Rome, life became more bourgeois and the emphasis shifted again to heterosexual relations, including those of the married couple. Whereas much 5th-century art is blatantly sexist, portraying women as sex

Tomb of the Bull (*Tomba dei Tori*), 7th–4th cent. B.C. Etruscan mural, Tarquinia. This painting reveals the powerful cross-fertilization of cultures in the Mediterranean. Created in Italy, it combines a Cretan-style bullfighting scene with the Greek tradition of using erotic images in a religious setting.

The Serpent Goddess of Knossos, c. 1600–1580 B.C.
**Terra-cotta with colorful decoration, 29.5 cm high,
Archaeological Museum, Heraklion, Greece.** Snakes
were a symbol of regeneration.

objects, a great deal of Hellenistic and Roman art suggests more mutual and enjoyment between men and women. It was probably also aimed at a female audience.

The Romans dated the founding of their city by Romulus to 753 B.C. As they expanded they came into increasing contact with the Greek world, which they absorbed into their growing empire in the second century B.C. The Roman attitude to Greece was always ambivalent, and an alternative legend has it that Rome was founded by Aeneas, a refugee from Troy and thus an enemy of the Greeks. Having conquered Greece by military means, the Romans found themselves nevertheless conquered by Greece in a cultural sense. From the second century B.C. onwards Greek ideas, philosophy, literary forms and gods steadily gained in status among the educated classes. This provoked repeated purist backlashes in favor of wholesome Italian customs against what were seen as decadent and licentious Greek practices.

Both Greek and Roman society were sharply differentiated by gender, class and legal status.

Freeborn citizens were distinguished from slaves and foreigners, rich from poor, and male from female, and very different sexual behavior was expected from each of these. Indeed, one's sexual behavior was part of what defined one's social status, and there were often severe punishments for behaving inappropriately. Though there was a steady concern with male and female procreative powers, the main categories of sexual behavior throughout Greek and Roman history were not so much male and female as active and passive, penetrator and penetrated. The dichotomy of penetrator and penetrated was linked to a sharply divided evaluation of power. Penetration through any orifice, whether vagina, anus or mouth, made the penetrator masterful and in control and the penetrated person weak or subservient. A male who allowed himself to be penetrated was supposed to be of a lower class than the penetrator. If he was from an upper class then it was considered that he was defiling himself. This feeling was at its most intense in the context of oral sex.

Amazons

The philosopher Aristotle used the word *gynecocracy* (women's rule) to describe not so much a political system like matriarchy, but a situation where women stand outside the control of men. This fear was clearly expressed in the myth of the Amazons, a tribe of female warriors whose name may mean "breastless", from their habit of removing one breast so as to be able to draw a bowstring more effectively. The Amazons mated only once a year with men from another tribe and then destroyed any male offspring they bore, thus maintaining an all-female society.

The Amazons were said to have invaded many parts of the Greek world and even to have attacked Athens, where their graves were still shown to visitors in historical times and their ghosts fed at annual rites. Male heroes vacillated between being seduced by these women, and killing them. Particularly in 5th-century B.C. Athens there are numerous carvings and vase paintings showing battles in which male heroes stab or club Amazons to death, the men often aiming for the breast while the Amazons aim for the men's genitals. It would be hard to imagine a more graphic expression of a war of the sexes. The Amazons were felt to be un-Greek in other senses too. They helped the enemy during the Trojan War and their queen Penthesileia was killed by the Greek Achilles, who tragically fell in love with her a moment too late, when his eye was caught by hers while he was plunging his sword into her breast.

Amazon jumps from the cliff, pursued by a Greek, 5th cent. B.C. Ashmolean Museum, Oxford. Although the Amazons were described as being breastless, classical aesthetic ideals meant that they were often shown as unmutilated.

Love charms

The art of making friends and influencing people, even political allies, was said only half-jokingly to be helped by the use of love charms. To those who specialized in the field of sexual attraction, such charms were taken very seriously, along with facial cosmetics and other aids in response to the intensely visual Greek and Roman sense of beauty. While these usually receive only passing reference in literary texts, other documents like the pieces of papyrus preserved in the dry climate of the rubbish dumps of Egypt give many spells and recipes. Many of these ointments and potions use plant and animal parts, often hard to obtain, such as crocodile teeth, weasels' testicles, drowned field mice, baboon dung, or the penis of a lizard caught copulating. They might be rubbed on one's own genitals or secretly given to a beloved to drink, whether to aid or prevent conception, or to produce erections in men and orgasms in women. Women were often thought to be specialists in such charms, and they also used them for their own needs.

Most powerfully, charms were used to produce an erotic obsession in the desired person, which matched one's own. One recipe explains how to make a wax effigy of the god Eros and bring it to life by offering it the life-force of sacrificed birds. The recipe promises that the effigy will then serve its owner by making them desirable to anyone they choose. It can pass into the loved person's house and enter their dreams. The infliction of pain and emotional turmoil on the object of one's love might be done both to win their love and as an act of revenge for one's own torment. The way in which the spells often portray the user as taking control of the beloved's emotions merely emphasizes how far the lover is in the grip of his own desperation.

The effect of being struck by the arrow of Eros was not so much the pleasure one felt in the beloved's presence, but the unbearable pain one felt in his absence. Sexual passion was seen almost in medical terms as a disease, a disorder of the crazed body and soul which is very difficult to treat and which distorts one's judgment and impels one to mad actions.

Woman Watering Phalluses. Detail of the decoration of a red-figure vase c. 430–420 B.C. British Museum, London. This may be an example of fertility magic or a love charm, or may have been part of a fertility festival.

Opposite: **Augustan silver cup, first cent. B.C. C. 12 cm high, British Museum, London.** Typically, in such scenes, the older man penetrates the younger. Cups such as these, and contemporary Arretine pottery on similar themes, reveal a Hellenizing influence on Roman culture.

Many poems and graffiti testify to this, and furthermore Latin vocabulary even distinguished the humiliating *fellatio*, the sucking of someone's penis, from the aggressive *irrumatio*, the thrusting of one's penis into another person's mouth. Male thieves and trespassers were sometimes punished by being raped anally or orally, and the widespread use of phallic boundary stones and gateposts as aggressive markers of territory embodied the implicit threat of this. In Athens, male adulterers could have a horseradish thrust up their rectum, perhaps symbolizing the penis of the outraged husband.

Implicit misogyny is inherent in these values. Since, owing to their anatomical structure, women can only be penetrated and never the penetrator, they are explicitly or implicitly given a subservient status. At the same time however, women were often seen as inherently lustful and their desires as dangerous for men. Evidence from this period tends to reveal strong male anxieties about controlling women's sexuality and ensuring their fidelity, while at the same time not being bound by such restrictions themselves.

Since the object of a penetrating male could equally well be a woman or another man, the categories of heterosexual and homosexual were not so clearly distinguished as they are in the modern world and the bisexual tone of much ancient literature does not seem to have been felt as in any way anomalous. There are many similarities in the ways in which boys and women are described and desired by men. But there are also some important differences, including, in Greek culture at least, the repeated assertion that boys are generally more desirable than women and that the desirable stage of their lives is much more fleeting. The 8th-century poet Hesiod advised that taking a partner was desirable if only to provide for old age, but that even the rare man who found a sensible wife would experience more evil than good. He also said that it was better to buy a woman than to marry her, because then it was easier to make her follow the plough.

Divine Sexuality

In the beginning, according to the Greek poet, Hesiod, who lived in the 8th century B.C., there was the void, or Chaos. Out of Chaos there arose five original elements: Gaia (the Earth), Tartarus (the Underworld), Erebos (the Darkness of the Underworld), Nyx (Night) and Eros (Love or Desire). Nyx mated with Erebos to produce Day and Aether, the upper atmosphere. Gaia produced Ouranos (in Latin, Uranus, the Sky), who in turn was aroused by Eros to fertilize Gaia with his falling moisture. Together they produced the Titans and various other races of giants and monsters.

In this account the early beings are so far removed from any human form that mating and procreation is almost the only animate quality they appear to have. But it is striking that even the most primeval and inchoate beings are still related to each other in family terms, showing that sexuality is there from the very beginning of the universe – even, it seems, in the absence of genital organs – through the principle of Eros. Ouranos feared that his sons would usurp him, so he confined them underground inside their mother Gaia and would not allow them to emerge. In revenge Gaia persuaded one of their sons, Kronos (in Latin, Cronus), to castrate his father with a sickle. The drops of blood from Ouranos' severed genitals fell to earth giving rise to races of giants and Furies. Where the genitals landed in the sea off the coast of Cyprus the semen they contained gave rise to white foam from which was born the goddess Aphrodite (the Foam-Born). Fearing the same treatment himself, Kronos devoured each of his children as they were born until his consort Rhea succeeded in hiding the baby Zeus from him and giving Kronos a stone to swallow instead. In time, Zeus (in Latin, Jupiter) did indeed dethrone his father and became the chief of the gods.

The Olympian gods who are produced in later generations become progressively less elemental and more human in form, and their sexuality more closely resembles that of humans. The

Zeus as a Swan with Leda, end of the 4th cent. Marble relief from Argos, British Museum, London. Classical depictions of the rape of Leda are most surprisingly coy, giving little indication of what an overpowering bird a swan can be. In this statue, indeed, it appears to be Leda who is taking advantage of the bird.

sexual morality of the Greek gods was not superior to humans. Indeed, they were able to indulge in sexual activities that were impossible for mortals. In telling stories about the love life of the gods, the Greeks were exploring themselves and their own limitations.

The ways in which these stories were told or interpreted changed considerably with the preoccupations of each generation. In the period of rapid social and political change from about 500 B.C. there seems to have been an upsurge of interest in the love-lives of the gods, as reflected in the large number of vase paintings which portray gods pursuing a wide range of mortals (though there seem to be no lesbian encounters). Male gods pursue women, as was done by Zeus on many occasions, or young men, as when Zeus pursued and abducted Ganymede. Goddesses pursue young men, as when Eos, the Dawn, fell in love with Tithonos, asking that he be given eternal life but forgetting to ask at the same time for eternal youth, so that he gradually shriveled up into a grasshopper. It is the seductions and rapes of mortal women by male gods which produced the half-human, half-divine races of demigods or "heroes", such as Heracles, who are so prominent in Greek myth. Interestingly, no god or goddess ever seems to be shown in the act of sexual intercourse in the vase paintings, nor any gods with their penis erect, which suggests that the myths always retained something more abstract, beyond literal sex.

Though he was married to his sister Hera in a *hieros gamos* (sacred marriage) that resembled those of the Near East, Zeus was also the most promiscuous of the gods. He adopted numerous disguises, both to deceive his wife and to get near the mortal women whom he desired. He abducted Europa by disguising himself as a bull, on which she unguardedly sat; and visited Leda in the form of a swan, and Danae in the form of a shower of gold.

Francisco de Goya, *Kronos Devouring his Children,* **c. 1508. Oil on canvas, 116 x 105 cm, Museo del Prado, Madrid.** Greek myths, with their dark and frequently licentious themes, provided inspiration (and creative freedom) for later artists.

When one woman, Semele, learned the identity of her seducer she begged to be allowed to experience Zeus' presence in his true form. Since he had offered to grant her any wish, Zeus reluctantly obliged and Semele was burned up, perhaps by the force of an orgasm on a divine scale. Zeus took the baby Dionysos from her womb and completed the child's gestation in his own thigh. In a similar way he removed his child by Metis (Wisdom) and himself gave birth to Athena who sprang, a fully-armed adult warrior goddess, from his head. Remembering the fate of his father Kronos and grandfather Ouranos, Zeus resisted the temptation of the nymph Thetis because it had been prophesied that any son she bore would be greater than his father.

One of the few beings whom Zeus was not able to seduce or rape was Aphrodite, the goddess of sexual passion known to the Romans as Venus. Zeus punished her for her rejection by forcing her to marry the lame and ugly blacksmith god Hephaistos (in Latin, Vulcan). She was constantly unfaithful to Hephaistos and in the epic poem the *Odyssey* Homer tells how her husband found her in bed with Ares (in Latin, Mars), the handsome and muscular god of war, after a tip-off from the all-seeing sun god Helios. Hephaistos forged a net of fine metal and cast it over the amorous couple to trap them, inviting all the other gods in to laugh at them. Another god remarked that he would willingly endure such humiliation himself for a turn in bed with Aphrodite.

Another aspect of sexuality was represented by the goddess Artemis (in Latin, Diana). Artemis was both a perpetual virgin and a hunter, two conditions which were normally not available to mortal women. Conceived along with her brother Apollo from one of Zeus' many seductions or rapes, Artemis was born first and assisted her mother to give birth to her twin Apollo. So appalled was she by the sight of her mother's suffering in childbirth that she asked Zeus to be allowed to remain a virgin. She became the patron goddess of midwives. This role linked her to the menstrual cycle, and she was later identified with the moon, while her twin brother Apollo became a god of the sun.

Some stories highlight the dangerous tension between devotion to the chastity of Artemis and to the voluptuousness of Aphrodite. The young hunter Hippolytus was so devoted to Artemis that he denied himself all sexual interest in women. Aphrodite was insulted and arranged for him to become the object of the forbidden lust of his stepmother Phaedra. Phaedra wrote him a letter confessing her feelings, at the same time claiming that she had become a devotee of Artemis and suggesting they went away together on a hunting trip in honor of the goddess. The chaste youth was horrified at the letter and rejected Phaedra, whereupon she hanged herself and left a note to his father Theseus claiming that he had raped her. On finding the note, Theseus banished his son and begged his own father Poseidon, the sea god, to attack him on his journey into exile. As Hippolytus was riding along the beach, a huge sea-monster reared up out of the water and stampeded the horses. Hippolytus was dragged along behind his chariot and killed. In his play based on this story, Euripides makes Aphrodite warn the audience, "All those who live within the bounds of Ocean and Atlas and see the sun, I grant them favor if they respect my power. But if anyone disrespects me, I destroy them."

Eros

Eros (Love or Desire), called Cupid in Latin, was sometimes portrayed as the son of Gaia, or else of Darkness or Night. The meaning seems to be that it was Love who brought order at the beginning of time to the elements that make up the universe, by motivating their desire to procreate. In some traditions, he was already on Cyprus when Aphrodite was born in the sea, and welcomed her ashore. In others, he is the son of Aphrodite herself. He is closely associated with her, helping and attending her in her bath.

Eros is often shown as a child, symbolizing both the youthfulness of the emotion for which he stands, but also its capriciousness and irresponsibility. In earlier representations he attacks his

Antonio Canova, *Cupid and Psyche*, 1796. Marble, 13 cm high, State Hermitage Museum, St. Petersburg. The story of Eros and Psyche can also be interpreted in metaphysical terms as meaning that the soul cannot manage without love but may not recognize it at first and attains it only after many obstacles and trials.

Opposite: **Titian, *Diana and Actaeon*, 1558. Oil on canvas, 129 x 180 cm, National Gallery of Scotland, Edinburgh.** Diana (in Greek, Artemis) was so offended at being seen naked by the hunter, Actaeon, that she turned him into a stag, whereupon he was torn apart by his own hounds.

victims with a whip, but from the 4th century B.C. onwards he is armed with a bow and arrows from which not even the strongest and most self-disciplined adult, nor even a god, is immune.

The most important story about Eros is his love affair with Psyche (the Human Soul), a young woman so beautiful that Aphrodite became jealous of her. She commanded Eros to punish Psyche for her beauty by making her fall in love with someone totally unsuitable, but Eros fell in love with Psyche himself. Without telling his mother he lifted her up with a gentle breeze and took her to safety. He secretly visited Psyche each night, making love to her tenderly and disappearing before daybreak.

Eros warned Psyche not to try to discover his identity, but one night, driven by her own curiosity and the goading of her envious sisters, she lit a small lamp and held it over him. In her excitement at his beauty, she spilled a drop of hot oil on his shoulder. Eros woke up and disappeared in a fury. Aphrodite then pursued Psyche with a string of impossible and dangerous tasks, even sending her on an errand to the land of the dead. Each time, the elements around her were so moved by her love for Eros that they helped her. First Eros and then Aphrodite forgave her, and finally Eros and Psyche were married on Mount Olympus and lived happily ever after.

Greek Marriage and the State

The Greek *polis* (city-state) was composed of a number of households, called *oikoi*. Just as cities engaged in warfare, so households competed for prestige and power through athletic and artistic contests, legal disputes, the holding of public office, the production of male children and the jealous safeguarding of their women's chastity. The head of the *oikos* was a freeborn citizen male, who also served as a warrior on behalf of his city. Such males were not supposed to engage in types of behavior, such as passive male homosexuality, which were only appropriate to lower categories. Non-citizen males (such as slaves and resident foreigners), as well as women of all classes, were expected to avoid any activity that could compete with the prerogatives of the citizen adult male.

Sexuality was also understood in hierarchical terms. It was widely viewed not as a mutual feeling of love between equals, but as a relationship between a desirer and an object of desire. This relationship was subject to social control. A male citizen could pursue other male citizens subject to certain rules, and female citizens with a view to marriage; but non-citizens and slaves of both sexes were considered freely available. Though little is said about this, it is likely that women could generally pursue other women.

The paradox was that a dominant desirer was dependent on the response of the beloved unless that particular object of desire was completely under his control, as perhaps with a slave or prostitute. He could also be said to be

"captured" or "enslaved" by the object of his desire or by the god Eros. This "enslavement" could be dangerous as it threatened his ability to function as a responsible, level-headed householder. Both women and boys (if free citizens) had to be courted or "persuaded". Often women were given gifts of jewelry, flowers, fruit and cosmetics, while boys were given gifts of hunting equipment, hares and roosters.

However, the ideal of a harmonious, loving relationship between husband and wife appears frequently as a counterweight to these ideas. In the *Odyssey* (Book 6, lines 182ff), attributed to the earliest known Greek author, Homer, Odysseus blesses the young princess Nausicaa with the words: "May the gods grant you all your heart's desire / A home, a husband, the sweet harmony / That everyone seeks. For there is nothing more consistently lovely / Than when a man and wife share their hopes and their hearth / Confounding the envy of their enemies and delighting their friends."

Mythology provided various models for human marriage. Odysseus's own wife Penelope stays faithful to him through a 20-year absence (during which he sleeps with other women, all the while pining for Penelope), fending off other suitors with her intelligence and initiative. There are also examples of passionate, even self-sacrificing devotion. Orpheus descends to Hades in an attempt to rescue his girlfriend Eurydice; Alcestis offers to die in place of her husband, so that he may live. When Hector's wife Andromache senses that he will die and begs him tearfully not to go outside the walls of Troy to fight again (Homer's *Iliad*, Book 6, lines 392–496), Hector is touched with pity at the sight of her and strokes her, saying, "My dear wife, do not grieve too much for me. No man will send me to Hades unless he is destined to do so." However, the marriage of Zeus and Hera, which was invoked in wedding ceremonies, must have stood as a model for many marriages among mortals: while he was constantly unfaithful to her by being with other women, she remained at home as goddess of the domestic hearth.

Marriage ceremonies varied in ancient Greece. In some areas, including Sparta, they could

include a mock reenactment of an abduction, suggesting that marriage by capture was sometimes practiced. But generally, Greek marriage was founded on the giving of a woman by one man to another for the procreation of children. Usually the closest male relative to the bride would arrange this transfer privately, but over time cities introduced laws to regulate marriage. In Athens, a male relative of the bride would formally give the woman to her husband, without requiring the woman's consent. Bigamy was illegal but a married man could keep a concubine, though her children would be illegitimate. Sending the wife back to her father's home, after which she could be remarried, effected divorce.

Through much of Greek history a man might be 30 or more before he married, while his wife might be only 15. As one of Euripides' characters puts it, "It is quite wrong to join together two persons of the same age. For the strength of man lasts far longer, while the beauty of the female body fades much more quickly." However, this could make the ideal of harmonious partnership difficult to realize. A textbook on household management by Xenophon (*Oikonomikos* 12–13) contains the following ironic dialogue:
– Is there anyone you entrust with more important matters than your wife?
– Certainly not!
– Is there anyone with whom you talk less?
– Hardly anybody, I must admit.
– And you married her when she was just a child and had seen and heard nothing of the world?
– That's right.

In Athens, the family of the bride acted together with that of the groom to perform the marriage ceremony. Preliminary sacrifices were made particularly to the goddesses Hera, as goddess of marriage, Aphrodite as goddess of sex, and Artemis as goddess of young womanhood. Water was brought in special jugs from a sacred spring or river in order to bathe the bride. The bride's father hosted a banquet at which the bride was unveiled and shown to the groom. In the evening she was led in a torchlight procession to the groom's house to the accompaniment of blessings shouted by the guests. On entering the house the bride and groom would go to the hearth where they were showered with dried fruit and nuts, as symbols of fertility, before retiring to the bedroom to the sound of marriage hymns.

According to law, the girl was supposed to be a virgin. Although it is not clear how often it was actually followed, the legal code drawn up in Athens by Solon (c. 640–c. 559 B.C.) stated that if a girl proved not to be a virgin, her father should sell her into slavery. Solon's laws also stipulated that a man should have sex with his wife at least three times a month, which sug-gests that many male citizens sought their sex-ual satisfaction outside marriage, either with boys or with non-citizen women.

In the upper classes marriage was a contract between families or households who invested a great deal of their prestige in the match. It was for this reason that so much emphasis was placed on the bride's virginity and her avoidance of

Coitus Scenes, Askos, c. 470 B.C. Clay, Kerameikos Museum, Athens. It is difficult to be sure whether Greek artists were more concerned with stimulating their audiences than with providing an accurate reflection of the sexual practices of their time. So rear-entry intercourse (in which there could be no doubt about what was happening), and face-to-face positions in which the woman's legs were raised (to display the male genitals) were especially popular.

adultery after marriage. A girl's father might even employ matchmakers. Matchmakers were women whose job it was to praise the girl's chastity, modesty and industry to the fathers of prospective grooms.

Women were largely referred to as the wife or mother of a given man and it is striking how few women can be identified by name today. In a famous speech, the Athenian leader Pericles is reported to have said that the greatest reputation for a woman is not to be talked about by men at all, even favorably.

The Athenians were both fascinated and appalled by the Spartan habit of training women to be fighters, and allowing them to appear naked. They also mocked the Spartan style of marriage, in which the man lived with his male friends and colleagues-in-arms, and only sneaked out on rare occasions to visit his wife by night. Later, in the first century A.D., Plutarch wrote of the Spartans that sometimes "a husband had children without ever having seen his wife by daylight." But actually Athenian husbands and wives did not have a great deal more to do with each other.

Citizen men lived a public life consumed with public affairs. In comparison, even citizen women did not have the right to vote and though they attended religious festivals and even the theater, they spent much of their lives indoors in houses which usually had no windows opening out onto the street. It has been suggested that there are significant parallels between the way in which women were shut off in dark internal spaces, and the Greek understanding of the inaccessible internal spaces of their genitals. Plutarch described how, in the 6th century B.C., wives who went outdoors had to be chaperoned, and at night were required to travel in carriages with lanterns.

In vase paintings of the 6th and 5th centuries B.C. there is a visible emotional distance between copulating couples that makes the women seem like sexual objects or slaves. In the later Hellenistic period, eye contact and emotional involvement are clearly portrayed, and some artistic styles even become what might be called romantic or sentimental. This corresponds to a much higher degree of freedom for women in a society that was becoming bourgeois. At this point in time manuals of sexual positions and pleasures began to be written, often claiming (implausibly) to be authored by women such as midwives who claimed a specialized knowledge of female sexuality. Erotic pictures showed heterosexual couples as equals surrounded by the comforts of home, bed and pillows, and a wide range of household items including women's mirrors. This continued into Roman times.

Cnidian Venus, Roman copy of Praxiteles's Aphrodite of Knidos (marble statue), c. 350 – 330 B.C. Plaster cast, 209 cm high, Musei Vaticani, Rome. Pliny described the original as the finest statue in the world.

Nudity

Male nudity was common in the context of athletics, where it was also often associated with homoeroticism. For example, literature contains many references to the arousing beauty of a youth's thighs. When the statues and paintings from that age are viewed today, one is struck by small men's genitals on the nude subjects. Athenian taste preferred the penis to be slender and neat. During athletic exercises the foreskin was often tied up over the glans (large genitals were attributed to barbarians, satyrs and other similarly inelegant or unrestrained creatures.) Respectable women were absent from athletic events, and in most situations the genitals were generally kept covered. The nude figures shown on vases, especially the pornographic paintings on the *kylix* (drinking cups) of the early 5th century B.C., would be unlikely to be seen by women. It was only later in the 5th century that paintings of naked women bathing moved from the exclusively male world of the drinking cup to vessels such as women's water-jars and other pots used on social occasions such as weddings.

The nude female statue did not develop until the second half of the 4th century B.C. The key work in this style was a famous statue of Aphrodite, now lost but often imitated, by Praxiteles. Many viewers found this statue sexually arousing, and ancient guides used to tell tourists that a small discoloration in the marble inside one thigh was caused by the semen of a young man who had become obsessed with the statue and had secretly ejaculated onto it.

Prostitutes, Concubines, and Courtesans

In the earliest surviving Greek literature, the *Iliad* and the *Odyssey* by Homer, there is no mention of prostitutes. Homer's heroes used female slaves, concubines and war captives for their sexual satisfaction. Although by the 6th century B.C. this situation had changed (the lawmaker Solon established the first Athenian brothel at the beginning of the 6th century), it is nevertheless true to say that for the male citizens of Athens, only slaves or foreign women were available outside of marriage. The relationships that men might forge with the various sorts of women could take only so many forms. These are summed up in a famous sentence from a speech against a woman called Neaera, who was accused of mixing up the different categories: "We have courtesans for our pleasure, concubines for our daily personal service, and wives to bear us children and manage our house faithfully."

The hetaera (courtesan) was a refined version of the general category of *porne* (prostitute). Prostitutes were either of the slave class (distinguishable on vase paintings by their short haircuts) or, if free women, then immigrants from other cities. They were owned or otherwise controlled by pimps and madams who ran brothels. Both prostitutes and their owners were considered to be carrying out an ordinary trade like any other, subject to similar kinds of taxation, and their fees were regulated by a system of clerks and magistrates. This lack of any moral condemnation was because they were considered to be outside the formal social fabric, and thus posed no threat to citizens' wives or the legitimacy of their children. Although they could never become a member of the citizen class, prostitutes could save up and buy their freedom, which they sometimes managed to do in later life. Others might be given their freedom by a male admirer.

After an early homosexual experience as an older man's boyfriend, a young citizen male's first heterosexual experience would probably be at a symposium, a men's drinking party at which prostitutes would also provide the music and dancing. Though the symposium could also include homosexual activities, there are many surviving scenes of vigorous heterosexual activity involving male clients and female prostitutes. These scenes are painted

Brygos painter, Erotic Group, Athenian red-figure cup, c. 480 B.C. Clay, Archaeological Museum, Florence. This is typical of the group-sex scene on the inside of drinking cups. Although the Greeks viewed the drinking of neat wine as barbaric, it seems that they drank enough of the diluted stuff to become greatly intoxicated, and uninhibited.

Opposite: **Tyrrhenian amphorae (detail), second quarter of the 6th cent. B.C. Clay, 41 cm high, Staatliche Antikensammlungen und Glyptothek, Munich.** Dark male figures, some displaying large phalluses, some in the act of intercourse with women, are depicted dancing as if in a procession.

Brygos painter, Symposium (Drinking Party) Scenes, Athenian red-figure cup, c. 480 B.C. Plaster, 32 cm in diameter, British Museum, London. A young prostitute dances at a party for a boy, who beats time for her on his knee. In his hands he holds a set of pipes.

especially on the *kylix*, a flat, shallow wine-cup. The outside of the *kylix* is often decorated with scenes that may show sexual activity but often only imply or promise it. The flat bottom of the inside of the cup then shows a more explicit sexual scene that would appear and become gradually clearer as the drinker emptied his cup.

There are scenes of group-sex and frequent portrayals of men penetrating women from behind. In a few paintings, this appears to be anal, but usually it is not clear whether the penetration is anal or vaginal. Either way, the imagery seems to epitomize male domination,

since it was widely thought that to be penetrated in any way, for either a man or a woman, was a sign of inferiority and a cause of humiliation. There are also pictures of prostitutes performing fellatio on men. The women do not always appear to be enjoying the experience, and this action is sometimes closely associated with images of men beating women with a stick or sandal, perhaps compelling the reluctant women to perform the act.

These scenes seem to represent a relaxation of normal social constraints, in tableaux which may or may not really have taken place at the symposium, but which probably did not take

place outside it. If at all, these activities and positions did not occur often between citizen men and their wives, and are in fact the same as those adopted in art by the most lustful of non-humans, the Satyrs. The depersonalized nature of such sexual contact is revealed by the contrast with those vases which instead portray sexual intercourse face to face. The women are still prostitutes, but there is a much greater sense of intimacy. Vase painters expressed this through eye contact between the participants. Often the man is on his knees, while the woman is on her back and with her legs around his waist or shoulders.

There are also paintings showing other signs of affection, such as couples embracing or kissing mouth to mouth, which was not done in public between married couples. One painting shows a prostitute tenderly supporting the head of a young client who is vomiting, presumably after drinking too much. There was always a risk of too much emotional involvement, and it was not always easy for a citizen using a prostitute to avoid becoming "captured" by Eros. The courtesan was a sophisticated kind of prostitute who developed a more elaborate relationship with her clients. Hetaeras (the word means "companion") were variously owned and hired out, and while many were treated like slaves and prostitutes, others became *pallake* (concubines), in effect secondary wives.

The life of a woman in any of these roles was precarious. As a prostitute she would have the protection of her pimp or owner, but was liable to be exploited and abused sexually and financially. Unless she managed to claw back a good part of her fees, she would face poverty as her physical beauty faded. As a hetaera she might be less crudely exploited, but she would still have to remain pleasing to the man or men who were supporting her financially. Thus in one comedy a character remarks that a hetaera is easier to live with than a wife, precisely because she lacks the wife's legal rights.

Even the most respected and influential courtesan was a kept woman, supported by men who had both the citizenship and the money. As a reminder of this fact, several *kylix* paintings show a purse in the background. If a hetaera's relationship with a man matured into a long-term concubine arrangement, she might well achieve financial security. Though still ultimately based on the man's power of free status and money, such relationships sometimes involved a degree of affection that was missing in many marriages. On the other hand, if a man tired of his concubine, he had the right to sell her to another master, or even to a brothel.

Temple prostitutes

There were several temples in the Greek world built for *Aphrodite Porne* (Aphrodite the Prostitute). Women would be dedicated to the goddess and work in the temples as sacred prostitutes, a practice which the Greeks said came from the Near East, especially Babylon. Citizens would sometimes offer their own wives or daughters to the goddess as a temple prostitute in return for salvation in a disaster. The people of Locri, in southern Italy, once offered their virgin daughters to Aphrodite for use as prostitutes if she would help them in a war.

One of these temples was at Paphos in Cyprus, where Aphrodite (the Foam-Born) first arose from the froth of the waves containing her father's severed genitals. Here, it was said that every young woman had to spend a period of time as a temple prostitute. The great centers of prostitution were seaports, such as Athens and Corinth. Of these, the greatest was Corinth, which supposedly had a thousand prostitutes. There was a saying, "Not every man gets to go on a voyage to Corinth." There is a record of a Corinthian citizen who won at the Olympic Games and dedicated a hundred women to the temple on a single occasion. Here, great processions of prostitutes would be held with prayers, sacrifices and feasting. These commemorated the occasion when the invading Persian army had tried to capture the citadel, but had been repelled after a crowd of prostitutes had prayed to Aphrodite for protection.

Pan painter, Red-figure mixing-bowl (*krater*), 470 B.C. Clay, Antikensammlung, Staatliche Museen, Preussischer Kulturbesitz, Berlin. One of the roles of the prostitutes in the Athenian festivals devoted to the wine god Dionysus was to carry massive phallic symbols.

***Aspasia*, relief of a chest from Pompeii, end of 4th–first cent. B.C. Bronze, National Archaeological Museum, Naples.** Apasia, one of the most famous courtesans and mistress of Pericles, is apparently teaching Socrates the woman's view of love and marriage.

The whores of Corinth were said to be especially skilled – and expensive. The orator Demosthenes sailed to Corinth just to meet one of the most famous, Lais. But when he arrived, he was deterred by the enormous fee she demanded of 10,000 drachmas.

Famous Courtesans

The more sophisticated hetaeras were a byword for intelligence and wit, perhaps because they were the only kind of women who could attend a symposium and take part in the conversation, rather than just turn up as sex objects.

Hetaerae adopted professional names or were given nicknames, such as Leaina (Lioness), from the crouching position she adopted, with her backside in the air, or Klepsydra (Water Clock), from the strict time limit she allotted each client. A work by the Greek satirist of the second century A.D., Lucian, called *Hetaera Conversations* reveals a very earthy world of bitchiness, humor, mutual solidarity and the exploitation of jealous clients.

The most famous courtesan was Aspasia, the mistress of the great Athenian leader Pericles (d. 429 B.C.). Although she had not been born in Athens, she was a free woman and so had the possibility of social mobility. Originally a hetaera and brothel-keeper, Aspasia became a concubine to Pericles after his divorce and stayed with him until his death. She appears to have been greatly admired by leading men of the day, notably Socrates, for her intelligence and political acumen, and was said to have composed the speeches which made Pericles' career.

Another famous prostitute, Neaera, was the target of a vitriolic law-court speech which has survived from the late 4th century B.C. Neaera (whose name means "belly") was accused of the serious offence of hiding her past and pretending to be a free citizen. The speech gives a fascinating insight into the low-life of ancient Greece and reveals, for example, how foundlings and other little girls were bought up and trained by brothel-keepers. Neaera was taken to Corinth, where she earned enormous sums for her madam before being bought outright by two men who wished to share her, as this was cheaper than renting her. They later gave her her freedom and she returned to Athens disguised as the wife of an Athenian client. Her many other adventures included blackmailing foreign clients by sleeping with them and then afterwards claiming to be the wife of an Athenian citizen, with whom they had unwittingly committed adultery. Tantalizingly, the outcome of the case against her is not known.

Lesbian Love and Female Autoeroticism

Portrait of a woman, known as Sappho, Pompeii, first cent. Frescoe, 31 x 31 cm, National Archaeological Musem, Naples. At the time when this image was made, much of Sappho's work still survived, in nine volumes of lyrics and one elegy that had been collected and republished in the second and third centuries B.C.

involved in local political in-fighting and Sappho was banished for a while along with her family. It seems that she was the head of a girls' academy, in her own words a "House of Muses", in which the girls studied poetry and music in particular, and perhaps also domestic arts. Their sense of togetherness may also have been fostered by participation in women's cults and in weddings of other girls. Some of these girls' names are known from Sappho's poems: Telesippa, Megara, Gongyla, Clais. One of Sappho's pupils, Damophyla, is said to have gone on to teach a further generation of girls and this may indicate the existence of an extensive tradition of girls' schooling.

It is not clear to what extent Sappho was homosexual or bisexual. There are several ancient references to Sappho's male lovers, and one source even claims that she pursued a beautiful ferryman called Phaon and leaped to her death into the sea when he rejected her. Certainly some of her poems are addressed to women in the kind of passionate sexual language commonly used by men addressing boys. This suggests a parallel to the kind of tutorial relationship so well-documented with male homosexuality, in which the older partner is both lover and teacher. At the same time,

Given the male domination in Greek culture, it is not surprising that references to Greek women's homosexual or autoerotic behavior are rare. Even Plato in his *Symposium* (360 B.C.) concerned with the origin of all possible sexual orientations, devotes only one sentence to the topic. This lack of evidence surely does not reflect an absence of such behavior, but only its exclusion from the male world of public life. Though male writers and characters in plays occasionally make fun of it, it is not seriously denounced, perhaps because it threatened the status less than other forms of sexual activity and did not affect the performance of any of the public roles expected of women.

The Greek word for a female homosexual was *tribas*, (hence the term "tribadism" of modern sexologists). The Athenians believed that Spartan women were especially prone to falling in love with young girls, but the place that historically became most linked with tribadism was Lesbos. The island was associated with general female licentiousness (perhaps especially fellatio) but the term "lesbian" gradually came to be used for female homosexual behavior because of the fame of the poetess Sappho of Lesbos, whose verse was popular as far afield as Athens, where her name appears several times on vases. Sappho's poems survive only in fragments that were written in a difficult dialect which is hard to understand and translate. Very little is known about her life. She was probably born around 612 B.C. and came from a local aristocratic family. At one point her family became

Roman oil lamp, first cent. A.D. Clay, 2.7 x 10 cm, Rheinisches Landesmuseum, Trier, Germany. Girl on the back of a crocodile about to sit on a dildo. This image may have been intended as a satirical comment on the excesses of Cleopatra.

however, her poems are also linked to a wider tradition in which a chorus of women would sing praises of other women, often in erotic terms, particularly in the context of a girl's marriage (and to texts composed by male poets).

In one of her best-preserved poems, Sappho appeals to the goddess Aphrodite for help "with what my heart's madness most desires". Aphrodite replies, "Whom shall I persuade this time to love you? Who is not treating you right, Sappho? For even if she runs away, she will soon pursue you, and if she does not accept gifts from you, she will be giving them. And if she does not love you, soon she will love you even against her will" (Fragment 1, lines 18–24).

The poem follows a typical Greek pattern of lover and beloved, pursuer and pursued, except that Aphrodite promises to turn this around to bring about the requital of Sappho's passion. But the satisfaction of Sappho's longings can-not always be guaranteed. In another poem she expresses jealousy and anguish on catching sight of another woman bestowing her loveliness upon a man. It has been suggested that Sappho may be addressing a young woman who is now moving on to betrothal or marriage and thus leaving the circle of Sappho's girls: "That man seems to me to be equal to the gods, who sits opposite you and hears from close up your sweet voice and your desire-arousing laugh. I swear it has set my heart fluttering in my breast. For whenever I glance at you, I become incapable of speech. My tongue is fixed in silence, and immediately a subtle fire runs under my skin. With my eyes I see nothing, my ears hum, a cold sweat comes over me, I am seized all over with trembling, I am paler than grass, and I seem close to death." (Fragment 31, lines 1–16) The fragment then breaks off with the words: "But I must endure it all."

Epiktetos, Hetaera with Two Dildos and a Basin, 4th cent. B.C. Cup fragment, Archaeological Museum, Naples. The women shown holding dildos in Greek art were usually entertaining men or taking part in festivals, rather than giving pleasure to themselves.

Dildos

The Greek dildo (*olisbos*) was long and made of leather. It was lubricated with olive oil before use. One humorous text (by a male writer) has women gossiping about where to obtain different makes and styles. The best were made in Miletus. In Aristophanes' play *Lysistrata*, first performed in 413 B.C., all the Athenian women's husbands are away at the war with Sparta, and since the war has stopped trade with Miletus, there is a shortage of "leather comforts". In another comedy a woman complains that a dildo resembles the real thing as the moon does the sun: though the appearance is similar, it has no heat.

Sapphic pleasure in girls' community of the Thiasos, 4th cent. B.C. Terra-cotta, British Museum, London. This is an extremely rare example of lesbianism being depicted in Greek and Grecian-influenced art.

Male Homosexuality

Sexual relations between men took various forms. In Thebes there was a "Sacred Band" of dedicated warriors made up of pairs of lovers who would fight and die together. In Homer's *Iliad*, the warriors Achilles and Patroclus may have also been lovers. But the main form that was sanctioned, and even developed into a major social institution, was pederasty (love of boys), between a mature man and an *ephebos* (immature youth) just past puberty. In the barracks culture of Sparta, every freeborn man was required by law to have young male lovers and to train them in their adult duties to society. The more mature partner was responsible for the behavior of his student-lover, and might remain in the role of teacher even after the boy had outgrown the sexual side of the relationship. In Athens, such relationships were especially prominent in the late 6th and early 5th centuries B.C. Among freeborn citizens sexual relations between age-equals, like prostituting oneself, was viewed with disapproval. While male slaves were sexually fair game and could be taken without ceremony, citizen boys were reserved for citizen men under strict rules of procedure and the relationship was part of a man's proper relationship with the state. The older lover was

perhaps a partial substitute for the boy's rather distant father, who spent a great deal of time out of the home. It was said that the older partner would "breathe" his love into a beautiful boy, thereby increasing his modesty and self-control. The relationship was developmental. The boy would lose his appeal to older men when he grew a beard, and he would become an older lover himself. The institution is thus comparable to initiation rites elsewhere.

The relationship was conceived in terms of pursuer and pursued, respectively the *erastes* (the older lover) and the *eromenos* (the younger beloved). This pursuit was not violent, but rather a form of *peitho* (wooing or persuasion) by the older partner. The *eromenos* was not considered feminine but manly, and his submissiveness was not one of character but of his stage of life. Whatever his feelings of affection, the young *eromenos* was not supposed to feel sexual desire for the older man. This explains the frequent lack of youths' erections on vases. In terms of domination, the language of "pursuit" can be read in reverse: the boys may often have controlled the feelings of their older lovers, who were thought to be "captured" by Eros.

An *erastes* competed with others for the more desirable boys and an *eromenos* might boast of his admirers or lovers. As Socrates is supposed to have said, "Beautiful boys get full of pride and conceit when they are praised and glorified." However, though this was a publicly sanctioned institution, there were ambiguities. It was also felt that an *eromenos* should conceal the fact that he had been seduced. This was especially so if the youth allowed himself to be penetrated, an act considered unworthy of a man and a free citizen, and one which could threaten his citizenship. Boys learned to expect gifts and favors, and if their behavior was judged to be actual prostitution they could be disenfranchised. Many surviving speeches from the courts of law revolve around this kind of accusation. In one story, a man met another man on the street and made reference to his *eromenos*, asking if the boy was pregnant yet. The *erastes*, enraged by the insult to his boy, killed the accuser.

Vase paintings are very clear about the correct sexual position, showing male citizen lovers as standing up and facing each other, not penetrating any orifice but with the *erastes* rubbing his penis inside the boy's thigh (interfemoral

Homosexual courtship scene, c. 540 B.C. Amphora. The beloved youth is shown without an erection. Xenophon said that, whereas women share a man's pleasure in intercourse, boys do not. He describes them as being "cold sober", compared to their lovers who were "drunk with sexual desire".

Man fingers a boy's penis, c. 480 B.C. Interior of a drinking bowl, clay, Ashmolean Museum, Oxford. Unusually in the idealized art of the Greeks, the youth reciprocates the affection of the older man.

Ganymede and the Eagle (Zeus), third cent. A.D. Roman mosaic. The divine model for male homosexual love was the story of Zeus' abduction of Ganymede. Zeus was so taken with the boy's beauty that he descended to earth and swept him up to Mount Olympus, where he became a wine-waiter to the gods. There were many interpretations, which varied with time. In a statue from Olympia, dating from around 470 B.C. Ganymede is a child, while the inside of a *kylix* shows him as a youth. In this later Roman version he seems just prepubescent.

intercourse). The decorum of this contrasts strongly with other kinds of couples. Heterosexual paintings are often wild and fantastic, involving fellatio and anal penetration of prostitutes who were slaves or foreigners. Male satyrs sodomize each other freely, but the acceptance of anal penetration was ridiculed and Aristophanes' plays contain numerous references to known "catamites" who do not face their partners. When one character asks another about the identity of a third, he is told: "You've certainly penetrated him, but perhaps you didn't recognize him."

As the structure of society changed, so did this ideal combination of homosexuality and manliness. In the 4th century male homosexuality came to be more associated with effeminacy. Heterosexual relationships became more relaxed. Men married earlier and with the disappearance of the fiercely independent and competitive city-states their lives became less militarized and athletic. Homosexuality came to be seen more as a special taste rather than as a necessary part of the process of education and acculturation of warriors. Society tended to keep boys away from homosexual contacts.

Platonic Love

The term "Platonic love" is used today to mean an intense relationship in which the participants forgo sexual fulfillment. However, in the works of Plato, *eros* (love) was given a mystical meaning which went far beyond this. Plato wrote his works in the form of dialogues, generally between his teacher Socrates and several of Socrates' students. The most famous treatment of love is in his *Symposium*, "Drinking Party".

At this party, instead of the usual entertainment by dancing girls and female flute-players, the drinkers (all male), who are poets, playwrights and philosophers, opt to have a serious discussion in which each member should deliver a speech in praise of love.

Each of the friends delivers his speech, whether humorous, philosophical or bizarre. But the serious message of the *Symposium* is contained in Socrates' speech which comes at the end. Socrates starts with the homosexual love for youths which is taken for granted in his circle, and which he himself felt keenly. But he takes it further. Love is a consciousness of a need for something one does not possess, and the object of love is beauty. A mature man should be susceptible to the beauty of a boy through experiencing the "madness" of love. Yet he should transcend physical desire and in particular avoid consummation since love is a desire, not for bodily contact, but for absolute beauty. The beauty of the *eromenos* (beloved boy) becomes the inspiration for the soul of the *erastes* (lover) in its upward flight towards the contemplation of absolute beauty and absolute reality – in short, for its flight towards divinity and moral perfection.

Socrates claims to have been taught this insight by a wise woman and diviner called Diotima, from the city of Mantinea. He retraces her explanation to him of how love gives one a kind of apprenticeship to the understanding of the Beautiful by leading one through increasing levels of abstraction, from the plurality of phenomena in the world to the absolute unity which underlies them (Plato's so-called *Theory of Forms or Ideas* (*eidos*). As Socrates explained it: So when a man starts from this world of the

senses and through the proper love of boys, starts to ascend and perceive that beauty, he has almost reached his goal. The right way to be initiated into the mysteries of love is to begin from examples of beauty in this world, and to use them as rungs on a ladder to ascend steadily with that absolute beauty in view, from one to two and from two to all beautiful bodies, and from beautiful bodies to beautiful morality, and from beautiful morality to beautiful knowledge, and from beautiful knowledge to end up at that supreme knowledge which is nothing other than knowledge of absolute beauty, and to know at last what true beauty is" (*Symposium* 211b–c).

Here we are in the language of religion and the Mysteries, in which devotees are initiated gradually to ever-higher stages of enlightenment. The guide on this path is the god Eros, who at this point is also equated with Socrates himself as a teacher. When confronted with the beauty of a youth, the uninitiated man will indulge like an animal in gross physical sexuality, while the more aware man will allow his soul to take flight in pursuit of the divine. The initiatory and educational role of the pederastic relationship means that the soul of the *erastes* overflows into the soul of the boy who is its source, so that he in turn is filled with *eros* (desire) to fly up to the truth.

It is unclear why Plato makes Socrates credit this wisdom and instruction to a woman, since women were excluded from this kind of philosophical quest. It may be that he wanted to give a disinterested view of male homosexual love. But it may also be because of the female associations of incantation and divination. The madness of being in love is said to be like the madness of diviners in a state of possession, a condition open only to women. The name of Diotima's city, Mantinea, contains a pun on the words for *mania* (madness), *manike* (possession) and *manike* (divination). The madness of love is the best of all forms of divine possession because it puts us in contact with the gods.

Brygos painter, attic red-figure cup from Vulci, c. 480–470 B.C. Greek ceramic, 74 cm high, 21.3 cm in diameter, Ashmolean Museum, Oxford. The scene includes a seated man and a young boy. From the man's stick hangs a strigal, a sponge, and an aryballos, inscribed KAVOE. The boy carries a string bag.

The Three Sexes and the Origin of Sexual Orientation

Among other speakers at the symposium, Plato makes the comic playwright Aristophanes tell a fable about the origins of humans and of their sexuality. At the beginning of the world, humans were not as they are today. They had four legs and four arms, two faces, and two sets of genitals. Their means of locomotion was by doing a sort of cartwheel. There were three sexes: all female, all male, and half and half, whom Aristophanes calls hermaphrodites.

These humans eventually became so proud that Zeus split them down the middle with a thunderbolt so that they came to resemble modern humans. But each being which is now recognized to be a person is really just a half of an original pair, and each one spends their life in the quest of their missing other half. Love is thus "the desire and pursuit of the whole". Those who came from a hermaphrodite original being seek members of the opposite sex, those from an all-female original seek other women, while those from an all-male original

seek other men or boys. This final category is the most noble.

Though this story is mythical and fantastic, it shows that the Greeks could also entertain a concept of a person's permanent and exclusive sexual orientation, as well as the more polymorphous or bisexual life experiences of most Athenian men (and perhaps women).

Festivals and Mysteries

The great religious festivals of the ancient Greeks were not merely to propitiate the gods or celebrate the unity of the state. It appears that many of them also provided an opportunity for the massive, collective release of tensions and frustrations, by means of drink, drugs, dancing and sex. The most famous and widely followed of the orgiastic gods was Dionysos (known as Bacchus to the Romans), whose name can be interpreted as either "son of god" or "tree god". He was an ancient fertility figure who may have originated in Thrace or Asia, but by the time he reached Attic Greece he was mainly renowned as a god of wine, orgies, madness and possession. His followers seem less concerned with ensuring a plentiful harvest than they do with attaining a state of personal rapture, during which, in some cases, the god would take over their bodies.

Makron Painter, Satyr with Leather-Dildo and Tail, c. 500 B.C. Red-figure cup, clay, Staatliche Antikensammlung und Glyptothek, Munich. Satyr players were actors in Bacchic dances and dramas – wearing fake horns and a strap-on phallus and tail.

Euphiletos painter, Dionysos Accompanied by Satyrs and Maenads, c. 530–500 B.C. Black-figure vase, clay, Museo Archeologico, Fiesole. Dionysos as a solemn god, unmoved by the celebrations of his retinue. In early representations, Dionysos is usually a dignified, bearded and somewhat aloof figure. Gradually, however, especially in Hellenistic and Roman art, he became more effeminate, and appeared to be as drunk as his followers.

The first step towards this goal was to achieve the condition of *ekstasis*, or ecstasy, which literally meant being beside oneself (or in modern parlance "out of one's head"). This was achieved by rhythmic, hypnotic dancing, and the chanting of hymns called dithyrambs, but more especially through drinking large quantities of wine. Though the Greeks had not discovered the process of distillation, and so their wine cannot have been especially alcoholic, but it is thought to have contained numerous fairly toxic, and in some cases hallucinogenic, herbal essences. To the uninitiated, large amounts could probably be lethal. Some classicists argue that the wine was not drunk haphazardly, but in a measured series of toasts, regulated by a priest who decided on just how inebriated the revelers would become. Because the goal of the ritual was to lose one's sense of personal identity, the drink would be accompanied by uncontrolled, orgiastic sex, in which men and women would often wear each others' clothes, or dress as mythical creatures such as satyrs, sileni and nymphs. The retinue of Dionysos – the *thiasos* – was thought to include all these beings, as well as centaurs, animals and more minor deities such as Pan. Once the worshippers had surrendered all self-control, a lucky few would move on from *ekstasis* to *enthousiasmos*, or enthusiasm: a form of frenzy that

meant they were possessed by the god. This state could last from a few hours to a few days. There were four major Attic festivals to Dionysos – the rural or Lesser Dionysia in December; the Lenaea in January; the Anthesteria in February; and the city or Great Dionysia which lasted for a week in late March to early April. Each had its own special character. Little is known about the Lenaea, but it is possible to surmise from the name that it was devoted to the Lenae, or Maenads – the wild female followers of the god. The Anthesteria was specifically related to wine, and was held to celebrate the new vintage. The rural Dionysia, coming in winter, was more specifically concerned with fertility than the others, and to this end included a phallic dance called the *komos*, in which the participants dressed up as satyrs.

Titian, *Bacchus and Ariadne*, 1522/23. Oil on canvas, 175.2 x 190.5 cm, National Gallery, London. Bacchus and his entourage, who are about to turn her into a Maenad, find Ariadne, abandoned by the hero Theseus, on the shore.

The Violent Death of Pentheus, first cent. A.D. Mural of the House of the Vettii, Pompeii. Pentheus is about to be killed by Maenads. One of his attackers appears to be wielding the Maenad's traditional weapon, a cone tipped spear known as a thyrsos. A pinecone was a ubiquitous fertility symbol.

The Maenads

Euripides' tragic drama, *The Bacchae* (or *Bacchantes*), written in about 406 B.C., tells the story of how Dionysos arrived in Thebes, dressed as a young holy man, with his retinue of female votaries (who are the Chorus of the play). He was rejected by the people and by the king, Pentheus, who attempted to have him arrested. In revenge, the god lured Pentheus into the mountains, where he had driven the king's mother, Agave, and the other women of Thebes into a state of Bacchic frenzy. They tore Pentheus to pieces, and Agave returned to Thebes carrying her own son's severed head.

The women that Dionysos is supposed to have driven into a state of divine madness were known as Maenads, Lenae or Bacchantes, and there is little doubt that they really existed. Plutarch and other writers describe how women would roam off into the wilderness during Dionysian festivals, dressed as men or draped with the skins of animals, ripping apart with their bare hands any living thing that crossed their path, and pausing only to dance, drink wine or eat the raw meat of their victims. It is likely that the activities of the Maenads were a remnant of organized human sacrifice, which is thought to have taken place in the early days of the Bacchic cult.

Eventually this practice led to the satyr plays which were the forerunner of Greek drama, both tragedy and comedy. Indeed, the word comedy derives from *komos*, and much of the innuendo, phallic imagery and slapstick of the rough, rural fertility dances survived into the works of the great comic playwrights such as Aristophanes. These festivals were all essentially local in character, but the great Dionysia attracted thousands of visitors to Athens and may have involved a thousand or more active participants. There were sacrifices, processions, poetry and drama competitions, as well as the drunken orgies for which the god was famous. In fact, by Roman times, the religious aspect of the great Dionysia was diminishing and it was coming to be mainly seen as a kind of arts festival.

The Dionysian cult was one of the sources of the mystery religion known as Orphism, which arose in the 6th century B.C. It was said to be based on the mystical writings of Orpheus, a musician so skillful that even the rocks danced for him, who was eventually ripped apart by the Maenads because he preferred Apollo to Dionysos, but whose still singing head floated to Lesbos where it became an oracle. The Orphics continued to use sexual motifs in their rituals, but with a different, more metaphysical emphasis. They were ascetics, who believed that the body was polluted, and little more than a prison for the soul (a view that, via the Gnostics, was to have a considerable impact on Christianity). The *likhnon* – a winnowing basket filled with fruit, with a towering central phallus – that they used prominently in their

Thesmophoria

The Thesmophoria, or "carrying of things laid down", was a festival to Demeter that took place over three days in the middle of October (In Attica the event was lengthened to five days.) It was restricted to free women, who were probably married, although they had to abstain from sex during the festival. The Thesmophoria mainly took place in darkness, by torchlight, to the accompaniment of raucous mocking among the women which was thought to be a magical way of promoting fertility. The central rite of the festival saw the bodies of piglets being thrown into an underground chamber called a *megaron*, which was filled with snakes. Phallic symbols such as pinecones and figures of men and snakes made out of dough were traditionally carried by the celebrants, and may also have been cast into the *megaron*. After three days the women would descend into the pit and bring up the rotting remains of the piglets, sometimes enacting symbolic intercourse by piercing the meat with pinecones, before laying it on an altar of Demeter and mixing it with the grains and seeds that would be sown in the new year.

Cult of God Ceres, first cent. A.D. Mosaic from Pompeii. Ceres (the Roman name for Demeter) crowns the newborn ear of wheat. This may be one of the few near-contemporary records of the Eluesinian Mysteries.

worship was not a symbol of fruitfulness, as it had been for the Dionysians, but a promise of a joyous afterlife.

Most of the mystery religions were rumored by outsiders to hold orgiastic rites. It was said that, in parts of Greece, followers of Athena, the goddess of wisdom, performed group-sex while wearing gorgon masks, and even the virgin goddess Diana was supposed to preside over orgies. Insiders generally said nothing. There is surprisingly little known about what went on at the Eleusinian Festival of the goddess Demeter, even though at its peak up to three thousand people would attend it each year. Demeter (Grain Mother) was a fertility goddess, whose daughter Kore was one day kidnapped and forced into marriage by Hades, king of the underworld. In retaliation, Deme-

ter made the land barren until Zeus negotiated a deal whereby Kore could spend part of the year with her mother, and part with her husband. Winter is the time when Demeter is without her daughter.

Initiates into the cult of Demeter were prepared at the Lesser Mysteries in Agrai, held in February–March, before proceeding to the Greater Mysteries at Eleusis, in September–October. They had to endure a ritual bath in the sea and three days of fasting before they were taken into the *telesterion*, Hall of Initiation, for the central rite. In the words of one authority, "something was read, something was revealed and acts were performed," but it is hard to be more specific than that. However, it is known that initiates experienced an overwhelming, often life-changing

vision, and the archaeological pharmacologist, R. Gordon Wasson, has suggested that this was related to the *kykeon*, or potion that they had to drink. He believes that the *kykeon* was made from an ergot (fungus) growing on barley, which would act much like LSD. Since Demeter was primarily a goddess of grain, and since the visions were produced annually, and to order, this is a plausible suggestion, but there is no way to be sure. Similarly, although Christian writers, attempting to brand the worship of Demeter as a pagan abomination, later accused her followers of mass promiscuity, the role of sexual intercourse in the Eleusinian Mysteries is unclear. It would be strange, however, if ritual sex did not play some part in the cult of a hallucinogen-wielding fertility goddess.

Hermaphroditus

The figure of Hermaphroditus has often been interpreted as an acknowledgement in Greek and Roman culture that each sex contains some of the characteristics of the other. The name of the god is an amalgamation of the names of Hermes and Aphrodite, and he-she was generally shown with a feminine face, female breasts and hips, but also with a penis.

There are various stories of the origins of Hermaphroditus. In one story, he is the offspring of a night spent together by Hermes and Aphrodite. Aphrodite tried to conceal his birth by giving him to the nymphs of Mount Ida to bring him up. But he grew into an exquisitely beautiful boy. The water-nymph Salmacis fell in love with him as he prepared to bathe at her lake. The shy youth struggled to resist her ardor and in her passionate embrace, the nymph begged the gods that they should never be separated. In response, Hermes and Aphrodite merged the two of them into one being combining both sexes. Salmacis dragged Hermaphroditus down into the depths of the lake, which afterwards acquired the property that any man who bathed in it would emerge effeminate.

There were no temples or public festivals for Hermaphroditus, but shrines with small statues were common inside the home and were probably associated with the married couple's sexual enjoyment. From the 4th century B.C., statues of Hermaphroditus moved beyond the private house to public spaces, especially the bath and the gymnasium, where large statues became common. As well as standing figures, many statues were carved of Hermaphroditus asleep.

Images of Hermaphroditus became especially popular in Roman times, where they were also used for titillation. In some Roman pictures, lustful satyrs uncover what appears to be a sleeping nymph, intending to rape her, and are comically taken aback at the unexpected sight of her penis. The hermaphroditic idea also appears in images of dancers and the male gods Eros, Dionysos and Priapus, all very directly associated with sexual energy, were often depicted with breasts and a female body shape in addition to their penis.

Hermaphrodite. German Archaeological Institute, Rome. Hermaphroditic images became common as lucky charms and talismans in the Roman world, and this statue may have had protective significance, similar to those of the phallic god, Priapus.

Pan flees from an hermaphrodite, first cent. A.D. Mural, Pompeii, National Archaeological Museum, Naples. The strangeness of the hermaphrodite is emphasized by showing how even Pan is shocked by his discovery. In some Roman art, however, the satyr is driven into a frenzy of desire by the hermaphrodite's appearance, and attempts to couple with what is, after all, a hybrid creature.

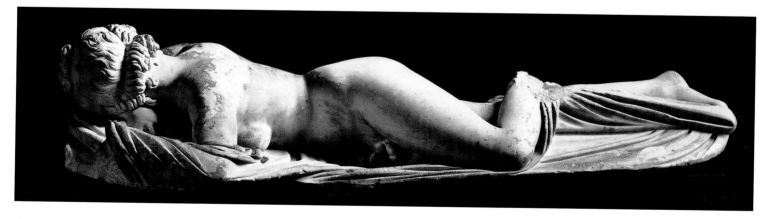

Sleeping Hermaphrodite. Marble, Palazzo Massimo alle Terme, Rome. This is probably a copy of a Hellenistic original. The delicacy of the reclining hermaphrodite reveals that these were not exclusively figures of fun, nor indeed purely erotic objects. The hermaphroditic form appealed strongly to the Classical aesthetic sense (as it would later also appeal to the artists of the Renaissance).

Roman Marriage

Roman tradition and law viewed marriage as undertaken for the procreation of legitimate children. Marriage was based on mutual consent "in divine and human law" and was considered to last so long as both partners maintained that consent. If either partner was under the legal control of their father, then that father's permission was also needed. Marriage was monogamous and an older married woman often commanded considerable authority. Divorce was common and not particularly censured. Remarriage was common, but the status of a woman who had been married only once was especially auspicious and such women had a special role in attending young brides at their weddings.

The marriage customs of the upper classes are well recorded. The day before the wedding, the bride would put away her young girl's garment and change into the straight white tunic of a mature woman. Her hair was arranged into six locks bound with strands of wool and she would put on shoes and headscarf of bright red. Members of both families gathered at her house and a matron of honor linked the right hands of both bride and groom. A pig was sacrificed, with the assembled guests shouting "Good Luck!" After a feast paid for by the groom's family, the bride would be escorted in a procession to the groom's house, where he would already be waiting to carry her across the threshold. This was done so as to avoid any possibility that she might stumble as she first entered, which was considered to be a bad omen – a custom which is still common in Europe in modern times. The bride would touch water and fire, symbols of the life of the conjugal home, while a choir sang a wedding hymn.

The aim of begetting legitimate children was linked to a strong moral code of chastity and puritanism. These were seen as typically Roman values, supposedly epitomized in a model of the rustic virtues of early Rome which later generations of moralists pointed to as a counterpoint to their own supposedly depraved age. This kind of evidence makes it hard to know what sexual life was really like in the earlier period, since the later accounts which survive generally have a nostalgically utopian ring and a contemporary political message. Perhaps the most famous and often-quoted incident from early history was the rape of the Roman Lucretia by Tarquin, the son of the Etruscan king. As later retold, Tarquin was so inflamed by Lucretia's conspicuous chastity that he entered her bedroom when she was alone. He threatened that if she did not submit to his advances, he would kill her along with her male slave and leave their naked bodies together to suggest that they had been caught in adultery. Her virtue was more important to Lucretia than her life, but this prospect was so shameful that she was left with no alternative. Later, when she told her father and husband, the Romans rose up in angry revolt and threw off the rule of the Etruscan kings. In this story, Lucretia dies in order to provide a founding myth for later Roman political structures.

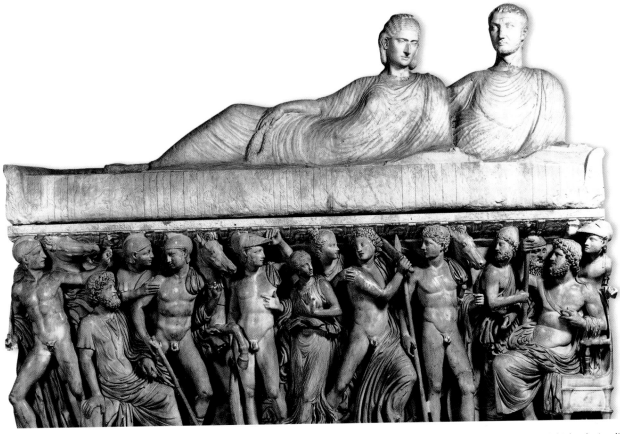

Achilles Sarcophagus, third cent. A.D. Marble, 131 cm high, Museo dei Capitoline di Roma, Rome. However fragile Roman marriages might be during life, they were inevitably immortalized on sarcophagi. Here, the dead man and his wife preside over mythological tableaux.

Titian, *Tarquin and Lucretia*, c. 1570. Oil on canvas, 190 x 121 cm, Fitzwilliam Museum, Cambridge. Significantly, Lucretia is described as making no sound during her ordeal, after her rapist addresses her with the words: "Be silent, Lucretia – I am Sextus Tarquiniius." In symbolic terms, Lucretia has been deprived of her voice, just like the people of Rome under the Etruscan rulers.

Ara Pacis Augustae (Altar of Peace, detail), c. 9 B.C. Marble, 157 cm high. Created to mark Augustus's return from the western Empire, the frieze shows the Imperial family presenting a united face of domestic order and bliss.

When her father and husband forgive her and try to comfort her, pointing out that it was only her body, not her inner will, which had been made impure, Lucretia insists on her own death, explaining, "Though I absolve myself from sin, I do not exempt myself from punishment. Let no unchaste woman in the future be able to claim me as her model."

Other important early stories repeat the same theme. The humble centurion Verginius killed his own daughter to save her from the shame of being violated by the magistrate Appius. The story was later told to justify and explain the abolition of the magistracy. This attitude continued into later times and lies behind the famous saying that Caesar's wife should be above suspicion. When his wife was implicated in a possible scandal, even though he believed that she was innocent, Julius Caesar divorced her saying, "My wife should not even be suspected of sexual impropriety."

At the end of the Republic in the first century B.C. and under the emperors from Augustus (31 B.C.) onwards, a burgeoning literature contains much discussion of licentiousness and shows an increasing preoccupation with forms of sexuality outside the monogamous heterosexual model. Even before this, the expansion of Roman dominion had led to increasing cultural influence from Greece (which Rome had conquered) as well as from Egypt and Persia. All these exotic "oriental" regions were portrayed as centers of decadence and vice, in contrast to the supposed purity and austerity of traditional Roman values. In particular, pederasty was presented as a Greek custom and passive male homosexual behavior as a Greek vice.

Roman law in all periods shows a great concern with adultery. The moralist Cato congratulated a young man whom he saw coming out of a brothel because it kept him away from other men's wives (although seeing him again a few days later, he added "But I only advised you to visit the brothel, not to live there!"). Various punishments were prescribed at various times for women and their male lovers, including the homosexual rape of the latter by the aggrieved husband or his slaves, or the thrusting of a mullet up their anus. These laws were often not enforced. Indeed, it is obvious from literary sources that such activities were widespread, so that these laws remained more a repertoire of possibilities to be drawn upon by litigants in the courts of law and politicians engaged in power struggles with each other.

The preoccupation with adultery was built on the ancient Roman perception of a link between marital breakdown and political decay. Especially condemned were sexual relations between high-status women and low-status men such as slaves, since this threatened the entire social

Jacques-Louis David, *Battle Between Sabines and Romans*, 1799. Oil on canvas, 385 x 522 cm, Musée du Louvre, Paris. Hersilia, the daughter of the Sabine leader, throws herself between Romulus and her father.

The Rape of the Sabine Women

Later authors tell the famous tale of the "Rape of the Sabine women" as motivated not by lust, but by the need to sustain the population of a new settlement made up entirely of male refugees from elsewhere. No local tribes were willing to enter marriage alliances with the earliest Roman settlers, so their leader, Romulus, the legendary founder of Rome, invited the Sabines to a grand festival for the god Neptune. At a given signal, the Romans seized the Sabine women and ran off with them. Having got them home they wooed their captives with loving words and convinced the abducted women that their own parents were to blame for being too proud. When the Sabines, under their leader, Titus Tatius, had rounded up their allies and returned for a full-scale war, their own daughters ran between the armies to hold them apart. Standing between their fathers and their husbands, they held up the babies which now bound both sides together into one people.

Neo and his Wife, c. 50 A.D. Wall painting removed from Pompeii, 58 x 52 cm, National Museum, Naples.
This double portrait reveals the relatively egalitarian nature of a Roman marriage at the time – the woman is in front of the man, and gazes out with complete self-assurance, holding a pencil and tablet to show her administrative skills.

Adultery became closely assimilated to treason against the state, with similar vocabulary and legal procedures. It was thus clearly a dangerous accusation which could be used effectively to ruin opponents. Various laws passed under Augustus prescribed that a father should kill his daughter as well as her lover if he discovered her committing adultery and required a husband who knew of his wife's adultery to divorce her within three days or himself be accused of complicity in the act. Women convicted of adultery could be forced to wear the clothing of a *meretrix* (prostitute). Informers could be rewarded and slaves could be tortured to force them to give evidence, a procedure which was normally reserved for crimes of utmost seriousness.

Other factors also lay behind Augustus's laws. The marriage and birth rates among the upper class of senators had been falling for some time, and Augustus enacted a system of penalties for those who remained unmarried and of rewards for those who produced children. The details of this are very revealing: given the high rate of child mortality, the minimum requirement of three live births per couple is still below the figure required to sustain a population at a steady level and shows how deep the demographic crisis in this class must have become after the civil war.

structure and called the position of elite men into question. Despite the examples of victims like Lucretia, our (almost entirely male) sources see uncontrolled female sexuality as a metaphor for political and social breakdown, especially among the upper classes of senators and knights. Men making speeches regularly linked political opponents with notoriously immoral women. These were not merely courtesans, but often their opponents' own wives and sisters.

Such rhetoric played on the deeply-rooted sense of the threat posed by female immorality to the stability of the state, in order to imply that their opponents were less than men because they were unable to control their women. This in turn suggests that such women may in fact have wielded great influence, a point which is highly debated among feminists and other historians.

The Republic broke down after a generation of civil war and the victor, Augustus, gave himself the newly-invented title of *imperator* (commander). As part of a wider drive to assert his control over every aspect of Roman life, he initiated a large-scale program of political and moral reform. Declaring that religion and public morals were both in decline, he restored temples and commissioned authors like Livy to write down early morality tales, such as the rape of Lucretia, for the edification of modern readers. He tightened state control over domestic morality, portraying himself as a "universal father", so that the whole state effectively became his household.

Birth Control

The Romans, like the Greeks, used contraception, abortion and infanticide when they wanted to limit the number of their children. They used spermicides of gum, vinegar, olive oil or brine and vaginal suppositories made of sponge or wool and coated with various substances, as well as using amulets, or changes of position. Abortion methods included violent exercise and probing with rods. It is not clear how frequently unwanted babies were left to die of exposure. This important in myth, where exposed infants often return in adult life, bearing a bodily mark or a piece of jewelry which was left by their side and precipitating dramatic events in the lives of their relatives who had believed them long dead.

The Vestal Virgins

There were several categories of priests in Rome who were surrounded by exceptionally strict taboos. These were among the earliest priesthoods in Rome and retained many very archaic features. They included the male priests of Jupiter, Mars and Quirinus, but also the six Vestal Virgins, who were priestesses of the hearth goddess Vesta.

These women were always recruited from upper-class families before reaching puberty. They were obliged to serve for 30 years and maintain themselves in a state of the strictest chastity, that is, throughout the period of a woman's maximum normal sexual activity. When their 30 years were up, they were free to marry but often they had become so accustomed to the way of life that they remained priestesses to the end of their days. The six Vestals lived together in a close community but were able to sustain normal social relations outside the temple, providing, of course, that they did nothing to compromise their chastity. Indeed, many of them became women of exceptional influence in Roman society.

The Vestal Virgins were the only women in Rome who had any kind of formal status and symbols of office, and they commanded awe and respect wherever they went around the streets of Rome. There is even a story of how one Vestal was insulted on the street by some men when returning late at night from a dinner party because she was not recognized at first. Such an apparently trivial event was clearly a source of horror to the Romans.

The duties of the Vestal Virgins centered on tending and preserving the fire which was consecrated to the goddess Vesta. Other duties included fetching water from a sacred spring and grinding the mixture of salt and flour which was an essential ingredient in all Roman sacrifices. The temple of Vesta was a small building of a very unusual circular shape, whose ruins can still be seen in the Roman forum. It contained no statue of the goddess, who was represented instead by the flame of the fire to which her priestesses tended, under a domed ceiling which represented the sky. Outside the temple stood an ancient oak tree.

Vestal Virgin, cast of a marble statue (time of the emperors, National Museum, Rome), Museum of casts of classical sculpture, Munich. The Vestals officiated at a number of festivals, including the Vestalia (7–15 June) and the Parilia (21 April).

VESTA - MATER (sacrifices of the Vestal Virgins), Reverse of a silver medallion of Julia Domna, 196–211 A.D. Silver gilt, 37 mm in diameter, Münzkabinett, Staatliche Museen, Preussischer Kulturbesitz, Berlin. Despite her early death, Julia Domna might already have been a priestess of up to nine years' experience.

At a Vestal's initiation her hair would be cut off and hung on this tree. Thereafter she dressed her hair in the style of a bride on her wedding day and wore the dress of a married woman. In addition to the goddess Vesta it seems that the fire also represented a male principle and the combination of the priestesses' celibacy and their clothing suggests some kind of marital relationship – mediated by the fire – with that principle. There are other signs that a Vestal's virginity also contained an implicit procreative power. In one legend Romulus himself, the founder of Rome, was born to a Vestal Virgin, Rhea Silvia, who had been raped by the god Mars. But in another, more suggestive version, he was born to a Virgin who had been instructed by a soothsayer to have intercourse with a phantom penis which appeared in the middle of the Vestal fire.

The Vestal flame was taken very seriously at all periods of Roman history, and represented the continuity and security of the Roman state. Any violation of the priestesses' chastity was thus seen as a treasonable attack on the state. If a Virgin broke her vow of chastity the flame would extinguish itself spontaneously. Vestals could also rebut accusations of unchastity by miraculously causing the extinguished flame to reignite. The punishment for a man who seduced a Vestal was to be scourged to death. For the woman the punishment was to be buried alive. She was screened in a litter and carried in a somber procession past the depressed and silent crowd. Plutarch wrote: "There is no spectacle in the world more terrifying, and in Rome no day of comparable horror." Still invisible to the onlookers, she was escorted into a specially prepared chamber provided with food and soft furnishings, earthed up, and left to die. This rite seems designed to deny the fact that the woman is actually being killed, and there may be some idea of regeneration and rebirth in the process, which is common to tomb symbolism – the grave is simultaneously seen as a womb. In the same way, the extinguished flame of Vesta must always be restored to life.

Such burials happened at times of political instability and anxiety, on two occasions after the catastrophic destruction of a Roman army by a foreign enemy. In 216 B.C. the Roman forces were wiped out in northern Italy by the Carthaginian general Hannibal who had come from North Africa across the Alps. In the panic which ensued at Rome, two Vestals were put on trial. One was buried alive and the other committed suicide to avoid punishment, while at least one of their supposed seducers was flogged to death. In 114 B.C. another Roman army was destroyed by tribesmen in Thrace. The trial acquitted the accused Vestals, but the political pressure to find scapegoats was so intense that they were retried in a determined attempt to find them guilty. This time three women were buried alive on separate occasions, in a frenzied wave of attempts to stave off a feeling of political collapse. In later times, especially under the emperors, many stories of uncontrolled licentiousness among prominent men centered on the rumor that they had seduced a Vestal Virgin. The symbolic value of these women was such that the Emperor Domitian had the Vestal Cornelia buried alive, apparently just to make his reign seem important. She defended herself by saying, "How could Caesar think I am unchaste when he has triumphed through my exercise of my sacred duties?"

Peristyle of the House of the Vestal Virgins with statues of the High Priestesses, first – 4ᵗʰ cent. A.D. Forum Romanum, Rome. The Temple of Vesta, Rome (ruins visible on far right). This is supposed to be one of the oldest sacred sites in Rome. Traditionally it was a round structure, to imitate a simple hut and symbolize a hearth.

Mystery Cults

Bacchanalian Festivity (Dionysian Scene), Roman sarcophagus, second cent. A.D. Marble, National Museum, Naples. The god is in the center, drunk and held up by satyrs.

The Romans were avid collectors of other peoples' gods, importing them with the captives and slaves that poured into the center of their expanding empire. One of the earliest and most important deities, however, was brought to Rome in response to an invasion attempt. When Hannibal attacked in 204 B.C., the Cumaean Sibyl prophesied that his armies would only be defeated if a mother goddess was imported from Asia. The black stone that was the icon of the Phrygian goddess Cybele was brought to Rome, along with the goddess's eunuch priests, and Hannibal was duly routed. According to one legend, a jealous Cybele drove her son, Attis, insane after he fell in love with a mortal woman, and in this state he castrated himself with his own hands before bleeding to death. During the festival of Cybele and Attis, which took place in late March, the priests, called *galli* or Corybantes, would flagellate themselves into a condition of frenzy. Men who had merely come along as spectators would be so carried away that they announced themselves as initiates for the priesthood by rushing out of the crowd and seizing a ceremonial sword. The historian Lucretius describes a typical initiate: "He takes it [the sword] and castrates himself and runs wild through the city bearing in his hands what he has cut off. He casts it into any house at will, and from this house he receives women's raiment and ornament."

Corybantes wore women's clothing, and were a common sight in Rome, marching through the streets singing and playing musical instruments. When the cult of Cybele first arrived in Rome, citizens were forbidden to take part in the Mysteries, but by the time of Augustus, the goddess was one of the most important, widely-revered deities in the city (Augustus thought his wife, Livia, was the living embodiment of Cybele).

Near-Eastern plaque on Altar of Roman period, c. 295 A.D. Cybele is drawn by lions towards Attis, who leans against a tree. Statues of the goddess were apparently drawn in this way, by trained lions, through the streets of Rome.

Other gods and goddesses, although popular among the people, earned the disapproval of the authorities. In 19 A.D., a Roman noblewoman called Paulina spent a night in the temple of Isis, where she imagined she was seduced by one of the Egyptian goddess's attendant male deities, the jackal-headed Anubis. There was a scandal after it was discovered that this was just one of the priests in a costume, and the Emperor Tiberius responded by crucifying the priests and deporting many of the worshippers to Sardinia.

In the first century B.C., the historian Livy described how, shortly after the war against Hannibal, the orgiastic Greek god Dionysos was imported into Rome as Bacchus. At first, said Livy, the Bacchic Mysteries were harmless festivals for women, presided over by respectable matrons three times a year. Gradually, however, men were admitted and the number of ceremonies multiplied until eventually there were five a month, all under the cover of darkness. The only aim at these ceremonies was to throw off all forms of restraint, and both men and women would fall upon initiates and debauch them by force. Anyone who struggled was murdered. The truth came to light when a young man called Aebutius told his mistress that, at the prompting of his mother and stepfather, he was about to become initiated. The mistress had experienced the Bacchic revels, and realized that the couple were trying to get her lover killed (they had been misappropriating his inheritance).

Because Aebutius's mistress broke her code of silence, there was a purge of the Bacchic religion and, according to Livy, 7000 Romans were arrested, many of them from wealthy families. The men were executed by the state, while the women were returned to their families, who were encouraged to punish them. It was claimed that the followers of Bacchus conspired with each other to commit other crimes, such as the forgery of wills. In 186 B.C. the Senate banned all celebration of the Bacchic Mysteries, but the cult could never be completely wiped out, and in 49 B.C. Julius Caesar lifted the ban, after which for a few years the worship of Bacchus became one of the most fashionable religions among the Roman elite.

The Lupercalia

Although the name of the Lupercalia festival probably derives from *lupus* (wolf), it is not clear where the ceremony itself originates. It was possibly intended to propitiate some ancient, forgotten god who protected sheep and shepherds, or it may have commemorated the she-wolf that suckled Romulus and Remus, the legendary founders of Rome. The god most closely associated with the Lupercalia, however, was Faunus, a rural fertility deity who was half man, half goat, and by classical times was being identified with the Greek god, Pan.

The festival was controlled by a band of priests called Luperci, and began with the sacrifice of two goats and a dog, after which two of the Luperci were led to the altar and had their heads smeared with sacrificial blood, which was then washed off with milk. At this point they were required to laugh. After a sacrificial feast, the Luperci cut straps from the skins of the sacrificed goats and ran around the city lashing out with them at any women who came near, an act which was supposed to confer instant fertility.

Concert of Pan and nymph. Frescoe, Museo Nationale, Naples. Faunus (Pan) was originally portrayed as a man in a goatskin, and it was only gradually that he took on goatlike attributes, such as hooves and horns. Faunus had a female counterpart, Fauna, who under the name of Bona Dea, was worshipped by an all-woman cult.

Priapus

Priapus was an early fertility god of the Roman world, and there were almost certainly crude wooden statues of him to be found throughout the countryside long before the birth of the empire. There are different mythical accounts of his birth, but he was usually considered to be a son of the wine god, Dionysus. Most of the existing statues of Priapus show him hitching up his robe to reveal his defining feature, a grotesquely enlarged, permanently erect penis. Roman aesthetics considered large genitals to be embarrassing, or simply ugly – classical male statues of the time were usually given slightly smaller genitalia than might be expected from their other proportions – and as a result Priapus was a figure of amusement rather than reverential awe.

Nevertheless, he was an important god, propitiated throughout Rome with the first fruits of the harvest. Many of the more subtle Roman statues of Priapus emphasize his role as a fertility figure by having him gather up fruits, or sometimes even children, in his clothing. In Isernia, near Naples, it was still common in the 18th century for people to buy votive wax phalluses which they presented as gifts to the saints, Cosimo and Damian. Despite its Christian patina, this practice can be placed in an unbroken tradition of Priapus worship stretching back to the days of the Roman Empire.

Because a god who guarantees good harvests must also be a protective spirit – warding off disease, birds, thieves and bad weather – Priapus became a popular deity of homes and gardens, with statues, lamps and other effigies placed around the house to keep away burglars and evil spirits. In the satires, *Sermones* (35/30 B.C.) of Horace, it was said that Priapus frightened thieves by threatening them with the "crimson stick stretching from his obscene groin". Priapus was not, however, the only priapic god honored by the Romans. He shared both his protective function and his outlandish genitalia with several other figures, including some aspects of Mercury, Faunus and Silvanus. These various deities were often conflated in the Roman mind. The early rustic statues of Priapus might have served the same function as herms – boundary markers in the form of the god Hermes (Mercury), which were thought to protect the ground where they stood, and Mercury-Priapus was an especially popular deity in the Celtic parts of the Roman empire, because he so closely resembled the Celts' own ithyphallic gods.

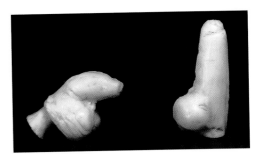

Phallic votives from Isernia, 18th cent. Wax, British Museum, London. Engravings of these phalluses appeared in the collector and antiquarian Richard Payne Knight's treatise, *A Discourse on the Worship of Priapus*, published in 1786.

Tintinnabulum, multiphallused Mercury, first cent. A.D. Bronze, National Archaeological Museum, Naples. This figure may have served to ward off evil spirits. The rings are for the attachment of bells.

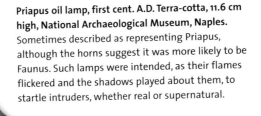

Priapus oil lamp, first cent. A.D. Terra-cotta, 11.6 cm high, National Archaeological Museum, Naples. Sometimes described as representing Priapus, although the horns suggest it was more likely to be Faunus. Such lamps were intended, as their flames flickered and the shadows played about them, to startle intruders, whether real or supernatural.

Opposite: **Priapus Weighing his Member, first cent. A.D. Mural of the Casa dei Vetii, Pompeii, National Archaeological Museum, Naples.** Priapus's role as fertility god is emphasized by the basket of fruit at his side.

The Secrets of Pompeii

The city of Pompeii received the first hints of its future destruction on 5 February 62 A.D., when it was partly demolished by a massive earthquake that, according to Seneca, also killed 600 sheep. The people of the city were undeterred, and rebuilt their homes, but on 24 August 79 A.D., after four days of earth tremors and the drying up of the water supply, Vesuvius finally erupted. First there was a hail of red-hot stones, thrown into the air by the volcano, which smashed down on the streets and buildings. This was followed by a cloud of poisonous sulfuric fumes that poured down from the mountain, and a rain of pumice-stone fragments that covered the ground to a height of about 6.5 feet to 10 feet (two to three meters). What was left of the city was preserved by a deep layer of ash which fell for two days and eventually hardened so that it perfectly preserved the outlines of bodies, food, plants and animals.

At its height, Pompeii had a population of 20,000, and it is estimated that one-tenth of them died under the ash of Vesuvius. The city was a popular venue for holiday villas built by the wealthy of Rome, but it is not clear whether the atmosphere there was a great deal more hedonistic than elsewhere in the Roman world. The beautifully preserved city of Pompeii is a snapshot of a particular time, rather than a particular place. The murals that cover the walls and floors reveal a powerful sense that life is fleeting and pleasure must be taken while it can. In addition to the erotic images, there are also a great deal of graffiti concerned with gambling (especially dice), the theater and the idolization of gladiators (one called Celadus was tagged "the man the girls sighed for", while another called Crescens was "Lord of the Dolls"). However, there were exceptions to this free and easy way of looking at life, even in Pompeii – at the so-called House of the Moralist, the dining room wall is decorated with injunctions such as "Don't be coarse in your conversation," and "Don't cast lustful glances, or make eyes at other men's wives."

The ruins of Pompeii were first discovered in the 16th century by the architect Domenico Fontana, but were only excavated haphazardly and often destructively until 1860, when the archaeologist Giuseppe Fiorelli was made director of the site. Over the years, a wealth of erotic murals, frescoes, sculptures and artifacts were uncovered. Many, however, were removed from the site and locked away in "secret collections" at the Museum of Naples and the British Museum, which remained closed to general visitors until late in the 20th century.

Oil lamp, Pompeii. Lamp-engraving, 9.25 cm in diameter, National Archaeological Museum, Naples. A lamp showing fellatio. Romans were obsessed with the idea of a clean mouth – the organ of speech and oratory. Fellatio was an act only expected of prostitutes, not respectable women, and when it is depicted, the man invariably has his hand on the woman's head, to push her down onto his penis. The man who practiced cunnilingus was especially despised – even more than the passive partner in a homosexual liaison.

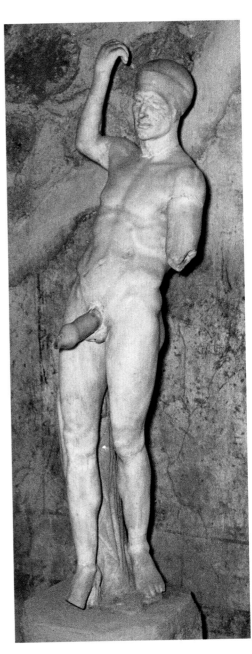

Priapic fountain-statue, Casa dei Vettii, Pompeii, National Archaeological Museum, Naples. This statue, whose phallus was a waterspout, came from the house of two nouveau riche freedmen brothers.

Suburban Baths, Scene IV, Camera secreta, 62–79 A.D. Mural Pompeii, National Archaeological Museum, Naples. Some of the most famous and beautifully erotic images of Pompeii were uncovered in the public baths.

The Villa of the Mysteries

The temples of ten different gods have been unearthed in Pompeii, though most of them are very badly damaged. The best preserved belong to the Mystery cults of Isis and Dionysos, and both contain frescoes showing rites of initiation. In the temple of Isis, a number of frescoes show the initiates taking part in a sacred dance, and receiving an urn of holy water, while others recount episodes from the life of Io, a Greek heroine who was equated with Isis. Arguably the most magnificent frescoes in all Pompeii, and the most complete record of a Bacchic initiation ever made, come from the Villa of the Mysteries. The images form a continuous narrative, showing the initiate lifting the lid of a holy casket, uncovering a winnowing basket that contains a large phallus, being whipped and deflowered, and finally dancing in ecstatic bliss.

Scourged woman and dance of a Bacchantian (detail), first cent. A.D. Mural, Villa dei Misteri, Pompeii, National Archaeological Museum, Naples. Whipping and beating were an rare theme in Roman erotic art.

Men, Women, and Beasts

In the words of one authority, "the Romans had a very catholic interest in animals." They admired them, collected them, trained them and hunted them; they incorporated animals into their pornography; and they also used animals in the arena, to execute criminals, fight gladiators and take part in extravaganzas of sex and slaughter for the general amusement. In the earliest games, which were staged some time before 200 B.C., the involvement of animals was minimal – horses took part in chariot races, while other animals were trained to perform tricks similar to those of a traditional 20th-century circus. There were also wire-walkers, boxers, theatrical shows and athletic displays. However, the tastes of the Roman crowds gradually became more bloodthirsty, and by the time the Republic was about to pass into the hands of the Caesars, Pompey (106–48 B.C.) put on a spectacle in which 600 lions, 20 elephants and 410 leopards fought against men armed with darts. The Emperor Trajan (c. 53–117 A.D.) celebrated his victory over the Dacians by slaughtering 11,000 animals in the arena.

The crowds were driven into such a bloodlust by these shows that women would masturbate themselves to orgasm in public view, and opportunistic men would sneak into the women's seats, where they might fondle or molest those who had become too excited to notice their attentions. The arenas were the most popular haunts for prostitutes, waiting for men whose libido had been stimulated by the sight of death and savagery. It was not just the slaughter of animals that provoked a sense of abandon in spectators. The chariot races in the Circus Maximus had a similar effect, creating their own form of ecstatic madness, which was known as hippomania. Women fainted, men bit themselves and performed wild dances, or, having lost all their money, bet away their freedom. A popular diversion at the games was the staging of mythological scenes, many of which involved the rape of a woman by some god who had taken the form of an animal. Nero famously staged the rape of Pasiphae (the mother of the Minotaur) by having an actor climb into a wooden cow, where another actor

Gladiators Fighting Leopards. Roman frescoe, Leptis Magna, Libya. The Roman appetite for the slaughter of wild animals was so great that the games were probably responsible for the extinction of big cats in northern Africa.

in a bull-costume mounted him. Eventually, the crowds bayed for more authenticity, and by the first or second century A.D., it seems that the *bestiarii* in charge of the animals were training them to rape women (who were usually Christians or criminals). In his story, *The Golden Ass*, written in the first person about a man transformed into a donkey by meddling with witchcraft, the second-century author Apuleius makes use of autobiographical and documentary elements. He provides one of the most graphic accounts of such a scene, involving the punishment of a woman who had poisoned five people in order to gain their property. She was sentenced to be torn apart by wild beasts (the Romans used lions, wolves, leopards, bears and dogs for this purpose, often at the same time), but was first tied to a fine tortoiseshell bed in the middle of the arena and raped by a mule, as an additional punishment and disgrace.

The Golden Ass also recounts an episode in which an aristocratic woman seduces the transformed Apuleius, and this type of liaison is a popular theme in Roman pornography. Images

of humans and animals copulating were intended to have a satirical and humorous purpose, but were clearly also meant to be arousing. Acts of bestiality are more common – and easier to bring about – between men and animals, but the vast majority of the Roman erotica dealing with the subject shows male animals coupling with human females, indicating that this was a form of erotica aimed at men. As in the arena, mythology provided a template for many of the images. Another recurring theme was the satyr, which in its sexual frustration was portrayed as attacking anything that moved. Following the tradition that had been established on Greek vases, however, the satyrs in Roman art are almost always shown being driven off successfully by women, and usually have to satisfy their appetites with goats or deer. The Romans also amused themselves with other pictures of cross-species mating – for example, showing a donkey mounting a lion, in a titillating parody of the normal relationship between the hunter and the hunted.

God Pan and a She-goat, first cent. B.C. Villa dei Papiri, Herculaneum, National Archaeological Museum, Naples. Herculaneum was destroyed by the same volcanic eruption as Pompeii. This figure is unusual for a sculpture in that it actually shows penetration taking place.

Roman Emperors

Gaius Julius Caesar, c. 50 B.C. Basalt with inlaid quartz eyes, 41 cm high, Antiken-Sammlung, Berlin. Despite his own wild reputation, Caesar divorced his wife, Pompeia, merely on the grounds that her morals were not "above suspicion".

Roman emperors were repeatedly accused by their subjects, opponents and chroniclers of licentious and perverted behavior. In particular, given the Roman habit of conflating non-standard sexual practices, they were generally accused of being both homosexuals and adulterers with women. This epitomizes a consistent Roman feeling that all forms of sexuality outside the standard marriage bond were equivalent to each other as a threat to civilized morality and the social values of the state.

Much of the information about the sexual behavior of the emperors comes from the Roman writers Suetonious and Tacitus. It is hard to be sure how far these are a factual account and how much they are political propaganda or written for titillation. There is sometimes a striking repetitiveness about the acts and tastes ascribed to successive emperors, as if there were a folk tradition in which they were necessarily portrayed as debauched. Significantly, the most intense levels of depravity are generally linked to the most uncontrolled exercise of political power, as with Tiberius, Nero and Caligula. By contrast, Claudius (10 B.C.–54 A.D.), who did not run a terrorist state, is portrayed as sexually weak and looking on helplessly at the debauchery going on around him. The most he was apparently able to do was to watch visitors to the palace being groped. Other weak emperors are similarly reported as being unable to perform sexually. Very often they are portrayed as impotent voyeurs, as passive homosexuals, or as the victims of other men's adulteries.

Julius Caesar (100–44 B.C.), in effect the first emperor, was notorious for his polymorphous sexual appetite and was called "every woman's husband and every man's wife". His affairs with numerous married women were a source of great pride among his soldiers, who used to sing while marching, "Citizens, guard your wives: here comes the bald lecher!" Nevertheless, the orator and political commentator Cicero remarked that he had not expected Julius Caesar to become such a powerful political figure because he had often observed him scratch his bald head with one finger. This was supposedly an effeminate or *mollis* (soft) gesture.

The Theater

With his father dead and his mother in exile, Nero had been brought up largely by a dancer and a hairdresser and was fascinated all his life by the theater. Actors were regarded in Rome with suspicion, both as effeminate and sexually depraved, and under the emperors as potentially outspoken critics of the regime from the safety of the stage in front of a large audience. Indeed, they were generally the only people outside the governing class who were in a position to make powerful public political statements. Members of the ruling class often expressed anxiety about the similarities between their own profession as statesmen and orators, and that of the actor. Playwrights closely sensed the mood of their audience and audiences frequently responded with the open expression of disapproval of an emperor. One actor, while uttering the lines "Goodbye Daddy, goodbye Mommy!", mimed the gestures of swimming and drinking as an oblique reference to the ways in which Nero had his mother and stepfather murdered. Caligula had a playwright publicly burned in the middle of the amphitheater for writing one line which had a critical double meaning. This silencing of opposition within the context of public display reappears in another incident in which a Roman knight loudly protested his innocence as he was being thrown to the wild animals. Caligula had his tongue cut out to silence him before returning him to the arena to be mauled.

Dwarf in the Act of Sodomy, second cent. A.D. Pavement mosaic. This mosaic is probably depicting part of a sex-show in which a dwarf sodomizes another performer. While they were ambivalent about serious drama, the emperors were extremely fond of more licentious, circus-like forms of theater.

Portrait of Augustus, 31–14 B.C. Marble, 42 cm high, Museo Capitolino, Rome. When Scribonia, Augustus's wife, began to complain about one of his mistresses, he divorced her on the grounds of "moral perversity".

Julius Caesar's successor Augustus (63 B.C.–14 A.D.), who converted the Republic into an Empire, launched a far-reaching moral crusade that brought the intrusion of state power into the bedroom. However, in his youth he too had been a famous adulterer. His enemies pointed out the inconsistency between his past conduct and his new policies. But his friends added that he had seduced men's wives, not because he was sexually uncontrolled, but as a way of learning their husbands' political secrets. As a young man, Augustus had written obscene verses as a form of political invective against opponents, as was the custom, but these opponents had not dared to respond in kind because they already understood the power he would later have to destroy them. Julia, the only child of Augustus, slept around freely with numerous men. Many jokes were in circulation which used her to satirize Augustus's moral program. When someone expressed amazement that such a promiscuous woman gave birth to children who resembled her husband, she supposedly replied, "It's because I never take on a passenger unless the ship is fully loaded." Julia's misdemeanors were so flagrant and so openly subversive of her father's policies that the exasperated Augustus was obliged to send her into exile. Whereas Augustus was a calculating and self-controlled person, it is possible to see Julia as only the first of many in the imperial family unable to handle the immense power which came with empire.

The exercise of unbounded power made some emperors legendary for their sexual depravity. Tiberius (42 B.C.–37 A.D.) had a villa on the island of Capri where he entertained himself with shoals of swimming naked boys and a specialized troupe of sexual acrobats. Depravity was often combined with sadism. Perhaps the most intemperate sadist among the emperors was Caligula (13–41 A.D.). When kissing a woman's neck he would say, "This lovely neck will be chopped off whenever I say so." Of one woman he would say that he would like to have her tortured to make her reveal herself, so that he could see why he loved her so much. Once at a banquet he burst into fits of laughter at the thought that he could have his consuls' throats slit with one nod of his head. On another occasion he asked an actor which he thought was the greater, himself or the god Jupiter. When the actor hesitated for an instant, Caligula had him cut to pieces with a whiplash. As the actor screamed for mercy, Caligula praised the musical quality of his voice.

Nero (37–68 A.D.) believed that no one was chaste or pure and that anyone who appeared to be so was just pretending. It seems that in his youth he had been tormented by the moral dilemmas of power: the first time he ever had to sign a death warrant he remarked "I'm sorry I ever learned to write." Later, however, he seems to have sought out the most extreme taboos in order to break them, as when he was alleged to have had sexual intercourse with the Vestal Virgins. He was said to have "married" a male favorite, to have kept brothels of boys and of married women, to have sexually abused prisoners tied to stakes, and to have killed partners, including his stepbrother, after committing every conceivable sexual act with them.

Roman Emperors **233**

Contemporary portrait of Nero. Marble. Some contemporaries believed that the greatest corrupting influence on Nero was Ofonius Tigellinus, the emperor's chief adviser from 62–68 AD. Tigellinus was prefect of the Praetorian guard, and actively encouraged Nero to be violent and debauched.

Otho (32–69 A.D.), who became emperor after Nero, made the mistake of praising before the emperor a woman he admired, named Poppaea. Nero's desire for Poppaea was inflamed and she herself saw an opportunity to become empress. She played cleverly on Nero's weaknesses to such an extent that Nero banished Otho. Poppaea taunted Nero by calling him a mamma's boy and Nero had his own mother Agrippina murdered. He had been very attached to his mother and after her death he was haunted by the sound of mourners wailing around her grave. The conduct of emperors frequently stirred up the hostility of the populace. Nero's wife Octavia was popular with the public and news of her return from a spell of banishment induced a crowd to crown her statues with garlands and knock down the statues of her rival Poppaea. Again under Poppaea's influence, Nero had his wife murdered. For all the emperors, the public opprobrium of the Roman populace was difficult to face down. Caligula is recorded as saying that he wished the Roman people had one single head so that he could slice it off and silence them more easily.

Hadrian and Antinous

The emperor Hadrian (76–138 A.D.) was in love with a beautiful youth called Antinous. Antinous was one of many boys with whom Hadrian was associated but the relationship seems to have been one of exceptional devotion. Antinous died under mysterious circumstances while they were traveling together in Egypt. There were sinister rumors that the emperor had been experimenting with black magic and that Antinous had been offered as a sacrifice to prolong Hadrian's life. This echoes a long-standing Greek notion of erotic devotion in which a lover offers him or herself up to the gods of death as a substitute for someone else. The emperor mourned him "as a woman mourns", and established a city on the site which he called Antinopolis. He had statues of Antinous set up in every city of the empire and identified his soul with a new star that appeared in the sky. Local cults in Egypt identified Antinous with the Egyptian god Osiris. Like Osiris,

Sir Lawrence Alma-Tadema, *The Roses of Heliogabalus*, 1888. Oil on canvas, 132 x 214 cm, private collection. Heliogabalus's homosexual orgies outraged the sensibilities of the Roman people. He constantly sought new ways of keeping himself amused. One of the emperor's more famous practical jokes was to release tons of rose petals from a canopy above his guests, gradually suffocating them beneath the weight.

the priests of the cult ritually reenacted Antinous's death and resurrection every year.

Heliogabalus

Heliogabalus (204–222 A.D.) was a boy emperor from Syria who introduced his own Middle Eastern cult to Rome. He was a youth of exceptional beauty who dressed only in the finest silk, despising the wool of Greek and Roman clothing. Predictably, Romans linked his oriental manners to sexual depravity, referring frequently to his effeminate way of walking and dancing, to his excessive use of make-up, and to the phallic nature of his cult. Heliogabalus seems to have thought of himself as the sun

Heliogabalus on his Chariot Drawn by Women. Cut gemstone, Bibliothèque Nationale, Paris. Unlike shown here in his sexual relationships, Heliogabalus often took the female role.

god. He built a huge temple to the sun and every morning at sunrise would conduct elaborate ritual dances with mass sacrifices of sheep and oxen. When impersonating the god he married a Vestal Virgin, an act that outraged Roman opinion.

Heliogabalus had been put on the throne by the army for political reasons, but his mincing oriental style did not long please the gruff Italian soldiers. Military and palace intrigues conspired to replace him by his much more sober twelve-year-old cousin Alexianus. After Heliogabalus attempted to assassinate Alexianus, the soldiers rebelled and killed him along with his mother, who was thought to be his controller.

Love Poetry

Roman love poetry looked toward earlier Greek models but developed them in a fresh and distinctive way. Imagery from the Greek world is often used to create a romantic and voluptuous atmosphere, with boys and women given pseudonyms that are taken from the shepherds and shepherdesses of early, pastoral songs and odes. These figures were sometimes imaginary but often served as a thin disguise for a real-life lover, possibly the wife of another man. Even when it is conventional or fantasized, Roman love poetry claims to be intensely autobiographical, and even self-analytical.

From having been a lower-class craft, by the first century B.C. writing poetry had become a respectable activity for well-born men, and there is increasing ambiguity about the social status of the people to whom the poems are addressed. The women referred to by poets such as Catullus (84–54 B.C.) and Propertius (55/43–after 16 B.C.) under pseudonyms such as Lesbia and Cynthia were respectable, even married women rather than courtesans. Part of the thrill conveyed by the poets lies in the illicit nature of the affairs they describe, as when they play footsie under the table with women who pretend to be completely uninterested.

The work of some of these poets forms a cycle which takes the reader from the earliest stages of love, as when Propertius opens with the line, "It was with her eyes that Cynthia first captivated me and made me helpless," through tiffs, periods of despair and reconciliations. Catullus writes to Lesbia (poem 6): "Let us live, my Lesbia, and let us love … / Suns may set and rise again, / But for us, when our brief light sets just once, / There is a perpetual night to be slept through. / Give me a thousand kisses, then a hundred, / Then a second thousand, then a second hundred, / Then yet another thousand, then a hundred. / Then when we have totted up many thousands. / Let's scramble the figures so that we won't know, / And no ill-wisher can envy us / By finding out the total of our kisses." Two poems later (poem 8) he is writing: "Poor Catullus, stop being a fool, / And accept that what is gone is gone. Suns shone brightly for you once … / Now she does not want you, so you can also play hard to get … / You'll be sorry, Lesbia, when nobody asks you out. / What life remains for you, you wretch? / Who will seek you out? Who will find you attractive?… / Whom will you kiss? Whose lips will you bite? / But you, Catullus, stand firm and don't give in."

Love poems are addressed equally to women and boys, but always from the perspective of the mature, freeborn male. The social status of boys is rarely specified, but they were generally slaves because the desire for freeborn boys was not acceptable and for much of the time was illegal. This makes the young male figures in the poems romanticized, idealized sex objects. As in Greek love poetry, boys are often portrayed as more desirable than women for various reasons, including the fact that they will swiftly outgrow their desirability. Whereas unresponsive women are chided with threats of old age, boys are chided with mentions of their impending hairiness. Thus a boy's period of desirability is much briefer.

Simon Vouet, *The Death of Didon*, c. 1642. Oil on canvas, 215 x 170 cm, Musée Municipal, Dôle, France. It seems a paradox, but in epic poetry like the *Aenais*, which concerns huge historical events and political destinies, the erotic feelings of women are explored more fully than in love poems, as part of a well-developed plot. But here too women's desire ultimately becomes subordinated to male destiny. Dido, the Queen of Carthage, succeeds in detaining Aeneus in her bed until the gods command him to continue on his mission. The torment of "unhappy Dido" is described at length before she kills herself. As Aeneus says when he later visits her ghost in the underworld, "It was against my will that I left your shore."

Workshop of Perennius, Roman terra-cotta vase (detail), late first cent. B.C. Clay, Museum Arezzo. Perrenius produced remarkably tender and realistic erotic art, even by the standards of the time.

The Art of Love

Ovid's *Ars Amatoria* published in 1 B.C. contains two books giving sometimes explicit sexual instruction to men. A third book was added, Ovid mischievously says, in response to his women readers who asked for something similar for themselves. Ovid knew that he was heading for a dangerous confrontation with Augustus' new legislation on adultery and emphasized that his poems were about courtesans, not married women. He also included flattering references to Augustus himself. However, the context of these remarks was so salacious that Augustus inevitably linked this work to the adulteries of his own daughter and granddaughter. He exiled Ovid to a remote and desolate marsh at the mouth of the river Danube. The sophisticated and witty Ovid was miserable in this barbaric backwater and so sent back to Rome a stream of new verses designed to secure his pardon and return. However, he never did return and Roman love poetry never recovered from his banishment. This was partly because of Augustus's regime and the changed emotional tone of imperial society after him, but also because Ovid's own wit was so ironic and self-conscious that he made it difficult for any successor to treat love poetry seriously without seeming naive.

There is no insight into the boy's point of view or what may be attractive to him about the older man. With women, there is often an acknowledgement of mutual attraction. Catullus's Lesbia is clearly a match for him, and Ovid in his *Ars Amatoria* (The Art of Love, 1 B.C.) pays unusual attention to the achievement of simultaneous orgasm. However, much of the poetry makes it clear that the women are prostitutes or are at least orchestrating the situation for the physical pleasure of the man. Though many of the women in love poetry have fairly complex characters, these are revealed primarily through their actions in response to a man's advances, and in their ability to reduce their lovers to despair. Descriptions of physical beauty are conventional, focusing on a woman's sparkling eyes, small feet, or smooth white neck, breasts and thighs. In one poem, written in Greek, the poet recounts how he was asked to judge between the naked thighs of three women, who are described in voluptuous detail. He concludes, "But knowing exactly what happened to Paris when he made his judgment, I immediately crowned all three goddesses at once!" There is a striking omission of female genitalia as a place of physical beauty. By contrast, in those poems which continued to be written in Greek there are many references to the beauty of a boy's anus, which is sometimes described as a rosebud surrounded by growing dark thorns as the boy's pubic hair starts to sprout around it.

Love scene in the bedroom of an upper-class Roman house, first cent. A.D. Mosaic, Centicelle, Antikensammlung, Kunsthistorisches Museum, Vienna. In all love poetry the man is portrayed as the rugged pursuer, in contrast to girls and boys, who are delicate and fragile. Though many of the women have fairly complex characters, these are revealed primarily through their actions in response to a man's advances, and in their ability to reduce their lovers to despair.

Erotic Items and Jewelry

Many everyday objects were shaped in sexual form or decorated with sexual scenes. These were not simply erotic playthings, but were often charged with sacred power and used for ritual purposes. Vases shaped like a phallus with scrotum were widespread in the 6th century B.C. in Greece and among the Etruscans in Italy, and the phallic motif survived into Roman times. Such vases were used as containers for perfumed oil and often dedicated to gods or buried in tombs. Phallic jewelry was also common. Many Romans wore a phallus of bronze or gold as an amulet, and a phallus was often carved on a wall, either as the trade sign of a brothel, or just as a symbol of good luck. Upper-class children wore small rings with a phallus carved on them for protection on either a chain or finger. Adults wore pendants of coral or bronze, sometimes in the form of the phallus of a bear or a boar, which was presumably linked to the animal's virility and power.

In the 6th and 5th centuries B.C., erotic scenes on Greek vases were largely intended for male use in settings like the symposium. But from the 4th century onwards and into Roman times, these increasingly appeared on household objects such as water-jugs, lamps, mirrors and the handles of knives and other tools. The houses of upper- and middle-class families were decorated with frescoes showing men and women engaged in sexual intercourse. Many of these clearly represented a married couple. This shows how far sexual desire had become domesticated and brought openly into the domain of women.

Erotic jewelry. British Museum, London. This complex Roman bronze amulet is of a well-known type, incorporating three lucky symbols, the hand, phallus, and crescent.

Roman lamp handle, second cent. A.D. Terra-cotta, British Museum, London. The penis was not the only sexual organ used to ward off bad luck. Vulvas also appear in this context, albeit more rarely.

Roman knife handle. Bronze, British Museum, London. The couple is shown lying on their side, with the man penetrating the woman from the rear. This was an especially popular position on vases, medals and houseware, because it presents an extremely good view of the genitalia of both parties.

Tintinnabulum from Pompeii and Herculaneum, National Archaeological Museum, Naples. The tintinnabulum was thought to ward off evil with the tinkling of its bells, and its power could be enhanced by making it in the shape of a phallus, often with wings or legs to emphasize its beastlike ferocity.

Tintinnabulum, Herculanum, first cent. B.C. Bronze, 21 cm long, National Archaeological Museum, Naples. This humorous variant on the theme of the protective or talismanic wind-charm suggests the aggressive, unpredictable nature of the penis. It takes the form of a gladiator attacking his own penis.

When Desire
Turns to Sin

**Hieronymus Bosch, *The Garden of Earthly Delights*
(detail), c. 1500. Oil on panel, 220 x 389 cm, Museo del
Prado, Madrid.** The triptych depicts heaven and hell
on its two wings, with earth in the center. While the
left-hand wing shows the chaste Christian union of
Adam and Eve, the center panel (see detail) presents
human vices and the sensual desires of the flesh in a
moralizing, but highly imaginative, manner. Once in
hell (on the right-hand wing), the sinful souls are subject to torments without any prospect of salvation.

The Love Feast

Constantine (c. 285–337 A.D.) was the first emperor to be converted to Christianity, although his motivation has never been clear. Some say it was a political maneuver, others that he had a genuine and profound spiritual conviction. However, there is no doubt that the Christian Church had developed a large and impressive bureaucracy which was a useful adjunct to the somewhat derelict imperial administration, especially in the West. Perhaps he hoped that by encouraging the Christian Church, he could give the Roman Empire a new lease of life. Certainly in the short term he succeeded, although many historians have argued that in the long term, Christianity did as much as anything to undermine the stability of the Empire. Certainly, within 150 years, there was no Empire in the West – but there was a flourishing Church.

Where secular governments contented themselves with controlling men's behaviour, the Church wanted authority over their minds and souls. This ambition was rationalized by basing it on one of Jesus' most far-reaching moral innovations – his claim that any man who gazed lustfully on a woman had already committed adultery with her in his heart. The idea that thoughts and not just actions could be sinful was much more rigorous than anything in Jewish tradition, although of course Jesus balanced this with his central message, that of forgiveness, which was in marked contrast to other rabbinical moralists – as outlined to great effect in the parable of the Prodigal Son, and demonstrated by his reaction to Mary Magdalen and the woman caught in the act of adultery. Indeed, many of the early Christian communities were extremely tolerant. Some of them, based on the idea of a universal, non-sexual love, were called Agapetae, after the Greek word for chaste love *agape*. Unmarried men and women celebrated communion together with the so-called "love feast", a meal that preceded the Eucharist, and lived in communal houses without any impropriety, a practice that gradually earned the mistrust of Church authorities. One Agapetaean group, the Carpocratians, were said to indulge in indiscriminate sex, while Valesian men, by contrast, were accused of castrating themselves (an operation condemned in the Old Testament) to ensure their chastity and also to emphasize their common humanity with women – the Church regarding the latter goal as the greater perversion. Saint Chrysostom, bishop and patriarch of Constantinople since 398, wrote a polemical text, *Against Those Who Keep Virgins in Their Houses*, in

Voluptas, c. 1300. Stone sculpture, Minster tower, Freiburg. A woman in Christian iconography personified Voluptas, or Lust. She was depicted naked, or sometimes riding a goat or wearing its pelt. Because of its sexual stamina, and its links to the devil, the goat was one of her familiars.

which he railed: "Our fathers only knew two forms of intimacy, marriage and fornication." Now a third form had appeared: men introduced young girls into their houses and kept them there permanently, respecting their virginity. Somewhat unexpectedly, he thought this a "violent and tyrannical" pleasure. The objections men like Chrysostom and Saint Jerome had to Agapetae were based on their own conviction that women were weak, and given to temptation, and that their weakness was contagious. They particularly objected to the fact that women could be deacons in these communities, and gradually the Agapetae were broken up and dispersed. In later centuries, any groups that tried to organize themselves upon similar lines, such as the Cathars, were automatically branded as heretics.

Many of the early Christian thinkers were converts from paganism, and their writings show the strain of trying to reconcile their new convictions with their earlier lives. At the same time, in their missionary work, they had to assimilate pagan ideas so as to win over new converts. Most of the Church's views about the evils of sex derive from ancient Greek and Egyptian Gnosticism – which

taught that the body was little more than the prison of the soul – and Persian Manichaenism – which held that flesh was inherently evil. And the most corrupt flesh of all belonged to woman, who, as the Severians taught, was made entirely by the devil (as opposed to man, who was only the devil's work from the waist down).

The Eastern Orthodox Church, which split from the Latin Church in the 11th century A.D., has in many ways perpetuated attitudes towards women and sex that even Roman Catholicism abandoned centuries ago. Menstruating women are not allowed to take communion, kiss holy images or clean behind the sacred doors of the church for fear of contaminating it. Young men have to seek atonement even for spontaneous nocturnal emissions, and, in the Greek Orthodox Church, crosses are forbidden in the bedrooms of married couples, since it would be sacrilegious to have sex in their presence. However, the Orthodox Churches, like the Protestants, allow their parish clergy to marry. In addition, although some Orthodox rules concerning sex are very strict, they have been less pervasive and arguably less harmful than the

Anonymous, *The Baptism of Christ*, beginning of the 6th cent. Dome mosaic, Battistero degli Ariani, Ravenna. Some early Church paintings allow for the possibility that Christ was baptized naked.

strictures of Rome, because the Patriarch of Constantinople always tacitly accepted the authority of the Eastern Emperor, and never sought the absolute power that was coveted by generations of Western popes.

F. Morellon la Cave, Christian Nudists (Adamites) (detail), 18th cent. Engraving, private collection. Like most heretical sects, the Adamites were accused of sexual license, sodomy and other officially condemned perversions, although in fact, like modern nudists, they actually discouraged sexual thoughts of any kind at their meetings.

Baring the Flesh

The baptisteries of Ravenna contain mosaics showing Christ being baptized in the nude, and in the early days of the faith this was the common custom for adults as well as children. Pope Hippolytus, writing at the beginning of the third century, insisted that only the naked could be baptized. However, the pope's support did not extend to some sects, variously referred to as Adamites, who believed that the sinless perfection of Adam before the Fall was the result of baptism, and that, similarly cleansed, baptized Christians should also go without clothes. The first Adamites appeared in the second century and were persecuted into extinction by the 4th century, although Adamite groups reappeared after the Middle Ages in the Netherlands and Germany – one of the last was suppressed in Bohemia in 1849. In the 20th century, the Dukhobars, a Russian Christian sect most of whose members now live in Canada, pioneered the use of nudity as a form of religious and political protest.

Sin and Shame

The Jewish tradition is opposed to celibacy. In the Bible, God instructed the first people to "be fruitful and multiply" (Genesis 9:7), and procreation within marriage is regarded as a sacred duty. Yet when Jesus preached about the coming Kingdom of God, he specifically included one of the lowest and most reviled figures in Jewish society – the barren woman. On another occasion, he was asked his opinion of divorce. The rabbis believed that women who did not make good wives should be discarded, although they disagreed as to the criteria that should be applied. Some thought that adultery and infertility were the only proper reasons for divorce, while others taught that a man could put aside his wife for burning his dinner.

Jesus took a different stance: "But from the beginning of the creation, God made them male and female. For this cause shall a man leave his father and mother, and cleave to his wife. What therefore God has put together, let no man put asunder." (Matthew 19:4–6). This extraordinary, for its time, elevation of the state of marriage above the demands of procreation should have had a liberating effect, especially for Christian women. But it actually set the stage for centuries of repression. For Christ also praised celibacy, and his early interpreters, freed of the necessity to regard procreation as an absolute good, ended up despising all sex.

The man who was instrumental in this transformation was Saint Paul – though when using the word "transformation", we must remember that Paul's letters were almost certainly composed before the Gospels. Paul was born in Tarsus in Asia Minor, and grew up as a Greek-speaking Jew. As a young man he was an enthusiastic persecutor of Christians, until he was converted after seeing a vision of the risen Christ on the road to Damascus. Paul's views on sex are out of line with modern thought. Another difficulty is that our source of information, the Letters to the Corinthians, comprise largely ad hoc answers to specific questions put to Paul by the local Christians. They were a group of recent converts living in Corinth, one of the most decadent cities on earth, at a time when it was commonly believed that the world was about to end.

So on the one hand he decried the Corinthians' belief that sex was just exercise for the genitals, and told them that it was a unique form of commitment and self-revelation (a position that was conveniently ignored by generations of Churchmen, and had remarkably little influence on Christian thought). Yet he also taught that, although marriage was tolerable for the weak – because "it is better to marry than to burn with desire" (1 Corinthians 7:9) – it was always a poor second-best to celibacy, and that

Anonymous, The Creation of Eve, 12th cent. Mosaic, Cupola della Creazione, S. Marco, Venice. Eve's position as an inferior being was reinforced by the idea that she had been made from Adam's rib – therefore, not only was she subordinate to him, but was also a lower creature, having been created from corruptible flesh.

The Sin of Sodom

The Bible is vague about exactly what went on in Sodom. In Genesis 19 it is said that the Lord sent two angels to investigate its wickedness, and that they were offered hospitality by Lot, but the men of the city surrounded his house and shouted: "Where are the men who came to you tonight? Bring them out to us that we may know them" (Genesis 19:5). The word translated as "know", *yadha*, occurs nearly 1000 times in the Old Testament, but on only 15 occasions does it definitely have sexual connotations. The rest of the time it means, "to become acquainted with". It is likely that the men of Sodom were more curious than aroused. The Israelites originally used sodomy as a catchall sin that included pride, adultery and blasphemy. It still has this original, useful versatility – the anti-sodomy laws of 20th-century Virginia banned all forms of oral and anal sex, regardless of the participants' gender. Nevertheless, following Philo of Alexandria in the first century A.D., the Church began to identify sodomy more and more as a homosexual sin. By the beginning of the 4th century, baptism was denied to homosexuals. In 538 A.D., the Emperor Justinian equated sodomy with blasphemy and blamed the two sins for the existence of earthquakes, famines and pestilence. Nevertheless, from about the 6th to the 12th centuries, homosexuals were treated little more severely than heterosexuals who practiced contraception. All this changed with Saint Thomas Aquinas in the 13th century, who declared once and for all that the destruction of Sodom and Gomorrah could be blamed on homosexuality, and decided that sodomites were damned for all eternity.

Anonymous, Naked Male Couple, Marginalia from Psalter and Book of Hours in Latin and French, last quarter of the 13th cent. Northeast France, probably Arras. Parchment, Pierpont Morgan Library, New York. Erotic images, including the occasional, albeit rare, homosexual scene, can be found on the fringes of medieval sacred art – whether in book marginalia or on the corbels, bosses and misericords of ecclesiastical architecture.

"neither fornicators, nor idolaters, nor adulterers, nor effeminate, nor abusers of themselves with mankind … shall inherit the kingdom of God" (1 Corinthians 6:9). Paul's mistrust of marriage grew into outright hatred among the Church Fathers of the 4th century. Saint Jerome thought it was only tolerable because it peopled the world with virgins for him to convert. Like his near contemporary, Saint Augustine, Jerome was a man of violent passions, who often seemed to be wrestling with his own urges as much as with the issues of theology.

After Saint Paul, Augustine was perhaps the most influential Christian thinker on the subject of sex, perhaps a result of an early life that was anything but pious, and is described in exhaustive detail in his *Confessions*. Although Augustine believed that even infants at the breast were guilty of sin, including gluttony, he relates that he was 15 years old when he became possessed by the "madness of lust", an appetite that he took every opportunity to slake among the "lawless loves" of Carthage, where he went to study. In his youth, Augustine felt himself "boiling over" in his fornications, and

Hans Baldung Grien, *Aristotle and Phyllis* (detail), 1513. Woodcut, 23.8 x 33.3 cm, Staatliche Museen, Preussischer Kulturbesitz, Berlin. The Greek philosopher Aristotle was one of the greatest influences on Christian thought. The allegorical print is intended to mock the power that the passions have over the intellect.

Confession

The confessional was one of the most powerful, and most widely abused, methods of social control ever devised. Initially, Christians had to make only one public confession, which lasted a lifetime. By the 8th century, however, the Church was already insisting on regular acts of contrition. Chrodegang, the bishop of Metz, ordered monks to confess every Saturday, and laymen to confess twice a year, at Lent and in the autumn. At this time it was possible for laymen to hear each others' confessions – although they could not grant absolution – but in 1215 the Lateran Council made it compulsory to confess to priests, who by this time were no longer content to listen passively to their flock: from about the 10th century they had been encouraged to interrogate penitents aggressively, often accusing them of specific sins in order to get a reaction. The power to grant or withhold absolution was regularly used to extort sexual favors. Given its antipathy to sex, the Church was astonishingly lenient with priests who abused their power in this way. For example, in 1535 a cleric called Valdemar was tried in Toledo for seducing two women and refusing absolution to another unless she slept with him, and was fined just two ducats and ordered to spend 30 days in seclusion in his church, after which he was free to take up his duties again. Some dioceses even came to the conclusion that it was perfectly innocent to give a woman a love-letter in the confessional, so long as it was not intended for her to read it immediately and give her answer before being absolved. Until 1714, men who confessed to fornication had to name their partner, affording the priest even more opportunities for sexual blackmail.

Tree of Vices, 12th cent. Studienbibliothek, Salzburg.
In medieval iconography the Tree of Vices grows from Superbia (pride) and branches out into the principal vices, each of which has seven subsidiary leaves. Luxuria, or sensual pleasures, at its crown, has more forms and more dangers than any other vice.

famously prayed to God: "Give me chastity and continence, but not yet." When he was 17 he took a long-term mistress, whom he loved for many years, and with whom he had at least one child. Yet even this apparently wholesome relationship was later described by Augustine as a defilement. Despite his appetites, Augustine was drawn to the philosophy of Manichaeanism, which held that flesh was intrinsically evil. This attitude was to infect all his later writings, even after he had apparently renounced and refuted the Manichaeans' teachings, and been converted to Christianity.

What horrified Augustine most about sex was the loss of control. In his *Confessions*, he wrote: "It is the keenest of all pleasures on the level of sensation … at the crisis of excitement, it practically paralyses the power of deliberate thought." After his conversion to Christianity, in 386 A.D., Augustine became obsessed with the question of why such a debilitating force as lust had been introduced by God into the World, and decided that in fact it had not.

There was no lust in Eden, and Adam and Eve had sex only occasionally, in an uninvolved way, with Adam ejaculating from a limp penis by pure force of will and with the sole object of procreation. Lust was introduced into creation by Eve, when she ate the apple from the tree of knowledge, and this original sin stained every subsequent generation at birth, even those born within wedlock. Moreover, because death also entered the world with the Fall, lust was responsible for mortality.

From the 4th century, the Church became ever more involved with regulating marriage, even though it fundamentally disapproved, and finally declared it a sacrament in the 12th century. It strictly regulated when marital intercourse was allowed, forbidding it on Thursdays in memory of Christ's arrest, Fridays (for his death), Saturdays (in honor of the Virgin Mary), Sundays (to mark the resurrection) and Mondays (to remember the departed), as well as the Tuesdays and Wednesdays before communion and the 40 days before Easter, Pentecost and Christmas. But even as it gained more power over lay marriage, the Church was struggling to control the sex lives of its priests. Pope Siricius had tried to stop his deacons sleeping with their wives in 386 A.D., but without success. By the time of Gregory VII, in the 11th century, the papacy was powerful enough to issue an edict banning clerical marriage and establishing the principal of clerical celibacy (although the German priesthood announced

that they would rather give up their lives than their wives). Principle only rarely translated into practice, however, and many priests continued to keep concubines. When the Bishop of Liège was deposed in 1274 he had fathered 65 illegitimate children, and in some villages the lay authorities petitioned the Church to allow local priests to retain their mistresses, as this kept them away from the townspeoples' wives. The Reformation of the 16th century attacked the whole idea of clerical celibacy and monastic vows of chastity, which Martin Luther insisted were only for "peculiar" individuals. Although Luther retained some Catholic guilt and ambivalence about marriage, calling it a "hospital for the sick", John Calvin wholeheartedly praised copulation as a state that was honorable and holy. Protestant Christianity became increasingly pragmatic about sex, concentrating its fire on practices that seemed to threaten marriage, rather than on marriage itself. So even the puritans believed that a man and his wife should have a healthy sex life, while continuing to persecute adulterers, homosexuals and masturbators. Nevertheless, procreation remained the true goal of sex – the Anglican Church did not officially approve contraception until the 1960 Lambeth Conference.

Giotto, *The Last Judgment* (detail), 1303–1310. Fresco, 1000 x 840 cm, Scrovegni Chapel, Padova. Scenes of the Last Judgment frequently depict the sufferings of those damned for their sexual peccadillos. In Giotto's *Last Judgment*, the damned can even be seen suspended by their genitals.

Ascetics

The ascetic spirit can be summed up in a story told by the 13th-century Cardinal Jacques de Vitry, about a monk who loved a woman so much that his longing for her remained even after she died. As a cure, he dug up her corpse and "filled his nostrils with that putrefying flesh, and the stench of it cured him henceforth of all concupiscence". The early ascetics were trying to overcome their sexual appetites by distracting their minds and bodies with privations. Despite the trials they put themselves through – solitude, starvation, prolonged meditation, self-administered beatings and wearing rough hair-shirts or going without any clothing at all in harsh environments – they were only ever partially successful. The 4th-century Church Father, Saint Jerome, admitted that as he sat in the desert: "Sackcloth disfigured my misshapen limbs, and my skin had become as black as an Ethiopian's … Yet I, who from fear of Hell had consigned myself to that prison where I had no other companions than scorpions and wild beasts, fancied myself among bevies of dancing maidens … my mind was burning with the cravings of desire, and the fires of lust flared up from my flesh that was as that of a corpse."

Because of their harshness and isolation, the deserts of Palestine and Egypt had always been popular with Jewish and pagan ascetics.

Dominique Louis Papety, *The Temptation of Saint Hilarion*, 1843 /44. Oil on mahogany panel, 47 x 59.7 cm, Wallace Collection, London. Hilarion was a 4th-century mystic who founded the Christian monastic tradition in Palestine. Like other hermitic desert dwellers, such as Jerome and Anthony, he fantasized that demons appeared to him, tempting him with the promise of food, drink, and sex.

Sebastiano del Piombo, *The Martyrdom of Saint Agatha* (detail), 1520. Oil on panel, 13.1 x 17.5 cm, Galleria Palatina, Florence. The Christian appetite for overcoming sexual urges by inflicting pain also manifested itself in the huge number of virgin martyrs celebrated by the Church, whose sufferings in defense of their purity were often described and depicted with sadomasochistic relish.

Like-minded Christians first began to migrate up the Nile valley in 270 A.D., and their numbers were swelled by the persecutions of Diocletian in 303. Although Saint Jerome and the other desert hermits were ostensibly trying to free themselves from lustful thoughts, it is easy to see that their austerities often drove them into a state of erotic hallucination. The same is true for later mystics, such as Christina Ebner (1277–1356) who spent two years torturing herself – by cutting out a cross of skin over her heart, for example, and then ripping it off – before experiencing a series of visions in which she felt Jesus embracing her, and imagined that she had borne Him a child. There is a long list of canonized nuns who behaved in a similar way, such as Saint Mary Magdalene dei Pazzi, who vowed herself to chastity at the age of four, and had a fondness for rolling in thorns and having herself tied to a post to be insulted. When she was put in charge of the novices at her convent, she had one of them stand on her

mouth to whip her. She was canonized in 1668. Some men undertook the ultimate self-mortification in an effort to overcome their desire, and had themselves castrated. Origen of Alexandria was one of the most powerful and original thinkers in early Christianity, but was never canonized because of the Old Testament injunctions against men with injured testicles. It is possible that when he castrated himself in 206 A.D., at the age of 20, he was responding to a slur that he had slept with his female students. There are, however, other explanations. Origen's philosophy held that the body was only the "waxen imprint" of the soul, which was, or should be, constantly in the process of evolving closer to God. Therefore, as the soul developed, physical attributes, including sexuality, should become fluid and indeterminate. Origen, unlike other ascetics, may not have been trying to conquer his desire at all – he may have made himself neuter as a sign of his soul's advancement. In 364 A.D. the Council of Nicea

The Skoptsys

In 18th-century Russia, a peasant called Kondrati Selivanov announced that salvation was only possible by suppressing all sexuality, and that to prove his point he would go through a "baptism of fire" and have himself castrated. His action prompted a sense of awe among the common people, and he attracted many followers, although the Russian Orthodox Church thought him mad. The admiration of Czar Alexander meant that Selivanov and his group – the Skoptsys, or castrated ones – were at least temporarily safe from persecution. Skoptsy men were generally allowed to father some children before undergoing their own baptism of fire, while the women often cut off their own breasts or nipples as a symbol of their own commitment. The Skoptsys survived into the 20th century – it was estimated that there were 2000 in the Soviet Union in 1929, although they were soon decimated by Stalinist purges, and the last documented castration occurred in 1951.

confirmed that self-castration was a sin, but some in the Church continued to regard it as the only conclusive way to achieve continence. The so-called pierced chair of the Vatican was designed to ensure that no eunuch ever became pope, by giving cardinals an opportunity to see the papal testicles. However, a symbolic form of self-castration (which was also popular in ancient Rome) survives in the tonsures of monks. As the agonies people would put themselves through to attain the holy life became ever more imaginative and extreme, some ascetics came to regard themselves as "athletes for God", competing among themselves in the austerities they could endure, or the temptations they could resist. One popular strategy was to sleep with beautiful women, but avoid touching them by an effort of will. In the 9th century, Saint Brendan reproached his colleague, the Irish monk Saint Swithin, for sleeping with two beautiful virgins. Saint Swithin replied that he did so in perfect innocence, and challenged Brendan to do the same. Although Brendan could resist the temptation, he found that he was unable to get to sleep all night.

A number of heretical sects, such as the Albigensians, or Cathars, also encouraged men and women to sleep together chastely. The Cathars – the "pure ones" – believed that the spirit was trapped in the body, and that creating more bodies by procreation was therefore an evil act that only increased the power of Satan. Animal husbandry was to be avoided for the same reason. A fully-initiated Cathar was not only expected to abstain from sex with his or her spouse, but to avoid eggs, meat, milk and cheese as these were all, directly or indirectly, the products of reproduction. Because Cathar men and women slept together but had no children, the Church accused them of sodomy – a charge habitually laid against any and all heretics, including witches and the Knights Templar. The Cathars became enormously popular, especially in southern France, and were seen as such a threat to the authority of the Church that they were mercilessly wiped out during the Albigensian crusades declared against them by Pope Innocent III.

Penitents and Flagellants

The first known penitential books appeared in Wales in the 6th century, and were imported by missionaries to the European mainland. They were lists of sins and their appropriate penances, which gradually became more complicated and punitive throughout the Middle Ages. They were not under the central control of the Vatican, and varied from place to place. The most common penance was a period of fasting – avoiding all sex and self-indulgence, and taking no food or drink except for bread and water. In one penitential, which is typical of the 6th to 9th centuries, nocturnal emission calls for seven days fasting, and masturbation requires 30. Some of the most serious penances were for contraception, including the use of "poisons creating sterility" and anal intercourse, which required fasts of between three and 15 years.

In the 13th century, the Franciscans began to extol self-flagellation as a form of penance. By 1259, a mania for this practice had developed in northern Italy. Penitents – some as young as five years old – would form into groups and march through the streets, whipping themselves. Magistrates expelled the flagellants from their cities, and eventually the movement died down, only to flare up again whenever some natural disaster spread panic through the populace. During the plague, the Black Death,

in the mid-14th century, the flagellant movement spread to Austria, Germany, Switzerland, the Netherlands and England, with thousands sometimes taking part in a single procession. Their goal was to atone with their bodies for the sins of the world, but when flagellant groups started calling themselves the Brethren of the Cross, and claiming that the ministrations of the Church were not necessary to attain salvation, they were declared heretical in 1349 and driven underground.

Some ascetic groups, although frowned on by Church authorities, have shown more longevity. In 15th-century Spain and Portugal, encouraged by the apocalyptic preaching of Saint Vincent Ferrer, lay brotherhoods began to form, which were dedicated to the practice of self-flagellation. Despite the hostility of the Church, which repeatedly tried to ban them, these brotherhoods flourished and held long public processions and whippings, especially during Holy Week. The tradition was taken to America, where it still survives in New Mexico and southern Colorado, among the Penitentes (*La Fraternidad Piadosa de Nuestro Padre Jesus Nazareno*). The Penitentes not only whip themselves, but also carry out a range of other austerities, such as wearing loincloths lined with pieces of cactus, and reenacting the crucifixion by having their wrists tied to a wooden cross.

Opposite: *Procession of Penitential Flagellants*, illustration from a Book of Hours, 1408. Parchment, Bodleian Library, Oxford. The Italian mania for flagellation lasted barely two years – it was banned by the Church in 1261, although not actually declared heretical. However, members of the movement fled to Germany, where they attracted a devoted following.

Pedro Berruguete, *Auto-da-fé*, c. 1495. Oil on canvas, 154 x 92 cm, Museo del Prado, Madrid. The painting depicts the execution of two Cathars. By emphasizing the power of the devil in the material world, the Cathars unwittingly made it easy for the Church to compare them to Satan-worshipping witches, and dispose of them in the same way.

Faces of the Virgin

For the Church Fathers after Saint Augustine, all women were tainted with the sin of Eve. In the words of Tertullian: "Do you not realize that Eve is you? The curse God pronounced on your sex still weighs on the world … The image of God, the man Adam, you broke him … You deserved death, and it was the son of God who had to die." It was Saint Paul, in his letters to the Corinthians, who first suggested that Jesus was the new Adam, the being through whom everything was reborn in a pure state. But Saint Irenaeus and Saint Justin Martyr extended this idea, independently, in the second century to include Mary. In their formulation, just as a virgin, Eve, had conceived sin and become the fleshly mother of all subsequent generations, another virgin, Mary, had redeemed sin and become the spiritual mother of all humanity.

If sex was a sin, and celibacy an ambition and a state of grace, then the noblest natural condition was virginity. The early preachers were eloquent in their praise of virgins. Saint Jerome in the 4th century called them, "roses from the thorns, the gold from the earth, and the pearl from the shell". Especially skilled at converting the young, wealthy maidens of Rome, the charismatic saint even managed to imbue the state of chastity with a special, intensified eroticism, by describing virgins as the brides of Christ. Writing to Eustochium, one of his young female converts, he advised, "Let the seclusion of your own chamber ever guard you; ever let the Bridegroom sport within you. If you pray, you are speaking to your Spouse … When sleep falls on you, He will come behind the wall and will put His hand through the hole in the door and touch your belly. And you will awake and rise up and cry, 'I am sick with love'."
It followed that, if virgins were the brides of Christ, any man who slept with one was not merely fornicating, but committing the much more serious sin of adultery. A hundred years before Jerome, Saint Cyprian had already formulated this bizarre doctrine: "If a husband come and see his wife lying with another man, is he not indignant and maddened? … How indignant and angered then must Christ our Lord and Judge be, when He sees a virgin, conse-

Anonymous, Christ and the Virgin, 12th cent. Mosaic in the apse, Santa Maria in Trastevere, Rome. Christ and the Virgin Mary portrayed as husband and wife. Mary was wed to Christ not only because she was a virgin, but also because she represented the body of the Church.

The Black Madonna of Montserrat

Black Madonnas are considered to be especially exotic and magical. They can be found all over Europe, most famously at Chartres and Orléans in France, in the Santa Maria Maggiore in Rome and at Montserrat, the site of one of the oldest cults of the Virgin Mary. There are many explanations for their existence. Some say they represent not only Mary but the beloved in the Song of Solomon, who declares: "I am black, but comely, O ye daughters of Jerusalem" (Song of Solomon 1:5). The figure in the Song is often taken to be the Queen of Sheba, who had magical and prophetic gifts. More simply, it has been suggested that their blackness is a patina from the smoke of votive candles: over the centuries, the clothes were cleaned, but the faces left untouched out of reverence.

The Madonna of Montserrat was supposedly carved by Saint Luke and brought to Spain by Saint Peter. Shepherds rediscovered it after the Moors had been driven from the region in 888 A.D. The site is now a favorite shrine for newly married couples, and draws so many that in the 20th century the monks had to build a large new hospice to accommodate them. The Madonna of Montserrat is supplicated on matters of sex, pregnancy and childbirth. One of the more famous miracles attributed to it was the barren woman who gave birth to a lump of dead meat, but prayed to the Black Madonna until it turned into a baby boy.

Anonymous, Black Madonna, late 12th cent. Silver, Monasterio de Montserrat, Barcelona. Despite all the legends that surround its manufacture, the Madonna of Montserrat is probably, in fact, a statue of Byzantine origin.

Fra Angelico, *The Annunciation* (panel painting, central section of an altarpiece), c. 1430/32. Oil on panel, 194 x 194 cm, Museo del Prado, Madrid. Fra Angelico's painting also contains a scene of the expulsion from Eden, emphasizing Mary's status as the second Eve. Christian artists, poets and musicians made great play of the fact that angel Gabriel's greeting to Mary – "Ave" – was the reverse of Eve (or Eva), and marked the moment when her curse was also reversed.

crated to His holiness, lying with a man ... She who has been guilty of this crime is an adulteress, not against a husband, but against Christ." On the other hand, by remaining pure, women could to some extent avoid the stigma of original sin – and just as importantly, they could avoid passing that stigma on to yet another generation. For the early Church Fathers, it was obvious that Christ himself was free of sin, and it seemed that this could only be true if his mother, Mary, was a virgin, a claim they were also anxious to make for more pragmatic reasons.

The first Christians were taunted with rumors about Mary, which they were desperate to refute. Among the Jews it was said that she had conceived Jesus when she was seduced by a Roman centurion called Pantherus, and in Alexandria the story went that she had formed an incestuous union with her brother. In addition, so many pagan gods and heroes – from Bacchus to Alexander the Great – claimed virgin birth that it almost seemed a job requirement for any divine being. Jesus' credentials as a holy leader would be seriously damaged by a normal birth. Ironically, in one of the earlier texts of the New Testament – a letter to the Galatians, written in about 57 A.D. – Saint Paul was keen to stress just the opposite: that Jesus was fundamentally human, and "made of a woman" (Galatians 4:4). The New Testament evidence for Mary's virginity occurs in the Gospels of Luke and Matthew, but not in the narrative of Jesus' teachings, so the source is questionable. Matthew says only that Mary was "found with child by the Holy Ghost" (Matthew 1:18) and that an angel appeared to reassure Joseph of this, but he does link the birth to an Old Testament prophecy of Isaiah: "Behold a virgin shall be with child and shall bring forth a son." (Isaiah 7:14). However, Matthew was using a Greek translation of the text, in which the Hebrew *almah* (meaning only a girl of marriageable age) had been translated as *parthenos* (which implies a physically intact virgin). Luke describes the Annunciation more thoroughly, as when the angel Gabriel appears to Mary to tell her that she will have a son, to which she replies: "How shall this be, seeing I know not a man" (Luke 1:34).

Mary and Child, illustration from *Hours of the Virgin (Hours of Cecili Gonzaga),* 1470. Pierpont Morgan Library, New York. Not all images of Mary and Christ were suffused with awe. Some were irreverent in a way that, even today, would be surprising. In this Italian Book of Hours the baby Jesus appears to have an erection, which, on closer inspection, proves to be the Virgin's pointing finger.

But there are also difficulties in this gospel. In Luke 2:48 Mary refers to Joseph as Jesus' father, and when Jesus says he must be about his real Father's work, neither Mary nor Joseph understand what he is talking about. The generally held belief that Mary remained a virgin (miraculously intact) after the birth of Christ is supported by even less biblical evidence (in fact, despite its popularity, the Vatican Council of 1964 refused to con-firm it as an article of faith). Indeed, there are numerous references to Jesus' brothers, although the Church argued that these were either children of Joseph from a prior marriage, or merely cousins and other close relatives.

Nevertheless, the cult of Mary continued to grow. The first prayer addressed specifically to her appeared at the end of the 4th century, and around this time the Western Church decided that she was incapable of sin (the Eastern Church continued to hold her guilty of several venial sins such as vanity). Saint Augustine declared that she was even free of

original sin, but he never actually said that she had been conceived without sexual intercourse. There is no biblical evidence for the Immaculate Conception of Mary, and the first suggestion that the Virgin herself was the product of a virgin birth is probably found in the apocryphal Book of James, written in the second century. Nevertheless, this was the view that came to prevail in the Catholic Church, although the Immaculate Conception of Mary did not become official doctrine until 1854, when Pius IX decreed it in a papal bull.

As Mary became ever more purified in the eyes of the Church, she seemed to become an object of ever-greater erotic fantasy in the minds of her dedicated followers. In the Middle Ages she inspired the love songs of the troubadours and the feverish dreams of the love mystics. Plays and poems tell of Mary marrying her votaries – who would symbolically slip a ring onto one of her statues – and damning them to hell when they were unfaithful to her by marrying flesh-and-blood women. At the same time she was said to protect adulter-

ous women from discovery by taking their place in the marriage bed. The healing miracles attributed to the Virgin also acquired a sexual frisson. One of the first monastic compilations of such miracles describes a monk afflicted with an ulcerous and rotting mouth who was left for dead by his colleagues. After he called out to Mary in the words of Saint Luke's gospel, "Blessed is the womb that bare thee and the paps which thou didst suck" (Luke 11:27) she appeared and brought about a cure by sprinkling him with milk from her breast. By the end of the 12th century, when this story was retold by the monk and composer Gautier de Coincy (1177–1236) in his composition *Les Miracles de Notre-Dame*, it had become extremely sensual: "With much sweetness and much delight, from her sweet bosom she drew forth her breast, that is so sweet, so soft, so beautiful, and placed it in his mouth, and gently touched him all about and sprinkled him with her sweet milk." The milk of Mary in fact became such a powerful symbol of healing – both physical and spiritual – that phials of it appeared as relics all over Europe.

Virgin Healing a Sick Man with Her Milk, illustration from a Queen Mary Psalter, early 14th cent. 17 x 28 cm, British Museum, London. The Virgin is healing a monk of his mouth ulcers by squeezing milk from her breast.

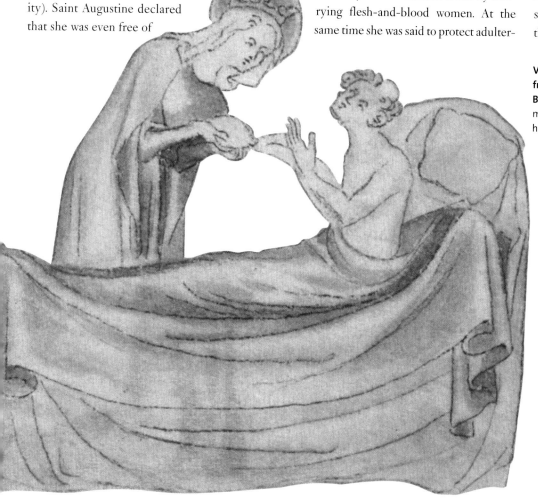

Love Mystics

The greatest self-advertising triumph of medieval Christianity was the way in which it described the chaste life in such blatantly erotic language. From about the 12th century, the writings of the Church's greatest visionaries are colored, to a greater or lesser extent, by nuptial mysticism – the idea that the soul of the believer is the bride of Jesus, and can unite with Him in a state of overwhelming ecstasy. This tradition, also called love mysticism or bridal mysticism, can also be detected in the writings of comparatively sober figures such as Julian of Norwich in the 15th century and Thomas a Kempis in the 16th.

The common thread that links many of the love mystics, from Saint Bernard of Clairvaux, who died in 1153, to Saint John of the Cross in the 16th century, is their obsession with the Old Testament Song of Songs, which they interpreted as a dialogue between Jesus and the Church, or Jesus and the individual soul (Saint John, who was put to death by the Church after he was accused of seducing nuns, had the Song read to him in the final hours before his execution). Through his many sermons on the Song of Songs, Bernard evolved a complex erotic mysticism, in which he preached that "if anyone once receives the spiritual kiss of Christ's mouth he seeks eagerly to have it again and

Filippino Lippi, *The Vision of Saint Bernard* (detail), 1486. Fresco, Badia church, Florence. Legend has it that Saint Bernard was reciting an Ave at the church of Saint Vorles in Châtillon-sur-Seine and when he reached the words, "Show thyself a mother," the statue of the virgin let three drops of milk fall from her breast onto his lips.

Alchemy

At the same time as the love mystics were striving to unite their souls in passion with the Godhead, another esoteric group was attempting to achieve its own mystical marriage between disparate elements. The alchemists were trying to fuse substances with very different properties – such as mercury and sulfur – to create the philosopher's stone, an object capable of transforming base matter into gold. In a number of written accounts of their experiments, however, it is clear that the philosopher's stone is only the symbol of a sense of exaltation – and divine power – that the alchemists were trying to create within themselves, by combining the body with the spirit to make a new, purer substance.

The 20th-century psychoanalyst Carl Gustav Jung was fascinated by alchemy, and saw its procedures as metaphors for integrating and harmonizing the different aspects of the personality. Each alchemical element had its psychological counterpart, so that tin was nobility, for example, while the volatile mercury which made all transformations possible was the collective unconscious – the store of archetypal memories shared by the whole human race.

The Hermaphrodite Crowned, illustration from the manuscript *Tractatus qui dicitur Thomae Aquinatis de Alchimia*, c. 1520. University Library, Leiden, Netherlands. A hermaphrodite – a common alchemical image and, in Jung's analysis, a marriage of the animus and anima, or male and female parts of the psyche.

again," and that "love is the very being of the Bride. She is full of it, and the Bridegroom is satisfied with it. He asks nothing else." But although Jesus was the Bridegroom, his attributes were not confined to the male sex. Bernard also advised those visionaries who claimed to have kissed the wounds of Christ: "Suck not the wounds, but rather the breasts of the crucified. He shall be as a mother to you and you as a son to him."

Bernard's near-contemporary, Saint Hildegard of Bingen (c. 1098–1179), was more consistent in portraying God's love as being feminine and maternal. But she also compared the Trinity to what she described as the three components of sexual intercourse: strength, desire and consummation. Hildegard was among the first of a long line of noted female love mystics, not all of who were ordained as nuns. Saint Mechthild of Magdeburg was a 13th-century beguine – an unmarried woman who wished to live a spiritual life embracing poverty, chastity and service, but without entering a convent. For Mechthild, the sacrament meant receiving "God's body" in the bread, so that "God's manhood mingles with our flesh." She advised "all virgins to follow the most charming of all, the 18-year-old Jesus!" and described herself as "sick with love for Him". Like many mystics, Mechthild was also prepared to reject conventional morality in pursuit of her vision. She writes of God as waiting for her in her bedroom and advising her to cast off fear and shame, as well as "all exterior virtues". Instead she must be guided only by her "noble desire" and her "insatiable hunger", which God promised to "satisfy eternally".

Not surprisingly, nuns were especially prone to sublimating their natural desires in fantasies of holy union. One of the most famous – and one of the last of the great love mystics – was Saint Teresa of Avila, who died in 1582. Teresa was the founder of the Carmelite Reform, which introduced a stringent asceticism into convent life. Her meditations, however, were voluptuous. She wrote of her communion with "an angel in bodily form . . . and very beautiful . . . In his hands I saw a great golden spear, and at the iron tip there

appeared to be a point of fire. This he plunged into my heart several times so that it penetrated to my entrails . . . The pain was so severe that it made me utter several moans. The sweetness caused by this intense pain is so extreme that one cannot possibly wish it to cease, nor is one's soul content with anything but God . . ."

Giovanni Lorenzo Bernini, *The Ecstasy of Saint Theresa*, 1645–1652. Marble, 350 cm high, Cornaro Chapel, Santa Maria della Vittoria, Rome. Teresa had a bitter falling out with her fellow mystic, Saint John of the Cross, when he warned her that perhaps not all her visions were acts of God.

Troubadours and Chivalry

The troubadours were minstrels, composers and poets who originally came from the region of Provence – and more specifically the court of Duke Guilhem of Aquitaine – in the early 12th century. Indeed, it was the Duke himself who wrote the first poems of courtly love for which the troubadours have become famous. Guilhem, the most powerful noble in Christendom, with more lands than the king of France, was an inveterate womanizer, who felt stung by a number of sermons against adultery that were being delivered by the preacher Robert d'Abrisel. Where d'Abrisel promised the torments of hell to adulterous wives, Guilhem responded with a series of poems praising love as a divine mys-

tery, and the woman who inspired it as a goddess, worthy of adoration. Troubadours became so obsessed with the idea of an ennobling love for a well-born lady that each one chose the wife of a feudal lord and devoted all his songs and poems to her. He would address her as Midons or My Lady, and the very concept of the mistress – a woman in a long-term, non-marital relationship with a man – began with the troubadours. Until this time it had been an offence – and sometimes a capital one – to address a love song to a married woman, because it was seen as a type of enchantment. But the troubadours sidestepped this charge by insisting that what they loved in their mistress was not just her beauty, or her nobility, but also her virtue, which had to be unassailable.

Their love, they insisted, was meant to be unconsummated – all that they wished was to catch a glimpse of their mistress, to be acknowledged with a nod, or receive a token such as a glove. Some troubadours did sing about undressing and caressing their mistresses, but even they never suggested that the troubadour-lady relationship (known as *donnoi*) should ever lead to intercourse. When Andrew the Chaplain wrote his definitive and widely translated *Treatise on Love* in 1186, he advised that *donnoi* "goes so far as the kiss and the embrace and the modest contact with the nude lover, omitting the final solace, for that is not permitted to those who wish to love purely." Even at the time, many people doubted that courtly love was truly innocent, but there are few references in the literature to the illegitimate offspring of minstrels, and husbands were happy to invite troubadours into their castles, and even ennoble them, which suggests that they had no real fear of being cuckolded. Andrew the Chaplain pragmatically advises the courtly lover to satisfy his lust with lower-class women, so that he can keep his love for his

Master of the Prise de Tarente, *Six Legendary Knights as Devotees of a Triumphant Venus,* **first half of the 15th cent. Oil on polygonal panel, 51 cm in diameter, Musée du Louvre, Paris.** In the romance tradition, Arthur and the Knights of the Round Table became exemplars of chivalry and courtly love. In this painting they are shown gazing in adoration at the goddess Venus.

An Unarmed Knight is Handed a Lance by a Lady, book illustration, Zurich, c. 1310–1340. Pen-drawing on parchment, subsequently colored, 25.3 x 35.2 cm, **Grosse Heidelberger Liederhandschrift (Manasseh Codex), University Library, Heidelberg.** In medieval tournaments, a knight would compete as the champion of his chosen lady. He would signify this by wearing a token from her, such as a handkerchief. In this illustration, the lady goes further, and actually arms her knight.

mistress pure. By the 13th century, more and more troubadours were giving up on real women altogether, and addressing their songs to the Virgin Mary.

The troubadour movement spread to northern France with the marriage of Guilhem's granddaughter, Eleanor, to Louis VII in 1137. It also found an enthusiastic following in Germany, where the minnesingers passionately extolled the practice of chaste love (*minne*). Under the influence of Eleanor and her daughter, Marie de Champagne, the courtly ethic was also combined with tales of action and heroism to create the *romans*, "romances", which heralded in the age of chivalry. Until this time, knights had been brutal, murderous, opportunistic and mer-

cenary – little more than robber barons. With the romances, a new type of knight was born, who considered loyalty to be the greatest virtue – to God, to the king and to his own lady, usually, but not always, in that order (sometimes the lady was elevated above the king). He was expected to defend his lady's honor at all costs, to ride into battle and conquer in her name, and to expect no reward greater than a word of praise.

Once again, it is unclear how closely the reality follows the myth. Certainly, romances like Chrétien de Troyes's Arthurian story, *Eric and Enide* (12th century), indicate that knights and their ladies were expected to enjoy a rumbustious love life. *Eric and Enide* also suggests that, when knights jousted, their ladies were little

more than spoils of battle, to be enjoyed by the victor. In practical terms, it was obviously easier for first-born sons, who would inherit their father's wealth and title, to conform to the ideals of chivalry, while younger sons – who had to find themselves rich wives as a matter of necessity – might have been more practical and calculating. However, even in the real world, there are accounts of knights such as Ulrich of Lichtenstein (c. 1200–1275/6), who fought maniacally for his lady's name, bathed in her bath water and cut off his finger to prove his love. Once Ulrich even rode from Italy to Bohemia in blond plaits and dressed as Venus, the goddess of love, challenging all comers to joust in honor of his lady.

Witches and Witch-hunters

At one time the Church actively protected people from accusations of witchcraft. In 785 the Synod of Paderborn issued a ruling that any person who burned another for being a witch should themselves receive a death sentence. The position of the Church at this time was that witchcraft was nothing more than a superstition, and bishops were ordered to excommunicate anyone who believed in the power of witches. John of Salisbury, who was Archbishop of Canterbury in the 12th century, confidently stated that anyone who claimed to be a witch was suffering from delusions, and added: "As late as 1310, the Synod of Treves was able to declare: 'Let no woman allege that she rides through the night with Diana and Herodias, for it is an illusion of the Demon'," but within 150 years the view that witches flew through the darkness to attend black sabbaths far from their homes had become official Church dogma. The first steps from scepticism about witches to wholesale persecution of them were taken by Pope John XXII in the 14th century. His bull, *Super Illius Specula*, warns about the power of witches to damage crops and cause illness and death. Gradually however, in a succession of later papal edicts, the emphasis shifted towards sex, and the way that witches tempted and enslaved men through lust, or cast spells that caused impotence and sterility.

All these accusations were enshrined in the 15th-century bull *Summa Desiderantes*, issued by Pope Innocent VIII at the request of Heinrich Kramer and Jakob Sprenger, two Dominican inquisitors who were so overzealous that they had lost the support of the clergy in their native Germany. The pope, however, was won over, and gave them plenary powers so that they could now demand assistance even from bishops. After this bull, it became heresy not to believe in witchcraft. Having gained the approval of the pope, Sprenger and Kramer prepared a handbook for witch-hunters, called the *Malleus Maleficarum*, or *Hammer of Witches*, which was published in 1486. Sprenger and Kramer spend a whole chapter describing why women are more likely to be witches than men, the main reason they gave being that "all witchcraft comes from carnal lust, which in women is insatiable."

In places the *Malleus Maleficarum* reads like a textbook of sexual malfunction. Any and all cases of impotence, childlessness or sexually-related fantasies or manias were taken to be, self-evidently, the result of sorcery. First the "victim" was invited to denounce his (or sometimes her) tormentor. If he or she refused, or was unable to supply a name, the citizens of the town were asked to do so instead. The accused was arrested and almost always tortured into

Bernard Picart after Francesco Mazzola Parmigianino (c. 1530), *Witches' Sabbath* **(detail), 1732. Engraving, private collection.** The now-traditional witch's broomstick actually used to be a hobbyhorse, or a pole, which in some cases was said to be used as a dildo, and inserted into the devil's backside.

making a confession, before being burned at the stake. Hot irons, boots designed to crush the bones of the feet, beatings, spikes, scalding lime baths and various forms of water torture were all approved methods of extracting a confession. The inquisitors even deluded themselves that they were torturing people for their own good – there would be no possibility of divine forgiveness without the confession. Some extremely cruel forms of interrogation were not even considered to be torture – one popular way of finding a witch was to probe the body with a long needle or bodkin, searching for an area that was insensitive to pain, which would in itself be enough to prove that a person had diabolical powers. Unsurprisingly, the genitalia and breasts were probed most assiduously.

The inquisitors spent much of their time dreaming up sexual crimes that they could accuse witches of committing. Sprenger and Kramer, diagnose three different kinds of impotence that were caused by witchcraft.

There was the inability to get an erection, the inability to produce semen and the inability to find one's own penis because it had been rendered invisible and intangible. They include a story about a youth who had suffered from such a *glamour* (an old word for spell which reveals a lot about the link between magic and desire) until he confronted his old girlfriend and accused her of hiding his penis from him. It was only when he began to strangle her with a towel that she touched his groin with the words, "Now you have what you desire," and he felt his member restored. Sprenger and Kramer quote this tale as fact, but are amusingly anxious not to appear too gullible: "It must in no way be believed that such members are really torn away from the body, but that they are hidden by the Devil through some prestidigitatory art, so that they can be neither seen nor felt."

In 1400 the Church decreed that sex with the Devil was a capital crime and the agents of the Inquisition, convinced as they were that witchcraft originated in lust, always included this as one of the accusations against any woman they were investigating. Witches, they charged, would fly through the air to congregate at a black sabbath, where they summoned up the Devil and greeted him with the so-called "obscene kiss" on his backside. In the words of one investigator, the flight itself was a powerfully erotic experience, especially when a witch passed over water when "it was like someone having intercourse with them in a most voluptuous way".

Although the various accusations made against witches were clearly fantasies, the would-be witches themselves often shared them. There are surviving recipes for ointments, intended to be rubbed on to a witch's body so that she could fly to the black sabbath, which contain belladonna and atropine, the active ingredients of deadly nightshade. Absorbed through the skin, these chemicals can produce vivid hallucinations.

Father Urbain Grandier Dies at the Stake, first half of the 17th cent. Woodcut, Bibliothèque Nationale, Paris.
The illustration shows the confessor at the Ursuline convent in Loudun, being burned at the stake after the mother superior and some of the nuns falsely accused him of summoning demons to possess them.

Executions in Europe in 1600
(figures refer to present-day geographical areas)

Country	Execution	Population
Ireland	2	1,000000
Portugal	7	1,000000
Iceland	22	50,000
Estonia	65	no data given
Russia	99	15,000000
Slovenia	100	no data given
Finland	115	350,000
The Netherlands	200	1,500000
Sweden	300	800,000
Spain	300	8,100000
Liechtenstein	300	3000
Norway	350	400,000
Belgium/ Luxemburg	500	1,300000
Hungary	800	3,000000
Czech and Slovak Rep.	1000?	2,000000
Austria	1000?	2,000000
Denmark	1000?	570,000
Italy	1000?	1,3100000
Great Britain	1500	6,500000
France	4000?	20,000000
Switzerland	4000	1,000000
Poland/ Lithuania	10,000?	3,400000
Germany	25,000	16,000000

Although anyone could be accused of being a witch, those most commonly denounced were women aged 14 and upward. King James VI of Scotland wrote a book called *Daemonologie* in 1597, in which he estimated that 20 women were executed for every one man, but other contemporary estimates put the ratio as high as 100 to one. After a series of purges in the German bishopric of Trier, two villages were left with only one surviving female each. The sheer scale of the witch-hunts in Europe is staggering. A history of the Inquisition written in the 16th century boasted that, in the space of 150 years, the Church had burned more than 30,000 witches. If anything, this may be an underestimate. A single bishop was responsible for burning 500 people in Geneva in only three months, and at one mass trial the Senate of Savoy condemned 800 in a single day.

While some countries – such as Germany, France and Switzerland – suffered appalling persecutions, others largely escaped the witch-craze. In Italy, women accused of witchcraft could often escape with a small fine. Occasionally, even in countries that had persecuted witches, sanity would prevail. In Spain, there was such a wave of denunciations in 1611 that the authorities set up an investigation, which concluded that, out of 1300 accusations, not one was genuine. This mass hysteria, it was concluded, could be blamed on the priesthood and its preoccupation with bringing witches to light.

The numbers tried as witches in Europe and America fell dramatically from the end of the

Right: **Francisco José de Goya, *Witches Sabbath*, 1797/98. Oil on canvas, 43 x 30 cm, Museo Lazaro Galdiano, Madrid.** The black sabbath was always thought to involve an orgy, possibly with the sacrifice of children, and concluded with each witch being sodomized by the Devil, despite the "freezing coldness" of his member. In some accounts, the Devil's phallus was double pronged, so that it could penetrate vaginally and anally at the same time. If the Devil was not present, witches were supposed to couple with their familiars – personal demons that had taken the form of animals such as cats or frogs.

Below: The mark of the beast was branded on Aleister Crowley's women disciples. This girl, Edith Y, he used to call "The Mother of God".

Robin Ray, Demonic Entity of Succubus Attacks a Sleeping Man, date unknown. Engraving. One popular tradition held that the incubus and its female version the succubus, were actually the same demon – after collecting the seed of a man by sleeping with him as succubus, the creature would change its form and use the stolen seed to impregnate a woman.

17th century. However, the relevant laws often remained on the statute books – the last witchcraft law was not repealed in Britain, for example, until 1954. Although the vast majority of people tried over the centuries were certainly not witches, it is likely that various pagan religions survived on the fringes of the Christian world, worshipping horned fertility gods and ancient mother goddesses, such as the Egyptian Isis. Modern witchcraft movements tend to trace their ancestry back to what they claim are these unbroken traditions, although their rituals are often improvised, or derive from the inventions of 19th- and 20th-century magicians such as Eliphas Levi, Aleister Crowley, or Gerald Gardner. Sometimes these magical gurus, when they wanted to invent rituals that would shock outsiders and cow their own followers, might even find inspiration in the fantasies of the witchhunters. One of Crowley's spells involved sacrificing a goat by cutting its throat as it copulated with one of his mistresses. Another, which required the magician to masturbate himself to a climax while reciting the names of supernatural beings, was actually called, in a nod to the Inquisition, "The Congress with Demons". These rites, all invented by Crowley, owe just as much to the witch-hunters as they do to any ancient pagan magical traditions.

Incubi

The incubus was a male demon, which existed only to seduce women. Even in the Middle Ages, incubi were something of a joke to the sophisticated. Geoffrey Chaucer, the author of *The Canterbury Tales*, c.1390 pointed out that the rumors of demon lovers had greatly decreased since the appearance of *limitours*, or wandering friars, who took their places in the beds of married women. Reginald Scot, in his *Discoverie of Witchcraft*, 1584 mentioned an incubus that visited a woman and made "hot loove unto hir" until she cried out in protest. When her household searched the room they found the demon hiding under the bed, having miraculously transformed itself, the author sharply observes, into the shape of a lecherous local bishop. Scot also, acutely, pointed out that incubi visited women with "melancholie abounding in their heads", that virgins and widows were much more susceptible than housewives and that nuns were the most common victims of all. Enlightened doctors were able to treat incubus visitations, and the phantom pregnancies that often went with them, by persuading the victims that they were only fantasizing. None of this stopped the Inquisition from believing in them.

Even when there is no reason to fear legal action, most witches have preferred to keep their activities a secret for fear of arousing hostility and misunderstanding. They also feel a need to avoid the attentions of the prurient – although rites differ from group to group, many are conducted in the nude and some may involve sex magic that calls for ritual intercourse.

The Popes – Myth and Reality

The first Bishop of Rome was a married man, before and after he became a disciple. Saint Peter even took his wife with him on his apostolic travels, although some claim that he was a widower by the time he reached Rome. Surrounded by pagan religions – with which they had to compete – and vying for the patronage of often-licentious Roman nobles, Peter's immediate successors were often opportunistic in their attitudes to sex. While some advocated complete celibacy, others were succeeded by their own sons. Innocent I, who established the primacy of the Roman See and is sometimes described as the first true pope, came to power in 401 on the death of his father, Pope Anastasius I. About a thousand years later, the reign of Innocent VII – who lavished gifts and positions of influence on his 16 illegitimate children – was known as "the Golden Age of Bastards".

Even those popes who advocated celibacy were usually revealed as hypocrites. The 4th-century pope, Damasus, who wrote that "intercourse is a defilement", was accused by a Jewish convert of adultery and forced to stand trial before a synod of 44 bishops. He was only saved from execution by the intervention of the emperor, Gratian (359–383).

Other popes were more resourceful in their own defense. Accused of seducing a nun in 440, Sixtus told the biblical story of the woman taken in adultery, and dared his judges to cast the first stone. Symmachus, charged in 501 with adultery, was the first – but by no means the last – pope to claim that, as pontiff, no human court could judge him. Even the pope could not escape natural justice, however, and several – including both John XII and his successor, Benedict V – are said to have died at the hands of jealous husbands.

Even children were not immune to the corrupting influence of the papal throne, and the near-absolute power that came with it. When John XIX died mysteriously in 1032, a 12-year-old boy was installed as his successor, taking the name Benedict VIII. According to Saint Peter Damien, who wrote an 11th-century text on sex and the priesthood called *The Book of Gomorrah*, from the beginning of his career the boy "feasted on immorality". He was a bisexual with a fondness for sodomizing animals, practiced witchcraft and murder, threw homosexual orgies and opened the greatest brothel in Rome within the Lateran Palace. This was not unusual. Sixtus IV (1414–1484), for example, helped fund his war against the Turks, as well

Pope Joan

The first written accounts of a female pope appear in the 13th century. The most popular, by Martin of Troppau, tells how a woman calling herself John Anglicus became pontiff after the death of Leo IV in 855. According to Martin, John was born in Mainz, and first dressed as a man to accompany her lover to Athens. She was elected pope after impressing all Rome with her piety and learning, but after nearly two years in office became pregnant by the same lover. Her secret was finally revealed when she gave birth during a papal procession. Martin says she died in childbirth, but other authors have her put to death by being dragged behind a horse, or retiring in peace to raise her son.

Over the next 300 years, the story of Pope Joan, as she came to be known, was almost universally accepted as a fact. She was even included among the busts of the pontiffs completed for Siena Cathedral in 1400, although she was later removed by order of Clement VIII.

It was not until the Reformation, when Protestant writers used the idea of a female pope to attack the Church, that Catholic commentators began to dismiss Pope Joan as nothing more than a legend. The story of the papal sex test sprang up some time after the 10th century, independently of the legend of Saint Joan. After his election, it was said, the pope would sit in a "pierced" or "groping chair", with a hole cut in its seat. The youngest cleric present would then feel his genitals, before announcing, "He has testicles," to which the others responded, "God be praised." Early chroniclers said that this was not so much to prove that the pope was not a woman, as to prove that he had not been castrated. Eunuchs were not allowed to hold high church office.

Anonymous, Pope Joan Giving Birth to Her Child, 16th cent. Italian woodcut. The Via S. Giovanni, where the birth was supposed to take place, was shunned by papal processions throughout the 14th and 15th centuries. The street is said to have once held a statue of Pope Joan, suckling her child.

as the building of the Sistine chapel named after him, by opening a *lupanar*, or brothel for both sexes, and levying a weekly tax on every prostitute in Rome.

The most notorious of the popes was the Spaniard, Rodrigo Borgia, who became Alexander VI in 1492. He was famously licentious. When he met his long-term mistress Vannozza Catanei – who bore him four children – he had already slept with her mother and probably her sister. After the death of Innocent VIII, he used his enormous personal wealth to bribe his way into office. Cardinals were given castles, abbeys and mule-loads of silver. The clinching vote, however, belonged to a Venetian who wanted only 5000 crowns and a night with Rodrigo's 12-year-old daughter, Lucrezia. The deal was done in a moment. It was widely believed that Lucrezia had already been deflowered by her own father, and the existence of an incestuous relationship between the pair was the most common of the many accusations made against Alexander.

There was a temporary period of papal sobriety from the reign of Paul IV in 1559 to the death of Pius V in 1572, but mistresses and prostitutes returned to the Vatican with Pius's successor, Gregory XII. It was only at the end of the 17th century that popes consistently began to practice what they preached, or at least began to be discreet about their indiscretions. Even during this period, however, rumors clung to some of them, such as Gregory XVI (1831–1846), who kept the wife of his former barber in an apartment next to his own, and was said to have fathered several children by her.

Above: **Anonymous, Caricature of Pope Alexander VI, represented as a syphilitic, c. 1500. Woodcut, private collection.** Alexander VI was a favorite target of the Protestant Reformation, which held him up as the prime example of all that was rotten about papacy. His sexual appetites were formidable – he famously organized orgies during which his favorites raced whores as if they were horses. He even invited his daughter Lucrezia to attend his debauches.

Bartolomeo da Veneto, Idealized Portrait of a Lady (the so-called Lucrezia Borgia), between 1502 and 1546. Mixed technique on panel, 43.5 x 34.3 cm, Städelsches Kunstinstitut, Frankfurt/M. Lucrezia Borgia was married off three times in the service of her family's political ambitions. After the failure of her marriage to Giovanni Sforza, Lord of Pesaro, she began to appear in public with a young child named Giovanni, who was recognized in two successive papal bulls as the illegitimate son of first her brother, Cesare, and then her father.

The Ordained

Anonymous, *Nun and Monk*. Klinger Collection, Nuremberg. Saint Dunstan, the 10th-century bishop of Canterbury, decreed that any nun or monk who fornicated with another would be subjected to a ten-year fast, with perpetual lamentation and abstention from meat. His penance was widely adopted in monastic orders, but to little effect.

"The monk is chaste when he's in the pulpit," so the saying goes. Because religious institutions have imposed such strict regulations on the lifestyles of secular people, infractions on the part of the clergy have been a popular target for critical commentary through the centuries. At the beginning of the modern age, Giordano Bruno (1548–1600) wrote of "swinish monkery". In the German language, one who lived licentiously was said to "whore like a Carmelite", and in some regions of Germany a hot water bottle was referred to as a "monk". With regard to nuns in convents in particular, their thoughts and feelings were supposed to be focused on the love of God, not on worldly love. Already under Charlemagne (742–814) the few nuns who could read and write were forbidden to copy love poems. Nevertheless, they did have dealings with love. Naturally, their transgressions came to light more easily than the monks' dissipations. Some convents supposedly resembled birthing houses more than cloisters for celibate women.

"Yes," wrote the German aphorist Georg Christoph Lichtenberg (1742–1799), "nuns haven't only taken strict vows of chastity, they also have strong bars on their windows." At that time, the bars were necessary, since many of the women hadn't taken the vow of their own free will. Many a hard-to-marry maid was forced to take the veil. The Italian Giacomo Casanova reported in 1755 that many of the women who became nuns did not want to live the pious life that they felt was being forced on them when they entered the cloister. They schemed to obtain a little freedom, and were often successful, especially during carnival time, when they dressed up as ladies or gentlemen and let courtesans disguised as nuns take their place for a while. They were "Brides of Christ", but they seem to have had lovers from monasteries. Especially in 18th-century France, the younger sons of noble families who were put in cloisters had no desire to stay there and live a chaste life. The clergy's excesses were and still are an important theme in erotic art. However, at that time putting their conduct on public display wasn't only voyeuristic; it also had political

Anonymous, *Confessional and Discipline*, c. 1700. Copperplate engraving. A confessor aroused both by the words of his female penitent, and the possibility of punishing her. Originally, the penance for sexual sins involved mostly fasting, self-denial and prayer. Self flagellation became an acceptable alternative for monks during the 11ᵗʰ century, and the laity began to receive whippings by the parish priest shortly afterward.

motives, which are easily overlooked centuries later. Especially during and after the Reformation, the secret sexual lives of the clergy were popular subjects for caricature and critique. Individual cases of supposed "immorality" were presented as typical, and this immorality was used as evidence of flawed doctrine.

One should be skeptical of one-sided interpretations that portray these exposures as attempts at liberation from hypocritical constraints. In some respects, the reformers wanted to be more Catholic than the pope, to be the better Christians. They could only accomplish this by denouncing the secret lusts of "the others". The Protestants permitted even those in God's service to have sex-lives. Yet this freedom didn't contribute to greater sensual enjoyment, since Protestants, regardless of origin, had to strive for the blamelessness that the Catholics only pretended to. But penitence led to a very peculiar lust, one that was neither goal-oriented, genital nor orgasm-centered. Many nuns and monks lived out their sexuality in

good, that is to say, purified, conscience. Excessive rites of penance, wearing hair shirts or chains and, above all, self-flagellation, commonly replaced obvious sexual dissipations.

Sexual transgressions, of all things, were supposed to be atoned for through corporal punishment. Differences were made between so-called "upper" and "lower" penance, the latter of which was reserved for nuns and other female penitents, as it was in Spain as late as the 19ᵗʰ century. Supposedly women couldn't endure blows on their upper backs, so instead they had to expose themselves to the father confessor from the navel down to receive their birch strokes. That offered the Dominicans and Jesuits a welcome opportunity to enjoy a voyeuristic sight and some sadistic activity.

In some convents, stinging nettles were grown for the sole purpose of whipping penitents. This burning treatment has functioned since antiquity as an effective means of strengthening erotic desires. Thus the criticism came again and again: the discouraged sensuality is

further stimulated by precisely the penance practiced in cloisters. The beating of the lower body especially would lead to enhanced circulation and sexual desires.

It's no accident that the followers of today's sadomasochistic scene aren't entirely unlike the penitent bishop. Perhaps without realizing it, they are part of a long tradition. Whereas clergymen searched for the lust hidden in pain, today's sadomasochists have discovered that pain can be a lust in itself.

For centuries spiritual and sexual longings have been diametrically opposed in the West. As British Nobel Laureate Bertrand Russell noted, the church has done everything in its power to make the only permissible form of sexuality – monogamous sex between husband and wife – as devoid of enjoyment and as full of suffering as possible. Thus, the statement a clergyman made in conversation with the British physician and sex researcher Henry Havelock Ellis (1859–1939) remains a baffling exception, claiming as he did that his entire being went out to certain people who excited him so much that he ejaculated from the excitement of simply sitting with them, yet without having any sexual thoughts at all. The ejaculation, he claimed, resulted from the joy of his soul, which made his whole body glow with health.

Illustration on musical pocketwatch, early 19ᵗʰ cent. Gold and enamel, 57 mm in diameter, Christie's, London. In Protestant controlled countries, and in Catholic countries at times of great social strife, baiting the Catholic clergy for their sexual antics was such a popular activity that satirical sketches were even used to decorate watches.

Marquis de Sade

"What do I care about the victims? There will always be victims." Not only did the Marquis de Sade describe his cruel fantasies in works like *Justine, or The Misfortunes of Virtue*, 1791, but in *The Story of Juliette*, 1797, and *The 120 Days of Sodom*, first released in 1904, he glorified sexual violence against women and children. This son of a venerable French aristocratic family, like many of his contemporaries, actually tried to realize his fantasies. However, according to today's understanding of sadism, de Sade would not be considered a sadist but a sadomasochist: he liked to be whipped until he bled just as much as he liked to do the whipping. He composed his long-banned works during the total 27 years of his life that he spent in prison, of necessity long phases of forced abstinence. But it was precisely this abstinence that, in his own words, inspired his "pipe-dreams" (which is what he named his erotic fantasies), as well as his desire to realize them. His readership can be divided into two groups, the "philosophers" and the "practitioners". The former group included the Spanish and French

Marquis Donatien-Alphonse-François de Sade, allegorical sheet with portrait, c. 1830. Hand-colored etching. In his will, de Sade wished that his remains be scattered, and his memory effaced from the minds of men.

surrealists of the 1920s and the existentialists of the 1950s who regarded his writings as libertinistic philosophies. Albert Camus (1913–1960) once said that de Sade made Reason realize that it was not omnipotent. And Simone de Beauvoir (1908–1986) posed the question, "Must we burn de Sade?" only to refute it definitively. But that which the "philosophers" sought and discovered in de Sade's works is of little interest to his second group of readers, the "practitioners", who are more interested in de Sade's variations on sex, and who usually enjoy the illustrations in his books more than the writings. In prison, de Sade had enough time to analyze this unbridled arousal. His admirers herald the fact that he unmasks a thoroughly depraved society with his work and interprets it primarily as an obscene outcry against the hypocrisy of his time.

Some people regard de Sade as a "sex fiend" while others esteem him a "divine Marquis". He maintained that it is legitimate to find pleasure in the degradation and maltreatment of other human beings. As the prototype of "sadists", a term coined by Richard Freiherr von Krafft-Ebing (1840–1902), the Marquis turned his fellow human beings into mere sex objects. In his writings, de Sade tried to disprove the existence of God by creating a cynical anti-world in which only wickedness was rewarded. Thus, he created a variation of the then-popular motif of "persecuted innocence" and tried to destroy the "ridiculous idolatry of virtue". There is no God, he professed, and if there is, then it is a God who is indifferent to its creatures; otherwise wickedness could not triumph. In de Sade's narrations *The Crimes of Love*, 1800, even the Ten Commandments of Judaism and Christianity prove to be invalid. The excesses described in this book are thus always a form of blasphemy as well. The fact that he radically challenged and disputed the Christian world-view earned him many admirers, especially among his successors. 19th-century writers like Baudelaire (1821–1867), Flaubert (1821–1880) and Dostoevski (1821–1881) highly respected his work. Philosophers of the 20th century like Thedor W. Adorno (1903–1969) and Max

***Justine*, still from the film by Jesús Franco, 1969, Romina Power as Justine and Horst Frank as De Bressac.** *Justine* illustrates the stupidity of trying to be virtuous in the face of a cruel universe, and the suffering of those who try.

Horkheimer (1895–1973) also interpreted de Sade's writings as a shrewd critique of the consequences of Enlightenment-era rationalism. In his prefaces to de Sade's works, French philosopher George Batailles (1897–1962) once noted that this anti-Enlightenment author had realized "the visionary and intoxicating aspect" of lascivious outbursts of sadism. At the age of 23, the Marquis married Renée-Pélagie Cordier de Launy de Montreuill, one year his junior, with whom he is said to have had three children. A few months into their marriage the Marquis was arrested for a sexual offense. Five years later he brutally abused a beggar woman. She pressed charges and de Sade was imprisoned for a short time. The next hearing came in 1772 after he partook in an orgy with four young women and his male servant in Marseille. Charged with sodomy and poisoning someone with the aphrodisiac "Spanish fly", he fled to Italy with his sister-in-law, who was his mistress at the time. In his absence he was sentenced to death and burned in effigy. Five years later – his sister-in-law had passed away by then – he was finally arrested. In the meantime, however, the death sentence had been rescinded. In 1789, de Sade was sent to prison for partaking in revolutionary activities, and in 1790 he was released.

His wife tolerated his excesses for a long time and helped him to escape again and again. In her own words she professed to "idolize" him and sent passionate letters to him in prison. It was not until 1790, after 27 years of marriage, that his wife, who had in the meantime become religious, finally filed for divorce.

In 1801, de Sade was again incarcerated after disparaging Napoleon in a *roman à clef*. On March 14, 1803, he was sent to the penal institution, Bicêtre, and on April 27 of the same year he was transferred to the insane asylum, Charenton-Saint-Maurice, in Paris. Eleven years later, in 1814, he died at the age of 74, still not a free man.

Left: **Illustration to *Juliette* by de Sade, attributed to Binet, 1797. Copperplate engraving, black-and-white, Bibliothèque Nationale, Paris.** The novel *Juliette* is a counterpart to *Justine* and, arguably, a more complete exploration of de Sade's philosophy. Its heroine undergoes many of the same pornographic adventures as the virtuous girl of the better known book, but uses them to educate herself and unleash her own darker instincts and appetites.

***The 120 Days of Sodom*, still from the film by Pier Paolo Pasolini, 1975.** De Sade wrote *The 120 Days of Sodom* while imprisoned in the Bastille, on a roll of paper twelve meters long. When Pasolini made the story into a film, he updated it to create an allegory of Fascist Italy.

Double Standards in Victorian England

William Acton (1813–1875), the author of several works about prostitution and venereal diseases in 19th-century England, once stated that the ideal English wife and mother is "friendly, considerate, self-sacrificing, sensible, and of such pure heart that she is oblivious to sensuality". However, the Victorian ideal of the asexual woman was created and exemplified much less by the aristocratic upper class than by the bourgeois middle class. But it was the exploited lower class, in particular, that fell victim to this double standard.

During this seemingly prudish era, both men and the women themselves were ideally supposed to forget that they possessed legs and other shameful body parts. Women of decency were not even supposed to wash their private parts (at least not before marriage). The mere mention of them was an offense to propriety. Once this anti-body upbringing had taken effect, women were for the most part anesthetized to sex.

Premarital sex education was often just an allusion to coming injustices, and certainly not to the joys of sexual love. Mothers advised their daughters to concentrate on something else during their wedding night and the many nights to come, and that they should, for example, "close their eyes and think of England!" Frigidity was thus not yet a reproach, but a social expectation and the product of "successful" sex education.

Dante Gabriel Rossetti, *The Beloved (The Bride)* (detail), 1865/66. Oil on canvas, 76.2 x 82.5 cm, Tate Gallery, London. The Pre-Raphaelites typified Victorian attitudes to young women – they painted them so that a veneer of innocence hung over a powerful promise of sensuality, exoticism and often even depravity.

Queen Victoria

Even today, she remains the epitome of prudery: Queen Victoria, who was born in 1819 and who, in 1840 at the age of 21, married her cousin of the same age, Prince Albert of Saxe-Coburg. In 17 years the Queen gave birth to nine children, spending almost seven years of her long life being pregnant. She chose her prince consort herself after seeing him and finding him attractive. In her diary, she described the man who made her heart race as having "broad shoulders and a narrow waist".

Contrary to the opinions held about motherhood at the time, the Queen did not enjoy anything that had to do with pregnancy and birth. For her, the consequences of marital intercourse represented the dark side of marriage and sent her into long bouts of depression. Birth seemed to her to be an animalistic, unaesthetic occurrence. She felt that her pregnancies hindered her from executing the duties of her office. After the death of the Prince Consort in 1861 (at the age of only 42) she lived and reigned for another 40 years.

Queen Victoria with her grandchildren, Prince Arthur (b. 1883) and Princess Margaret of Connaught (b. 1882), April 1886. Private collection. As her letters to her daughter reveal, Victoria felt little exultation in women's motherly self-sacrifice. Her resentment of women's physical sufferings led her to be among the first to use chloroform for anesthesia in childbirth, thus making the practice respectable for other women.

The widespread opinion of the eroticized Victorian era was that men lose strength through sexual intercourse with women. Instead of feeling relaxed after the sex act, they feel exhausted. This profound mistrust of sexual activity was expressed in the lectures of Henry Varley, among others, who in 1887 branded even marital sex as a form of wastefulness.

The fact that homosexuality abounded in Victorian England is often seen as a reaction to the idealization of women as wife and mother and the simultaneous devaluation of women as sex partners. But maybe it was also the other way around. Wasn't the asexual wife simply ideal for the man who really loved men but had to enter into a bourgeois marriage for societal reasons? In any case, it was exactly this attempt to ignore everything sexual that led people to be overly attentive to anything that was even remotely suggestive, from oysters to chair-legs.

Frank Harris, 1890.

Frank Harris and Anonymous "Walter"

British journalist Frank Harris (1856 –1931), a friend of the poet Oscar Wilde who was imprisoned in England, published his extensive memoirs *My Life and Loves* between 1923 and 1927. Although a whole generation had passed since the reign of Queen Victoria, her moral standards were still in effect. In his writings, Harris described his love life very openly and thus was censored in the United States as well as in Great Britain. But he was not the first Victorian to proudly own up to his erotic indulgences. Frank Harris's most famous predecessor had already published his erotic memoirs around the turn of the century in an extensive, three-volume edition entitled *My Secret Life*, which appeared in the Netherlands and later in France. In it, the author (whose identity remains a mystery) gives a detailed and creative description of his 1200 experiences under the pseudonym "Walter". A picture is painted of a society in which morality has in no way triumphed over indecency. Women of all classes and social standing appear equally familiar with all conceivable sexual deviations. These memoirs are considered to be one of the most important documents about the Victorian period in England. However, his stories were even seen as extremely offensive when they were published in his British homeland after the beginning of the sexual revolution. "Obscenity" was the British court's judgment against the company that published Walter's memoirs in 1969, almost a century after the described indulgences had taken place.

Matt Morgan, *The Girl of the Period! or Painted by a Prurient Prude*, illustration from *The Tomahawk*, 1868. Despite their obvious, theoretically admirable, probity, spinsters were often figures of fun in Victorian popular art. They are portrayed as jealous, unhappy and twisted by their sexual frustration. It is said that in some of their households, even the legs of the furniture were covered because they were imagined to be threateningly seductive.

Transgression and Carnival

"Carnival" sometimes refers to a general public jolification, not connected to any particular time of the year. The word derives from the Latin *carne-levare* (to take away meat), which later became *carne-vale* (goodbye, meat). Traditionally carnival is a celebration to make the most of things before the long Lenten fast. It starts six days before Ash Wednesday, the first day of Lent, in the world's great carnival centers, Venice, Rio de Janeiro, and the Rhineland. Carnival is not a festive beginning, but a final blow-out in the face of a coming sacrifice. In keeping with the word's derivation, carnival originated as one big farewell party.

Until the late Middle Ages, carnival was under the guidance of the Church. It is believed that the festivities originated in monasteries and convents. One theory is that they were an attempt to eclipse or blot out heathen rites that were performed at that time to drive out winter. While Roman orgies were aimed at achieving a catharsis, a purification of passions by breaking boundaries and pushing limits, carnival was acceptable to Church superiors only if it led to a spiritual hangover – to a bad

conscience and increased willingness to repent. Carnival is often symbolized by a young man bursting with life, while Lent, on the other hand, is represented by a withered old woman. However, carnival is not just meant to counterbalance Lent but also the rest of the deprivation-filled year. In cities, carnival was initially celebrated with feasting and dancing. It wasn't until the 15th century that long-nosed, horned devil and witch figures began to appear more frequently at masked processions. In the years before the Reformation, starting in 1490, carnival became a welcome opportunity to mock church institutions, which were coming under more scrutiny. Clergy members were not living up to the expectations and demands that were being placed on them.

Protestant reformers, however, fulminated against the "Christian Bacchanalia". In 1509, the reformer Erasmus witnessed the Italian carnival festivities for himself and found them to be "un-Christian". He remarked that society was just taking advantage of the opportunity to "give free rein to immorality". In England, the Puritans extinguished the old tradition altogether since they rejected everything that served the purpose of entertainment.

The merriment that couldn't be contained was tamed. Theatrical productions replaced the excesses in the streets. From the 15th century, carnival in Florence was organized and run by the court of the Medici. Ruling families in Rome and Venice soon did the same. It was not until the second half of the 17th century that this type of carnival celebration reached Germany. In the Rome of Goethe's time, as described in his *Italian Journey* (1786–1788), the street stopped being a street. According to him it became a ballroom – an enormous, decorated gallery. By the 18th century, carnival was being celebrated in India, czarist Russia, and the European colonies in both North and South America.

Although these annually reoccurring excesses were a thorn in the Church's and later the State's side, they stabilized the existing order much more than they threatened it. Carnival provided an outlet for the oppressed. It was a

Gerda Wegener, *Erotic Trio in Fancy Dress*, illustration from *The Pleasures of Eros*, 1917. Pen and ink, watercolor, Stapleton Collection. The masks and costumes of carnival provide license to act in any way the wearer desires – whether they wish to indulge in violence, sex or gourmandizing. Even if the identity of the masked wearer is known, it is customary to feign ignorance to protect his or her notional anonymity.

time when the boundaries between gender, age, and class dissolved. Year after year, people would practice reversing the status quo in jest, but they would never attempt to make the reversal permanent. Carnival was conceived to be completely transitory. Even before the celebrations begin, everyone knows that they will be over on Ash Wednesday.

Every year in fiery sermons, the priests would chastise those shameless men who would deny themselves and their masculinity by dressing up and acting like women. At the same time, women were amusing themselves by parading in men's clothes. Women who normally spent the whole year in the house now romped in the streets. Notably, it was even often perfectly acceptable for masked people to invade other people's private apartments.

Sex Rituals in France, Germany, and Italy

In the rural areas of Germany, rules were not broken; they were made to be enforced. The atmosphere in the rural areas was much less open and permissive than in the cities. Legal organizations referred to as "courts of reprimand" would assemble to pass judgment on the village people's sexual misconduct particularly during carnival. In France especially, satirical

court proceedings or *causes grasses* would be held. Young and/or hen-pecked husbands sitting backwards on donkeys would be led through the streets under the supervision of the "Great Prince of Mardi Gras". This was a form of public humiliation that was customarily performed throughout the year.

Many carnival rituals seem to symbolize the act of fertilization, like men throwing or spraying various liquids at women. In the Venetian *Gioco degli Uova,* men dressed as devils throw eggs filled with cologne up to the windows of the women they desire. On the other hand, women standing on their balconies would drench the men below with liquids that weren't always crystal-clear water. The throwing of candy, corn or eggshells can also be interpreted as "sowing the seed". In the 1700s, in the town of Trani in southern Italy the rituals were even more blatant. The people there would carry the *Santo Membro,* the holy member, around in a ceremonial procession during carnival. The *Santo Membro* was a priapic wood statue with a chin-high, erect phallus. In Florence, the key makers would serenade the women on the balconies, singing, "Our tool is handsome, new, and useful / We always carry it with us / It's good for everything. Whoever wants to can hold it in their hand."

Above left: The Sydney Gay and Lesbian Mardi Gras is the largest of its kind in the world, and has been embraced enthusiastically by Sydney's heterosexual community. It is the culmination of a month-long festival of music, art and films.

Above right: **Levilly,** *Ash Wednesday,* **c. 1780. Lithograph.** It was customary in Rome, and several other Cathedral cities, for penitents to begin their public penance on Ash Wednesday, when they were sprinkled with ashes and segregated from the rest of the Christian community until the Thursday before Easter.

Rio de Janeiro – Carnival. Two of the most famous carnivals in the world occur in Rio de Janeiro, Brazil, and in Trinidad. They share many features, including extravagant but extremely fancy costumes that may cost many times the average local weekly wage.

Mardi Gras in New Orleans

In North America, carnival has a long tradition in only one port on the Mississippi Delta: New Orleans. Year after year, thousands upon thousands of tourists flock to the city, especially on the Monday and Tuesday before Ash Wednesday which are referred to there as Lundi Gras and Mardi Gras. The majority of the people who live in New Orleans are descendants of African slaves and Creoles. Catholic immigrants from Europe imported carnival to the area around the middle of the 19th century. Mardi Gras is also celebrated, for example, in the French port of Nice. The North American carnival is a mixture of rituals from several different continents. One famous spectacle in particular is provided by the Zulus, descendants of black slaves, who appear in the parades on "Fat Tuesday" in brightly colored feather costumes. In New Orleans, Mardi Gras does not just refer to a few individual festival days but to festival weeks that extend from the sixth of January to the beginning of Lent. During this whole time, imaginatively and elaborately costumed revelers organize parades that are accompanied by brass and Dixieland bands. Music and rhythm set the scene.

Since the 1950s, homosexuals have played a special role in the festivities. At a time when scarcely a single man in the US could admit to being gay, and long before there was a Christopher Street Day, gays were dancing in the French Quarter of New Orleans and attracting admiring looks, even from heterosexual men who often just didn't notice that the splendidly dressed women weren't really women at all. On the balconies of the French Quarter prostitutes present themselves. All other women who appear in a window during this time will also hear the cries of "Show us your tits!" from the people in the streets. Even "normal members" of society willingly respond to the request by baring their breasts. Women in the streets must also expose themselves if they want a cheap strand of the beads that are traditionally thrown – similar to candies in Germany – in the parades. While bodies in European carnival parades usually remain covered and hidden under cos-

tumes and masks (if nothing else because of the cold), the dancers in New Orleans disguise themselves with the mask of nudity.

Fascinated by the *joie de vivre* that is expressed in the carnival festivities of warmer regions, Central Europeans are now trying to imitate the parades and processions of southern cultures. Thus we see attempts, as in Berlin, to start multicultural celebrations of life and Dionysian movements – held at the end of May when warmer temperatures can be expected – completely unconnected to Lent. Whilst they too have dancers doing the samba on floats, the longed-for orgies don't materialize. Evidently, revelers need the right temperament as well as the right temperature.

Mardi Gras in New Orleans. The French name, Mardi Gras or Fat Tuesday, comes from the habit of using all the fats in the house before Lent. During the festival, New Orleans's incredibly diverse immigrant community, comprising large Irish, German and Italian contingents, join together for an Afro-American-inspired party.

Privacy and the Law

For centuries, it was church and state institutions that determined what was sexually permissible. Everything that was labeled sinful in the Bible was punishable by law. Any practices that were performed purely for pleasure and not for the purpose of reproduction were also forbidden. Every union that was not legitimized by the church was regarded as a sexual offense. This didn't change until the introduction of the civil marriage brought about by the French Revolution.

In Germany for example, the laws regulating sex differed from state to state. However, when these were all compiled and standardized, it was by no means the liberal laws that prevailed. Thus, homosexual acts were punishable by law in the whole country after the establishment of the German Empire in 1870. On the other hand, in the Kingdom of Bavaria after 1810, a law set forth that a mutual act between two adults, like the exchange of money for pleasure (in other words, prostitution) was an offense to the moral code but was not punishable by law. (There was a similar law in force in France.) These laws prevailed in Germany until the criminal law reform of 1973, i.e. for more than a century.

The concept of having an erotic private life did not exist until at the earliest 1800, starting in France. It was and still is a middle class privilege not available to all adults. Since sex that takes place in front of "unwilling witnesses" can always be regarded as an offense to public decency, only those that have their own room or rooms will be able to enjoy an undisturbed private life. The offense of "gross indecency in public places" is unlikely to ever disappear and occurs when sexual acts are carried out without regard to the embarrassment of a third party.

In the past, all persons, who were housed in institutions, for example, had to give up intimacy. In Prussia in 1851 a law was enacted which forbade sexual contact with sick or helpless individuals in institutions. Although this law was actually meant to protect these individuals, it essentially constituted a ban on sexual activity for the patients and inmates themselves.

As sex laws in Europe are modernized, the word "indecency" is becoming more and more obsolete. Now the essential factor in judging sexual activity is whether it is by mutual consent. If all parties involved in sexual acts are expressly willing, then it is none of the lawmakers' business. Otherwise it is considered to be a violation of a person's right to sexual self-determination, and is not a sexual offense but a crime of violence.

In various states of the United States however, laws governing sexual acts still exist today which are based on religious tenets. This is especially true in states located in the so-called "Bible Belt". Sex outside marriage is forbidden in Idaho, Utah, Mississippi, and South Carolina, to

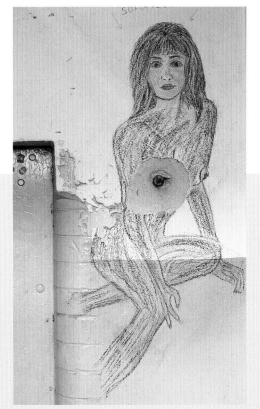

Prisoner's Erotic Fantasy. For imprisoned men, their pinups take on an extra significance, as symbolic of the little freedom they possess.

Sexuality and Imprisonment

Depriving prisoners of the opportunity for sexual activity has always been an unspoken part of the punishment. Groups who portray the inmates as victims of society have denounced this from the beginning. The critics of imprisonment claim that only regular heterosexual intercourse guarantees the sexual health of an adult and the stability of society. Behind the minimal sex life granted to married couples by liberal-minded European administrators of penal institutions is the dread of "forced homosexuality" – sexual molestation and rape, especially of the younger prisoners – which is not uncommon. There is also the ongoing secret fear of masturbation causing damage, and the acknowledgment that stable relationships minimize the probability of recidivism.

From this point of view prisoners are in the same desolate situation as hospital patients, the mentally and physically disabled, confused and elderly people in old-age homes and others in similar establishments. Until well into the 1980s they were also denied any kind of privacy, and, even today, this is the case inside many institutions. Any sexual encounter takes place potentially in public view. Those who go ahead regardless are categorized as "obscene" or "shameless" and discredited as "anti-social".

Illegal Sex Practices in the USA (1995)

- adultery
- prostitution
- homosexual oral sex
- all oral sex
- sex/marriage with cousins
- homosexual anal sex
- all anal sex
- sex outside marriage
- cohabitation
- visible erection
- child pornography
- obscene pornography

name but a few. In New Mexico and Virginia, unmarried couples are not allowed to form their own household. Each state has its own laws about sex. In one state you might get sentenced to life imprisonment for something that is legal only a few yards away in the next state. At the end of the 1970s, Hawaii and California were considered to be models of liberalism. In many US states however, every sexual activity that does not serve procreation is punishable by law. In principle, anal and oral sex are still punishable by law in the United States, even between married couples. Alfred Kinsey had already pointed out at the beginning of the 1950s how unrealistic the existing laws were. Since the majority of citizens feel this way, these laws are not usually enforced. However the "religious right" has an extremely strong lobby. Nobody dares to challenge the outdated laws, even though only a small minority of the country supports them. Many people could be targeted as repeat offenders and blackmailed or ruined through deliberate campaigns. It is ironic, though, that if these laws were enforced, it wouldn't just be a small minority that would be found guilty. It would be the broad majority.

The Mann Act

At the end of the 19th century, the International Bureau for the Suppression of Traffic in Women and Children was founded in London. This led to the enactment of the infamous Mann Act in the United States in 1910. This law made it illegal for a man to take a woman over state lines for "indecent purposes". Whether the woman was accompanying the man voluntarily or not was irrelevant.

In 1912, the first black World Heavyweight Champion in boxing, Jack Johnson (1878–1946), became a famous victim of this ruling as he and his white girlfriend, to whom he was not yet legally married, were traveling to one of his fights. Found guilty of violating the Mann Act, his only hope of evading the one-year prison sentence was to flee the country. A law that was intended to help women and children who had been abducted to be forced into prostitution was then misused, in this case for racist reasons, to make "undesirable" relationships more difficult. Disguising himself as a member of an all-black baseball team, Johnson escaped to Canada and from there made his way to Europe, where he lived as a fugitive for seven years.

Most American laws on sexual behavior exist on the statute books, because attempting to remove them would cause a fundamentalist right-wing backlash, but nobody ever expects them to be enforced. The only laws that are regularly employed concern themselves with public or quasi-public acts, such as using a prostitute, exposing oneself in public, or distributing pornographic material.

Sex Murderers

Today, only a historian would know who was the British Minister of War in 1888, but almost everyone would recognize the nickname of his contemporary, the murderous Jack the Ripper. His claim to fame? He brutally butchered and disemboweled several streetwalkers in London. There are more than a hundred books and just as many theories about the Ripper. Anti-Semites suspected a Jew, critics of the church suspected a member of the clergy, and opponents of the monarchy suspected a scion from the British royal family. Public outrage spread rapidly at the police's inability to solve these murders that were practically committed in broad daylight. The London Police Commissioner was forced to resign. Even years after the series of murders, a letter to a newspaper alleged to be from Jack the Ripper sent the newspaper's sales soaring. This was exactly what the writer of the letter, a journalist, was

Bottom left: **James Maybrick.** Maybrick, a Liverpool cotton broker who died of arsenic poisoning in 1889, was controversially identified as Jack the Ripper in 1992, after the discovery of a diary that was claimed to belong to him. It was signed "Jack the Ripper" and contained gruesome descriptions of the Whitechapel murders.

Bottom right: **Fritz Haarmann.** Haarman exemplifies a theme common to a number of cannibalistic sex killers, including the American mass murderer Jeffrey Dahmer. He chose victims he envied, and wished to resemble, and ingested them to absorb their qualities.

M, **still from the film by Fritz Lang, 1931.** "Who is the murderer?" asks the poster. Peter Lorre stars as a serial child-murderer, who in a chilling confession claims that he is not responsible for his actions, and cannot control the "evil thing" inside him. The film is based on the life of the Düsseldorf child-killer Peter Kurten.

banking on. The budding tabloid press had found in the mysterious murderer its first usable subject. The dubious, posthumous fame of criminals has nothing to do with the number of their victims. It is much more the circumstances surrounding the crime that make a murderer unforgettable. In the United States around 1890, Herman Webster Mudgett promised about 200 women that he would marry them. As soon as they made him their sole heir, he murdered and dissected them. But Jack the Ripper is more famous to this day because he remains the "great unknown". Moreover, he killed women who had placed themselves in danger and thus, as the morals of society dictate, they paid the price.

Between August and November of 1888, in the lower-class district of Whitechapel, Jack the Ripper slit the throats of at least seven prostitutes and removed their innards, especially their inner reproductive organs. His methods not only led people to believe that he had anatomical knowledge, but also that he was a sex murderer, he murdered to attain sexual satisfaction.

However, very few so-called sex murderers actually kill for sexual satisfaction. Much more often, they take their victims' lives to cover up a rape or to eliminate troublesome witnesses (of a sex crime). Wives, mistresses, and especially prostitutes fall victim to men who are impotent in their presence and thus feel humiliated and become enraged. Other perpetrators may kill their victims during a robbery, notice their arousal in the process, and defile the corpse.

Even mass murderers whose names are remembered centuries later may have killed with pleasure, but not for the sexual thrill of it. Gilles de Rais was executed in France in the 15th century because he was said to have cruelly murdered numerous children at satanic masses. The Hungarian "Blood Countess" Elisabeth Bathory, who died in prison in 1614, took baths in the blood of young women to preserve her youth.

For the real sex murderer, the act of killing itself, as well as dismembering, impaling, and cutting open the bodies (and especially the sex organs) of their still living, dying or already dead victims, is the focus of their desire. These acts are specifically needed in order for the killer to experience sexual satisfaction.

Whole generations have grown up in the dark shadow of infamous murderers – Jack the Ripper, the French serial killer Henri Landru who was born in 1869 and executed in 1922, or Fritz Haarmann (1879–1925), who killed and sometimes ate a considerable number of young men in Germany in the 1920s. The German child murderer Jürgen Bartsch (1947–1976) massacred four young boys as a youth. Some English murderers, such as John Christie in the 1950s, Dennis Nielsen in the 1980s and Fred West in the 1990s, achieved additional notoriety by disposing of the corpses in and around

their own homes, giving rise to grisly but spectacular exhumations by the police.

The sex murderer preoccupies the mind of the peaceful citizen much more than other mass murderers. Sex murderers tend to commit murders compulsively even though they are aware of the fact that killing is against the law. This is exactly why people find them such monsters or beasts, the incarnation of evil. Sex murders inspire not just horror but profound hate, especially in those who themselves suffer from murderous impulses but not from the compulsion to realize them. Numerous artists

René Magritte, *Les Jours Gigantesques*, 1928. Oil on canvas, 116 x 81 cm, Kunstsammlung Nordrhein-Westfalen, Düsseldorf. Magritte sometimes used direct and even brutal imagery in his paintings. *The Rape*, for instance, makes a woman's head out of her torso, with breasts for eyes, and the vulva as her mouth. In *Les Jours Gigantesques* he seems to be suggesting that a deep psychological kinship exists between victim and attacker, by fusing them onto the same body.

have satisfied their deadly fantasies by making a sex murderer the focus of their work. One theory explains that they experience the terrible deeds vicariously through their creations.

War and Eros

The destructive effect of war on erotic culture has long been a controversial topic. Some people even refer to the passionate liaison between the Greek god of war, Ares, and the goddess of love, Aphrodite, as an indication of a certain harmony between aggression and eroticism. As late as 1930, a scientific German work on sexuality still emphasized the notion that in the past, women were the main spoils of the victors and even willingly became their possessions. Mercenaries were even recruited with, among other things, the promise of being allowed to rape the women of the conquered peoples.

During the First World War when the German Federation for the Protection of Mothers tried to establish legal abortions for women who had been raped, their efforts were met with great resistance. Even though it was only meant to be an emergency law to help the girls and women who had been violated by members of the enemy army during the war, the women who fought for this legislation were suspected of having unpatriotic intentions. They were supposedly just using the events taking place as an opportunity to accomplish what a few feminists had been striving for: the right of women to control their own bodies.

Sexual violence against an enemy nation's women is unfortunately still practiced in wartime today as a way of humiliating the nation's men. Women who consequently become pregnant are often faced with strict religious doctrines. In 1999, Pope John Paul II warned that the women of Kosovo who had been raped would be committing murder if they removed from their bodies the product of the crime committed against them. In addition to this, it is also common for men to be raped by the victors. The Treatment Center for Victims of Torture in Berlin, among others, drew attention to this in the summer of 1999 in connection with the war in Kosovo. Rape against men is not made public nearly as often, since men are even more ashamed to talk about it than women.

In addition to the violence that occurs against them in wartime, women's loyalty to their nation is always questioned. This is due to the fact that in all wars, women from the home front have become involved with prisoners of war – and the more foreign the men looked, the greater the national outrage. Even the German *frolleins* of the allied troops were subjected to fierce hostility and decried by their fellow Germans as "GI-sweethearts" or even "GI-whores". However, the soldiers themselves certainly didn't only visit army brothels. They also entered into sexual relationships with the "respectable" women of the occupied countries. During the Second World War soldiers of the German army fathered several thousand

Heinrich Zille, *In the Flemish communications zone (Place d'Armes), Queuing at Mme Aline Florimond's.* Drawing.

children in Norway and Denmark alone. Once the Allied forces retook the countries, the "Germany-loving sluts", who had become involved with members of the occupying forces, either out of spite or affection, were subjected to extreme humiliation by their fellow countrymen. In France their heads were shaved and they were then driven through the streets to be ridiculed by the public. (Head-shaving has a long tradition as a form of public shaming. Around the end of the 18th century, the prostitutes of Vienna were also threatened with the loss of their hair.)

Even after the Second World War, the notion persisted – and this was even propagated by scientific works about sex at the time – that women of a conquered nation could not wait to be ravished by enemy soldiers. It is always only the enemies that are brutal and sexually unbridled: along with the reproach that enemy troops murder little children, it is also claimed in the war propaganda of all nations that enemy troops commit systematic, mass rapes – with the officers' approval.

During the First World War, families were often separated for years, and home leave was

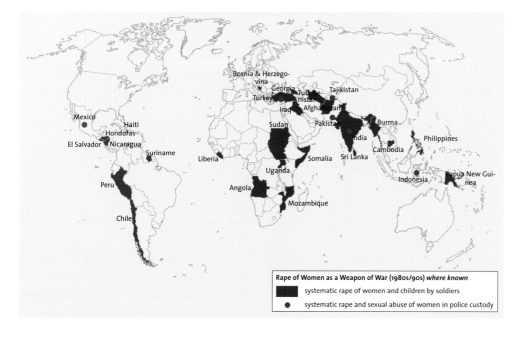

Rape of Women as a Weapon of War (1980s/90s) *where known*

■ systematic rape of women and children by soldiers

● systematic rape and sexual abuse of women in police custody

Rape is about power not desire. When soldiers rape in war, they are exerting both individual male privilege and organized male domination.

Francisco José de Goya, *They Don't Want to* from *The Disasters of War*, 1820. Etching, 14.0 x 19.4 cm, Museum of Fine Arts, Boston. Although Goya retained his position as court painter after the Napoleonic invasion of 1808, he recorded his response to the horrors he witnessed in a dramatic series of etchings, called *The Disasters of War*, which were first published in 1863.

seldom granted. While on the front, the sex lives of the soldiers were put on hold, but their sexual desire was not. Since homosexual contact and masturbation were disapproved of and wives were many miles away, lines formed at the army base brothels. Although this was not looked upon too highly, it was seen as the lesser of two evils. Unlike haphazard, unregulated prostitution, visits to the brothel could be monitored by regularly conducted examinations of the soldiers as well as the prostitutes. But despite all attempts to bureaucratically regulate sexual intercourse, the number of people affected with venereal diseases continued to rise throughout the war.

In her memoirs, American madam Nell Kimball (1854–1934) commented laconically on the behavior of soldiers after the United States entered the First World War, noting that sometimes it wasn't even about lust; it was more of a kind of "nervous breakdown that could be only be cured by a girl between the man and the mattress". The women serviced the men like objects on an assembly line. Only the officers had their own brothels and were able to satisfy their sexual needs at their leisure. The men in the ranks were advised to prepare for the brief moment that they would get to spend with a woman by helping themselves along with a few hand motions while they were waiting in line.

When the soldiers were reunited with their wives after the war, they often had marital problems. Commonly, the couples had become strangers to one another. This would remain the case long after the war was over. For many men, impotence was an additional consequence of war trauma. Women sometimes contributed to the marital problems by assaulting their husbands who returned home disabled from the war. During and after the First World War the women of Nagyrev, a small Hungarian village on the river Tisza, even began poisoning their "useless" and "boring" spouses, so that they could take more virile husbands and lovers. More than 100 men were poisoned between 1914 and 1929.

Sex Education and Upbringing

Erasmus of Rotterdam

Before about 1750, sex education as we know it today did not exist. In Antiquity and the Middle Ages, sexuality was a regular part of life; it was not some extraordinary, problematic issue that required any special attention. Children did not live in their own protected world; they gathered their own sexual knowledge like anyone else. Neither the well-to-do nor the poor had any real private sphere. Families usually bathed in front of one another and slept naked, and several family members often shared one bed. Courtship, pregnancy, and birth were a part of everyday life. Young people were considered to be of marriageable age as soon as they reached puberty. This changed little with the beginning of the modern age, as the urban middle class gained the ability to circulate important knowledge in printed form. In text books, like *Colloquia Familiaria* by Erasmus of Rotterdam (1466 or 1469–1536) which was published in 1522, sexuality is discussed openly and simply as a permanent part of everyday life. Gradually, however, the topic of human sexuality became a well-kept secret. By the time Jean-Jacques Rousseau published his book *Emile* in 1762 with its educational concepts about the "facts of life", sexuality had already become a mysterious and highly confusing sphere of human existence.

Jean-Jacques Rousseau

With his educational novel *Émile*, Jean-Jacques Rousseau (1712–1788), who was born in Geneva, had the greatest influence of all philosophers from the pre-French Revolution period on the thoughts and impressions of the coming century. But also in his work *The New Heloise*, published in 1761, he stressed the importance of emotions for the human constitution – a divergence from the philosophies of the Enlightenment. According to Rousseau, human nature is essentially good. He believed everything is good as it proceeds from the hands of the creator of all things; humans ruin everything. In terms of sex education, Rousseau advocated being honest and factual above all. He believed that the educator should answer a child's question with utmost simplicity, without secretiveness, without embarrassment, without a smile. He stressed that it is much less dangerous to satisfy the child's curiosity than to keep him in suspense, and that answers should always be serious, succinct, definite, and should ensue without hesitation.

In his *Confessions*, published posthumously in 1782, Rousseau confessed, among other things, to his erotic desires. Sacher-Masoch's inclination could definitely have been termed Rousseauism instead. A beating given to him once by a young female teacher made a lasting impression on him. For the rest of his life, he

Hans Holbein the Younger, *Erasmus of Rotterdam*, 1523. Oil on panel, 42 x 32 cm, Musée du Louvre, Paris. Erasmus was a humane scholar who argued against both the claims of the papacy and the predestination of Luther. He believed in the power of the intellect, but ironically accepted that the world was ruled by passions, and that, in his own words, even the wise man must become a fool to make a child. He wrote a text book for children where he openly spoke about sexuality as part of human life.

Maurice Quentin de Latour, *Jean-Jacques Rousseau*, 1753. Pastell, 46 x 37 cm, Musée d'Art et d'Histoire, Geneva. For Rousseau, innocence granted total license.

dreamed of women who would dominate him. Many of his contemporaries were outraged by this autobiography. But no matter how unpopular he became, there were always enough women of society who were willing to use their influence to save him from imprisonment.

Before he finally married the laundress Thérèse Levasseur in 1768, he had already lived with her for a quarter of a century. Rousseau placed all five of their children in an orphanage – an ironic fate for the offspring of an educationist.

Bertrand Russell

While doctors, psychiatrists, and jurists in the 19th and early 20th centuries were primarily occupied with the question of whether that which the Christians considered sinful really wasn't just pathological, writers and philosophers were developing a much more optimistic view of human sexuality. Sexual desire is not the ruin of human beings but instead an inherent, positive force. Especially during phases of sexual liberalization, more and more people in all countries of the Western world began to endorse this understanding and appreciation of erotic love that was foreign to typical occidental thought. And this change of consciousness was certainly influenced by philosophers like Bertrand Russell (1872–1970).

As an older man, philosopher and mathematician Russell was asked what he thought about marriage, since he was considered to be against it. A lot, he answered, after all, he had been married four times, hadn't he? All throughout his long lifetime, he longed for love, "because it delivers us from loneliness, that terrible loneliness in which a single, shuddering soul peers over the edge of the earth into the cold, lifeless, unfathomable abyss". For him, deliverance from loneliness could also be achieved through sex. Love, however, could only thrive if it were free and spontaneous. In 1929, Russell published his book *Marriage and Morals* wherein he defended his (at that time) highly progressive sexual ethics. He believed that if a marriage had brought forth children, the mother and father should try to maintain their bond for the rest of their lives if possible, but without ruling out other sexual relationships. According to Russell, complete fidelity could not be expected from most married couples, but despite their affairs, spouses should still try to stay committed to each other. Though even in an open marriage, as he saw it, the wife should only have children with her own husband. However, Dora Black, Russell's second wife, who was married to him from 1921 to 1936, didn't want to have children by him alone. Thus, his theories didn't always correspond to reality. Russell did not define "free love" as random sexual intercourse with changing partners. He professed that free love should remain romantic, and women should be hard to get. While emphasizing the practiced importance of marriage, Russell did not believe that sex needed deep love for its fulfilment.

At a time when innocence was often still equated with sexual naiveté, Russell stressed that inexperience could never lead to correct behavior; people must be informed about the "facts of life". He maintained that especially the Christian teachings about the sinfulness of sexuality could be inexpressibly harmful to an individual's character.

Eleven years after his theories were published, they were still being held against him. In 1940 he planned to accept a position as a visiting professor in New York. A Protestant bishop objected, saying that it would be unacceptable to hire as a professor a foreign atheist who supported "free love". Russell did not get the job.

Russell, aged 90, with his fourth wife Edith Finch. Despite his socially and sexually utopian ambitions, when Russell died he left behind two deeply embittered ex-wives and a son driven into a state of schizophrenia by his emotionless practice of "scientific parenting".

Freud and His Successors

Very few sex theorists have made such a lasting impression as Sigmund Freud (1856–1939). Originally, however, Freud, who was born in Moravia in 1856, wasn't even interested in human sexuality. The subject is not discussed in any of his earlier works. At the age of 30, when he finally wanted to marry after being engaged for four years, he was not earning enough through his academic work to support a family. Reluctantly, he opened a neurological practice. Soon Freud noticed that many illnesses were the manifestation of unfulfilled sexual desires. His patients were ashamed of or disgusted by what they craved. Their illness was the only escape from their pressing desire for something that they believed to be immoral, repulsive or forbidden. Psychological processes that completely eluded mere self-knowledge influenced their behavior.

With this discovery, Freud joined the ranks of Copernicus and Darwin. While these two scientists robbed humans of the illusion that they were the center of the universe and the crown of creation, Freud takes the credit for generating a third fundamental uncertainty: humans were not even "lord of their own castle".

The illness-inducing process begins long before the onset of puberty, because the striving for pleasure, the libido, is much more comprehensive than the desire for genital sex. Every boy sexually desires his mother, and every girl her father. Each would most like to violently eliminate their same-sex parent – their hated rival. It is an aggressive impulse, which in turn leads to feelings of guilt and angst. As Sigmund Freud stressed, sexuality and genitality are by no means identical: the former is much more diffuse and also includes actions and sensations that do not involve the genitals at all. This important distinction was ignored by many of Freud's critics, who vehemently contested the idea that children were sexual beings. In 1939, when Freud died in forced exile in London at the age of 82, his works were not only frowned upon by Nazi Germany, but also by Stalinist Russia. In the Soviet Union, psychoanalysis, the form of therapy that Freud developed to solve psychosexual conflicts, had

Sigmund Freud at the age of 16 with his mother Amalia, 1872. Sigmund was the eldest of Amalie's eight children, and always her favorite. She called him her "golden" Sigi, and prophesied greatness for him. Freud later pointed out that any man who has been the indisputable favorite of his mother feels like a born conqueror, and goes through life with a confidence of success that often becomes a self-fulfilling prophecy.

been outlawed since the late 1920s. Even late into the 1970s it was claimed that Freud's form of therapy played no small role in corrupting children and adolescents. The emphasis that he placed on sexual problems would supposedly lead to moral perversion and contribute to the premature development of an interest in sex – an opinion that was already expressed by Rousseau in a somewhat different context.

But treatment with psychoanalysis certainly does not lead to a sexualization of the patients, which some people hoped and others feared. Insight into the motivations and causes of sexual desire doesn't necessarily stimulate it. Freud himself studied and dealt with sexual desire – more theoretically than practically – all his life, yet claimed to have concluded his active sex life in his early forties.

In the 1990s, there was a vigorous revival of the debate on child abduction and its disastrous consequences. Criticism was then leveled at Freud for changing his theory about child abuse. It was claimed by some that in order not to endanger his career Freud had rejected his earlier finding that patients really remembered childhood seductions.

Freud and Feminism

Women in particular criticized Freud's phallocentric theories about sexuality. Are little girls really envious of their little brother's penis? Do they really desire to have a child as compensation, as a vicarious penis, because they cannot have that of their father's? Isn't it more likely that men envy adult women for their ability to bear children?

For Freud, the clitoris was just a stunted penis. Freud believed that women had two independent erogenous zones, the vagina and the clitoris. However, he deemed the clitoris as inferior, claiming that all orgasms that were reached without the phallus (in other words, orgasms achieved through clitoral stimulation) were infantile and immature. According to Freud, mature women have vaginal orgasms and women who only had clitoral orgasms are frigid.

Helene Deutsch (1884–1982) contested Freud's theory as early as 1944. She maintained that the clitoris was for pleasure and the vagina was for reproduction.

In 1963, American psychiatrist Mary Jane Sherfey also stressed the sole importance of the complex clitoral system for a woman's pleasure, saying that it is a decisive factor in the high potency of the uninhibited woman. Unlike men, she pointed out, women can have multiple (complete) orgasms in rapid succession.

Alfred Ernest Jones

The fact that psychoanalysis is so well-known in the Anglo-American world can essentially be attributed to Alfred Ernest Jones (1879–1958). After first reading Freud's work in 1905, this founder of the British Psychoanalytical Society wrote his main work of three volumes, *The Life and Work of Sigmund Freud* from 1953 to 1957. When he was still just the director of a psychiatric clinic in Toronto, Canada, Jones – who would later become President of the International Psychoanalytical Association – organized the first psychoanalytical convention in Salzburg, Austria with Carl Jung.

After 1933, he played an active and influential role in the integration of scientists who were forced to leave Germany as a result of the Nazi persecution of the Jews and any intellectuals who publicly disagreed with Nazi ideas. It was also thanks to Jones that Freud was still able to emigrate out of Austria in 1938, the year before his death.

La Ronde, still from the film by Max Ophüls, 1950, Anton Walbrook and Simone Signoret. In his buoyant, erotic play *Reigen*, 1900 (as a private limited edition, 1897) Arthur Schnitzler constructs ten scenes, each forming a link to a sexual chain of changing partners. The circle is formed when a prostitute, Leonada, who appears in the first scene with a soldier, reappears in the last with an elderly nobleman.

The Artist and the Scientist

The Austrian novelist Arthur Schnitzler (1862–1931) was the son of a physician. He studied medicine and practiced it for much of his life, taking a particular interest in psychiatry, which no doubt helped him to write the critiques of eroticism and morbidity for which he is most famous. In plays such as *Reigen* (filmed in 1950 by Max Ophüls as *La Ronde*) and stories such as *Traumnovelle* (filmed in 1999 by Stanley Kubrick as *Eyes Wide Shut*) he dissected the sexual mores of the Viennese bourgeoisie.

Freud believed that Schnitzler had divined the same truths as himself about the human mind, but through a poet's intuition rather than through scientific analysis and the laborious study of other people (a disingenuous claim when so many of Freud's insights resulted from introspection). As such, he perceived Schnitzler as a kind of doppelganger, and took pains never to meet him.

Carl Gustav Jung – The Crown Prince

After intensive collaboration in the beginning, a fierce rivalry would often develop between Freud and many of his students, which would usually lead to a parting of ways. Many of Freud's successors founded their own schools of thought and are still famous today. One of them was Swiss psychoanalyst and psychiatrist Carl Gustav Jung (1875–1961), who for many years was expected to follow in Freud's footsteps. The two men met in 1907, but six years later they parted company because Jung defined the libido differently from his teacher. For Jung, the libido did not represent the striving for pleasure but the striving for the meaning of life. Jung's assessment of the significance of sexuality was thus completely different from that of the founder of psychoanalysis. Unlike Freud, Jung was not primarily interested in a scientific explanation for psychological conflicts. Instead, he became increasingly interested in a spiritual one. He was fascinated by the symbols and archetypes of human thought, the correlation between Classical myths and psychotic fantasies. The soul, he believed, provides on the one hand a condensed image of everything past, and with this, on the other hand, an image

Carl Gustav Jung, 1955. Jung's reputation was fiercely guarded by a coterie of female followers, known to outsiders as his "Valkyries".

of the realization of everything to come. In this respect the soul, itself, creates the future. He regarded dreams as an expression of the "wisdom of the unconscious". Jung's teleological interpretation was comparable with his preoccupation with the occult, parapsychology, and astrology. The collective unconscious was just as important to him as the unconscious of the individual, if not more so.

Even when a patient dreamed of sexual symbols, Jung believed this could mean something completely different than repressed sexual desire. He also believed that the unconscious, represented in men by a female figure, the anima, and in women by a male figure, the animus, complements the conscious and makes it whole.

Wilhelm Reich

Wilhelm Reich, who was born in Galicia, Poland (1897–1957) studied medicine at the University of Vienna after the First World War. Of all Freud's students, he was especially politically active. In the 1920s he published the writings entitled *What is Class Consciousness?* and later *The Mass Psychology of Fascism* under the pseudonym of Ernst Parrell. Although he tried to create a synthesis between psychoanalysis and Marxism, he was expelled from the Communist Party in 1933 as well as the Psychoanalytical Society in 1934.

In contrast to Jung, Reich defined the concept of sexual desire much more specifically than the founder of psychoanalysis. According to him, all striving is aimed at the orgasm, the release of desire and the natural pulsation function of the complete living organism. Thus, for Reich, it was not about the sublimation of sexual desires. Neuroses as a product of sexual repression were for him quite clearly the socially dictated consequences of sexual oppression. And especially the Oedipus complex would not be a biological fact but in the end an effect of private property.

After emigrating from Germany in 1933, Wilhelm Reich lived in Norway for six years and then from 1939 in the United States. There, he dedicated himself to his "science of the vital energies". In 1954, his theories were fiercely

attacked and a ban on his scientific work was called for. When he was in his mid-50s, he was declared insane after refusing to let jurists judge issues of natural science. 20 years earlier, doubt had already been expressed about his mental condition by his ex-wife, Anni, and some of his colleagues from the time when he was still interested in psychoanalysis. At the end of 1957, he died in a state penitentiary; his writings were demonstratively destroyed. His followers today still believe that his incarceration was the work of a conspiracy of representatives from the pharmaceutical and nuclear industries. Reich's attempt to explain everything based on a single cause was insane for some and fascinating for others. According to Reich, there is a strange life elixir, the orgone, which can be accumulated in so-called orgone accumulators. This energy was in his opinion a panacea, since it can be used to treat all illnesses and can solve all philosophical and religious problems.

Reich believed that authority, in whatever form it may take, gains control over us because we suppress our instincts. Humans only submit to others because the profound fear of sexual arousal is in the end the neurotic fear of freedom. Reich localized this fear in a tension of the body musculature. He referred to this as "armoring" and believed that it hinders all orgiastic gratification, even in people who are not obviously impotent. For Reich, this sexual blockage was the energy source of neuroses.

When instinct frees itself from culture, the liberated orgasm will help society in a reverse process to achieve liberation from fascism and oppression. Even if Wilhelm Reich did have a one-track mind, he was anything other than an eroticist. His interest in sexuality was limited to climax and thus to the reliable dispersion of desire. Among other things, he developed massage techniques to help break down this armor. However, these were not meant to increase, but to eliminate desire.

Given their political implications, his writings, especially *The Function of the Orgasm*, 1927, received much attention in Germany during the student rebellions in the 1960s. Resolving problems that one had with reaching orgasm suddenly took on societal importance. The true

revolutionary was, or would at least claim to be, completely uninhibited when it came to sex. Reich believed that the force of attraction that one human being exerts on another endangers the rational way of life. Prolonging pleasure was not part of his concept; a direct course should be set towards orgasm. This is why French philosophers Pascal Bruckner and Alain Finkielkraut in the 1960s described Reich's ideas about sex as an "apotheosis of functionalism". They maintained that all Reich was interested in was killing desire and pleasure.

Johann Heinrich Fuseli, *The Nightmare*, 1790. Oil on canvas, 76.5 x 63.5 cm, Freies Deutsches Hochstift, Goethehaus, Frankfurt/M. Fuseli's macaber and fantastic paintings provided fertile ground for analyses by early psychiatrists, especially those, who preferred to apply psychoanalytical techniques to art, folklore and literature than to living people.

Great European Perversion Experts

Richard Freiherr von Krafft-Ebing. Terms like sexual dependence and masochism are part of the everyday language of today. They were coined by Krafft-Ebing.

Underwear fetishist. Most fetishists are men, and for all of them, true sexual satisfaction becomes virtually impossible in the absence of the fetish.

Richard Freiherr von Krafft-Ebing

Born in Wiesbaden, Germany in 1840, this psychiatrist – or "lunatic doctor" as members of his profession were called in those days – worked as a psychiatric expert at trials in Heidelberg after studying medicine. When he was still very young, Krafft-Ebing (1848–1902) was granted a chair at the University of Strasbourg. In 1886, his main work *Psychopathia Sexualis* was published and read with great interest – by more than just members of the psychiatric community.

As the first sexologist, he described the various forms of sexual satisfaction. He gathered his material from his own patients and those of his colleagues who did not want to publish their observations under their own names. Court testimony and older medical textbooks supplemented his collection that described almost every conceivable type of deviation from "normal sexual intercourse". He was the first to refer to the phenomenon of sexual dependence and coined the terms "masochism" and "sadism" which are in general use today.

Readers without a classical education eager to learn about erotic topics were disappointed when they read *Psychopathia Sexualis*. They could at best only guess what perversions of love were being described. Whenever Krafft-Ebing went into detail, he would discreetly switch to Latin or French. In the late 1960s, versions for laypersons were published in the United States, which fed readers' demand for sensationalism. Whoever bought this book expected sex and scandal.

Even today, some people are appalled after reading this book, perhaps because they find cases reminding them of their own preferences. Are they "morally degenerate" or "hereditarily burdened" like the mentally ill individuals described in the book? Whether intentionally or not, Krafft-Ebing reinforced the (uneducated) reader's idea that basically every sexual variation is cause for alarm.

Like the majority of people in his generation, this sexologist found masturbation in particular to be pernicious and advised drastic methods for suppressing it. As an expert witness, one of the issues that Krafft-Ebing spoke out against was the criminal persecution of male homosexuality, which he referred to as an "antipathic sexual instinct". This was by no means motivated by his sense of liberalism; for him, homosexuals were neither sinners nor criminals, but rather sick people who were not of sound mind.

In 1889, three years after the publication of his major work, he was appointed Professor in Vienna, where he continued to work in his specialized fields of criminology, neurology, and psychiatry. The question of when a criminal is legally responsible for his acts occupied him until the end of his life. It was his opinion, for example, that if a man's main reason for repeatedly stealing aprons was not material gain but only the compulsive desire to possess his fetish, then he was not a criminal. However, his sexual deviation – whether he was deemed sick or criminal – would ostracize him from society.

Henry Havelock Ellis

The English doctor Henry Havelock Ellis was born in 1859, during the 22nd year of Queen Victoria's reign. Born almost 20 years later than Krafft-Ebing he was a child of the same generation as Sigmund Freud. Like Freud, he believed that adult sexual desire is very strongly influenced by parental behavior, upbringing, and early childhood experience. In a society where almost everything sexual was associated with shame, Henry Havelock Ellis

Henry Havelock Ellis, 1931. Ellis was an early champion of women's emancipation, contraception, changes to the divorce laws and sex education for children.

dedicated the first part of his main work, which was published in 1897, to the development of the feeling of shame. He drew his information from a variety of sources – Casanova's manuscripts, studies conducted by anthropologists on the customs of several Indian tribes, as well as reports about Islamic prostitutes in Turkey. Unlike many women from Christian countries, these prostitutes would display their bodies completely in the nude, but carefully cover their faces with a veil. For more than three decades, between 1897 and 1928, Ellis completed and published his *Studies in the Psychology of Sex*. Much earlier than other researchers, he described masturbation by men and women of all ages as a completely normal phenomenon. At the same time, he felt that apparently normal phenomena needed to be explained just as much as deviant ones. Accessible only to experts of the profession until 1935, his writings had to be published abroad.

Whereas his contemporaries could not imagine a person who was completely oblivious to sex-ual arousal and passion, Ellis pointed out that people with no sexual desire do exist. As an example of this condition, Havelock Ellis cited the famous German painter Adolf von Menzel (1832–1905). This state of so-called erotic apathy is now clinically widely recognized. Like Krafft-Ebing, Henry Havelock Ellis was a fanatical collector; he, too, archived all variants of human sexuality. But his interest in perversions was marked by empathy and understanding. He did not want to categorize and ostracize the "others", the "perverts"; he wanted to understand the reasons behind the peculiarities. Unlike Krafft-Ebing, he did not portray all deviations as being equally dubious. Quite the contrary, he stressed that the various expressions of sexuality are all possible variants. Thus, from a contemporary perspective, he is perceived as being not only much more modern, but also more philanthropic than his German counterpart.

Ellis's own preferences were defined by peculiarities. Ever since childhood, the sight of women urinating in a standing position fascinated him. On through old age, sexual intercourse with a woman was not the focus of his erotic fantasies. Nevertheless, he had intense and long-lived love affairs with a great number of very intelligent women, often writers.

Blue. **Woman's Body Played on by Water, partial shot.** In one of his studies Ellis examines Undinism, a term for the fetishistic role of water. There are people who reach orgasm through swimming.

From Preference to Fetish

Austrian satirist Karl Kraus (1874–1936) once joked that there is no creature under the sun more pitiable than a fetishist "who longs for a woman's shoe and has to put up with the whole woman". In one of his works, the French pornographer Restif de la Bretonne (1734–1806) wrote that he "pressed his lips to one of the treasures while using the other in place of a woman". Having a shoe fetish also used to be called "restifism" after Bretonne.

Many men develop a marked preference for certain lingerie items or women's shoes, but still find a woman arousing without this accessory. Some couples wouldn't miss a fetish party where the dress code stipulates some special get-up made out of rubber, leather or another material. They, however, are not fetishists in the strict sense of the word. They are simply searching for new, modern sources of excitement. In fact, this is exactly what the fetishist does not do. When it comes to his fetish, he is very conservative. He is not interested in new fashions, but instead in the erotically effective details as they were when he first discovered their special attraction. When the pageboy look became popular in the 1920s, proponents of the old image of femininity were not the only ones who protested. Ponytail fetishists suffered too. A real fetishist does not have "preferences". He is indeed only interested in one specific thing. Because there seemed to be a similarity between the phenomenon of sexual fetishism and the devotion that African tribes exhibited towards their fetishes, the term "fetish" was first used by French psychologist Alfred Binet (1857–1911) in the late 1870s.

A fetishist can deem himself lucky when all he has to do for his happiness or arousal is to look at or wear used women's clothing. Some fetishists adore objects while others are obsessed with certain materials like rubber, leather or fur – things that they can collect and surround themselves with. At best, the fetishistic cult of object worship is something like a sexually charged piousness.

If the fetish is inevitably connected to a living human being (as in the case of the foot fetishist) then the fetishist will find himself in a dilemma

similar to that of the masochist. He cannot get rid of the rather pleasure-killing human without simultaneously losing the object of his desire. This is why fetishism really has more to do with the attempted escape from the opposite sex, at least according to psychologists like Wilhelm Stekel (1868–1940). Particularly precocious children, who develop strong erotic desires at a young age but are not allowed to direct them towards the closest members of their family, divert their desires towards inanimate love objects. Everything, even the average housefly – and this has been documented – can become somebody's erotic fetish.

Less obvious is the fetishism of those who are not primarily interested in material things. Some people react erotically to very specific situations, like being laced up tightly in something, or conditions, like extreme cold. Their obsession does not always give them away. There are people who have a fetish for emaciation or obesity that could never fall in love with a person of average build. The ballerina Fanny Elssler in the 19th century – with her undeveloped hips and her breasts, in the words of the contemporary critic, Théophile Gautier, "no fuller than a hermaphrodite of Antiquity" – seemed to be the ideal woman for such people. More than 100 years later they made an icon out of the supermodel Kate Moss. Those who like thin people just seem to be interested in a certain type of person – just like everyone else. The fetishistic character of the relationship doesn't become obvious until the woman – who has been insanely adored up to this point – changes slightly and is then all of a sudden found to be completely unattractive.

Anti-fetishists are probably more common than fetishists, but they are much less conspicuous. They are less particular and may like blondes just as much as brunettes. However, the women cannot have any specific characteristic – like large breasts, for example – otherwise the anti-fetishist's interest will wane immediately.

Psychologists argue about how such fixations originate. Sigmund Freud claimed that every fetish is associated with the last moment in which a young boy still believes that all humans have a

Drawing of a foot fetishist, c. 1900. For the foot fetishist, everything about the foot is delightful – not just its appearance but also its scent and its flavor. Washing the foot only diminishes the pleasure.

Carlos, *Catalogue Général* of the Librairie Générale, 1930s. The Kinsey Institute for Research in Sex, Gender and Reproduction, Inc., Bloomington. In clothing fetishes, the fetishized item of apparel takes on an erotic life of its own, so that a boot, for example, is sexually stimulating regardless of whose leg is inside it, or indeed whether or not it is worn at all.

penis like he does. When he makes the shocking discovery that mother does not possess this organ that he holds so dear, he can only imagine that his father has forcefully robbed it from her. So he sees himself as being exposed to this same danger. For the rest of his life, the last thing that he perceived before making this shocking discovery will be more important to him than any human being. As controversial as this theory may be, it does seem strange that there aren't very many women who are true fetishists.

People in Uniform

The pre-1914 officer ideally was a figure whose irreproachable inner attitude found perfect expression in his outer bearing. If you were a "dashing" officer this enhanced your chances with women. Uniform fetishes are said to be a more common occurrence among women than among men. The outer casing gives its wearer an eroticising aura of power.

Until the First World War the clothes of an officer, especially in full-dress uniform, were far more colorful than those of civilians. The eroticizing of the uniform was also caused by the fact that it did not suffer from the tyranny of fashion changes: the intimate objects of desire – the officer in uniform as a target for fetishism, particularly through his accessories and flourishes – which were vividly remembered from childhood were still available in the everyday world of adulthood.

After the Second World War the erotic symbolism of the uniform dwindled significantly, since it became a purely practical item of clothing. Nonetheless military uniforms continue to play a major role for particular groups of homosexual men who find an erotic fascination in the symbols of power and submission.

The fetishist attraction of women in uniform is also obvious with women who are obliged to wear a certain costume in their jobs. Unlike the officer uniform, which armor-plates and sheaths the body, the light clothing of, for example, a nurse evokes a fantasy of accessibility. A 1982 American survey emphasized that in 73 percent of the films between 1930 and 1980 nurses were portrayed as sex objects. In the male sexual fantasy a woman's uniform symbolizes a certain power. The nurse can force patients to submit to various unpleasant procedures. In contrast to this sadistic version she might alternatively appear in a serving role. Many customers in so-called massage salons demand that the women dress in classical nurse gear. For them the outfit with its cap and apron is a sign of the willingness to serve.

Gil Elvgren, *Now Don't Ask Me What's Cookin'*, 1949. Oil painting, 60 x 75 cm, private collection. This image neatly elides the two conflicting messages that are sent by the nurse's uniform. She is boiling something, so she is domesticated and subservient. Yet at the same time there is a flirtatious, veiled threat that the boiled object is a bandage or poultice about to be applied, painfully, to the onlooker.

Masochism

Austrian-born Leopold Ritter von Sacher-Masoch (1836–1895) was first and foremost a respected writer. His contemporaries compared his novels to those of Russian author Ivan Turgenev; literary specialists studied the similarities between his portrayal of women and that of German author Thomas Mann. The latter made only obscure allusions in his literary work to his erotic obsessions. Since Sacher-Masoch was more candid, he is still remembered more than a century after his death as being the apparent creator of a certain perversion. Especially in his work *Venus in Furs*, from the year 1870, which is still famous today, he describes quite clearly what he is fascinated by. His creativity was inextricably linked to the fulfillment of his unusual erotic fantasies. For this he required a very specific woman, a woman named Wanda, who is still today the focus of many masochists' dreams. What we know today as "masochism" already existed long before the psychiatrist Krafft-Ebing (1840–1902) first associated this paradoxical sexual orientation with the name of his contemporary – an association that never died. Earlier it was somewhat poetically called

Anonymous, *The Domina*, beginning of the 20th cent. This sketch for a stained glass window was commissioned by a fan of this erotic deviation.

"remorseful bliss". What this refers to is the tendency to derive one's own personal sexual pleasure from being tortured, used, and humiliated by a desirable person. Even though psychologists regard masochism as a feminine quality, the most well-known case studies involve almost exclusively men.

As paradoxical as it may seem, masochists do not want to suffer. The sexual pleasure that they experience from subtle to intense torture is in no way unconditional; it is tied to very specific requirements. In many cases – as in the case of the unwitting eponym of this erotic passion – the pleasure the masochists get from

Opposite: **Carl von Stur, *Viennes Figaro/His Muse*, 1879.** Because Sacher-Masoch never hid his tastes, but advertised them widely, he was a popular subject for caricaturists, who found him an easy target. They could lampoon him simply by illustrating his own stories.

Torture belt with adjustable handcuffs, replica 1875, sadomasochistic accessories from the Erotic Museum in Barcelona.

their own submission is not just dependent on the performance but also on the presentation of the torturer. Sacher-Masoch personally drew up the contract that obliged his wife Wanda to wear a fur whenever she was cruel to him. This excited him, and not just sexually. Later, when they got divorced, he realized to his dismay that the whole secret was the fur, and not Wanda. Usually it is the male masochists who make the rules about the conduct they find satisfying. They are the directors of their own experience. Only a woman who does not dominate – but never lets that show – will be able to "master" them. Krafft-Ebing described a man who suffered from an attack of masochism one or two times a year. He would rent an apartment and instruct the "personnel" what was to be done with him. Whenever he visited the apartment he was undressed, masturbated and flagellated as ordered. He pretended to offer resistance, and begged for mercy; then, as ordered, he was allowed to eat and sleep. But in spite of protest he was kept there, and beaten if he did not submit. Thus the affair would go on for some days.

When his attack was over he was dismissed, and he returned to his wife and children.

"Unconditional submission" is nothing but a sexual code. The people who actually fantasize about it and act it out don't give themselves up or let themselves go at all, but instead want to meticulously control the conditions of every erotic encounter. Somebody other than Sacher-Masoch may not have required Wanda to wear a fur. And instead of having to try to make him jealous by flirting (ineffectively) with another man (Sacher-Masoch's favorite, the "Greek"), she may have had to let him drink out of her chamber pot. A masochist's supposed longing for "domination by a woman" is usually pure fiction and is completely overshadowed by his barely concealed contempt of women – which explains why Sacher-Masoch also wrote for a magazine entitled *The Misogynist*.

It is the "domina" who is always expected to satisfy the often very high demands of the slave. It is only when the woman is a true sadist that she will treat him correctly. But if she truly is a sadist, she will also exploit him, wear him out,

and leave him. Only a dominatrix in that one high-priced moment of intensity is the exact incarnation of a masochist's dreams.

The dilemma that arises in a long-term relationship between a submissive man and a dominant woman is usually irresolvable. If she does really despise him, then she will probably end up leaving him. If she doesn't really despise him, then he will leave her. For the masochist, the contrast between her magnificence and his insignificance can never be great enough. If the mistress turns out to be a plain old person, less cruel and unpredictable than the masochist had hoped, then his ideal crumbles.

The situation didn't become easier for erotic deviants until the 1990s, when sadomasochism became socially acceptable – at least in the larger cities of the Western world. As opposed to the way it used to be, people can now act out their fantasies freely in a role-playing game at the weekend, where they will sometimes play the dominant role and other times the servient role. But this so-called "switching" isn't for everybody; not everyone longs for this type of flexibility.

Prostitution in the Western World

A Job like Any Other

Jan Sanders van Hemessen (with Jan Swart), *Wayfarer in a Brothel*, c. 1545/50. Oil on panel, 83 x 111 cm, Kunsthalle Karlsruhe. Every possible impropriety that the whores in the brothels practiced, such as theft, rude conduct (for example emptying chamber pots over suitors), or quarrelsomeness, were represented in paintings and drawings time and again. But the images say nothing about the associated health risks. The elderly visitor's gesture of refusal on this painting can be seen as one of the few visual hints to the dangers houses of pleasure posed to one's health.

At the beginning of the 20th century social critics remarked that the struggle against prostitution bore similarities to Don Quixote's battle against windmills.

However, not everyone took part in the hopeless struggle, and it certainly did not involve all social circles. It was inspired by a black-and-white view of the world, with the respectable and upstanding living on one side, and the dishonored and fallen on the other. But for a long time it was consistently overlooked that the former, in particular where the upholding of sexual mores was concerned, were fundamentally dependent on the latter.

For centuries the Church sat in judgment over prostitutes. According to the Scriptures it was Woman who tempted Man. Women who sold themselves were sinners. They would and should repent of their unchaste behavior and find the faith; if not in youth, then in old age. This led to the saying: young whore, old churchgoer. Anyone who returned a prostitute to the path of righteousness by marrying her was doing a good deed.

The Christian Church's renunciation of sexual passion was one expression of the rejection of all those desires which distracted attention away from the hereafter and directed it at the here and now. The pursuit of virtue involved far more than the renunciation of the "desires of the flesh". The brothel was regarded as a place of depravity because the people there were seeking pure pleasure. Whoring wasn't the only activity offered; many men also indulged in gluttony and card and dice games. From the beginning of the 19th century attitudes towards prostitution were shaped not so much by clerics as by lawyers. Women working as prostitutes were now considered criminals and were dealt with accordingly. They were held almost entirely to blame for the spread of venereal diseases such as syphilis, which still posed a deadly threat well into the 20th century. Owing to fear of disease and its spread, from the middle of the 19th century the medical fraternity wielded increasing influence over social values. Only "degenerates" were found amongst the prostitutes, and their descent from families which had produced drunkards, gamblers, and criminals was emphasized. Prostitutes were also seen from this perspective as "bad people".

Finally, social critics and community reformers were concerned with the rehabilitation of prostitutes rather than of prostitution. As victims of society, they said, these women were not to blame. They did not provide sex for money because they were corrupt, but because of financial hardship.

While it was considered to be a mark of destitution – something that was effectively beyond her control – the life of a prostitute could have no redeeming features. Its image began, tentatively, to assume some positive connotations only after society started to accept that a woman's own sex drive – and not mere economic necessity – might be a valid reason for her turning to prostitution. Thus it was only towards the end of the 20th century that the extremely varied self-images of the prostitutes themselves entered the public debate. Some of them saw themselves as social workers who

took pleasure in their career. Others described themselves as victims of exploitation and violence. Nevertheless, the "red-light trade" remains a world that seems especially prone to mystification.

In the Western world the centuries-old debate about the value of prostitutes continues as before without reaching a conclusion. This is reflected, among other things, in very different ideas on regulation: should men be prevented by law from offering women money for sexual favors, or will the eventual decriminalization of prostitution be brought about if prostitutes are no longer stigmatized and socially isolated?

Only one thing is certain: the influence of prostitution on the economy cannot be overestimated. In material terms countless people make a profit out of the so-called oldest profession in the world. Owners of brothels are often "respectable" people. However, the biggest profit is made by the state, which claims billions in taxes from the sex industry. Prostitutes are liable to taxation like any other worker, but are not granted the same rights.

Top: **Vittore Carpaccio, *The Courtesans* (detail), 1495. Oil on panel, 100 x 70 cm, Museo Correr, Venice.** Prostitutes and courtesans turned up frequently in paintings that were meant as allegories or fables. They were often used, for instance, to illustrate the transitory nature of youth and beauty.

Left: **Alexandre François Xavier Sigalon, *The Young Courtesan* (detail), 1821. Oil on canvas, 110 x 120 cm, Musée du Louvre, Paris.** The skillful courtesan could have the best of both worlds – wealthy admirers who provided for her material needs, and young lovers who provided at least the illusion of romance.

From Streetwalking to Luxury Bordello

Irma la Douce, **still from the film by Billy Wilder, 1963, Shirley MacLaine as Irma, Jack Lemmon as Nestor Patou**. Irma was set up in her own apartment, so that her "benefactor" could visit her whenever he wanted.

The car is not just a convenient way to cruise for prostitutes, it often provides an alternative to renting a hotel room.

Whore Organizations

In much the same way that homosexuals have given a new positive meaning to the word "queer", used pejoratively since the 1930s, many confident prostitutes are now referring to themselves as "whores". From the mid-1970s onwards, in nearly all Western countries, they formed lobbies similar to other civil rights movements. In London, for example, there is "Pussi" (1975), later renamed PLAN (Prostitution Laws Are Nonsense), and the ECP (English Collective of Prostitutes). In 1977, in Spain, prostitutes founded a trade union of sex workers *(Sindicato de la trabajadores del amor)*. Poland also has organizations concerned with looking after disenfranchised prostitutes, for example "La Strada", formed in the 1990s. In 1978 the civil rights group PLRA (Prostitute Law Repeal Association) was set up in Sydney, Australia. In addition to lobbies, prostitutes also band together for International Whore Congresses, which have been held since 1975, with Paris hosting the first, and Berlin the 24th (in 1999). The agenda included, among other items, the formation of "Whore Schools" and the recognition of whoring as a profession. "We Provide Training!" mocked a cartoonist in a conservative newspaper.

Although the political voice of prostitutes has been growing louder, only a minority of the women earning money for sexual services put themselves in the spotlight. Those few have recently reconstructed the image of "the prostitute", but in reality there are enormous differences within the profession. For some it is a trade, requiring an apprenticeship which they pass down through the years and decades, often well on into a ripe old age. For others it is a job reluctantly done, initially with the vain hope of being able to give it up at some point.

In order to find clients with expendable income, prostitutes sometimes have to be willing to relocate to a different country from their own. In Germany the proportion of prostitutes from abroad is steadily increasing, and because of this some organizations have recently been formed which represent the interests of women from particular countries. For example, *Ban Ying* is a Berlin advice center especially for women from Southeast Asia; amongst other services it provides a secret safe house.

"Zones of Tolerance"

In some parts of Europe "zones of tolerance" is a euphemistic expression for a red-light district. In all towns in which prostitution is legally restricted to an area of a few streets, it follows that this is where one will find a concentration of prostitutes and their clients. Zones of tolerance are justified with the claim that they "protect public morals". No one need be offended by the sight of prostitutes in busy shopping areas and town squares.

Homeowners in zones of tolerance who are unable to move away, however, are out of luck: the value of their property will decline.

The question of whether it is reasonable to attempt to banish the phenomenon into invisibility is a matter of heated debate. Allegedly the creation of a sex ghetto makes it possible to assess and therefore control the problems associated with prostitution. Those who oppose the idea of delineated areas point out that this is the very kind of regularization which encourages prostitution. They say whoever officially regulates the sale of sex at the same time institutionalizes the poverty and oppression of women. This was the objection put forward at the start of the 1980s by Carola Bustelo, the then-leader of the Spanish Women's Institute, to the Mayor of Madrid's proposal to designate a part of the city as a zone of tolerance.

Eros Centers

A modern variant on the delineated zone is the Eros Center, originating from the end of the 1960s, a type of super-brothel with seemingly self-employed small entrepreneurs. The apartments are apparently ideally suited for the sex trade, but many women who are not directly involved, especially immigrants, can also find themselves living there. Sometimes the prostitutes in an Eros Center walk the streets in search of clients, but a more consumer-friendly method is to turn the center into a kind of sex-mall, possibly with receptionists and "sales staff", in which clients can make their selection from books containing the pictures, descriptions and prices of the women present. Several women may club together to take a single room, which they occupy in shifts, but a common – and more traditional – practice is for one person to hire a room and act as a sort of small-scale "madam".

Top: Paris, Rue St. Denis – In red-light districts, where the interest of visitors can be taken for granted, many prostitutes find it more convenient to advertise themselves through cards in windows and doorways, rather than by standing out in the street.

Five-star bordellos like the Yab Yum in Amsterdam are only available to an exclusive clientele. In this atmosphere, where sexual lust is only one of the things for sale, the prostitutes have their price.

On the "International Day of the Whore", in Berlin, 1999, prostitutes put on fancy dress and demonstrated for their right to the same legal status as other workers.

Prostitution in Germany

The trade is plied in different ways, not only in the various federal states within Germany, but also in the various cities. According to statistics from the 1990s, Hamburg, which is a seaport, had one prostitute for every 210 inhabitants, while landlocked Dresden had only one for every 4800 (seaports traditionally have a disproportionately large number of prostitutes). In Berlin – the only city in which there is no so-called zone of tolerance – prostitution is predominantly based in apartments. In Hamburg quite a few prostitutes stand waiting for their next john on the street.

Current estimates of activity within Germany are at strong variance with each other in every respect: there are between 150,000 and 400,000 prostitutes working in Germany, out of a total population of more than 80 million. 60,000 of these are registered with the health authorities. A working woman will be visited by, on average, 140 men per month.

It stands to reason that the better the establishment, the greater the demand for attention by the big-spending clientele. There the cost unit is the hour, not the quick screw. About every eighth woman working in the German sex trade could be categorized as a high-class prostitute. A prestigious companion for the whole night is expensive. At the end of the 1990s a client would have had to spend up to 2000 German marks for such a service – a month's salary for many.

As in other countries, the picture is different as far as streetwalkers are concerned: if only sexual relief is wanted, it can be had cheaply. The cheapest woman with a drug habit – every twelfth prostitute is in this position – needs more than ten customers every day to finance her addiction. Usually, however, she also has to support the habit of her pimp. Needing the money immediately, she is open to negotiation over the price as well as over the request, frequently made by the clients, for unprotected sex. Most of the prostitutes in Germany – two out of three – work in bars and brothels. It is common for bars to impose an unwritten rule that for every half hour spent in a private room, a bottle of champagne automatically gets put on the bill. Many women then drink all those bottles which have been paid for, leading some of them into alcoholism. The alcoholics age rapidly, and once they pass the age of 25 they are often in financial ruin. Unless they have regular customers their outlook is bleak. Once past the age of 30 many cross over into the world of bondage, discipline and sadomasochism, where the age of a prostitute usually is of less importance.

The 1975 Whore Strike in Lyons, France

Since the 1970s prostitutes have no longer left it up to those who lead totally different existences from themselves to pass judgment on their way of life. In June 1975, during the International Year of the Woman, 150 prostitutes in the French city of Lyons, with lively media participation, occupied Saint Nizier Church and called for a general strike. Many of their colleagues had been murdered in the previous years and it appeared as if the police were making little effort to find the perpetrators. Moreover, the prostitutes argued that they were being harassed by police. At that time in France there was a misdemeanor called "behavior inviting sexual offence" (R 34 of the French Penal Code). As soon as a prostitute allowed herself to be seen in public she was hit with a fine of 150 francs (with an average annual income of 49,000 francs in France at that time); frequently this happened several times a day. Above all, however, there was the threat that repeated offences would lead to a prison sentence.

The (government-led) fight against the syndicates of pimps had the gravest implications for the women, because even the hoteliers who let out rooms to prostitutes were classified as pimps. Women who wanted to rent an apartment together were liable to be charged with procurement. However, prostitutes wanted to be allowed to practice their trade anywhere. They were not interested in the reopening of the French brothels, which had been closed in 1945. They wanted to be in business on their own account.

From the prostitutes' viewpoint the French government was the biggest pimp of all. In other French cities, such as Marseilles, Grenoble, and Montpellier, churches were also being occupied, and finally even in Paris, where (in 1975) 6000 registered prostitutes lived. The occupation of the churches was forcibly brought to an end after ten days, on the grounds that the highly publicized strike, according to police, had been organized by pimps.

Lack of Rights

No matter what big differences there were and still are between the cities in Germany, the selling of sex for money was considered immoral everywhere. The prostitutes could not enforce payment of their sexual wages. Only in 1999 did female politicians support the abolition of a few absurd laws. For instance, although under the 1973 reform of Germany's criminal law prostitution was no longer prohibited, there was a ban on "the promotion of prostitution". Every brothel-keeper who created humane working conditions was open to prosecution, for, after all, he should have made the lives of his employees as difficult as possible in order – in accordance with the pious hope of the lawmakers – to discourage them from this profession. He was allowed to issue bed linen and towels as required, but if he checked that condoms were always within reach he committed a crime.

In short, the more undignified the working conditions, the more legal the brothel. It was forbidden to provide either official conditions of service or a written contract of employment. However, this may be changing rapidly – as of the year 2000 in Germany, "prostitute" is a recognized profession and has ceased to be an "immoral trade".

Bad though the situation is for local prostitutes it is still worse for the foreigners with no right of residence. Their numbers are rising steadily and in many cities they have been the majority for quite some time. Asians, Africans, and East Europeans are for the most part smuggled in by slave-dealers and work illegally. If they dared to report the person who was confiscating their earnings they would themselves be threatened with criminal proceedings.

Bargain Hunters or Cross-border Relations

Women are "cheap" if the clients and prostitutes originate from neighboring areas with wide economic disparities. In the last decade of the 20th century that was the case especially in the border regions of central and eastern Europe.

After the collapse of the communist states, men, especially from Germany and Austria, were on the lookout for "bargains" of every kind from beyond the former Iron Curtain. They found them – after 1989 – particularly in the Czech Republic and in Poland. Even someone who could not afford much in his home country would discover that a few miles away, on the other side of the border, he was a man of means. In 1999 in Slovakia a female seamstress, for example, earned only about 75 US dollars a month. The best known cruising strip is the Europa Route E55 which runs through, among other areas, the northern parts of the Czech Republic. When, in 1996, streetwalking in the vicinity of the town of Dubi (population of 8000) was banned, bars were opened with big windows facing on to the street, so that the customers could take their pick from outside. By 1997 no fewer than 50 clubs were already established on the E55.

The young women working there mostly originated from Russia, Belarus or Bulgaria. Others came from the Ukraine where (in 1999) 72 out of 100 unemployed people were women. The prostitutes working in the border areas are frequently transported by pimps from one area to another after a short time. This leaves the clients with the satisfying sensation of repeatedly discovering new girls.

Russia

In Russia, as early as 1843, there already existed a well-organized system of official and medical supervision of prostitution. In 1890, 22,674 prostitutes were registered by the Russian state. Every sex worker had to surrender her pass and received in its place a "yellow card" incorporating her photograph. No one took exception, except for the great Russian writers who denounced the situation of these women. In *Crime and Punishment* Dostoyevsky even portrays the whore Sonya Marmeladova as a kind of saint who shows the wayward Raskolnikov the true path. Katyusha Maslova in Leo Tolstoy's *Resurrection* plays a similar role. After the October Revolution of 1917 the Soviet state tried to ban prostitution on the grounds that there was no place for it in a socialist society. The result was that it continued to exist in secret. One of the first indications of *perestroika* was the article about illegal prostitution which appeared in the newspaper *Moscow Komsomolets*. In the meantime *MK* has become the most popular tabloid, in which can be found numerous advertisements for *dosug* (recreation). Nowadays, this Russian word stands for all possible sexual services.

The E55 between Zinnwald in Germany and the Bohemian town of Dubi has become the longest continuous cruising strip in Europe since the fall of the Berlin wall in 1989.

Courtesans

The King's Mistress

The royal mistresses of France were remarkable women – powerful and politically adept – but their influence was almost universally disastrous. Louis XIV was one of the most feared monarchs in Europe when he married his mistress, Madame de Maintenon, in 1685. She was controlled by the Jesuits, and at her prompting thousands of Protestants were driven from the country. Louis' great-grandson, Louis XV, was under the thrall of the most famous of all royal mistresses, the Marquise de Pompadour, who effectively controlled the state for 20 years until her death in 1764. Her successor, Madame Dubarry, was no less ambitious, and extracted 180 million livres from the treasury between 1769 and 1774.

François Boucher, *Portrait of the Marquise de Pompadour*, 1756. Oil on canvas, 157 x 201 cm, Alte Pinakothek, Munich. Madame de Pompadour was one of France's most important patrons of the arts, and the hedonistic Boucher was her favorite painter.

A street prostitute is to a courtesan as a conveyor-belt worker is to an artist. The "cheap" whore spreads her legs, opens her mouth, or, alternatively, holds out her hand. In the jargon the latter is called "pushing a trap", i.e. creating an impression of penetration for the client. As soon as the negotiations are over the prostitute gets down to work. As soon as the men come, she goes. The business takes a matter of a few minutes, at worst a quarter of an hour. Some of the streetgirls' customers allow more time for their daily visits to the toilet than for their genital excretions.

The man with more time and money, to whom eroticism is more important than rapid relief, would in former times have been able to afford a courtesan and today makes use of an especially stylish call girl. The prostitutes of the higher classes are also paid for their sexual services, but by no means do they limit their repertoire to the production of orgasms. Quite the contrary. The more renowned and expensive they are, the less direct their approach to the job. A mistress of the art will specialize in erotic delaying tactics. Some give their customer what he obviously wants: the impression

that they are not with him because of the money, but because he is such a good lover.

The word courtesan originates in "lady of the court". Indeed, many courtesans were of noble birth. Tullia di Aragon (1510–1556) was the granddaughter of a ruler (Ferdinand I) and the daughter of a cardinal. She and her colleagues understood how to conduct themselves in the highest circles. Imperia da Ferrera (1481–1512) self-confidently nicknamed herself "the noblest whore of Rome" (*nobilissimum Romae scortum*). In *Raimond Sebond* the French essayist Michel de Montaigne (1533–1592) expressed his surprise at the courtesans of Venice by noting that they can be seen in large numbers, and that they spend a princess's fortune on furnishings and clothes. The many well-to-do Venetians wanted to be surrounded by desirable women who were not only cultivated but frequently also better educated than most men and women of their time and who mixed with artists and rulers.

In the 15th and 16th centuries Rome and Venice formed the centers of the Italian courtesan empire; in the 17th century Paris took over their role. For wealthy customers to spend time with a courtesan and pay for it was an honor and an

erotic pleasure rather than a purely sexual pleasure. From time to time especially favored courtesans were promoted to the rank of mistresses, i.e. kept lovers of the rich and powerful.

Ninon de Lenclos (1620–1705)

The majority of famous courtesans died young or spent their twilight years in poverty. This was not true of Ninon de Lenclos, to whom the French statesman Cardinal Richelieu (1585–1642) offered 50,000 livres for her favors. Even when advanced in years, she was still very beautiful. Her own son is said to have fallen in love with her and to have killed himself when he found out that the object of his desire was his mother.

Ninon de Lenclos was a very educated woman and remained at the center of a free-thinking circle until she reached old age. She was known as a friend not only to men but also to women of social standing. She financially supported the playwright Molière (1622–1673) and is said to have bequeathed the eleven-year-old Voltaire (1694–1778) the sum of 2000 livres to build a library. She became well-acquainted with him when his godfather, Abbé François de

Châteauneuf, then fifty years of age, became her lover on her 77th birthday.

Rosemarie Nitribitt and Christine Keeler

Since the association with expensive prostitutes is not limited to hurried sexual contact, the courtesan or call girl frequently gets an insight into affairs of state and economic decision-making. Some prominent customers like to emphasize their own importance through name-dropping.

For this reason high-class prostitutes often become central figures in intrigues or in political or economic scandals. With intimate knowledge in their possession, they are in a position to expose, betray or blackmail powerful men. The more incredible it seems that a (married) politician should indulge in paid sexual contact, the greater the outcry as soon as the client list of a particularly sought-after prostitute is made public.

"Die Nitribitt", or "Countess Mariza" as she called herself, was during her lifetime well-known only to her circle of clients. However, this circle was quite varied, consisting of politicians and industrialists, Greek officers, and Turkish businessmen. She started her career at the age of 21 during the postwar reconstruction phase of the Federal Republic of Germany. Since she had a good eye for solvent customers, she led an extravagant life in Frankfurt on the Main during the three years of her work as a high-class prostitute. She stood out amongst her contemporaries, for she was able to afford a Mercedes Coupé 190 SL. However, she became famous only after her murder. On 1 November, 1957 the body of the 24-year-old was found, thus initiating one of the biggest scandals of Adenauer's chancellorship of the Republic. The judicial authority was nevertheless successful in stopping any details of her professional contacts from reaching the public domain. In 1959 and in 1996 films were made of her life under the title *A Girl Called Rosemarie.* A film was also made immediately in the wake of the so-called Profumo Affair, the scandal of the century which rocked the United Kingdom in 1963. The affair ended with the resignation of a minister, the weakening of Harold Macmillan's government, and the suicide of osteopath Stephen Ward, who had introduced Miss Keeler to Profumo. In the 1964 film *The Keeler Affair* Christine Keeler played herself. Her love life provided her with a similarly wide range of contacts as Rosemarie Nitribitt had enjoyed. That was the undoing of the British Secretary of State for War John Profumo. At the time the young woman was sharing her favors between him and Yevgeny Ivanov, the deputy naval attaché of the Soviet Embassy. It was suggested that the minister might have passed state secrets through her to the Russians.

28-year-old Heidi Fleiss was given a three-year sentence for procurement, which was subsequently lifted in 1996. She also had to appear before a Federal Court on charges of financial irregularities.

Heidi Fleiss, the *Hollywood Madam*

The notorious American sex scandal of 1994 involved not high class prostitutes themselves, but their employer. Heidi Fleiss ran an exclusive call girl ring in Hollywood, whose clientele included numerous Hollywood bigwigs and movie stars such as Charlie Sheen. He, for example, ordered 27 women within 15 months for whom he forked out 50,000 US dollars, as was revealed during the trial. The ring was busted when Fleiss provided call girls for three undercover investigators. In 1995 Nick Broomfield made a documentary film about Heidi Fleiss, in which he presented his own personal, inside view of the young lady. Years later, her former customers still fear that their identities could be made public. In January 2000 it was rumored that Fleiss wished to reveal the names of various actors, sport stars and businessmen in an internet interview.

The death of the prostitute Rosemarie Nitribitt (1934–1957) caused a major scandal in postwar Germany.

Pimps and Madams

Of the women who voluntarily work on the streets, many start out only because of the seemingly big money involved. The sheer financial turnover is indeed immense and is especially attractive to female drug addicts.

However, even without a drug habit the majority of whores keep only a fraction of their takings, since few work on their own account. Those who share their earnings, i.e. the pimps and the brothel-keepers, maintain that the whores are in their debt, because they supply everything the women need to work or survive. The pimps promise protection, brothel-keepers make the necessary premises available and where addiction is involved dealers supply the lifesaving drugs. What they all have in common is that they rake in lots of money in return for their "services".

When a whore begins to sell herself "out of love" for her pimp, it is he who financially profits most from her work. It is not just her income that belongs to him but also her body and soul. Even when the bond on his part is a purely financial one, for the woman who lets herself be exploited, the bond consists of affection, servility, and fear.

Most traditional pimps hold sway over a certain number of women who stand on the streets for them and finance their lavish lifestyle. At regular intervals the "protector" puts in an appearance in his domain, usually in a conspicuously expensive car, and checks whether the women are at their allocated spots selling their wares and, above all, whether they have been earning enough.

However, modern western European pimps see themselves as managers. They are less obviously to the fore and do more background organization. They run sex-clubs or Eros Centers in which prostitutes are supplied with their own rooms for rent, paid on a daily basis, of a couple of hundred dollars.

Here, unlike the set-up with traditional pimps and their women, the relationship between earner and taker can be purely economic on both sides. Although some women become psychologically dependent on their "manager" and turn over all their earnings to him, it is not a foregone conclusion. At any rate, even if there is no psychological dependence on her pimp, the prostitute must still turn over a portion of her earnings to him. Most prostitutes then give some of what is left to the men they love and/or their families. In the case of prostitutes who come from poorer countries, any surplus is often sent back to relatives in their homelands. Therefore the first cut of the prostitutes' earnings goes to those who own the prostitutes, and the second cut to those to whom they feel they belong. Sometimes it is difficult to tell these two groups apart.

The more consistent the effort to free prostitutes from the criminal world, the more the pimp uses the smart businessman as a model. In the Netherlands there have been attempts since the mid-1990s to shift prostitution out of the criminal environment and into the general world of business. As a result only respectable businessmen, who at least on the surface have a clean record, are allowed to open such establishments. The brothels are also checked as to whether the women have "normal" working conditions. The more restrictions a country places on the merchandizing of sex, the more this lucrative business becomes the exclusive domain of those who also break the law in other ways, such as drug-dealing, violent crime or gun-running.

Félicien Rops, illustration to *Les Cousines de ma Colonelle* attributed to Guy de Maupassant, 1882. Etching, 16.4 x 10.8 cm, Musée provincial Félicien Rops, Namur, Belgium. The illustrations to Maupassant's works have usually been more explicit than the text.

Procurement

The procuresses had their heyday when it was still considered improper for respectable women to go around unaccompanied in public. In offering an unmarried couple the opportunity for an intimate liaison, they laid themselves open to prosecution. Professional procuresses arranged the assignations between the suitors who were prepared to pay and those women whom (older) men could otherwise not have met undisturbed. It was not unusual for the go-between to be related to a young girl who was looking for a "good match". Through her "good aunt" she would be put in touch with an "admirer".

The boundaries between this type of behavior and slave-trading were fluid; the assignations were not always entered into voluntarily. There were also procuresses who took on the guise of employment agents and supplied "fresh meat" directly to the brothels.

The procurement of young women has nowadays become a predominantly historical phenomenon if one excludes the passing on of telephone numbers and addresses, which a hotel porter, for example, might provide for a guest.

Another phenomenon is the procurement of children for pedophiles, which – especially in poorer countries – goes on to this day. There was a big scandal in Vienna in 1822 when minors were offered by their own parents using box numbers for contact.

Otto Dix, *Pimp with Two Whores*, 1922. Oil on canvas, 70 x 55 cm, private collection. Underlining the fundamental brutality of the scene the artist makes use of the typical grim realism of the *Neue Sachlichkeit*.

Félicien Rops, *The Examination*, 1878–1881. Pencil, ink, native chalk, black chalk, 16 x 13 cm, Musée Royal de Mariemont, Morlanwelz, Belgium. The madam of a brothel is inspecting new recruits for her establishment.

The Madam

The huge numbers of procuresses, female organizers of call girl rings, and madams show that plenty of women also made and still make money from prostitutes. Sociologically speaking, their number increases if the activity is semi-legalized, so that restrictions are more easily circumvented by skillfully bribing government officials than by brute strength.

Unlike the males attached to the whore business, the "madams" for the most part had simply promoted themselves. They were often former prostitutes who had learned their trade and worked their way up, essential in the sex business. As former specialists, in later life this was one of the only lines of work at which they could succeed. The madam of the old school held her "family" together with motherly firmness. Today even she has been replaced by the versatile businesswoman, who does not care whether she earns her money in real estate, the sex business or share dealing.

"Every girl is sitting on her own goldmine; she just has to exploit it." As a child Nell Kimball (1854–1934) learned this theory at her aunt's knee. In her old age she published her memoirs *Her Life as an American Madam by Herself*. In her time Nell was one of the best known brothel-keepers in Storyville, the New Orleans red-light district which was closed down in 1917. Brothel-keeping was (and is) one of the few lucrative occupations available to older women who in their youth were themselves prostitutes. However, some deny ever having done the same work as their employees. The madam organizes, regulates, advises, pays, where necessary – and cashes in, where possible. She needs influential friends and satisfied customers within the police force and the town council.

Kimball's sober, confident conclusion was that a cathouse is just as difficult to run as a steel-mill. She was a success at the job, even though in her day it was necessary to bribe official-dom, pay protection money, and nevertheless hold at bay well-meaning "protectors" who would have liked to have relieved her of some of her profits.

Particularly in the 18th century, the brothel was above all a meeting place. Because of this, unmarried women looking for a "good match" for themselves were sometimes there to be found. They needed procuresses to introduce them to the right men – and a place for the action. Skilled seductresses from poor families were seeking social advancement, and they sometimes succeeded.

Only since the 19th century have the brothels which were banned in many countries – but continued to exist nonetheless – been organized in the same way as workshops. The women working there have to make themselves available to the clients at certain times. It is therefore up to the madam to ensure that the staff are conscientiously fulfilling their duties, to provide the catering, and to advise the regular customers who might request "novices".

The Gray Zone – Casual Prostitution

In the 1990s there was no longer a basic contradiction in being a prostitute as well as an upright citizen. This innovation is intrinsically linked to sexual liberalization in some Western countries: a woman with sexual experience, perhaps even well-versed in love (a "woman with a past") is no longer as exposed to disgrace as she used to be. Even a history of many changing affairs, in principle, no longer makes her a social outcast for all time. Altruistic, self-sacrificing love has long since ceased to be held up as an ideal for modern young women.

In sexually liberated states, especially in the Dutch metropolis of Amsterdam, from around the beginning of the 1990s quite a few career-conscious young students – and they openly admit this – no longer look to the ever-dwindling number of vacation jobs in factories to finance their studies. They can get enough money in return for sex, and their few regular customers can only get sex with young attractive women if they part with money for it. As intelligent, young and experienced playmates – neither stale nor embittered – they are much in demand with well-to-do customers. These women have a choice: they only take a client on if they like him. They don't have to accept everyone and thus they remain more or less independent.

However, this freedom is often illusory: after the completion of their studies they do not always manage to cross over to middle-class life. Nonetheless the lot of the casual hooker has nothing in common with the sufferings of the woman who is forced all day and all night to accept anyone who comes her way and who every year receives less and less money for what she does and for what is imposed on her. Even today her spiraling descent serves as a warning to many people who have great trouble in living "respectably" that "a life of sin" (in the long term) is not worth it.

In centuries gone by the only chance of upward social mobility for women from impecunious families lay in their physical attractiveness. They could use it to smooth their path to a good marriage – or, at least while they were young, to an income which they would never otherwise have attained.

Those with nothing to lose, not even a good name, were readier to turn to prostitution. The daughters of the petty bourgeoisie were not given this chance; they had to protect their purity in order to secure husbands for themselves. Their scorn was therefore all the greater for a woman who "gave herself" before marriage. In their eyes she was no better than a prostitute – someone about whose life they knew absolutely nothing, assuming that, in accordance with custom, they were completely inexperienced in erotic matters. Only one thing was clear: a prostitute was a woman whom they must not acknowledge. It was unthinkable that they should speak to such a person. She belonged to another caste. It was unthinkable that a woman from a good home should have a changing circle of male acquaintances if she ever aspired to a better future for herself. At the outside it would have to happen in secret. Indeed, it did happen on occasion, especially in the 19th century, that financially dependent middle-class women would make an arrangement with gentlemen of standing, if they found themselves unable to pay the milliner's bills which they had run up behind their husbands' backs. It is unknown how widespread this method of stretching the housekeeping budget was. Possibly those rumors also served a specific purpose: they gave apparent credence to the popular male fantasy that when

Gerda Wegener, *Modern Prostitution Business*, c. 1920. Drawing. At the beginning of the 20th century street cafés were popular places for casual amorous encounters.

it gets down to basics every woman is a potential whore – their own mother, excepted, of course. In the 19th century most of the women who sold themselves now and again were underpaid servants and waitresses, such as are described in the tales of the Frenchman Guy de Maupassant (1850–1890), or the Austrian Arthur Schnitzler (1862–1931). In order to survive they had to market all their possessions or skills.

The members of the middle-class community of that time and the professional prostitutes had a common enemy: those women who used sexual favors merely to earn a little on the side. In the eyes of health officials such women presented an even greater risk to public health than the "registered" prostitutes who had to undergo regular checks. Any woman who was prepared to make herself sexually available to more than one man was regarded as a potential prostitute. Even a woman who did not keep her virginity until she was married was held in scorn: as soon as an unmarried woman slept with a man, she deserved society's condemnation. Not until the early 1980s did casual prostitution start to come in from the cold.

Anonymous, Shopgirl Uses Boutique as Cover for Her Activities, c. 1890. This sort of camouflage was doubly profitable – after selling herself to a man, the shopgirl could usually persuade him to buy a gift to take back to his wife, and assuage his conscience.

Théophile Alexandre Steinlen, *Three Seamstresses as Occasional Prostitutes*, c. 1900. Color etching, 14.9 x 22.5 cm, Staatliche Museen Preussischer Kulturbesitz, Berlin. Seamstresses, maids and milliners were so badly paid that some of them resorted to occasional prostitution in order to make ends meet.

Forced Prostitution

The slave trade in Europe has never been completely abolished. Usually very young women (predominantly between 18 and 25 years of age; around one in twenty a minor) or their relatives are told a story of a distant land (in the past it would be a richer area of the country, normally a big city) where, working as waitresses, dancers or domestic servants, it is possible to earn more money than can be made in decades working in the old country or in the local region, if indeed paid employment is available there for women at all.

As a rule the contact is made by ostensibly trustworthy fellow-countrymen who act as go-betweens. In the last decade of the 20th century increasing numbers of women distinguished themselves in this way; in 1999 in Berlin every fifth person suspected of involvement in the slave-trade was female.

In reality the young women are sold like cattle, auctioned off at a price ranging from 1500 to 5000 German marks (with an average annual income of 70,000 German marks), considerably

more in individual cases. More rarely, rather than being enticed away with false promises, a girl is forcibly abducted. Both methods produce a thriving business: Interpol estimate that a single prostitute can earn 210,000 German marks per year. Therefore low fines are not effective deterrents.

After their arrival in foreign parts, many of these women are systematically raped, held in captivity and put at the disposal of men in exchange for money. In Germany alone, where in 1999 three out of four prostitutes already come from foreign countries, 10,000 women are said to languish in forced prostitution. (In 1997, 1200 victims of the slave trade were picked up; 87 percent came from the East.)

It's a similar story in Austria: four out of five employees in Viennese sex clubs are from the East. Meanwhile in the big cities of France such as Paris or Nice seven out of ten prostitutes have likewise been "imported". However, as in France, forced prostitution is punishable in Austria by up to ten years' imprisonment. Therefore the slave trade is less in evidence there than in other Western European states.

While some young women are pumped full of drugs, others are threatened that something bad might happen to their families back home. With little knowledge of the local language and, as "illegals", more vulnerable to persecution by the police than their tormentors, it is almost impossible for them to get help. At the most they have a visa to stay for three months; by that time the pimps have earned enough through the women's

Hans Baluschek, *He – She – It*, from the cycle *Victim*, 1906. Charcoal drawing on card, 10 x 6.9 cm, Staatliche Museen, Preussischer Kulturbesitz, Berlin. This scene, showing a pimp, a whore, and her mother, is taken from the streets of Berlin at the turn of the 20th century when economic conditions were strained.

efforts to replace them with fresh supplies. If they are picked up in a raid they face immediate deportation. They are then unavailable to take the stand either as plaintiffs or as witnesses.

This leaves the traders in human flesh. Thousands of new prostitutes annually are introduced into Berlin alone. There, between 1992 and 1995, only 40 charges were brought in 188 cases covering human trafficking.

Only since 1993 in the Netherlands and since 1995 in Belgium has support been given to "illegals" who are prepared to speak out against the traffickers. In return they receive immunity

Striptease contestants in Moscow waiting for their turn, 1995. Competitions such as this lure contestants with the false promise of contracts to dance in Western nightclubs.

A Respectable Profession

Among the women who come from abroad there are a few who know what they are getting themselves into. But even when they have to hand over almost everything, a little is still left over for themselves and their families. Are they sacrificing themselves for their families – or are they being sacrificed by their families? In places where women meet increasing difficulties to find any paid work – for example in the countries of the former Eastern bloc – working as a prostitute seems a desirable prospect to a growing number of even well-educated women. In 1990, when asked in a school survey about their choice of career, a considerable number of girls had already decided they wanted to be prostitutes, or, alternatively, headmistresses. Meanwhile prostitution is thought to have become the most frequently named career choice, and for many the only career with a future. Their education is of no value; their only assets are their attractive bodies.

from prosecution and legal support. For the first time in the Netherlands, five Albanians caught trading in women were given five-year jail sentences in May 1998.

In Germany regulations favoring the women are being torpedoed by conservative politicians. They fear that if the victims went to court they would be entitled to social welfare. The protection of the state from immigration seems to be more important than the protection of women.

Nowadays the trade in human flesh is especially prevalent in countries such as the Netherlands and Belgium with liberal provisions for pimping. The contemporary trade in girls, with its mafia-like structure, concentrates on these countries. It is from there that, at the start of the 21st century, many young women, mainly from Eastern Europe, are shipped overseas. Not until 1997 did the 15 states of the European Union agree to a common program.

Even such women as are not being held as slaves are given the impression that they are in debt to their "owner". He claims that he has had to put a large sum of money up front – in individual cases anything up to 20,000 US dollars – to pay for false papers for the entry and the flight. This debt, they say, just has to be worked off, for example through 12-hour shifts in the course of which the reluctant prostitute has to accommodate anyone who approaches. The brothel-keeper skims at least 70 percent of the takings; frequently even all of it.

Because the women, at the same time, are billed horrendous sums for bed and board, months and years pass by before they are free of debt. By that time most of them are completely burnt out, assuming that they have not already been picked up in a raid and deported.

Free Choice

Even the experts are not able to agree whether such a thing as voluntary prostitution can exist at all. On the affirmative side, in particular, are the activists. They contrast the normal sex industry with a Utopian picture: pleasure houses concerned with more than just the duties of the girls and the pleasure of the clients. It is

John Collet, *The Victim*, 1780. Mezzotint engraving, 33 x 25.4 cm, private collection, London. Orphanages and the homes of the poor have always been a rich source of children who could be pressed into the sex trade, usually after some cosmetic tinkering to make them appear more presentable.

possible, they claim, to prostitute yourself out of a sensual desire. They demand palaces instead of squalor. Prostitutes who are experienced in the media, reinvent themselves as designers of "temples of lust" where the trade is carried on humanely.

The difficulties in bringing about such a vision are revealed when the prostitutes themselves – for example in Frankfurt on the Main – want to open a brothel-cooperative. This has been tried since the second half of the 1990s by the organization *HWG* (*Huren wehren sich gemeinsam* – whores defend themselves collectively; or *Häufig*

wechselnder Geschlechtsverkehr – frequently changing sexual intercourse). These plans are opposed not only by politicians but also – militantly – by those who have hitherto profited most from the sex industry.

Also, prostitutes are increasingly coming to the fore who maintain no woman would prostitute herself voluntarily. If there is no current pressure, they say, such as addiction or debts to prevent the prostitute's immediate escape, then there must be unknown reasons in her biography, such as sexual abuse in childhood.

Alternative Brothels

Since time immemorial brothels have served as locations for the fulfillment of desire. They were places of excitement, where men could seek pleasure and make up for any sexual deficit in their everyday lives. At least this was and still is the expectation generated and reinforced by those who work in the industry. Even when the customers return sobered by their forays into the demimonde, their erotic urges will soon make themselves felt once more and draw them back.

In the days when "decent" middle-class married women – simply from fear of pregnancy – were rarely prepared to have sexual intercourse, the "public women" were available. However, it has always been the case that many customers demanded not only "normal" sex, but other practices as well. Unlike nowadays, most men did not expect their wives – as long as they considered them "decent" – to let themselves in for anything else beyond the regular fulfillment of their "marital duty". Sexual flamboyance only dates from the end of the 1960s, when emphasis was put on the importance of sexual experimentation for a happily married life.

Some men may find that not all their desires can be fulfilled in the marital bed. Often the wives are supposed to fill a quite different role for their husband than that of the perfect erotic playmate. When a couple live and work together for years on end other qualities are essential. Yet the erotic urges continue. They may well have to be satisfied in different surroundings.

A second function of prostitution which is becoming more and more important with the increase in tolerance towards sexual variation is the fulfillment of those sexual desires which

for the self-confident clientele are "unusual" or "unconventional". However, from the point of view of those who consider the urge for frequent sex a strange habit, such desires may appear deviant or perverted.

Some, from curiosity, want to try everything at least once, perhaps so that they can contribute to the conversation when the subject of alternative sex crops up. Everyday voyeurs, exhibitionists, sadomasochists, and fetishists seek out and find the "extraordinary" in alternative brothels. Perhaps a man secretly dreams of having an adolescent girl or else a female form where from under the unmistakably feminine clothes a man emerges at the last instant. Such persons – and uniquely equipped facilities

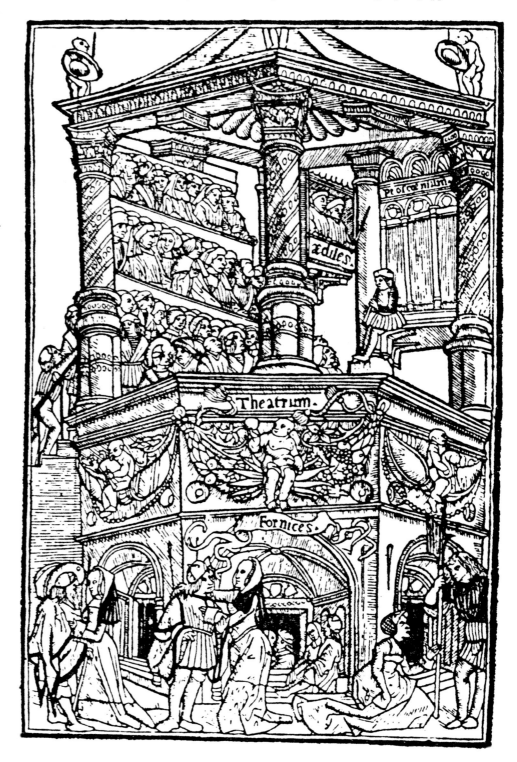

Open-air Theater, late 15th/early 16th cent. Woodcut, Italy. Theater and prostitution were traditionally closely linked in European history. Both theaters and bordellos used to be condemned as places of licence – the theater was a place where prostitutes solicited their clients while bordellos have always catered for their customers' tastes by enacting erotic dramas or mises-en-scènes. The proximity of theater and bordello is shown on this woodcut of a medieval house of ill fame where the stage is on the first floor and the bordello on the ground floor.

where fantasies are acted out, such as "hospital rooms" or rooms with oversized playpens for grown-up toddlers – are only to be found in alternative brothels.

When garter belts and stockings are no longer enough to conjure up forbidden fruits, ever more emphasis is put on staging fantasy scenes which cannot be performed within a domestic context. In Japan, married couples may visit specially furnished "Love Hotels" in order to enjoy each other in unfamiliar surroundings. But in the Western world the idea of husbands and wives going together to establishments which serve as playgrounds for their favorite fantasies is still widely deprecated. In the West, as a rule, men go alone to such places and seek out a suitable lover, which often means a prostitute who specializes in acting out their desired fantasy.

For centuries anyone who prefers watching to doing has been able to enter alternative brothels in which the spectacle he finds most arousing will be staged for him. It might involve flagellation by housemaids or elaborately staged orgies. He can watch all those scenarios, therefore, which the observer would not get to see in the normal course of events, but which might nonetheless be constantly recurring in his erotic imagination. Even though the immediate proximity of the action can increase the excitement, the widespread use of video cassettes means that such shows are nowadays predominantly enjoyed within one's own four walls. Those who only want to watch rather than participate prefer to stay home alone with the arousing pictures.

There are also films *about* voyeurs, e.g. *Belle de Jour*, 1966, by the Spanish director Luis Buñuel, who shows how a voyeur, or indeed an initiated prostitute can use one-way mirrors or peepholes to watch or eavesdrop on a typical scene.

Secret prostitution has always attracted the special attention of the vice squad. Because the main purpose of the brothels lay in providing satisfaction for the paying male customer, sometimes it is not only sexual intercourse which occurs in those places. Desire finds fulfillment in different ways. As long as a definite idea prevails of standardized sexuality and of what should or should not give sexual satisfaction, such places come across as even more suspect than normal brothels. Anyone turning a trick here has to be really twisted.

To this day in the newspaper advertisement sections there are notices which are fronts for sexual services and which only an ever-dwindling number of naïve and ignorant readers misinterpret. Massage parlors could indeed be establishments where the customers undergo powerful pummeling, but also places where men enjoy being masturbated. Frequently they serve a clientele who are inclined towards fetishes, and who particularly like the workers there to be made up and dressed as "nurses" complete with cap and unbuttoned uniform. In the big brothels of turn-of-the-century Paris there were said to be wardrobes containing anything to gladden the heart of a fetishist or a transvestite. The customers in those brothels did not hire a woman for themselves but rather their favorite objects to satisfy their longings.

Although the "mistress" in a sadomasochistic brothel tries to appear sexy, she is usually not in fact selling sex, but the possiblity of experiencing pain, humiliation or servitude.

Johns

A woman who occasionally uses her physical charms to earn money does not only work as a prostitute, she is one, and remains one in the accepted sense, even when she has not been involved in prostitution for decades and has long since grown old. A different attitude prevails toward the man, especially the male white collar worker who has used prostitutes on a casual basis for decades. Surely it would be absurd to claim that this man is nothing but a john. According to information collected by prostitutes' organizations, three out of four men use a whore at least once in their lives. For others, paying for contact with women is the most important aspect of their sexuality.

Brothels and street prostitution have always functioned as points of initiation for young males. But since the beginning of the sexual revolution, at the latest, when the value of virginity was questioned and even "respectable" women acknowledged their sexual needs, there has been a decline in the number of young men who had their first sexual experience with a prostitute. Nonetheless the importance of lust as a marketable commodity has not diminished.

From the cycle *Love Life – Pictures with Irene*, photographs by Roswitha Hecke, beginning of the 1980s. In Germany, in the early 1980s, the average john was aged between 20 and 40, visited a brothel about every three weeks for between 30 minutes and an hour at a time, and paid 159 German marks to have sex with a prostitute whose average age was 29 (with an average annual income of 47,000 German marks).

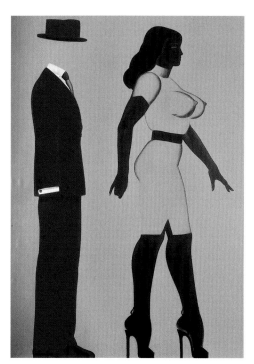

Allen Jones, *Maid to Order III* (detail), 1971. Oil on canvas, 182.8 x 139.7 cm, Waddington Galleries, London.

Even today, plenty of young men resort to a prostitute for their first sexual experience. Every day, in Germany alone, a million men treat themselves to purchased sex. While marital sex is the favored option by night, buying sex is particularly popular during the day. As many go in for the sex-siesta during their lunch-break as for a quickie right after work. A lot of these men turn into regular johns: that is, they like coming back to one particular prostitute and stick relatively faithfully to her. Even the regular pay-outs seem small to them, compared with what they would have to invest in a permanent mistress – not only materially, but above all emotionally. Johns are men who buy their freedom from all the commitments which usually seem to be tied in with sexual liaisons. For the john, a big advantage is the simplicity of the purchased sexual act. All his qualms – fear of rejection, the need for courtship – are swept aside. Thus his fear of failure is considerably reduced. Many men are sexually potent

only when they approach a prostitute. Writing about this kind of neurosis (among others), Freud declared that where there is love, there is no desire, and where there is desire there is no love. Many men love and respect their womenfolk and therefore do not like to ask them for the sex they dream of and of which they are ashamed. Others never love and always desire – and do not get the chance as often as they would like. They, too, are clients of the prostitutes, although they are not necessarily grateful for it. They bear a grudge at having to pay for their lust. It is only for a few men that contact with a prostitute is a substitute – for a great number it is an independent, additional sex-game which they would not want to do without. The clients of streetwalkers keep out of each other's way: their biggest fear is that they could meet someone they know. Only a few acknowledge that, for example, visiting a drug-addicted streetwalker is part of their lifestyle. Their shame is caused less by the sexual transaction than by its

Prostitute and john on the street. According to a study done in Berlin in 1997, for which 260 prostitutes were questioned, 70 percent had tried to quit after five years, more than half felt nausea when approached by a john, and over 40 percent admitted to feelings of hate.

misery. Those with more money to spend on their desires are more confident about letting themselves be seen. Such johns parade within the intimate circle of the brothel as men of the world. Some large companies have a special budget for important customers and top employees; what better venue for celebrating a successful end to negotiations than a high-class brothel?

The John in the Role of Criminal

Towards the end of the 20th century the first attempts to criminalize johns were made. San Francisco was once considered the most sexually liberated city in the United States. Since around 1995 however, there has been an intensive campaign against johns, using undercover police officers. By way of example, in March 1999 four women officers dressed up as prostitutes in extremely provocative clothing and posed in the Polk Gulch industrial quarter. The 43 men who tried to approach them were arrested on the spot.

As first offenders, they had to pay 500 US dollars and agree to take part in an aversion therapy course in a so-called "John School". Unless they took part they would acquire a criminal record.

The fees paid by the participants, who have meanwhile grown in number to over 3000, are used to finance the employees of SAGE (Standing Against Global Exploitation), former prostitutes who now vehemently confront the public with the shady side of prostitution.

Civil-rights groups from Vancouver in Canada, such as "Sex Workers' Alliance" and "Coyote", resolutely oppose the idea. They argue that through such courses prostitutes and clients are being ostracized.

Since the mid-1990s Sweden has also blazed new trails in the fight against prostitution. After there was a 44 percent female intake into the Swedish Parliament the female members have increasingly tried to stand up for women's rights and therefore also for prostitutes. Since 1999 prostitution is no longer a crime; the criminal is the john who wants to avail himself of a prostitute's services.

Illustration from *Romance of Alexander*, 1338 – 1344. Bodleian Library, Oxford. This scene is perhaps one of the oldest illustrations of a brothel, showing a john offering a coin to the brothel-keeper.

Men for Sale

When one talks of prostitution one thinks as a rule of male johns and female prostitutes. However, there have always been men who "put a price on their bodies", albeit predominantly to members of their own gender, much more rarely to well-heeled women. In fact, even in ancient Rome there were male prostitutes, who also serviced women. Eunuchs, men who had their testicles removed, were also said to have been popular. The sexual services they provided could not lead to an unwanted pregnancy, to the enhanced delight of the female clients.

The relative rarity of male prostitutes is explained more readily by women's lack of economic power than by their lack of interest in sex. Historically and in an international context, only very few women have had control over enough money to splurge on extravagant pleasures of this kind. Even when they were married to rich men and every other luxury was placed at their disposal, the husbands would be reluctant to pay the price of sex.

Only those with financial means beyond the necessities of life can afford to pay for sex. This is particularly true of women: for potential female clients there is no male equivalent to the cheap addict-beat from which the johns derive such questionable pleasure. To hire yourself a gigolo is and has always been a luxury.

Even though at the end of the 1990s a newly opened establishment on the Hamburg Reeperbahn received numerous applications from men who deemed themselves potent enough to satisfy rows of women, such piece-workers represent a small minority amongst the male tarts. Frequently, the male prostitute is an attractive, potent young man who is ready and willing to be kept by only one rich woman. For female sex tourists, exotic lovers from South America or Africa are in demand, and are patronized by various women during the different holiday periods.

Towards the end of the 20th century a lot of women had more money at their disposal than many men – not the men in their own countries, but in developing countries. Women therefore started to travel from the United States and western Europe to the Caribbean,

A. Reebrocky, *Saloon for Ladies*, **1920s. Drawing.** A street scene from Algiers. In fact, men were as likely as women to frequent these saloons.

Kenya or South America. If they were no longer able to find an attractive lover in their homeland they would still appear desirable in foreign countries. Unlike male sex tourists who get through five different sex workers in the course of a single trip, the female johns are usually satisfied with the first one who conveys the sensation they seek, which means that he embodies their desires. Unlike male tourists they romanticize the affair and claim that their bond with the exotic man has a much wider basis than mere sex.

By providing sex services to unsatisfied women whose husbands spend all their time on their careers, many gigolos, particularly in Germany, kept their heads above water throughout the period of mass unemployment after the First World War.

In Paris and other European cities between the two World Wars there were – exclusively for higher-class women – brothels in which they found the fulfillment that would otherwise pass them by. At the end of the 1920s professional French women even demanded the provision of "institutes of philogeny". This phenomenon was interpreted by the male sex researchers of the time as "a most unpleasant development" and as a modern "symptom of the defeminization of women". They argued that the female

Marcel Vertés, *The Gigolo*. **Etching.** Gigolos were frequently former army officers, the financially embarrassed scions of respectable families, or at least men who had taught themselves how to behave well in polite society. Even a lady could afford to be seen with them in public.

American Gigolo, **still from the film by Paul Schrader, 1980, Frances Bergen as Mrs Laudner and Richard Gere as Julian.** The main character Michelle must decide whether to risk her reputation or to provide her gigolo with an alibi when one of his clients is killed.

At a *maison close,* or brothel for women in Paris, this handsome "male escort" entertains clients in the "Midnight Chamber".

johns separated sexuality from emotions and saw the sex act as no more than a hygienic exercise.

At the start of the 19th century there was a big demand from wealthy women for male prostitutes as well. In the years when Queen Victoria, later known for her prudishness, was still a child, Mary Wilson reigned in England as "Queen of Prostitution". This alternative kind of monarch published pornographic novels and opened a series of tastefully appointed broth-els in London. Her customers had at their disposal a refined erotic library, which they could use to whet their appetite for anything they would later want to experience. If they took more pleasure in paintings than in books they could look at the splendid obscene pictures in the salon. The resourceful madam and porno-grapher also had plans to establish a brothel aimed at female clientele – for it was not yet unthinkable that women should get to know and enjoy erotic desires. Well-to-do women were supposed to be able to literally subscribe to lust with Mary Wilson's pornographic nov-els. According to the plan of this madam, who held sway in the second and third decades of the 19th century, the subscribers, without being seen themselves, would be able to take their pick from amongst the men – who would be totally naked – in the ladies' brothel. However the times and the moral climate then changed rapidly, so the idea never became reality and the erstwhile celebrity died destitute.

Women of Easy Virtue

The social exclusion of the "fallen woman" is the mirror image of the idealization of women. Particularly in the 19th and early 20th centuries prostitution became the central theme of art. Even while in real life they were frequently banished behind the scenes, prostitutes played an important part in books, dramas, operas, paintings, and later in films. In this context it should be remembered that the definition of a "fallen woman", according to the ideas of the time, applied to any woman who had had an affair with more than one man – or perhaps only with one, but outside marriage.

19th-century artists often "lived in sin" with their lover for years and decades without being able to legitimize their relationship. In this respect their preoccupation with the theme of the "fallen woman" is also an indication of the social restrictions of the time. In the world of art, while the middle-class woman, at best, lived a virtuous life only because of the prevailing conventions, the warm-hearted prostitute became a good woman. If her conversion is not acknowledged by society she is ruined. Those are the terms in which rebellious young men interpreted the situation. At the same time, many artists, such as Charles Baudelaire (1821–1867), endured a love-hate relationship with their mistresses, despising them for their availability even while desiring them.

Édouard Manet (1832–1883), born into a middle-class home, was only able to marry his piano teacher, Suzanne Leenhof, in 1863, after the death of his father. By that time she had been his mistress for 13 years. One of Manet's most famous paintings, *Olympia*, dates from the year of the wedding.

Some artists idealized the unvarnished honesty of wretched figures and preferred it to the hypocritical, make-believe world of the bourgeoisie. The whore became both, muse and model for them. Some of these are long forgotten, but there are many renowned artists besides Toulouse-Lautrec (1864–1901) who were regular visitors to houses of ill repute, including the painter Paul Gauguin as well as his colleagues Vincent van Gogh, Georges Seurat, Claude Monet, Camille Pissaro, and Auguste Renoir.

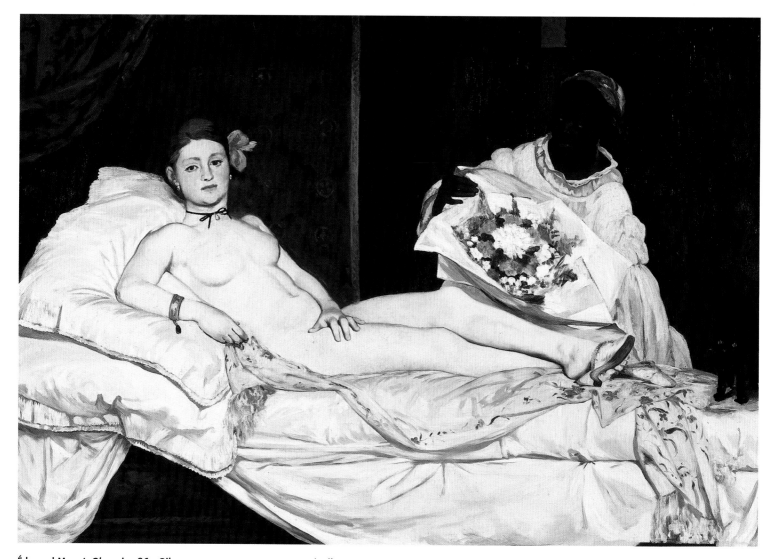

Édouard Manet, *Olympia*, 1863. Oil on canvas , 130.5 x 190 cm, Musée d'Orsay, Paris. The bourgeoisie was particularly shocked by Manet's painting because it parodies similar portraits by Titian and others by placing a prostitute in the position normally occupied by a goddess.

Henri de Toulouse-Lautrec, *Reine de Joie par Victor Joze*, 1892. Charcoal sketch, poster, Kunsthalle Bremen. Victor Joze was the pseudonym of the Polish writer Victor Dobrzky. The poster also served as the cover of the book.

The Paris Bohemian and Painter Henri de Toulouse-Lautrec

Drinking, drugs, gambling, depravity, and erotic desire – these secret practices shaped the lives of many members of the 19th-century bourgeoisie. However only bohemians admitted to such unconventional stimulations, particularly in Paris in the second half of the 19th century. Outsiders from various backgrounds met up in the bars and dives of the metropolis.

In their rejection of the middle-class way of life the demimonde and the bohemians had a common cause. The artists did not differ from their middle class contemporaries so much as they perhaps would have liked. They too sought diversion from everyday life by seeking out the whore, whom they saw as a complement to the virtuous woman, whom they could not live without. However, they would never have admitted to this fascination.

With his posters, Henri de Toulouse-Lautrec brought world renown to the Paris pleasure district of Montmartre and, in particular, to the Folies-Bergère and the Moulin Rouge, founded in 1889, with its can-can dancers and cocottes.

Born of aristocratic stock, the painter was crippled in his youth by two bad riding accidents. For a while only art and alcohol kept him alive. He lived and worked in the brothel and met his friends there, because (or so it was claimed) the women's will to live with degradation reflected his own experience. Their portrayals were not prettified – but they convey the fascination which they held for him and others.

Cover of the Ricordi piano version of the opera *Manon Lescaut*. The novel inspired among other composers Jules Massenet (1884), Giacomo Puccini (1893), and Hans Werner Henze (1952).

Édouard Manet, *Nana*, 1877. Oil on canvas, 154 x 115 cm, Kunsthalle Hamburg. What the public objected to in works of art such as the novels of Zola and the painting of Manet was not primarily their erotic content, but their realism. Audiences still wanted their erotica dressed up as romantic fantasy, as in the paintings of Jean-Auguste-Dominique Ingres (1780–1867).

The Story of the Chevalier Des Grieux and Manon Lescaut

There is a long tradition in Europe of criticizing the conventional morality of calculating reason. Even before Jean-Jacques Rousseau, the French writer Abbé Prévost (Antoine François Prévost d'Exiles) defended the legitimacy of *amour passion*, love in its natural state, as a thing of passion and fate. And what could be less rational than loving an unfaithful woman?

In his youth and his old age Prévost turned to religion; for twenty years in between he lived as an adventurer. The only one of his works (out of almost 200) still read today is to be found in the seventh volume of his *Mémoires et Aventures d'un Homme de Qualité*. Published in 1731, it is the sentimental story of the love affair between the prostitute Manon Lescaut and the chevalier Des Grieux.

Des Grieux is prepared to sacrifice his career in order to satisfy his passion. The family of the aristocratic youth try to break up the attach-

ment to Manon Lescaut; she is sent by her own family against her will to live in a convent "in order to drive out of her the urge towards worldly pleasure". Manon flees to Paris along with her lover, where, compelled by financial need, she gives herself to other men. Involved in theft and intrigue, they are both sentenced. Manon is to be transported as a criminal to New Orleans. When her bid for freedom fails, her oft-betrayed lover accompanies her into exile, where she dies, profoundly mourned by him.

Nana

In 1880 the naturalist Émile Zola (1840–1902) published his cocotte novel *Nana*. He portrayed the society and the demimonde in the days of the Second Empire in merciless detail. Zola's eponymous heroine does not follow the romantic tradition of true love and is not represented as an alternative foil to the corrupt bourgeoisie. This scheming and voluptuous *femme fatale* is no better than those men who fall for her and are thereby ruined.

The career of the heroine begins on the streets and ends there – she dies of smallpox on the eve of the Franco-Prussian War of 1870–1871. Zola depicts the persecution of women who dare to appear alone in public, the behavior of the prostitutes and their appraisal of the affluent men who seek their services.

The Lady of the Camellias and *La Traviata*

Based on the real Parisian courtesan Marie Duplessis, the character in both the novel and the stage version who is known as "Marguerite Gautier", better known as the "Lady of the Camellias", is the archetypal endlessly generous tart with a heart of gold.

She loves an upper-class gentleman and sacrifices herself for him, for her lover's family honor forbids him to form an attachment to a former courtesan. To avoid ruining his life she appears to return to her old trade. Her lover contemptuously rejects her and, too late, realizes the sacrifice she has made for him. She dies – in the novel as in real life – all alone, of a lung disease which she has picked up from one of her customers. Every day Marguerite wears a camellia on her dress; usually a white flower, but a red one during menstruation. On those days she could not be hired. (So it is no accident that a well-known European brand name for sanitary napkins was also named after the camellia.)

A young author, one of Marie Duplessis's lovers, was not rich enough during her lifetime to maintain the demanding "Lady of the Camellias". Through her death he became rich and famous: the author Alexandre Dumas *fils* (1824–1895). He was born in the same year as the *dame aux camélias* and he wrote his first novel in the year after her death. In 1849 there followed an (initially banned) stage version. Because the insurmountable conflict between respectability and passion was still fascinating in middle-class circles, the book, the play and Giuseppe Verdi's opera *La Traviata*, performed in 1853, became lasting successes.

When the theatrical production, banned for over three years on moral grounds, had its premiere in 1853, Giuseppe Verdi, who was also "living in sin", attended the performance along with his mistress. Moved by the story, he at once composed, to a libretto by M. F. Piave (1810–1876), his opera, in which the central character was renamed Violetta. First performed in Venice, *La Traviata* remains today one of the most popular operas worldwide; in Germany alone 230,000 people every year go to see this particular work. The story has also been filmed, in 1937 as *Camille*. Greta Garbo played the tragic courtesan creating in her audience what the French critic Roland Barthes called "the deepest ecstasy … where the flesh gives rise to mystical feelings of perdition."

Maria Callas in *La Traviata* at the Royal Opera House, Covent Garden, London, 1958. Violetta was a familiar role to Callas who felt particulary drawn to tragic characters. The first ever performance of this opera in 1853 was famously mocked, as the robust and abundantly well-fed soprano, Fanny Salvini Donatelli, unsuccessfully tried to convey that she was dying of consumption.

The Oldest Profession

The church father Augustine, Bishop of Hippo Regius in the 4th century, did not differentiate between the *copula carnis* of married couples and the *copula fornicatoria* between man and whore. He damned both as sinful. On the other hand he admitted in his *Confessiones* that if prostitution was banned "an unrestrained lust would destroy the community." The religious philosopher Thomas Aquinas (1225–1274), who was canonized in 1323, is credited with the statement that prostitution was as much part of society as the cesspit was part of the most glorious palace. Without both, each would become impure and noisome. So while in the Middle Ages sex-for-sale was regarded as an evil, the necessity for its existence was not questioned. Before the spread of syphilis, prostitutes were regarded as sinners, but not as criminals. In medieval societies it was recognized that social stability was not feasible without the sale of sex. Those whose sexual needs were not provided for, particularly the many traveling merchants and officials, had to be given an outlet for their "wicked desire". The brothel was therefore seen as a place of purification.

In 1435 Emperor Sigismund sent a letter of thanks to the town of Ulm, Germany: during his stay there the town brothel had been put at the disposal of him and his entourage. In the same year the prostitutes of Vienna came naked to greet him at the city gate.

Peter Lenk, *Imperia*, 1993. Concrete, 10 m high. The statue is to be found in the town of Constance on Lake Constance, Germany. The prostitute carries the devil on one arm and the pope on the other.

Clothing Regulations

In the Middle Ages, just as for other professions, there was a wide range of different kinds of apparel designated for prostitutes; this varied from town to town and region to region. Jeanne I, Queen of Naples and Countess of Provence, in Avignon, reportedly decreed in such words: "In the year 1347, on the eighth day of the month of August, our good Queen Jeanne has given approval for the opening of a special house of sin in our town. At the same time she forbids all the wicked women from plying their trade in the town, and when they go out they should wear red braiding on their left shoulder." Sometimes definite markings were required, usually in red or yellow, the colors of sin and of the sun. In Bergamo, Italy, they wore yellow coats, in Vienna yellow cloths under their armpits. In Strasbourg, where there were so many brothels of all sizes that you could bump into prostitutes in the very towers of the cathedral, they were required to wear a white veil on a small black hat and were given the nickname "tower swallows". In 14th-century Florence and Ferrara they had to draw attention to themselves by wearing bells on their hats, in the same way as jesters. The distinguishing marks served a double purpose: the good-time girls must not be confused with honorable ladies or men and had to stand out. In many municipalities the prostitutes were positively urged to attract the attention of men. The courtesans of Venice had to sit at their windows with their breasts exposed in order to attract customers. They were strictly forbidden to wear the so-called "pudding-bowl haircut" of the men. If they tried to look like males and enticed men to participate in illicit acts, they would be threatened with flogging and high fines for "sodomy".

Whores' Outfits in the Middle Ages. The four originally colored paintings show the insignia for prostitutes of various medieval towns. In Switzerland, Bern and Zurich whores had to wear a red bonnet, in the Austrian city of Vienna a yellow scarf, in the Italian province of Piemont a horned cap was required, and in the French city of Lyons they were forced to wear a red armband.

Between 1350 and 1600 most houses of pleasure in Germany belonged to the cities. Everything was strictly regulated. Married women and nuns were not allowed to enter the brothels. The licenses were often granted as levies, and popes and kings also made a profit out of the duties. In Toulouse the city authorities split the takings from the houses of pleasure with the university. In Mainz, Germany, around the middle of the 15th century Archbishop Dietrich launched an official complaint against the citizens on the basis that he alone had the right – for a suitable fee, naturally – to grant licenses to run whorehouses. Pope Clement VII decreed in 1523 that upon the death of a prostitute, half of her estate should be surrendered to the Church. The money went to a convent for penitent female sinners.

At first the staff in the houses of pleasure mainly consisted of "traveling women". In the 14th and 15th centuries, if the wandering prostitutes were successful and remained settled, they lived under the protection of a well-organized tradeswomen's guild. In the late Middle Ages the so-called "Brothel Queen", after having been chosen as overseer by the prostitutes in a free vote, was sworn in and endorsed by the town council. Prostitutes who did not belong to the guild, the *Böhnhäsinnen* (freelancers in the prostitute trade), were run out of town as unwelcome competition.

The prostitutes who belonged to the guilds (and only they) enjoyed certain privileges. In several towns they were invited to wedding festivities and receptions. And they were given rights: no one was allowed to harm them or to refuse to pay their fees – as was the case by the end of the 20th century.

Traveling Women

From the early medieval period on, destitute, orphaned, and widowed women wandered as vagrants through the country. Among them, too, were the daughters of men who had "dishonorable" trades such as gravediggers or hangmen, and who therefore were not allowed to marry. The only asset at the disposal of these women was their bodies.

Master with Revenue Seals, *In the House of Pleasure,* **mid-15th cent. Copperplate engraving.** The Catholic Church prohibited sex between married couples on so many holy days that men felt driven to the brothel.

Frans Brun, *Soldiers' Whores in the Baggage Train,* **1559. Copperplate engraving.** Up to the beginning of the 20th century prostitutes were transported with the army, just like any other provisions.

In Germany, the so-called *Landstörzerinnen* offered their services by the side of country roads and traveled from place to place. Wherever there was a big assembly of men – at church councils, trade fairs, carnivals and *Reichstags* (parliaments) – traveling women were to be found and were even tolerated during these events.

In most medieval towns the "locals" were prohibited from working in the brothels. In the years 1414–1418 alone, during the Council of Constance, there were said to be 800–1500 (figures vary) vagrant "merry women" in town. In time of battle, especially, the warriors could count on the same treatment. A horde of women followed every baggage train, so that the lansquenets' sexual needs were catered for alongside their material needs. These traditions only began to change with the introduction of standing armies and finally came to an end with general conscription in the 19th century.

Brothels in the Wild West

In some ways the "old countries" carried out a regular human trade with women who, in their homeland, had perhaps breached society's moral code. Although they may have been outcasts in their birthplace, in their new domiciles they were welcome, needed, and there was a looser moral code.

In the so-called Wild West, where the building of the railroads led to a rapid growth of the towns, women were a scarce and desirable commodity. On a day-to-day basis women were more conspicuous by their absence than in other male-dominated communities. They were needed for just one reason: to satisfy sinful desires of every kind.

Unmarried females, often descendants of those disadvantaged women who had come to the New World not of their own free will, later ended up in the saloons as dancers, hostesses, and croupiers. They had a bad reputation. Any amusement, including gambling and drinking, was regarded with suspicion and as incompatible with the respectable way of life. If they worked as waitresses or in the gambling halls, erotic contact with the customers was frowned upon. They were not supposed to sate the appetites they aroused. However the sheer proximity of such women, who embodied a world completely different from their everyday lives of deprivation, engendered even more recklessness amongst the men at the gambling tables.

For purposes of "fornication" another class of women, who were prohibited from entering the saloons, had to be resorted to. For one hour during daylight only, they were allowed to show their faces in the town streets. In the settlements which were, at first, very small and rudimentary, there were always three important places, which in a way represented the cultural centers of the emergent frontier towns: the church, the saloon, and the brothel. It was there that all the important municipal decisions were made. For example, a town such as Abilene in Kansas was founded only in 1861. After the arrival of the railroad six years later it underwent an economic boom. More and more prostitutes moved into the town and found work and a livelihood. In the following years

Transporting Prostitutes

By no means were all the Europeans who settled in America after 1620 die-hard Puritans. The very people who had come into conflict with the rigid moral attitudes of the ruling majority in England also arrived – often against their will – in the New World. A large proportion of the new inhabitants of North America were transportees or the dependants of transportees.

Deportation was almost tantamount to a death sentence, because many unfortunates did not even survive the long, arduous sea voyage to the New World. Those sentenced to transportation were very poor. Only young women of "easy virtue" had anything of value to offer the male members of the crew.

Anonymous, *The Sad Departure of the Girls of Joy*, 18th cent., France. Etching, Public Library, New York. The European states, especially England and France, used to deport thieves, beggars and prostitutes to their colonies right up to the 20th century.

The women employed in this brothel in Creede are gathered around the recently invented gramophone which is undoubtedly the main attraction of the establishment.

Opposite: **Cora Pearl in the 1890s.** One of the best known madams during the gold rush was Cora Pearl of San Francisco. Her establishment was notorious for its virgin's room where gullible johns were conducted to a professional virgin and to the delectation of hidden spectators gave of their best.

increasing numbers of illegitimate children were born, who grew up either in church homes or along with their mothers in the houses of pleasure. In the church orphanages they died "like summer flies in the cold wind", as the madam Nell Kimball critically observed in her memoirs.

Nonetheless women who worked in brothels as prostitutes were less stigmatized in the Wild West than in other contemporary societies. If they got to know a man through their work who no longer just wanted an occasional visit, they would get married to him. It was taboo to allude to the past of a former prostitute; now she was a "respectable" woman.

According to the size of the frontier towns there were single brothels or complete red-light districts – with a motley crew of clients: pan-handlers, trappers, railroad workers, soldiers, cowboys, and settlers. Apparently the trappers and hunters soon adopted the relatively free sexual attitude of the native Indian population. Settlers from a more puritanical background, however, continued to apply the Victorian double standards. If they approached prostitutes they considered that a moral lapse and blamed their sin on the depraved hussy.

Many pioneers resolutely differentiated themselves and their "respectable" lifestyles from those of cowboys and prostitutes, while at the

same time envying the nomad riders. The moral life and the free life fell into an unbridgeable opposition. The free life involved a more easygoing attitude to matters of the body, to nudity, and to sexuality.

The lifestyle of the unattached wanderer, just like that of the sailor, also lends itself in the erotic sphere to myth and romance. Even today the sexuality of free-living individuals provides a fantasy world for those who do not have such opportunities.

The 30,000–50,000 cowboys were mostly unmarried. In contrast to the settlers, who had to depend on an everyday basis on hard-working undemonstrative women who embodied effort and sacrifice, the cowboys wanted female companionship of a different kind. The "public women" obviously belonged to the world of freedom, pleasure, and extravagance. Whenever the opportunity arose, particularly during the winter months, the cowboys were on the loose, forming bonds for a few weeks or months. No decent woman could have agreed to this. The half-nomadic men lived two separate lives. In winter they indulged without inhibition in pleasures which they abstained from in summer. But as johns they were more tolerable than those guilt-ridden settlers whose consciences continually plagued them even during their furtive brothel visits.

Mary Magdalen

Donatello, *Saint Mary Magdalen*, 1453 – 1455. Wood (polychrome), 188 cm high, Museo dell'Opera del Duomo, Florence. When Mary became a hermit she had no need of clothes because her hair grew to cover her.

Few women play an important role in the New Testament. Characteristically enough, up there alongside the Mother of God and Virgin Mary, is a prostitute: Mary Magdalen. Ever since 1037 Vézelay, in Burgundy, where the relics of the saint were supposedly found, has been a much-visited place of pilgrimage. In nearby Auxerre she has even been revered since the 6th century. However, Mary Magdalen, who is honored as a repentant prostitute, is in fact a compilation of three female figures. In Mark's Gospel it is written how Jesus drove seven demons out of one Mary Magdalen. This woman later witnessed his death and resurrection. After the Ascension there was a certain Maria of Egypt, who had spent nearly two decades in brothels before the first adherents of the Christian religion took her with them to Jerusalem. As a convert she took a vow of chastity and lived for another 47 years as a recluse in the desert. It was she, rather than the follower of Jesus, who became the patron saint of repentant prostitutes. The Italian artist Donatello (1382/86–1466) in his famous wooden relief, today to be found in the Museo dell'Opera del Duomo, portrays her as a very old, completely emaciated hermit.

Luke, in his Gospel (7: 36–50), mentions a nameless female sinner, who washes Christ's feet with her tears, dries them with her hair, and then anoints them. There is no evidence that this "sinner" was a prostitute. The cathars, a medieval sect, took her for Jesus' wife or mistress. While in the Middle Ages Mary Magdalen was still mainly presented as a disciple of Jesus, after the Counter-Reformation the penitent

Mary Magdalen grew in significance. Artists used the rare opportunity to portray a young, Christian, female saint half-naked, with flowing reddish-blond hair. This erotic symbol was just as much part of the iconography of Magdalen as her jar of ointment.

All the same, whether pensive, penitent or ecstatic, Mary Magdalen's portrait also remains one of temptation, and the devotion which her pictures conveyed was not necessarily of the pious kind. From the start of the Italian Renaissance contemporaries often recognized in these pictures famous courtesans who had posed as models. Mary Magdalen had become an excuse for religious pornography.

The religious community of beguines, also founded in the 12th century, made an effort to redeem prostitutes, especially in the Netherlands. At the start of the 17th century the government took over responsibility for the Magdalen-houses. However, the workhouses or spinning factories, which the government then turned them into, bore a greater resemblance to penitentiaries than to houses of repentance.

The title page of a book of rules for a refuge in Paris depicts Mary Magdalen surrounded by repentant prostitutes, c. 1500.

Magdalen-houses

Magdalen-houses, originally endowed in the Middle Ages for the conversion of prostitutes, were frequently financed by well-to-do elderly courtesans. The Order of the Penitents of Saint Mary Magdalen has, since 1200, spread across Germany and into France, Spain, and Italy. Magdalen-houses were correction institutes, convents, and asylums which were administered by Church authorities. The inmates were prohibited from leaving the homes. If they returned to their trade they were threatened with death. For the "penitent sinner" the only possible route back to normal life was through marriage. No one was allowed to insult with impunity a woman who had found refuge in a Magdalen-house.

Louis Finson after Caravaggio, *Madeleine in Ecstasy*, c. 1613. Oil on canvas, 100 x 70 cm, Musée des Beaux-Arts, Marseilles. In a number of 16th- and 17th-century paintings and sculptures, religious ecstasy is almost indistinguishable from the rapture of orgasm.

The Erotic Muse

Art and Artifice

Sleeping Satyr, so-called Barberini Faun (provided with fig leaf for the exhibition), c. 220 B.C. Greek original, marble, Glyptothek, Munich. Around 1860, the "nakedness" of the classical sculptures in the Munich Glyptothek was covered with fig leaves, the consequence of prudish legislation which came into force about 100 years after the figures in the Vatican Sistine Chapel and many other European collections had been similarly covered. The fig leaf, the first "garment" recorded in the Bible, and the sign of sexual shame after the Fall, became a means of censorship.

The Pleasure of Observation

an active agent, projecting fantasies onto female figures that do no more than reflect male desires. Many painters have also recognized the voyeurism implicit in their work, and have even made it explicit by placing an observer within the painting who stands as surrogate for all those who are outside, looking in. On the most basic level, this internal observer, by his presence (it is almost invariably a male), is giving the real spectators permission to join him in looking at the woman, but he is also acting as a mediator between the erotic object and the outside world, coloring and shaping the possible range of responses. Sometimes this figure is intended to legitimize both the artist and his audience. In the numerous paintings on the theme of the Judgment of Paris, for example, the goddesses Hera, Athena and Aphrodite have been reduced to posing and simpering to win the approval of a mortal. The figure of Paris is not only an invitation to the spectator to appraise the goddesses, but a statement of

Jean-Honoré Fragonard, *The Swing,* **1767. Oil on canvas, 81 x 64.2 cm, The Wallace Collection, London.** Fragonard was given very little freedom when commissioned to paint this work: it had to show his patron's mistress on a swing that was being pushed by a bishop. The patron himself, the Abbé de Saint-Non, was to be shown on the ground, looking up the woman's skirts.

No work of art, whatever its content, can become erotic without the activating force of the spectator's gaze. And any work of art that is intended, despite its distance and passivity, to arouse observers, automatically invites them to assume the role of voyeurs. Sigmund Freud wrote that all art appreciation is founded in the same impulse as voyeurism. For Freud, it was only when this natural voyeuristic impulse was sublimated – or "shifted away from the genitals onto the shape of the body as a whole" – that it became one of the engines driving a so-called "disinterested" love of art.

Because the naked female body is the most common erotic object in Western painting, much feminist criticism has attacked the way in which the male gaze is always presented as such

Lucas Cranach the Elder, *The Judgment of Paris,* **1530. Oil on beech panel, 35 x 24 cm, Staatliche Kunsthalle, Karlsruhe.** Cranach was an expert at partially covering his female nudes, in the process making them more erotic than if they were completely naked.

Jacopo Robusti Tintoretto, *Susanna and the Elders*, between 1555 and 1556. Oil on canvas, 146.5 x 193.6 cm, Kunsthistorisches Museum, Vienna. Sometimes the lecherous gaze of a man is even represented as a form of illumination, bathing a naked woman in its glow, as in this painting, based on the biblical story of Susanna and the Elders. Stories such as this and David and Bathsheba were popular sources for artists seeking a biblical context as an excuse to portray nudes.

the artist's power as an arbiter of beauty. Perhaps even more interesting are the paintings in which the artist recognizes and even mourns the unbridgeable gulf between the watcher and the watched. This is most often done by emphasizing the inhumanity of the pictorial observer, such as the bestial satyrs that Renaissance painters liked to show spying on the goddess Diana. And in the 20th century Picasso depicted himself as a Minotaur, gazing with desperate longing at a beautiful girl but unable to make any real contact with her. He also put himself into many of his later etchings in the guise of a grotesque or foolish old man, watching a young couple making love. In works such as these, the artist recognizes the impotence which, as well as the magus-like power, is inherent in being an observer.

The Camera's Eye

As Susan Sontag and other critics have suggested, the camera's ability to capture an image instantly and objectively makes photography a supremely voyeuristic medium. Although a photograph may be as much a piece of artifice as any painting, it can easily seem to be no more or less than an authentic record of some event, unmediated by an artist's sensibilities. For this reason, and because they can be reproduced so easily, photographs create in observers an especially powerful sense that they own – or at any rate have access to – the thing depicted. The invention of digital and video cameras, the seamless computer doctoring of pictures and the uncontrollable proliferation of images on the Internet are all helping to create a world in which the boundaries between the public and private are dissolving.

Paradoxically, however, the sense of voyeurism becomes especially acute in a public arena – the cinema – as the spectator sits hidden in the dark, watching a private, untouchable world revealing itself in the distance. Films such as Michael Powell's *Peeping Tom*, Alfred Hitchcock's *Rear Window*, Krzysztof Kieslowski's *A Short Film about Love* and Patrice Leconte's *Monsieur Hire* have deliberately exploited this sense of being a secret, helpless, yet intrusive watcher.

Charles Gatewood, woman masturbating with onlookers, 1970. For many men, to watch a woman masturbating is more arousing, and more transgressive, than to watch her having penetrative sex, because masturbation is the more solitary act, and witnessing it is more of an invasion of privacy.

Censorship, Aesthetics, and Arousal

Pornography is, in many ways, a Victorian invention. The word itself comes from the Greek *porne*, "street prostitute" and *graphos*, "writing", and entered general usage in the 1800s, when the well-to-do gentlemen of Naples, Paris and London needed a term to describe the collections of ancient erotic art they were accumulating in the locked rooms of their museums. When excavations began at Herculaneum and Pompeii in the 18th century, the archaeologists and trophy hunters involved were appalled by the amount of erotic material they uncovered – especially by the profusion of erect phalluses that confronted them from almost every wall, corner and pediment. They revered the Romans and Greeks as the fathers of civilization, but felt betrayed by the sheer volume of erotica before them. They believed that to put these objects on public display would be a threat to society itself, but were serious enough as scholars to balk at the thought of destroying them.

It was Francis I, Duke of Calabria, who suggested in 1819 that all the erotica should be locked away in a single room at the Museum of Naples, which was called the *Gabinetto degli Oggetti Osceni*, "Cabinet of Obscene Objects". It eventually became popularly known as the Pornographic Collection, or more simply the Secret Museum. Entrance was restricted to "persons of mature age and proven morality", which invariably translated as wealthy men. Women, children and the lower classes were all forbidden entry. The Neapolitan approach was adopted by great museums throughout Europe, leading to collections such as *L'Enfer* in Paris, and the Private Case of the British Museum, all of which can be seen as a paradigm of censorship. In each case it is assumed that gentlemen – those with wealth, education and above all power – are incorruptible, whereas everyone else, possessing a weaker mind and more fragile sense of morality, is in constant danger of being depraved by scenes or descriptions with sexual content. In many ways, the often-quoted distinction between the erotic and the pornographic is drawn along similar lines, and is every bit as artificial: erotica is something that the cultured will savor, while pornography is something that the vulgar will abuse.

As a result, the difference between erotica and pornography often depends on little more than

A wall painting showing a couple with a satyr from the secret collection of 206 paintings, sculptures and other objects drawn from the excavations at Pompeii and Herculaneum.

Guglielmo Marconi, *Académie* Figure, c. 1870, Uwe Scheid Collection. Marconi was a photographer at the Art Academy in Paris between 1869 and 1874. He probably began making nude studies for professional artists in 1870. This impeccably tasteful academic study is modeled on a painting, *The Rokeby Venus*, by Diego Velázques (1599–1660).

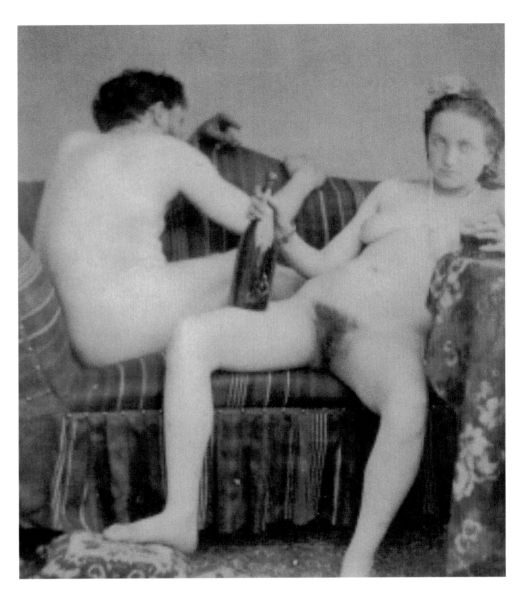

A confiscated image in the archives of the Paris police, 1862. Louis Daguerre revealed his new invention, the Daguerreotype, to the Academy of Sciences in Paris in 1839, and almost immediately the first nudes were being created. Called *académies*, they were legal, and supposed to emulate the life studies of artists. Many of them copied the poses of acknowledged masterpieces. However, by 1855, the first exhibition of the newly-formed *Société Française de Photographie* was already announcing, "nudes in general, and without exception, will be refused." By this time, pornographic prints in their thousands were being produced and traded. When in 1852 it was decreed that prints must be registered with the Paris Police Department, almost half the pictures submitted were *académies* (a figure that was itself dwarfed by black market images). In 1855, the Paris Police set up an archive of photographs seized in raids on private homes.

how many copies there are. A painting or a limited edition, seen by a select few, is erotic, while an identical photograph is obscene. This knee-jerk distinction was comically exposed in Hamburg in 1881, when the police confiscated photographic reproductions of various Titian Venuses because they were seen as being pornographic. Those who consider themselves an educated elite try to stop images they regard as suitable for themselves from getting into the hands of the proletariat via the means of mass production. In this light, censorship can be seen as a struggle for power, rather than for moral standards. One of the earliest recorded acts of censorship was the banning of Aristophanes's play, *Lysistrata*, in 411 B.C. Although the play was about women denying sex to their husbands, and was as ribald as might be expected, it was banned not because of its sexual subject, but because of its satirical jibes against the state of Athens. To those with the power of censor-

ship, subversion has always represented a greater threat than sex. However – correctly, as it turns out – the authorities have always seen subversion and pornography marching hand in hand. Throughout history, pornographers seem to have had an appetite for transgression that does not stop at the purely sexual. It is as if they are duty bound to oppose any and all social norms, and satire and parody, however weak, have always been a staple ingredient of porn. Indeed, leaving aside debatable moral positions, or spurious aesthetic arguments, the best definition of pornography seems to be "that which converts all other human interactions – including politics, warfare, family, contracts and the ownership of property – into the currency of sex, and interprets them in the language of sex." Just as Aristophanes used bawdy jokes to attack the Athenian state, so the pamphleteers of pre-Revolutionary France in the 18th century attacked their rulers by depicting them as sex-

ually incontinent, and often incompetent (if the king's scepter – his penis – was weak, then clearly so was his rule; if the queen was promiscuous, the paternity of her children, and therefore the legitimacy of the monarchy itself, was called into question). It has been estimated that two-thirds of all the printed literature which was being read at the end of the *ancien régime* was forbidden by the state, with a considerable amount of it being pornographic. Growing concerns about the power of the king also marked another golden age in the history of pornography, the English Restoration.

If anything, the Church was an even more popular target for pornographers, and ever since the Council of Trent (1545–1563) there was a papal censor responsible for compiling and administering the Index of Prohibited Books, 1559, which existed until 1966, and included some of the world's most distinctive literature, like Immanuel Kant's *Critique of Practical Reason*

Marcantonio Raimondi, *Posture 4*, 1524. Wood engraving. This engraving is accompanied by a sonnet by Pietro Aretino (1492–1557), printed in 1527. Aretino, the "Scourge of Princes" and the "Pimp to Popes", wrote a sonnet to accompany each of Raimondi's Positions. There appears to be only one surviving edition of the 1527 book that combined the sonnets with wood engravings of the Raimondi prints. The book was unique in the West, as possibly the first time that illustrations and text – each as scandalous as the other – were married together for public amusement. The collaboration between Oscar Wilde and Aubrey Beardsley centuries later is only one of the more celebrated examples of the tradition started by Aretino and Raimondi.

***The Kiss*, still from the film by William Heise, 1896, May Irwin as Widow Jones and John C. Rice as Billie Bikes.** When *The Kiss*, one of the earliest ever pieces of film footage, was first shown, publisher Herbert S. Stone demanded police action. It seems that whenever a new invention gives the public greater access to, and control over, images and information – the most notable examples being print, photography, cinema and the internet – there is a new frenzy of debate about censorship. The People's Institute of New York set up the National Board of Censorship to review films as early as 1902. Similar bodies were established in Germany in 1908, in Sweden in 1911 and in Britain in 1913. Later, in the 1930s, Hollywood opted for a form of self-censorship by agreeing to the Hays Code, which contained such ludicrous edicts as the one forbidding two people to sit on a bed, even fully clothed, unless each had one foot on the floor.

and Jean Jacques Rousseau's *Émile*. At first, the papacy was more concerned with anti-clericalism than with sexual representation. Boccaccio's *The Decameron*, which first appeared in manuscript form in 1371, had become one of the most popular books in the world after the invention of printing in the 15th century (by 1500 there were 300 different editions). When the Church authorities expurgated it, they allowed the racy stories to remain, but changed the copulating nuns, monks, priests and abbesses of Boccaccio's stories into aristocrats and entertainers.

Although the Counter Reformation did signal a backlash against erotic art, it was directed more against the new, mass-produced, printed images than against original, one-off artworks. In the 1520s the artist Giulio Romano is said to have drawn 16 pictures of copulating couples on the walls of the Sala di Constantino in the Vatican. In 1524 the engraver Marcantonio Raimondi copied them and began offering them for sale as the *Sedici Modi* (Sixteen Positions). Although Romano's originals no longer exist, the artist himself was free to go on painting explicit images for his patron, Duke Federico di Gonzaga of Mantua. Raimondi's work, on the other hand, attracted the attention of the papal censor, Cardinal Giberti, who ordered all the plates and existing prints to be destroyed, and the death penalty for anyone who tried to reprint them. Raimondi himself was thrown in jail. Once again, what was at work here was fear of the erotic getting into the hands of the masses, rather than fear of the erotic itself.

Although the Church could point to its concern for the health of the soul as a justification for its interest in pornography, it was only in the 18th century that the secular courts codified their own right to interfere in people's enjoyment of the erotic. In 1727, in England, a Mr. Justice Probyn ruled against Edmund Curll, publisher of a book called *Venus of the Cloister: or, The Nun in Her Smock*, declaring that "morality is part of the law of the land as Christianity is" and that any act "destructive of morality in general" should be punished in the same way as blasphemy. This hugely influential ruling – the basis for many censorship laws worldwide – was reinforced in the wording of the 1859 Obscene Publications Act in Britain, which defined obscenity as that which was liable to "deprave or corrupt". A new Act, passed in 1959, allowed artistic or literary merit as a defense, which was successfully exploited by the publishers of *Lady Chatterley's Lover*, written

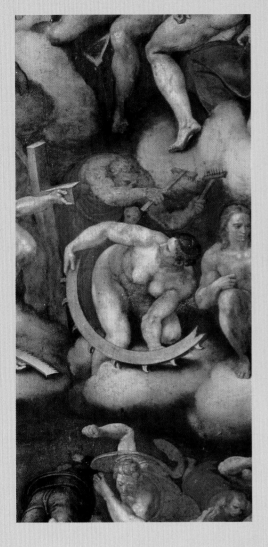

Adulterating Masterpieces

The power of great art to arouse is often ignored or forgotten, but the Renaissance biographer Giorgio Vasari (1511–1574) describes how a painting of Saint Sebastian by Fra Bartolomeo, created in 1514, had to be removed from its place in church when women confessed to having sinned while contemplating it. When Biagio da Cesena, the papal master of ceremonies, first saw *The Last Judgment* on the ceiling of the Sistine Chapel, he told Michelangelo that he was doing "a very improper thing to paint so many nude forms". He was promptly painted into hell by the vengeful artist (Biagio is the one having his genitals bitten by a serpent). In 1564 the Council of Trent decreed that many of the offending body parts should be covered up with pieces of cloth, a process that continued until the 18th century. A black market in copies of the original, unadulterated version thrived as a result.

Left: **Michelangelo, *The Last Judgment* (detail), 1537–1541. Fresco, 1370 x 1220 cm, Sistine Chapel, Vatican. *Right:* Marcello Venusti, *The Last Judgment*, Museo di Capodimonte, Naples.** *The Last Judgment* as we know it today, and a copy by Marcello Venusti (c. 1512–1579), indicating how this masterpiece was altered. Among the grosser changes, Saint Catherine has been clothed, and Saint Blaise's head twisted so that he is no longer looking at her in what could be interpreted as a lustful way.

by D.H. Lawrence, who were prosecuted and acquitted in 1960.

The struggle for the control of public morals continues. Even during the 20th century, copies of *The Decameron* were being seized by US postal workers, and burned in Britain by Court order. The US Presidential committee set up by Lyndon B. Johnson in 1967 eventually reported – after three years' work – that all extant pornography laws should be repealed. They cited the case of Denmark, which had been the very first country to decriminalize pornography in 1969, and had experienced an almost immediate drop in sex crimes in general. President Nixon ignored the recommendation. Another pornography committee, the Meese Commission, was set up by Ronald

Reagan in 1985, and was headed by anti-porn zealot Edwin Meese. Its conclusions were diametrically opposed to the earlier report. It is still not possible, it seems, to divorce the erotic from the political.

Because of the inability to separate the erotic from the political, situations arise like that of the trial of a Cincinnati museum for showing the work of the internationally famous photographer, Robert Mapplethorpe, and the unanimous vote by the Supreme Court of Canada in 1992, allowing the victims of sex crimes to sue the makers and distributors of pornography. At the other extreme, there is the Manhattan jury that acquitted the maker of a film showing sex between two men and a dog, on the basis that it was so disgusting it could not possibly arouse

any normal person. As the judge said: "If you're not aroused, it's not obscene." The clash of public and personal that exists in pornography, and erotic art in general, does not seem to allow for any universal values. That is its subversive, eternally disquieting power.

The Naked Body

In the last years of the Roman Empire, artists began to reject the Classical ideals of balance and proportion that had dominated aesthetics since the ancient Greeks. They lived at a time when civilization itself was crumbling around them, and responded with a sensibility that reveled in the expressive, the unusual and sometimes the grotesque. When they turned their attentions to the human figure, they were less concerned with capturing some imaginary perfection than with exploring the character within, and elements that did not further this cause, such as the hair or the extremities, were sometimes only sketched in. By contrast, heads were often woefully large by Classical standards.

The eastern Roman Empire, centered on Byzantium, survived much longer than the empire in the West, and by the 6th century most Christian artists were in thrall to Byzantine ideas of art, which emphasized icons and abstract patterns, and had little room for the naked body. As a result, the nude became less important in Western art. It almost disappeared completely after the Iconoclastic Crisis of the 8th–9th centuries, when Pope Leo III decided that the crucified Christ was not an appropriate object of veneration, and had images of crucifixion replaced with the unadorned cross. Because the Church held that the body was a vessel of sin, the medieval nude was not an

François Boucher, *Nude on a Sofa (Louise O'Murphy)*, 1752. Oil on canvas, 59 x 73 cm, Alte Pinakothek, Munich. In female nudes from the 17th–19th centuries, the buttocks of a woman were the most conspicuously eroticized parts of her body. The genitals were usually hidden, but could occasionally be glimpsed. The focus on breasts is very much a 20th-century phenomenon.

Peasants Treading Grapes, 4th cent. A.D. Mosaic, Santa Constanza, Rome. This mosaic is a typical combination of Christian and pagan influences, superimposed on scenes of ordinary people at work and play.

object of delight in itself, but usually appeared only to enforce some moral point, or illustrate an allegory. Within religious art, the only fit subjects for nude portraiture were Adam and Eve (rarely other biblical characters) and the dead, whether being judged or resurrected. The bodies shown were typically ugly, emaciated or suffering the torments of the damned. In the 13th and 14th centuries, tiny naked figures also began to appear in the marginalia of prayer books, and these were often scurrilous or satirical in nature. Texts about the mythical Golden Age could also be illustrated with nudes, and these provide some of the few occasions in medieval art when naked people are shown enjoying themselves, without some dire threat of retribution looming in the background.

There is good reason to believe that most female nudes painted during this period were executed from memory, and the imagination, rather than life. They are usually high-waisted and long-legged, with small breasts and protruding stomachs – exactly the build that was hinted at by the fashionable ladies' clothing of the day (the shape given to women by art has always had more to do with fashion than physiology). This particular ideal female form survived into the Renaissance, in the work of French or German artists such as Cranach the Elder (1472–1553), but the period is more famous for the rediscovery – chiefly by Italian artists – of the Classical form, and of the naked

Anonymous, *Bathsheba Bathing and King David*, Hours of Marguerite de Coëtivy, 15th century. Parchment, Musée Condé, Chantilly, France. Apart from Adam and Eve, Bathsheba being watched by David, and Susanna being spied on by the Elders, were the two biblical stories that gave late-medieval artists the greatest license to paint nudes.

male body. The sculptor Nicola Pisano was already experimenting in both areas by the 13th century – his pulpit in the baptistery at Pisa, made in 1260, includes a nude allegory of strength based on the figures of Hercules that were sometimes found on Roman sarcophagi. However, it was not until the 15th century that the interest in Classical prototypes became a

full-blown artistic movement. Some of the most influential artists of the Renaissance – including Cellini, Donatello, Leonardo and Michelangelo – were homosexual or bisexual, and they responded most passionately to the Classical tradition of the heroic nude male. Michelangelo was famously inept at portraying naked women, usually producing, in the words of one critic, "men with udders". Another reason for the early Renaissance painters' greater interest and therefore assurance with the male figure was that artists then were still organized into all-male workshops, with a master, journeymen and apprentices, many of whom would model for each other. The Church was fiercely opposed to women entering a workshop, and several of the early sketches for Raphael's Madonnas, for example, were modeled from boys.

However, it would be wrong to suggest that Renaissance art was in any way uniform in its inspiration or its aesthetics. For Leonardo, the nude was a scientific exercise in proportions – it had to conform to the dictum of the first century B.C. architect, Vitruvius, that a man with arms and legs outstretched would fit perfectly into the two basic geometric shapes, a square and a circle. At the same time, it had to conform to the Golden Mean, according to which if a line is divided into a longer and a shorter portion, the relationship of the shorter to the longer should be the same as the relationship of the longer to the whole. (Leonardo was too good an artist to follow these precepts slavishly; Dürer, who made the attempt, produced many clumsy nudes before learning to temper his mathematical tendencies.) On the other hand, Botticelli's rhythmic, sinuous command of line transformed his Classical nudes, turning them into figures that looked back to the organic spontaneity of the Gothic cathedrals, and forward to the decorative exuberance of the Baroque. In his various paintings of Venus, the *Primavera* and so on, he also made extensive use of the license granted by pagan mythological subjects – it is hard to imagine the army of naked gods and goddesses painted by Titian, for example, without Botticelli's example.

Under the influence of Titian, and later Rubens, the naked female form evolved into the most popular subject in the whole of Western art. It also changed shape with the dictates of fashion, becoming softer and more voluptuous. By the time of the French Rococo, two approaches to the nude emerged which would, in various guises, dominate art for the next 150 years. On the one hand there were the romantics and fantasists, epitomized by Mme Pompadour's favorite, François Boucher (1703–1770), who delighted in playful, openly erotic female nudes whose poses occasionally prefigure the early pinup photographs of the 20th century. On the other there were the real-

Jacques-Louis David, *Leonidas at the Thermopylae* (detail), 1814. Oil on canvas, 395 x 531 cm, Musée du Louvre, Paris. After the Renaissance, there was a lapse in interest in the male nude until the Neoclassical movement, which was inspired by the homosexual German scholar, Johann Joachim Winckelmann (1717–1768). David was among the most enthusiastic converts to Winckelmann's ideas, and produced a series of paintings that emphasize the heroic male in a Classical setting. However, a new bourgeois audience for art was developing which placed more emphasis on hedonism than on education, and which tended to prefer the female body. The reemergence of the male nude in the 20th century is largely linked to the explosion of a widely tolerated homosexual culture.

ists and moralists, such as Diderot's choice, Jean-Baptiste Greuze (1725–1805), who, when he wasn't painting po-faced genre pictures, produced slightly unnerving shots of pubescent girls, accompanied by some obvious prop, such as a broken jug, suggestive of the loss of innocence.

In the first half of the 19th century, this opposition was expressed in the diverse approaches of the realist, Courbet, and the orientalists, Ingres and Delacroix, who liked to paint nudes in harem or other exotic settings. Curiously, it was the realists who attracted the greatest censure. Although the pose was borrowed straight from Titian, a scandal ensued when Manet painted his *Olympia* (1863), because the model was so clearly a flesh and blood woman, and moreover a prostitute. (Incidentally, this was another reason for the increased appearance of the female nude in the 19th century – artists were finding more women willing to pose for them as the demimonde became ever more visible and was itself swelled by the growing ranks of the urban working classes.) Impressionism, the major

Donatello, *David*, c. 1440. Bronze sculpture, 158 cm high, Museo Nazionale del Bargello, Florence. Like many Renaissance artists, although Donatello embraced the Grecian model of the heroic male, he made it considerably more androgynous. His David is slimmer than its Classical antecedents, and the body is held differently. Whereas the Greeks had treated the pelvis as the main pivot of the standing torso, Donatello's David, setting the pattern for most subsequent Renaissance nudes, puts more emphasis on the waist.

artistic movement towards the end of the century, had little interest in the nude figure – both Manet and Renoir painted fewer nudes when under the influence of the impressionist circle than at other times in their careers. However, one of the impressionists, Degas, had a profound effect on representations of the nude, through his dislike of conventional beauty, and the conventional poses used to show it off. He often preferred to twist his models into strained, uncomfortable positions, and portrayed them from strange angles.

The distortion of the body became a staple of 20th-century art, from the cubist *Les Demoiselles D'Avignon* (1907) of Picasso to the surrealist experiments of Magritte and Dalí. It was left to photography (and, to a lesser extent, to carica-

turists) to preserve and celebrate the changing norms of the female form, from the flat-chested 1920s flappers to the well-fed, glowingly healthy, cantilever bra-ed pinups of the 1940s. By the 1950s, Willem de Kooning was producing abstract expressionist paintings of women, which, however scarified, clearly borrowed from the pinup tradition, a trend that grew even stronger in the 1960s, with the arrival of the pop artists who self-consciously borrowed from popular culture. Some of the most confrontational nudes of recent years – such as the pictures taken by Jeff Koons of himself and his porn-star wife of the time, La Cicciolina – have exploited the tension between photography and painting, and between so-called high and low art.

Tom Wesselmann, *Nude*, 1975. Pencil and liquitex on paper, 45 x 73 cm, private collection. The series of Great American Nudes is among the most aggressive appropriations of girlie magazine clichés, even by the standards of Pop Art, reducing the image to little more than genitals, nipples and tongues.

Cult of the Castrati

In harems in the Orient, especially in China, it was normal to employ eunuchs who had been robbed of not just their testicles, but of their penises as well. In the Christian West, those who were castrated for the sake of their singing lost "only" their testicles.

The first authentic report of the castration of singers dates from Roman Antiquity. In his extensive Roman History (book 75, chapter 74), senator and consul Cassius Dio Cocceianus (late-second–early-third century) from Asia Minor mentions that a favorite of Emperor Septimus Severus (146–211) had boys, youths and men castrated not only to provide his daughter with servants, but also with singers. Castrati appeared for the first time in the service of Christian sacred music in the 12th century in Constantinople. From there they began their slow victory march to the West. Pope Clement VII (1523–1534) was the first to substitute castrato voices for women's voices in the Capella Pontifica, the Papal chapel choir. In his time there were supposedly already approximately 4000 castrated boys in Italy. The tradition of capons, as the commoners referred to castrated singers, continued in the West for almost 400 years. Pope Leo XIII (1878–1903) was the one who finally put an end to the tradition. The 1902 and 1904 recordings of the Papal castrato Alessandro Moreschi (1858-1922), the so-called "Angel of Rome", can still be heard today. Castration reached its greatest popularity in the 17th and 18th centuries. Spurred on by the great success certain castrati had in the newly emerged and very successful operatic genre, numerous poor parents had their sons castrated in the hope of paving their ways to wealth and honor. Innumerable boys were unmanned for this reason but never became notable singers. Although castration was officially strictly forbidden in Italy, once the operation was performed, it wasn't hard to state that it was the result of an accident. However, everyone knew what was really occurring; famous singers were hailed with the enthusiastic cry *Viva il coltello!* "Long live the knife!" The little Umbrian city of Norcia even gained the dubious reputation of being the castration capital of Europe.

Although no one remembers the thousands of boys who were mutilated by the practice but who never achieved fame, the biographies of about 40 castrati are known. One of the most famous castrati was the extremely tall and thin

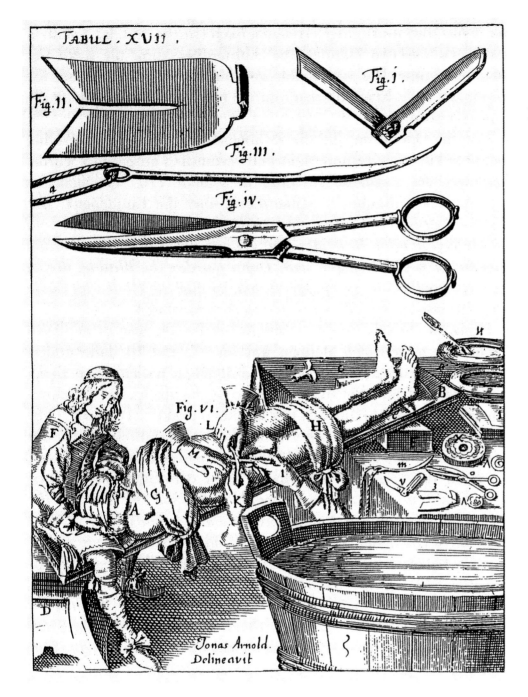

Johannes Scultetus, *Castration or Testicle Removal*, 1666. After castration a boy's larynx stopped growing. The result was a small larynx with short vocal cords – producing a high-pitched voice – above the chest, the strong lungs and the facial structure of a grown man.

Antonio Maria Zanetti, *Giziello*, 1750. Drawing, 28.5 x 19.4 cm, Fondazione Cini, Venice. Castrati often suffered from deformation in their development. They were a frequent subject of caricature, portrayed as either excessively fat or inordinately tall and thin.

Filippo Balati (1676–1756), who left behind an autobiography in verse. Another well-known figure was Gaetano Majorano Caffarelli (1710–1786), whose city mansion, built near the Teatro San Carlo in Naples in 1754, is still a wonder to behold. Mozart wrote several arias especially for him. As famous as they were in their time, they were all surpassed by Carlo Broschi Farinelli (1705–1782), who was immortalized in the 1990s by Gérard Corbiau in his film *Farinelli: il Castrato* that freely mixed truth and fiction. As the private singer of the melancholy King Philip V of Spain, he virtually became the Spanish prime minister, attaining tremendous wealth and honor.

Bach, Handel, Mozart and many other composers wrote numerous works for castrati. Giacomo Meyerbeer (1791–1864) conceived the last castrato opera *Il Crociato in Egitto* (1824) in honor of Giambattista Velluti, whom he highly esteemed. Velluti died at the age of eighty in 1861.

While castrati were celebrated as kings of the European stage by their audiences, in their private lives they were excluded from society at the insistence of the church, in part because they presented a special temptation for "libertine" women: sexual enjoyment with them could not lead to pregnancy. Bartolomeo Sorlisi (1632–1672) is a prime example of a cas-

trato barred from normal life and sent to an early grave by society. In 1662 he sang in the first Italian opera performance in Dresden. In 1666 he was made a noble, and in 1667 he married Dorothea Lichtwer. This marriage led to a long ecclesiastical debate about whether capons were allowed to or even "able" to marry. By the time the comprehensive work *Eunuchi Conjugium* (Capon Marriage) appeared in 1685, Sorlisi was long since dead. The Church forbade marriages with castrated men as they could not father children.

The Significance of Clothing

Lucas Cranach the Elder, *Adam and Eve*, early 15th cent. Oil on panel, 81 x 52 cm, Östergötlands Länsmuseum, Linköping, Sweden. In his knowing, seductive way, Cranach uses the leaves to tease the observer as much as to hide the modesty of his subjects.

Protection from the hazards of hostile nature may have been the initial reason for the invention of clothing, but the desire to decorate the body and emphasize certain body parts may have also played a role. Another important motive for being wrapped up in clothes, one that has not changed since prehistoric times, is that nakedness is, next to death, the greatest equalizer. The clothes make the man: garments establish superiority and determine the "pecking order". Clothing must suit the position, be it a doctor's white coat, a judge's robe, priestly vestments or a military uniform.

According to the Bible, Adam and Eve grasped fig leaves the moment they became aware of their nakedness – their exposed genitalia caused them shame. "And the Lord God made for Adam and for his wife coats of skins, and clothed them," recounts Genesis (3: 21). Thus the second wardrobe of the original couple came straight from the hands of God, setting man apart from the animals.

The veiling of the body with clothing is supposed to civilize Man by controlling desire and suppressing sexual drives. Paradoxically, it can also do the opposite. Sigmund Freud believed that "the covering of the body that accompanies civilization arouses constant sexual curiosity."

The male silhouette has remained remarkably constant in men's fashions. The classic triangle formed by broad shoulders and narrow hips, first valued by the Babylonians and the Egyptians, is still admired today. In the history of Western men's fashion, the only exceptions made to the desired triangle shape were the Greek chiton and the Roman toga. Women's clothes, however, have been subject to constant change since the beginning of modern history: from flat chest to swelling bosom, from overflowing garments with padded hips to smooth, close-fitting dresses. Every social era links its own ideal of beauty, which is achieved through or at least supported by clothes, with its moral values. Interestingly, the higher a woman "stands" in society, the more seductive and lavish her clothing becomes.

The true importance of clothing as fashion began in early medieval times. Despite their renown as kings of fashion, the French were the first to outlaw and penalize unreasonable fashion creations. For women, the length of a train or the plunge of a neckline were precisely prescribed. The color, fabric, and cut of a dress corresponded to a woman's class. In addition, clothes had to be appropriate to the occasion –

a rule still observed today. Women were viewed as erotic creatures, as decorative adjuncts to men, skilled in emphasizing or veiling their charms according to the demands of the moment. Naturally, men determined the prevailing ideal of beauty. Hosts of tailors and hairdressers created the image of Woman to subordinate her sexuality.

One means of subordinating women was to create the appropriate packaging to limit their freedom of movement. Female bodies were bound with harmful corsets, locked into hoop skirts made of whalebone and wood, or covered with abundant padding, as was the fashion in medieval times, or the *Cul de Paris* of the *Belle Époque*. Heavy fabrics and uncomfortable shoes made walking difficult. Clothing fashions remained consistently highly unnatural and unfriendly to the body except during a few liberal phases. As late as 1900, getting dressed was still an extremely involved procedure that a woman couldn't manage without assistance. A lady's handmaid had to fasten the countless hooks and eyes of a corset, which was made as tight as possible. Next the lady's hair was piled high and held with innumerable hairpins, clasps, and combs. Then came the petticoats, pads, the basket-like framework for her bosom and backside, and finally the dress itself with frills, flounces, and draperies. It was a perfect

prison. Men, on the other hand, strutted around stiff and aloof in high, white stand-up collars, tailcoats, and top hats, all of which were supposed to express the wearer's strong character and high morals.

The fashion became increasingly more body-friendly in the decades that followed. There has been a significant relaxation in clothing styles and dress codes since the 1960s. Along with "the pill" and the sexual revolution in the West came the victory march of blue jeans, miniskirts, and transparent tops. Even men's fashion acknowledged a change in style. Men began to wear clothes with brighter colors and patterns, often made of synthetic fabrics. As leisure grew in importance towards the end of the 20th century, clothing became more casual and comfortable. It became acceptable to wear a polo shirt, a sweater-vest, or even a pullover with a suit. Blue jeans were topped by a T-shirt, the erotic potential of which was first explored in 1952 by a muscle-bound Marlon Brando in the film *A Streetcar Named Desire*.

Especially among young people, clothing helps blur gender roles. Cross-dressing isn't just a fashion statement; at the beginning of the 21st century androgyny in clothing is also rather utopian. The second skin doesn't so much protect one from fickle nature as from all-too-certain sexual and social classification.

A Streetcar Named Desire, **still from the film by Elia Kazan, 1951, Marlon Brando as Stanley Kowalski.** Marlon Brando set a new trend in that underwear was considered so sexy as to became overwear.

The Man in the Gray Flannel Suit: or, How Men's Clothing Ceased to Be a Means of Self-expression

Change in Western men's fashion began with the end of the divine right of kings. With the introduction of property rights and the rise of the middle class, the modest garb of the Puritans became the sign of masculine superiority. Accordingly, opulent and richly decorated fabrics fell out of favor. First the embroidery disappeared. By the mid-19th century the previously colorful suits started to become dark and simply cut. Little has changed since then. Members of the middle class have dressed themselves soberly in gray, brown or dark blue suits, as if to compensate for their feelings of inferiority by dressing like their superiors. Business suits are the uniform of the people, of the faceless army of 20th-century office workers. The man dressed in gray flannel has come to embody the conformity of the middle class and its search for security. Men in business clothing symbolize the uncritical acknowledgment of the dominant social order. Only the necktie, a solitary, phallus-shaped banner, signifies that some individuality remains.

In the cutthroat world of the City, conformist clothing helps provide the illusion of team spirit.

Accentuating the Body

The stricter the dress code and public morals, the more sexual attractiveness was both stressed and obscured. Especially in women's fashion, an endless variety of ornaments, belts, epaulets, seams, pockets, clasps, zippers, Velcro, buttons, ruffs, folds, and frills, as well as countless patterns and colors, fabrics and cuts, emphasize the body's best features. There are still more unusual means of accentuating the female form. Padded shoulders refer indirectly to breasts and buttocks; the suggestive groove between the toes, visible in low-cut shoes, is reminiscent of exposed cleavage.

Dictated by fashion's whims and the ever-changing ideal of beauty, new ways of catching the male eye with breasts, legs, waist, and buttocks are constantly developing. Occasionally grotesque forms emerge, like a short-lived fashion in late-19th-century England, when enormous breast pads ("pouter pigeons") blocked a woman's view of her own feet and gave her a strikingly pigeon-like silhouette. Other fashion curiosities include medieval pointed shoes and the artificial calves men stuck in their stockings to keep their legs from looking scrawny and spindly.

Agnolo Bronzino, *Eleonora of Toledo with Her Son Giovanni de' Medici*, 1544. Oil on panel, 96 x 115 cm, Galleria degli Uffizi, Florence. Padded shoulders refer indirectly to breasts and buttocks, and the string of pearls worn by this lady also draws the attention to the breasts which have disappeared under the tight bodice.

Pointed leather shoe from the Gothic period, c. 1420. The phallic poulaine was worn by the rich and powerful, its length denoting the wearer's precise status.

Western fashion has developed quite a few peculiarities since it freed itself from Classical influence. Greek and Roman men and women had worn essentially similar garments. From the Middle Ages onward clothing became gender-specific and thus charged with sexual meaning. Men of the upper class adorned themselves richly, while the women veiled themselves in pleated but otherwise simple dresses. They wore narrow sleeves, lavish headwear (in place of a veil), and trains of a length proportional to their social standing. In addition, they padded their backsides, foreshadowing the *Cul de Paris* of the 1880s. But the most important new development – though it remained for some time the privilege of the aristocracy – was the décolletage, the low neckline that revealed the upper curve of the breasts. The division of the female body had begun, and very little was altered in the centuries that followed. Below the navel lay a mysterious region, cloaked by a flood of heavy fabric, while the bosom, robbed of all natural roundness by the corset, was reduced to an abstract cone. On the chest were placed one or two semicircular strings of pearls, recalling the lost form of the breasts.

Nobility, wanting to distinguish themselves from the commoners, primarily dictated the dress code of the Middle Ages. The first medieval fashion decrees came from Aragon, Castille, and France, reaching Germany in the mid-14th century. In order to reinforce the social structure, colors, patterns, cuts, and fabrics, as well as hairstyles and accessories, were established for each class. Not everyone,

The Pneumatic Bosom, from a picture postcard. At the beginning of the 20th century, air-filled rubber balloons were used as false breasts.

hanging breasts toward the neckline for display. While showing the fully-bared breast was for the most part the business of prostitutes, it was also customary at Catherine de' Medici's social events in the late Renaissance. The bare-breasted look was very popular in the French court at around the same time. It reappeared briefly in late-17th-century England, where ladies even danced at balls with their breasts bulging out. The artificial breast first appeared on the market near the end of the 18th century. It was made of wax or flesh-colored leather. Veins, which were painted on, made them remarkably realistic. One model even had built-in springs that gave it the natural, rhythmic undulations of a real breast. But wearing artificial breasts was risky; an accident could always expose the trick. Once introduced, however, new versions followed – from padded metal frames to the rose-scented rubber models of the late 19th century.

After the American ideal of bombshell breasts took the world by storm following the Second World War, and the monstrous busts of Jane Russell and Jayne Mansfield surged over the silver screen, the days of the conventional padded bra came to an end. Suddenly there were inflatable models, or rubber balls that one could stuff into conventional bras. Then there were the so-called "falsies", with their especially pronounced nipples. They were made entirely of rubber and were worn over the bra itself. It is rumored that even Marilyn Monroe used them. After the sexual revolution of the 1960s discarded the old dress codes and freed the female body, conspicuous body-accentuating "aids" like brassieres, corsets, padded girdles, and push-up pantyhose have only been worn when they have matched a woman's own self-image. This image bears the mark of individual sexual fantasy, the true motor of late-20th-century fashion. Its rapid change indicates potency, fantasy, and the never-ending search for the perfect expression of one's feeling of the moment, the feeling that fuels individual creativity. In the vanity market at the beginning of the 21st century anything goes, from Madonna's aggressively pointed conical brassieres to gel-padded "Wonderbras" that promise the most natural contour possible for larger-looking breasts. Whether it's a question of fashion jewelry, piercings, tattoos, transparent blouses, or rubber miniskirts, in the end the wearer's own inventiveness has the leading role in the ever-provocative play of sexual signals.

Jakob Seisenegger, *Emperor Charles V*, 1532. Oil on canvas, 203.5 x 123 cm, Museum of Fine Arts, Vienna.

though, followed the scheme; restraining individual creativity is not an easy task. Suppressing the ambition to rise above one's class is even more difficult. The moneyed merchant class, aspiring to nobility, started to dress the part.

A century later, prescribed dress could be justified on religious and moral grounds, by barring women in low-cut dresses from mass. But the fashionable staging of sexuality was always one step ahead of the moral watchdogs. The laced corset entered the scene, defiantly lifting the

Masculinity on Display: The Codpiece

The exaggerated codpiece of the Renaissance is one of the most absurd means of emphasizing the male genitalia ever devised. Clothing for the legs had previously been divided into an upper part, something like "breeches", which in the Middle Ages were knee-length, and the so-called "hose" from the knee to the foot. As fashion whims made the "breeches" shorter and shorter, the stockings (hose) climbed higher. Jackets were getting shorter at the same time, so the lower body was no longer fully covered. In order to avoid indecency, everything was sewn together as a pair of tights. A flap provided additional covering for the genitalia, but such flaps functioned like fingers pointing at what they were supposed to conceal. Consequently, some men stuffed them in order to arouse women's curiosity. The result was the padded, stiffened codpiece, which was sometimes even decorated with ribbons and small jingle bells. Over time it took on ever larger proportions until it became either a large testicular globe or a lengthened, penis-like brayette. These obscene articles of clothing were worn up to the 17th century precisely because of the controversy they caused and were particularly popular with men who were vain about their sexual prowess. Professional soldiers, military leaders, and men of high standing had themselves represented in portraits with prominent brayettes.

Sculpting the Body

Silhouettes have varied effects on the beholder. Deviations from the natural symmetry and the ideal of the "golden section" are disturbing but at the same time more provocative than balanced body forms. The towering hairdos of the 17th and 18th centuries sent deliberately asymmetric signals by making the head appear oversized. A similar intention underlies wearing high heels. Oversized hips, padded shoulders, and extensive trains emphasize the salient gender-specific characteristics of the conventional mating scheme: the buttocks, waist, and bust of the woman, and the broad shoulders and chest, strong arms, and narrow hips of the man. Through exaggeration, natural charms become even more erotic. The Cretans knew this 4000 years ago. Among the artifacts from the Palace of Knossos were figurines of women in flounced dresses that could be seen as forerunners of the crinoline. These dresses had a high, tightly-laced waist that literally made the breasts bulge from the low-cut neckline. Hoop skirts and bodices for shaping a woman's body features are apparently not modern inventions. The feminine hourglass figure was carried to an extreme in the 19th century. A delicate, fragile-looking body was important in the German Biedermeier (1815–1848) and English Victorian (c. 1850–1900) periods. Everyone was devoted to the ideal of "beauty as artifice". Like women, men wore corsets, which had employed wood, metal, and whalebone stays since the 18th century to ensure the "perfect" torso. A narrow waist suggested fragility and drew attention to what was essential: the lower part of the body. In the course of the 19th century the waist reached a minimum circumference of 35 cm (13.8 inches) – the circumference of the average calf.

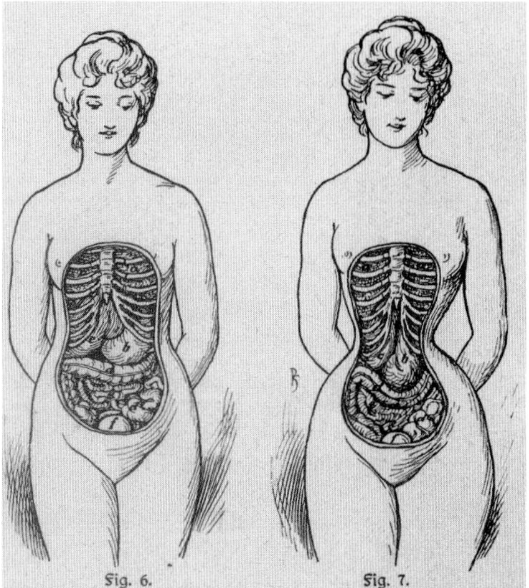

In the 19th and even well into the 20th century no woman would appear in public without a

Right: The dire consequences of tight corsets on the internal organs are shown in this drawing, which appeared in M. Platen's *The New Way to Health* in Berlin in 1905. Due to this shifting of the internal organs, the liver and spleen are so constricted and hindered in their function that they can no longer purify and refresh the blood properly.

Fig. 6.
Normale Lage der inneren Organe.

Fig. 7.
Verlagerung der inneren Organe durch die Korsettpressung.

Amelia Bloomer fought for emancipated dress around 1850. Her Turkish harem pants which were bound together at the ankles were especially spectacular.

Panties

There is a persistent belief – possibly fueled by male fantasy – that women wore no kind of pant-like garment under their skirts until the 19th century. In fact the evidence suggests the opposite. Elizabeth Pepys, the wife of the famous 17th-century English diarist, certainly wore what were known then (and until quite recently) as "drawers", and to judge by other literary allusions, their use was common even then.

During the 19th century, "rational dress" enthusiasts attempted to shorten skirts and lengthen drawers; one exponent of the fashion was Amelia Bloomer, who gave her name to the resulting garment, which was widely ridiculed.

Drawers seem to have had no erotic appeal (hence the name "passion killers") until Parisian cancan dancers embellished them with red ribbons and ruffles and displayed them to considerable effect. In 1918, breathable one-piece combinations emerged, supporting women's new self-confidence. Light, lacy, fine fabrics transformed utilitarian underwear into tender lingerie. Finally the radical shortening of skirts in the 1960s resulted in a corresponding abbreviation of the garment beneath, giving us the "panties" we know today.

corset. It was a necessary item to have on for her to consider herself properly dressed. Costly models were custom-tailored to the particular woman's body and not only provided elegant contours, but "countenance" – as a mirror of inner worth. Less affluent women were forced to either buy shoddy, mass-produced corsets or make their own, if they wanted to keep up with the rich. The unhealthful waspwaist was responsible for permanent lace furrows, squashed organs, and deformed ribs. In order to further the desired silhouette, some women even had ribs surgically removed.

This extreme, not to say fetishistic bondage reached its height in prudish late-19th-century Victorian England. It wasn't just a sadomasochistic practice of prostitutes; even bourgeois housewives prized the lust a tight corset could evoke. It made the female body a sculpture and, in its most extreme and rigid form, extended from the breasts to the thighs. These unhealthy and uncomfortable restraints were cursed by women and their doctors. The dress reform movement, born in the United States during the mid-19th century, demanded freedom from all pressure and constriction, lighter clothing, and the distribution of weight on the shoulders and hips, as well as the banning of trains. With loose flowing robes, the American Amalia Bloomer set out for emancipation, saying that abandoning the body-constricting fashions of the time would foster solidarity among women by reducing envy. Additionally, it would free up the time women spent studying fashion magazines. Hope springs eternal!

True reform began in the 1920s when the corset split into three parts: the elastic girdle, stockings, and the brassiere. After the Second World War Christian Dior as part of the figure-intensive "New Look" rediscovered the corset. Its function, however, was different from its 19th-century role. At the beginning of the 21st century, corsets, along with stockings and garter belts, are pieces of erotic lingerie.

Monsieur Belle Taille or *L'Adonis du Jour*, **fashion plate engraving, 1822.** Men have, at various times, been expected to subject themselves to much the same tortures and indignities as women in the quest for a fashionable appearance.

Getting dressed in the era of the crinoline, 1865. At first the crinoline was hailed by women as a relief from the heavy layers of petticoats, some stiffened with horsehair, which had previously provided their skirts with bulk. But crinolines made it hard to sit down, indecent to bend over, and dangerous to stand near the fire.

The modern corset is not underwear but overwear, stressing in a fetishistic way the artificiality of the silhouette.

Bathing Fashion

European bathing culture began around 1770 in France and England: one took a dip in the sea for one's health. At the new seaside resorts of the time, those who were brave enough were pushed out into the water in a small cart toting a cabana to a spot where a tent was erected above the surface of the water. Under the tent's cover the bathers could glide into the water, dive under a few times, and then get dressed again in the cabana. At the time, not even sailors could actually swim. Less than fifty years later, at the beginning of the 19th century, splashing around in the open had become a social event at seaside resorts. But of course, not an inch of skin was left exposed; a long tunic and baggy trousers prevented it. In 1890, this attire was worn over a corset de bain, a bathing corset, along with the inevitable black stockings and espadrilles.

Fun on the beach at Shanklin, Isle of Wight, 1928. From 1920, the bathing suits of both sexes became more similar and liberal – people wanted to swim and tan. To allow the sun access to as much skin as possible, sleeveless one-piece suits were preferred. The body-shaping whalebone stays were discarded. With the help of a flat swimming ring, a lady could bathe in full make-up. Gentlemen wore sleeveless bodices with knee-length pants made of dark cotton jersey.

Top left: In late-19th century France, fashionable bathing-costumes, consisting of jacket or long blouse and long pants, were made of flannel (those illustrated have red ruffles) or light woolen fabrics.

Top right: **Ernst Heilemann,** *Voice in the Background,* *"Damn! I'd like to see them at the court ball"* **from the German satirical magazine** *Simplicissimus,* **1 August 1906.** To prevent this kind of involuntary exposure, it was customary to test bathing gear before buying it. The wet fabric wasn't supposed to shrink or stick to one's skin.

"SLIX" appeal

SWIM WEAR

Left: **Swim Wear by Slix Ltd., 1950s. Robert Opie Collection, Museum of Advertising & Packaging, Gloucester.** The bathing fashion of the 1950s demanded a swimming suit with a chaste little skirt. As shown on this poster, it still emphasized the figure, though now without whalebone.

Right: The staging of the body in film was an art mastered in Hollywood. Unknown screen actors used all kinds of tricks to catch the eyes of agents looking for new talent. A good-looking figure in a bathing suit helped a lot of would-be hopefuls, such as Johnny Weissmüller, the gold-medal winner of the 1924 and 1928 Olympics in swimming. His muscular body adorned the official poster for the 1932 Olympics in Los Angeles. In the same year, dressed in a leather loincloth, he swung himself through his first Tarzan film and became a screen legend. He was the first athlete ever "discovered" for film: the athlete turned Noble Savage.

Above: Already at the beginning of the 20th century, Lehr, a lifestyle reformer from Freiburg, Germany, introduced a two-piece bathing suit for women. It consisted of a porous, translucent fabric that exposed the skin to sun and air. Only a few, though, dared to wear it while taking a plunge. In 1946, the Frenchman Louis Réard introduced the actual bikini – here presented by the nightclub dancer Micheline. This had an effect similar to that of the American nuclear tests on the Pacific atoll of the same name. For the first time, the navel and buttocks were left exposed. The bikini displayed the "bullet breasts" of the "bombshells" perfectly and unleashed so much protest that it was immediately prohibited in many countries. Its more demure successor required a lot more fabric. Yet by the end of the 1950s, the two-piece had asserted itself in Europe. During the 1960s, it even conquered the prudish U.S.

Left: The string bikini and the thong have long existed in numerous African and native American tribes. But when Brazilian beauties discovered them for themselves in 1974, string bikinis became fashionable all over the world. They became more and more scanty until only the nipples and pubic hair remained covered. A mere string ran between the buttocks. Everyone questioned how far clothing could be reduced before the body was considered naked. Compared with the fabric-rich bathing costumes of the 19th century, the modern ones seem to de-eroticize the female body. On the other hand, those last tenaciously-held threads draw attention to the few body parts still covered. They still conceal secrets, and these remain as erotic as ever. Despite fancy cuts, which emphasized the genitalia, the thong didn't catch on as bathing suits for men.

The Erotic Language of Hair

Hair has always fascinated mankind – probably because Man is the only naked "ape". Our lack of hairiness has always been a feature that distinguishes us from the beasts. In addition, what hair we retain tends to be concentrated most thickly on the head and around the genitals. As a result, by association, head-hair has been seen as a signifier of character and intelligence in general, and sexuality in particular.

Curly hair is regarded as a sign of volatility, while straight hair represents calm, goal-oriented thinking, emotion, and behavior. The popular Elizabethan motto, "Bush natural, more hair than wit," enshrines a popular prejudice that has survived to the modern day – that people with a full head of hair are somehow less intelligent, and more bestial, than average. It is no coincidence that an abundance of hair is often regarded as a sign of potency and sexual freedom in both men and women. For most of the Middle Ages, men wore their hair loose and flowing over their shoulders. Women on the other hand braided and arranged their hair in artful hairstyles, sometimes interwoven with jewelry. Additionally they partially concealed it under caps, hats or scarves. Cutting off a woman's hair served as punishment and meant she lost her honor. When entering a convent, the shorn head stood for the rejection of vanity and a vow of chastity. The language of hair is sometimes contradictory, however – virgins, for example, were allowed to wear their hair loose. In medieval iconography, Mary Magdalen's wild mane clearly signaled sexual desire before she was saved, but after she wandered into the desert as an ascetic it became a symbol of modesty by hiding her nakedness.

Not surprisingly, wigs become more popular during periods of long or ornate hairstyles. The Egyptians probably invented wigs, weaving them out of human hair or vegetable matter, treated with beeswax. Wigs have variously been used as marks of status, age and profession. In ancient Rome, prostitutes could be spotted by their yellow wigs. In sexually repressive times, wigs become less popular – the Victorians used them only secretively, to disguise baldness. By contrast, in 18th-century Europe, there were 110 recorded styles of wig for men alone, the largest being the 48-cm (19-inch) high horse-hair macaroni.

Long or extravagantly arranged hair is often associated with periods of sexual freedom.

Anonymous, *Independence Hairdo*, or *The Triumph of Freedom*, c. 1778. Colored copperplate engraving, Musée de la Coopération, Blérancourt, France. In her search for an amusing and provocative hairline – perhaps to show off her patriotism in the face of increasingly fierce, pro-Republican criticism – the French queen Marie Antoinette had the victorious warship *La Belle Poule* modelled on her head, complete with billowing sails.

One advantage of the beard in all forms – even the three-day-beard (sported here by film actor Pierce Brosnan) – is that it provides an instant semblance of a jawline – and a strong jaw is one of the characteristics that women traditionally look for in a mate.

The Beard

For men at the end of the 20th century, facial hair is a question of image. Whoever strides purposefully through life is usually clean-shaven. He renounces the symbolic hair that might identify him as free-thinking, eccentric, foppish, or sexually repressed. Facial hair can signal many things, and thus there is no one typical form of beard and moustache, but countless variations across peoples and periods: from English mutton-chops (worn during the Biedermeier period), to Adolf Hitler's toothbrush; from Clark Gable's beguiling pencil moustache to Salvador Dalí's twirled handlebar; from Lenin's goatee to the allegedly erotic three-day-stubble worn by models at the beginning of the 21st century – a living advertisement for a plentiful supply of testosterone and a lifestyle that need not bow to conventional ideas of neatness and professionalism. Beards have a controversial history. They have been used as symbols of wisdom and nobility – so much so that sometimes they have even been offered as proof that women could not be genuinely noble or wise. The German philosopher Immanuel Kant (1724–1804) denounced learning in a woman, declaring that she "might just as well have a beard, for that expresses in a more recognizable form the profundity for which she strives." Yet within decades his countryman, Arthur Schopenhauer (1788–1860), was railing against the beard by saying that it only amplified man's animalistic qualities and indicated that the wearer was unfit for higher intellectual pursuit. Unlike in the past, the neatly trimmed goatees and sideburns popular with the younger generation at the end of the 20th century had little or no ideological content. Inspired by "cool" pop stars, they were simply supposed to indicate self-confidence and masculinity.

A. Grévin, *Beautiful Hair*. Drawing. Men are as liable to comment on the scent of their beloved's hair as on its appearance, often comparing its aroma to apples, lavender and other blossoms or even, more abstractly, to "spring" itself. The scents invoked are invariably redolent of youth.

Following a phase of close-to-the-head hairstyles, mid-18th-century women began to wear their hair "up" again – way up. They attached their hair to horsehair and wool-filled pillows or wire frames which reached heights of up to three feet. Artificial hair was also worked in, and everything was smeared with pomade and powdered white. On top sat the most unbelievable objects: feathers, ribbons, pearls, and even miniature windmills together with pet zoos or gardens of real or fake flowers. Even in more repressive ages, the popular sex symbols – whether artists, poets or rock'n'roll stars – are often distinguished by their ostentatious hair-

cuts. In the 1950s, Elvis Presley wore a quiff and greasy sideburns. So-called "rowdies" followed the example of actor James Dean, slicking their hair back with brilliantine into "duck tails". Just a few years later, in the midst of the sexual revolution, everything was different: men and women both wore their hair long and loose, as an Afro or as a wild hippie-mane. Whether long or not, androgynous hairstyles are another marker of social and sexual revolution. Following the First World War, the 1920s brought radical change in the ideal of feminine beauty, paralleling women's new position in society. To suit her new active lifestyle she

dressed boyishly in the garçonne style and bobbed her hair. The hairdo supposedly resulted from a whim of a friend of Coco Chanel, who was inspired by it, and soon millions of women worldwide followed suit. As a clear sign of women's emancipation, "the bob", as the radical haircut was called, was hardly met with universal approval: the Protestant Church of Germany denounced it as "un-German", while the Japanese government felt it was hostile to the state. China and the Philippines even considered taxing it.

The color of a person's hair – especially that of a woman – also speaks volumes to observers.

Among its other connotations, dark hair is also frequently seen as a mark of low birth. The early models for erotic photographs were usually working class, or prostitutes, and when they were suitably cleaned up and sanitized, as seen in this picture by Leopold Reutlinger from the 1880s, their squalid origins provided an extra thrill for the bourgeois gentlemen who were the photographers' chief clients.

The European ideal of beauty has always been blond hair – at least since Homer described the hair of Aphrodite as *xanthe*, or "golden". Blondness is both biologically and symbolically linked to innocence. A woman's hair is naturally at its palest when she is young and nubile, and most fairytale princesses – on the brink of their sexual maturity – are blondes. In the 20th century this innocence has been stigmatized in the person of the "dumb blonde", and many women who change their hair-coloring claim that they are taken less seriously by both their male and female acquaintances when they lighten their hair. But whether radiating innocence or lack of intelligence, it appears that a large part of the

blonde's attraction for men is that she makes them feel more mature, protective and "manly". It is telling that the most iconic blonde of all, Marilyn Monroe, was as attractive for her vulnerability as for her beauty, and that many of her male fans wanted to protect as much as possess her.

On the other hand, dark hair makes a woman chic, dangerous – a femme fatale – probably because among pale-complexioned peoples it contrasts her skin most dramatically. Dark hair tends to frame the face and accentuate the eyes, which gives an appearance of watchfulness and (often secretive) intelligence. Another, socio-biological, explanation for this perception of

brunettes is that a woman's hair darkens as she grows older (before she starts going gray). So to the subconscious male mind a dark-haired woman appears experienced, sexually as in other things. Language, literature, religion and the power of the symbolic imagination all serve to reinforce such prejudices. The word "blond" appears to relate to the Latin *blandus*, or charming. In Old English and related tongues, the word "fair" was originally a noun, meaning a beauty, which became an adjective meaning without blemish, before it began to refer to complexion. In the process it retained all its earlier, positive connotations. Poetically, blond hair is compared to gold, honey, sunlight –

things that are bright and sweet and of the daylight. Dark hair is compared to night and ravens' wings – objects of mystery, magic and darkness. Perhaps the hair color that has suffered most from this kind of metaphorical thinking is red, or ginger. Redheads are traditionally described as passionate, unpredictable people with a violent temper and often unbridled sexual appetites. The heat of the person's coloring is translated into a subliminal expectation of a hot-blooded temperament. In various northern European countries, these expectations have taken on a more sinister aspect, and red hair has been seen as a sign of the witch, the vampire or the demon. During the 20th century, red hair regained a more positive image, as it became more socially acceptable for a woman to be adventurous and aggressive, inside the bedroom and outside. In addition, a few film stars, most notably Rita Hayworth, managed to portray themselves as vivacious rather than dangerously passionate, which removed some of the sting from the redhead's persona.

Of course, Hayworth was not a natural redhead, just as Monroe was not naturally quite that blond. While many women who color their hair attempt to emulate a more or less natural shade, others deliberately opt for the artificial, such as the peroxide blondes – the most famous among them being Jean Harlow – who became one of the greatest sex symbols of 1930s Hollywood. This sends out many complicated messages. By wearing their hair almost as another piece of clothing, or jewelry, they advertise their independence, and make a statement that they will not be taken for granted – tomorrow they may be something completely different. Peroxide blondes also create a powerful sense of sexual ambiguity. The artifice parodies the innocence of the natural blonde in a way that is clearly very knowing.

Sandro Botticelli, *The Birth of Venus* **(detail), c. 1482. Tempera on canvas, 172.5 x 278.5 cm, Galleria degli Uffizi, Florence.** Like many artists, Botticelli was influenced by Homer's description of Aphrodite's hair as being golden. However, his choice of model had hair that was much less yellow than that favored by his contemporaries. This idealized woman features in several of the artist's other paintings, including Venus and Mars (in which the goddess smiles calmly at her sexually exhausted lover, confident of her power over him).

Edvard Munch, *The Vampire,* **c. 1893/94. Oil on canvas, 91 x 109 cm, Munch-Museet, Oslo.** Red hair was the mark of the vampire in Eastern and parts of Northern Europe. Munch saw vampirism as a sucking away of sexual energy, rather than a literal draining of blood.

Depilation

As sparse human "fur" is, in the genital area it is thicker than a chimpanzee's. The way this hair is dealt with in a society depends on culture, moral attitudes, and fashions. Some African tribes depilate the genitals in order to keep the body free of animal nature. Religions that view women as "unclean", such as orthodox Judaism and Islam, still require the removal of a woman's body hair before ritual cleansing can proceed. In ancient Egypt, both men and women depilated themselves for aesthetic and hygienic reasons. Depilated genitals also aided sexual stimulation. Although the Mediterranean peoples are among the most hirsute, ancient Greek and Roman statues and illustrations of athletic bodies show no trace of chest, armpit, or pubic hair. The body's beauty was portrayed entirely unveiled, an ideal that took eternal youth and sensuality as its themes. The inclusion of hair would have destroyed the enticing sight by making it "soiled". In the Renaissance, the beauty of idealized nature became a recurrent theme in literature and was also a central tenet of art, which imitated the classical portrayal of naked, hairless bodies. Only the naked body has timeless beauty; fleeting fashion can make it look ridiculous. Many consider Leonardo da Vinci's drawing of a naked man whose extremities trace the outlines of a circle and square a portrayal of the Classical ideal. The drawing is not meant to show intimacy or even a particular person. Nakedness here is a symbol of purity.

But what role did body hair play in everyday European life? In the Middle Ages, the crusaders promoted the oriental ideal of the woman without body hair among the European aristocracy. Removing a lady's pubic hair was a duty of her private maid and doubtless served sexual stimulation.

In other places and times forced removal of pubic hair served as punishment or humiliation. According to the Old Testament, the Israelites shaved the pubic hair of their captured male enemies to place them on par with

Standing Youth from Anavyses, Attika (grave statue for a warrior, named Kroisos), c. 520–530 B.C. Parian Marble, 194 cm high, National Museum, Athens. This marble statue shows no trace of hair as hairlessness was an ancient Greek ideal.

their women, who were required to pluck their pubic hair. The entirety of an accused witch's hair was removed during torture, so that nothing remained concealed. During the German Nazi regime, even the hated homosexuals were spared from a particular humiliation the Nazis practiced on Jewish women in concentration camps. In front of an audience, the women were forced into degrading postures and depilated from head to toe.

Many psychological factors play a role in the exposure or concealment of the vulva. One factor, which has found expression in many of the world's myths, is man's fear of the ravenous *vagina dentata*, a sharp-toothed vagina that threatens the penis. Perhaps a hairless mound is less frightening, more reminiscent of virginal innocence. The argument against this exposure is the general sense of shame felt by both sexes with regard to genitalia. It results from the fact that the genitals do not have an attractive appearance since, as behaviorists remind us, they are so close to the excretory organs. Given how often intercourse took place (and still takes place) in total darkness, it seems that

Bangelithy, *La Toilette de Vénus*, c. 1795. Colored copperplate engraving. Despite the large number of genre paintings produced in the 16th–19th centuries of depilated ladies at their toilette, few show the woman actually shaving. In fact, the art critic John Ruskin (1819–1900) was shocked to discover that his wife had pubic hair.

many people would rather explore each other's genitals by touch than by sight. Thus, feminine pubic hair is the last defense against prying eyes. The feelings of shame and vulnerability that can arise from genital depilation are individual and are eroticized according to a society's conventions and morals.

Islam still insists upon the removal of female body hair. In Asia, especially in Japan, showing pubic hair in films or print is considered obscene. One can only avoid censorship by showing depilated or discreetly covered genitals. At the beginning of the 21st century, Western films and advertising increasingly favor bodies free of hair. Women in the United States and Great Britain especially follow this trend. In these two countries, 90 percent of modern women remove hair from their bodies. In France, the figure is 66 percent. It is primarily the underarms and lower legs that get depilated, and, mainly in the summer, the "bikini line". Uncontrolled tufts of hair are still seen as a sign of animalism and aggressive sexuality. But there are those who regard a sharp contrast between hair and skin as chic and sexy, so some women like to trim their pubic hair in the form of a narrow strip or a heart. Very few dare to get rid of it entirely. Many probably associate this ultimate nakedness with vulnerability and a peculiar return to childhood. In addition, hairless pubic regions have acquired quite a different meaning: it suggests a readiness for sexual experimentation, for which the exposed vulva has heightened sensation.

Interestingly, the male "inner animal" has also been suppressed. More and more male models are displaying hairless, muscular upper bodies and winning female approval. A man who does not have a naturally hairless chest and who subscribes to this ideal has to extend his daily shave to reach his navel.

For those who wish to eliminate unwanted body hair, there are two distinct forms of hair removal: depilation and epilation. Those procedures which allow the regrowth of hair are known as "depilation". These include hair removal by chemical means (depilation creams and gels), or by mechanical means like razors,

tweezers, cold or hot wax or pumice scrubs. The roots of the hair are unharmed by these methods, so the removal is only temporary. Epilation, on the other hand, is a procedure which results in permanent loss of hair due to the destruction of the roots from which the hairs grow.

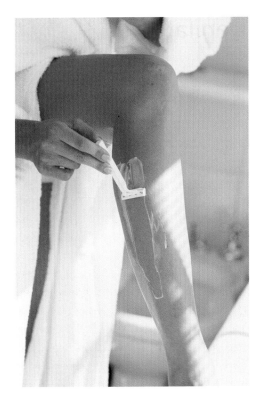

Right: The American ideal of beauty demands smooth, naked skin. Shaving is one way of achieving the desired effect.

An advertisement for depilatory cream in the 1920s aimed at women with active, busy lives, who have no time for the laboriously dangerous business of shaving.

Skin Signs

Prior to the time when clothing completely concealed the body and in warm climates where clothing was superfluous, people primarily used their own skin to indicate their social standing or their membership of particular groups. Skin painting, ornamental scarring, and tattooing with soot and plant pigments marked rites of passage or sexual maturity, functioned as amulets of protection against hostile powers, and enhanced one's strength, invoking helpful spirits. Not only does one find tattoos on the skin of the 4000-year-old mummy of a pharaoh's child, but also on "Ötzi", the Stone Age traveler found recently in a glacier. Curiously, not all of the symbols on Ötzi's skin were in obvious or openly visible places, so they must have had some private meaning as well. Almost all aboriginal peoples let their skin speak for them, especially in the Pacific, where the hot climate makes a complicated dress code absurd. In this enormous region many skin decoration techniques have developed, and symbols have taken on the most diverse functions, not just aesthetic or erotic ones. As soon as a female Japanese aboriginal got married, she got a blue tattooed moustache. It symbolically stated that from that point on she spoke through her husband's mouth. Those who did not want to undergo this procedure had to remain single and were banned from festivals and ceremonies. Still today, the Dyak women of Borneo tattoo themselves with the darkest of pigments, since they believe that everything

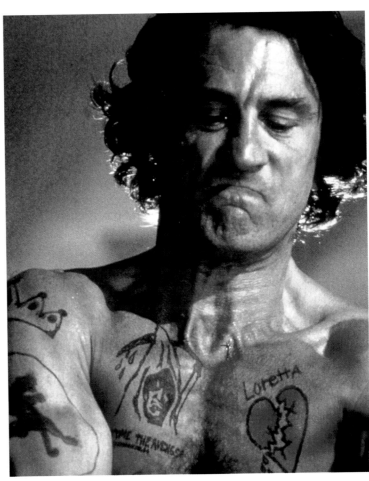

Cape Fear, still from the film by Martin Scorsese, 1991. Robert de Niro in the role of the psychotic but wrongly convicted felon Max Cady. De Niro's character makes his own skin a testament to his inner rage.

will be reversed in the afterworld. The skin a woman now colors black will shine brightly, lighting her dark path into the afterlife. Only Dyak men are allowed to carry torches on this journey. The motifs she prints on her skin must exactly match the traditional family pattern, otherwise the woman is sent back to earth as a ghost. Similarly, the unique, circular facial tattoos of New Zealand's Maoris were also very

complicated. Not only did they recount the life story of the wearer, but those of his ancestors as well. This is perhaps why, after death, the head of the deceased was cut off and kept.

The English word "tattoo" originates in Polynesia and is onomatopoeia for the sound of a sharpened bone tool being driven into the skin with a stone. The grand masters of tattooing are the Japanese. Since the beginning of the 19th century, the whole-body tattoo, the so-called "Japanese bodysuit", has developed into a decorative figurative art. The decorated skin had to compete with the costly silk of kimonos. A strict dress code placed the most precious fabrics "off-limits" to the members of the wealthy businessman class. At this point these men began to flirt with tattooing, previously restricted to fringe groups. The decorated skin was so prized that they were even left to family members as inheritance. Various well-preserved skins are displayed in Japanese museums. The designs juxtapose heroes fighting monsters with famous figures from mythology and history, as well as Kabuki-inspired ghosts,

Traditional Maori patterns have influenced Western tattooists and body-painters.

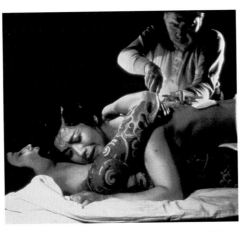

Irezumi, still from the film by Yoichi Takabayashi, 1982, Tomisaburo Wakayama and Harue Kyo.

Illustrated from head to toe: La Belle Angora, c. 1900. The tattooed lady was a popular feature of traveling sideshows. Most could make their tattoos move in amusing or suggestive ways.

Whores and Sailors

When Captain Cook (1728–1779) and other Pacific voyagers discovered the artful tattoos of Polynesia, and Oceana, they collected souvenirs of these earthly paradises on their skin. On their return, the "illustrated" sailors created a sensation, kindling the European and American tattoo traditions. Despised by the bourgeoisie, 19th-century European nobility, world travelers, and American naval officers decorated themselves with tattoos. Those on society's fringe – prostitutes, criminals, and convicts – displayed their tattoos at fairs. They were covered with pictures from neckline to toe but were nevertheless modestly dressed. The American "La belle Irène" was one of the first to get her skin almost entirely covered with butterflies, flowers, snakes, bugs, and Indians.

Others, too, had fanciful stage names, like her compatriot "Lady Viola", who had six presidents portrayed on her thorax, or "Anetta Nerona" of Germany who had Goethe, Schiller, Bismarck, Wagner, and Kaiser Wilhelm II romping across her skin. Men displayed themselves less and less as more and more women came on the scene; the sensation of catching a glimpse of usually well-covered female skin won hands-down. Tattoos held an additional attraction in that these women often worked as prostitutes on the side, as mistresses of the art of undressing. A special role for tattooing emerged among some of the prostitutes of late-19th-century Paris: the designs could cover up the signs of syphilis.

centration camps. Most were marked by a combination of branding and tattooing. Christians in non-Christian societies tattooed crosses on their wrists as a sign of belonging to the faith. Prior to their conversion to Christianity, the Greeks, Gauls, Britons, Thracians, and the Germanic tribes also wore ornamental tattoos, partially as charms and partially as identification. Tattooing was also part of group initiation rituals. Those belonging to some professions, like blacksmiths and bricklayers, wore tattoos as encoded marks of membership, as did members of secret societies.

Through sailors during the Age of Discovery, tattooing won renewed popularity in Europe. During the 19th and 20th centuries, tattooing in the West was characterized by domestic, religious, and nationalist motifs – hearts, crosses, anchors, ships, and swastikas, as well as oaths of vengeance or love, including the beloved's name. Young hoodlums and loose girls put permanent signs of devotion on their bodies in the hope that their love wouldn't die before they did. If their adoration waned, there was always the painful resort of acid, or later laser treatment, to remove any marks.

In the 1990s the negative image of tattoos changed, and the designs became more aesthetically meaningful. Through punk and American youth culture, tattooing had reached the point where art and taboo meet, a sensuous interplay of refinement and primitivism. Complex, artful images or traditional designs from the Pacific emphasize the body's forms, guide the eye of the beholder to hidden parts, and awake curiosity. In addition, they reveal something about the person who wears them: their readiness to undergo a painful procedure and their ability to choose designs that will be with them for the rest of their lives. As true today as yesterday, tattoos are best suited for initiation and proof of masculinity. They are signs of strength, which women are increasingly discovering for themselves. Like piercing, tattooing is supposed to express individuality, independence, and self-confidence, with undercurrents of provocation, rebellion, and adventure – all of which have subliminal erotic connotations.

flowers, and animals. In the Japanese film *Irezumi*, the heroine, Katsuko (Harue Kyo) undergoes the tattooing of her whole body to please her lover, which is carried out by the old craftsman Kyogoro (Tomisaburo Wakayama). By using a special technique, Kyogoro's assistant, Harutsune, succeeds in uniting Katsuko's feelings of lust and pain, and in so doing, giving her a new awareness of her body and a new consciousness of her "self". In modern Japan tattooing has spread to all levels of the population.

The patterns are not exclusively traditional and even comic-book heroes and pop-stars are frequently portrayed in this form of body-art.

Europe lacks an analogous tradition since the church had forbidden tattoos and piercings. This prohibition of strange cult practices is found in the Bible. Leviticus 19.28 states: "Ye shall not make any cuttings in your flesh for the dead, nor print any marks upon you." The only people who were marked were slaves, heretics, soldiers, criminals, and prisoners in Nazi con-

Piercing

The more extreme forms of tribal piercing, as seen here in Brazil 1999, have still not been widely adopted in the West.

They've been a standard part of the Western metropolitan street scene since the mid-1990s: men and women, mostly young, with piercings. Their appearance seldom causes a stir any more, unless the metallic shimmer of rings and studs covers their faces entirely. Piercing is in vogue, part of a body cult that wants to demonstrate willful experience of pain: whoever endures this uncomfortable procedure can cope with worse things – the ever more impersonal monotony of everyday life, or thoughts of an impending apocalypse.

Perhaps this need for piercings in the era of hyper-reality comes from the wish to "be sure of" one's body. These mutilations paradoxically draw attention to and destroy the body's perfection at the same time.

Piercing, like tattooing, has its origin in so-called primitive cultures. The high priests of the pre-Columbian Maya (c. 1500 B.C. – 1540 A.D.) pierced their tongues in order to humble themselves before the gods. Even today in certain parts of India and Indonesia, holes in the cheeks are a symbolic means of honoring gods. In other locations around the globe animal teeth, shells, wooden plates or pegs, feathers and stones are driven into the skin and the holes gradually enlarged. Certain Amazon Indian tribes wear stone pegs or wooden plates in their lower lips and push wood sticks through their nasal septa. These practices belonged to a mythic cult dedicated to gaining supernatural power, but whose meaning has since been forgotten. Today such marks don't just indicate the bearer's social standing or ancestry, they also establish the stage of life the bearer is in, beginning with ritual initiation. The mutilation of the unscarred body symbolizes entry into adulthood. Whoever can rise above the pain is old enough to assume the rights and responsibilities of the next phase of life.

With the age of colonial settlements, the Europeans got to know "primitive" cultures through travelers' accounts, illustrations, and genuine "savages" brought back for show. But except for ears nothing was pierced. At the beginning of the 19th century piercing began to find favor on society's fringes – homosexuals, fetishists, and sadomasochists. This changed in the 1970s when punks mutilated themselves demonstratively with razor blades and put rings through

Earrings

Since the dawn of history, men and women have decorated their earlobes. Besides being relatively insensitive, these body parts are highly visible and therefore predestined for decorative erotic signals. Earrings emphasize the body's symmetry, accentuate the length of the neck, and sparkle with fire and temptation when decorated with gems or rhinestones. Ear piercing, at least those of female infants, was common practice in Mesopotamia, on the Iberian peninsula and the Greek islands and mainland in the second millennium B.C. As earrings took on the function of amulets which were supposed to protect the wearer from magical irritations as well as the widespread eye-diseases among the early cultures, they became popular with both sexes. By the 18th century earrings had achieved wide popularity as everyday jewelry. Special designs were worn as emblems of various guilds, especially in Switzerland, signaling membership. In the 19th century, earrings were increasingly seen as barbaric relics, with effeminate connotations and became taboo with the majority of men. Aristocrats, artists, dandies, soldiers and sailors continued to wear them. Sailors often acquired an additional earring each time they crossed the equator. In the 20th century, members of fringe groups continued to wear them, emphasizing their unconventional attitudes. In the early 1970s a ring in the right earlobe served the gay community as a means of recognition. But signs and significance changed rapidly in the 20th century, and within a decade their meaning disappeared.

Fulani Woman, Mali. The earrings worn by this woman are called "Kwottenai Kanye". They were given to her by her husband at marriage as part of the bride-price.

Those who have themselves pierced tell those around them: "My body belongs to me!" That is why rings, rods, and studs are placed in obvious spots: nose, tongue, eyebrows, lips, nipples and navel.

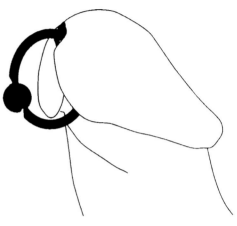

The Prince Albert, so-called because, as legend has it, it was invented by the consort of Queen Victoria to prevent smegma buildup under his foreskin.

their noses, brows, and lips, and literally perforated the arches of their ears with metal. For the punks it was a form of social protest, whose uncompromising force fascinated the *haute couture* establishment. Fashion designers began to use this protest for their own gain and have popularized, via the catwalk, an extravagant elegance centered on pierced body parts and sadomasochistic eroticism.

At the same time, the West Coast in the U.S. witnessed the birth of another phenomenon, the Modern Primitives, a subgroup of the Los Angeles sadomasochistic scene. Fascinated by aboriginal peoples' mutilation rituals, they adopted some of them, most prominently the piercing of private parts. The Modern Primitives are interested in the self-determined "re-creation" of their bodies, heightened sexual stimulation, new aesthetic experiences, and the pain-altered states of consciousness reached through tattooing, piercing, branding, ornamental scarring, and other mutilations.

For sadomasochists, piercing is nothing new. At the beginning of the 20th century, nipple piercing was already popular with both sexes as a means of making these erogenous zones even more sensitive. Piercing the sex organs is also supposed to heighten sensitivity. Men have

rings and studs put through the skin folds of the scrotum (hafada), between the scrotum and anus (guiche), through the frenum, through the foreskin (oetang), and over the base of the penis where it meets the groin (pubic), but they also get pierced in the area of the head of the penis (glans). Accessories worn here include the "ampallang", a shaft pushed sideways through the head of the penis; the "dydoe", a large ring worn through the underside of the glans of circumcized men; and the "apadravya", a rod-shaped accessory already mentioned in the *Kamasutra* pushed through the urethra to the underside of the glans, its name essentially meaning "substitute", and is particularly intended for impotent men.

Before piercing, the skin is disinfected and numbed. It is then fixed in a special piercing clamp, and pierced with a hollow needle, which leaves a small plastic tube behind when removed. A ring or stud is then put through the tube and capped with a ball. Larger or thicker rings can be worn through the hole after it has healed.

For the so-called "Prince Albert", the penis is pierced vertically, through the urethra, and decorated with a ring. It was supposedly especially popular with dandies and soldiers during

the Prince Consort's lifetime. They fastened their penises to their trouser buttons so they always appeared erect. The ring must be at least 30–32 mm (1.18–1.26 inches) in diameter and 3.2 mm (0.12 inches) thick. If it is too loose it can injure the partner, and if too tight an overly enthusiastic tug can tear the glans in half down to the frenum.

The Changing Shape of the 20ᵗʰ-century Ideal Woman

Although the idealized female shape has always varied according to the whims of art or fashion, it probably reached a peak of volatility only in the 20ᵗʰ century, in response to the kaleidoscopically changing flood of media images unleashed by photography, cinema and a growing popular press. The trend to rapid and sweeping changes was exaggerated by the formation of a modern, intensively capitalized fashion industry, which, like all such industries, has constantly to create or exacerbate the demand it exists to satisfy.

The wasp waist suggests fragility and at the same time emphasizes the hips and backside. In the 19ᵗʰ century, all attention was drawn to the lower body: a round belly, broad hips, and wide buttocks. At the beginning of the 20ᵗʰ century, the s-shaped silhouette of the British actress Camille Clifford came to represent the perfect figure.

Above: The flapper look of the 1920s was itself an attempt to create an androgynous, boyish shape – enhanced by a shorter haircut. The emphasis was on a woman's freedom to do anything that a man might do, and on her ability to lead an active life, unencumbered by her clothing. It was said that there were only two costumes a woman needed – sportswear for the day and a dance frock for the night.

Right: During World War I, thanks to the emancipation movement, androgynous, narrow lines became fashionable. Women adopted masculine role models – Marlene Dietrich wasn't the only woman who wore a man's suit.

Since the 1950s, Hollywood stars, or rather the movie studios, have defined fashion and the image of woman. Extremely low necklines showcased Jane Russell's bombshell breasts and Marilyn Monroe's dangerous curves. Europe found one of its own new sex symbols in the Italian actress Sophia Loren (photo).

Left: The 1960s were the age of the sexual revolution. They belonged to pop music and its iconography, at the top of which stood the slender, boyish shape of the English star model, Twiggy. In 1967, the 17-year-old presented Mary Quant's mini skirt. Her childlike upper body and her endless, spindly legs reflected the proportions of a pre-pubescent girl. Her short hair and the girlishness of her face, which she exaggerated with "twiggies" – painted eyelashes under the lower lid, reinforced this impression.

Right: During the 1990s, supermodels such as Naomi Campbell, Claudia Schiffer, Elle MacPherson, Linda Evangelista, and Cindy Crawford celebrated the cult of the perfect body. However, a new face quite suddenly emerged from the masses and became designer Calvin Klein's star of the young generation. Kate Moss, a skinny, mistreated-looking, strangely raw creature, marked the beginning of a new trend, which elevated physical imperfection to the beautiful. The scandalous British designer Alexander McQueen (Givenchy) went further still by having a model with artificial limbs walk the catwalk for the first time – Aimee Mullins (photo) was born without lower legs. Flaunting physical shortcomings is turning into a means of emphasizing individuality – in an age of anonymity nothing seems more desirable.

The Beauty Business

Women finally succeeded in the 1960s in closing the book on kids, kitchen, and church and the accompanying "little woman" image. But no sooner had they started taking "the pill" with confidence and winning their way into the "man's world" of the workplace, than they fell under the spell of the beauty myth promoted by film and advertising. Suddenly it was no longer enough to be competent, diligent, and dependable. Something else determined a woman's professional development that didn't affect a man's – sex-appeal.

At the end of the 20th century, men had also begun to groan under the weight of this myth. Nakedness and perfect bodies are everywhere. Pornography, advertising and film are marketing an ideal of beauty to both sexes which is getting further and further from nature, thanks in part to the influence of computer simulation. The new reality which is evolving has little to do with the traditional art of body care and make-up. The Greek word *kosmetikos* means "skilled in arrangement or adornment", but derives from *kosmos*, which means "order". In almost every culture, beauty-care is closely connected to religion as well as medicine – health is beautiful and thereby a sign of heavenly order.

Make-up and fragrances were closely connected to religion because they originally served religious purposes. But 5000-year-old finds in Egypt indicate that fragrances and make-up have long had more profane uses. Even then these items had found their way into daily life, enhancing well-being and increasing sexual attractiveness. By the end of the 20th century, cosmetics broadcast a complex picture of beauty that combines the moral sensibilities of current cultural circles and individual self-definition.

Cosmetics aim primarily at face care and make-up, which crown the image that body and clothes help to create. Among the many possibilities, women can choose that image which corresponds best to their type, mood, self-image and perhaps also to the demands of fashion. Simply put, make-up has two contradictory motivations, to follow socially accepted trends in order to conform, but also a desire to be different leads to individuality.

Mummy mask of a young woman with braided hair, Egypt, first/second cent. A.D. Stucco, painted with eyes of colored glass, Egyptian Museum, Berlin. The ancient Egyptians believed that some cosmetic chemicals had magical properties, so that when a woman applied her make-up she was, literally casting a spell.

"Red Lips Are for Kissing"

A made-up face is full of symbols, but does make-up emphasize what is natural, or is it a mask? Should it hide the intellect or the emotions? The surface is crucial. An unblemished complexion is like a blank sheet of paper on which one sketches one's face of the day, one's new self, matching the wardrobe. The better it's done, the more mask-like the result, provided the face remains motionless. This emptiness is supposed to signal passionlessness, modesty, and an unassuming nature. It was already an ideal in the Middle Ages when it was achieved by depilation of the eyebrows, temples and hairline. The ideal of beauty in the 1930s and 1940s was based on a similar naïve, childlike look that was supposed to waken the man's protective instincts: narrow, plucked eyebrows arched in astonishment over enormous wide eyes. Now and then, the eyebrows themselves were entirely removed and drawn again above their natural position with an eyebrow pencil. Heavily made-up eyes were central to silent film due to the limitations of the medium. Dark and mysterious, they gleamed against the porcelain-white skin. Eyes, the windows to the soul, emphasize the upper half of the face, where the spirit is supposed to reside. The lower half is the domain of instincts and passion. With color film came the exaggeration of red tones, which Marilyn Monroe's lips and Brigitte Bardot's pout pushed into the limelight. These erotic signals cannot be clearer – the redder and glossier the lips, the more sensual they appear to be.

Innumerable women's magazines and beauticians give make-up tips for every type of woman and for every occasion. These spreading tentacles of the cosmetic industry have taken hold of the faces of many people in the Western world. Though there have always been

Kohl and similar substances have been used for millennia to darken and apparently thicken eyelashes. Modern mascaras even claim to enrich the lashes by providing them with extra protein.

Pétit after François Boucher, *Le Matin*, 18th cent. Copperplate engraving, Bibliothèque Nationale, Paris. Artificial beauty spots were made of black velvet, silk or paper-thin leather. Every position on the face had a special meaning. Worn close to the mouth, the decoration signaled a readiness to flirt.

Case for beauty spots, 18th cent. Wella Museum, Darmstadt. Many cosmetic boxes had decorative flies on their lids, alluding to the French word, "mouche", for beauty spot.

beauty aids – the kohl that rimmed the eyes of Egyptians, both men and women; the golden hair dye used by Venetian women; the henna with which Indian women decorated their hands; the belladonna drops that dilated eyes in the Middle Ages; the beauty marks in the shapes of moons and stars as well as the 18th-century powdered faces and wigs – the freedom to choose one's appearance has never held more importance for career and sexuality than it does at the beginning of the 21st century. In his 1976 book *Symbolic Exchange and Death*, the French philosopher Jean Baudrillard proclaimed that signs had become more real than what they represented.

Twenty years later, the body appears to be merely a product of cosmetics, diet, exercise, and cosmetic surgery. The cosmetic industry is finally in step with fashion: each season has its special color. Haircuts, wardrobe, even fragrances change with the season. Body and face have to harmonize – as wrinkle and fat-free as possible. Countless anti-wrinkle creams, peelings, hair products, anti-cellulite products, and make-up utensils promise eternal beauty and surefire seduction, ensuring the cosmetics industry billions of dollars of business every year worldwide. In Germany alone in 1996, body-care products had a turnover of 15.8 bil-

lion German marks (approx. 8 billion dollars). The 1990s saw the development of permanent make-up, which is commonly used to trace the contours of the lips, eyelids, and eyebrows. Dye is injected, as in a tattoo, but not as deeply into the skin. It's not a risk-free undertaking: wrongly placed or poorly chosen colors can disfigure, and nothing is said of the color changes, inflammation, or allergies that are possible. The chic beauty aids that reflect certain eras are much better suited to the game of fashion. They regularly reappear: false eyelashes, glue-on fingernails, lip-gloss, beauty marks, and unplucked brows.

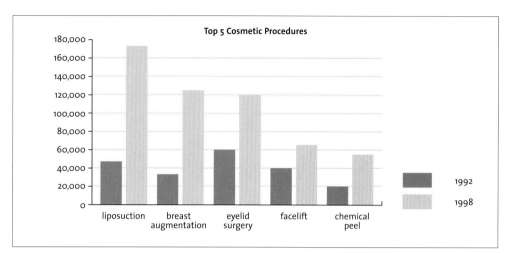

Top 5 Cosmetic Procedures

Legend: 1992, 1998

Top 5 cosmetic procedures. The diagram above shows the most common beauty surgery for men and women in the United States of America (excluding breast reductions). People risk financial hardship, physical discomfort and even personal danger in their quest for physical "perfection". Within a period of six years the number of these operations has more than doubled.

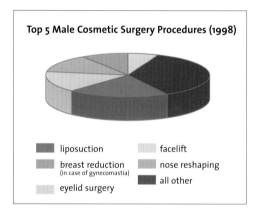

Top 5 Male Cosmetic Surgery Procedures (1998)

- liposuction
- breast reduction (in case of gynecomastia)
- eyelid surgery
- facelift
- nose reshaping
- all other

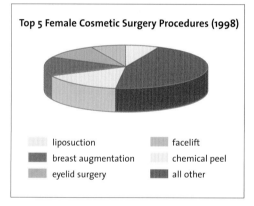

Top 5 Female Cosmetic Surgery Procedures (1998)

- liposuction
- breast augmentation
- eyelid surgery
- facelift
- chemical peel
- all other

Top 5 male and female cosmetic surgery procedures (1998). Surgery opted for both by women and men. While beauty surgery used to be restricted to women it is now becoming popular with men as well. But with a total of just over 99,000 operations in 1998 men are still far behind women. Many Western women find it hard to resist the pressure to conform to a standardized form of beauty. By 1998 947,000 American women had undergone cosmetic surgery.

The Cosmetics Industry

Once wrinkles have a foothold, they become ever more often a case for plastic surgery. During the First World War, the Berlin surgeon Jacques Joseph performed today's most common face operation for the first time: the face lift, popular with politicians and stars, men and women. The operation isn't always successful; the German actress Hildegard Knef (b. 1925) was mocked after her operation. People called her "Miss Piggy". The American entertainer Liberace (1919–1987) endured so many skin-tightening face-lifts that, by the end of his life, he was unable to shut his eyes at all. Confidants have described how eery it was to enter a room and find him dozing with his eyes open. Grotesquely, Liberace also spent a fortune on plastic surgery for his male lover, in an effort to make the young man look more like himself.

Other surgical procedures improve the appearance of noses, chins, and prominent ears, or build up cheeks by implanting plastic cushions on the cheekbone. Lips can be made larger or smaller to order by injecting collagen or grafting skin. In Japan the most sought-after cosmetic operation makes narrow oriental eyes rounder and more "Western" (blepharoplastic). The "dream figures" of the actors and actresses from TV and film can be desired as much as

Bleaching Black Skin

Christian mythology, colonialism and racism are responsible for making generations of blacks uncomfortable in their own skin, regardless of whether they have grown up in Africa, America or Europe. The color black itself has negative connotations even at the end of the 20th century. Blacks are still almost automatically considered criminals by some whites, and they are still generally discriminated against. The ideal of spotless white skin has damaged the self-esteem of many dark-skinned people. They have seen that wealth and privilege are associated with white skin, and even the "Black is beautiful" movement of the 1960s could do little in the face of this experience. The desire for posh pallor, through which "blue blood" pulses, is present in many dark-skinned ethnic groups. Buying into the white ideal can be so extreme that a "person of color" may consider others inferior just because their skin is darker than his or her own. Some black women try straightening their hair, dying it blond, and lightening their skin. A few go to more extreme measures. Experiments with zinc, saltpeter, sulfur pastes, and even with white lead and mercury chloride have led to burns and serious injury.

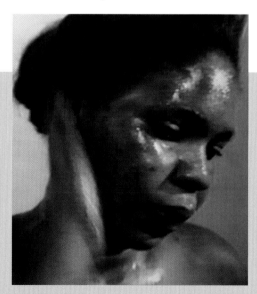

Bleaching of the skin by means of hydroquinone. This promises "reversible depigmentation". Sunscreens are an essential additive.

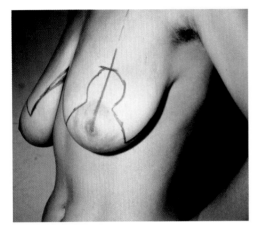

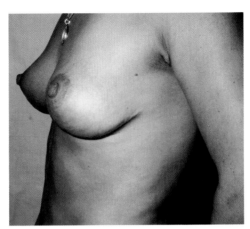

Breast surgery: The new position of the nipples must be determined when the patient is standing because the breasts move to the side when she is lying down. The operation lasts two to three hours on average.

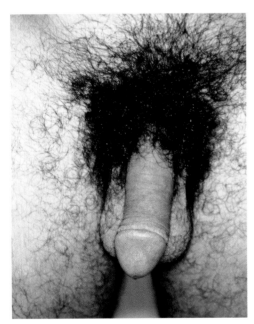

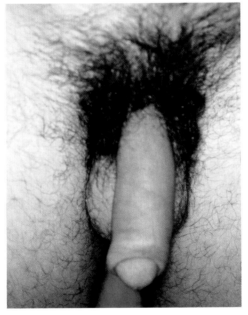

A popular form of penis enlargement involves implanting fat cells from elsewhere in the man's body. He must abstain from intercourse for five to six weeks in order not to injure the newly implanted cells. The increase in length is often combined with an increase in circumference.

any face-altering surgery. Ideal measurements create longings and lead to distorted relationships with one's own body: bulimia, anorexia, misuse of laxatives and addiction to exercise. Who really has the perfect breasts, the well-rounded buttocks and the trim waist of highly paid models? Only a few of them are genuine. Still, Pamela Anderson Lee, shapely ex-star of the American series *Baywatch*, won't be the last to have her breasts enlarged. The end of the bosom cult is not in sight, although the enormous bust does not accord well with the cur-

rently favored athletic figure. Even Pamela Anderson Lee has had surgery to reduce her bust to its former pre-implant proportions. In fact many women have breast reductions rather than enlargements, not just for the sake of their appearance, but in the interests of health. Large-busted women, especially as they grow older, can find the weight of their breasts putting an unbearable strain on their backs, affecting their posture and sometimes causing great pain. The American actress Roseanne (b. 1952) reported a vastly improved quality of life after

her well-publicised breast reduction. Nevertheless, there are many women who want a breast volume of 250 to 350 cubic centimeters (15 to 20 cubic inches). For some even that's not enough – the French glamour model Lolo Ferrari (1969–2000) had breasts the size of soccer balls. Together they weighed over six kilograms (13 pounds) and won her the nickname "Miss Airbag".

Conventional breast enlargement, as performed since the 1960s, involves the implantation of cushions of silicone gel. Silicone, which was developed for the U.S. Navy as a caulk and sealant, has the disadvantage of hardening at some point. As a consequence, enlarged breasts lose their shape after a certain time and begin to hurt. The implants make breast examinations difficult, decrease the sensitivity of the breasts, and can even burst, poisoning the body. Due to their negative health impact, silicone breast implants were removed from U.S. markets in 1992. In 2000 they are still permitted in Europe. Currently, one can choose to have implants filled with soy oil and hydrogel, which pass harmlessly through the kidneys in the case of a rupture. Implanting a plastic cushion can also reshape a flat bottom. It is placed in such a way that one does not have to sit on it.

Yet another chapter is the surplus fat layer that, since the 1970s, has been removed by scalpel. Through a small incision in the chin, neck, upper arm, chest, belly, hip, thigh, knee, or ankle a small suction tube is inserted and the fat sucked out. This process is known as liposuction. The results of the early procedures were unpredictable, and often a corset had to be worn during the long healing process. In today's improved version of the operation, the outer portion of the fat tissue is also removed, resulting in better skin contraction. The body doesn't replace the removed fat cells.

A curiosity of the beginning of the 21st century is penis-elongation surgery for men who have complexes about this issue. Since the full length of the erectile tissue doesn't lie outside the body but rather partially between the legs, this portion is detached and pushed further out. It is a very painful and sometimes dangerous operation.

Scent and Sensuality

When Marilyn Monroe was once asked by a journalist what she wore in bed, she famously replied: "At night, I don't wear anything – except a few drops of Chanel No. 5." With these coquettish words she not only fueled the erotic fantasies of millions, but also brought the tight liaison between scent and sexuality into focus. Mankind has known for a long time that the sense of smell plays an important role in choosing a mate, even if it is done unconsciously. In terms of evolutionary history, the olfactory sense is the oldest. Yet depending on the morals and fashions of the time, the conscious play with smells may be frowned upon, since civilized societies consider sniffing and snuffling animal behavior.

In literature, the sense of smell is repeatedly described as the origin of emotion and memory. For Jean-Jacques Rousseau (1712–1778), it inspired fantasy and aroused lust. At the beginning of the 21st century, scientists have proved that both man and animal instinctively register by smell which genetic type is suitable for mating. In terms of survival of the species, he or she whose body tissue structure differs most from one's own, smells most desirable.

Not everyone's personal body odor has the same aphrodisiac effect as Rasputin's (1871–1916) goatish sperm stench, which allegedly placed women at his mercy. Thus perfumes play an important role in the history of the art of seduction. The first modern eau de toilette based on ethereal oils and alcohol originated in 1370. It was called *Eau d'Hongrie*, and it entered history as a special guarantor of seduction: hardly had the 72-year-old Elisabeth of Hungary sprinkled herself with a little of the fragrance (made especially for her), when the King of Poland fell in love with her.

By the end of the 16th century, the company of Florentine René on the Pont-au-Change had become one of the most important Parisian addresses for fine fragrances. Strong-smelling essences were modern, and not just for covering up the stink that tanned leather gloves left on the hands, or to veil the strong body odor of the wearer. Doctors also recommended heavy fragrances in the belief that the stronger one smelled, the less vulnerable one was to typhus, plague, cholera and, above all, syphilis. At Versailles in the time of Louis XIV and XV, with 10,000 courtiers and 25,000 lackeys, strong perfumes were necessary to cover up the stench of the ubiquitous excrement. It was only after the French Revolution that hygiene came back into vogue. A good citizen cherished bouquets of tender flowers; the fresh, volatile scent of the famous "Eau de Cologne" fitted the time perfectly. French soldiers brought it home from Germany after the Seven Years' War. Developed in 1714, it was originally a health tonic that one drank. Animal fragrances, however, including musk, ambergris, and civet, returned with the empire. Napoleon loved dousing himself and his wife Josephine with them.

French perfumes, especially from Guerlain, had their heyday in the 19th century. In 1828 Guerlain opened his shop in Paris in the Rue de Rivoli, and by 1842 he was the supplier to the Grand Duchess of Baden and the Queen of Belgium. The discreet scent of his perfumes was appreciated by the Prince of Wales and King Ferdinand of Bulgaria. His perfumes were often made for a specific woman and a special event. They emphasized her individual personality and were a sign of extravagance that only the very cream of society could afford. An increasing number of middle-class women were developing a taste for perfumes, but as a rule they had to be satisfied with what they could get at the town market. The virtuous woman smelled of innocence: pure as a rose and as modest as a violet. The real perfume boom came with the *Belle Époque* (c. 1890–1914) when countless fragrances and body-care products were developed. Perfume became the expression of feeling, of love, of personality, and the woman who wore it became a desirable creature of luxury.

Girl pouring perfume, c. 63–14 B.C. Fresco, Villa Farnesina, Rome, Museo Nazionale Romano delle Terme, Rome. The Romans learned the art of perfumery from Egypt.

"Chanel No. 5", the legendary floral bouquet, came on the market after the First World War and was the most expensive perfume of all time. Its fragrance isn't particularly sensual. Like most fragrances from fashion designers, it is closely coupled to the world of "haute couture": those who can't afford the expensive clothing can get a taste of it through the associated perfume.

At the end of the 20th century, androgyny, being more than a mere fashion statement, has invaded the world of perfumes as well. In the 1970s the earthy leather and spicy smells of men's fragrances gave way to more feminine components. Conversely, more and more women started favoring masculine fragrances. Not as pretentious, sweet, and capricious as typical women's perfumes, they exude a career-conscious, sporty, active image. In addition, by playing with masculine attributes creates an eroticizing sexual ambiguity. It suits the women who no longer accept traditional gender roles and express this in their clothes and hairstyles. Studies have found that the nose rules at job interviews as well: women who wear men's cologne get further in the selection process. It should come as no surprise that some late 20th-century fragrance manufacturers have abandoned the traditional separation of men and women's perfumes in favor of various images and scent "directions".

Every perfume goes through phases in which it gives off different notes. It combines refreshing, stimulating, and narcotic essences. The first should awaken the tired senses and draw attention to the sense of the smell itself. The narcotic ingredients intoxicate the intellect and overcome all kinds of inhibitions, allowing fantasy to unfold. Erogenous scents are reminiscent of body scents and thus act directly on the limbic system, the part of the brain that controls emotions and sex drive. This last category includes beguilingly heavy and sensual perfumes with animal products like musk (originally a glandular secretion from a type of Asiatic deer; now manufactured), ambergris (a rare secretion of sperm whales, which washes up on beaches; today substituted), and civet (a secretion of the wild Ethiopian civet cat) as well as balsam, moss, exotic flower essences and wood.

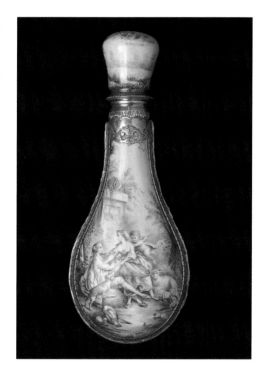

Porcelain flask with pastoral scene, 18th cent. Gray tone paint. Richly decorated and extravagantly shaped bottles (this one would have needed a stand) add to a perfume's illusion of hedonism and luxury.

Below: **Nicolas de Larmessin, *Perfume Man's Costume*, 1695. Copperplate engraving.** This perfume maker's dress is both clothing and carry-all.

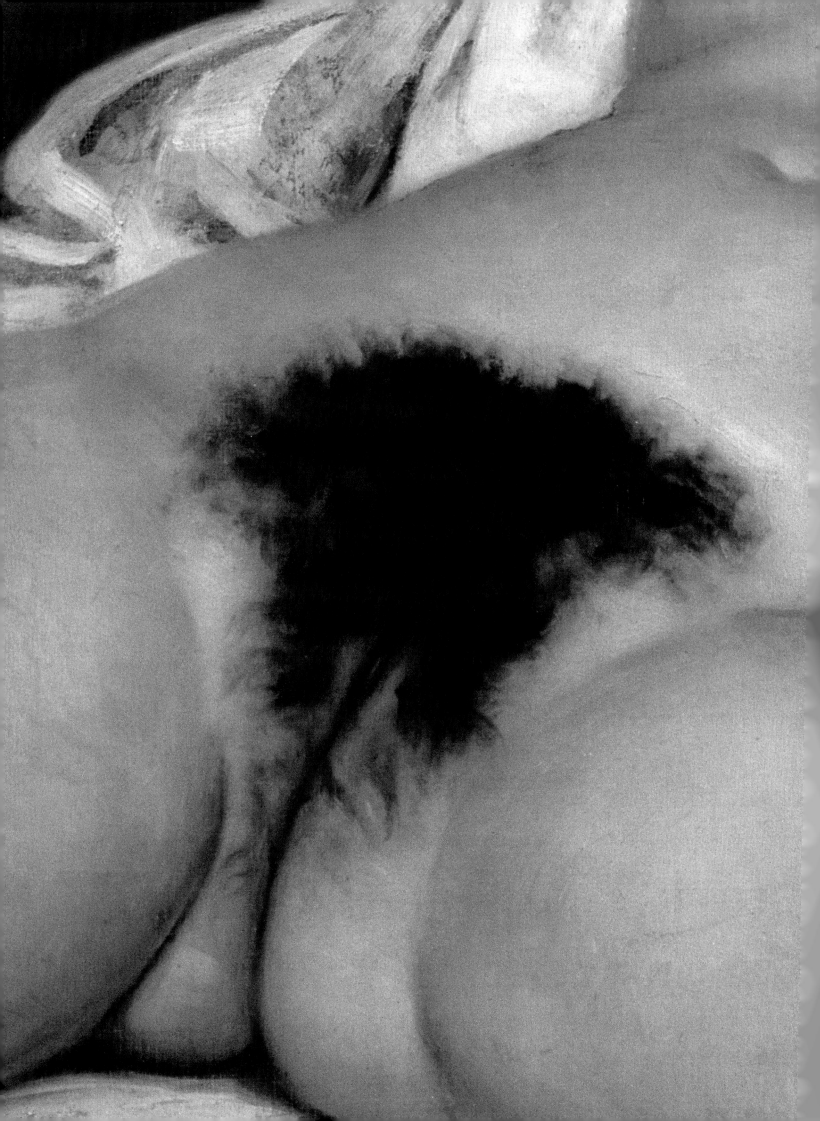

A Culture
Steeped in Sex
Europe and the USA

Gustave Courbet, *The Birth of the World (detail)*,
1866. Oil on canvas, 46 x 55 cm, private collection.
This picture was concealed from the public for
almost 130 years. Only in the late 20th century was it
placed on view in the Musée d'Orsay. The public display of the naively exhibitionist *Birth of the World*
demonstrates the "seizure" of the female body by
the gaze of the beholder, which, alongside the
development of erotic photography, sexually fixated
psychoanalysis and the revolutionary abandonment
of taboos, characterizes the whole 20th century.

The Pleasure Taboo

Dirck Santvoort, *Group Portrait of Three Generations of a Family in the Grounds of a Country House*, 17th cent. Oil on canvas, 129 x 185 cm, Johnny van Haeften Gallery, London. Protestant puritans retained the Catholic ideal that sex was mainly for reproduction.

A few decades ago the question "What is sex?" would have seemed easy to answer: sex is something that only married couples are allowed to have. Sex is what happens if a man and a woman "sleep together". In the Christian Western world sexuality has always played an important role, because for centuries it was condemned as a "sin". Today, whether denigrated or approved, it is still the key element of Western thought and emotion.

The insistence upon erotic desire was seen as being a diversion from the path of righteousness. At the age of 18, on becoming King, Henry VIII married his brother's widow, Catherine of Aragon. Like most royal marriages, this had little to do with love and much to do with politics. Like most kings, Henry had mistresses on the side, but when his marriage failed to produce a male heir (and Henry never considered the possibility that the failure might be his), he decided he needed to marry his current lover, Anne Boleyn, in order to legitimize any offspring. As the Pope for good political reasons refused to annul his marriage, Henry nationalized the English church, which obligingly did the necessary. Thus the Church of England, which still disapproves of divorce, was founded to rubber-stamp a king's breach of the prevailing sexual rules. Henry VIII is famous for having had six wives – but curiously, apart from that with Anne Boleyn, none of his marriages seems to have had much of an erotic foundation. The Reformation brought with it an illusion of sexual liberalization when, after the dissolution of the monasteries and convents, celibacy was no longer required of the Protestant clergy. In reality people were encouraged to channel their erotic urges into worldly asceticism. In the Western world for centuries there was a strict dichotomy between the functional sex life within marriage and all other forms of useless and therefore sinful lust. The latter were considered expressions of disease, depravity or faulty upbringing. Everything from masturbation to extramarital intercourse to homosexual contact was regarded as an offence.

Most rigid of all were the ideas of the reformer John Calvin (1509–1564) whose specific type of Protestantism defined itself by its narrowness. In 1536 he was forced to leave France because he supported the cause of the Protestants. From 1536 onwards he lived, with some interruptions, in Geneva. He slept little, worked a lot and lived a chaste life. It was true that in 1540 he married the widow Idelette de Bure, but it was not in the hope of at last enjoying worldly love. "If I take a wife it will be so that I will be freed from many tasks of drudgery and therefore better able to consecrate myself to the Lord." He understood the Church to be "the community of the chosen" which had to excel through iron discipline. Later, owing to the fact that many successful traders in Holland, France and Scotland were Calvinists, their strict religion spread across the entire Western world.

By the mid-17th century, in Calvinist Geneva, a change had set in as far as the birth-cycle was concerned. There was an increasing tendency for siblings to be born at intervals of four or more years so that each could be nurtured properly. The believers seem to have realized that enhancing their descendants' chances of survival was in their hands, not those of Divine Providence. In Catholic France birth control was promoted for the first time in the wake of the French Revolution.

The religiosity of the English Puritans developed in a particular way. Alternative fundamentalists in today's terms forced the closure of all public theaters in England in 1642, because they regarded them as dens of iniquity. In fact, as far as they were concerned, all sources of worldly pleasure were sinful. From the beginning of the second half of the 16th century, the Puritans carried out a church reform movement, which aimed for a pure, unspoiled doctrine. This involved a radical breakaway from the Catholicized forms of the Anglican cult. Anything of worldly significance was to be replaced by inner contemplation. Saints should not be objects of veneration; rather believers should themselves live like saints. Self-control and firmness were held up as ideals.

In the Puritan philosophy, morality and lifestyle are identical. Of course, good qualities such as honesty and reliability are encouraged, but interestingly, because everyone has to be an example to the rest, intolerance, self-opinionatedness and prudishness are amongst the qualities to be cultivated.

According to the Puritans, all human energy, including sexual energy, should in the last instance serve the demands of economic and military power. Human sexuality was subjected to a clear purpose: the production of legitimate offspring whose well-being or failure would be a proof of divine grace just as much as the parents' material success. Proper sexuality was reduced to a functional, limited sexual act, which started with vaginal penetration, ended with the orgasm of the married man, and might lead to the impregnation of his wife. Thus, for example, a woman who could no longer have children but was sexually attracted to a man was considered ridiculous or even suspect. In addition, particular attention was given to stamping out masturbation amongst children and young people.

The Puritans believed the sum of all ambition should be the glorification of God, who was represented as an implacable father figure. In accordance with his unfathomable will the living were divided into those who would share in God's grace and those who would never attain this state. Believers had no influence over whether or not they were chosen, but they could uncover the truth. If they met with success in earthly affairs, they were amongst the chosen. Thus true believers had to compulsively check by measure of their worldly success whether they were blessed in this way. However, at the same time, all resistance to the ascetic rules put up by the socially excluded appeared only to prove their fundamental depravity. Any sensual desire, any lustful urge, was an indication of such depravity.

These Puritan ideals, which were imported with the Puritans when they arrived in the New World, still impact North American thinking about sex. The Puritans generally took the eroticism out of love and differentiated between "indecency", which they of course rejected, and godly love, of which they had to constantly prove themselves worthy. That led, as the German publicist Sebastian Haffner (1907–1999) put it, to rendering the sexual life "unromantic, objective and brutally isolated".

When the descendants of the Puritans called for sexual revolution in the 1960s, they simply took the Puritanism of their forefathers and stood it on its head, operating with the same idea of, so to speak, abstract, isolated sex. Only now they were no longer against it, but in favor of it.

Penitentials

Public punishment by populist methods was meted out to persons guilty of sexual offences ("indecency"), to serve as a deterrent to those whose sins still remained undiscovered, and

Top: **Anonymous, Punishment of Two adulterers by Nude Procession Through the Town, 13th cent., illustration from the *Livre juratoire d'Agen*. Bibliothèque Municipale, Agen, France.** The punishment of adulterous women was often highly public and demeaning. Unlike shown here the punishment of the lover, which was widely considered a private matter of honor, to be dealt with by the cuckolded husband.

Above: **Convicts in Vienna, who have been Sentenced to Sweeping Alleys (standard measures taken by the chastity commission against the *Grabennymphen*), c. 1770. Copperplate engraving, private collection.** *Grabennymphen* was a euphemism for whores streetwalking the *Graben*, the Viennese equivalent of the *Champs Elysées* in Paris or the *Kurfürstendamm* in Berlin. Here, they are being sentenced by the Austrian chastity commission to perform menial tasks such as sweeping the streets. The first stage of the women's punishment is the cutting of their hair.

for the delight of those who craved sensation. Many towns in Europe had their own preferred methods of punishment. The best-known example of a penalty for dishonor – meant to humiliate sinners – is the pillory for women who had dared to indulge in premarital sexual intercourse. Whoever had been without shame would be shamed and exposed. The culprit would be stripped naked and made to face the scorn of the mob; in the 16th century this included being forced to ride a donkey backwards through the streets. Additional forms of punishment included being dragged through the town in the "whore-cart", or having to carry a heavy burden, the so-called vice stone, symbolizing the illegitimate child. Adulteresses were pulled through water in baskets or dunked repeatedly into the river until they almost drowned. The "indecency of the female" always became apparent if she became pregnant outside marriage. In the case of "free love" the Magdeburg church rules of 1685 prescribed public penance in church. The chastity commission set up by Maria Theresa, Empress of Austria, sentenced those who fell foul of it to public labor. Flogging was also a popular punishment, customary in Europe and the USA into the 19th century. In order to avoid the penalties, many women turned to infanticide. The above punishments were often combined with some form of mutilation. Cutting off the hair was a widely-practiced form of punishment for offences of honor. In order to permanently stigmatize the offender, the face was often disfigured. Adulteresses and procuresses would have their noses or their ears sliced off. Removal of sex organs was also prevalent for men and women. Men found guilty of rape could be put into the "Iron Maiden", a hollow case with spikes on the inside which, when the case was closed, bored into the body of the person shut inside. Many forms of physical punishment involved mutilation with a phallus-shaped object. As sadistic and masochistic tendencies have always been a widespread phenomenon, public retribution always drew large crowds of people. This could even involve a fetish about executions, which Casanova, among others,

described in his memoirs. Ironically, the scene of an execution was regarded as an excellent hunting ground for seducers, on the basis that the sight of violent death would "quicken the blood" of any woman present.

David Chodowiecki, *Flogging of Unmarried Mothers*, 18th cent. Colored etching, private collection. From the 16th to 18th century flogging was a popular punishment for unmarried mothers, unlicenced whores, and unmarried couples caught in the act.

The Wild West

At first Wild West society was almost exclusively male. Apart from the religious settlers, emigrants to America were predominantly adventurous young men. Even if they were perhaps already engaged or married, they took the chance to start what was in every sense a new life. In 1869, in Wyoming for example, there were six times as many men as women.

Amongst the voluntary emigrants who went west as pioneers, the desire for erotic variety was far less prevalent than amongst the men of today. The exotic gave rise to fear rather than lust. Many settlers were afraid to get sexually involved with "natives". Therefore, many tried to initiate a relationship with a woman from their homeland, from the poor regions of Ireland, Scotland, Germany or Sweden. A favorite way was through newspaper advertisements. From many thousands of miles away, the women had to commit themselves without ever having met their betrothed. However, once in America, it was usually too late for any disenchanted women to return to Europe. If a woman decided to leave the man she came to America to be with, she quickly slipped into prostitution, and some of the new arrivals chose this route. Those who did not yield to the temptation to leave demanded respectable behavior from

Cosmopolitan Saloon in Telluride, c. 1910. This early photograph taken in the wealthy mining town of Telluride in Colorado shows the marshall watching gamblers, but the portrait on the wall of a local whore suggests the establishment also offered other attractions.

their husbands. The success rate of this demand was patchy, because so-called respectability prohibited literally everything that had eased the hard life led by the men: swearing, smoking, chewing tobacco, watching dancing girls and gambling. Alcohol was especially taboo.

Some of the female advocates of abstinence were completely adamant when it came to promoting their ideals. In the Wild West they had the possibility to wield political influence and tried to push their opinions on a communal level. In Wyoming, for example, in order to attract more women into the state, they were given the right to vote in 1869, at a time when in Europe this was still unthinkable.

If, in the final reckoning, having a hard-working, resilient and respectable wife was more important to the men than dissipation, then they obeyed with reluctant grace. However, the men could not afford to be choosy. Although these immigrant women had had little chance on the marriage market back home, so long as they were strong and tough enough to survive, they were in demand in the Wild West. Their capacity for work was urgently needed.

Among the religious settlers, every form of contraception was frowned upon, even *coitus interruptus*. It was thus advantageous if a women felt no erotic desire and severely restricted her husband from satisfying his urges. Certainly, children were highly welcome as extra workers; but at the same time frequent pregnancies and childbearing were a threat to the productivity of the mother. Women had to be able to resist strangers who could not control themselves as well as their own husbands. However the strictly monogamous men in reality lived in serial monogamy, because they usually survived several wives. Often it was a plain-looking woman who perhaps would have otherwise become an old maid who married a man with numerous children from previous marriages.

The only way for both men and women to survive in the hostile environment was for them to be ready and willing to make great sacrifices. For this reason self-sacrifice was extolled as a virtue and soon was no longer seen as plain necessity but as a personal quality and a sign of decency.

Calamity Jane, dressed as scout of Crook's troops, c. 1882.

Calamity Jane (1848/52–1903)

In the 1880s, a woman dressed in men's clothing was stylized as a heroine of the Wild West: Martha Jane Cannery (or Canary), still famed today under the name of "Calamity Jane". She had barely left childhood behind when she set off with her family on a five-month trek to Virginia. Her mother died on the journey, her father a short time later. By this time, she already had acquired a reputation as a good rider and sharpshooter. Calamity Jane wore women's clothing until 1870, when she went to work as a scout for Confederate generals Custer and Mile. It was in this role that she wore men's clothing. Supposedly, her prior jobs included being a cook, a dancer, a mail-coach driver, a nurse, and also a prostitute. When she was 24 she moved to Deadwood, South Dakota. When she made stage appearances later in her life, she related that gold prospectors there had to be defended from attacks. She found fame because of an alleged affair (which must have been very short-lived) with one of the best-known fast draws of the Wild West, William Hickock, nicknamed "Wild Bill". He was shot in 1874. Whether Jane's illegitimate daughter, whom she gave up for adoption, was a result of this affair is disputed. From 1895 she toured with Wild West shows. Even by this time the recent past had become the subject of myth. Calamity Jane was blind when she died. At her own request she was buried beside the gunslinger "Wild Bill".

Sexual Utopias

The Shakers

Ann Lee (1742–1784) was an apostate Quaker from Manchester, England. In 1774 she emigrated with other alienated coreligionists to New England where she formed the United Society of Believers in Christ's Second Appearance whose members also became known as "Shakers". Ann Lee rejected all carnal lust and demanded celibacy from her disciples. However, the believers did not lead lives completely devoid of devotion. Learning to live with their desire, they managed to rise above it. Ecstatic, agitated dancing marked their religious gatherings, which gave their community its name.

In 1784 the charismatic founder died. In the first third of the 20th century there were still approximately 4000 Shakers in 18 settlements in the Midwest and New England. Obviously the Shaker way of life was more attractive to women than to men: at the turn of the 20th century three out of four Shakers were women. At the beginning of the 21st century a tiny group of Shakers are living in Maine: six women and two men.

The Mormons

Joseph Smith (1805–1844) was 25 when he founded the Church of Jesus Christ of the Latter Day Saints, whose followers have also been known as "Mormons" since the beginning of the 20th century.

From 1846 Smith's successor, Brigham Young, played a significant role in forming the image of the Mormons. He organized a trek to the West where the group settled in what is today the state of Utah. From 1850, as the land was progressively wrested away from the native Indians, Young became the secular and spiritual ruler over a growing number of believers.

Mormons believe that there are "waiting hordes" of unborn children, spiritual beings, who are waiting to receive a body. It therefore seems imperative to have as many children as possible. In 1852 Young proclaimed the duty of polygamy, which five years later led to armed struggle with the government. It was this instruction, more than any other factor, which caused the rage and hatred of monogamous Americans towards the sect.

With the coming of the railroad in 1869, Utah was no longer as geographically isolated as before. This immediately increased the pressures on the non-conformists. In 1877, after the death of Brigham Young, the religious community was dissolved and its possessions seized by the American government. As a reaction to this the then World President of the Mormons, Wilford Woodruff, revoked the instruction for polygamy in 1890. The region of Utah (which to this day is approximately 70 percent Mormon) became the 45th State of the Union only six years later, after several decades of having its application for statehood rejected.

Even during the nearly fifty years that polygamy was a religious duty, only a fifth of the men, most of them tending to be from the governing class, actually had a large number of wives. Even though Brigham Young married 27 women, the majority lived in traditional monogamy. Today, some Mormon groups in Utah and in northern Arizona secretly continue the practice. Despite the concerns of various feminist groups, who see polygamy as a form of socially sanctified slavery, polygamists are rarely prosecuted.

Oneida

The Oneida Community (1848–c. 1884) advocated absolute communal ownership. After more than thirty years the commune was transferred into a still existent trading company that turns out steel traps and silverware.

In the Oneida Commune, which at its height numbered over three hundred members, every male member was the husband of every woman. Sex was regarded as a sacrament. The specific type of "complex marriage" lent itself to strong group bonding. However, since the women never took the initiative, there were clear distinctions between the younger and more desired partners and the older ones. The Community's founder, John Humphrey Noyes (1811–1886), favored a strict separation of the social and reproductive components of sexuality – a very unusual idea for the 19th century. During puberty, the rising generations – the boys right at the start of puberty, the girls a few

The Shakers, one of the sects derived from the Quakers part of whose worship services involved a trembling dance, c. 1840. Lithograph, Staatliche Museen Preussischer Kulturbesitz, Berlin. The dancing that gave the Shaker community its name is an extension of the trembling that sometimes gripped participants in a Quaker meeting, when they felt they were seized by the holy spirit. Although men and women were celibate, some partnerships were recognized by the community. However, the couples' contact was extremely limited, and they were only allowed to converse with each other from a safe distance, at communal meetings. Rooms, such as the meeting hall, that were shared by men and women had separate entrances for either sex.

In memoriam Brigham Young. "And the place which knew him once shall know him no more". The members of the sect of Mormons were relentlessly attacked, libelled and ridiculed by their compatriots as shown in this caricature at the death of their leader Brigham Young in 1877.

The Oneida Community. Group activities with the "common" children of the community played an important part in the life of the Oneida members.

years later – were initiated into sexuality by older and more spiritually experienced members of the sect.

The men had to learn to have sexual intercourse without ejaculating. They were supposed to be able to copulate with a woman for over an hour without achieving orgasm. During the first two decades of the commune only one or two children were born every year. The withholding of semen not only served contraceptive purposes; another reason was the then much-discussed danger that spilling his semen led to the loss of vitality in a man.

After 1869, when it transpired that the integration of new members into the firmly-established group was becoming difficult, couples with particularly good qualities were permitted to reproduce "according to scientific criteria" (in this context it is impossible to overlook the influence of Charles Darwin's teachings on genetics – his book *The Origin of Species* was published just ten years earlier). In the following decade approximately 60 children were born, who remained in the care of their birth mothers only while they were infants, after which they were raised in the community. This was another attempt to prevent close bonding between individuals. Lovers were on principle kept apart.

In 1879, Noyes fled to Canada, because he feared prosecution. He advised the members remaining behind to refrain henceforth from the practice of "complex marriage".

David Koresh and the Davidians

The "Adventists" live in the immediate expectation of the Second Coming of Jesus Christ. The sect, one of many revivalist movements falling back on early Christianity, originated in 18th-century America. In 1934 a small group, the "Davidians", split off from the Adventists. At the end of the 1980s David Koresh, just thirty years old, took over their leadership. Like many charismatic leaders of this kind of sect Koresh tried to sever every link to the outer world and to minimize bonding between members. The Davidians were prohibited from initiating erotic relationships with each other. However, the aim was not celibacy, but rather to focus the attention on the "divine leader". Thus any sexual contact with the "Messiah" was regarded as honorable for the object of his desire. David Koresh was said to have sired 18 children.

His disciples trusted him blindly and in April 1993 followed him to their deaths. For more than seven weeks the FBI and the Davidian sect were involved in a standoff at the sect's compound in Waco, Texas. The FBI went to search the complex for illegal weapons and arrest Koresh, but the ranch had been turned into a fortification. Then, after a bloody shootout in front of the cameras of the world, the settlement went up in flames along with its inhabitants. More than 80 people met their deaths, among them the "divine leader".

Davidian Sect, leader David Koresh in front of his followers, 1990s. For Messianic leaders such as Koresh, gaining control over another's sexual practices is a sign that their power has extended beyond the public sphere, and that they now control the minds and inner worlds of their followers.

The Sexologists

Four American sexologists polarized the debate about sexuality in America in the second half of the 20th century: Kinsey, Masters and Johnson, and Hite. However different the focus of their research might be, they had one thing in common: their conclusions gave rise to great interest and vehement rejection when their surveys brought to light a considerable discrepancy between the ideal of the "upright American" and reality.

Alfred Charles Kinsey. After studying psychology Kinsey gained a doctorate in entomology. From 1920 onwards he was a biology lecturer at the University of Indiana, where in 1946 he founded and directed the university's Institute for Sex Research. He remained in this position until his death in 1956.

Alfred Charles Kinsey (1894–1956)

A biologist, Kinsey was 43 years old when he received an offer to conduct a new university course about sexuality and marriage. When he established how little scientific (by this he meant statistically watertight) knowledge there was about human sexuality he dedicated himself to the relevant research. First of all Kinsey took stock thoroughly. Quantitative sexual research was by and large unknown until the 1940s. Sexual relations had been evaluated, but not measured. The then-recent analysis of no fewer than 4600 short interviews with unmarried men, gathered from medical examination centers in New York and Baltimore at the beginning of the 1940s, had concluded that only three to four out of every thousand respondents had had homosexual experiences. However, it was not in the interest of any of the young men to disclose deviant behavior, because this would have prevented their voluntary enlistment for the war.

Through their well-considered interviewing technique Kinsey and his colleagues uncovered different results. They did not ask, "Have you ever masturbated?" but "When did you begin masturbating?" signaling that such practices were regarded as completely normal.

In 1948 Kinsey and his team published their findings in *Sexual Behavior in the Human Male* and in 1953 there followed the corresponding report on the sexual behavior of women. The reports were based on interviews with around 5000 white subjects. The interviewees comprised residents of all the American states, married and unmarried, from all age groups, levels of education and religious affiliations. One of the conclusions was: even in the middle of the 20th century people had a sex life before marriage. On average men had experienced 1523 orgasms during intercourse before marriage – as many as they (again, on average) would experience in the first 15–20 years of married life. Women had experienced only 223 orgasms on average before marriage. The high degree of premarital satisfaction horrified and fascinated Kinsey's contemporaries. Some attacked his findings as being statistically unreliable

(Kinsey himself thought that he needed 100,000 subjects to make a proper study – at the time of his death, only 18,000 people had been thoroughly interviewed).

But considerably more fury was unleashed at the findings on male homosexuality: four percent of Americans had sexual contact exclusively with other men, and no fewer than 37 percent of the interviewees had had a homosexual experience. One in two had in the past been aroused by someone of their own gender.

William H. Masters (b. 1915) and Virginia E. Johnson (b. 1925)

Without the knowledge gained from their research laboratory in St. Louis, Missouri there would be no sex therapy in the Western world. At first the subject of their research was the physiology of sexual arousal. In eleven years they documented and analyzed around 10,000 sexual acts (involving both individuals and couples). In this way they established that women and men reacted more or less the same way during sexual arousal – regardless of whether they were masturbating or copulating. The collation of their findings appeared in 1966 in their book *Human Sexual Response*.

In 1970 they followed it up with a book about human sexual inadequacy. In it, the researchers

Masters and Johnson. The gynecologist William Masters and the psychologist Virginia Johnson began their work in the 1950s. After more than 15 years they married each other. One of the many things proved by the couple was this: scientifically based knowledge about the reliable methods of producing sexual harmony is no guarantee of marital stability. In 1993 they split up after 22 years together.

demonstrate how, through solid information on their own and other people's arousal, help can be given to patients who associate sexuality with fear or pain. Nonetheless, at the start of the third millennium in Europe sex therapy is still regarded as comparatively exotic.

Shere Hite (b. 1942)

As early as 1976 Hite published the much-discussed first volume of *The Hite Report. A Nationwide Study of Female Sexuality*, which was translated into 30 languages. The book evaluated the responses returned to the more than 100,000 questionnaires she had sent out. The women had to answer 130 questions, such as when, where and how they had experienced their first orgasm. It was very rarely through

normal sexual intercourse. Hite questions the Freudian model of mature vaginal sexuality and proclaims that women can well do without penetration. Because of this she made herself enemies, especially among men. At the same time many women received the survey with great delight. Her next three best-selling reports *On Male Sexuality*, 1978, *Women and Love*, 1987 and *On the Family*, 1994 were also the subject of controversy.

Shere Hite, 1987. Born in St. Joseph, Missouri, Hite studied history and music and became involved in the women's movement. From 1978 she headed her own research institute in New York and wielded considerable influence over the debate about female sexuality – hitherto predominantly defined by men.

The Sexual Revolution

Nude Revue, 1975. After being a hit in London and New York, the musical "Hair" was produced in Paris in 1975 under the name of *Lève-toi et Viens*. Here the cast kneel for the nude finale at the Taverne d'Olympia, Paris.

From the beginning of the 1960s it was the massive debate about "the Pill", in particular, which set the scene for sex to be discussed in the open. Doctors and theologians warned against the looming sexual "frailty" of women who no longer had to be afraid of pregnancy. Men, on the other hand, appeared disappointed if the women remained as reserved as before; it was true that they were more ready to consent to sex, but they seldom took the initiative. It was not long before feminists noted that the new freedom was no freedom at all. Old pressures had been replaced with new ones. Women who rejected advances were now regarded as prudish or old-fashioned. "But you are a modern young girl" was the phrase many "progressive" men considered a convincing argument when they were rebuffed.

The 1960s are remembered as an extremely politicized and sexualized period. It was still a bone of contention where one should start in order to obtain the desired freedom in all its aspects. Could sexually inhibited people solve political problems? To Dieter Kunzelmann (b. 1938), the cofounder of Commune I in West Berlin at the end of the 1960s and a member of the extra-parliamentary opposition, is attributed the remark, "What does the Vietnam War matter to me, when I find it difficult to have orgasms?" Unlike in the 1990s, the struggle for a change in sexual behavior was not solely motivated by hedonism. The increased lust had to serve a social purpose. Only then did it appear permissible to tinker about with the long-held taboos. The "new morality" made high demands: anyone who was more sexually balanced and less frustrated would be less susceptible to unfortunate political thoughts.

The family was regarded as the vehicle of sexual moral pressure. To many, liberty seemed possible only within other structures such as communes that would practice non-hierarchical social living. All possessions would be held in common, whether it were books, clothes, or sexual partners. Monogamy and also couple relationships were above all expressions of bourgeois possessiveness. And that was the very thing that you had to distance yourself from. It was said that you were part of the establishment if you had slept with the same person twice. Thus the desire for sexual variety was shored up on ideological grounds as well. Promiscuity had become a political demand.

However, the representatives of the revolutionary consciousness were not the only ones who wanted more sexual freedom. Their middle-class contemporaries, who on any other issue adopted a very different stance from student revolutionaries, were also interested in this. To the "bourgeois" faction it was all about converting marital duty into the more stabilizing marital lust. They were decidedly in favor of monogamy, but against monotony. A refined eroticism full of variation was to strengthen the bond between the married couple.

Swappers and Swingers

The 1960s and 1970s were a great turning point in terms of sexual liberation. Yet the percentages in surveys on adultery during this period did not yield higher numbers than those conducted by sexologist Alfred Kinsey in the 1940s and 1950s, with the exception that women indulged their extramarital urges more than they had done before. But by far the most significant liberation was evident in premarital sex among women, made possible by the advent of the contraceptive pill. With icons like Holly-go-Lightly (Audrey Hepburn) from the film *Breakfast at Tiffany's*, 1961, in their minds, women became more relaxed about brief and frequent sexual encounters. It was understandable therefore that the newfound sense of sexual freedom might continue even after marriage.

One manifestation of this was found in the practice of "wife-swapping", later called "swinging" to avoid implication of a power dynamic. In general, a group of friends met at a private home to exchange partners for the night. In order to achieve a "safe" or impartial pairing, the husband was required to drop his keys into a receptacle placed by the entrance. It was from this that the practice got the name "key clubs". Toward the end of the evening, the wives picked up a key and claimed the owner for the night. At least two reports conducted on the subject in the early 1970s revealed that those who indulged in "swinging" were of all ages and came from diverse backgrounds and religions. They were deemed "normal, well-adjusted" people, as well as having good social and professional status. Their reasons for swinging and sharing was to avoid sexual repression by allowing experimentation in a safe and trusting environment, and to deal with the standard negatives of married life such as boredom, jealousy and waning sex drive. Swingers fall into two categories: the "utopians" who believed that love and its consummation could counteract evil, including violence, materialism and jealousy and the "recreationals" who simply saw it as an alternative to conventional social activities such as card games and conversation around a dinner table.

Another sexual diversion associated with the swinging Sixties was the orgy, reputedly popular in sleepy suburbia where there was little local entertainment to be found. As with key clubs, it demanded the sharing of partners. There was a greater degree of freedom, however, with individuals joining couples already in *flagrante delicto* or advanced stages of foreplay. Unlike the paradoxically "conventional" rules of the key clubs, orgies included group sex, anal sex and, possibly to reflect a change in the law, homosexual pairings between men and between women. Describing "parties" of this kind, the author of the book *Happy Hooker*, 1971, Xaviera Hollander (b. 1943) wrote that the only reservations were from men who felt uncomfortable about kissing women who had been involved in acts of fellatio.

Though residual reservations about "free sex" are still found even in industrial societies, premarital sex is generally acceptable in the Western world. The thigh-slapping, beer-swilling "ladette" culture of the new millennium allows a young woman to "pick up" a sexual partner for the night as easily as a man may. Gone are the stereotypical expectations of women: it is said that women can now enjoy sex in the way that men do – by turning away and falling asleep after intercourse, or getting dressed and leaving immediately after achieving orgasm. The encounter demands no commitment of any kind and is merely a mutual act

Rehearsal in Hamburg's first Erotic Theater, 1970. Rehearsal of the play *MMM, Why Did Sharon Tate Have to Die?* under the direction of the Frenchman René Durand, also known as the "King of Sex".

Bob & Carol & Ted & Alice, **still from the film by Paul Mazursky, 1969.** Filmmaker Bob (Robert Culp, second from right) and Carol (Natalie Wood, second from left), a sophisticated couple, attend a therapy group and become more liberal in their sexual thinking and behavior – an outlook to which they eventually convert their best friends Ted (Eliott Gould, first from left) and Alice (Dyan Cannon, first from right).

Sandstone

In the 20th-century experimentation in the field of free sexuality has been a phenomenon mainly since the 1960s. In Topanga Canyon, California, Barbara and John Williamson organized a sex club during that time. The clientele consisted mainly of self-employed professionals, and membership cost around 250 dollars per year. Several times a week the house was opened up for the 400-odd couples. However, there were never more than a few dozen present. They ate together, played music, chatted and tried to overcome any residue of their puritanical upbringing. Nudity was desirable, but not compulsory. All kinds of communal contact, unlike in nudist camps, were sought after, and this expressly included sex. Above all, sex was not to take place in secret. Those who did not take part could watch. In the mid-1970s the owners sold Sandstone.

Feminism

Along with other emancipation movements, the 19th century also saw the beginnings of a rebellion by women who no longer wanted to be treated as children. Women were not legally competent, they had no vote, and they could not obtain professional qualifications. Husbands were often chosen for them, and once

Businesswoman and businessman conferring in the stock exchange. Despite their greater access to the business world, women still speak of the "glass ceiling" – an upper limit to their career prospects which does not apply to their male colleagues.

married, there was no divorce. Married women could not own property, and they had little control over how many children they would have. And if economic necessity forced them to go out to work, they were accused of neglecting their family.

There was never one unified women's movement. Right from the start there were two separate strands. The proletarian women's movement concerned itself with the interests of those who went to work to bring in an extra wage. For them the social question was more important than the "gender question". The middle class women's movement involved itself with the situation of the "wife and mother". This group did not feel privileged, but rather imprisoned in the "dolls' house", as described as early as 1879 in the play of that name by Norwegian playwright Henrik Ibsen (1826–1906). This group was mainly concerned with the problems arising between the economically dependent wife and her husband. The "New Women's Movement", which has since the end

of the 1960s defined the image of feminism, grew out of this point of view.

Many adherents of the earlier women's movement defined a woman by her capability as a mother. They emphasized the gender difference and highlighted the social necessity of despised female qualities. They did not want to be like men; from their perspective the professional world outside the home belonged exclusively to the male sphere. The gainful employment of women was accepted, at best, as a transitional measure while the men fought at the front.

Both World Wars were of significance to the women's movement since women were faced with new responsibilities while the men were away. After the wars, when the men wanted to have their hands on the helm once more, they were met with considerable resistance from those women who had become independent.

The women's movement took on a fundamentally new aspect only when the Pill severed the link between sexuality and procreation. In contrast to communist countries, in which

Simone de Beauvoir

Simone de Beauvoir (1908–1986), among others, provided the catalyst for the development of the New Women's Movement after the Second World War. In 1949 Beauvoir published *The Second Sex*, which for many women became the Bible of the new movement. "One is not born a woman, one becomes a woman" she wrote. Her central thesis: man is complete in himself – woman is not. In order to avoid letting love lead her into deadly danger, woman has to become like man. For him even a beloved woman is, at best, one among several treasured objects, never the be-all and end-all. For the woman, on the other hand, love is total self-sacrifice. Beauvoir's book put a question mark over the sanctity of the family. In 1956 her work was placed on the Vatican index of banned books. Her own relationship with the Existentialist philosopher Jean Paul Sartre which began in 1929 and lasted until his death in 1989, was a famously free and open one, a situation which seemed to cause her more emotional distress than it did him.

March of the suffragettes promoting their publication *Votes for Women*, c. 1905. The Women's Social and Political Union, whose members became known as suffragettes, was formed by Emmeline Pankhurst in 1903. Their tactics included open-air rallies, direct action which resulted in imprisonment, and hunger strikes.

Lesbian couple at the annual Gay Pride march in London 1993, promoting gay and lesbian rights. Many radical lesbians have a particularly tough appearance and often display attributes associated with S&M.

abortion was an element of socio-economic control, women in the Christian West are still fighting for the right to choose for themselves whether to carry a conceived child to term. The Catholic Church especially has proven itself to be a mighty opponent to those women who have been asserting since the 1970s, "My womb belongs to me!" While one section of the women's movement was proclaiming motherhood as a major obstacle for emancipation, the other section was presenting the ability to bear children as a specifically female form of potency, a view their opponents criticized as raising the birth-act to the status of super-orgasm and breast-feeding to that of social potency.

Since 1975 the debate about violence against women has played an ever-bigger role in feminism. Susan Brownmiller's book *Against our Will: Men, Women, and Rape*, which came out that year, eliminated the suggestion that rape is about sex. According to her it stems from systematic intimidation, whereby men in general try to keep women in a state of fear and terror.

The American Andrea Dworkin (b. 1945) and the German Alice Schwarzer (b. 1942) attacked pornography for its presentation of women as willing objects of male lechery. In the British Parliament in 1986 Clare Short initiated a major debate on whether or not pictures of naked women should be banned from tabloids. The pictures involved rape fantasies, which eventually translated into reality. Finally this debate led to a conundrum about sexuality, in which there were only male perpetrators and female victims. By the 1990s this tendency met with resistance: women joyfully acknowledged their capacity to become protagonists themselves. Naomi Wolf in her book *Fire with Fire*, 1993 presents a very different kind of woman who would not dream of letting herself become a victim. Young American feminists like her emphasize very strongly that the allegedly inborn docility and motherliness of women is a social construct. Sexual characteristics develop out of attributed responsibilities, not the other way round. The old models are questioned radically, especially by the faction of lesbians, small in number but active in the media, who are against the coexistence of the sexes. In 1990 the lesbian activist Sheila Jeffreys published her book *Anticlimax* in Great Britain. She wrote off the sexual revolution as "a call-up to heterosexual sex for all single women". What turned a woman into a lesbian was not her erotic inclination towards women. A lesbian (activist) was someone who in every respect could do without men and who defined all social relationships in terms of the feminine infrastructure.

Cover page of the *Stern* No. 24/1971 "We've had abortions". This cover of the German magazine *Stern* brought together a number of women – many of them in the public eye and among them internationally known actresses like Romy Schneider and Senta Berger, as well as top models of the time like Veronika von Lehndorff – who openly admitted to having had abortions earlier in their lives.

Sexual Correctness

Sexual correctness developed in the wake of political correctness. At California universities, where a large percentage of the students were members of non-white races, the start of the 1980s brought growing irritation with the way in which teaching materials were dominated by "DWM" (dead white men). There was no place on the curriculum for the cultural identity of the "individual". At first the opposition movement concentrated their fire on the "w" for "white", then feminists (predominantly white) turned it on the "m" for "men". They criticized the disregard for the cultural identity of women and felt oppressed by sexual standards which were determined by the men's wishes and not their own.

Until the 1970s society assumed that there was a tacit agreement between two sexual partners. Feminists, however, emphasized the problems inherent in a tacit agreement by pointing out that frequently an agreement didn't exist at all, especially wherever relationships of dependency existed – as in a working or educational environment. One of the results of this argument was that at a few American universities permission had to be obtained before a partner was allowed to make a move in a sexual context. This permission was received by asking a clearly articulated question such as, "May I give you a kiss on the right cheek?" and getting the answer, "Yes, you may give me a kiss on the right cheek!" Anyone disregarding this verbal contract was open to charges of molestation. Escalations were also possible: a written contract for the next five minutes could be concluded before witnesses. The basic requirement for any contract was that the woman must be in full possession of her faculties. In practice only a few concerned themselves with such tiresome regulations. In Europe especially, they were and are met with very little understanding, since they run counter to the image of sexual spontaneity and, above all, they run counter to the new female self-confidence, which takes as one of its forms the right to cross over to the side of the erotic lead player.

Sexual Harassment

By the beginning of the 1990s sexual harassment had become a socio-political topic in the West. Feminists fought not only against the blatant presentation of naked women on magazine covers, be it at newsstands or supermarkets, but also against sexual harassment in the workplace by male bosses or colleagues. An inappropriate touch or remark can constitute sexual harassment, but so can gestures, expressions or looks. In certain social situations it can lead to unresolvable conflicts. For example, if a female student is closely observed by her instructor, who wants to get an idea of her academic performance, the look could be misinterpreted as

"Simply gigantic", billboards in Hermsdorf, Germany, 1999. A large part of the sexual and political correctness movement is directed not at personal behavior but at public use of images and language. Just as some words are circumscribed, so are sexually provocative images. However, advertisers and salesmen have always relied on sex to sell their products, and were quick to use humor and irony to deflate any charges of incorrectness made against them.

harassment. Lack of attention, on the other hand, could be seen as discrimination. In the past the male perpetrator's testimony was given more credence than that of the female victim, but in the last decade of the 20th century the voice of the victim has found an audience.

Date Rape

Date rape, so called since 1982, is indecent assault in the context of a social engagement, a phenomenon occurring more frequently in the USA than in Europe. The culprits are male acquaintances who don't take it seriously when a woman expressly says: "I don't want intimacy!" The greater spread of date rape in the USA does not seem to be due to the greater propensity for violence of American men, but to the sexual codes that encourage as many dates as possible with members of the opposite sex. Feminist Andrea Dworkin's solution is simple: she advises against taking part in the "dating system" in the first place.

Public images of male nudes, as here in Australia, 1996, are still comparatively rare, and are almost always deployed in the form of a joke. A partially naked woman on a billboard or hoarding will still, usually, be an object of desire. A partially naked man will often be a figure of fun.

Victims of sexual harassment at the work place can suffer for a long time without complaining, because although they feel that there is a genuine problem, they are worried that they may be misinterpreting perfectly innocent gestures. Experienced harassers are careful to make their actions ambiguous for this very reason.

The Language of Sex

For a long time ordinary people were allowed to discuss sexual matters, if at all, only in the confessional. In public few specialists were allowed to talk and write about such things, and then mostly in Latin or in the biological, medical or legal jargon. Thus, in the legal world, a couple had "coitus", "premarital sexual intercourse" or were "carrying out their marital duties". From the world of medicine came terms such as vulva, vaginal lubrication or penis. This last label for the male sexual organ, current at the start of the 21st century, does not appear even once in the repeatedly banned 1749 novel *Fanny Hill* or *Memoirs of a Woman of Pleasure* by John Cleland. Instead more than 50 metaphors are used for what we nowadays prosaically refer to as a "cock", or "prick".

Particular sexual aspects will always remain concealed in a standard language. For a long time the jargon used in front of children masked the fact that erotic matters are by no means only spiritual, but also corporeal. If a woman and a man "sleep together" then that is exactly what they are not doing.

With the exposure of standard language as a concealing instrument of power in the 1960s, colloquial terms long regarded as vulgar appeared not only more appropriate but also livelier and more sexually effective than the standard language. In order to counter double standards and hypocrisy there was particular emphasis on the technicalities of the sexual act. It was more liberated to be "screwing" rather than to be "having intercourse". Sexual slang

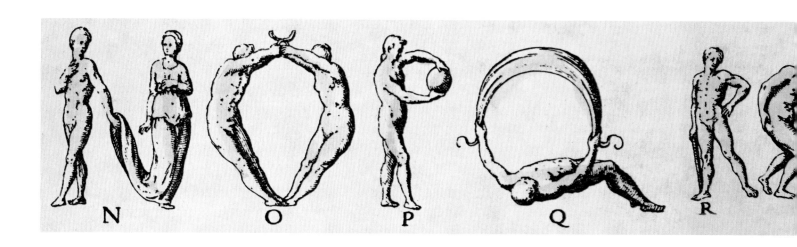

G   H   I   K   L   M

has always gone straight to the heart of the matter. "Banging" and "fucking" existed in the language even when the act as well as the terms were regarded as extremely coarse.

Scholars such as the German Ernest Bornemann (1915–1995) took the trouble to make a comprehensive record of the "language of the gutter". It reads like a set of instructions for DIY enthusiasts: one gets nailed, drilled and screwed. Military jargon also offers (especially for men) a rich fund of sexually useful expressions as do the vocabularies of farming and butchery.

The verb "to have sex" is supposedly an invention of Mae West (1892–1980), who was famed for her direct way of talking. Since the beginning of the 1990s people have spoken equally directly about sexual matters in many of the talk shows on TV. The high sexual connotations of formerly "forbidden" or "dirty" words are weakened, as the old taboos disappear. At the beginning of the third millennium sexual concepts have hardly any provocative effect, even if they are not part of the active vocabulary of the majority. In this context it is, for young adults at least, only moderately arousing to announce that they are horny or that they feel like fucking. Solely in pornography is language still deliberately phrased in order to increase arousal – albeit in a way which comes across as extremely comical to everyone not in its thrall. In the feminist lexicon, sexual metaphors and imagery, which are indicative of (undoubtedly existent) aggressive tendencies in erotic desire, are increasingly scorned.

Johann Theodor and Johann Israel de Bry, *Alphabeta et Caracteres*, **1596. Copperplate engraving, 24 prints on paper, private collection.** It is generally supposed that the history of written language involves a form of evolution from picture-writing, through hieroglyphics and culminating in the development of the alphabet. There is something delightfully concrete, primitive and counter-cultural in retracing these steps, and fashioning letters into pictures. Nevertheless, the artists involved would often be working to a highly sophisticated code, in which the bodies not only had to represent the shape of each letter, but also had to be performing an activity that captured an imagined, symbolic quality of the letter (such symbolic schemes were often based on mystical traditions, including the Jewish Kabbalah).

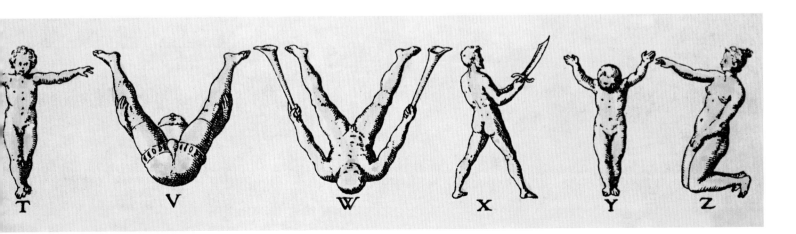

T   V   W   X   Y   Z

Telephone- and Cybersex

The human voice can be erotic, and the disembodied telephone voice even more so. However, it also depends, of course, on what the voice is saying. The fact that phone calls can be an erotic pleasure not just in bourgeois circles can be demonstrated by the phone calls between Prince Charles and his mistress Camilla Parker Bowles which became public after the line was tapped. "Dirty talk" is exciting when the horny words are whispered directly into someone's ear. Fantasy and technology surmount any distance. Erotic phone conversations can be held even between Canada and Capetown.

American author Nicholas Baker described exciting erotic chat in his novel *Vox*, 1992. The protagonists Abby and Jim find each other through a contact service, in order to set up, for mutual pleasure, an exchange of tele-erotic fantasies. In real life, however, the pleasure is mostly one-sided, because just as in the case of sex bought at close quarters, there are many female telephone sex operators who indifferently utter the sentences which paying listeners wish to hear. In Robert Altman's film *Short Cuts*, 1993, the character played by Jennifer Jason Leigh changes her baby's diaper while vocally carrying out a completely different role. After all, the caller is picturing a completely different scene. If horny action is requested, she moans down the telephone. If, on the other hand, she is supposed to be a small frightened girl showing terror at the sight of a huge penis (which the party at the other end of the phone pretends to have), the phone sex operator goes along with it and lets the customers hear what they want to hear. She helps to enliven dried-up images, which the callers still like to evoke. All the while a safe distance is kept. Those afraid of AIDS or other sexually transmitted diseases can breathe a sigh of relief: one cannot tele-erotically catch a virus.

Nevertheless, now and again there is a scandal, not on moral grounds but for financial reasons, if it becomes known that erotic conversations, which can be quite expensive, have been carried out from local authority or government offices. In the 1990s Italian taxpayers, particularly, became very incensed over this.

While in the 1990s the German courts were still divided over whether or not telephone sex was a service which must be paid for, another group of long-distance sex addicts were on the hunt for fully-virtual playmates. The internet facilitates any erotic exchange and typing replaces the spoken word. In cyberspace one can change sex and age and adopt new identities – a great chance for anyone who wants to escape from their everyday world. In virtual chat rooms one can fulfill all of one's desires. Here, a small number of insiders, who are familiar with the right codes, obtain virtual satisfaction.

If spelling things out is too abstract for some people, they can get interactive playmates on the VDU. Lara Croft is only one of many virtual sex icons who crowd the screen and influence the erotic imagination. Compared with them, everyday flesh-and-blood women seem increasingly boring and complicated. Suitably programmed, with behavior ranging from submissive to violent, they transmit to the real viewer the thrill of virtual power or – just as much in demand – powerlessness. At last there is a woman who, at the touch of a key, obeys her virtual "master".

Increasing employment mobility places new demands on partnerships. Many couples only rarely come within actual seeing and touching distance of each other. Some of those who are miles apart during the working week hope to use technological innovations to bridge the distance between them. Pictures and sounds are not the only effects that can be transmitted from far away. Touching, too, is nothing but electrical impulse. Couples will be able to do some tele-tactile cuddling – and even the already primed erogenous zones can be precisely targeted. At present, such stimulatory transmission is still dependent upon the use of expensive technology. However, this will certainly change in the near future.

Mike Masoni, Cyberoutfit. Cybersex technology is still relatively primitive, relying on a series of electronically-triggered inflatable devices – much like the cuffs used to measure blood pressure – to simulate the experience of being touched.

Mayumi Kubota, Virtual Woman. In cyberspace we will all be able to choose the form we take, as well as the means by which we can be stimulated.

Out of the Bedroom

The sexual life of the majority of people may take place in bed, but is the bed also the most favored erotic place? In a 1999 survey, a German tabloid newspaper found that three out of four Berliners have fantasies about a quickie in an elevator. Other common fantasies involve having sex in a bathtub or in a meadow.

For some people, the possibility of being discovered while making love heightens the thrill. Having sex in a public place is frequently experienced as breaking a taboo. Because they expect an increase in their lust for each other some couples even pounce on one another in churches or cemeteries.

Sex in public places, has, however, always also been a sign of penury. Prostitutes of the lower kind used to wait for a quick spot of trade on the riverbank under the arches of bridges. Others made off with their johns into dark passageways. In Venice the gondolas offered secret meeting places, and in 19th-century Paris there was the *bordel ambulant*, a special coach without any windows. It was used by prostitutes and their johns, but also for illicit liaisons. Vienna was famed for its coaches, whose drivers had coined their own expression for such trips: "porcelain fares", meaning slow, careful, totally aimless journeys through the town. With the comfortable sleeping cars of the great international railway lines – which were, however, not exactly cheap – the railway compartment became an important erotic venue.

Western sexual life entered a new dimension with the industrialized mass production of the

The hazards posed by rough, hard outdoor surfaces can modify the positions and the sexual techniques that are employed.

Albert Guillaume, *The Watchful Eye of the Law*, 19th cent. A policeman checks the licence of a Parisian whore plying her trade in a *bordel ambulant*.

automobile at the beginning of the 20th century. The range of options ranged from the German BMW Isetta "Lovebug" of the 1950s, to the small Italian cars which attracted attention by their violent rocking as immortalized by Federico Fellini in his film *Roma*, 1971, to the Russian taxis serving as a refuge to the Muscovites who had to produce their marriage certificates when wishing to hire a hotel room, to the oversized American limousine with the broad back seat, an important prop for American love life.

"Where there's a will there's a bush!" That German saying from the 1970s is probably still true

worldwide today. Those "other" places, for example the cornfield, the snow-covered park bench or the back row of the cinema, tend to remain in the memory. However, only those who could freely choose whether they wanted to gain their sexual experience at home or in unusual places will fondly recall such events. For those with no choice the special place that is the subject of their erotic dreams remains – the bed.

As a "locked space" the bathroom plays a big part in the sexual lives of many people in a modern urban setting. For children it is often the only place in the home where they can be alone and unobserved. And it is the only place where young men can quickly get rid of the traces of "self-abuse". Many prudish parents forbid locking the bathroom door. Anyone who spends too much time in the bathroom comes under suspicion.

For many the connection between excretion and sexual opportunity appears to hold good even past puberty. There is hardly a wall in a public restroom that is free from crude sexual drawings, offers from the chronically unsatisfied such as "Stallion seeks horny mare – I am here every evening at six o'clock," and from holes drilled in the dividing walls so that voyeurs can look into the neighboring cubicle. As public conveniences especially for sexual liasons, so-called "cottages", are seen as meeting points for extremely promiscuous homosexuals who seek anonymous sex. They were portrayed, for example, in Frank Ripploh's film *Taxi to the Cottage*, Germany, 1981. At the urinal they cast sidelong glances to check whether any neighbor might be interested. Cottages are usually well-known locally, if not notorious,

and there is little need for discretion. However, if two new acquaintances decide not to share a stall, but to disappear into neighboring cubicles, then it is most important that there should be a hole bored in the dividing wall which is bigger than one required by a voyeur.

Although nowadays outdoor sex is purely recreational, it was common until the 17th century in parts of Europe to encourage young lovers to copulate in the fields as a form of fertility spell.

Sex Shops

The Beate Uhse corporation and Ann Summers Ltd are two companies in the same business, with the same goals – to liberate and encourage the sexuality of both men and women. Although operating in different areas of Europe both pursue a similar strategy of moving away from the seedy back-street image of the sex shop and making it an acceptable part of the high street.

Beate Uhse, founder of the Beate Uhse corporation, Germany, began her mail order business back in 1948, supplying informative literature about sex and contraception, at a time when the country was still recovering from the Second World War. The mail order business grew and grew, and by 1952 there were more than 50 products on offer in the catalogue, including not only informative writings but also erotic literature. Ten years later, in 1962, the first sex shop in the Beate Uhse empire was opened. In 2000, there were over 52 Beate Uhse stores and 40 chain outlets distributed throughout central Europe, in addition to the booming mail order business and the company-owned film production unit.

Ann Summers Ltd. is a relative newcomer on the scene. The original Ann Summers store in Bristol, England, was acquired by the Gold Group International in 1972. Since then the company has expanded greatly, now encompassing over 30 stores throughout England, Scotland, Wales and Ireland (and also one in Sydney, Australia), as well as an extensive mail order business and the highly successful party plan network, which allows women to choose from the wide range of Ann Summers products – including everything from lingerie to erotic literature and sex toys – in a relaxed party atmosphere among friends.

Beate Uhse has achieved household-name status in Germany, which Ann Summers also enjoys in the United Kingdom and Ireland. This is due, in no uncertain terms, to the strong personalities of the women who run the companies.

Beate Uhse with stock certificate. Beate Uhse entered the stock market in 1999.

Exhibitions of Lust

Contemporary exhibits of the Erotic Museum, Berlin. The Erotic Museum in Berlin was opened in 1996 by Beate Uhse in commemoration of the firm's forthcoming 50th anniversary.

Even in previous centuries private individuals and rulers such as Duke Philippe IV of Orléans, the czarinas Elizabeth Petrovna, Catharine the Great, the czars Nicholas I, Alexander II and Alexander III collected erotica for their personal enjoyment. The collection of erotic rarities of Napoleon's step- daughter Hortense, Queen of Holland from 1806 to 1810, was unique in so far as she had all the scenes from de Sade's *Justine et Juliette* formed in wax. There is also the large collection of erotic art owned by the Vatican, which is not open to the public. Many of the early popes were enthusiastic collectors of erotica and pornography. However, when the museum, in the middle of the 18th century, began to turn into a center for communal instruction, the exhibition of erotic items was assiduously left out. Items relating to "sexual offences" and "decadent lifestyles" were not to be shown.

At the beginning of the 21st century, however, there are museums specializing in erotica in the majority of European capitals, for instance in Copenhagen, Amsterdam, Paris and Berlin. The various "exhibitions of lust" emphasize very different aspects. Some museums concern themselves with "everyday culture" (i.e. pornography); the others give themselves artistic airs, such as the Erotic Art Museum in Hamburg, founded in 1992. The Copenhagen Erotic Museum, also launched in 1992, has already moved from the seedy area near the train station where it was originally housed, to the pedestrian zone. The Tourist Information Bureau promotes the new attraction in the same way as it does the Little Mermaid, for erotic exhibitions are always well attended; today's open-minded international public is far from being embarrassed about its preferences. Some "museums" attract customers with the promise to provide insights into culturally interesting aspects of erotic everyday life, although it is a promise they often fail to keep. For example, in the middle of the red-light district of Amsterdam, where one can see real women sitting practically nude in windows, a few guilders will buy entry into an old house where visitors can see a dummy from a window display, dressed as a prostitute waiting for customers. The educational value to the visitor is limited to learning where in Amsterdam it is possible to purchase tools of particular interest to S&M enthusiasts. Two decades after the sexual revolution, by the end of the 1980s, sex found its way into regular museums, especially in Northern Europe. Monuments are erected and museums are opened to memorialize something which today is no longer restricted to dwindling enclaves. Therefore, exhibitions of erotica could also serve as an indicator of the gradual decline in fascination with sexual matters.

The Gay Museum in Berlin

For over a hundred years Berlin has been considered an "Eldorado" for homosexuals. It was there, in 1985, that the first and until now only museum in the world catering for this sexual minority was founded. The Gay Museum, cramped for space as it is, is much more than just an exhibition site for changing photographs and drag gear depicting homosexual life. In 1987, in the course of Berlin's 750th anniversary, an exhibition about "750 gay Berliners" was shown. The year 1995 brought the exhibition "Queens – Queers – Bull Dykes" with a whole century of transvestism in films. The heavily attended exhibition shown in 1997, "100 Years of the Gay Movement", had to take place in the Berlin Academy of Arts, because there was no longer enough space in the museum. The organizers see the Gay Museum as a social museum, an institution for exploration and (self) portrayal of homosexual life in all its manifestations. It is supported through voluntary work and patrons. The museum contains a comprehensive archive, where personal effects donated by gays and material relating to the history of the Gay Movement, are hoarded. A leaflet proclaims, "We collect everything!" Posters, films, sound recordings, newspaper articles and documents from the gay subculture are as welcome as donations. Lectures and film shows are on offer to a specialist audience.

Golden phallus in the entrance hall of the Museum Erotica, Copenhagen. Unlike many museums of art where phallic representations are hidden away, the museum in Copenhagen chooses to use this phallic symbol as its logo.

Pinups

Even before the Second World War there was widespread circulation within the US of pictures of nice, young – never exotic – "girls" with beautiful long legs, so called "cheesecakes", which could be looked at in "girlie magazines". The desire for such pictures reached new heights during the war, when there were no women for the soldiers to make contact with.

Unlike erotic postcards, the pictures, which were popular in the USA and also in Europe in the 1950s and 1960s, could not be hidden in a jacket pocket. They were of a large format and mainly adorned the lockers of workers and soldiers. They were supposed to have a motivating effect in reminding young men of what they stood to lose if they did not prove themselves efficient enough at work or war.

Because of this, the classic pinup girl is not an unattainable dream woman. On the contrary, it is the idealized and pepped-up girl next door. In the 1950s the iconography changed: half-shut eyes and a half-opened mouth were supposed to signal erotic willingness.

Any pinup aficionado has a relationship with the picture: its subject could be his lover who tempts him and waits for him. The drawing or photo shows and at the same time generates a moment of expectation. She belongs completely to him; or rather, she "would" belong completely to him, if he could only spare the time for her right now.

Polygamous dreams are also made real with the help of pinups, because the picture can always be changed for another. Or it is part of

Summer fashion, London, 1997. The designer Gianni Versace probably did as much as anyone to invent the concept of the supermodel when, in the 1980s, he invited four of the most expensive catwalk clothes-horses in the world – Naomi Campbell, Cindy Crawford, Linda Evangelista and Christy Turlington – to appear together in one of his shows. Since then, the term has become ubiquitous – randomly applied to any woman who appears on a top magazine cover – and so-called supermodels have taken over from film stars as the icons of glamor in the 20th and 21st centuries.

Robert Doisneau, *Dreams of a Tattooed Man*, 1952. The photographer Doisneau used to wander the streets of Paris, searching for those on the fringes of society. He intended this picture of a docker, lying on his bed and daydreaming about his pinups, as a parody on conventional masculinity.

a whole harem. When contemplating it, the owner is alone with the subject of the picture; no other person, in particular no man, blocks his field of vision. The picture is intended to stimulate, to have a "tingling" effect, but not to such an extent that the voyeur would have to seek relief right away. As opposed to the nude study, erotic pictures and pinups preferably depict a state of half-undress. It always appears as if the subject is going to show more. While pornographic pictures show everything in crude clarity, the erotic picture, like the strip show, fires the viewer's imagination and provides it with more scope. If only the girl would turn around a little more, then…

The pinups of the virtual age are, as before, snapshots of women dressed in skimpy costumes. However, in modern times they often move about in a house especially rented for the purpose which is rigged up with cameras that transmit streams of pictures via the internet. Around 15,000 men are supposedly in perpetual pursuit of the changing poses of various young women in the hope of seeing more than they are being offered. As unobserved voyeurs, they watch these "girls next door" go about their virtual daily business.

Moments to Regret

It seems that scarcely a year goes by without some celebrity being confronted by embarrassing videotape, or photographs, from his or her impoverished, anonymous past, or indiscreet present. A pirated home video of Pamela Anderson having sex with her husband became, in the late 1990s, the most popular piece of download material on the internet. Madonna appeared in a soft porn thriller before she became famous and Gerri Halliwell posed for tabloid newspaper style topless pictures before she joined the Spice Girls, but this is not a new phenomenon; in the early 20th century, Hollywood stars such as Hedy Lamarr and Joan Crawford both appeared in films that they later tried to suppress for the sake of their careers. Crawford's case was the most potentially damaging, because she did not appear in some vaguely erotic soft-core venture, but having unsimulated sex in a full-blown stag film.

Some stars turn to the law to protect their image, others try to buy up negatives and copies. In the modern age, perhaps the most sensible laugh it off and accept the free publicity. The public appetite for seeing their favorite stars in compromising situations is such that there are magazines and websites devoted to nothing else. In the age of computer trickery, many of the supposed exposés are faked, with celebrities' heads being superimposed onto models' bodies.

Playmate Marilyn Monroe, 1950. Marilyn Monroe posed for this photo in 1948, but it was published as the first ever *Playboy* centerfold in 1953, when it could potentially have damaged the career of an actress who had already starred in *Niagara* and *Gentlemen Prefer Blondes*. In the event, it only increased her popularity.

Striptease

In the late 19th and early 20th centuries one could go to see a show where women dressed in flesh-colored leotards danced behind transparent veils, giving at least the appearance of nakedness. Although this type of dancing was erotic, the excitement it caused observers was different from the excitement created by the slow, artistic unveiling of a beautiful body. Striptease had many origins. The French cancan and the burlesques in American red-light districts were responsible in equal measure for linking erotic dance with a ritual unveiling of the body. The movements and poses of striptease were borrowed from Arabian belly dancing. Without the thumping hip movements and the pelvic thrusts (the "bump" and "grind") and a huge number of other prerequisites, the simple removal of clothing is not striptease (in the narrow sense). Without stylization, public "undressing" remains artless and awkward.

For some this enactment is a ritual to be followed with rapt attention. To others it appears as kitsch. This difference of opinion is perhaps due to the fact that the stripper undresses herself in a suggestive way and produces, through alienation, a scenario with erotic elements. All those who do not become erotically involved with the performance therefore find such displays mostly embarrassing and tasteless. At any rate, this kind of erotic show rarely produces an indifferent response.

"Nudity for the sake of nudity" or *Le nu pour le nu*, was before long regarded as too simple. As

Scenery for a connoisseurs' theater, 18th cent. Before the 20th century, sex shows tended to be privately organized affairs, whether in amateur theaters, gentlemen's clubs or even at the court. Commercial theater was subject to rigorous censorship and control.

a result the strip was embedded in a fake erotic plot that enabled members of the audience to identify with the imaginary partner to whom the woman (sometimes apparently against her will) succumbed. In the final "scene" the stripper enacts a sexual encounter.

From the beginning, striptease gained an especially wide following in the United States, perhaps due in part to puritanical attitudes which attempted to suppress it. According to American historians the striptease developed between 1820 and 1860, when the settlers were moving West. Officially the first striptease show is supposed to have taken place in New Orleans in June 1861. Since the beginning of the 20th century the Columbia Theater on Broadway in New York, in particular, has dis-

Banana dance, c. 1925. Josephine Baker (1906–1975), who was born in Missouri, caused an international sensation when she went to Paris and introduced her *danse sauvage* at the Théatre de Champs-Elysées in 1925. She went on to be the star of the Folies Bergère, where she danced semi-naked in a skirt of bananas. A hero of the Resistance during the Second World War, Baker was awarded the Croix de Guerre and the Légion d'Honneur by the French government.

Burlesque

The burlesque was a review show that featured slapstick, songs, comic routines and lots of female flesh, exposed during chorus numbers and solo dances. Although it was a great American tradition, burlesque was introduced to the United States in 1868 by a group of English chorus girls called Lydia Thompson's British Blondes. By the early 20th century there were two major national circuits, as well as permanent shows in some major cities, the most famous being at Minsky's in New York. Nevertheless, burlesque was never considered respectable, and police raids were a common occurrence. Florenz Ziegfield modified the burlesque show and took it upmarket to create his Ziegfield Follies in 1907, which became the model for all subsequent glamorous review shows.

tinguished itself with striptease performances. During the Second World War part of the morale-boosting program for the troops included the provision of strip-shows. It was only after the Second World War that the American term "striptease" took root in Europe too.

In order for a stripper to be good at her craft, she has to have a vast wardrobe. The more single items and props there are for her to discard, the more she will capture the attention of the audience. Objects traditionally loved by fetishists – fishnet stockings and high-heeled shoes for example, kept on until the end, are the stripper's props. However, famous strippers turn everyday articles, such as ropes, into fetishes.

Although in the past a few inches of skin – the nipples and especially the genitals – had to remain concealed by a cache-sex or a G-string, it has already been quite some time since, at many venues, the last veil has been allowed to fall. Moralists are not the only ones to find this a source of regret. When someone recalls his first erotic memory of a stripper whose nipples were hidden behind tassels and who knew how to set those "pom-poms" artfully into circular motion, he will probably find full exposure somewhat disappointing.

Georgia Southern was well known for offering her audiences not only intoxicating movements, but also stimulating screams of lust. It was this extension of the performance into acoustic stimulation that again and again attracted the moralizers. After all, a sexual act should not be presented in too obvious a way.

In 1960 specialists in erotic pantomime were so much in demand that not only did a "striptease university" spring up in Los Angeles, but Europe was also scoured for women showing talent. In the Viennese "Lido im Maxim", a school for strippers was opened in 1962 which aimed at training women who wanted to perform in the USA.

Nevertheless, the end of striptease was predicted over and over again. In the 1960s *Variety* magazine announced that striptease was on its last legs. No more could be shown without

those involved risking arrest. However, less could not be shown either, or the audience would get bored.

The transition from striptease to live sex shows is fluid. The undressing may escalate to the point where the dancer masturbates on stage with a vibrator. In the 1960s and 1970s in particular strippers were considered very narcissistic and possessed by exhibitionist tendencies. Rumor had it that many were not just simulating the scenes of masturbatory orgasm.

Now that women have learned to see themselves as erotic beings, they also enjoy the voyeuristic pleasure of being part of the audience. Chippendale dancers and other male strip troupes perform in front of delighted female audiences worldwide. Peter Cattaneo's film *The Full Monty*, 1997, deals with completely normal men being given the opportunity to attract attention by taking their clothes off. The result here, though, is comical rather than erotic.

Despite all the flesh on show, strippers and their modern-day equivalents, lap and table dancers, are all agreed that the secret of a good performance is maintaining the illusion of eye contact. This inevitably also results in the biggest tips from satisfied punters.

Peep Shows

The first modern peep shows were established in a place where, to this day, prostitution is officially prohibited: in the United States. The distributors of pornographic films quickly realized that their clients might prefer private booths to public or semi-public cinemas, so that they could masturbate unselfconsciously. As a spin-off from these intimate screening rooms, the proprietors of sex shops began to provide small booths with built-in, shuttered windows, which for a small fee would open onto a real, live striptease or sex show. At regular intervals the shutter threatens to block the view, and will only rise again on the payment of a few more coins. The profit for the sex shop lies in the fact that hardly anyone requires only one look for lasting arousal.

In the solo-cabin there is an effect of apparent closeness since the man can not only see the woman, but he can also talk to her, usually by telephone or through a slit in the viewing wall. Arousing visions are supplemented by exciting conversation. Some use this to make "dates" for after closing time. However some of the women are not interested in closer and better-paid contact. They work there precisely because they don't want to get involved in prostitution. In Germany and other Western European countries in the 1980s – and in Eastern European countries such as the Czech Republic more than a decade later – women could earn several times more working in a peepshow than they could expect from more "respectable" menial labor.

Sex shows come cheaper to voyeurs on a group basis. If the woman lasciviously stretches and dances in the center for a whole group, each one only now and then gets the glimpses which he lusts after. Nevertheless a visit to a peep show takes only a matter of a few minutes. The men remove as little clothing as if they were going to a urinal and touch themselves as routinely as if they were passing water. Around a third of the visitors are regulars.

The peep shows first established in Europe in 1976 have been banned as "immoral" since 1982 when German judges pronounced that the single cubicles encouraged "the possibility of masturbation and its exploitation". In Germany there were then already 50 "wankotheques". The courts made the decision based on female dignity. It was regarded as an affront to a woman's dignity if, behind a pane of glass, she was to be used as an incitement to masturbation. However, for her to be "personally" used by johns was not. Visual sex has since been given a boost because of the fear of AIDS.

Some visitors find it relaxing to let their sperm drain out in a peep show. This method puts no strain on their imagination. What they otherwise have to make an effort to try to imagine lies there – prostrate – before them and yet remains as inaccessible as a picture in their minds. Grown men who are accustomed to having sex in the dark may gain some enlightenment here.

Elisabeth B., a German sociologist who in 1982 danced in New York peep shows and secretly photographed the visitors, emphasizes that many men could not get enough of looking at the orifices of the female body. For the visitors, being shown the orifices was more effective and more interesting than any sophisticated costume or seductive gesture.

Many customers enjoy imagining (as one "reviewer" asserts in the *Austria Sex Guide*) that they could have any one of the girls they wanted. The man is in control at the coin slot. As soon as he has had enough he can let the curtain fall and go. No one will want anything else of him. The men in their cubicles are safe. They can be quite sure that no one will barge into their cubicle or remonstrate with them. However, they have to pay up. Those who are especially thrifty start masturbating before they catch the first glimpse of the woman undressing herself.

Those who do not patronize peep shows claim that the customers are men who "have something lacking". The women in the shows, however, know better: the customers are completely average men – just like other johns. But unlike the latter, peep-show patrons can respond to the suspicious interrogation of their wives and girlfriends with an honest assertion that they haven't touched another woman.

The Raree-show, 18th cent. Copperplate engraving. The peep show is not a modern invention. The *raree-show* mentioned in the title was a kind of traveling museum, which offered customers a glimpse of badly reproduced copies of famous works of art. Some entrepreneurial spirits, however, recognized how much more profit they could make by exhibiting real women, instead.

Opposite: The single most common complaint made by women who work in peep-shows is the boredom of waiting around for their customers to appear, which is alleviated only slightly by the chore of having to perform for them. Some respond to this situation with a listless performance, while others put on an extravagant show, as much for their own amusement as anyone else's.

Pornography and Erotica

Aristophanes of Byzantium acquainted the ancient Greeks with pornographic representations such as the 135 biographies of whores. Like group sex, they recommended this literature as a cure for impotence. In the Christian West descriptions that were capable of arousing the reader were regarded as indecent and harmful to the well-being of the soul. Nonetheless erotica have been created and circulated down through the centuries. The more strongly sexuality which is not aimed at reproduction is considered taboo, the more readily erotic literature or art is regarded as pornographic. Thus even literary works were "edited for young readers", i.e. purged of erotic elements and those "dirty parts" which young people – and others not so young – gravitated towards. If those elements were not merely incidental, but rather the subject matter of the book, the work in question would be banned.

As long as sexually arousing pictures and texts were prohibited on moral grounds, an approval of pornography could be equated with the battle against censorship. British sex guru Alex Comfort maintained in 1972 that pornography was a term for any kind of sex literature that someone would want to ban. In his opinion the majority of normal people get pleasure out of looking at sex books and reading sex stories, therefore abnormal people have to spend much time and money on banning them.

In the second half of the 20th century the censorship debate shifted to the subject of violence. There were ever more frequent altercations between those who described pornography as a safety valve and those for whom pornography was, so to speak, a behavioral element, because it influenced the dealings the sexes had with each other.

Pornography has a polarizing effect; and yet strange coalitions form with people whose political convictions on all other matters would be radically different. Religious fundamentalists, feminists and communists find common ground in the fight against pornography. The stance taken by the former Austrian Federal Chancellor Bruno Kreisky (1911–1990) was a rarity: "I am not all that horrified about a bit of

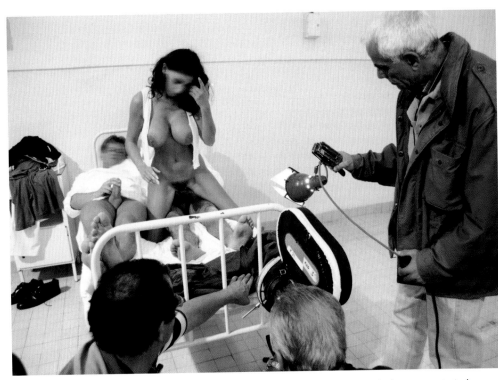

Shooting of a porn film, France, 1996. Ever since the earliest stag films, pornography has concentrated on intrusive angles and close-up shots, revealing more of the genitals than the participants themselves would be able to see. The authenticity of the sex on view is guaranteed by several conventions, the most prevalent being the "money-" or cum-shot.

pornography, because to me pornography is more agreeable than murder and such things. When all's said and done, pornography serves life and the others serve death."

To be sure, he was referring to soft porn and not to the so-called snuff movies. What is shown can – depending on the viewer's taste – have either an aesthetically appealing or a sterile effect.

Pictures and printed material which do not place sexual behavior within a social context, are regarded as pornographic. The protagonists have no personalities, no private history. They are nothing more than smoothly functioning sexual bodies. However, the so-called p-value is dependent on context. In an experiment, subjects were shown the same film scene, but the first time were told the scene depicted was a meeting between strangers, while the second time they were told it was a marital act. The effects on the viewers were completely different. Only the unknown and the unforeseen are exciting, even if the ending in a porn movie is totally predictable. Legal sex offers little in the

way of thrills, even if it is otherwise no different from sex between strangers.

When the legalization of soft porn came up for debate in West Germany around 1970, enthusiasts argued that a preoccupation with arousing pictures was an outlet for sexual urges and therefore contributed to the prevention of sexual offences. Although it is not certain whether there is a connection between pornography and sex crime, the anti-pornography camp returns again and again to the suggestibility factor: what the pictures show is what the viewers themselves would like to put into practice. Anyone spending too much time with pornography of a violent nature would be more inclined to regard women and children as mere sex objects. "Pornography is the obviously humiliating portrayal of women and girls, whether played down or glorified, in pictures and/or in text," was the message in the PorNO text of the German feminist Alice Schwarzer. Many feminists considered pornography a direct incitement to violence against women. "Pornography is the theory, rape the practice," asserts the American feminist Andrea Dworkin. She also points out that the porn industry has a higher turnover than the profitable music and film markets put together. Women have not always spoken out so decisively against pornography. However it is conspicuous that the producers as well as the consumers of pornography are overwhelmingly men. Alfred Kinsey discovered that most texts allegedly composed by women about their own love lives came from male authors. And the description of the sexual greed of women might be just a bit of wishful thinking on their part. At the beginning of the third millennium, however, the story is being put out once again that women are gagging for it: private TV stations give a lot of airtime to porn actresses who compellingly promote their profession and sing its praises. Millions of men are only too willing to hear it confirmed that there really are naturally lecherous women who want to do nothing but have sex. Clever porn stars market themselves accordingly. Annabel Chong, who set a "world gangbang record" in 1995 by having sex with 251 men, claimed to have done it for the pleasure rather than for the camera.

Pornography appears to have its own set of conventions, which are repeated endlessly, reducing everything to the level of the basic, the artless and the banal. However, fashions change in porn, just as anywhere else. A late-20th-century trend was for the so-called "gonzo" film, made on cheap equipment and often shot from the point of view of the male performer, who is also the filmmaker. In contemporary porn movies people appear in full view only when a whole group are engaged in a bang. An old porn movie from the early days of the film industry, screened in the plush second auditorium of the Copenhagen Erotic Museum, reveals how times have changed. There is less concern with physical perfection – the man is 50, and pot-bellied – and the scene is filmed almost like a theater auditorium, with a still camera taking in the whole of the action. And, because there is only one, live, take, the characters appear more human with all their fumblings and failings exposed to the world.

Men's Magazines

Until the 1990s, anyone who purchased a women's magazine expected to read articles about child rearing, recipes for Christmas cookies, but not about sex. It was a different kettle of fish with "Men's Magazines" or "Gentlemen's Magazines". Anyone wanting to purchase *Playboy* looked for it within the "erotic" section. 14 different editions of the monthly periodical appear in 200 countries worldwide. There are men living in every corner of the globe who proudly carry the Bunny trademark around with them and secretly buy the glossy magazine.

However, *Playboy*'s main readership is based in the USA: nine million out of a total of 15 million *Playboy* consumers live there. The journal promises to provide information on all the issues of interest to men. However, there is never anything published in it about DIY and seldom anything about computer problems. Men who are "playboys" are interested in cars and "girls". They are not interested in women. For decades the nudes depicted have looked like clones of each other and have come across as cute rather than vampy.

These "girls" are "bunnies", after all. And these "bunnies" attract the men that pay the bucks. This fact draws criticism from feminists who regard the few pictures in the journal as pornographic and misogynistic. Although there is a high proportion of text, in the end it is the pictures that sell.

The negative effect of these highly-stylized pictures of the lavishly portrayed "Playmate of the Month" is that they make wives and girlfriends look less attractive. All normal everyday women compare badly with the magazine lovelies. Those were the findings of research carried out in 1983 at Arizona State University. This conclusion comes as no surprise. There are no pictures of men in heterosexual men's magazines, so the *Playboy* reader himself is beyond any comparison.

Since 1975 there has been the international women's magazine *Playgirl* running alongside the international men's publication. The female readership, however, does not seem to be so interested in naked men unless they are rich and famous. *Cosmopolitan* magazine has been experimenting with nude photos of men since the beginning of the 1970s, and at first it selected specimens who were not outstandingly good-looking. Even though that has changed in

the interim and women have long since claimed to have discovered men as sex objects, no comparable change can be detected in men's magazines: powerful women are not in demand. However, the circulation does go up if the women are pretty and famous. In particular, athletes such as the German figure skater Katarina Witt cause a stir when they display unclothed skin and muscles.

The women of the magazine *Penthouse* present themselves as rather more untamed than the stuffed toys of the rival journal. The "Pets of the Month" show the gentle reader their mounds of Venus, shorn to appear pre-pubescent, and permit deep insights into their cracks and crevices, while at the same time appearing to ogle the reader. Women of untamed and dominant demeanor are found only in cartoons. In *Penthouse*, as in *Playboy*, there is a preponderance of text and stale jokes which male buyers find more humorous than their female companions.

Bob Guccione first published *Penthouse* in 1965 in Great Britain, and four years later it could also be found in the US. From 1970, more and more pubic hair was displayed, but from the start of the 1980s less and less. It was by then permitted, at least in the US, to expose what the hair was concealing. The American magazine *Hustler* specializes in pictures that could also be of interest to a gynecologist.

Hugh Hefner, who founded the *Playboy* magazine in 1953, arrives at London Airport, June 1966. As he grew older, Hefner became more reluctant to leave the comfort of the *Playboy* mansion, which he filled with models from his magazine.

Erotic Film in Europe

The erotic imagination of the 20th century was defined in the beginning by movies and later through television. When moving pictures were first developed in 1895, it seemed an especially enticing idea to make visible things that were on an normally remained unseen. So, at first, erotic films were often made from the keyhole perspective: the viewers were secret voyeurs. The first period when pornographic films flourished was from 1904–1908, when the new medium was not yet subject to police observation. Most erotic films were produced in Buenos Aires, Argentina, and smuggled from there into Europe. There was a market for these films in France, Russia, and the Balkan states, in addition to Germany and England. However, only the wealthy had access to the films, usually within private circles.

At that time, a film needed to show neither naked bodies nor sexual acts in order to be erotic. After the Second World War however, films were classed as particularly titillating and erotic (or, from another point of view, indecent and pornographic) whenever naked skin was on display. At the Prague première in 1934 of Gustav Machatys's film *Extase* or *Symphony of Love* there was a scandal when a nude female

Brigitte Bardot. Born Camille Javal, Brigitte Bardot was a model-turned-actress who was catapulted to fame as the archetypal European sex-kitten after appearing in her husband, Roger Vadim's film, *And God Created Woman*.

swimmer was briefly to be seen. Pope Pius XI immediately put his veto on the performance. Shortly after the production, the female star Hedwig Kiesler (later Hedy Lamarr) married Fritz Mandel, a wealthy Austrian, and an admirer of her art. Out of jealousy Mandel

Extase, **still from the film by Gustav Machaty, 1932, Hedy Lamarr as Eva.** Although many people remember this famous shot of young Hedi Lamarr, it is often forgotten that the film also features a close-up of her face during orgasm, which caused just as much controversy.

attempted, without success, to buy up and destroy all the copies of the film.

It was also highly daring when the German actress Hildegard Knef was seen naked for a few seconds in the 1951 film *The Sinner*. The churches in Germany encouraged their flocks to demonstrate against the film. A slow acclimatization to on-screen nudity began only in the wake of the sexual revolution of the 1960s, after which nudity became the norm. Since the 1950s French and Italian directors have been to the fore in the production of erotic films. The European sex-symbol best known internationally during the 1950s and 1960s, Brigitte Bardot, also known as B.B., was presented by her husband, director Roger Vadim, as a precocious child-woman.

In the 1970s simple nude scenes were no longer enough to arouse rage or interest; sexual intercourse would have to be shown, i. e. "hard sex". On October 14, 1972 *Last Tango in Paris* had its première, with Marlon Brando and Maria Schneider in the leading roles. In the original version the two stars have no common language: he speaks English, she speaks French. However, the dialogue was unimportant. The film, by Italian director Bernardo Bertolucci,

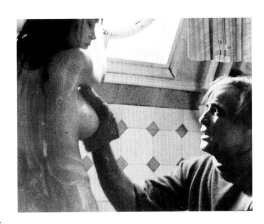

was banned in his own country on the grounds that the portrayal of anoymous sex had a pornographic effect. The sophisticated 1966 film *Belle de Jour* by Spanish director Luis Buñuel is also set in Paris. Catherine Deneuve plays a bored middle-class woman who eventually puts her masochistic fantasies into action when she goes to work in a brothel as a "Beauty of the Day".

Italian director Pier Paolo Pasolini, murdered by a male prostitute in 1975, devoted himself especially to the themes of sexuality and violence. He had filmed Boccacio's *Il Decamerone*, and his last film was de Sade's *120 Days of Sodom*.

*Top left: **Last Tango in Paris**, still from the film by Bernardo Bertolucci 1972, Marlon Brando as Paul and Maria Schneider as Jeanne.* This work about the growing obsession of an aging man for a young woman was hailed at the time as a crossover film that would make pornographic material acceptable in arthouse and mainstream cinema.

*Top right: **Belle de Jour**, still from the film by Luis Buñuel, 1967, Cathérine Deneuve as Séverine Serizy.* Cathérine Deneuve plays a bored housewife who takes a job in a brothel. In this, one of the many fantasy scenes from the film, she is tied up before being pelted with ordure.

Love as a Parlour Game, still from the film by Oswalt Kolle, 1972. In Germany, 50 million people saw Kolle's film in the 1970s (100 million worldwide).

Sex Education Films

In Germany, after the November Revolution of 1918–1919, film censorship was temporarily abandoned. During those years the first sex education films were made. The aim here was, however, not the promotion of an erotic culture, but the desire to warn of the dangers of sexuality (venereal disease and prostitution). However, since purely documentary films did not appeal to the public, the silent movies had to be moderately erotic. This strategy worked to fill the cinemas, but marketing interests and educational intent were basically incompatible. All that mattered to the viewers was that they could sit with their partners in the dark enjoying something exciting, and under those unusual circumstances they would feel inclined towards intimacy. Soon critics were predicting that the films would encourage exactly the kind of behavior they were supposed to warn against.

In the wake of the sexual revolution of the 1960s, sex education films were produced once again. The goal of informing the viewers was the same, but this time around it was not about the negative aspects of sexuality. Sex had, after all, in the meantime been defined as "socially valuable". Now it was all about the variations, positions and desires, which were supposed to guarantee marital bliss.

Just as before, it was alleged experts – mainly white-coated doctors, but also social scientists and lawyers – who described, evaluated and classified the sexual behavior displayed, for example, by schoolgirls, housewives or other groups. The sex scenes were so grotesquely overdone that a few decades later they had only comic appeal.

Sex in Hollywood

Hollywood never set out to portray the world as it is. Until 1966 what was shown was a fairy-tale world, which for the majority of consumers was – and was meant to be – the stuff of dreams: clean, healthy and optimistic. So anyone who did not like Hollywood films described them as kitschy and phony.

Only in the mid-1960s – when many American citizens had long been experimenting with partner swapping – did the pressure of competition from television force a loosening of the rigid rules. A few decades earlier there was conflict between business interests and the moral code of the ideological lobbyists, who put sex almost on the same level as crime. In 1934 more than eight million Americans followed the suggestion of the country's Catholic bishops, joined the Legion of Decency movement and signed a pledge to boycott "indecent" films. As in Europe, where in some places it was the responsibility of the village police to sanction a film after the initial showing, so it was in the USA: decisions about the offensiveness of

Lover Come Back, **still from the film by Delbert Mann, 1961, Rock Hudson as Jerry Webster and Doris Day as Carol Templeton.** Rock Hudson and Doris Day starred in a number of romantic comedies together, including *Pillow Talk* and *Send Me No Flowers*. They were portrayed as the perfect wholesome couple, despite Hudson's homosexuality, which was one of the most closely guarded secrets in Hollywood until his death from AIDS in 1985.

The Hays Code

Hollywood's first self-regulating code, 1927.
It is understood that those things included in the following list shall not appear in motion pictures irrespective of the manner in which they are treated:

1. Pointed profanity – this includes the words God, Lord, Jesus Christ (unless they be used reverently in connection with proper religious ceremonies), S.O.B., Gawd, and every other profane and vulgar expression.
2. Any licentious and suggestive nudity – in fact or in silhouette; and any lecherous or licentious notice thereof by other characters in the picture.
3. The illegal traffic in drugs.
4. Any inference of sexual perversion.
5. White slavery.
6. Miscegenation (sex relationship between the white and black races).
7. Sex hygiene and veneral diseases.
8. Scenes of actual childbirth – in fact or in silhouette.
9. Children's sex organs.
10. Ridicule of the clergy.
11. Willful offence to any nation, race, or creed.

It is also understood that special care be exercised in the manner in which the following subjects are treated, to the end that vulgarity and suggestiveness may be eleminated and that good taste may be emphasized:

1. The use of the Flag.
2. International relations (avoid picturing in an unfavorable light another country's religion, history, institutions, prominent people and citizenry).
3. Religion and religious ceremonies.
4. Arson.
5. The use of firearms.
6. Theft, robbery, safe-cracking and dynamiting trains, mines, buildings, et cetera (having in mind the effect which a too-detailed description of these may have upon the moron).
7. Brutality and possible gruesomeness.
8. Technique of committing murder by whatever method.
9. Methods of smuggling.
10. Third degree methods.
11. Actual hangings or electrocutions as legal punishments for crime.
12. Sympathy for criminals.
13. Attitude toward public characters and institutions.
14. Sedition.
15. Apparent cruelty to children and animals.
16. Branding of people or animals.
17. The sale of woman, or a woman selling her virtue.
18. Rape or attempted rape.
19. First night scenes.
20. Man and woman in bed together.
21. Deliberate seduction of girls.
22. The institution of marriage.
23. Surgical operations.
24. The use of drugs.
25. Titles or scenes having to do with law enforcement or law enforcement officers.
26. Excessive or lustful kissing, particularly when one character or the other is a "heavy".

The Seven Year Itch, still from the film by Billy Wilder, 1955, starring Marilyn Monroe. Monroe's sensuality was always unthreatening. The image she created – or that was created for her – was that of an innocent, spontaneous child of nature, always acting on a whim.

Russ Meyer

Russ Meyer (b. 1922) is one of those men who would answer the question "Do you suffer from sexual obsessions?" with "No, I enjoy them!" In his autobiographical film *The Breast of Russ Meyer* he demonstrated what fascinated him about actresses such as Kitten Natividad. Born in California in 1922, the sex-film producer who consistently ignored the outdated Hays Code is also a hate-figure to many feminists. Starting his career as a war correspondent, he later worked as a photographer for *Playboy* magazine; since 1959 he has been producing low-budget films. Later works (*Lorna*, 1964 or *Faster Pussycat...Kill! Kill!*, 1966) were notable for bizarre acts of violence, and for depicting the grotesque and exaggerated: he would never portray a radio talk show host without making a fool of them; defenders of law and order are, on principle, vain and stupid; all women have busts measuring from 111–132 cm (44–52 inches) and are not merely willing as in conventional sex films but violently rapacious. Interestingly, there are no wonderful studs in Russ Meyer's films. The men may be ready to accommodate the masterful desires of the female protagonists, but they are usually impotent, fixated or are, for example, only able to have anal intercourse. For a long time Russ Meyer's films, such as *Beneath the Valley of the Ultravixens*, 1979, have had cult status, and even intellectuals acknowledge the ironic dissociations that the "King of the Nudies" employs. Since 1971 there has been a collection of some of his works in the New York Museum of Modern Art.

Cherry, Harry and Raquel, still from the film by Russ Meyer, 1969, Uschi Digard as Soul. Vixen is a favorite word in Russ Meyer's vocabulary. It was the success of *Vixen!* in 1968 that led to the Fox Studio's offer to direct *Beyond the Valley of the Dolls*, 1970 and he returned to the theme in the 1970s in *Supervixens*, 1975 and *Beneath the Valley of the Ultravixens*.

films were made at local level. Therefore, in order to avoid falling foul of the local censor, producers practiced self-censorship. The duration of a kiss was measured out in seconds. Passion was not allowed on the screen. Marriage beds were not allowed to be shown in a rumpled condition. The censor could raise an objection the moment a married couple were both lying in their beds at the same time – even if the beds were separate. In "decent" films, moreover, nobody was allowed to swear. Above all, however, "perversion" – and that, of course, included homosexual behavior – was hushed up. Interracial love affairs were also classed as perversion. At the age of 42 William Hays (1879–1954) was president of the Motion Pictures Producers and Distributors of America Inc.; at 66 (in 1945) he became spokesman for the film industry. For decades the Presbyterian nice guy decided all questions of morality in films. The film produc-

tion code, which was obligatory from 1930 to 1966, got the name Hays Code, after him. The code concerned itself with "wholesome" entertainment for the entire family. Even before the happy ending the whole course of the film had to be slanted in such a way that no support whatsoever for nonconformity could squeeze through. Absolute conformity was the overriding rule.

It was this very code that led to the ambiguity of Hollywood films: naïve audiences only saw the "morally uplifting" fare, but the educated elite understood the subtle sexual allusions in dialogues and gestures. Instead of eroticism the directors fell back on erotic symbolism. The insinuating nature of the supposedly "clean" films was apparent, however, in distant lands. For a long time American films were not allowed to be shown in Red China on the grounds that they were only about eroticism – seen by the Chinese as a waste of time.

Scandinavia, a Sexual Wonderland?

Ever since 1944 homosexuals in Sweden have been free to "follow their inclinations" as it is put in Dr. Richard Wunderer's 1967 book *Hothouse of Eroticism*. Filmmakers such as Ingmar Bergman contributed to the sexually liberated image of Scandinavia through the international attention paid to their works, for example *The Silence*, 1963. The film became famous for a scene, in which a woman longing for a sexual relationship masturbated.

In the 1960s the Scandinavian vice laws were not concerned with prostitution and other "victimless crimes". But at the start of the 21st century Sweden makes headlines in the world press by passing legislation which looks anything but liberal: potential johns are open to prosecution if they try to make contact with a prostitute.

The positive image of Scandinavia can, however, also be traced back to the work of the Swedish psychiatrist and sex reformer Lars Ullerstam who referred to the legitimacy of sexual lust and portrayed "normal sexuality" no longer as sinful, but as "healthy" and "encouraging" for a marriage – a revolutionary attitude outside of Scandinavia in the 1960s. With his book *The Erotic Minorities*, 1965 Ullerstam wanted sadists, masochists, homosexuals, exhibitionists and other sexual minorities to be granted their right to happiness, health and unhindered erotic fulfillment – with government support. Deviating from the majority of his fellow-countrymen, the young psychiatrist gave no credence to the seduction theory. He therefore demanded that nobody should be prevented from seeking suitable partners through newspaper ads. Only the well-to-do could put into practice those inclinations that were not tolerated by society and thus ease the psychological tension between them and their environment. According to Ullerstam such opportunities should be available to everybody else, too. His trust in the Swedish social bureaucracy unbroken, he proposed the setting up of government mediation centers, supervised by medical experts, which could help "deviants" in finding the partner of their desire. He wanted a "treatment center for erotic minorities", where "deviants" were not to be forced to conform to the norm, but where they could find satisfaction. Article nine of his proposed sexual reforms ran, "Set up clubs where exhibitionists can strip in front of a selected audience!" Ullerstam also planned to provide personal caterers for those with disabilities, "erotic Samaritans", who would look after the sexual needs of the patients. The fact that his liberal and democratic ideas met with violent attacks by the press shows that there was by no means wholehearted approval of his plans even in his own country.

La Dolce Vita, **still from the film by Federico Fellini, 1959.** Anita Ekberg is the archetype of the Scandinavian sex-bomb, as much for her spontaneity and uninhibited sensuality as for her physique and blond hair.

Ellen Key (1849–1926)

Key's book *Love and Marriage*, translated into twelve languages, created a lot of hostility toward this Swedish author. Some of her ideas were perceived as revolutionary, others as conservative. Genuine love, according to Key, needed no institutional confirmation. Women criticized her unconditional idealization of motherhood; conservative men accused her of blasphemy because she encouraged civil weddings instead of ones blessed by the Church.

Swedish Eugenics

The tolerant, or even to some, utopian Swedish attitude to people with non-standard sexualities was not always extended to non-standard people in general. After coming under increasing pressure from within and without its borders, the Swedish government finally agreed, in April 2000, to launch a full investigation into a four-decade-long policy of enforced sterilization, under which more than 60,000 people who had been deemed "genetically inferior"

had been sterilized without their consent. The first involuntary sterilization law was passed in 1934. It initially applied to the mentally ill, but was soon being used against many who merely showed antisocial tendencies, or who had otherwise been classified as possessing congenital handicaps.

Men's camp in Egholm, Denmark. The popularity of the naturist movement in Denmark has, paradoxically, contributed to its image as a sexual utopia, even though its naturists themselves strongly play down the sexual connotations of nudity.

Iceland

Apart from syphilis, which came to Iceland only at the end of the 19th century with the Industrial Revolution, the inhabitants had been spared little in the course of their sexual history. The Lutheran Church forbade dancing and worldly festivities. Weddings were celebrated in great style by the upper classes, though servants had no right to marry. Thus it was almost impossible for lower-class women to become mothers in an honorable way. Many of them were executed, usually by drowning or being buried alive, for infanticide, concubinage or having babies by their brothers or fathers. It was even classed as "adultery" or "incest" when a widow married her single or widowed brother-in-law. Death sentences for vice-related offences were handed down until 1869. Nevertheless today in Iceland "immorality" has struck back with a vengeance. In 1998, 21.6 percent of all live births were illegitimate. Officially recognized partnerships between homosexuals have been possible since 1996. The Lutheran Church, to which 97 percent of the population belongs, is still split in its attitude to homosexual marriage. However, the first gay couple to get married received a church blessing.

But public evidence of sexuality and eroticism is still rare. Neither sex shops nor peep shows are to be seen in the towns and hamlets. Nonetheless in Reykjavik in August 1997, the world's first Museum of Mammal Penises was opened. Since the opening of the first strip clubs in 1995 this industry has been booming, and it is not just confined to the capital, Reykjavik. However, those involved behind the scenes of the strip clubs are met with suspicion. When some dancers for various reasons sought help from a women's refuge, a committee was formed involving the cooperation of three State Departments, which was to tackle the question of workers' rights for strippers. If the current laws prove insufficient, parliament will be involved. With regard to prostitution, the law prescribes that pimps are not allowed to make a profit and that the prostitute must not practice the trade as her or his main occupation.

The world's only penis museum in Reykjavik. The penis of the whale (on the right-hand wall at the back) is proportionally much smaller and shorter than the penis of human males, even when undried. The Penis Museum in Reykjavik is based on its founder's lifelong collection of mammal penises.

Russia – "We Have No Sex"

Saint Paraskiva Piatnitsa, Crucifixion scene **(detail from a Pskovian icon showing scenes from the saint's life), mid-16th cent. Museum of history, architecture and art, Pskov.** Russian icons are generally more ascetic than Western religious paintings. All attention of the painters is concentrated on the face and especially the eyes of the saint. Nude or semi-nude body images like in this scene showing the martyrdom of a female saint are extremely rare.

During one of the first live television chat-shows between the United States and the USSR in the early 1990s, answering a question about Soviet sexual life, one Leningrad woman said: "We have no sex." This phrase immediately became proverbial.

The historical and anthropological descriptions of Russian sexual culture have always revealed a wealth of conflicts. Medieval and early modern Russia was a patriarchal society, where women were brutally suppressed and oppressed both in social and domestic life.

Wife-beating was considered an expression and proof of conjugal love even by the women themselves. The gender inequality, aggravated by centuries of serfdom, is abundantly reflected in folklore and literature. At the same time, Russian culture has always had a "powerful woman syndrome". In Russian fairytales there are not only militant Amazons and faithful wives but also an unusual, by Western standards, image of a wise woman – known as Vasilissa Premudraya.

Equally contradictory were Russian attitudes to nudity and the rules of decency. In opposition to Western materialism, pragmatism and body-boundedness (*telesnost* – the idea that the self is largely defined by, and equated with, the body), the Russian national character and mentality were often represented as, predominantly, a realm of spirituality (*dukhovnost*). The ideal of disembodied spirituality, with the corresponding denigration of the body, is most clearly implemented in Russian Orthodox religious art. Whereas Western religious art from the late Middle Ages presents a view of the entire human body as living flesh, with only genitals covered, in Russian icons only the face is alive, while the body is fully covered or outlined in an emaciated, ascetic form. Orthodox icon painting, made according to the Byzantine canon, is much stricter and more ascetic than its Western counterpart, while secular nude painting appeared in Russia much later and under more stringent control than in the West. Whereas Italian painters were portraying the nude body in secular settings during the Renaissance, Russian artists only gained that right in the late 18th century. Even the extravagant Soviet prudery of the 20th century, with its bans and ideological campaigns against any kind of body display in art and everyday life, was historically rooted in this traditional religious mentality.

On the other hand, everyday life and popular culture and language have always been anything but modest and sexually prudish. Foreign observers in the 17–19th centuries expressed surprise and shock at the Russian custom of mixed bathing in bathhouses and rivers, although the sophisticated Giacomo Casanova, who

Geoffroy, after P. Iw., *Les Bains Russes*, 1845. **Engraving.** Russian mixed family baths were often used in Europe for hypocritical accusations of depravity. This engraving, taken from the russophobic book by Frederic Lacroix *Les Mystères de Russie*, 1845 had also been interpreted in this way. But it seems clear that there is nothing licentious in the scene, only peasants' naturalism.

visited a Russian mixed bathhouse in 1767, found it absolutely non-erotic. According to Casanova, this absence of shame was a result not of the licentiousness but of a "natural innocence".

The exaggerated opposition between body and soul is further projected into a perceived incompatibility between romantic love and carnal lust (sexuality). The widely-approved image of love in classical Russian literature is extremely inhibited, chaste, spiritualized and opposed to sexual, carnal pleasure. Russian 19th-century literature created a wonderful language of romantic and sentimental love, yet it also bore a strong imprint of what Sigmund Freud believed to be a fundamental contradiction of male, especially adolescent male, sexuality: it could not perceive a link between tender love and sensual attraction. Its moral emphasis was generally on self-control and restraint. Carnal passion, "love for sex" had to be sacrificed either to the spiritual "love for person" or to a serene marital "love for wedlock", especially in women. Alexander Pushkin's Tatjana (from *Eugene Onegin*) and Masha (from *Dubrovsky*) are typical examples.

In contrast, Russian folklore, language and everyday peasant culture has always been openly and crudely sexual. The famous rich-ness of Russian obscene language (*mat*) is a permanent object of national pride. The so-called erotic tales and proverbs describe naturalistically and in detail all kinds of sexual acts, as well as glorifying the sexual exploits of polygamous heroes, which include the possession of a sleeping beauty, "dishonoring" (i.e. raping) a young woman in revenge for her refusal to marry the hero, and so on.

These internal contradictions of Russian sexual culture can be explained historically. According to Russian historian Vassilii Klyuchevskii (1841–1911), the history of Russia is that of a country in the constant process of colonization, extension of borders, and conquest of new territories. The Christianizing of Russia, stretched over several centuries and all the while involving new territories and peoples, was slow and in many ways superficial. In popular belief, rites and customs, Christian norms not only coexisted with pagan norms, but also frequently incorporated them. A few phallic symbols are represented even in medieval Orthodox cathedrals.

The sexual behavior and mores of non-Russian ethnic groups were even more diversified. The Russian Empire was far too big and socially and culturally heterogeneous to be effectively controlled or "civilized" by administrative means. Because of this inability to exterminate the innumerable and immensely varied vestiges of paganism, the Russian Orthodox Church had either to incorporate certain practices or to turn a blind eye to them. Some pre-Christian lifestyles and attitudes to sexuality and the body continued to exist under the surface and on the periphery of official public life both in Czarist and Soviet Russia.

Regional and ethnic diversity was intensified by the enormous cultural gap between the educated and Westernized nobility and gentry on one side, and the illiterate and enslaved peasantry on the other. Serfdom, which was used also for sexual exploitation (gentry men could take any number of serf-mistresses), was abolished in Russia only in 1861.

The "civilizing process" in the 18th century, often called the "Europeanization" of Russia, featured the emergence of new forms of social control over sexuality and the body, and the introduction of new rules of propriety and "good manners", often originating in the Imperial court. Because of the all-embracing Russian absolutism, these new forms of socializing

Phallic Lion, relief around the center window in the west facade of Saint Demetrius' in Vladimir. Like in most other cultures, old Russian art contains some phallic images. The typical ancient Russian phallic symbol – an animal, usually the lion, with a long tail or sexual organ – is represented even in the ornamental church architecture.

and etiquette were not introduced merely as examples of more or less voluntary imitation, but as arbitrary and compulsory prescriptions. They came under close administrative supervision, and were enforced with the utmost contempt and disregard for individual preferences and tastes (famous examples include Peter the Great ordering the compulsory shaving of the boyars, and the obligatory Court assembly dances).

The individual's vulnerability to State interference was aggravated in local peasant communities, which were especially intolerant of any kind of non-conformity. An important psychological correlate of the imposed social control was a deep-rooted mass conviction that all aspects of personal and especially sexual life could and should be strictly regulated, and that everything was definitively either right or wrong (just as earlier it was either a sin or a virtue).

Russian Eros

The conflict between the naturalistic sexuality of the folk culture and the idealistic spirituality of "high" culture is reflected in the history of Russian erotic art. These two cultural poles formed different traditions that sometimes intersected with one another, but never coincided.

Traditional Russian folk ditties (*chastushki*), sung at community festivals, have been always sexually explicit and irreverent. Equally free and sexual have been primitive folk prints (*loubok*). Sometimes relatively decorous pictures were accompanied by less than decorous texts.

This tradition, combined with the influence of French "libertines", was continued in an outpouring of 18th-century underground obscene poetry, initiated by Ivan Barkov (1732–1768). This openly sexual and often anti-clerical poetry (later the best examples were published abroad) had important political meaning, as a challenge to government authorities and to the established religious order. But it was completely outside the mainstream of literary production and aesthetic criteria. Academic art of the early 19th century did portray some nude or semi-nude bodies (in the work of Karl Bryulov, Alexander Ivanov and especially Alexander

***Joseph and Potiphar's Wife**, 18th-century loubok.* This folk print depicts the Biblical image of the seduction of a young man by a married woman.

Venetsianov) but it could not yet be openly erotic. Censorship, imposed by both State and Church, was strict and all-embracing. Erotica were considered both corrupt and alien, and were attacked from both sides as having nothing to do with the Russian national heritage. While the conservative right censured eroticism for undermining religious and family values, the populists and social democrats could not fit it into their grand ideal of giving up all their energies and efforts to the liberation of the working classes. Any artist or writer who attempted to deal with sexual reality came under withering attack simultaneously from both right and left. This seriously hampered the emergence in Russia of the lofty, refined erotic art and the corresponding language and vocabulary which had emerged long ago in Western Europe, and without which Russian sexuality inevitably appeared base and sullied. The predominantly negative attitudes towards sexuality, the body and erotica began to change only in the last years of the 19th century and around the 1905 revolution, when "the sexual question" (*polovoi vopros*) became one of the most urgent issues in philosophy, education, politics and the arts. The nature of Eros, sex education, androgyny and homosexuality were intensively discussed. Yet the early-20th-century Russian philosophy of Eros was more metaphysical than phenomenological. Philosophers tried to rehabilitate an abstract concept of Eros, yet as soon as their deliberations turned to real

Lev Bakst, illustration for a Russian folk-tale, 1922. Male potency and penis size is glorified in some Russian folktales. For example, the hero of one folktale was given a fairy ring which could enlarge his penis until it reached his knees, but he had put the ring too deep on his finger, and his penis went up "seven miles in the sky".

bodily enjoyment, a barrier immediately arose. Poetry and the visual arts were much more expressive than philosophy, and Sergej Diaghilev's ballets in particular were real festivals of the human, especially male, body.

Like their European counterparts, Russian erotic artists at the beginning of the 20th century could be openly decadent. Their enchantment with unusual, strange and "perverted" sexualities was liberating but at the same time repulsive and shocking. It was not always easy to differentiate the arrogance of the experimental avant-garde art from the shamelessness of commercial erotica. To many prominent intellectuals, they formed a single and terrifying "sexual Bacchanalia".

Communist Sexophobia

The Communist regime, established in 1917, was strongly anti-sexual and repressive, despite the fact that Soviet legislation and policy on issues of marriage and procreation in the 1920s was progressive. Women were accorded equal rights with men. Church marriage was abolished and abortion was legalized. Yet the costs associated with the resulting breakdown in marriage and family patterns – unwanted pregnancies, fatherless children, the spread of prostitution and venereal disease – were enormous. As attempts to improve social conditions failed, the government turned to more and more restrictive social policies. The aim of adapting social conditions to the needs of individual human beings was gradually transformed into the task of adapting human behaviors, and even feelings, to the extant poor and inhuman social conditions. Social control took the place of individual freedom.

Ultimately, the regime had two alternative strategies with regard to sexuality: acceptance or suppression. The more liberal viewpoint, which had been formulated by the writer and diplomat Alexandra Kollontai (1872–1952), was always marginal. Lenin was adamantly against the theory of "free love": even when his own lover Inessa Armand advocated it, Lenin considered it "petty-bourgeois" or "anarchistic". The more rigid and dogmatic stance, taken

Boris Michailovich Kustodiev, *Russian Venus*, 1925–1926. Oil on canvas, 200 x 175 cm, State Museum of Art, Nizhny Novgorod. The woman depicted represents a traditional, classic type of Russian female beauty – big, plump, and with full breasts. Contemporary Russian beauty contests give prizes to the more slim and subtle bodytype. But the national ideal is still alive.

by Aron Zalkind, admitted the existence of a biological sexual drive in human beings and the harm of "sexual self-corking", but proposed a complete subordination of sexuality to the "class interests". Despite their extreme sociological vulgarity, these ideas were more appealing to the totalitarian mentality. The sole practical message of the Soviet state about sexuality was: don't do it!

Stalinist sexophobia was an important element in the general cultural counter-revolution of the early 1930s, aimed at liquidating social and cultural diversity and at establishing total con-

trol over the individual's personality, its most important steps being the recriminalization of homosexuality (1933), and bans on pornography (1935) and abortion (1936). In order to ensure absolute control over the personality, a totalitarian regime endeavored to destroy its independence and emotional world. The link between sexophobia and deindividualization was well recognized by Russian Soviet writers such as Mikhail Bulgakov, Yevgeny Zamyatin and Andrei Platonov in the 1920s and later, in the 1940s, by the British author George Orwell. Sexophobia also helped to confirm the fanatic

Aleksandr Aleksandrovich Deineka, *Lunch Hour in the Donbas*, 1935. Tretyakov Gallery, Moscow. Male nudity was under even stronger taboo in Stalinist times than the female nude. The only acceptable context for the naked male body was sport and physical exercises. Men had to be strong, masculine and always in motion.

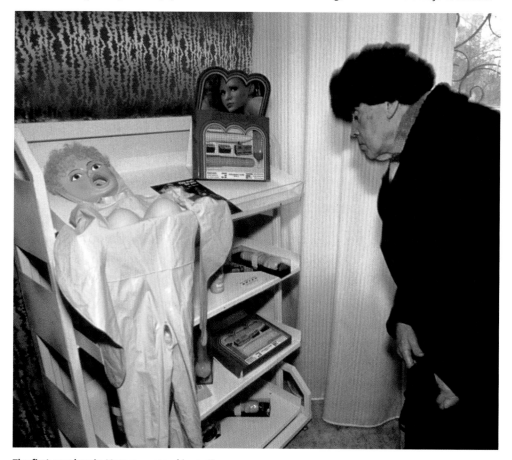

The first sex shop in Moscow, opened in 1998.

cult of the stern, moralistic father figure (i.e. Stalin) and performed some "applied" political functions; the party frequently used accusations of sexual perversion and decadence against its political opponents and dissidents.

The liquidation of sexual culture, including erotic art and sex research, produced not a "desexualization" of life but its impoverishment and vulgarization. Sexuality, driven underground and degraded to the level of a "sex instinct", became wilder and potentially aggressive. Enforced silence strengthened traditional hypocrisy, which, in turn, was easily transformed into cynicism. The forbidden erotica became a strong anti-Communist symbol.

The Second World War caused serious disorganization in marital and family relationships and gave rise to innumerable temporary liaisons and children born out of wedlock. After the legalization of abortion in 1955, the Soviet Union soon led the world in the number of terminated pregnancies. The penitentiary system also had an ongoing negative effect on sexual life. Not only were millions of people torn apart from their families and deprived of normal sexual lives for years, but they also had to put up with the terrible cruelty – including sexual abuse – of the camps. This certainly affected their subsequent sexuality.

After Stalin

Gradual liberalization and the transformation of the Soviet regime after Stalin's death from totalitarian to authoritarian altered its sexual policy from one of brutal suppression to one of awkward taming. Until the 1960s, sexuality was practically unmentionable; there was not a shred of public information available about it. Yet as soon as life became slightly freer, it became clear that the values and sexual conduct of Soviet youth were moving in the same direction as those of their counterparts in the West, featuring: earlier sexual maturation and awakening of erotic feelings among adolescents; earlier onset of sexual life; growing social and moral acceptance of premarital sexuality and cohabitation; weakening of the "double standard" of sexual conduct for men and women; enhanced significance of sexual satisfaction as a factor in making and sustaining a happy marriage; resexualization of women; an increase in public interest in the erotic; rising tolerance with regard to unusual, variant and deviant forms of sexuality, particularly homosexuality; and a growing gap between the generations in terms of sexual principles, values and behavior.

In the 1950s and 1960s a few progressive Soviet education experts, doctors and psychologists began to talk of the need for some sort of "sex education" for adolescents. Yet it was conceptualized primarily as moral education; no one dared to contemplate the idea of acquainting adolescents with the fundamentals of contraception, for example. The erotic art and literature that had been completely banned in Stalin's time began to reappear in the 1960s and 1970s. But it still was mainly underground; avant-garde art was ideologically unacceptable to the Communist Party, and any nude body was considered as pornographic.

Sexual Revolution and Counter-revolution

The collapse of the Soviet regime has brought the Russian people their long-awaited sexual liberation. But, as was also the case with the economy and politics, sexual freedom immediately transformed into anarchy and became an object of political struggle. Since 1987 sexuality has become visible: it is openly discussed and represented in mass media and advertising. A lot of erotic publications are available. People have become much more outspoken about sexual issues. A few voluntary associations for the promotion of sexual knowledge and safe sex practices, including a Russian Family Planning Association (RFPA), have been formed. Thanks to their efforts, the number of unwanted pregnancies and abortions has somewhat dropped in recent years. In 1990, 11.4 percent of women aged 15 to 49 had had abortions; in 1992 9.8 percent. By 1995 the figure had sunk to 7.4 percent. Nevertheless the Russian abortion rate at the beginning of the 21st century is still one of the highest in the world.

After long debate, homosexuality was decriminalized in 1993. Despite a high level of homo-

Male transvestites are very popular now in Russian show-business. This picture of three Russian drag queens in the Ptyuch Club in Moscow appeared on Gay.ru – Russian National Gay, Lesbian, Bisexual and Transsexual website. The Ptyuch club is famed for its transvestite shows.

phobia, same-sex love is no longer a taboo topic, and public tolerance is growing, especially among younger, better-educated and urban people. Gay men, lesbians and transsexuals have their own organizations and are represented on the internet.

Yet the liberalization of sexual morality has a lot of negative consequences. The average age of adolescent sexual initiation has dropped considerably since 1993, and this trend has corresponded to an increase in all forms of sexually transmitted diseases, especially syphilis, which have reached dangerous levels. The country is on the verge of an AIDS epidemic. Prostitution, especially child prostitution, is growing, as well as sexual violence and rape. Many young Russian girls are recruited and sold to Western bordellos. Mass culture is completely commercialized and Americanized, and the new Russian porn industry – which is barely regulated – is booming as Western distribution companies find it cheaper to commission their products from former Eastern Bloc countries than to hire technical crews and performers in the West. All kinds of legal and illegal "sexual services" are openly advertised in mass media.

All this is very frustrating for parents, teachers and intellectuals, and provides ammunition for political campaigners. In early 1997 the Communists and Russian Orthodox Church jointly initiated a new crusade against sexual culture, including women's reproductive rights, sexual and erotic materials and sex education. They say that sex education, birth control, abortion, masturbation and homosexuality are exclusively Western, non-Orthodox, anti-Russian subversive phenomena, and are deliberately imported for the final demolition of Russian national culture and the physical extermination of the whole nation. Antiponography slogans are used against freedom of the press and artistic expression.

In the long run, this crusade is doomed. Current sexual attitudes and practices in Russia are highly diversified according to age, gender, education and regional, ethnic and social background. Any attempt by the State, Church or local community to forcibly limit sexual freedom is set to fail, and will undermine the authority of the institutions making such attempts. In the meantime, the politicization of sexuality is highly detrimental to public health and education.

The Art and Science of Sex

India and the Himalayas

Lady with her maidservants waiting for her lover.
Lakhnau, late 18th cent. The *Kamasutra* is anything
but an Indian sex manual. Only one of the seven
parts is concerned with the techniques of physical
love. The rest is a systematic textbook whose intention is to define the relationship between man and
woman in its whole spectrum, from courtship to
equipping the kitchen. In this way, educated town-
dwellers were to be given the opportunity of attaining love as one of the three Hindu goals in life
(alongside making money, and religious duties).

Conflict and Fusion

The Indian subcontinent is home to more conflicting ideas about sex than any other place on earth. Sensualists, taboo-breakers, otherworldly ascetics, traditional joint families (several generations living in the same house and pooling their resources), Western-style nuclear families and promiscuous, guru-like visionaries who view sex as a road to spiritual power can all be found, often living shoulder to shoulder.

This diversity stems not only from the wide range of indigenous faiths, but also from the way in which they have grown out of and influenced each other. Archaeological finds in Harappaa, Pakistan and elsewhere suggest that the roots of all Indian spirituality lie in a pre-Hindu, Indus-valley civilization that worshipped a mother goddess and the power of the phallus. It is likely that early Hindus disapproved of phallic worship, but that the practice was adopted and revived by a wave of Aryan invaders, thought to be the ancestors of the modern Brahman, or priestly, caste of Hindus. The scriptures known as the *Rig Veda* suggest that, by 2000 B.C., Vedic Hinduism regarded monogamy as the only acceptable form of marriage, although some interpretations suggest that several brothers could marry the same woman (a practice still existing among some peoples such as the Nepalese Nyinba today), or at least that a younger brother may have had some sexual rights in connection with an elder brother's wife. However, women were generally allowed to choose their own husbands, and were free to experiment sexually until they made their choice.

The situation of women gradually became less enviable until, according to various documents including the *Atharvaveda* scriptures of about 1000 B.C., men were allowed to have several wives, whom they might offer to guests in a gesture of hospitality, and widows were expected to either remarry immediately or throw themselves on their husband's funeral pyre because widowhood was considered an impure, outcast status. The practice of self-immolation, known as *sati*, continued into the 20th century, long after the British colonial government officially banned it. Widows sometimes threw themselves onto the pyre voluntarily, either in genuine grief, or because they could not bear the outcaste status, but there are many accounts of women being forced into the flames against their will.

Around 500 B.C., religions such as Buddhism and Jainism became popular as a reaction to the rigid, caste-bound thinking of the Hindu ruling classes. They were the first organized faiths to preach celibacy as a virtue. Whereas even Hindu priests were married, all early Buddhists were enjoined to shun sex – to see it as a distraction from the contemplative life, which alone could bring nirvana; as a way of becoming emotionally attached to another human being, and therefore to the illusory material world; and as a potential cause of children, which would bring further ties and make it even harder to attain non-being. Sex was

Seal from the Indus Valley civilization, c. 2000 B.C. National Museum, New Delhi. The central figure is dressed as a woman, yet it also clearly displays testicles and an erect penis. Thus the ithyphallic transvestite figure may well be the forerunner of the god, Shiva, who is today commonly worshipped in the form of a phallus, or *linga*.

Modern Jain ascetics. In the first century B.C., the Jains split into the Shvetambara (white-clad) sect, who wear clothing and accept that women can achieve salvation, and the Digambara (sky-clad) sect, who believe that men must go naked to emphasize their abandonment of the material world, and to lessen the chance that they might accidentally kill insects and other minute forms of life.

regarded as bestial, and women as a constant source of danger. It was said that a monk would be better off plunging his penis into a fire or a snake than into a woman's vagina. Nevertheless, by the process of cross-fertilization that has always gone on throughout India, Buddhism and Jainism gradually relaxed their precepts, at least for the laity, and began to absorb Hindu sexual attitudes and symbols. Buddhism especially has always been an intensely practical, tolerant faith, and while preaching celibacy has accommodated a wide variety of sexual practices. There are even some phallic-worshipping branches of Buddhism, which interpret the *linga* (holy phallus) of the Hindus as a lotus, within which one of the Buddhas, the Aadhi-Buddha, revealed himself. In these traditions, the mantra, or holy chant, *Om mane padme hum*, can be translated as "Hail the jewel in the lotus," and refers to an act of divine intercourse between the individual soul and the godhead. Similarly, although Jainism is an extremely ascetic faith, perhaps a third of the famous erotic temple carvings at Khajuraho are of Jain origin, and the largest temple of all is devoted to a Jina ("conqueror", or Jain holy teacher) called Parshva.

The mingling of faiths is demonstrated in the way that Hindu Brahmans acted as chaplains to Jain laymen, and officiated at their ceremonies of birth, marriage and death. A Jain layman was expected to take a vow of chastity, which was interpreted to mean that he should be faithful to his wife, once married, that he should not seek out a liaison with a woman he could not marry for some reason, and that he should not consummate marriage with a child. However, the definition of a child varied from group to group. Most sects married off their daughters at the age of 14 or 15, but the Digambara (sky-clad) sect would marry off daughters as young as ten. Jain women were not kept in seclusion from men, but, in yet another example of religious mongrelization, many of them adopted *purdah* – took the veil – after the Muslims invaded India, both as a means of protection and as a sign of social status.

The spirit of renunciation that can be found in much Indian religion is anathema to some later groups, such as the Sikhs, which were founded in the 15th century by a warrior-caste Hindu, Guru Nanak. Much of the modern appearance and custom of Sikhism goes back to the tenth Guru, Gobind Singh, who founded a group called the Khalsa ("the pure") to fight Muslim oppression. Where Buddhist monks shaved their heads, a Sikh of the Khalsa was required to wear his hair uncut, as a symbol of virility. Where Buddhist, Hindu and Jain ascetics renounced all ties, the Sikhs declared that the Khalsa was a brotherhood and Gobind Singh was their father. Women could also be initiated. They were not secluded and did not wear veils. In 1945 the Sikh shrine committee approved a document which reveals how much Sikhism is a reaction to Hindu ideas – it rejects the idea of castes, ritual pollution and child-marriage.

The Sikhs, especially those who were initiated, developed their own form of marriage sacrament, which acknowledged and respected the rights of the woman. In 1910 it was accepted by state governments in India. Although a prospective bride has to be acceptable to the whole family, Sikhs prefer to talk about "assisted" rather than "arranged" marriages.

Buddhism, although it repudiated caste distinctions and gave women more freedom, nevertheless thought that women were inferior beings, and meant to be the possessions of men.

Mihuna figures (detail) from the frieze along the Lakshmana temple (built in 950) in Khajuraho (Madhya Pradesh, India). Even some of the sacred temples of India are decorated with relief carvings of groups engaged in acrobatic sex, often in the presence of onlookers.

One authoritative early text lists ten different kinds of wives: those who were bought for money, those living in the home voluntarily, those to be enjoyed or used occasionally, those who had given cloth in their dowry, those who brought water, those with a cushion that allowed them to carry vessels on their heads, those who were slaves, those who were artisans, those who were prisoners of war and those who were only temporary. The family arranged the marriage, and although women had a greater say in the choice of partner than in a Hindu household, it was still the father who had the ultimate power to give his daughter away. The wedding itself took place in the bride's home, and was a civil ceremony, without priests.

Hinduism fought back against the popularity of Buddhism by placing a new emphasis on passionate, personal devotion to the gods Vishnu and Shiva, and to their incarnations or avatars, especially Krishna. The first systematized book of Hindu ritual laws, *The Laws of Manu*, had appeared by 100 A.D., and includes numerous rules about sexual conduct. One declares that a man who has had "intercourse in water, or with a menstruating woman, shall consume cow urine, cow dung, milk, sour milk, clarified butter and a tea of kusa grass, and fast for one day and one night". The most severe punishments are reserved for men who commit adultery with the wife of their guru, or spiritual teacher. Anyone who performs such an act must sit on a red-hot iron plate and cut off his penis with his own hands. For those who could not bear the idea of such an ordeal, there was an alternative, of more practical benefit to the priestly caste – the guilty man could lay down his life for a Brahman.

The Laws of Manu spawned a host of laws, all having something to say about sexual conduct. The commentator Mahaanir-Vaangat stated that fellatio should be punishable by death, and other lawmakers decreed that sexual misdemeanors were as serious as the crime of murdering a priest. However, it is typical of the contradictory Indian approach to sexuality that any pilgrims to temples such as Khajuraho and Konarak could see the very acts these authorities were railing against glorified in stone. Even in its holy places, Hinduism celebrated the things that it was forbidding.

A more serious threat to eroticism in the region came from the Islamic invasions that began in earnest in the 12th century and within 300 years resulted in the Mughal Empire. The Muslims were opposed to any realistic icons, let alone those showing nudity or sex. One ruler, Aurangzeb (1618–1707), is credited with destroying more than 200 temples in a single year. However, even the Mughals were eventually seduced by the manners of their new country, and some of the most celebrated Indian erotic art of the 17th century emanated from, or was inspired by, their courts. Ultimately, it took British rule, and the anglicization of the native ruling classes, to make Indians ashamed of their own erotic traditions, which had flourished for thousands of years.

A priest at the festival Durga Puja before the image of a ten-armed warrior goddess. Female divinities are among the most popular in Hinduism.

Castes and Pollution

There are four basic castes in orthodox Hinduism, though each is split into numerous groups, called *jatis*. Traditionally, each jati was reserved for a particular occupation, and occupied its own place within the social pecking order. Of the castes, the Brahman or priestly caste is highest, followed by the Kshatriya or warrior caste, which included kings, soldiers and scribes. Next is the Vaishya caste, of merchants and farmers, and lowest is the Shudra caste of laborers. There are also *harijans*, or untouchables, so-called because any contact with them defiles a caste-member. Upon independence, the Indian constitution made untouchability illegal, though it still goes on.

The idea of ritual pollution informs many aspects of Indian sexuality. A woman, when she is born, is pure, but then, through puberty, marriage and childbirth, passes through several stages of pollution until she at last becomes a widow, one of the lowest of the low.

Semen is considered to be a pollutant that contaminates both the man shedding it and the woman receiving it, but whereas he can wash off the corrupting element, she is thought to absorb it permanently, and is therefore more badly and irreparably damaged. This attitude has been used to explain an apparent hypocrisy in relations between the castes, namely that men are allowed to have sex with lower-caste women, because they can cleanse themselves afterwards, but a woman who has sex with a lower-caste man is tainted for life, and will therefore be expelled from her own social group.

Mihuna figures (detail) from the frieze along the Lakshmana temple (built in 950) in Khajuraho (Madhya Pradesh, India). Humorous depictions of acts such as bestiality can be seen on the temples of Khajuraho – near the base of the temple, where the details, such as the onlooker peeping in the background, could be appreciated.

Mythical Archetypes

Indian school, Hannyman worshipping Rama, while Sita and Lakshman look on. Miniature, Victoria and Albert Museum, London. A miniature showing Rama and Sita enthroned in exile. Rama was the seventh incarnation of Vishnu, and his relationship with Sita forms a model for most Indian marriages: she was docile, pure and obedient, even when he banished her.

When the pale-skinned Aryans invaded northern India in the third millennium B.C., they categorized those they conquered as having black complexions, no noses, an unintelligible language and no religious ceremonies. However, archaeologists working in the Indus valley have uncovered a number of cone-shaped objects, which indicate that the pre-Aryan Indians worshipped the phallus as a source of power and fertility – a belief system that gradually found its way into the faith of the new rulers. Many of the conquered peoples' gods also reemerged in Hinduism, after disappearing for a while under the new regime. There are so many rough terracotta figures of naked women in the ancient cities of the Indus – thought to be representations of a mother goddess – that it is likely that every home kept one in order to ensure the fertility of the household women. There is no powerful mother goddess in the Vedic scriptures of the Aryans, but such a figure was to reappear in many forms from about the first millennium B.C. – as the daughter of the mountains, Parvati; as the warrior goddess, Durga; and as the bringer of life and death, Kali. Archaeology has also uncovered a number of small, engraved seals showing an ithyphallic, horned figure with three faces, sitting naked in a yoga position and surrounded by wild animals. Clearly a fertility and nature god, this being has been called the Proto-Shiva, forerunner of the great Hindu god who is also called Lord of Yoga or Lord of the Beasts, and is often shown with three faces and worshipped in the form of an erect phallus. Just like the mother goddess, there is no mention of Shiva in the Vedic scriptures, and the first references to him appear in the *Shvetashvatara Upanishad*, where the first principles of yoga are also laid down. At that time, however, he was merely an aspect of the Vedic god, Rudra. His name meant "kindly" or "auspicious". The mythology of Shiva was developed in the epic poem, the *Mahabharata*, and in the Purana tales, where he appeared as one of the most important gods. His nature has always been enigmatic – instead of having one definite virtue, responsibility, or attribute, he always embodies contradictions. He is the god of virility and the god of destruction; at the same time a master of yogic restraint and a superhuman sexual athlete. Sometimes he is said to wear a garland of *yonis* (vaginas), and sometimes one of skulls. Despite his asceticism, Shiva is the only god to have a wife who is his

Standing, ithyphallic Shiva with his consort Parvati as Loving Couple (fragment), 4ᵗʰ cent. Mathura-Stone, 103 x 60 x 22 cm, Russek collection, Switzerland. The two figures are sometimes also seen combined into one – a hermaphroditic divinity called Ardharanishvara, whose right half has the attributes of Shiva – matted hair, part of a third eye on the forehead and snakes as ornaments – and whose left half has the attributes of Parvati – a rounded breast, half of a red dot, or *tilaka*, on the forehead, sumptuously combed hair and a body dressed in girdles, silks and an anklet. One explanation of the figure is that it shows the inseparability of male and female. Reference is also made to the legend in which Brahma, the creator of the world, made only males, and did not realize his error until Shiva appeared before him in his androgynous form.

equal. Vishnu's bride, Lakshmi, is always shown as docile and subservient, and the wives of most gods are no more than reflections of their masters, bearing the same name with a feminine ending, such as Indrani, wife of Indra. However, Shiva's consort, who may have many names, is always some aspect of the great mother goddess, Shakti, and is often described as the more potent and active of the pair.

It is said that Shiva had been sitting in the mountains for many centuries, meditating and living the life of an ascetic. When Parvati, the daughter of Himalaya, spotted him, she

decided that she wished him to marry her. Although her father disapproved of her choice, he agreed to help by sending along Kama, the god of love, to pierce Shiva with one of his arrows and fill him with desire for Parvati. Shiva was so outraged that he opened a third eye in the middle of his forehead and burnt Kama to ashes (although he revived him later). However, his interest was aroused, and he decided to test Parvati by appearing as a priest and describing all Shiva's bad qualities – his nakedness, his three eyes, his garland of skulls and fondness for cremation grounds, and smearing himself with ashes. When her love was unshaken, he agreed to marry her, although he caused a scandal by appearing naked at the wedding. The couple made love for a thousand years, and the friction of their intercourse was so great that the other gods became afraid and sent Agni, the god of fire, to interrupt them. Eventually, though, Shiva felt his sexual powers waning and had to revive them by going off into a forest for a period of ascetic meditation. The way in which *tapas* (asceticism) and *kama* (desire) constantly ebb and flow, each giving way to the other, in the story of Shiva demonstrates the Hindu philosophy that they are not, in fact, opposites, but just different, mutable forms of energy.

The Linga and the Yoni

There are different accounts of how the Shiva-linga – the phallus of Shiva, often carved from stone – became the common form in which the god is worshipped. In one, he was wandering as an ascetic, dancing, naked and with an erection, when the wives of some sages fell in love with him and began to follow. The jealous sages placed a curse on him so that his penis fell off, but it immediately became a linga of fire, so huge that the gods Vishnu and Brahma could not find the top or bottom of it. Shiva only quenched the flames when the sages agreed to worship his phallus. Another account says that the gods visited Shiva when he was having sex with Parvati. They refused to stop for their visitors, who cursed them both so that they died entwined. Shiva announced that henceforth his new shape was the linga, or phallus, and Parvati's was the yoni, or vagina. The pair are often worshipped together, in the form of the linked yoni-linga.

Adornment of Shiva-Linga. A stone Shiva-linga within a yoni near the River Ganges. A linga is often anointed with milk and ghee (clarified butter), and draped with flowers or sweets.

The Many Heads of the Creator

There are numerous Vedic and Hindu creation myths, but in almost all of them sexual energy is seen as the origin of the universe. In one, the universal male spirit, Purusha, burst from a cosmic egg but, finding himself alone, cut himself in two, one part male and one part female, and from their congress came the world.

In one version, the female part was afraid of sex, and kept changing herself into different forms to escape from the male. However, whatever shape she assumed, he matched it and copulated with her, creating all the species on earth.

Another version says that the original self-existent spirit called Kama (desire), began to stir and created Brahma, the visible creator of the universe. Brahma originally had one head, but when he copulated with Maya (illusion) and she gave birth to his daughter (variously called Savitri, Satarupa, Srasvati or Gayatri), he developed an uncontrollable passion for the girl. She tried to escape from him, but whichever way she ran, north, south, east or west, he grew a new face so that he could observe and lust after her. When she flew up into the sky he grew a new face, pointing upwards. Eventually he had his way with her, and their union produced the human race. A disapproving Shiva, though, cut off the fifth face as punishment.

A sculpture at the Kesava temple in Somnathpur, 13th cent. showing Brahma the creator, the first god of the Hindu trinity. The three great gods, Brahma, Vishnu and Shiva, are all thought to preside over one of the three stages of the cosmos – Brahma is the lord of creation, Vishnu the lord of preservation and Shiva the lord of destruction. There are comparatively few temples to Brahma in India, because after creating the universe he had little more to do with it.

Scholapur Dekkani, Krishna, late 18th cent. Krishna sits in a tree impervious to the anger and shame of the *gopis* whose clothes he has stolen while they were bathing in the river Jamuna. He refuses to return their saris until each of them has given him a kiss.

From about the 5th century B.C., the Brahman priests had been losing converts to newer faiths, such as Buddhism, because they were increasingly seen as elitist, inflexible and divorced from the real world. The passionate personal devotion that worshippers felt for Shiva played a big part in the revival of Hinduism from about the 5th century A.D. Another factor in this resurgence was the popularity of several incarnations of Vishnu. This preserver-god is often described as having a much simpler iconology than Shiva, but in fact there are also many contradictions in his character. In his early myths he was a trickster and deceiver – he would take on female form to seduce his enemies and cause them to bring about their own defeat. For example, when Shiva unwisely granted the demon Bhasmasur his wish that anyone upon whose head Bhasmasur placed his

hand would turn to ashes, the demon began by trying to test out his new power on the god. The terrified Shiva fled to Vishnu, who transformed himself into the ravishing Mohini and persuaded the demon to dance with him. Soon Bhasmasur was aping all Mohini's movements. When Mohini flirtatiously put her hand on her head, the demon followed suit and burnt himself up. There are many other Mohini legends along the same lines.

The most popular incarnation of Vishnu, however, is Krishna (the black), who appeared in the *Bhagavad Gita*, a part of the *Mahabharata*, as the supreme god and teacher of morality. The Purana tales describe him as an incorrigible prankster, and a favorite theme in poetry and painting is the occasion when he stole the clothes of some *gopis*, "cowgirls" while they were bathing, and made him come to them with their arms held aloft to retrieve them. This is widely interpreted as an allegory of the nakedness of the soul before the god. He would lure cowgirls – married and unmarried alike, in defiance of convention – with his flute playing, and entice them into groves to seduce them.

Once again, this story is regularly interpreted as the soul leaving everything behind in pursuit of the divine.

Krishna's favorite *gopi* was Radha, who left her husband for him. Their passion and her willingness to overturn convention for him became major themes in the cult of Krishna. The *Brahmavaivarta Purana*, from about the 10th century, is typical in the way that it emphasizes the eroticism of their love: "Krishna pulled Radha with both his arms and stripped her of her clothes. Then he kissed her in four different ways and the bells of her girdle were torn off in the battle of love. Then Radha mounted Krishna … and later Krishna adopted eight different positions and tore her body with biting and scratching until she was unable to bear any more and they ceased from the battle." Krishna's love for Radha did not mean that he neglected the other *gopis* – although there were 900,000 of them, he satisified each of them by transforming himself into an equal number of Krishnas. It was imagery such as this, allied to a philosophy of *bhakti*, "personal devotion", that spread the cult of Krishna throughout India.

Asceticism and Semen-power

देवनागरी script in image:
ૐ श्रीराधाका गन; गोपल्लरागनी सन्ह्रेगवे

Just as traditional Hinduism divides life up into four castes, and four great aims (duty, prosperity, pleasure and escape from the cycle of birth and reincarnation), so there are also four stages in the ideal life of a man, at least for the upper castes. After his childhood, a boy was supposed to be presented with a sacred thread as a mark that he had been twice born, once biologically and once into society. From this point until the age of 20 he was a student, expected to be obedient and celibate. Then he passed into his maturity, when he would marry and become a father. Lastly, when his own children had become parents, he was expected to leave his home and assume the life of a homeless wanderer, to free his soul from the chains of the material world. A woman cannot be a *sannyasi*, a renouncer, or seeker of salvation. To undergo this quest she must first live through her current life and then hope to be born again as a man. Naturally, many men choose not to follow this pattern. Others embrace the life of a voluntary, wandering beggar-ascetic much earlier in life. However, the classical tradition illuminates the Indian attitude that asceticism need not be a lifelong commitment. Indeed, one of the key advantages of sexual renunciation is, paradoxically, that it creates greater sexual powers, which may in turn manifest themselves as magical abilities and enormous physical strength and stamina. Some of these powers come from a system of austerities and contemplation, which reveals the illusory nature of the world (and the body), and thus gives the ascetic power over it. However, just as important to the ascetic regimen is the idea that semen is a vital substance which, if retained in the body, is capable of transmuting ordinary flesh into a purer and more rarefied material. It is thought to be distilled at a very slow rate from the blood – one Hindu Brahman estimated that it took 40 drops of blood, thickening and refining itself in the body for 40 days, to produce one drop of semen. Anyone who did not waste his semen,

Workshop in Bundi, Rajasthan, *Gauda Malhara Ragini*, c. 1680 –1700. Pigments and gold on paper, 21.5 x 12.5 cm, Museum Rietberg, Zurich. Occasionally a woman may decide to adopt the life of a male ascetic.

but instead stores it up (in a special reservoir, near the head) is capable of becoming a super-human. Mahatma Gandhi (1869–1948) is known to have practiced sexual renunciation (to test himself he slept, chastely, with 19-year-old girls) because, he believed, it gave him the power to influence political events. He thought that his celibacy might help him quell the riots caused by the partitioning of Bengal.

Semen-power is not restricted to ascetics, however. To increase their internal stock of the precious fluid, ordinary Hindus do as much as possible in their everyday lives to preserve the semen produced. In traditional homes they try to avoid foods that they categorize as hot, such as garlic, because it is believed that they lower the production of semen. Ayurvedic medicine, the ancient Hindu philosophy of health, recommends anything made from *ghee* (clarified butter), milk and sugar, as well as dried fruits, rice, pulses, mustard oil and, more exotically, saffron, gold dust and pearl dust, as being good for semen-production. Marijuana is also considered a semen-strengthening substance because, it is thought, it sustains an erection and allows intercourse to continue longer without ejaculation. Ayurvedic notions about hygiene include the theory that an oily skin is beneficial to a man, because the oil will eventually seep into the glands and find its way to the reproductive system, where it will nourish the semen.

As part of his *brahmacharya* (practice of celibacy), and as a yogic feat, an ascetic winds his penis up on a stick.

Panel of the Lakshmana temple in Khajuraho, c. 930–950. A carving showing an ascetic being aroused by courtesans, who probably worked at the temple.

The Ascetic and the Apsaras

The early ascetics described their austerities as a form of internal sacrifice, replacing the sacrificial fire of Vedic Hinduism with the inner fires of contemplation (called *tapas*). The spiritual power of asceticism is described as a form of heat, or dryness. Its complement can be found among the *apsarases*, the heavenly nymphs, who attend Indra, king of the gods, each of whom is the embodiment of a river. The courtesan is considered to be an earthly equivalent of the *apsaras*. In myths, the presence of a drought is often ascribed to the existence of too much chastity, and furthermore the breaking of the drought is linked to the seduction of an ascetic.

The story of Risyasringa, told in the *Mahabharata* and the *Ramayana*, is typical. It begins when Risyasringa's father, himself an ascetic, spots an *apsaras* so beautiful that, despite his discipline, he ejaculates into a pond. A doe drinks the water and gives birth to Risyasringa, who grows up in the forest with his father, living an austere life without ever casting his eyes on another human being.

When there is a drought in a nearby city, the king sends an old prostitute and her daughter into the forest. The daughter pretends to be a hermit, plies Risyasringa with delicacies and lures him to follow her to the city. There, the king houses him in the women's quarters where he is repeatedly seduced, whereupon Indra sends the rains.

Sacred Prostitutes

Apsara sculpture. Stone, Chittaugarh, Rajasthan, India. On temple walls, prostitutes are explicitly equated with the handmaids of the gods.

A girl dances for Krishna. Even though prostitution has been driven from most of the temples of India, dance itself remains as a symbolic form of sexual intercourse with the gods.

Temple prostitution has thrived in India longer than in any other country. Archaeological evidence suggests that there may have been prostitutes working in the temples of the Indus valley more than 4000 years ago. In the 11th century A.D., the Rajarajeshvara temple in Tajore employed 400 prostitutes, and it is likely that, in holy centers such as Konarak, temple prostitution formed a significant part of the area's commerce. When the missionary Abbé Dubois was writing about sacred prostitutes in the late 18th century, he recorded that "every temple … entertains a band of them, to the number of eight, twelve or more." Although he, like most Europeans, condemned them ("A religion more shameful or indecent has never existed amongst a civilized people") he acknowledged that they were hardly comparable to the whores of Europe. "Shameless as the dancing girls of India appear to be, they will not venture, upon any occasion, to stop a man on

The Hijra

Homosexuality is illegal in India, but a blind eye is often turned in the case of the hijras, transvestite males who often make their living as prostitutes. Like the devadasis, hijras are considered to be impure but auspicious – a necessary nuisance. They are regularly called upon to sing and dance in the home of a newborn male child, as a form of blessing. In some parts it is still considered extremely lucky to have a hijra attend one's wedding ceremony. Although traditionally a hijra is supposed to castrate himself as a sacrifice to the goddess Bahachura Mata, most hijras claim that they were in fact born with deformed genitals.

Because they are thought to have sacrificed their own fertility, hijras are considered a magical source of fertility in others.

the streets, or to take any indecent liberty in public." He also noted: "These prostitutes are the only females in India who may learn to sing, to read and to dance. Such accomplishments belong to them exclusively, and are, for that reason, held by the rest of the sex in such abhorrence, that every virtuous woman would consider the mention of them an affront."

In these lines, the Abbé appears to be blaming the *devadasis*, handmaid of the god, for holding up progress in India, especially among women. This was an attitude that would be echoed by many English-educated Indians, keen to Europeanize their country. In 1892 a group of them founded the Madras Hindu Social Reform Association, aimed at promoting female education, marriage reform, the eradication of "such manners and customs as are injurious" and the amalgamation of castes. One of the conditions of membership was "not to invite a nautch-woman or other fallen woman for singing, dancing or other purposes." "Nautch" is an anglicized form of various Indian words for dance. One of the duties of the sacred prostitutes was to dance for the god of the temple when he was ritually fed each day, and prostitution and dance were virtually synonymous in India until the 1920s. The reformers wanted to

abolish prostitution – especially temple prostitution – as one of their "injurious" customs, and gradually their movement spread throughout India as the "anti-nautch campaign".

Madras was the first state to prevent girls from becoming temple prostitutes, in the hugely influential 1947 Madras Prevention of Dedication of Devadasis Act. It is to be noted that it was not illegal to be a *devadasi*; taking the pledge to be one was the crime. This reflects the usual Indian way of dealing with prostitution – it is not outlawed in itself, but many of the things associated with it are, such as soliciting in a public street, or carrying out prostitution in a prohibited locality or premises (laws inherited from the British).

Nevertheless, even towards the end of the 20th century there were still temple prostitutes at various sites, although their numbers were dwindling. When the state government took over the running of the Jagannatha temple in Puri from the king in the 1950s, there were 30 *devadasis*. By the early 1980s there were nine, aged from 35 to 75. Most were poor girls offered to the temple by their parents, although in parts of India any woman from one of the four pure castes could become a temple prostitute and enter a new life in which she was said

to have no rank. Widows would also become sacred prostitutes, rather than being treated as unclean and worthless by their own families. *Devadasis* are earthly counterparts of the heavenly courtesans who surround and entertain Indra, king of the gods and master of the rains. In this world they are exclusively for the pleasure of the earthly manifestations of the gods – the king and the Brahman priests – and are not supposed to sleep with anyone else. This rule is rarely adhered to, although the king has an officer who polices the sexual relationships of the devadasis, and punishes them if they have sex with men from an impure caste, or with outsiders. They are regarded as being married to the temple deity, and as such they cannot marry a mortal man. If they want children, they are expected to adopt (usually a girl, to provide the next generation of *devadasis*) rather than give birth.

Although married to the god, they are never allowed into the inner sanctum of the temple. They are auspicious – indeed one of their titles is "the auspicious women" – because their activities guarantee the fruitfulness and prosperity of the land, but they are nevertheless thought of as being impure: a kind of spiritual and social compost heap, unclean in itself, but a source of life, wealth and goodness.

The Kamasutra

By the time of the great epic poem, the *Mahabharata* (begun in the 4th century B.C.), there were four great aims to which every Hindu should aspire. The last of them – to escape from the endless cycle of death and reincarnation – was beyond the individual's direct control, but might be attained by paying proper attention to the first three. These were *dharma*, *artha* and *kama*. *Dharma* can be translated as duty, and it is different for everyone, being determined by the individual's sex, caste and profession – just as it is the warrior's *dharma* to fight, it is the prostitute's *dharma* to give pleasure. Fulfilling one's *dharma* brings freedom from the accumulated sins of previous lives. *Artha* is the responsibility to prosper for the sake of one's family, but it must always be regulated by *dharma*, or it will become opportunism. *Kama* (which is also the name of the Hindu god of love) means any form of pleasure that can be experienced through the senses, not merely those of sex. *Dharma*, *artha* and *kama* are to be pursued simultaneously and harmoniously. In the *Bhagavad Gita*, a part of the *Mahabharata*, the god says: "Where *dharma* does not forbid it, in all creatures I am *kama*." Although the epic tends to place an emphasis on *dharma*, in some of its most popular tales it is *kama* that is described as the womb which gives birth to the other two great aims. It is the innermost core of the world. The *Kamasutra* (Aphorisms on Pleasure), was written in India between the third and 5th centuries A.D. and is attributed to a sage named Vatsyayana. Although it is famous as a sex manual, only one of its seven books (the second) is concerned with the techniques of physical love. The others deal with a general philosophy of life, society and love; methods of courtship; aspects of marriage, such as running a household, how to have an affair with another man's wife (including how to break into a harem); the life of a courtesan; and love magic. Vatsyayana's aim was to provide a complete picture of the relationship between the sexes, and his work, he claimed, was only the latest phase in a tradition that stretched back to Prajapati, the creator of humanity, who first taught men and women how to lead moral, mutually satisfying lives. Nandi,

Rajput School, Rajasthan, a prince and his lover in a state of sexual arousal, c. 1900. Gouache on paper, miniature, private collection. A woman with a narrow *yoni* applies ointment which will help her receive her lover. This could be made of clarified butter and honey, or the resin of the sal tree, which is recommended in Ayurvedic medicine to the present day.

the bull that guarded the palace of Shiva, passed on the *kama* teachings. They fell like flowers from his lips during the thousand years that Shiva and his consort Parvati were locked away inside, making love. The first human being in this apostolic line was Svetaketu Auddalaki, who is thought to have lived around 1000 B.C. He wrote a massive treatise on *kama*, which was condensed by the 5th-century B.C. sage, Babhravya of Panchala. However, all these books – none of which have survived to the present – were so massive they were unusable, so Vatsyayana wrote the *Kamasutra* as a workable summary of all that had been taught up to his time.

The prose form chosen by Vatsyayana, the sutra, or aphorism, is the briefest possible statement of an idea. It was popular among authors who were aspiring to make scientific or legal texts (Panini's rules of grammar and the yoga instructions of Patanjali were both written in sutras), and Vatsyayana spends an enormous amount of time classifying and codifying attitudes, physical types and sexual techniques. He lists nine ways of moving the *linga* (penis) inside the *yoni* (vagina), eight stages of oral intercourse and eight kinds of love bites; four kinds of mild embrace and four that are extremely passionate; three kinds of kisses that a man can give to an innocent girl, and four angles from which he can attempt to give them. The *Kamasutra* often compares sex to a pleasurable battle, or a quarrel. It recommends a whole repertoire of blows to different parts of the body, and even classifies eight different kinds of scratch that can be left by the nails. Some of the recommendations in the *Kamasutra* alarmed its readers. The sage Suvarnanabha is quoted as recommending, "that they first be practiced in the bath", in order to avoid possible injury.

Some of the most detailed classification is concerned with the compatibility of couples. Men are organized by the size of the penis, and women by the size of the vagina. A man's *linga* would identify him as a hare, a bull or a horse, while the depth of a woman's *yoni* would make her a deer, a mare or a cow elephant. The perfect unions were a hare with a deer, a bull with a mare, and a horse with an elephant.

Vatsyayana was not some desiccated pedant, however, doing little more than ordering, labeling and footnoting the work of earlier teachers. He questioned the traditions that had been handed down to him. For example, he disagreed with Auddalaki's opinion that there is no such thing as a female orgasm. Vatsyayana believed that the best way to achieve pleasure as a couple was for the man to consider the woman's satisfaction before his own. He also pointed out that, for those who were in love, no special techniques or rules were necessary.

Mogul, late 18th cent. Miniature. Vatsyayana wrote as much about courtship as he did about sex, and much of his advice emphasized cunning and stratagems. Here a lover elopes with his princess after riding his elephant through a lake to an unguarded part of her palace.

Sutras and Commentaries

A sutra is so succinct that, to modern eyes at least, it appears meaningless, and all sutra texts are meant to be read with extensive commentaries. The most popular commentary on the *Kamasutra* is the 10th–11th-century *Jayamangala* of Yashodhara, which may be printed alongside the original or incorporated into translations of the work. For example, the sutra that describes the *vadavaka* sexual technique would be rendered literally as: "Like a mare cruelly gripping. That is the mare, learned only by practice." With the aid of the *Jayamangala* it becomes clear that the woman is trapping the man's penis and "milking it", that this requires a great deal of practice, that the woman should stop kissing the man when performing this, and that it is a specialty of women from Andhra.

Orissa, 19th cent. Miniature. Fellatio and cunnilingus were clearly popular in 10th-century India, if the temple carvings of Khajuraho are any indication. However, during the following centuries such practices were largely discouraged by Hindus, at least in print. By the time of the Mughals, more liberal sexual attitudes were once more on the ascendent.

Malwa, c. 1680. Miniature. The matchmaker is a popular theme in Indian art and literature, and performs many functions. This one was sent by a king called Amaru to apologize to a woman he did not wish to marry.

Haiderabad, 18th cent. Miniature. Three elegant courtesans from Haiderabad drink wine on a terrace. The best-educated prostitutes were talented singers and dancers, and could recite vast quantities of poetry in both Urdu and Persian. They were far too expensive for any ordinary man, and were mostly the consorts of princes. Vatsyayana writes in detail about the lives of such courtesans.

Basohli, early 18th cent. Miniature. A woman protests her devotion after having sneaked into the house of her lover, accompanied by two attendants who noisily support her. Breaking and entering, and how to lie to a lover when one was being unfaithful, were two of the many subjects on which Vatsyayana gave practical advice.

Pahari, Sikh School, 19th cent. Indian men preferred, and were expected to be, on top, so the *purushayita*-positions, in which a man assumes a subordinate position, were considered to be extremely adventurous. Vatsyayana devotes part of his chapter on role-changing to a selection of these daring experiments.

Koka Shastra and Ananga Ranga

There were a number of medieval texts that imitated the *Kamasutra* of Vatsyayana, some of them slavishly, although none with the same rigor. They were written in (often florid) verse, rather than the super-condensed prose, or sutras, used by Vatsyayana, and the authors seem to have given free rein to their fantasy when inventing some of the sexual positions that they recommend. One of the most famous of the medieval sex manuals was the *Ratirahasya* (Secret Doctrine of Love's Delight) of Pandit Kokkoka, which became better known as the *Koka Shastra* (Koka's Treatise). According to his own personal legend, Koka's fame became established when a nymphomaniac appeared at the court of his patron and threw off her clothes, stating that, because gods, men and demons were incapable of satisfying her sexual needs, she intended to wander the earth naked. Koka asked his lord for permission to try his hand with the woman, and when it was granted he took her with such strength and skill that she fainted from a surfeit of orgasms.

Whatever his skills as a lover, Koka was an appallingly careless plagiarist. He even copied out Vatsyayana's passage about the sexual tastes of the women of Pataliputra, although in his day the city itself had been lying in ruins for four hundred years. In general, the *Koka Shastra* sticks to the same recipe as the *Kamasutra* – classifying people according to the size of their genitals and including advice on love magic and courtship. It does go into more detail about sexual positions, although several of which only a contortionist would attempt. Nevertheless, the needs of Koka's audience were different from those for whom the *Kamasutra* had been written, and alleviating boredom among married

Rajput School, Jaipur, 19th cent. Miniature. Two women prepare to lower another onto the penis of the man. From here she could be raised and lowered, or more likely swivelled. This is probably the artist's interpretation of a position called *Utkalita* in the *Ananga Ranga*.

Mankot, Punjab, Lovers in extravagantly open posture, not mentioned in the Kamasutra, mid-18th cent. Gouache on paper, private collection.

couples had become more important than providing practical advice for young lovers.

When Vatsyayana wrote the *Kamasutra*, it seems that women were not secluded, and that there were plentiful opportunities for unattached (or relatively unattached) members of the opposite sex to meet. By the Middle Ages, society had become much more rigid and rule-bound, opportunities for premarital and extramarital sex had dwindled, and child-marriage had become commonplace. These changes are reflected in the 15th-century *Ananga Ranga* (Stage of the Bodiless One) of Kalyana Malla. This became one of the most important of all medieval sex manuals, in part because the author was in the service of a Muslim nobleman, and as a result his book was translated into Arabic and widely disseminated throughout Islam. Kalyana Malla, who grandiloquently described himself as "the Prince of Poets" set out with the intention of showing how a married couple "may pass through life in union", without ever looking for sexual partners outside the marriage. According to Kalyana Malla, the cause of adultery was a "want of varied pleasures", and so he set about providing a mass of rules and prescriptions for varying them. Much of the material is based on the *Kamasutra*, but with greater emphasis given to the various systems of classification, mixed in with a mélange of information about palmistry, astrology and amateur psychology. Whereas the *Kamasutra* restricts itself to the physical and sexual consequences of having a certain penis size, the *Ananga Ranga* draws conclusions about the owner's temperament and likely fate. Curiously, at one point it concludes: "The man whose penis is very long will be wretchedly poor. The man whose penis is very thick will always be lucky. And the man whose penis is short will be a king." The *Ananga Ranga* is as pedantic as it is copious. Because the pleasure principle migrates around the body according to the phases of the moon, there are even detailed descriptions of what a husband must do to particular parts of his wife's body – even including the big toe – for each of the eight watches of day or night throughout the lunar calendar.

Udaipur, 19th cent. Following the *Ananga Ranga,* this picture labels a woman's body parts, and gives instructions as to how they should be treated at different times throughout the lunar cycle.

The Battle of Love

"The blandishments of love are a manner of battle," says Kalyana Malla, "in which the stronger wins the day." He lists four types of blows that the husband and wife might deliver upon each other (although they are gentler than those in the *Kamasutra*), including "*Sampatah-asta*, or patting with the inner part of the hand, which is slightly hollowed for the purpose, like a cobra's hood;" seven different *dashanas*, or ways of applying the teeth, including *kand-*

abhrak, "the cluster or multitude of impressions made by the husband's teeth upon the brow and cheek, the neck and breast of the wife" which will "add greatly to her beauty"; and seven *nakhadanas*, or ways of titillating and scratching, which include the *mayurapada* (peacock's claw), made by "placing the thumb upon the nipple, and the four fingers upon the breast adjacent, at the same time pressing the nails until the mark resembles the trail of the peacock, which he leaves when walking upon mud."

A Universe of Desire

Chinnamasta, the goddess of wisdom, c. 1800. Gouache, 20 x 15 cm, private collection. The goddess is standing on the copulating bodies of a divine couple, decapitating herself to feed her disciples. According to the Tantras, Chinnamasta herself is only one of the vibrations generated by the love play of Shiva and Shakti.

Tantra or Tantrism is a collective term for a wide range of mystical traditions, whose beliefs often contradict each other. The Tantras themselves are a set of texts dating back to the 6th or 7th century A.D., although many of them claim that the ideas and traditions they contain are very much older, and even predate Vedic Hin-

duism (c. 2000 B.C.). There are both Hindu and Buddhist Tantras, and each has its own elaborate secret language, with multiple sets of codes, metaphors and allusions. A fundamental idea found in most of the Tantric sects is that the entire universe is sexual in nature. It is continually created and recreated by the goddess Shakti as she copulates with the impassive, unmoving god, Shiva. The sexual throes of the divine couple generate a series of vibrations – like the harmonic series in music – which become progressively less subtle and perfect. What is perceived as the material world is only one of the coarser vibrations thrown off by the lovemaking of the gods.

Because the universe is born of desire, Tantric disciples (called Tantrikas) do not try to subdue their own sexual instincts. Unlike the ascetics of Buddhism and Hinduism, they attempt to use their sexuality as a tool to achieve enlightenment by fine-tuning their bodies so that they become sensitive to ever more subtle vibrations emanating from Shiva and Shakti. Tantrikas use ritualized sexual intercourse to emulate the divine couple, although devotees of the so-called Right-hand Path of Tantrism believe that actual physical sex is not required. They claim that the Tantric rituals should be sublimated, and performed purely in the mind as acts of meditation. Left-hand Path Tantrikas accept that this is an ideal to be aimed at, but believe that only one or two gurus in each generation might be capable of achieving it. For most disciples, physical love is the best way of approaching enlightenment.

Ritual sex, or *maithuna*, is only part of a fivefold ceremony called the *panchamakara*, or five-Ms, which also involves partaking of *mamsa* (meat), *matsya* (fish), *madya* (wine) and *mudra* (parched grain). The use of marijuana or some other drug, such as datura, may also play a part in the five-Ms, but the details of the rituals vary from text to text. Some say that *maithuna* should only be performed between married couples, after the woman has been properly initiated as a Tantrika. Others state that the male disciple should seek out the lowest caste woman he can find, and preferably have sex with her while she

Erotic posture of Lord Shiva with Shakti the goddess. Members of Tantric sects believe that the lovemaking of the god and goddess generates vibrations, one of which is perceived as the material world. Because the universe is sexual in nature, Tantrikas use sexuality in their attempt to achieve enlightenment.

is menstruating. One of the reasons for this is that the Tantrika must be prepared to disregard the mores of conventional society, if necessary making himself an outcast in the process. In the words of more than one Tantric sect, "One must raise oneself by that which causes one to fall." The 18th-century text known as the *Yoga-Karnika* takes this advice to extremes, advising the disciple to penetrate his own mother, while resting his feet on his father's head and fondling his sister's breasts. It continues: "He who worships, day and night, an actress, a female-skull-bear-

er, a prostitute, a low-caste woman, a washer man's wife, he truly becomes the blessed Shiva." Another scripture, the *Niruttara-tantra*, says that adultery is a necessary prerequisite to gaining spiritual merit. However, the Tantras warn that *maithuna* is a dangerous process which should only be attempted by someone who is a *vira* (hero) – someone free of doubt, fear or lust. A true adept, apparently, might be expected to work his way through 108 women in a single night, although he would do little more than touch many of them.

Tantrikas believe that there is a complicated system of internal channels and energy points, called the subtle body. Sexual intercourse awakens a powerful source of female energy (called the *kundalini* serpent), which lies coiled at the base of the spine, and drives it up through the body to the crown of the head (known as the seat of Shiva). Since the *kundalini* energy is generally identified with Shakti, the Tantrika is using sex to achieve enlightenment by reenacting the union of the god and goddess within his or her own body.

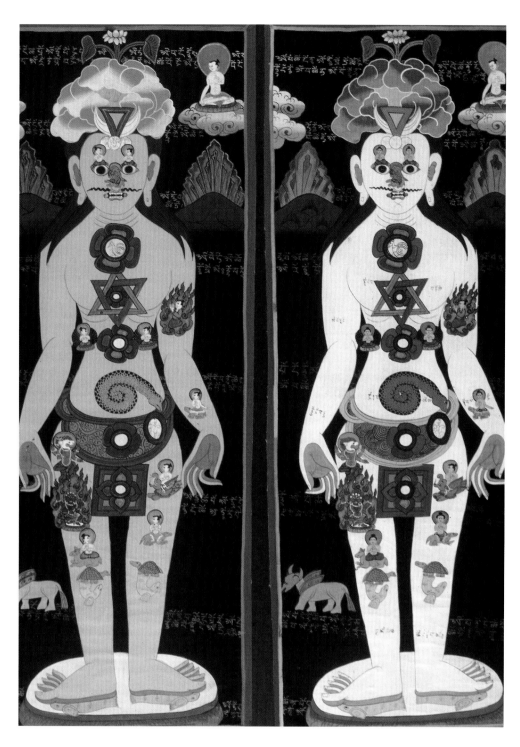

Cosmic men (purusha), 18th cent. Painting in Nepalese style. Each of the body's energy centers, or *chakras* is described as a lotus of a certain color, and with a specific number of petals. There are also two channels linking the yellow, four-petaled lotus at the base of the pelvis with the celestial, thousand-petaled lotus, or seat of Shiva, at the top of the head. The *ila* runs to the left of the spinal cord and carries the female creative energy in the body. The *pingala* runs to the right of the spinal cord and carries the male creative energy. When the *kundalini* energy is activated at the base of the spine, it combines with unshed semen to produce a substance called *bindu*, which forges a new, asexual channel in order to rise to the head.

Breaking the Greatest Taboo

Many of the early Tantrikas are thought to have come from the lower castes of Indian society, and this may be the reason why so many of the rituals and recommendations of Tantrism appear so perverse: they were adopted deliberately as a way of breaking taboos and offending the rigid, hierarchical order of society. Perhaps the most profound taboos of all surround death, and Tantrikas are often advised to make their home or at least perform their most secret rites in cemeteries. When a Tantrika copulates among the rotting corpses of a cemetery, he is offering up a sacrifice composed of his own disgust and sense of shame. The act is also seen as a form of meditation on the impermanence of the material world, and as a way of alienating the disciple from the conventions of a society that he must learn to flout if he is to achieve independence and enlightenment. At the same time, he must learn to see all the faces of the goddess he worships. She is not only Shakti, the life-giving creatrix, but also Kali, taker of life, who tramples on the corpse of Shiva even as she impregnates herself with his erect phallus.

Strictly speaking the man and woman should not move during *maithuna*, and the man must avoid ejaculating, because his semen is an important vehicle for transporting the *kundalini* energy. The woman, on the other hand, is encouraged to experience a conventional orgasm, because this increases the flow of her *rasas*, or vaginal secretions, which an adept male Tantric is said to be able to absorb through his penis, after which it enriches his hormonal system and helps to bring about the marriage of male and female elements within himself.

In several Tantric rituals, there is not even any need for the presence of a woman, so long as there is a supply of her *rasas* on hand, which will have been collected earlier on the surface of a leaf. The disciple dresses himself in women's clothing and, while reciting a series of mantras (or prayers), mixes the *rasas* into a bowl of pure water before drinking the contents. *Maithuna* is frequently referred to in the Tantras as *yoni-puja*, or the worship of the vagina, and some Buddhist texts, such as the *Subhasita-samgraha*, state that "Buddhahood abides in the female organ".

A group of Rajneesh's followers holding an ecstatic prayer meeting at the Rajneeshpurum, an "ideal city" built on a ranch in Oregon, which contained luxury hotels and a central hall that could hold 25,000 people.

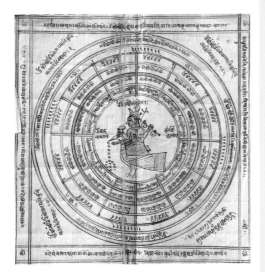

Tantric paintings, School of Rajasthan, 19ᵗʰ cent.
Because much of the material has been accessible only since the 1940s, the study of Rajasthani paintings is still in its early stages. The style evolved from illustrations in the manuscripts of Western India. The paintings were intended to be kept in albums or boxes, and they were viewed by being passed from person to person.

Gurus and Popularizers

The most difficult task a would-be Tantrika faces is finding a good teacher, or guru. The Tantras, despite the security afforded by their esoteric language and secret codes, make it clear that there are some secrets that cannot be written down at all, and must be handed-down personally from adept to initiate. However, precisely because these secrets are not recorded, the initiate has no way of checking the credentials of a guru. In addition, true gurus tend to be outcastes, or antisocial, and are more likely than not to reject prospective disciples.

Nevertheless, many people have declared themselves to be Tantric gurus, and often won themselves enormous followings. The Bhagwan Shree Rajneesh, who arrived in the United States in 1981 and was deported again four years later, professed to teach a form of neo-Tantrism, which used sexual intercourse to free the individual from guilt, inhibitions and neuroses, and thereby pave the way to a higher state of consciousness. One of the accusations against Rajneesh, who died in 1990, was that he abused his position to dupe young women into having sex with him. Other self-styled adepts, such as Aleister Crowley's secretary, F. I. Regardie, and authors such as Nik Douglas, have also introduced variants of Tantric practice to the West.

The Erotic in the Arts

The *Kamasutra* and the later Indian sex manuals had a profound influence on erotic art, both literary and visual. It even affected the nature of devotional verse. The 12th-century *Gita Govinda* (The Song of the Cowherd) written in Sanskrit by the Bengali poet Jayadeva, describes the love affair of Krishna and Radha in terms that allude clearly to the *Kamasutra*. When the god Krishna returns to Radha, after dallying with her friends, the couple kiss, scratch and reach a state of bliss by adopting what Vatsyayana, the author of the *Kamasutra*, called role reversal. Here, the woman takes the part of the man, either because he is tired or needs extra titillation. During her reconciliation with Krishna, the *Gita Govinda* describes Radha as the active partner, "lying over his beautiful body, to triumph over her lover." The *Gita Govinda* subsequently became one of the most popular stories among artists and illustrators, and frequently appeared decorated with miniature paintings. Some of the finest examples came from the Punjabi and Kangra schools. The educated men and women of Vatsyayana's time were advised to keep painting materials in the bedroom, for when an artistic mood came over them, but it was only in the 16th century that painting miniatures on paper became commonplace. Until then, they would have been executed on palm leaves, cloth or smooth stones. Many of the rules of composition remained constant through the centuries, however, having been set down in the *Vishnudharmottara Purana* and the *Natyashastra*, both of which date from the second century A.D. The *Natyashastra* is more famous as a treatise on dance and drama, but it was said that without knowledge of these subjects, the rules of composition and painting were impossible to understand. The *Natyashastra* also advised that eroticism was best conveyed by fairly dark tones, and recommended the addition of birds, bees, musicians, flowers and moonlight to heighten the mood. It is no accident that this text also influenced Vatsyayana, and was a powerful source of inspiration to the authors of medieval sex manuals in their tireless search for new sexual postures.

The erotic images of India are not restricted to paintings, or to the secular sphere. A wave of temple-building swept through the region from about the 9th or 10th century A.D., and it is highly likely that the *Kamasutra* was a reference for the erotic carvings that frequently adorned the walls.

India had always had sexual imagery in and around its temples. The most abstract forms – the *lingas* and *yonis* representing the phallus or vagina of a god or goddess, were usually to be found inside. The more explicit images were to be found on the exteriors, and it has been

Krishna adorning Rasha's breast, from the *Git Govinda* series, attributed to either Kushala or Gandhu, Kangra, Himadal Pradesh, Pahari School, c. 1780. Gouache on paper, miniature, private collection. The essence of a work of art, according to the *Natyashastra*, was its flavor or feeling, known as its *rasa*. Each *rasa* had its cast of characters and typical settings, appropriate actions and morals and complementary moods.

suggested that these figures (which are often at eye-level, and more crudely executed than the strictly religious scenes) were an advertisement for the services of the temple prostitutes. The most celebrated of the sexually-decorated holy sites are at Konarak and Khajuraho. They have wave after wave of deities, dancing girls and copulating figures, rising up to the heavens in a shape that, it has been suggested, is meant to resemble Mount Meru, the home of the gods. The extravagant positions adopted by some of the couples, trios and quartets on the temple walls has led some people to believe that they are actually meant to be lying down, and are only shown upright because of the limitations imposed by architecture.

With the arrival of the Mughals, the emphasis in Indian art switched from divine eroticism to portraiture, hunting scenes and ceremonials. The 16th-century emperor Akbar (the third of the Mughal rulers) is credited with overcoming the traditional Islamic revulsion towards the representation of living creatures. The Mughal style can be seen clearly in miniatures from Rajasthan, and in the illustrated sex manuals that began to appear, often called *Koka Shastras*, after the famous Medieval text. These showed Indian princes copulating as one of many possible "acts of life", so they would be smoking, riding elephants and camels or hunting wild animals while at the same time engaged in sexual intercourse. The all-around virility of the man was constantly being advertised by these paintings. In contrast, when European men appeared in Indian erotic miniatures, they were regularly presented as a source of ridicule. Even when otherwise naked they would still wear their hats and wigs, and would appear in far less demanding positions than the local princes.

Kandariya Mahedevo temple, Khajuraho, c. 10th–12th cent. An inscription on one of the walls describes the shape of the temple as being like "the snowy peaks of the Himalayas", lending credence to the claim that the temples of Khajuraho are meant to resemble the holy Mount Meru.

Linga of Shiva, from a temple in central India, 5th or 6th cent. Sandstone, De Young Memorial Museum, San Francisco. A phallus such as this, with an image of Shiva carved on one side, is known as an *ekamukha linga*. It is thought to be a compromise between the iconic and the abstract representations of the god.

Panel of the Lakshmana temple in Khajuraho (detail), c. 930–950. The Lakshmana temple is typical of 10th-century North Indian temple sculpture, with its profusion of angular, decorated shapes.

ागरधांत्रासननामःःाछंदसुरिहःाबनमेंत्रगरांसत्रा
बतुहैःनरनारीसुंजोगजनाबतुहैःासुरसामंत्रगसुंचोटक
दैःविन्त्रासहिकेंकंरबंदूकधरदैःाा५३॥

Bundi-Kotah, Rajput School, Rajasthan, 1790.
Gouache on paper, 22.9 x 13.3 cm, private collection.
Even while making love, the prince finds time to
bring down a deer with his bow and arrow.

The term that was disparagingly used for them was "dunghill dicks", in reference to their lack of imagination, flexibility and stamina. The Europeans got a measure of aesthetic revenge by vulgarizing and Victorianizing the great tradition of Indian miniatures, turning them into glossy objects that would make amusing souvenirs. The result, the so-called Company Style, probably originated in Bengal before spreading to Lucknow. There are still thriving schools of miniature painting, especially at Udaipur, but many of them are satisfied with imitating the past, with an eye on the tourist trade.

Opposite: **Bundi, Rajput School, Rajasthan, a European man makes love to a girl while she is playing with her cat, 1790. Gouache on paper, 22.2 x 16.5 cm, private collection.** This Indian woman is so unaffected by the European man's lovemaking that she finds time to play with her pet. The fact that the man is still wearing his coat and hat is also intended as a sly comment on European sexual performance.

Modern India

One of the most far-reaching pieces of legislation in modern India was the Hindu Marriage Act of 1955, which attempted to emulate English customs, and outlawed polygamy and child-marriage. The attempts to create a European pattern of marriage in India had only limited practical success, however, and the Act was widely ignored. Tradition is still the governing force in many people's sex-lives. The caste system, for example, retains a profound influence on Hindu marriage, despite continual attempts by the Indian government to minimize its importance. There are theoretically four main castes – the Brahman, Kshatriya, Vaishya and Shudra – but new ones are constantly coming into existence, both by a process of cross-marriage, and because they are specially created (the so-called scheduled castes) for tribal groups which have become Hinduized. By the end of the 20th century, there were more than 3000 different castes in India.

Although these traditional injunctions survive in modern India, it is increasingly true that the education of a prospective mate carries more importance than his (or more rarely her) caste. A graduate is considered a valuable addition to the family, and often one worth paying a high price for. In most of India marriage still involves an exchange of money or goods. The dowry paid for a well-educated bridegroom can be exorbitant, and the members of several lower-caste groups, who formerly adopted the bride-price system, are increasingly switching over, after first sending their sons through college.

However, in the cities at least, all forms of dowry system are under threat from the tendency for young men and women to marry in civil ceremonies, without the consent of their parents – a trend that has been encouraged by a succession of laws raising the age at which people are allowed to marry. Increasingly in urban India, marriage is between adults who have received some education, seen a bit of life outside the home, and know their own minds. The attitude towards premarital sex, though, is no less confusing now than before. On the one hand, virginity is highly prized, or even expected, in a bride. On the other, men are supposed to bring some sexual experience to the marriage bed, and it is widely thought that real pleasure is only possible with a worldly, knowledgeable woman. One Hindu tradition even holds that it might be harmful to sleep with a virgin.

The situation is somewhat more straightforward in many tribal societies, where boys and girls are expected and even encouraged to experiment sexually. Groups such as the Nagas of Assam, the Santals of Bengal, the Khonds of Orissa and the Mannans of Travancore employ a system of communal dormitories for this purpose, which are shared by pubescent boys and girls. The best-organized communal dormitories are found among the Murias of Madhya Pradesh, who call them *ghotuls*. There are several types: in one, the *jodidar*, a boy and girl are paired off and are considered to be "married". They are expected to be faithful to each other while they are in the *ghotul*. In another, the *mundi-badlana*, which is more widespread and

Population Control

The first census to be taken after independence revealed that India had a population of 361 million, with a disturbing annual growth rate of 2.16 percent. As a result, India became the first country in the world to institute a government-backed birth-control campaign. A five-year-plan was drawn up which aimed to educate the population about the need for birth control, open clinics in rural areas and provide contraceptive devices. More controversially, at least to human rights groups in the West, sterilization was also introduced. The IUD became the official national contraceptive method for women in 1965, and the first "vasectomy camps" for men were opened in Kerala in 1972. Couples were given financial incentives to be sterilized, but in many cases also found themselves lied to and bullied by over-zealous bureaucrats who were desperate to achieve the official targets that had been set by the Ministry of Health and Family Welfare. The Ministry's goal was to reduce the birth rate from 35 per thousand in the early 1970s to 25 per thousand by the end of the decade. The marriage age was raised to 21 years for boys and 18 years for girls, and although there were no national statutes making sterilization compulsory after three children, individual states were allowed, or encouraged, to pass such laws themselves. At times, the sterilization program has been carried out with an almost military fervor. Unmarried boys and elderly people were operated on indiscriminately, and against their will. Yet despite the most strenuous efforts, India at the end of the 20th century still had to cope with one of the fastest growing populations on earth.

Divorce

To the orthodox Hindu, marriage is a sacrament, not a contract, and as such can never be broken, even by death. Before the Hindu Marriage Act of 1955, even a woman who was accused of adultery and stripped of her caste and her status would not be divorced: the husband would simply get himself another wife. The Marriage Act prohibited such easy acquisitiveness on his part, while making it easier for both parties to get a divorce. Even so, the break-up of a marriage is still more common among the lower castes. Among the Doms of Tehri-Garwhal it occurs by mutual consent, while in Uttar Pradesh a husband can divorce his wife either verbally or in writing, and insist that the next man who takes her pays double the original bride-price.

Divorce is still more prevalent among the tribal groups than in Hindu society. The Bhils allow it under any pretext. The husband calls together the village council and tears a piece off his turban, hands it to his wife and tells her that her conduct has been bad and that from this day forward she will be as a sister to him. For the Parojas of Orissa the procedure is even simpler. A woman can walk away from her marriage if she pays the man five rupees – the man can leave if he pays the woman one.

traditional, a couple is allowed to spend no more than three nights with each other before having to form fresh liaisons. A *ghotul* will typically hold 20 adolescents, and often a head boy or girl draws up a rota. The Murias say that they discourage long-term attachments in the *ghotul* because it makes conception less likely, and because "too much love before marriage will mean too little after it."

Opposite: **The Holi festival.** A relic of an ancient fertility rite, Holi is a riotous festival during which caste divisions are traditionally ignored. It is also a time when, by custom, male and female in-laws are allowed to behave in a flirtatious manner. A man may chase his sister-in-law through the streets and, when he catches her, rub colored powder over her cheeks, back and breasts, while she similarly smears his cheeks and hair.

Betrothal of children. A ten-year-old from the Kot Khawadar district of Jaipur takes milk from his mother's breast as a symbolic gesture to mark the end of childhood. He is about to take a bus-ride with the men and children of his village to the home of a seven-year-old girl, who is to become his bride. Returning to the village alone, while his new bride remains with her family until she reaches puberty, he will nevertheless enjoy the status of a grown, married man.

Bollywood – The Indian Factory of Dreams

When the British Broadcasting Corporation (BBC) launched an internet poll for the millennium to choose the biggest and best-loved film star in the world, the winner was not Harrison Ford or Sean Connery or Brad Pitt. By a clear margin, the world's favorite film star was 55-year-old Ambitabh Bachchan, from Allahabad. The Bombay film industry, known affectionately as Bollywood, is larger and more prolific than its American namesake, turning out more than 1000 films a year for an audience that potentially numbers more than a billion in South Asia alone, not to mention the 25-million-strong Asian diaspora. In 1998, two films, *Dil Se* and *Koch Kuch Hota Hai*, became the first unsubtitled foreign language films to break into the British cinema Top Ten at the box office, and Bollywood movies play to huge audiences in China, Russia, Africa and the Middle East. The top Indian stars are worshipped almost as gods, providing lessons in how to live properly

as well as entertaining their audience. The hero, however much in love, is always sexually continent (which means he does not have sex with more than one woman), the villains are lechers, and from this basic flaw all their other moral defects flow. Indeed, the Bollywood films have been claimed as the finest, or at any rate the most thorough, examples of the precepts laid down in the second-century A.D. *Natyashastra*, which aimed to teach the principles of aesthetics, dance and drama to ordinary people so that they could worship the gods better and learn how to live properly.

Although Indian cinema has always had its share of highly-respected art-cinema directors, such as Satyajit Ray (b. 1921), Gautam Ghose (b. 1950), and Adoor Gopalakrishnan, (b. 1941) popular Indian cinema is based on a clearly-defined formula of rhetoric, morality tale, spectacle and romance, with generous servings of song and dance. In a country where arranged

marriages are commonplace, the cinema is obsessed with the idea of romantic love, borrowed from the West but also based on Sufi mysticism and Urdu poetry. Typically, boy meets girl and falls in love at first sight. The couple declare their intention to marry, only to encounter a series of obstacles to their romance, usually put in their way by puritanical parents or relatives. However, all problems are overcome, the relatives have a change of heart and acknowledge the unstoppable rightness of young love. The climax in the film is the marriage, or the preparations for it.

This appears to be similar to the Western romantic comedy, but with the difference that the couple's ambitions are clearly to enjoy each other sexually. The Indian cinema acknowledges sex more than its Western counterpart, while being unable to explicitly show nearly as much. Nudity is forbidden, and even kissing scenes are banned. Instead, Bollywood film-

Madhuri Dixit, perhaps the biggest female Bollywood star in the 1990s, embodies an independent spirit without moving too far from the traditional Indian feminine virtues of chastity and obedience.

The confusion of categories in Indian popular life, and the iconic status of film stars, can be seen on almost any urban billboard.

Hindi Film Set, Bombay. Actress Madhuri Dixit and Saroj Khan rehearse, while director Chimpu Kapoor turns his attention elsewhere.

makers use a number of well-worn devices to get sex onto the screen. There is the tribal costume, which exposes swathes of skin, especially near the pelvic region. Even more popular are the wet sari scenes – Bollywood heroines are forever getting caught in torrential downpours – and the dream sequences, in which women who must conventionally be demure, such as recent widows, are allowed to be transformed into singing, dancing coquettes.

The musical numbers are the main vehicles for the films' sexual content. In at least one of them the heroine has to come out from behind a pillar, column or tree, behind which she disappears again at some stage – the Bollywood equivalent of a striptease. Another convention is for the hero and heroine to vanish behind a

bush together for a moment, emerging again with the woman wiping her lips. Although innocent enough to Western eyes, this has been compared to the feudal tradition whereby a woman displayed the love-marks from her sexual initiation. The most explicitly sexual moments in a Bollywood film, however, occur in the lyrics of the songs. Usually performed by so-called backing singers (sisters Lata Mangeshkar and Asha Bhosle have between them recorded more than 20,000 songs in at least 15 different languages), the lyrics are filled with descriptions of the kissing that cannot be shown on screen, along with allusive references to lips, eyes, breasts, bedding and the ecstasy of sexual gratification. Nevertheless, even in the songs it is sometimes possible to go

too far. When the hero of the film *Khalnayak* sang to Madhuri Dixit, *Choli Ke Peeche?* (What's Behind Your Blouse?), it may have helped make her one of the foremost screen goddesses of the 1990s, but the song was banned from national radio and television.

Wives and Brothers

Polyandry – the marriage of one woman to several men simultaneously – is quite rare worldwide, but relatively common in the Himalayas. Among various Nepalese groups, such as the Nyinba, a woman is expected to have several husbands. Normally, she marries a group of brothers and moves into their home. She is sup-

Wedding ritual to "destroy evil". In Spiti, western Tibet, the ritual cake *torma* is consecrated and burned in order to ward off evil influences from the bridal couple and the family.

posed to show equal affection for all of them, and any displays of favoritism are frowned upon as a threat to the stability of the group. If a man is an only son, he will usually have a wife to himself, but women frequently say that they prefer being married to several husbands because of the extra economic security that such an arrangement provides.

The Nyinba are a Tibetan-speaking group, surrounded by Hindus, and the marriage customs they preserve are typical of Tibet, where polyandry has existed since at least the 10th century A.D. It also used to be popular in Bhutan (although traditionally not more than three brothers would share a wife), but was made illegal in the 1960s.

The Sherpas of Nepal also have a history of polyandry, with normally only two brothers involved in the marriage. It is often said that polyandry is a response to the harsh, unforgiving environment of the Himalayas – it pools the labor of several men in support of the family, while limiting the number of children that can be born. However, it is more likely to be a way to avoid dividing land and property among a number of brothers – only half the Nyinba practice polyandry, and they tend to be the wealthier members of the community. A rich man without brothers may instead practice polygyny (one husband with several wives), while those with no wealth to divide are likely to favor monogamy.

This wide diversity of alternative, acceptable marriage-styles is typical of cultures that allow polyandry. Occasionally, so-called oblique marriages are also encountered, in which a man and his son may marry the same woman – an arrangement that is considered perfectly respectable, and is known in Tibet as *kammagdang*, or "half-beam-half-rafter". More rarely, a man and his nephew will marry the same woman, or a woman and her daughter may marry the same man. All these types of union seem designed to reconcile the demands of a hierarchical system with the need to preserve an undivided family unit.

The principle of hierarchy also plays its part in polyandrous marriages. Only the eldest brother has any say in choosing the wife, and only he is

Tibetan Marriage. During a wedding ritual in western Tibet bride and groom are blessed by the Lama Spirit.

actually wedded to her, in a single ceremony. To avoid having to divide property, younger brothers may be sent to a monastery. Later they may share the eldest brother's wife. This is thought to indicate the harmony of the brotherhood. The younger brothers are then considered as de facto husbands. Any children are counted as belonging to the eldest, whoever their biological parents may be. Although another man might theoretically be brought into a polyandrous marriage, this occurs only rarely, because it is a potential threat to the fraternal group. Usually, however, when a younger brother sets himself up with a separate wife, home and land, he loses any rights to his elder brother's woman and property. The union of brothers is so important in Tibetan culture that, on those occasions when unrelated men are married to the same woman, they are regarded as *spun-zla*, or sworn brother-cousins. The polyandrous marriage can also be seen as a form of protection, or insurance, for the eldest brother. In its absence, an eldest who remains childless, or who fathers only daughters, may be supplanted as head of the family by one of his younger brothers. In some cases, the younger may, in the process, even take over his brother's wife. Whenever a man who has retained his position as head of the family dies leaving only a

daughter, she inherits everything and marries a man who takes her name and lives in her home. He is known as a *go-mag*, or "husband/son-in-law", and has a status little higher than that of a serf. The purpose of the *go-mag* is seen as being little more than to ensure the line of succession. Tibetan religious and social customs have survived successive waves of Mongol and Chinese rule since the 13th century. However, the most recent Chinese invasion – by the People's Liberation Army in 1951 – led to the merciless suppression of local traditions. An influx of Chinese into Lhasa made the Tibetans a minority in their own capital. The Dalai Lama fled the country in 1959, religious buildings and structures were destroyed, and under Chairman Mao's orders, agricultural land was collectivized and men taken by force into labor camps. The existence of collectives and the lack of men conspired against the practice of polyandry. However, in the 1980s, under Deng Zhao Ping, a process of liberalization gave villagers the chance to dissolve the communes, and return to their old ways of land ownership, inheritance and distribution.

Tibetan Marriage Rites

The indigenous religion of Tibet is Bon, which probably existed in the region before the intro-

duction of Buddhism in the 8th century A.D. Since about the 12th century, however, the two faiths have developed many common elements, with an abundance of fierce local deities and demons. There is no single wedding ceremony that is common to all Tibet, and customs can change enormously from village to village. However, many modern marriages – even among Buddhists – seem to be based on old Bon rituals and stories, with ceremonies that are modeled on the first ever marriage between the gods and men, which united the two groups for all time.

The bride might be brought to the wedding by seven boys, representing the groom, known as "buyers". Girls who sing riddles bar the way, only relinquishing the bride once the boys have sung the proper answers. During the marriage ceremony, a woolen thread is tied to the groom, representing the cord that connects earth to heaven, and another is tied to the bride, representing the good fortune that she brings with her into the house.

The priest presents the groom with a gold ring, known as his soul-gold, and the bride with a piece of turquoise, known as her soul turquoise. The couple is seated together on a white carpet, covered with a swastika of barley grains, and the service concludes with the priest's prayers for good fortune.

Divine Consorts

In Tibetan philosophy, the nature of the Buddha is often thought of as possessing both male and female elements. To reflect this, the iconography of Tibetan Buddhism is filled with images of Bodhisattvas (beings who have attained enlightenment, but chosen to remain in the material world as teachers, saviors and protective deities) who are shown with female consorts, often in the act of sexual intercourse. The consort is the "power" or the "wisdom" of the Bodhisattva. She is also the ultimate form of the dakini – a mighty female, either human or demonic, with the power to initiate men into the secrets of Tantric magic. The initiation always involves a real or symbolic act of copulation, and has lain at the heart of Tantric thought for many centuries.

Padmasambhava (also known as Guru Rimpoche), the Indian sage who spread Buddhist doctrines throughout Tibet in the 8th century and founded the Red Hat Sect, received his first lessons in magic from the dakinis who haunted a cemetery. By the time he was invited to Tibet by King Trisrong Detsen (742–797), Padmasambhava had traveled throughout India and the neighboring Buddhist countries, learning different occult techniques from a succession of gurus and dakinis. Tellingly, in a number of cases, he had to rape a dakini to gain her knowledge, and the link between esoteric knowledge and sexual violence is a common element in Tibetan mysticism. As Padmasambhava was trying to enter Tibet, the goddess Mutsame, one of the country's twelve guardians of the mountain passes, turned herself into two cliffs and tried to crush him between them. Padmasambhava paralyzed her by sticking a phallic dagger into the ground, and the humbled Mutsame offered the sage her heart. In return he gave her a new secret name, Indestructible Mistress of the Snow Peaks, and made her a Buddhist protective spirit.

In stories like these, sexual and magical powers are seen as being essentially the same thing. The 11th-century saint, Milarepa, was famous for conquering dakinis, and making them sexually subservient to him. It is said that Mount Labchi, in the south of Tibet, was the home of flesh-eating dakinis until it was exorcised by Milarepa, who took one of the dakinis of the Zullekang La pass as his consort. The gods of Labchi sent an avalanche of boulders down on the saint, but his consort and the other dakinis came to his aid, making a safe winding path for him between the falling stones. The path is still there, and is used by pilgrims to the mountain. In popular folk-tales, dakinis have become the fairies, elves and witches of Tibet, where they are known as *khadomas* (sky-walkers). One of Tibet's famous pilgrimage sites, Mount Tsari, at the southeastern end of the Great Himalayan range, is particularly famous for its *khadomas*, and there are many tales associated with the place. One of the first holy men to climb it – the Indian sage Lawapa – had reached the Dorje Phuk cave, high in the mountain, when he turned and saw 21 virgins dancing in the valley below. He sent his disciple, Bhusuku to fetch one, but by the time Bhusuku returned the woman had turned into

Vajrasattva in union with Visvatara the supreme wisdom, Tibet, 18th cent. Bronze and jewels, 25 cm high, Philip Goldman Collection, London. Vajrasattva is the supreme Buddha, and in his hands he holds thunderbolts. The embrace with his wisdom, Visvatara, is known as *yab-yum*.

a radish. Lawapa ordered his disciple to make the radish into soup and, drinking it, he floated up into the sky to stay with the sky-walkers. Dakinis may appear as ordinary women, as beautiful maidens – naked, luxuriously clothed or draped in a loose mail made from human bones – or as hideous toothless hags. Of the dakinis who first initiated Padmasambhava, some had five heads, and swam in a sea of blood; others rode on the backs of birds while eating human entrails; the most terrible had many hands, in which they carried corpses, their own decapitated heads and their own plucked-out hearts. A number of flesh-and-blood women have also acquired the status of dakinis. One of the best known, who lived in the 8th century, was Chosa Bonmo, a fantastically strong woman who could tie a sword into three knots. Even the greatest Tantric sages did not necessarily restrict themselves to supernatural consorts. In addition to his many demon guides and conquests, Padmasambhava had five earthly dakinis, including the youngest bride of King Trisrong Detsen.

Dakini, Tibetan God of Seduction, late 18th/early 19th cent. Copper, 126 x 62 x 40 cm, Musée Guimet, Paris. Some Buddhist sects in Nepal and Tibet still carry out initiations by placing a statuette of a dakini over the lap of the initiate in an act of symbolic intercourse.

Stupa on Lake Manosawar, Nepal, Solu Khumbu, Namche Bazaar. *Stupas* or *chortens* act as repositories of spiritual power. They may mark the spot where a great sage meditated, guard a mountain pass, imprison a demon or hold the bones of a holy man.

Pinning Down the Demoness

Every mountain and rock in Tibet seems to house a spirit or god, but more than this, the whole of central Tibet is a massive demoness, lying supine with her shoulders to the east of Lhasa and her hips to the left, and her limbs spread-eagled through the border provinces. The lake in the Plain of Milk in Lhasa is her heart's blood, and the three hills rising from the plain – Marpori, Chakpori and Bonpori – her breasts and pubic mound. The demoness is the source of all the hostile elements, and is boundless in her lusts and her bestial appetites. In order to subdue her, the 7th-century king, Srongtsan Gampo built a series of palaces, temples and *stupas* (monuments of brick or stone) intended to pin her down and make her powerless. Every new *stupa* built in Tibet helps to immobilize the demoness even further.

Forbidden Zones
China and Japan

Woman Looking at Erotic Drawing (detail), from the album *Jin ping mei*. Color on paper, 37 x 32 cm, Bertholet Collection. Under the decadent and barbaric rule of the Manchus, China saw an age of demureness, prudery, and double standards. The popular erotic albums of an earlier age were banned. The novel *Jing ping mei* was also forbidden, but continued to circulate "under the counter". Here we see one of the characters, the cruel Pan Jinlian, studying erotic picture albums.

China – Secrets and Misconceptions

To Westerners, the relationship the Chinese have with sexuality and eroticism is mostly viewed only in terms of stereotypes. To this day, its image is dominated by partly erroneous fragments of information taken from the tales told by Western travelers of centuries past. Furthermore, wildlife protection organizations, which defend China's animal and plant life under threat of extinction, further focus the public's attention on the production of miracle aphrodisiacs made out of rhinoceros horn or tiger bones. Books emphasizing the erotic or pornographic comment on the sexual practices of Daoism, and paintings and woodcuts depict downright acrobatic acts. The ideas one has regarding the role-specific behavior of communist China, as they are contemporary, are thought to be judged correctly, yet they aren't. That of pre-modern China, on the other hand, because of the complex background of sources – philosophical writings, poetry, novels of manners, legal texts and precedents, medical literature in the Chinese language and reports by Western Christian missionaries and other travelers – is difficult to comprehend, let alone judge. Since sexuality pertains to the most personal domain of everyday life, foreigners were discouraged from getting too close. The Italian painter Giuseppe Castiglione (1688–1766) complained of having to produce, unseen, the portraits of the concubines of the Emperor. Immanuel Kant (1724–1804), who himself never left Königsberg, opined that the Chinese were exceptionally composed, reserved, wily, efficient in business and traditional. With regard to the females he mentioned their small feet and added: "She always lowers her eyes, never shows her hands and is, by the way, sufficiently white and beautiful." Marriages were arranged by the parents, he wrote, the bride was to all intents sold. There were no bachelors; polygamy depended upon financial standing. Kant's views reflect the Western sources which were available to him. Evariste Régis Huc (1813–1860), a Chinese-speaking Christian missionary from southern France, who was a longtime resident in China, produced an extensive travel guide in which he portrays it as a man's country. From childhood on the man is prepared for the role of *pater familias*, ruling over women and children as well as his own social inferiors. The women, on the other hand, live from cradle to grave in suffering, deprivation, contempt, misery and oppression. Confined, deprived of joy and entertainment, uneducated, valued as nothing more than chattels that can be beaten or traded within the conditions of polygamy, they are often driven to despair and suicide.

In 1865 another Westerner, the German archaeologist Heinrich Schliemann, traveled through China and Japan. He reported that in the countryside it was the women who did strenuous physical work, that in Beijing – unlike Shanghai – no respectable upper-class woman went to the theater and that feminine beauty was measured by the minuteness of the feet: "A young girl, pockmarked and gap-toothed, or with thinning hair, but with a little foot no longer than three and a half thumbs, is considered a hundred times more beautiful than one who, by European standards, would

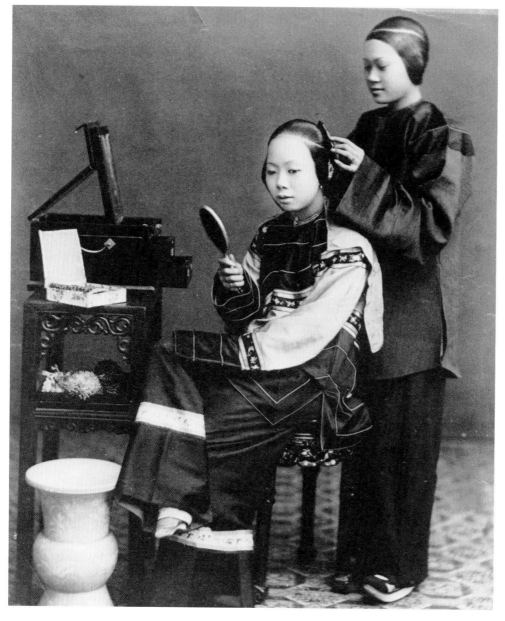

Chinese Lady with Servant, c. 1868. The young lady is wearing traditional costume with elaborately embroidered borders and a pair of trousers beneath which her delicate feet can be seen.

be considered exceptionally lovely but who has a foot four and a half thumbs long." Schliemann knew that only Chinese women had such deformed feet; Mongolian women (he probably also included Manchu women in this group) did not. From his writings, one gathers that he was permitted to see bound feet naked – an outrageous privilege. After a digression about shoe fashions he criticizes the fact that the women who had been mutilated in this way waddled like geese. The so-called "lotus feet" were achieved by binding the outside three toes, from childhood on, towards the ball of the foot, whereupon the instep became malformed into a pronounced curve.

Neither Huc nor Schliemann make any mention of erotic, illustrated handbooks. A scholarly debate, transcending clichés, about sexuality and role-specific behavior originated with what has hitherto been a seminal work on the subject of the relationship between men and women in China, their married lives and the art of physical love: Robert van Gulik's *Sexual Life in Ancient China*. The book was released in the early 1960s, during the sexual revolution in the West. However, van Gulik's bashful treatment of quotes from his sources stands out in marked contrast alongside the extensive analysis of

classic Chinese texts taken from philosophy, poetry and novels. In his introduction he comments: "Since this book will be freely available in the trade, all realistic passages have been put in Latin."

Van Gulik's outline embraces more than 3000 years (1500 B.C.–1644 A.D.) of Chinese customs and sexual history. Such historical knowledge is indispensable for the evaluation of developments from the Manchu Qing Dynasty (1644–1912) until the establishment of the People's Republic (1949). In addition there are the texts about the role of the women, inspired by the emancipation movement, or the analyses of newer archaeological finds which shed light on the pre-historical era. The latter include the female torsos of the Hongshang culture (3500 B.C.) and the clay figures, dating from the Qujialing culture (c. 3000 B.C.), which have been interpreted as oversized phalluses.

Role-specific behavior and sexual attitudes have not only changed in historical terms, but they also have clearly varied within a given period due to China's fifty different ethnic groups. In the 1990s the Han, the majority, comprised 94 percent of the population, and then there were the so-called national minorities: ethnic groups such as the Moslem Hui (0.8 per-

Female Torso, Hongshan culture, c. 3500 B.C. Fired reddish-brown clay, 7.8 cm high, Museum of History, Beijing. The find shows the very exact observational talents of these early sculptors, because both correct proportions and movement are reproduced. Today the sculptures are seen as proof of the existence of female deities, venerated at an altar in Dongshanzui, and of a matriarchal social order.

cent of the total population), whose gender roles are anchored in their religion, or the Miao (0.7 percent in 1990) in South China with their strict matriarchal social order, who have preserved the custom which allows girls to choose their husbands freely. (Furthermore, he may be sent back if he does not please her.) Likewise, the status of a Mongolian or Manchu woman within the community, as measured by her right to make her voice heard, was historically always higher than that of a Han Chinese woman living at the same time. Communism marked the first attempt to break down this hierarchical structure.

However, it is notable that in China there were no painful male initiation rites and no circumcisions of male or female children. During Imperial times, the act of defloration was not considered dangerous for the man, as it was in many Asian countries, such as Cambodia. Homosexuality, though not a matter for punishment, was looked upon with suspicion. Sexual infringements such as rape were subject to prosecution and strict punishment. Until the 13th century people in every social stratum wrote and spoke frankly about sexuality; later the references were veiled. This may explain why the subject seemed taboo to the first Europeans, who made initial contact with Chinese culture in the 13th century and only had closer contact from the 17th century onwards.

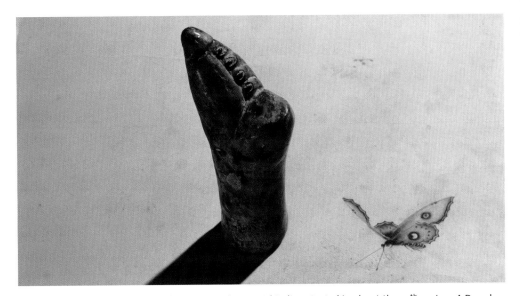

Model of a "lotus foot", private collection, London. Foot-binding started in about the 10th century A.D. and was not forbidden until the 1912 Revolution. A connection between this ideal of beauty and a woman's ability to become sexually aroused has often been postulated but never medically proved. The custom affected the Han Chinese elite on the one hand, and prostitutes on the other. This clay model of a "lotus foot" was possibly used for teaching the binding of girls' feet.

Sex and Tradition

China's major philosophical schools of thought, Confucianism and Daoism, both founded in the 5th century B.C., developed essentially different role models and ideals as well as clearly divergent attitudes to sexuality. Before the evolution of these philosophies, during the Shang Dynasty in the second millennium B.C. and earlier, Chinese society was organized along matriarchal lines. Although China's creation myths tell of a male Maker, Pan Gu, who put together heaven and earth, the human race was molded out of clay by a female goddess Nü Wa, in her own image.

It was during the Zhou Dynasty (11th century B.C.–221 B.C.) that the social system changed into one based on patriarchy and feudalism. Imperial China (from the third century B.C.) developed a strictly regulated multi-caste social system based on the teachings of Confucius (5th century B.C.) and their documentation and interpretation by scholars through subsequent centuries. Master Kong constructed a virtuous ideal – a model of Confucian morality combining *ren* (human kindness), *yi* (righteousness), and *xiao* (filial piety). The thought was that if everyone lived in accordance with such an idealized morality, this would lead to prosperity for the individual, the family, the people and the ruler, and to peace throughout the land. The political content of his teachings amounts to the demand for peace, unity and rule by the most able person. The most able person, according to him, was the one who lived most purely by his ethics. This philosophy first showed a broad effect during the Han Dynasty (206 B.C.–220 A.D.), when Confucianism was established as state etiquette. Until the end of the Empire in 1912 its sway was never challenged. The role-specific behavior and sexual relations based on the so-called Confucian doctrine would dominate the lives of the ruling elite (beyond the walls of their private quarters) until the foundation of the People's Republic of China in 1949.

In Confucianism the family was seen as a reflection of the state in microcosm. The father assumed the role of the ruler: to the wife fell the lot of the servant. The family as the smallest social unit was governed by a hierarchy defined by age and sex: the old commanded the young, Man commanded Woman. There were set rules of behavior for all minor and major occasions in public and in private life. By adhering to *li* (rites) and *yi* (etiquette) people could be certain that they were living in harmony with the universe. The ancestor cult and male descendants ensured the biological immortality of a clan.

The status of the woman and the pattern of behavior expected from her include unquestioning obedience, fidelity, modesty, chastity, cleanliness, restraint and subordination. Since they were not allowed to carry out ancestral rites or receive an inheritance, girls were of little value in the community. Ban Zhao (c. 40–120 A.D.), daughter of an official of the Han court and sister of the famous historian Ban Gu, was a member of the privileged elite. She produced a guide to bringing up a girl-child so that she would grow up, according to etiquette, into a demure married woman. It is true that she did not deny the girls' right to an education, but its aim should be to make them aware from childhood on of their lowly status within the community. The wife was to be the keeper of the home, faithfully caring for the male descendants, serving the husband and her in-laws, totally submissive, obedient, modest and without the right to participate in discussions about official matters.

Because boys were seen as having greater value than girls, one or more concubines could displace a wife who did not bear a son. Men had a right to polygamy and promiscuity, because they could thereby guarantee the continuity of their ancestral line and fulfill the duty of filial piety. A woman who bore no children could also be sent back to her parents.

Marriages in China were arranged by the parents, with the help of a matchmaker. The latter checked up on the exogamy of the couple, the virginity of the bride, the suitability of the horoscopes of bride and groom and the amount of the dowry. Often a girl would be betrothed while still a child and a boy while still in puberty.

Usually the children of a household were brought up together until puberty, after which the strictest segregation of the sexes was applied. The girls would be included in the life of the women's quarters, trained in feminine skills such as sewing, embroidery, or the playing of musical instruments. Virginity for the girls guaranteed a

Anonymous, *The Lotus Blossom Brings Forth Costly Seed*, late Qing period (1644–1912). Chinese Print, 60 x 106 cm, State Hermitage Museum, St. Petersburg. Until well into the late Qing period woodcuts with various blessings were hung up or given as presents at New Year, weddings, and births. Particularly popular were wish-formulas for the birth of a son. The pictorial elements – lotus blossom, mouth-organ (in the middle boy's hand), cinnamon twig, and pomegranate – contain a coded wish: "An uninterrupted series of respected sons."

Anonymous, *Bringing Home the Bride*, 19th cent. Chinese painting, Victoria and Albert Museum, London. In a splendid procession, the bridegroom fetches the virgin bride, clothed in red and borne in a closed sedan chair. The bearers of the red parasols of honor can be seen on the left, the magnificent chair in the middle.

good match, in fact it was a prerequisite for becoming a first wife. The boy, on the other hand, would have his first sexual experiences through visits to a brothel or by way of (tolerated) intercourse with the household maidservants.

The strict segregation of the sexes led to the development of separate lives for men and women, which was reflected in everything from architecture to furniture. The portable folding screen was an essential requirement for women who wanted to take part in festivities; they could remain unseen. The life of the nobleman and, later, that of the scholar, contrasted with the life led by his wife and her maids in their private rooms and sleeping quarters. While the men could take part in discourse with colleagues and go on nature excursions, the only break in the monotony for the women was a visit to the temple, which, although the women

would be carried there in closed palanquins, often gave rise to suspicion. Only female visitors such as medical practitioners, priestesses of the oracle or nuns were allowed to visit them. If a male doctor appeared, he would treat them from behind a curtain. These strict rules persisted until the last dynasty.

The sexual union of husband and wife was regarded as a microcosmic parallel to the macrocosmic duality of the universe. People were aware of the necessity of sexual intercourse for the wife to conceive. Ideally coitus led to the fathering of male descendants. Just as life was strictly regulated, so too was sexuality: it had to be moderate and timed correctly. Sickness was deemed the consequence of excessive surrender to lust. Fever was regarded as the result of sexual activity during the day. Social etiquette demanded that men must never spend any time

during the day in the living quarters of their wives. Nevertheless the man had to take care to satisfy the sexual needs of his wife or wives; so decreed the *Liji* (*Book of Rites*). Sexual neglect was a serious infraction of protocol. Only in old age was the man released from his conjugal duty.

With regard to beauty, young women were regarded as making the most attractive wives if they met the ideal standards: soft hands, tender skin, long white neck, beautiful eyebrows – which when they smiled took on the shape of butterfly antennae. From about the 10th century on there were the additions of the willowy waist and the bound feet.

The Challenge: Daoism

The ideal of a life regulated by rites and decorous behavior was questioned at the latest in the second century B.C. by the expanding search for immortality. Daoism was a significant movement in China and an independent religious philosophy in the widest sense. It altered ways of living and working together, especially those of its learned disciples, but also, in its populist form, those of a broad spectrum of the population.

Daoism involved a search for physical immortality, which, as it is understood today, means the longest possible extension of life on earth. Living in the spirit of Daoism involved disregarding the dictates of society and instead allowing changes to evolve unhindered; *wuwei* (non-action) was seen as the ideal. This hostility to social regulation brought with it a rejection of hierarchies. The Daoist scholar withdrew from public life and sought communion with the flow of the world, which to him was most manifest in mountains and rivers. Alongside the highly-educated scholars of this school of thought, self-appointed gurus with alleged specialist knowledge burgeoned. Teachers of specific breathing techniques aimed at increasing longevity competed with alchemists who were trying to sell drugs which promised immortality: mushrooms, vermilion (or mercury) or the elixir of life made from precious ingredients such as silver, gold and pearls. For those taking the potions the outcome was often the opposite of that envisaged;

in fact sudden death from lead, mercury or arsenic poisoning resulted. Certain sexual practices were also recommended for extending life. Even in the tombs of the Han period, signs were found of the all-pervasive spread of the belief in sexual alchemy. Thus, for example, the royal grave of Liu Sheng (c. 113 B.C.) contains several bronze phalluses. The Han rulers were, almost without exception, devotees of the elixir cult and of lengthening their life-spans through sexual alchemy.

In the course of the second century, because of the competition from Buddhism, a hierarchical Daoist State church and Daoist monasteries were established. The head was a magician who had allegedly discovered the elixir of immortality. In the monasteries sexual techniques were taught and put into practice during orgies. Zhang Daoling (first century A.D.), an important intellectual leader and patriarch of the Daoist religious community, is supposed to have advocated sexual union as the way to the forgiveness of sins (i.e. transgressions against the ideal of *wuwei*).

The striving for immortality gave way to the striving for as long and healthy a life as possible. Chinese medieval doctors were of the opinion that a healthy measure of sexual satisfaction was necessary for a healthy body. This concept is repeated in all sexual handbooks.

The Arrival of Buddhism

Buddhism arrived in the first century A.D., bringing with it, for its adherents, new promises of salvation, but also new religious obligations. The teachings of Buddhism spread into China through traveling traders and craftsmen and were promoted throughout the country under imperial patronage, after scholars were sent into Buddhism's land of origin. The doctrines represented a marked contrast to Confucianism but also opposed Daoist ideals. The renunciation of a domicile, the retreat from family and society, as well as the celibate lives led by monks and nuns, attracted suspicion from the Confucians. The suppression of human desires and sensual needs alienated the Daoists. Refraining from evil, doing good and keeping the spirit pure brought the promise of entry into the Buddhist paradise, the escape from the cycle of reincarnation. Sexuality was classified as one of the desires which should be overcome through abstinence. Sex was denounced as a sea of pleasure in which people drowned themselves. Only with Tantric Buddhism (from the 8th century) was the experience of sexual fulfillment given new validity, which was reflected also in the new duality of the deities: to every male Bodhisattva there was assigned a female companion.

Ladies' Biographies (detail), attributed to Gu Kaizhi, 4th cent. Ink and color on silk, 25 x 470.3 cm, Palace Museum, Beijing. Representation of the wife of Duke Ling of Wei, famous for her wisdom. When drinking with her husband, she concluded from the quietness that followed the passing of a coach that it was the minister Boyu, to whom all were bowing in silence.

Sexual Alchemy

The notion that sexual practices would extend life was based on the theory that during sex the *yin* powers occurring in the woman's body fluids would be absorbed by the man who would thereby be able to strengthen his own life-force, i.e. his *yang* powers. The alchemists therefore applied the ideas underlying the production of the elixir of life (the gold-cinnabar *pill jintan*) to the sexual act. Lead (seminal fluid) and cinnabar (vaginal fluid) were mixed in a vessel, which represented female genitalia. A furnace (coitus) and a predetermined cooking time (sexual technique) then produced the elixir. Daoist speculation about the magical powers of sexual union was applied to man and woman who were both supposed to profit from the exchange of active agents and juices. There are several traditions of sexual vampirism in which one partner, by way of special practices, could extract the other partner's essence without giving up his or her own. Also there are known to have been sects that promoted mass orgies. Soldiers believed themselves to be rendered invulnerable or invisible by way of specific sexual practices.

A Court Lady Receiving Instruction (detail), attributed to Gu Kaizhi. Ink and color on silk, 25 cm high, British Museum, London. The virtuous lady wore a number of flowing robes which left only the face and fingertips exposed. Hair decoration in the form of ribbons or pins was the mark of a married woman. "To arrive at the hairpins" was a metaphorical expression for the first menstruation, i.e. puberty.

Anonymous, *Contemplation of the Yin-Yang Symbol* (detail). Ink and color on silk, hanging scroll, British Museum, London. Daoism sees in the cosmic forces of *yin* and *yang* a duality which keeps the world on its course by cyclically building up and destroying each other. One cannot exist without the other. *Yin* is the predominant force of the woman, *yang* of the man. The black-and-white circle symbolizes this duality. Sunk in contemplation of this symbol is one of the highest deities of the Daoist pantheon, the god of long life *Shoulao* – recognizable by his pilgrim's staff and bald head with its marked bulge. Beside him stands a stag, symbol of immortality because of his constantly renewable antlers.

Harems and Courtesans

The first references to prostitutes can be found in literature as far back as the Zhou Dynasty (11th century B.C.–221 B.C.). The idea that a finite amount of *de* (potency), was granted to each person (women were given more *de* than men) and that by way of intercourse the woman's juices could add to the strength of the man's *de*, led to the conclusion that intercourse with numerous women should certainly not be banned; on the contrary, it was to be encouraged. However, it was important that only the woman should have an orgasm, not the man.

Aristocrats, scholars, high-ranking officers and, from the beginning of the Song Dynasty (960–1279) even merchants, often set up their own harem with a great number of women of various ranks. In any case, they had at least a first wife and a few concubines.

Within aristocratic circles, the wives were ranked by number. The higher the hierarchical rank, the lower the number of women having that rank: *hou* (first wife), *furen* (secondary wife), *bin* (wives of the second rank), *shifu* (wives of the third rank), and *yuqi* (concubines). They all lived within reach of their lord. The

The Night Entertainment of Han Xicai (detail), attributed to Gu Hongzhong, 10th cent. Handscroll, ink and color on silk, Palace Museum, Beijing. Gu Hongzhong followed and documented – presumably on behalf of the Southern Tang Emperor – the lifestyle of the scholar and partygoer Han Xicai. Here we see a detail showing Han with a ladies' orchestra.

Three Ranks of Brothels

Texts from the Song Dynasty describe social differences between brothels. Zhou Mi (1232–1308) mentions simple brothels, *washe*, for the underclass and the soldiers, *jiulou*, (wine-houses), and "high-class entertainment as offered by the houses of courtesans". The former were state brothels; among the wine-houses there were state as well as private enterprises, recognizable by red lanterns in front of the doors. The guests were offered drinks and private rooms with female entertainment. The houses where the visitors could experience music, dancing, intelligent conversation and high-class eroticism – *geguan* (song courts) or *chafang* (teahouses) – brought together educated and skilled courtesans. The clients of such houses were mostly high officials, rich merchants, literati or artists. Visits to brothels in this category were expensive, because for every service, from the bowl of wine to the sexual union, there was a fixed charge.

higher the rank of the wives, the less frequent he had sexual relations with them, but the longer they were allowed to share his bed (it could be anything from minutes to hours; only the first wife was allowed to stay the whole night through). The *Lienü Zhuan*, a collection of women's biographies from the Han period (206 B.C.–220 A.D.), mentions, for example, that the ruler was allowed twelve wives, the aristocrats nine, the ministers three and the officers two. Polygamy was permitted until the end of the Qing Dynasty in 1912, and the number of wives was frequently a question of means and status. The harems of the aristocracy were guarded by eunuchs. The eunuchs of China no longer had any sexual organs; the penis as well as the testicles had been removed. They could therefore provide no competition at all. Complete castration was the only operation carried out in Chinese medicine, for physical completeness was an important requirement for life after death. In order to meet that requirement, eunuchs stored their genitals in little vessels so that they could be buried with their bodies.

Besides the harem the aristocrat would sometimes own a ladies' orchestra, which was com-

posed of musicians and acrobats. They were the forerunners of the official prostitutes of medieval China. The artistes were also sexually available to the lord and his guests. They were sold, given as presents or used as bribes. Providing sexual satisfaction was only a secondary duty for singing girls; their main role was as entertainers, but nevertheless they associated with many men and were not bound by the strict moral code.

As early as the Han Dynasty the warrior Emperor Wu (reigned 140–87 B.C.) established the institution of soldiers' courtesans, who lived in the garrisons in order to entertain the troops and strengthen their will to fight.

During the Tang Dynasty (618–906 A.D.) there were three groups of prostitutes who, for instance, worked in the public brothels which had been founded in the Han period: the *changlou* ("houses of singing girls"), later known as *qinlou* ("little green castles"). These establishments were registered by the authorities. Apart from these there were the so-called "official courtesans" who were employed by the civil service to entertain the guests of functionaries. They remained based at the same

Advice on How to Introduce a New Concubine to the Existing Women

There is a text fragment dating from around 1550 A.D., which gives advice on family life. The anonymous author wrote such *jia xun* texts for his sons, intending them purely as private instruction and not for general consumption. He asserts that keeping the womenfolk sexually satisfied was of particular importance, because they were forced to live in the seclusion and monotony of the women's quarters. The man would have to be a good lover, or else sexual frustration would cause quarrels and rebellion to break out in the harem. In order to avoid jealousy, whenever a new concubine was introduced the women should have the opportunity to take a close look at her and to be present during her defloration, so as to answer their question: "What's she got that we haven't?"

their brothel, which, moreover, paid its taxes as a regular business.

With the Yuan Dynasty (1279–1368) China came under the rule of the Mongols, which had no effect at all upon the prevalence of polygamy and prostitution. Marco Polo mentions the four main wives of Kublai Khan and his 22 sons and the 20,000 courtesans in the suburbs of the capital. Apart from their work as prostitutes they also sang, played music and acted in the theater. Numerous descriptions of red-light districts have come down to us from the Ming period (1368–1644). The *huafang* (colored boats), of Nanjing, Suzhou and Yangzhou were particularly popular. In their day, these three towns were centers of commerce, art and cultural tourism. Courtesans and prostitutes were in demand as never before from traders, mandarins and bohemians. They lived in houseboats on the town canals.

Although brothels were an important outlet for the prevalent double standards in morality during the Qing Dynasty (1644–1912), erotic books and pictures were banned. Chastity was regarded as the highest ideal. On the other hand, there were richly appointed brothels where even men's most secret sexual fantasies could be satisfied.

Throughout works of historical literature and *belles-lettres* indications can be found that upper-class men were also involved in homosexuality and kept boys in harems. Princes chose their favorites among ministers, and the term used for homosexuality in literature to this day, *longyang*, goes back to a minister of the same name, who in the 4th century B.C. had an affair with the Prince of Wei. Furthermore, during the Song Dynasty the streetwalkers included young men who would dress in women's clothes.

location even when their masters changed. The third group, as before, were the courtesans visited by the soldiers.

The girls were mainly recruited from the underclass. The brothel madams, their adoptive mothers, taught them the skills of singing, dancing and playing music, but sometimes also reading and writing. In the brothel quarters there were courtesans and prostitutes of diverse intellectual levels, from the untaught illiterate to the educated entertainer who was well versed in the basics of classical literature. The lyrical heritage handed down from the Tang period contains the unimaginably large number of around 50,000 poems; among them are also poems by famous courtesans such as Xue Dao or Yu Xuanji (both 9th century).

The courtesans were important in society since they were not chained to the house, but could, as companions to noblemen, officials, scholars or merchants, share their lives in the community beyond the home. Often their dancing, musical and poetical talents were regarded as more important than their beauty. Whenever prostitutes or courtesans had cause to fear threats, abuse or attacks from their clients, they could rely on the protection of

Anonymous, *Courtesan with Client*, Qing period (1644–1912). Gold leaf and color on black lacquer, 26 x 27 cm, Bertholet Collection. The courtesan is undressed apart from her red bodice and the love-play has begun. The brothel was a luxury establishment, to judge by the opulent furnishings. The courtesan's tiny feet are clearly recognizable.

Ming Erotic Novels

A new literary genre developed during the Ming period (1368–1644), which was based on the stories and farces of oral tradition; the novel written in everyday language, rather than in the very complicated literary register of mandarin scholars. Historical events, ghost stories and vivid descriptions of Chinese society and its sexual and erotic attitudes as well as exaggerated, deliberately grotesque plots were written down in an easily comprehended way. The erotic novels have become well known through translations and often through the history of their censorship. For example, the first German language edition of *Rou pu tuan*, a book ascribed to Li Yu (1611–c. 1680), was confiscated in Switzerland in 1959 and destroyed in 1961 on the grounds of its indecency.

In the second half of the 16th century, towards the end of the Ming period, erotic motifs were strongly favored by the urban population of the Jiangnan region. However, during the Qing period (1644–1912), which was much more restrictive towards erotic literature and picto-rial art, many of the stories were placed on the index of prohibited works.

All the surviving short stories and novels, as well as plays meant to be performed in a theater, demonstrate a certain double standard in their treatment of sexuality. Outside the boudoir one was bound by a centuries-old strict etiquette while within the boudoir desires were fulfilled by way of imaginative games. Nevertheless, the ending always brought a moral message: the dissolute may remorsefully enter a monastery, the women dishonored by their carnal desires may choose to take their own lives, the scholars may have to face the courts for having seduced another man's wife. The lecher is punished by higher forces and meets an untimely death, as Bao Yu does for excessive masturbation in the novel *Hong lou meng*, (*Dream of the Red Chamber*). The following summaries represent the different types of erotic literature: realistic, comic and erotic-vampirical. *Jin ping mei* (early 17th century), first and foremost a social novel, describes life in the boudoirs of the bourgeoisie, taking as an example the family of the exceptionally rich merchant Ximen Qing, who has six wives and never misses the chance to visit the brothel. The reader learns of the wives plotting against each other, of lust, frustration, grief and of rival wives murdering each other's children. Love-play between couples in the garden, or even group sex, enlisting the help of maidservants for sexual intercourse, is described with no holds barred and often in earthy terms: "Being in high spirits after the bath, Ximen Qing put Golden Lotus face upwards on the board which lay across the bathtub, spread her legs apart and, penetrating her, thrust to and fro well over a hundred times. That made a noise like crabs scurrying in sludge." Ximen's demise comes after a bout of excessive lovemaking, which he only succeeds in achieving at all after taking potency pills.

The plot of Li Yu's novel *Rou pu tuan* (1633) only provides the framework for numerous erotic portrayals and fantasies. Provocative,

Anonymous, *Kun Lun Robs the Girl in the Red Silk Gown*, bef. 1738. Colored woodcut, 27.4 x 28.6 cm, Kupferstichkabinett, Dresden. Woodcuts like this were sometimes printed in color, and sometimes colored by hand. Here a scene from the novel *Rou pu tuan* is illustrated. On the way to a rendezvous, the robber Kun Lun keeps the dog which is guarding the lady away from his friend Wei Yangsheng.

Anonymous, *Ximen Qing Goes to Bed with Gold Lotus and her Servant Chunmi* (detail), probably second half of the Qing period (1644–1912). Pen and ink on paper, 37 x 32 cm, Bertholet Collection. The *roué* Ximen Qing in the novel *Jinpingmei* is shown naked, unable to control himself on the way to the bedroom. The representation of naked figures is schematic. Women's skin is depicted pale, breasts are seldom emphasized; potent men are given a sallow skin color; they bear their anatomically clearly painted genitalia like spears before them.

earthy but nevertheless ending with a moral message, it tells the tale of Wei Yangsheng, who marries the most beautiful woman on earth, Jade Scent. However, she is prim and virtuous; he tries to overcome this with the help of instructive erotic albums. Unfortunately, by the time her desire is finally awakened, her father has thrown his son-in-law out of the house leaving no man to satisfy her lust. Wei Yangsheng, meanwhile, is whoring his way around the higher echelons of society. Thirsty for revenge, one of those he has offended tries to seduce Jade Scent and she surrenders to him. Pregnant, she takes flight and, abandoned by her lover, ends up in a brothel. When her husband appears at the brothel, she opts for suicide. Railing against his fate, Wei Yangsheng turns to religion. Even as a monk he is still tormented by his fleshly desires and finally castrates himself. The final chapter of the book reveals the moral of the story: "Time to call a halt to the self-indulgent high living of modern times."

Frequently, erotic descriptions are treated with humor and irony, for example when Wei Yangsheng learns from a friend that his own penis is tiny: "How was I supposed to know that you'd only been given such a miserable scratch-stick of flesh …" Wei goes to a miracle-doctor in the hope of having his penis enlarged. The doctor recommends an operation. For that Wei must make three sacrifices: after the operation he must have no intercourse for 120 days and after that only with women over the age of 20; also he is rendered infertile. The miracle doctor cures Wei's penis using the penis of a dog.

Passages like this anticipate the surreal erotic-vampirical descriptions which can be found in the *Zhu lin ye shi* (early 17th century). The protagonist, the lovely lady Jia, is an erotic vampire who has learned how to draw out the life force from her partners. She escapes earthly jurisdiction, because at the moment of her arrest she wins immortality through her erotic skill.

Goddess of the Luo River **(detail), attributed to Gu Kaizhi, 4th cent. Ink and color on silk, 21.7 x 572.8 cm, Palace Museum, Beijing.** *Goddess of the Luo River* is the title of a poem by the leading poet Cao Zhi (192 – 232) which sings of Cao meeting with a river goddess. The goddess enchanted him, yet he could not get close to her. The poem is interpreted as being addressed to Cao's love of his younger days. The famous painter Gu Kaizhi – or the early copyist – interprets the well-known poem showing the unreachable goddess hovering above the river and Cao and his fellow men.

Erotic Poetry

The poetry of China is among the oldest unbroken literary traditions. Texts of various literary genres from the first millennium B.C. have been handed down, the majority of them dating from as far back as the Han period (206 B.C. – 220 B.C.). Among the oldest poems of the *Shijing* (*Book of Songs*), we find not only war songs or poems about social life, but also numerous love poems. The themes are courtship, declarations of fidelity, descriptions of manners or the lament of the forsaken as well as the longing for a partner. From the region around the middle reaches of the *Changjiang* a great number of songs have come down to us, traditionally described by the collective name *Chuci (Songs from Chu)*, which also date from the period before Christ, but were nonetheless written down at a later date than those of the *Shijing*.

Apart from love poems which were composed by male poets albeit told from the viewpoint of both sexes, some poems in the last days of the Han period were written by courtesans. However, there are also many wives of high officials who lament their lot as a lover, as a discarded wife, as first or second wife married against her will or as a faithful widow. Princesses mourn their destiny as victims of political alliances, sent away into barbarous foreign lands. Loneliness, lack of refinements, waiting, the pain of separation, even the encroachment of old age and the loss of beauty – all these are topics for the ladies.

The poetry of the Tang period conveys interesting hints in its portrayal of sexuality. Thus it is possible to conclude from the poem *A Bushel of Pearls* that this was the price paid for the defloration of a young courtesan. The short stories and novels of the later periods frequently incorporate poems, which are far more simply expressed, using a very straightforward sexual vocabulary. The poem *The Cock Crows*, handed down from Qi, tells of a nocturnal liaison: "Alas, the cock has just crowed – morning has broken. / That was never the cock crowing – it is the flies humming. / O, already the east grows bright – day is breaking. / That cannot be the light in the east yet – it is the moonshine. / The mosquitoes are humming around the room – it is sweet to dream by your side; / Alas, just go quickly – so that none will envy us."

These poems are surpassed only by the drinking songs of the Qing period (1644 – 1912), although in the opinion of the educated elite of China, as shared by Western literary experts, they can scarcely be classed as literature.

Books for the Bedchamber

The first mention of handbooks of sexual practices is to be found in the chronicles of the Han Dynasty (second century B.C.), where they are classified as medical literature. All eight books that were listed at that time as being on the theme of the art of love, a total of 86 scrolls (i.e. chapters) are thought to be lost. However, one thing is clear: The art of the bedchamber, *fang zhong shu*, is regarded as the high point of human emotion and the epitome of *dao* (the correct way). A fulfilled sex life is good and a necessary requirement for inner peace, a long life and harmonious social behavior. The sources indicate that the books from that time onward found their way into every well-to-do household and possibly were even part of the bride's trousseau.

At the time of the Warring States and the Six Dynasties (581–220 B.C.) only four of the ancient handbooks were known to be in use; others were still being written. The texts were compiled by Ye Dehui (1864–1927) in an anthology *Shuangmei jing an cong shu*. He reconstructed and published them. For this Ye Dehui made use of medical handbooks, which had been preserved in Japan including the *I-Shin-po* (984).

Apart from the introductory remarks about the importance of sexual union for health reasons, the texts contain recommendations on foreplay, on how to perform the sex act in various positions, explanations about the therapeutic value of coitus, hints on how to choose the right moment, on eugenics, ritual preparations to be followed for the birth of a son, and even diet sheets for pregnant women, recipes and medication for problems of potency or for curing disease in general.

From the beginning the bedchamber books were met with a mixed reception. Admittedly the Confucians did not reject them, but their stance was different from the one taken by the Daoists, in that the Confucians emphasized that the handbooks ought to be guides to procreation and eugenics. For the Daoists the instructions were a means by which you could stay healthy and live forever.

The scientist and alchemist Ge Hong (alias Master Baopu, c. 300 B.C.) made no mention of immortality, but saw the art of love as the road to health and a long life. He uses quotations from a lost book as evidence that all evil and all the misery of humankind can be attributed to misunderstandings in the bedroom.

School of Qi Ying, Zhen Houzhou and Concubine Seeking Inspiration for Poem, late 16th, early 17th cent. Ink and color on silk, British Museum, London. The sex manuals recommended different frequency of intercourse at different ages. Here an elderly scholar with his wives can be seen. A robust sexagenarian was recommended to have one ejaculation every ten days.

Master Dong Xuan's text which, even to the reader of today, seems exceptionally modern, explains, for example, that both the man and the woman should move during the act, so that both of them get the benefit. The whole spectrum of strokes has to be applied during coitus: deep and shallow, slow and quick, direct and penetrating, not just those favored by one partner. Foreplay should take place in a seated position, with the partners caressing and kissing each other. As soon as arousal manifests itself, the partners are ready for coitus. The treatise mentions the names and methods of thirty different positions and movements involved in the love act. The original way – i. e. the position intended by nature – is considered the one where the woman lies on her back and the man on his stomach with his face turned towards her: the "close union" position. There are numerous variations of this, such as the "united kingfishers" wherein the woman should lie, relaxed, on her back and the man should kneel in front of her and embrace her hips, in order to press into her. "Flying white tiger" is a variation of the fourth basic position "fish sunning itself" in which the woman kneels with her face in the pillow, and her partner kneels behind her while penetrating her vagina. The basic position "unicorn" has the woman on top, and there are likewise variations on this. The frequency of sexual union is related to age; the healthy 30-year-old may do it once a day, but the 50-year old would only copulate once every five days.

The handbooks detail the art of "loving strokes" (nine different movements for the penis and six methods of penetration) and the signs that tell the man when the woman reaches orgasm. Sucking the female breasts and erotic kissing are likewise recommended as roads to fulfillment. Fellatio is first mentioned in handbooks from the Ming period. Dong Xuan's advises the man to always wait for the orgasm of the woman before ejaculating himself. The texts give warnings about the occasions that are inauspicious for conceiving a child: one should avoid intercourse during the day, at midnight, during bad weather, eclipses of the moon or the sun or after a heavy meal.

Anonymous, Olisbos as a Gift for Women, 19th cent. Ink and color on paper, 19 x 21 cm, Bertholet Collection. In a luxurious setting, a Ming scholar is shown with an ivory olisbos as a gift for his two wives. There were various aids for masturbation, which was only tolerated among women: olisboi, Burmese bells, also a penis-like fruit. However, the sex manuals urgently warned against frequent use.

Poetic Allusions

Chinese literature as a whole is rich in imagery, metaphors, euphemisms and allegories. The description of physical love and of sexual fulfillment clearly requires a coded language, whereby the author can raise a profane matter up to an intellectual level. The concepts applied in poetry, in medical language and in novels are taken from different vocabularies. Therefore there is not only one metaphor used for a particular concept, but many. The sexual act is compared with clouds and rain (or rain-play), a sun terrace or a high hall, even Mount Wu. Bound feet were glorified as golden lotuses or lotus lilies. The word peony not only refers to the flower, but also to the female genitalia. Likewise the words flower bud, noble entrance, and vermilion crevice refer to the vagina, and silver sickle to the labia. Jade arrow, obedient vassal, yak plume (a military standard) and flying paintbrush serve to describe the penis. The master of the paintbrush is not necessarily an artist, but rather an accomplished lover. Pussy willow refers to venal love. The bedstead gets the name flowering camp, *hua ying*; *ying* is borrowed from military vocabulary. A starlet, *xiao xing*, is a concubine. Playing the flute refers to fellatio. The Burmese bell is a tool for female masturbation.

Erotic Art

Chinese art has produced neither original nude painting nor nude art sculptures. Those kinds of purely pictorial works stand worlds apart from the traditional Chinese artistic vision, which regarded only the predominantly abstract forms of calligraphy and ink painting as true art.

For a long time Chinese erotic art was represented only by book illustrations which served a narrative or didactic purpose. Admittedly, scrolls often served as models for the woodcuts, but because of the low value put on them by the intellectual elite, these pictures have rarely been handed down.

Chinese literature accredits Haiyang, the son of Prince Qu, who lived in the Western Han period, with having initiated the art of erotic painting. The utterly depraved Haiyang, who carried on incestuous relationships with his sisters, was said to have had the walls of his palace covered with paintings of copulating couples. The Emperor Yang of the Sui Dynasty (589–618 A.D.), who has been denounced by historians, was also supposed to have favored a similar decor and to have had mirrors placed all around the room while he was sleeping with his concubines.

Up to now archaeology has not unearthed any paintings of this kind, not even from more recent centuries. The sexual handbooks of medieval times were partially illustrated, but have not survived in their original form. Erotic paintings on scrolls may well have existed from the 6th century on, but no pictures of the *bixi tu* (secret dalliance) genre have come down to us from the era before the 14th century.

Zhou Fang (8th century) supposedly painted a picture portraying a ruler copulating with a concubine while maidservants gave assistance. A composition of this kind went a bit further than the usual love-scenes, which had until then shown only couples.

The Chinese history of art places four masters to the forefront as painters of erotic themes: Zhou Fang, Zhao Mengfu, the court painter of Yuan and Qiu Ying and Tang Yin from the Ming period (1368–1644), who, reacting to contemporary taste, also produced pictures of naked women and copulating couples.

The painters presented idealized pictures of courtesans, harems and courting couples, but the message is often veiled. The artists who painted erotic figures during the early Ming period did not depict naked bodies, but rather couples on their wedding day watching ants or other small animals mating. A woman sitting at her embroidery with her husband by her side, or a scholar writing with a woman nearby – scenes in which one partner has already entered the personal sphere of the other – are to be interpreted in an erotic way.

Couple in the Act of Sex, Qing period (1644–1912). Porcelain sculpture, 13 x 9 cm, Bertholet Collection. This sculpture shows a couple having intercourse in a complicated position. The vagina is given marked emphasis. The attribution of the sculpture to the puritanical, pleasure-denying Qing period is based on the hairstyle: the Chinese had to wear a pigtail as a sign of their subjection.

Numerous erotic albums of paintings originate from the later Ming period; they are known as the Spring Palace Paintings. From their descriptions in novels it is clear that they served the purpose of instruction and arousal.

Tang Yin and Qiu Ying are regarded as masters of this naturalistic school of painting. They depicted nudity and were frequently copied by famous engravers as the urban public was eager for erotic art. Clearly visible male and female genitalia, all sexual positions mentioned in the handbooks, and richly decorated boudoirs encouraged feelings of lust and the joy of living. Erotic woodcuts had their zenith during the years 1570 to 1650; albums printed at first in four, then in five colors, show a picture and the accompanying text on a double page. During the period of foreign rule which followed the collapse of the Ming Dynasty, the art of producing multicolored woodcuts was forgotten. Moreover, magical qualities were attributed to the widely circulated erotic prints. The book traders of the Qing period (1644–1912) kept erotic woodcuts as charms to protect their shops against fire. The Qing period gave rise to erotic porcelain sculptures of an artistically simple form, which provided a complete antithesis to the prevailing standards of decency.

The porcelain wine-bowls of the Ming period were also decorated with erotic scenes, although very little of this material has survived. Addi-

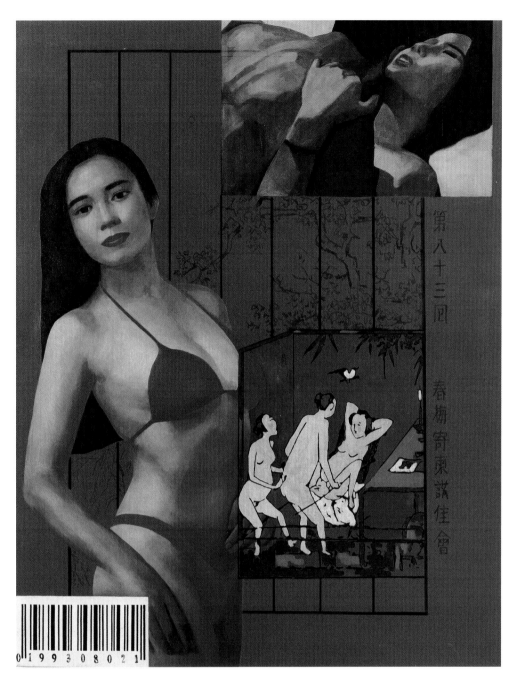

Lin Fengmian, *Female Nude*, c. 1955. Ink and paint on paper. 66.5 x 66.5 cm, private collection. Lin's artistic exemplar Henri Matisse is clearly recognizable.

tionally, the quality of the work did not reach the standards of other varieties of Ming porcelain, which were mostly commissioned under imperial patronage.

At the start of Chinese modernism, at the beginning of the 20th century, practitioners became involved in a discourse with Western art, a large part of which concerns nude painting. Traditional ink techniques were used to produce the first nudes. At the end of the 20th century, the ideas and the pictures of the young generation of artists were flouting the laws against pornography; their portrayal of naked women's bodies was clearly in breach of the regulations of the Communist Party, which demanded propriety.

Wei Guangqing, *Sensual Misunderstanding, chapter 83*, 1994. Oil on canvas, 160 x 120 cm, Stiftung für Kunst und Kultur e.V. , Bonn. Wei has painted a collage whose colors create a contrast between the art of the bedroom and everyday life. The gray reality of the present is set against the Ming illustration of love-play, and at the same time represents a stylized, desirable model of modern consumer mentality. Everything can be bought, as the barcode in the corner proclaims.

Decadence and Barbarism of the Manchus

Manchu rule (Qing, 1644–1912) brought with it a period of conservatism, prudishness and double standards. The new dynasty tried to compensate for its foreignness and – in comparison with China – its lack of refinement, by extreme adaptation. The Manchu became more Chinese and Confucian than the Chinese themselves. The literati wrote about every subject under the sun – to this day ambitious editorial enterprises show up in numerous anthologies and encyclopedias – but the topic of sexuality was strictly prohibited. Anyone who wrote on this subject, as Ye Dehui did in the closing years of the Qing period, was branded a black sheep among the literary community. The puritanism of the Qing rulers went as far as to revive old ritual regulations which decreed strict separation of the sexes even within the home – husband and wife should not even keep their clothes in the same chest. Female roles in theatrical productions were to be exclusively played by men. The erotic albums and erotic novels dating from the Ming period (1368–1644) and the early Qing period were placed in the index. The novel *Jin ping mei* was banned in the year 1687 by the Kangxi Emperor (reigned 1662–1722), but it continued to circulate on the black market. In 1708 it was even translated into Manchurian. The book was once again expressly prohibited in the year 1789 during the Qianlong era.

In spite of the purism of Confucianism the Qing epoch appears, in the light of its literature, to present a highly decadent image: indecent, pleasure-seeking, insatiable and contradictory. No epoch has left us more descriptions of depraved lives than the Qing period, although the writings themselves criticize this very depravity. The moral degeneration, which overtook the wasteful, lazy, gambling and brothel-crawling scholar class, is extensively pilloried.

The 19th-century novel *Precious Mirror to Evaluate the Actors* portrays another side of life in the community: pederasty and homosexuality. For a while visiting female prostitutes are said to have been completely "out". The plot is set in the world of actors – men acting in the roles of women are the objects of desire and the decadent scholars are

Anonymous, *Monthly Acitivities – the Twelfth Month* (detail), Qianlong period (1736–1795). Hanging scroll, ink and light paints on silk, National Palace Museum, Taiwan. The scroll depicts high-society life in winter. The ladies can be seen in the background buildings watching life from their windows and balconies, the children and the master's circle are busy outside and in their studios.

their clients. The novel mirrors social reality, for with the exception of the two heroes all the characters are historical figures. Han Bangqing (1856–1894) wanted his novel *The Prostitutes of Shanghai* to be taken as a moral lesson, so that the reader would learn the secret of the brothels and the prostitutes: pretence and falsehood, superficiality, hypocrisy and meanness.

Because the foreign rulers feared the individualism of the Daoists and tried ruthlessly to suppress them, the sexual insights of the medical handbooks were also consigned to oblivion, along with the right of women to sexual satisfaction. When the Daoist Kundan sect arose in the 19th century it was mercilessly annihilated under the pretext of its challenge to moral values. Its members, who had to join as couples, practiced group sex like those of a swinger club, although only under cover of darkness.

From the 19th century, however, a unique example of female determination is known, originating in the small-scale border region in the far south of China: the refusal of marriage. This movement, which was regarded with trepidation by the traditionalists and developed a bad reputation, was set off by the progress of industrialization and by the Western powers dominating the area around Canton. Writers of imperial historical sources are tight-lipped about the whole affair. It is only from personal reminiscences that we know of this movement, which, among other things, was based on the girls' fear of a mother-in-law's tyranny or of their total abandonment. Young girls refused to wed the bridegrooms chosen for them by their parents. They took flight to escape the wedding and afterwards lived in sisterhoods together with other women. If they were unable to escape the forced marriage they chose suicide or tried to get rid of their husband by a magic spell. The idea of the communal sisterhood was given backing by the Buddhist religion of the South as well as by Buddhist expectations of salvation. Through their attempts to lead pure lives, their voluntary avoidance of marriage and hence of impurity – pregnancy and parturition – the women hoped after their deaths to gain direct entry into Paradise. It was said that the women also formed lesbian bonds, but this has not been confirmed.

Through their activity in the silk production industry the women of the South constituted a

Xu Chu after Liu Songnian (c. 1200), *In a Chinese Pleasure House – Beating a Bound Woman on a Truckle Bed* (detail), second half of the 19th cent. Tempera on silk, Staatliche Museen, Preussischer Kulturbesitz, Berlin. Bound to a bed, a courtesan is being whipped. Pictures like this suggest that during the Qing period sadism was one of the services offered in a brothel. In the background, a voyeur is watching the scene.

significant economic force. Only unmarried girls were allowed to work in the factories, because of the obstinate prevalence of the idea that only women who had not yet borne children had the necessary purity for involvement with the silkworms. Under these circumstances, being single was even socially acceptable.

The Taiping Rebellion (1850–1864) against the Manchus, fueled by Christian influence, meant a further challenge to traditional sexual roles and attitudes. The whole of Middle China as well as parts of the South and the North were in the grip of the rebellion. The founder of the "God Worshippers' Society", who came from Guangdong peasant stock and was a reject of the imperial examination system, had a vision which led him to believe that he was the younger brother of Jesus Christ. His ruling ideology combined Christian precepts of loving your neighbor and equality with identical ideals held by the south Chinese minority. Rape and the selling of girls and women met with the death penalty, and the binding of feet was also a punishable offence. Female soldiers and generals marched with the Taiping troops. Women were allowed to sit the state examinations of the Taiping Empire. The strict separation of the sexes in the domestic sphere was maintained, however, so as not to endanger public order.

Anonymous, courtesan of the Qing period (1644–1912), 19th cent. Glass painting, 74 × 49 cm, Bertholet Collection. Pictures of this kind served as advertising placards for brothels and were designed to allow customers to make an informed choice from among appropriate ladies. The high-class courtesan shown here shows both her tiny foot and her opulent jewelry. In addition, she holds an opium pipe in her hand. Opium and sex could often be obtained under one roof.

From the Start of the Republic to the Present

Maoist Family, c. 1950. This family presents itself in front of a framed portrait of the Communist Mao Tse-Tung who introduced the so-called Mao look, a blue suit usually made from a coarse material for men and women alike.

The opponents of Communism sought to make a political campaign out of the right to a free choice of spouse, portraying it in their propaganda as "the right to free love"; they chanted slogans according to which, in the Communist controlled areas, women were collectively owned and sexual chaos prevailed. However, there was in fact no question of sexual permissiveness. In the fight against Japanese aggression and against the Guomindang, the Communist Party adopted an extremely prudish moral stance.

With the foundation of the People's Republic of China in 1949, the guidelines with regard to free choice of spouse, the freedom to divorce and the right of widows to remarry, which were already in place on a regional basis, were given the force of law throughout the country. Child marriage, foot-binding, concubinage and prostitution were finally prohibited. Despite this, the new marriage laws of 1 May 1950 brought a fresh danger for women: after divorce many were completely destitute, and there was a massive rise in the suicide rate.

Law enforced modernity, but traditional ideas and role models lingered obstinately in the minds of the people. The female author Ding Ling (1904–1986) summarized the dilemma which politically active women still frequently faced: unmarried women were ridiculed; being married, having children and being politically active met with disapproval; being married, having children and retreating from public life could make women into conservative yokels.

Equal pay for equal work was entrenched by law. The principle of equality, which meant that men and women worked side by side in front of a furnace, in the fields or in the army also led to a visual unification of the sexes. For decades the world of life and work bore the mark of the so-called Mao look, the high-necked blue working ensemble. Men and women alike wore this uniform, which many today still find practical. Only since the beginning of the 1990s, following the example of the West, did people start strolling out in their Sunday best, bringing new color to the city streets.

With the Revolution and the founding of the Republic came new laws, particularly against the unequal treatment of men and women. Progressive thinkers from the closing years of the Empire laid the groundwork for this.

Qiu Jin (1875–1907), China's first feminist – publicly executed at the age of 32 – encouraged men to recognize that women and men are equal by nature: beings with four limbs and five senses, wisdom, intelligence, strength and courage. The social reformer Zhen Tianhua (1875–1905) called on women to acquire an education and give up foot binding. The First Republic (1912–1949) was nonetheless ruled in 1913 by a Parliament consisting of 120 men. After 1919 mixed schools and kindergartens were established, and women, so long isolated within the family, emerged into the daylight. Birth control became an issue for discussion. In 1921 the Women's Union of China demanded equal rights of inheritance, the franchise for women, the right to education, the right to work and to self-determination with regard to marriage. Prostitution and concubinage were not yet forbidden. Another ten years were to pass before these demands were put into effect. At the start of the thirties, within the regions controlled by the Communists, arranged marriages, the selling of women, child marriages, concubinage and polygamy were banned. Divorce was permitted and women, who were often rendered economically dependent because of their crippled feet, were placed under the special protection of the State.

According to the law, men and women own an equal share of the sky, but women are still at a disadvantage. They are hardly represented in high political office; female cadres are responsible for child rearing, sex education, birth control and the overseeing of campaigns about hygiene. The five womanly virtues of thrift, harmony within the family, child-care, attention to health and hygiene, and eagerness to learn are only a rewording of the Confucian virtues.

Modern sculpture, propaganda posters and paintings portray strong women standing alongside men as equals, women straining towards the light of freedom, upright women to whom all professions present an open door. In spite of this women are still predominantly active in those fields which have been assigned to their gender since time immemorial: spinning silk, harvesting tea, growing rice, educating children. In addition there are the service and retail sectors.

With regard to personal relationships, men and women get to know each other through work, by frequenting meeting places or through state marriage bureaus. Once the couple agree to get married, friends and relations then get the preparations for the marriage under way. A wedding in China can cost up to two years' income.

At the universities, relationships between the students are strictly forbidden. However, one glance in the bushes around the campus parks tells the observant stroller that the ban is ineffective. The couples are aware of the risk they are running: if discovered, they can count on being assigned, after graduation, to posts far apart from each other.

Traditional customs, such as marrying in red since it considered the color of good luck, are slowly falling victim to social change and losing their meaning, while values such as the desire for male descendants remain intact. Because of the population explosion China has opted for strict birth control. The mantra goes *wan, xi, shao*: late, spaced well apart, few.

During the 1970s the country had the so-called two-child policy; at the start of the 1980s the one-child-marriage was established for those of Han origin. At the wedding ceremony the couples sign a certificate whereby they commit themselves to maintaining a one-child-marriage. National minorities are not included in this strict program. If you have one child you enjoy numerous privileges, if you have a second child you are stripped of these privileges and if you have still more children you are punished. Promotion at work will then also be more difficult, as will pay raises. Abortion is always available on the wishes of the parents and without having to give any medical reasons, particularly in centers of population. The stage of

Sex Education

While it is true that sex education is officially prescribed in China, only women are included in the state provision. That may have led to the situation that contraception has become a matter of concern only to women, while men are rather irresponsible in bed. Sex education consists of an explanation of the sexual organs and bodily functions. Sexual intercourse and possible techniques are excluded. Theoretically, sex-education literature is available to everyone, but the subject is still taboo. There is no sex education at school, since traditional taboos still make premarital intercourse unthinkable. The instruction of teenagers – if it takes place at all – is carried from mother to daughter or from father to son.

pregnancy makes no difference. In order to fulfill their duty to limit their family, many women opt for sterilization after giving birth to a child. However all kinds of contraceptives are available; condoms and birth control pills are given free of charge to married women. There are only a few unmarried mothers in China, because they are objects of social scorn.

Modern medical technology now allows the sex of a child to be predicted during pregnancy with greater certainty. Boys however still enjoy greater prestige in China, so girls are often aborted. Because abortion is always allowed at the request of the woman, this can be done at an official doctor's surgery. Nonetheless there is a high number of unrecorded cases where girls, who would have been capable of life, are

Canoodling on a park bench – an unusual picture, given that Chinese couples are usually extremely reticent in public.

Physical Contact

Many Chinese regard physical contact in films as something to be rejected in disgust. Only since the beginning of the 1990s have couples been seen in public, sitting close together, tentatively holding hands. Just as before, kissing and cuddling are forms of behavior reserved for children. Caresses between partners are far less prevalent than the affection expressed towards children. When young people of the same sex go about hand-in-hand this is taken as a sign of friendship, not as proof of homosexual inclinations.

The overcrowded living quarters limit physical contact in the private sphere, particularly when you have up to three generations sharing a home. In a 1990 survey on sexual habits it emerged that more than a third of married couples – out of around 20,000 respondents – had never seen each other completely naked.

Chinese woman with two children, 1998. Legally, having two children is either a privilege due to ethnic origin (non-Han) or due to the fact that at least two generations of the same family had one child only.

solute, superficial and mean. However, the idea of not getting married at all is as unthinkable as ever for the majority of Chinese.

The great traditions of the Chinese love life have been forgotten; at the start of the 21st century the sex act is performed in a fast and simple fashion. According to a survey conducted in the late 20th century, comparable to the Kinsey Report in the West, Chinese couples indulge in this mostly one-sided pleasure barely five times a month.

Taiwan, the Republic of China, has had to struggle with very different problems with regard to the social aspects of sexuality. There, the development, which started in 1949, was based on the general Confucian traditions of thought. Taiwan is one of the main importers of aphrodisiacs of unproven efficacy. So, on the one hand, the custom of parents selecting spouses and arranging marriages survives. On the other hand adaptation to the Western world has brought more open-mindedness.

The dark side of this is sexual abuse of children: widely-circulated pornographic material in the form of film and printed matter, and a disturbing incidence of rape. Through the endeavors of a large housewife union who have nailed their colors to the mast of an improvement in living conditions, these problems have been openly discussed in Taiwan since the 1990s. The women of the union are trying to have sex-shops removed from residential areas, to keep the mass media free from pornographic literature and advertising, and to offer young people a way out of prostitution. The union publishes books and produces theater shows, which are meant to warn children and explain the dangers to them.

Marriage

Today, after the abolition of parentally arranged marriages, love-matches only occur in the rarest instances. Marriage means comradeship. In Communist China the image of the ideal partner has constantly altered in accordance with political guidelines. During the anti-rightist campaigns a worker decorated with political medals was regarded more highly than a

declared to be stillborn. The corpses of female infants are also occasionally found. On the other hand there are increasing numbers of immensely proud parents of little princesses. However, today's generation of teenagers is for the first time showing a surplus of males.

Social checks in the area of birth control and distribution of contraceptives – for married women only – are the remit of politically organized women, such as the so-called neighborhood groups. They have the last say, after a public discussion, on whether to give permission for a pregnancy and it is also up to them to sort out irredeemably broken marriages. However, the suicide rate is rising amongst women, the reasons for which lie in the powerlessness engendered by all this social control. Even today a divorced woman is regarded as dis-

The Taiwanese Housewives' Association has been running an anti-pornography campaign since the early 1990s. All indecent material is given short shrift.

university teacher; sons of political activists were especially attractive on account of their privileges. Women experienced in the class struggle were desirable partners. Today that ideal has altered yet again. Many people now are drawn to the clichés of the beautiful woman, often adjusted by way of cosmetics and hair-perms to Western taste, and the male macho type who is successful in running his own small business. Even in the year 2000, the pattern of single living was still hard to grasp for many Chinese, because their main hope of being looked after in their old age depended on the child's duty of care, which is firmly enshrined in family law. Marriage law was amended in 1980. The earliest age for marriage is set at 20 for women and 22 for men. Local by-laws even set the marriage age for the woman at 25 and for the man at 29. Marriages between blood relatives or individuals with inherited diseases are prohibited. There is free choice of family name: the marriage partners can adopt identical names or retain the names they had when single. Marital partners are obliged to support each other and

their children. In addition there is an obligation for children to care for the elderly. Illegitimate children are given equal status with legitimate children (although there should not be any of the former, because of the rule of abstinence from premarital sex). Divorce requires mutual consent. The court fixes the settlement, in cases where partners fail to reach agreement. Obligations toward the children are unaffected by divorce. The children are given a free choice as to which of the partners they want to live with. Homosexuality is banned in China, and it is also forbidden to write about it. However, at the beginning of the 21st century it isn't persecuted any more but passed over in silence as long as it isn't openly shown.

Ban on Erotica

China has strict laws against the trade in erotica and against pornography. Foreign films are censored, and homegrown productions examined while still at the screenplay stage. Western publications are searched for indecent pictures and, if necessary, confiscated. However modern

art, for example, and the internet present a huge challenge. All the same, pornographic material is easily available on the black market, most of it from the printing presses of overseas Chinese. It is also not difficult to buy aphrodisiacs in the traditional pharmacies; that is to say, one gets, with the purchase of a medicine, a frank explanation as to whether it is also of use as an aphrodisiac.

Mass Wedding. Three hundred couples from all over China toast each other during a mass wedding ceremony at a park in Beijing, 10 October 1999. The wedding was organized by the All-China Women's Federation and was the third of its kind. The Western outfits of the brides and bridegrooms do not imply acceptance of Western ideas of marriage, but just shows that they are modern and up-to-date.

Japan – The Cultural Climate

Katsushika Hokusai, *Awabi Fisher and Octopus*. Color woodblock print, British Library, London. The octopus, common around the shores of Japan, is noted for terrorizing diving girls with its eight probing arms and its elongated, tube-like mouth. This is one of the most startling pictures in the rich history of Japanese art, which shows one of these creatures engaged in cunnilingus with a naked girl, the tip of one of his tentacles coiled around a nipple; a smaller octopus is penetrating her lips with his mouth. This image has been interpreted in some quarters as an elaborate allegory of female fantasy and masturbation. Far from terrorizing the girl, the octopus is her dream lover.

The famous Japanese writer Yukio Mishima (1925–1970) once described his country as a "crucible" – in which foreign imports are melted down and fused to generate something new, and in the process are so changed from the original form that they now appear quite native and at home. It is a process with ancient antecedents, but the first true cultural import occurred during the 7th century when Japan absorbed Chinese writing, bureaucratic organization, Buddhism, city layout and fashions in costume, housing, crafts and lifestyle – and over the next few centuries fused them into what would soon appear as native-born culture. Further waves have followed, culminating in the rapid "Westernization" that has totally changed the face of Japan since the end of the Second World War. But there is something at the core of the Japan-

ese soul that has not been imported, nor born of any "crucible fusion", and that is the native Shinto belief – a faith that has no doctrine or moral strictures, but shows respect and veneration for the mysteries of nature. The idea of original sin, or even ordinary sin, is completely alien to the Japanese mind. Shame is understood and discussed more than guilt, and although sexual acts are practiced within certain social restrictions of time, place and privacy, sexuality is recognized as just another appetite to be satisfied – like eating and drinking – and the satisfaction gained is considered necessary for a balanced life of health and happiness. Shinto recognizes members of the imperial family as direct descendants of the Sun goddess Amatesuru, as well as countless other *kami* (deities) which are often unusual objects of nature; a

Anonymous, *A Phallic Contest: The Competition* (detail), pub. c. 1870. Scroll, private collection. The earliest known *makimono*, or horizontal scroll, was called *The Phallic Contest,* and was attributed to the Abbot Toba, who lived between 1053 and 1154. It is now only known from later copies. Its intention appears to have been comic rather than erotic.

strange-shaped stone, or a giant, ancient tree. Of equal importance is the concern for fertility, and the orderly passing of the seasons – a concept that is never far from the minds of the Japanese, most of whom were involved with farming or fishing until the modern period. Fertility is connected with sexual images all Japanese were familiar with throughout most of history.

Sexual imagery is seen, thinly-disguised, in many figures of legend and folklore – often gods who can trace their ancient origins back to India, but are now so transmogrified and domesticated as to seem completely Japanese. Jurojin, the god of longevity, is always depicted with an elongated, bald head and carrying a ripe peach, and Otafuku, (also known as Okame), is the goddess seen everywhere with cheeks so plump that they resemble buttocks. She is often associated with good-humored licentiousness, and can be seen in the company of the phallic-nosed Tengu goblin, or Hyottoko, the country bumpkin with a mouth pursed into a tube like that of an octopus. Masks of these figures are seen at country fairs and festivals, and always raise knowing smiles. Stones associated with divinities and carved or weathered into the shape of genitalia are a regular sight in parts of Japan, and not just in rutal areas. The Oogata shrine near Nagoya is noted for a stone that naturally mimics the shape of a vulva. It is more common, however, to encounter phallic stones. One of the most famous is in central Tokyo, located on an island in Shinobazu pond in Ueno park, near the temple.

Anonymous, *A Phallic Contest: The Charge* (detail), pub. c. 1870. Scroll, private collection. As the *makimono* is unrolled, it tells the story of the contest. After the strongest men of the realm have presented their penises to be measured at the Imperial Court, they are mobbed by a group of women, anxious to test the competitors.

Anonymous, *A Phallic Contest: The Committees* (detail), pub. c. 1870. Scroll, private collection. Even the strongest and best-endowed of the men is no match for the sexual appetite and stamina of the women. As a result, the women are declared to have won the competition, and are presented with the Imperial prize.

Sasenasai Marumaru, *Mōzō*, illustration from *Fables of Coitus all Year Round* by Inraku-Doju. *Mōzō* refers to fantasy pictures, here with a markedly phallic component.

Momongā. **Illustration from the book** *Pictures of Ghosts that Walk by Night.* **The** *Momongā* **is in fact a hairy monster from Japanese ghost stories.** *Momongā* **has also, however, become a colloquial expression for particularly hairy female pudenda. In his illustration, the artist has created a visual** *double-entendre.*

Top left: **Sho-Zau,** *Tempestuous Couple*, **printed in 1860. Polychrome woodblock print, 15.5 x 10.5 cm, private collection.** Shunga prints often grotesquely exaggerate the male genitalia. The artist here could be making an ironic comment on this tradition, by suggesting that the man has to prepare the way for his penis, using his open hand.

It is devoted to the female deity, Benten. This goddess is a fearsome denizen of streams and seas, sometimes seen in a half-serpent form. She has been tamed and domesticated for her insatiable appetite for men. By the edge of the pond in Ueno park is a large rock which, from the front, bears an image which may be that of Enno Shokaku – a hermit-magician and one of Benten's many paramours. From the rear, however, the rock appears as an enormous penis. The area is a popular spot for lovers' trysts.

Animals, too, can show phallic attributes, and shrines of the fox-god are found all over Japan,

especially on top of new office buildings. These images all have enlarged, erect tails, often tipped with red paint just to emphasize the point. Their job is also to warn and protect. Even certain plants have found a place in the country's sexual vernacular because of their suggestive shapes or properties. Eggplants and cucumbers were often employed as dildos (although richer ladies preferred their sex-aids fashioned of horn or ivory), and in art they are usually depicted in a suggestive manner, often with a female symbol, such as a clam, nearby. The highly-prized and expensive matsutake mushroom is always a subject for ribald banter, and for teasing the girls, on account of its sexually explicit form.

The Japanese have always had an uncomplicated attitude towards sex and its imagery, and no family – from grandparents to toddlers – would be embarrassed to visit the famous museums of phalli that can be seen in Shimoda and Beppu. Until very recent times, even special tastes such as homosexuality or sado-masochism could be practiced without censure so long as good form was kept, no one was hurt, and one's obligations (marriage, children, looking after elders, and so on.) were not compromised. It is a liberal attitude that has long delighted single foreigners living in Japan, and one commentator has likened the country to a sexual Disneyland. On the other hand it has horrified others who were more deeply influenced by Judeo-Christian-Islamic concepts of behavior.

During the late 16th century, Portuguese and Spanish explorers arrived in Japan and soon brought Jesuit and Dominican missionaries with them, with a view to converting the country. Many of the newcomers despaired. They were horrified to find that the local Buddhist priests sodomized younger acolytes and were resolutely unrepentant about doing so. When instructed that such practices were mortal sins that would be punished by the eternal fires of Hell, the temple priests would laugh and point out that it was fun and caused no pregnancy, so what could be wrong with it? Japan has never been an easy posting for missionaries.

Strangely enough in recent years there seems to be a switch of sexual mores across the ocean, and although gynecologically-explicit pornography can now be easily found in Europe and America, in Japan it is still in a legal gray zone where the law is erratically applied. This is not to say that such material is unavailable – government departments responsible for such areas cannot control the vast amount of parcel post – but there is something paradoxical, and uniquely Japanese, in the practice of employing teenage boys, part time, to ink out the pubic areas of imported Playboy centerfolds.

Stone Gods of the Wayside

Until the modern period the roads of Japan were little more than footpaths, and as they led to and from the unknown they held real terrors in the minds of those who had to travel them. Stone phalli and other deities of the wayside were made in large numbers since ancient times (they are mentioned in texts dating from the 10th century), and placed at strategic positions to protect, warn and no doubt, delight. The traveler would be aware of the power of these stones, be reminded of pleasures behind or ahead, and while prompted to behave properly in the presence of deities, would also give the sense of being in familiar company, resulting in feeling less exposed to the dangers of the road.

The earliest roadside images were in the form of an erect penis, but these were gradually replaced with the yet more potent image of copulation, and images known as *dosojin* were erected along the roadsides of Japan for the same purpose. These images depict a man and a woman standing either side-by-side, or face-to-face, not always in an obvious sexual embrace, but one with obvious meaning in a society where there was traditionally very little public touching between the sexes.

The original purpose of warning and protecting the traveler was enhanced by these images, which now invoked the even more powerful, complementary forces of *yin* and *yang*. As centuries passed, it was only to be expected that such familiar images should extend their powers from making the roads safe to curing various sexual disorders, and providing babies for barren women. People from the countryside would show their gratitude by leaving offerings of an appropriate shape: daikon radishes, carrots, and long, mountain potatoes.

Despite their fortuitous attributes, few such images remain to be seen, partly because imported Buddhism sought to disguise those that were overtly sexual in appearance – to clothe them, as it were, with the more sophisticated manners of the mainland. So while these images still abound, they appear in less-recognizable forms. For example, they can be seen in the bald-headed, standing statues of Jizo, a bodhisattva deity who has chosen to postpone eternity in Paradise in order to stay and help other souls. Particularly, he is associated with children, and is often seen at the sites of road accidents, and in profusion at temples such as Hase-dera in Kamakura, where, in a country where abortion is a common form of birth control, the souls of aborted fetuses are remembered. From the back, his form looks distinctly phallic. A boat-shaped, symbolic vulva against which he is often seen standing, or a halo, poised to be penetrated by his head, further enhances the allusion to his ancient purpose.

Perhaps the main reason for the disappearance of these venerable stones can be blamed on sadly misguided government policy during the 19th century when, after having been sealed off from the outside world for so long, Japan opened up its borders to foreign influence. One of the more regrettable imports of the time was that of Victorian prudery, and in a drive to emulate their Western peers, the great and good made much effort to get rid of the offending stones, despite widespread protests by the country folk.

Dosojins, such as this from Kanagawa Prefecture combine a phallic symbol and a male-female duality. In some cases, even when the *dosojin* has been abstracted into a pure phallic shape, the phalluses occur in pairs.

Shunga – The Japanese Art of Love

Torii Kiyonobu, *Foursome* (detail), 17th cent. Mita Arts Gallery, Tokyo. Torii Kiyonobu (1664–1729) founded the Torii school, the only *ukiyo-e* school to have survived to the beginning of the 21st century. Torii designed numerous portraits of *kabuki* actors. *Shogi gacho* (Picture Album of Courtesans) and the two-volume *Furyu shisho byobu* (Portraits of Famous Actors), both printed in 1700, are his representative works.

Ukiyo-e prints and paintings, which depict the courtesans and proletarian life of Edo period Japan (1603–1868), have been well known in the West since the late 19th century. The word *ukiyo* literally means "floating world" and originally evoked a Buddhist sentiment of the fleeting transience of life, which, whether painful or pleasurable, is all too brief. By the late 17th century, it became intimately associated with the demimonde of prostitutes and actors. *Ukiyo-e* (*e* meaning picture) were images that depicted this colorful world of the kabuki theater and the pleasure districts which were becoming so celebrated in the booming cities of the period. Famous collections of these pictures were formed, and until recent years, most of the scholarship of *ukiyo-e* was to be found in Europe and America. What is not so well-known is that a surprisingly large percentage of the corpus of *ukiyo-e* is explicitly and uncompromisingly erotic, and that these works, known as *shunga*, (literally "spring pictures"), were made by all of the *ukiyo-e* artists from Moronobu in the 1690s through to the decadence of the mid-19th century – and even later (though more surreptitiously) into the Meiji (1868–1912) and modern periods.

Erotic art has been found from almost all periods of Japan's history: phallic imagery can even be seen in terracotta figures of the 6th-century Tumulus period. A law passed in 701 decreed that doctors should study illustrated sex manuals as part of their training. The manuals referred to were almost certainly Japanese translations of Chinese texts that had been in circulation for centuries, and gave detailed instructions on how to use sexual techniques to improve health and longevity. In the Daigo-ji temple in Kyoto, a hand-scroll dated 1321 depicts scenes of sodomy – a widespread pastime among the ranks of the priests and samurai. Although there are a few *shunga* that date from such early times, the majority of the *shunga* that have survived until now date from the past 300 years.

Mid-17th-century hand-scrolls painted by Tosa school artists, who were largely employed by the court, usually depict twelve different sexual positions – presumably one for each month of the year. However, these are not technically *ukiyo-e* as they frequently portray courtiers and their ladies: people who are several rungs up the social ladder from the courtesans and actors celebrated in the *shunga* dating from the following two centuries. It has often been supposed that such pictures were made to instruct virgin brides, or for courtesans to warm up a cool customer, but in fact they were used much as pornography is used today – as a stimulus for fantasy and masturbation.

The *ukiyo-e* genre evolved through the 18th century to reach an apotheosis in the 1770s with the development of the *nishiki-e* – skillfully made woodblock prints in a variety of colors. Suzuki Harunobu (1724–1770) was the leading master of this new medium and produced several hundred prints in the last years of his short life. Perhaps the greatest of all the *ukiyo-e* artists, his works show a mastery of line and color, and a sensitive interpretation of the mood of the moment. In his pictures, lovers seem cool – as if time were of no consequence, and each delicious moment could be enjoyed to the limit – instead of being spent in sudden passion. But artistically, the feeling of freshness and lyrical beauty in Harunobu's prints was short-lived, and in the works of later masters we see an encroaching decadence that seems to reflect the ever-more chaotic insecurity of life in Edo, as the capital was known.

All *shunga* are notable for graphic exaggeration of the genitals, but in the hand of Harunobu's

Kitagawa Utamaro, Mita Arts Gallery, Tokyo. Kitagawa Utamaro (1753–1806) displayed a marvelous ability to capture the expressions of women, especially the fickle nature of the courtesans of the pleasure districts. They handle their customers with professional skill, no doubt, but often it seems that their eyes are elsewhere – on another lover perhaps – or on the bleak future that comes only too soon when they reach their mid-twenties, and youth will fade.

successors this tendency was taken to such extremes that male members were shown as having the same girth as the man's arm. Perhaps a national sentiment for phallicism and fertility images is the explanation for such focus, but by the early years of the 19th century *shunga* pictures were becoming more gross than stimulating. One star stood above the rest – Katsushika Hokusai (1760–1849) – for his dazzling skill, brilliant lines, and fertile imagination. But his taste for the bizarre and grotesque in *shunga* showed a direction from which there could be no further development – at least in the world of *ukiyo-e*. By the mid 19th-century *shunga* were turned out in increased quantities, and in decreased quality, with coarse composition, crude lines and brutal subjects. In addition the authorities did their best to outlaw erotic graphics after the opening of Japan to the West. Paintings and editions of prints continued to be made in private, and circulated surreptitiously. As such they were almost always made anonymously, although attributions to known artists can sometimes be made on stylistic evidence.

Katsushika Hokusai, *Tempestuous Union*, c. 1810. Polychrome woodblock print, Oban format, private collection. Showing what was perhaps a less agreeable side of Edo life, Hokusai depicts in this print a young lady who is trying to resist the attentions of a rather unsavoury-looking character of the lower classes.

The Floating World and Pleasure Districts

Although in past centuries, prostitution was widespread all over Japan, there was perhaps no place where the trade reached such a level of splendor as in the famous Yoshiwara pleasure district of Edo (now Tokyo), which was located just a couple of minutes walk behind the great Sensoji Kannon temple to the northeast of the city. The pleasure district was established in the early 17th century and completely rebuilt in 1657 in what was then a rural area, and was approached along a raised embankment between the paddy fields. It catered for the men of Edo and Tokyo for 300 years, surviving fire, earthquake and war, until it was finally closed by a government edict outlawing prostitution in 1957. Today the area is a nondescript concrete sprawl, and almost nothing remains to remind one of its original purpose except for the occasional "Soapland" (Turkish bath), or a discreet, private *ryotei* restaurant – a place for secret liaisons.

During the 17th century, Edo was a rapidly-growing city – home of the ruling shogun and his court, and palaces of the regional *daimyo* lords, their families, retinues of servants, and

Anonymous, *The Gay Quarters of Kyoto*, 17th cent. Ink, paint and gold on paper, six-panel folding screen, 140.3 x 358.2 cm, Museum of Fine Arts, Boston. Although the Yoshiv are depicted, where elaborate manners were elevated to serious ritual. Based on a pun between floating and sorrowful, Ukiyo came from the Buddhist "sorrowful world" of *Oshiwara no Okagami* (The Great Mirror of the Yoshiwara). Artifice and role playing, he pointed out, were as important as the possibility of sex.

samurai warriors. The *daimyo* lords were required to alternate their time between their home fiefs, and their palaces in Edo, leaving family members behind them as hostage. By having their families divided at any one time, and by having to maintain two households in a style appropriate to their rank, the time and assets of the lords were almost totally consumed – a shrewd calculation by the shogun, so that little chance would be left for any anti-government mischief. But such magnificent style required a lot of support, and within a few decades the city was filled with craftsmen and tradesmen who not only catered to the great households but also spawned new fashions in order to generate more business. Together with the armies of servants, samurai, job-seekers and endless visitors from the provinces, they made Edo a city of bachelors on the loose; a potential source of unruly energies which the authorities wisely concluded were best dissipated by peaceful means. And so the Yoshiwara was built almost as a separate city, where the men of Edo could devote themselves and their funds solely to the pursuit of pleasure.

most extensive pleasure district in Japan, other cities also had areas devoted to bathhouses, tearooms and brothels. On this folding screen the pleasure quarters of Kyoto nd grief. One of the foremost guides to etiquette and traditions of the brothel district was compiled by Fujimoto Kizan (1626 – 1704), who took 20 years to write his

Kabuki theater in Tokyo: man examining the arm of a geisha for tattoos, to reveal her as a thief, and at the same time, a man, c. 1928/29. The *onnagata* is considered to represent the ideal of feminine grace, much more than any real woman could be.

Kabuki Theater

Closely associated with the Yoshiwara in the Floating World were the *kabuki* theater and its famous actors. Whereas drama was the chosen entertainment for the upper classes, with its themes of warrior ghosts and lovelorn princesses, it was *kabuki* – which is roughly equivalent to vaudeville or pantomime in the West – that became widely popular among the rest. This dramatic entertainment originally evolved from shrine dances that were performed at various festivals, but by the early 17th century, had become a cover for advertising prostitutes who would sing and dance suggestively on stage. The authorities deemed the theater to be an outrage to public morals and order, and female performers were banned from the stage in 1629. Nevertheless, one vice was replaced by another, and male actors, known as *onnagata*, took the female roles and still do in the *kabuki* theater to this day. They too, performed in such a seductive and suggestive manner that their after-hours attentions were being competed for by members of the audience. Once again, the authorities tried to ban the theater but it had become too popular, and so a compromise was reached. Young actors were required to shave off their forelocks, which were considered by aficionados to be one of a youth's more endearing features (along with a hairless bottom). They retaliated by wearing women's wigs even off-stage, causing as much mayhem as before, until a final compromise was reached, and they were obliged to wear a cotton cap over their shaved heads when not performing.

Within the great gate of the quarter, the rigidly-maintained social ranks of the outside world broke down, and a new pecking order was determined by looks, style and money. Although one's image was much enhanced by arriving as ostentatiously as possible, at the entrance to the quarter, palanquins and attendants had to be dismissed, and, in the case of samurai, swords and other weapons had to be checked-in until departure.

The Yoshiwara came alive at sunset when the lanterns were lit, and the courtesans dressed up in their finery ready to receive customers. On passing through the main gate, the visiting rake was faced with the Naka-dori – the central thoroughfare that was planted with cherry trees, with the grandest establishments lining each side. Branching lanes were also lined with brothels and teahouses that either enjoyed lesser prestige, or that catered to those with special tastes. On the ground floor of these houses, the courtesans would wait behind wooden bars, through which important details could be negotiated and agreed upon.

The *oiran* were the highest-ranking courtesans in the Yoshiwara, peerless in the art of handling men, skilled at suggestive repartee, cultured and exquisitely attired. They were obliged to deal with men of all social backgrounds and so had to be intimately familiar with the complex punctilio that went with their rank. It took at least three meetings for a suitor to even entertain a hope of being able to win the favors of an *oiran*. Being prepared to spend vast amounts of money went without question, but it was considered unseemly to appear to give this a second thought. After all, one was paying for the favors of a princess of the night. What was important was to impress the *oiran* with good looks and grooming, good dress sense and a level of wit to match her own – a reputation as an accomplished lover would also help. *Iki* was a word coined to denote the necessary qualities – a smart way with fashion and style: a clever combination of colors that reflected the season, an unusual weave of cloth that preferably showed painstakingly difficult workmanship (and hideous cost), or a daring, but successful pattern. An absence of this sense was *yabo* – out of style, boring and of churlish taste: "naff". A customer so afflicted would have to seek his pleasures on the side streets where a lady might be found who was less choosy.

There were never more than eighteen *oiran* in the Yoshiwara, and most visitors selected from the wide range of lesser-ranking girls on offer. Guides were available in the Naka-dori to explain the skills and qualities of each girl available, and to make the necessary introductions if the client was not already a regular visitor. Once inside the house, the client was entertained with food, sake, music and dancing, in a manner commensurate with his largesse, before retiring to spend the night with his chosen courtesan. No client was allowed to spend more than twenty-four hours in the Yoshiwara, and the morning light saw the opening of shutters, morning tea, the usual bustle of Japanese hostelries, and the short journey back to the city. Most of the working girls in the Yoshiwara were recruited by professionals known as *zegen*, who scouted areas of the country that had been particularly blighted by typhoons, earthquakes or bad harvests. There they would offer a small, but vitally-needed sum of money to some wretched family in exchange for "looking after" their daughter. All knew exactly what this meant. Other girls came from among the inevitable babies that were born and raised near to the Yoshiwara, and yet more were recruited from the higher social ranks, when an uncontrollably wayward girl was sent to the quarter as a punishment.

The girls in the Yoshiwara could expect just over a decade of employment before their careers would fade with the bloom of their youth. During this time they would try to catch the attentions of a lover who would buy them out of the Yoshiwara, and provide them with a more prosaic, but secure, life as a wife and mother. This could cost a lot; the lover would have to be ardent enough to repay all the expenses that the courtesan had incurred since she was first procured, such as food, and the costume and ornaments of her trade. With this end in mind, courtesans would find extra-curricular amusements in order to get closer to their chosen lover. The passing of the seasons provided continual festivals and amusements; cherry-blossom viewing and picnics in spring, gathering shellfish around Tokyo Bay in the summer, and viewing the changing colors of the leaves in autumn.

The worry of imminent insecurity was the price to be paid for a few short years of being desired, and for many the future was bleak. The lucky ones would be bought out and married, others would find a management position in one of the brothels, but many would leave the Yoshiwara to ply their trade in the streets and under bridges. Faced as ever with the high risk of disease, and a precarious income that diminished rapidly as they aged,

Hosoda Eishô, *Oiran*, 1790s. Mita Arts Gallery, Tokyo. This print shows a courtesan or *oiran* with two young attendants. The *obi sash*, tied at the front rather than the back, was a trademark of the courtesan.

Utagawa Kunisada, *Brothel in Edo*, c. 1840. Polychrome woodblock print, 18.5 x 13.2 cm, private collection. Despite paying to be in the company of a high-class prostitute, men still found themselves having to compete for her attention.

their deaths went almost unnoticed, and their bodies, unnamed, would be tossed into a common pauper's grave.

The idea that sexual desire was an appetite meant that there was little stigma towards homosexual practices (known as *nanshoku*), and in the right context, they actually fitted in with the political philosophy of the Tokugawa rulers. Such activities had long been almost imperative in monasteries, and in the ranks of the samurai – where they were less frowned upon than heterosexual relations with one of an inferior class. There are references to large numbers of what would now be called "rent boys", who were available for "quickies" in any of the cities, and a book published in 1643, known as the *Shinyuki*, sought to classify how homosexual behavior should fit in with the

Confucian ethics that were favored by the governing authorities.

Parallels can be drawn with the ideals of ancient Greece, since at least at the beginning of a homosexual romance, the attraction should be between a mature man and a *wakashu* (or handsome youth), who would benefit from his elder's guidance. The pursuit of such a youth was known as *wakashudo*, or *shudo* for short – which gives a rather lofty impression of following an artistic "way". Many other books were written to eulogize the subject, but looking at the images of *wakushu* in prints and paintings of the period, one sees that most of them were involved with the world of *kabuki*, and it can be assumed that their goals were as commercial as those of their sisters in the Yoshiwara – all characters on the stage of the Floating World.

The Influence of the West

In 1957, Japan was on its way to recovering from the devastation of the Second World War. The occupation had ended in 1952 and the country was busy reinventing itself as a modern, Western-style democracy, with the United States as its role model. A new law was passed making prostitution illegal, and from that moment on, sex – or at least commercial sex – was forced to change its face. Large numbers of women were at risk of becoming unemployed, along with their armies of pimps and supporters, and so in a country where form usually matters more than content, the problem was addressed by changing the name of the business. The grandest brothels had to close down as they were too traditional to cope with the adjustment, but the smaller, more adaptable establishments went through a little metamorphosis and were reborn as "Turkish Baths".

On the surface that is exactly what they were – and one could certainly visit such a place to have a good sweat and get cleaned up. But there were plenty of other services on offer – all described with different euphemistic names – and the girls had the added advantage of looking after a customer who was not only naked, but also being steamed – a rather defenseless position. In Japan, the "health massage" could be given with or without cream, and of course anything else could be negotiated. The real problem was that the business, no matter what it was now called, was criminal, and so fell under control of the underworld with all of its less desirable aspects: threat, coercion, and a distinct lack of quality control.

But some sort of accommodation seems to have been reached, and so long as these places stayed in certain locations, (preferably in the *asobi-machi* – the "playtown" of nightlife to be found next to every major railway station), the police would keep their distance. The establishments also changed their name again after an embarrassing incident when the Turkish Ambassador in Tokyo boarded a taxi, asked to be taken home, and ended up being delivered to a brothel. Complaints were made from high-up, and in response the nationwide Turkish Bath Owners Association decided that from now on, their establishments would be known as "Soaplands".

As Japan raced to become an economic superpower, businessmen from around the world descended on the country, and they too, had to be looked after in an appropriate manner. Great nightclubs were becoming a feature of the Akasaka area, close to the government min-

Tea ceremony, 1983. The extremely stylized relationship between the geisha and her patron, which has survived the influx of Western habits, is revealed clearly in the formality of the tea ceremony.

Love Hotels

The love hotels are one of Japan's great institutions, and can be seen close to all nightlife areas, as well as in clusters around the expressway interchanges and dotted throughout the countryside. Those located outside the cities all have parking facilities, with discreet plastic curtains that hide the rear license plate. The same attention to privacy is seen at the entrance, which is usually small and rather dark – the sort of approach that can be slipped into quickly without attracting attention. There is no long reception desk either, and the room rate is usually paid under an opaque barrier so that no faces are seen. A small sign out in the street will advertise the charges: one for an "honorable rest", that is, two hours, and the other for an "honorable stay over", which is from 11 p.m. until the following morning. Love hotels serve a much-needed purpose by providing privacy, which is a rare luxury in Japan, where houses are cramped and often have three generations living under the same roof. Not surprisingly, a large number of those who use love hotels are respectably married. Some establishments are famous for rooms which feature special toys and inspirations to fantasy: revolving waterbeds, rocket-shaped beds, vibrating beds, strategically-placed mirrors, video-equipment so that one's performance can be checked – and as one famous hotel behind the Russian Embassy in Tokyo has advertised – "an S&M dungeon if you feel like it".

Outside a Love Hotel in Dogenzaka (Love Hotel Hill) area of Shibuya. The larger love hotels are famous for their fanciful architecture, a mishmash of Corinthian columns, Turkish minarets and stained-glass windows – a particularly popular one is a concrete, landlocked copy of the ocean liner *The Queen Elizabeth*.

istries and headquarters of leading corporations, where "hostesses" – chosen from the most beautiful girls in the land – would make their visitors feel like a king. A shrewd lady known as Mama Cherry became one of the most important figures in Japan's postwar economic miracle for her skill in making foreign businessmen feel welcome – it is believed that many a businessman would sign a deal with his Japanese business partners while offering a prayer to be sent back to Tokyo again soon. Hostesses were not obviously for sale, and like the *oiran* of the Yoshiwara, they dispensed their favors discreetly – and for a great price. In the meantime they could charm customers into not noticing the outrageous drinks bill, which in any case would probably be paid for by his Japanese corporate hosts.

Geisha

Somewhere in the mythology invented by Westerners about Japan is the misconception that geisha are in the sex trade, but nothing could be further from the truth, and the very suggestion would be highly offensive. Geisha are entertainers, trained from girlhood in refined skills: singing, playing the *samisen* and dancing, as well as the etiquette of hospitality, tea ceremony and flower arranging. Furthermore, their career is most certainly not over when youth fades.

The *maiko* (apprentice) begins her training at about the age of ten and becomes a geisha at eighteen. She will be hired out to entertain at banquets and those exclusive *ryotei* restaurants used by politicians and high-ranking businessmen. In such places, geisha hear much, but they are famed for discretion. Their services are extremely expensive, and all earnings go to the mistress, who invested in their training and elaborate costume. Naturally, the entertainment of men with its inevitable flow of *sake* can hardly be entirely lacking in any thoughts of romance – however chaste the ideal – and with luck, a geisha will be able to find a wealthy lover, maybe even a husband, who will keep her in suitable style, and perhaps finance her into establishing her own business.

By the end of the 20th century there were only 17,000 geishas left compared with more than 80,000 in the 1930s. The astronomical cost of hiring a geisha has contributed to their decline, but also means that they are seen as valuable status symbols by those who can afford them.

In modern Japan, many top geishas find themselves adopted as the mascots of large companies, with whom they sign exclusive contracts. In their corporate role they also have to learn new skills, such as how to play golf.

Modern Japan

During the last decades of the 20th century, Japanese society went through such change that it would now be unrecognizable to anyone born a hundred years before. In the past, almost all marriages were arranged, not only with the intention of combining money and power, but also because experienced adults were considered to be more capable of judging what was a good match. If there was also love and affection, so much the better – but if not, for the man at least, it could be found elsewhere. In modern Japan young people either marry for love – or, as is more common at the beginning of the 21st century – they don't marry at all. While women still confront a "glass ceiling" in the climb to promotion within the Japanese corporation, sexual equality is becoming more and more a subject for discussion and action. Lawsuits are being filed for *sekuhara* (sexual harassment), one of which ended the career of the extremely powerful governor of Isaka City.

The divorce rate is also climbing, and while still behind that of Britain and the US, the gap is narrowing. Young women openly admit that they can enjoy an easy, rent-free life with their parents, and spend most of their incomes on

Now, as in the past, the geisha's hair is carefully raised to expose the nape of her neck, a part of the body that has traditionally been seen as a powerfully erogenous zone in Japan.

themselves. They have the freedom to find – and reject – a lover on a whim. Why, they reason, should they give up this lifestyle to share a life with a husband, whom they hardly ever see, and one or two children, in extremely cramped living quarters in a dreary concrete suburb? It would be difficult to deny that these young women have a point – but they are certainly worrying the government.

The gap between the old and new generations is stretched yet further by the dizzy transformation of physical appearance. Whereas the traditional erotic focus of a young woman was

Kitagawa Utamaro, *Lovers*, from the album *Uta Makura* (Poem of the Pillow), late 18th cent. Print, 25 x 38 cm, Victoria and Albert Museum, London. The exposed nape of the woman's neck makes this print erotic even though the rest of her body is covered.

the bare neck (the rest of the body being swathed in a form-crushing kimono), the Japanese have now converted to the Western tastes for bosoms and bottoms, which are bared almost daily on late-night television and in popular magazines. Perfection of features is now sought through plastic surgery – an art where the Japanese have excelled for some decades. The most popular operation alters the typical Asiatic mongoloid fold of the upper eyelids to achieve a more wide-eyed expression, redolent of the Western ideal.

Men, too, flock to clinics and beauty parlors for aesthetic tampering. Traditionally, the main artistic adjustment to the male body was the splendid Japanese tattoo, with its strong design links to those of *ukiyo-e* (*karashishi* lions snapping at magenta peony flowers, and so on). Such adornments used to be associated with lower-class guilds of workers such as carpenters, but they have become the hallmark of the *yakuza* (Japanese mafia) gangsters. Another practice of the same social classes, now dying out, was the surgical insertion of pearls under the skin of the penis – a procedure that gave the organ a rather suspicious, bumpy appearance – but that apparently provided their partners with great stimulation.

The *bishonen* (handsome youth) will sport bleached-blond hair and a year-round suntan in an Asian version of the beach-boy look. A little plastic surgery may be employed to remove the odd birthmark, or to bring ears, eyes and nose into the standard, accepted shape. Body hair will be removed by the occasional wax treatment. All this artificial modification of nature results in a rather androgynous look. One can surmise that their female peers like them to look less like men, and by deduction, less threatening. With the cross-gender fashion of baggy clothing, which make the women look more masculine since it hides their natural female shape, it can sometimes be difficult to tell one from the other.

But for providing sexual excitement in all its forms, the nightlife of modern Japan is uniquely varied – surpassing even the legendary Yoshiwara. All developed areas have their *asobi-machi* ("playtowns"), and in Tokyo, these are like cities within the city. The great conglomerations of Ginza, Ueno, Ikebukuro, Shinjuku and Shibuya, which are located next to the railway stations of the same name, as well as the more internationally-flavored Roppongi, are famous for their discos and beautiful foreign models. Broadly speaking, Ginza is for well-heeled adults, Shibuya is for the very young and Shinjuku is for students and those with more raunchy tastes, but within these areas, almost all preferences can be catered for.

Looking after those with Oedipus complexes are very private (and expensive) establishments

where businessmen can shed their clothes and stress at the same time, and revert to blissful babyhood in the arms of motherly hostesses. Diapers can be changed, bottoms powdered and patted, and a comforting breast offered. For those whose upbringing lacked discipline, there are plenty of places where the customer can enjoy refinements of ill treatment, such as enemas, dripping hot wax or whipping. Men are not the only ones being taken care of: to look after the lovelorn housewife with a rich, but absent husband, host clubs have appeared, staffed by handsome, debonair young men who will dance and flatter – and perhaps offer other services later. This is a useful way for a young student to pay his way through college, and some have done quite well, earning themselves Porsches and frequent trips to Hawaii.

The Japanese sex industry is nothing if not resourceful at inventing new titillations. The 1980s saw the proliferation of "art gekijo" – display theaters with a central stage and a performance that started with young ladies squatting at each cardinal point and displaying their private parts. (The English word "art" is always suspect in Japan – sometimes the meaning is the same as in the West, but more usually it is connected with the sex industry, for example "art massage" and "art dancing".) Then, free of charge, any member of the audience could climb on stage, strip, enjoy a foamy body rub, and, fitted with a compulsory condom, could have sex with one of the girls to the cheers of his companions seated below. Other diversions have included "no-pants kissa" (coffee-shops where the waitresses are nude from the waist down), and *terekura* (telephone clubs where all tables are equipped with phones so that calls can be made to lonely hearts at other tables). School uniforms are a widespread fetish in Japan – both boys' and girls' – and this is often combined with a passion for underwear. There is a trade in unwashed schoolgirls' panties, available both by post and from vending machines.

Nobuyoshi Araki, *Untitled (Tokyo Comedy)*. Photograph on baryta paper, 78.9 x 97.4 cm, Modern Art Museum, Frankfurt/M. Elaborate bondage scenes are a popular subject of Japanese erotica.

The gay world, while not quite so far out of the closet as in much of the West, is well represented, and a Playguide annual directory lists thousands of bars, bathhouses and areas for discreet public cruising throughout the country. Until recently, homosexuals were synonymous with effeminacy and known as *okama* – the traditional iron pot for cooking rice where the heat is felt in the bottom. This analogy is extended with the word *okoge*, which literally means the crusty, slightly overcooked rice that sticks to the bottom of the *okama*, and is used in popular speech to mean "fag-hags" – those women who enjoy the safe company of male homosexuals. Included under the same umbrella were the transsexuals and transvestites, known as *nyuu haafu*, "new half". These were once the source of great fascination, but after they protested in a sequence of television programs that they were not gay, but perfectly normal women who had unfortunately been born into the wrong body, their cause has slipped a little from current interest. These days, popular opinion has matured, and though it is still not as progressive as that of the US or Northern Europe, the younger generation at least are more easy going with gay members of their group. Society at large, however, still frowns on any public behavior that is at odds with that of the majority, and most who wish to succeed in corporate careers choose to lead a quiet, double life.

Still, in the areas which are rich in nightlife, the daytime defenses can be dropped for an hour or two. There are hundreds of gay bars in Tokyo and the other big cities, with the largest concentration to be found in the Nichome area of Shinjuku in West Tokyo. Many of these places cater for specific tastes or fetishes. There are plenty of noisy, crowded bars where the young can make new friends, as well as little-watering holes with maybe only five or six barstools, for mature types who prefer to have a quiet drink with like-minded friends. Such places are often rather exclusive and have a regular clientele .

Other bars are noted for their customers who have more singular tastes; some where foreigners like to meet Japanese and vice versa, others where the young like to meet more mature men – particularly those having an imposing, fuller build. Father-figures seem much in demand in a society where businessmen work (or at least stay out), until late at night, and rarely see their children. Even more specialized are those places

The *bulusela* shops in Shinjuku, Tokyo, sell young girls' underpants in vacuum packed plastic bags, labeled with the girl's name, age and the price of the garment. Underpants are generally costlier if they have been worn for some time without being washed.

for the rough leather crowd (acquired from the West through movies), and others that have a theme of traditional Japanese *matsuri* fetishes – particularly rope-like loincloths and short crew cuts. Sadomasochistic bars are also to be found, but there is no tradition of spanking or caning in Japan (corporal punishment is usually far more severe, and newspapers frequently report cases of teachers injuring pupils). Most activity in these places consists of refined bondage, with demonstrations of intricate knot-work.

In Japan as in the West, it is becoming far easier to select and meet partners for sex, and an enormous variety of magazines and pulp-comic books have pages of lonely-hearts advertisements. The internet too, has come to Japan, and the personal computer is being bypassed by intelligent cellular telephones which appear to be owned by everybody – at least if they are under 50 – making instant personal ads and swift liaisons a real part of modern Japanese sex-life.

The great artist, Hokusai, coined the word *manga* (meaning irresponsible pictures) in the

"Sushi restaurant". The young woman acts as a serving platter for wealthy businessmen to eat from.

19th century. It has since become the generic name for Japanese comics, and also for the animated films more properly known as *anime*. Manga heroes and heroines must possess *kawaii*, "cuteness" – their eyes are large, with big pupils, and they often resemble anthropomorphized baby animals. Nevertheless, the subject matter of *manga* is often subversive in the extreme, including scenes of violence and perversion, not just between human characters, but also involving bizarrely shaped monsters, aliens and machines. There are also categories of porn *anime* which, although explicit in their action, often have the genitalia digitized out. Lesbianism is widespread in Japan, but it would be difficult to say whether it is as a practice or an ideal. *Ukiyo-e* prints sometimes showed Edo women, whose husbands were often absent, satisfying each other with dildos. Today, *manga* comics for girls are full of stories of intense schoolgirl friendships with lots of uniforms and gym-mistresses. A wildly successful comic-book series called *Berusaiyu no bara* (*The Rose of Versailles*) launched a character named Oscar François de Jarjeyes – a woman who had been raised as a man to become the commander of the palace guards. The character soon had a nationwide fanclub of millions of romantic schoolgirls, and when in one issue of the magazine Oscar was shot, the grief caused nationwide hysteria.

Matsuri – Celebrations with the Gods

In every part of Japan, one or two days of the year are set aside especially for Matsuri-festivals when the deities are invoked to descend from Heaven and to join in boisterous celebration – a time when ordinary everyday life is transcended, and when people revert for a while back to a time when the orderly passing of the seasons was a matter of life and death, and the gods had to be kept in good humor.

Many of these Matsuri are conducted in a highly-charged atmosphere that is overtly sexual in nature, and characterized by youthful participants in festival attire – which may be just a simple loincloth – and a certain abandonment of normal, social decorum. The naked

festival at Saidaiji Temple in the Okayama prefecture takes place every February – the coldest time of the year – and sees hundreds of young men clad in loincloths scrambling in an orgiastic frenzy for a small wand that has been tossed into their midst by a priest. Despite the freezing cold, much heat is generated, and priests spray sake from their mouths onto the writhing bodies, causing clouds of acrid steam to rise up into the rafters of the temple. It is a time when new bonds can be made, and old scores can be settled in the *mêlée*, and although no weapons are allowed to be carried, each year sees its casualties: bloody noses, black eyes and broken bones.

It can be presumed that there were many festivals in historic times that were far more overtly sexual, but these have gradually been forgotten over the last 150 years or so as Japan has become more westernized, and society more middle-class and urban. Fertility has always been of more importance to the impoverished peasantry than to the higher ranks of society, and so as the country has developed economically, some festivals that were perhaps a little too lively for the changing standards of the gentility have unfortunately disappeared. One widespread custom was the famous Utagaki-festival that was celebrated in various parts of Japan, which started with a dance, helped along with *sake* – and ended with the participants pairing-off to copulate in the bushes. A variant of this was the *yami-matsuri* (dark festival), which was held until recent years in the Miyagi prefecture, at a temple of the goddess Kannon, who has long been widely associated with childbearing. There, during one night every June, women would roam the temple grounds to meet men of the village, who had disguised themselves by wearing straw mats over their heads and were considered as manifestations of deities which descended from Heaven into their bodies. In the Niigata prefecture, at the Ginzan-ji temple, lights were also turned out so that the young of both sexes could meet for sexual encounters. Parents were tolerant, even of ensuing pregnancies, since they had been through it all in their own youth. They were

Matsuri-festival in Nagoya, 15 March. The pilgrims pray for their descendents in front of enormous wooden phalluses. The giant "Dankon", the "root of man" is considered to be the symbol of life and is therefore the center of the festival. Although some phallic festivals survive, the custom is generally on the decline, and many have disappeared altogether.

just as understanding about the traditional practice of *yobai* where a young man disguised with a towel around his head would steal into the house of his chosen girl for seduction, quietly leaving before the first light of dawn.

One of the most famous dark festivals, which probably dated from the pre-Buddhist era, was the *nareai matsuri* (which roughly translates as the "festival of illicit intercourse"). This was held at the Rokusho Myojin shrine to the west of Tokyo, on 5 May each year – a date which is also the nationwide "Boys' Day" holiday in Japan, when carp-shaped flags (which are phallic symbols) fly over every house that has male heirs. Rokusho, the shrine's deity, was closely related to the wayside stone gods, Jizo and Dosojin, and was famed for his taste for the nighttime and its excesses. During the daylight hours, the young bloods of the town would roam the streets carrying a golden palanquin-shrine on their shoulders. But at sunset, the power supply to the town was switched off and

the festival continued in darkness, with the youth of the whole city forming a denser and frenzied crowd, consumed with sake and fervor, making its way to the shrine. Most certainly, there was license and excess, so much so that, after the festival having been celebrated each year for many centuries, the authorities banned it in 1953.

But, so long as any real excesses are carried out in private, festivals of a proudly phallic nature can be seen all over Japan even today. In the Kanagawa prefecture, not far from Tokyo, the *mara-matsuri* makes no attempt to disguise or even symbolize the *kami* – or divine being – that is being celebrated: the phallus, for which *mara* is a colloquial Japanese word. A giant replica of the real thing is exuberantly carried around the streets, while talismans of the same item, in all shapes and sizes, are sold at the festival stalls. In the mountains to the west of Tokyo, another Matsuri involves the nearly-naked young bloods of the village riding a giant felled tree

down a steep, mud-covered slope, in an obvious, if hair-raising, piece of phallic symbolism. There are often severe injuries and occasional fatalities, and every year the police and local authorities fret about allowing the festival to take place again. But for the locals, such accidents are seen as unavoidable – and they consider that these things happen when the gods are invoked.

Sexual Crucibles

Nanahuazin, **Mexican syphilis god, detail from Codex Borgia 10 (Kingsborough 29). Biblioteca apostolica Vaticana, Rome.** The figure's knees already show hints of pathological change and the round structures on the unclothed skin suggest the bulbous form of syphilis, which may not, as was often thought in the past, have been brought from America to Europe, but probably was already widespread in the Old World, if under a variety of other names.

Paradise Spoiled?

There is a depressingly familiar pattern to the encounters between Western explorers and the inhabitants of the lands they claim to have "discovered" (conveniently ignoring the fact that the natives clearly discovered them first). The Westerners begin by extolling their new find as a version of Arcadia – an unspoiled land of plenty, filled with people who are innocent, generous and often scantily clad and sexually uninhibited. Early travelers' accounts almost always brim with a sense of nostalgia for what they see as a pre-civilized state of nobility and simplicity, which was once enjoyed by all humankind. Then, inevitably, the newcomers set about exploiting the countryside and the people, whom they condemn and persecute for the very traits they found attractive in the first place.

Throughout the history of colonialism, a native people's sexual habits have provided a very convenient excuse for subjugating them. Either their nakedness and sexual freedom meant that they were primitive, and they therefore needed to be accorded no more rights than a wild animal, or their more "exotic" preferences – whether for sodomy, polygamy, ritual transvestism, oral sex or anything else that could be labeled a perversion – meant that they had to be taken in hand and saved from their depravity by the twin civilizing forces of strong government and organized religion. This pattern was repeated again and again by colonial forces in Africa and America, but the characteristic blend of fascination, nostalgia, misunderstanding and condemnation can be seen most clearly in Southeast Asia and, especially, Oceania.

The very earliest Western accounts describe the South Sea Islands as idylls, sexual and otherwise, populated by beautiful, naked, compliant women who would swim out to sea in their eagerness to meet visiting sailors. Their favors were easily gained – the crew of the *Bounty* traded iron nails for sex. However, it is likely that this was an organized form of sexual diplomacy, designed to keep foreigners peaceful, and that respectable or high-ranking women were kept carefully hidden away from the sailors. In addition, some of the behavior interpreted by sailors as wantonness was religiously motivated –

the Ariori society of Tahiti for example was dedicated to the god of fertility, and its members would travel from island to island, singing, dancing, putting on sex shows and having intercourse with almost anyone who wanted them. Although on many islands premarital promiscuity was tolerated or even encouraged, in practice complicated incest laws meant that opportunities were limited, and on some smaller atolls everybody was so interrelated that emigration (or foreign visitors) provided the only opportunities for premarital sex. Nevertheless, the legend of the South Pacific as a place of unlimited sexual licence grew, and with it grew the determination of colonial governments and missionary organizations to stamp their own restrictive morality on the people of the islands.

However, the impact of the missionaries was always unpredictable. Often they successfully abolished the local sexual customs, but failed to establish Christian attitudes in their place, which had the effect of increasing sexual activity rather than decreasing it. In New Guinea and elsewhere, attempts to make women cover their breasts only created a new generation of men who found breasts erotic, which their fathers never had. The so-called moral teachers could themselves have highly dubious morals – at least one 19th-century Australian Anglican bishop was open in his admiration of Papuan youths who, he said, had the character of Saint John and the physique of Apollo.

Anti-colonial movements often focused on, and parodied, the activities of the missionaries. Initiates into the Mambu Movement, which sprang up in Papua New Guinea at the end of the 1930s, had to have their genitals baptized with holy water, after which they gave up their grass skirts for European clothing.

Even when trained anthropologists began to visit Oceania, it seemed that they were chasing fantasies rather than trying to establish facts. The Polish anthropologist Bronislaw Malinowski (1884–1942), under the influence of Sigmund Freud in the 1920s, traveled to the Trobriand Islands trying to find the universal core of human sexuality. He found what he

Theodor Galle after Jan van der Straet, *Columbus Discovering America*, plate 2 from *Nova Reperta (New Discoveries)*, c. 1580. Engraving, private collection. The New World has been represented, allegorically, as a vulnerable, naked, virginal woman. She is both innocent and ripe to be taken by her conqueror.

Paul Gauguin, *Te Arii Vahine – The King's Wife*, 1896. Oil on canvas, 97 x 130 cm, Pushkin State Museum of Fine Arts, Moscow. Gauguin was bewitched by the philosophy of the noble savage – the belief that civilization was a corrupting influence on human nature – which lured him to Tahiti, where he painted some of his most famous works, and helped reinforce the image of the island as a sensual paradise.

expected, a society rife with neuroses. Unlike many who preceded him, he realized that observing customs and accumulating anecdotes was not enough – he had to listen carefully to what the people themselves said about their own sex lives. However, like many later anthropologists he went, if anything, too far in this direction, failing to distinguish sufficiently between what people said and what they actually did. For example, when the Trobrianders told him that they believed men played no part in procreation, and that women were fertilized by spirits, he accepted this unquestioningly, perhaps because it chimed with his own convictions about the sexual ignorance of "savages", as he referred to them. Trobriand beliefs are actually more complex, and similar to those of Australian aborigines – a spirit fertilizes the woman, but a man's sperm is necessary to nourish the fetus. Another famous anthropologist who went to the South Pacific in the 1920s, Margaret Mead

(1901–1978), disagreed with Malinowski about human sexuality. She thought that it would differ profoundly from society to society, and portrayed Samoa in terms that would have been familiar to the early travelers, eagerly searching for an unspoiled paradise. She said premarital sex was guiltless and easy, and that there was no rape or frigidity. However, it seems that she was as guilty as Malinowski of seeing what she wished to see, and unquestioningly believed what she was told by unreliable informants. In 1983, after several years fieldwork, Derek Freeman wrote a book called *Margaret Mead and Samoa: the Making and Unmaking of an Anthropological Myth*, claiming that rape was endemic and female virginity a matter of almost pathological concern. The alien, it appears, will always seem exotic, and in trying to understand the sexuality of others, we must guard against the great danger of turning it into a repository for our own fantasies and fears.

Pre-conquest Peru

Although a certain amount of erotic pottery has been found in Mexico and Ecuador, the great focal point for pre-Colombian sexual imagery was on the northern coast of Peru, particularly in the Mochica or Moche culture, dating from about 100 B.C.–900 A.D. Burials containing such pots have been found either in open ground or under the floors of houses. A grave was sometimes a simple pit and sometimes an entire chamber with walls and thatched roof, according to the status of the deceased, and some bodies were buried with up to 130 pots, gold ornaments and finely woven cloaks, as well as other goods including basketry, gourds and copper discs. The erotic pots contained water or a maize beer called *chicha*, and the common form of double-holed stirrup handle would allow the liquid to flow smoothly out through one tube while air entered through the other. The bones of llamas and guinea pigs have also been found in graves, and it is clear that the pottery forms part of a wider cult of death, sacrifice and fertility.

The range of sexual imagery found in the graves is extensive. On some of the pottery, living persons are embraced by skeletons, whose sexual organs are however still intact. On others, figures perform various acts of masturbation, fellatio and sodomy. Llamas, rats, toads and other animals are also shown engaged in sexual intercourse and in one case a male mouse presents a nut to his partner while mating with her. The portrayal of human genitals is extremely accurate, reproducing precise details of labia, clitoris, pubic hair and the circumcised penis. Women are shown lying on their back, side or front, or sitting on top of a man, while their partners stroke their lips, chin, breasts or vulva. Frequently the man and woman are masturbating each other, and on other pots women are sometimes shown alone using a dildo. Though there seem to be few representations of homosexual intercourse, many of the women are being penetrated anally. There seem to be no representations of sex involving children or adolescents.

The interpretation of these pots is extremely difficult since they are accompanied by no texts or living oral traditions. Archaeologists (to say nothing of sexologists, among whom Alfred Kinsey took a great interest in such artifacts) have had to interpret them in terms of internal evidence as well as the contexts in which they were found, but because of their lascivious subject matter much of the pottery has ended up in museums and private collections with scant information about their setting or how they were placed within the grave.

Modern interpretations have at times been bizarre, such as the theory that the ancient Peruvian practice of binding skulls to elongate them led to sexual "deviance" because of brain damage. Other interpreters have tried to distinguish between moods or types of pot. For example, masturbating skeletons or skeletons copulating with living persons are supposed to represent the need to conquer sexual desire, while others such as vases which can be drunk from only through a figure's genitalia were taken to represent the ancient Peruvians' sense of humor.

Double-chambered ceramic vessel depicting an act of homosexual fellatio, 14ᵗʰ cent. Ceramic, private collection. Such homosexual acts are rare in this tradition of pottery.

Indian woman with exagerrated genitalia, pre-Columbian drinking vessel. Liquids could only be drunk from the woman's vagina. Note the clearly marked clitoris.

Pre-Columbian figurine, copulating couple with baby. Museo Arqueologico Rafael Larco Herrar, Lima.
The presence of the baby suggests that the sexual act may have a ritual purpose, perhaps of protection or strengthening the child.

Late Mohican/Chimu-culture, stirrup-spouted jar depicting sexual intercourse and skeletal figures fighting or dancing, 700–1400 A.D. Ceramic, private collection, New York.

Acts of sodomy were interpreted as a technique to avoid conception. All these ideas are controversial, and other theorists have seen the skeletal figures not as dead ancestors but as living shamans undergoing some mystical experience. Since the pots are also found in the graves of children, they cannot simply be representations of the sex life of the deceased while alive. The soundest avenue for interpretation remains firmly in the awareness that these objects were interred with the deceased in tombs. Accordingly, we need to try to understand the meaning that death, fertility and the role of ancestors may have had in these cultures. Much of the imagery suggests a cyclical connection between death and birth, in which the ancestors play a key role in continuity and the creation of new life. Pottery that combines a shape of a penis and an ear of maize demonstrate clearly the interlacing of human and agricultural fertility. This may also explain the pottery with copulating llamas, since domestic animals were probably also included in this cycle of life-force and even today some communities in the Andes "marry" their llamas to each other in order to ensure their fertility. This would leave unexplained the frequent portrayal of anal penetration of women, but would explain the skeletons with intact genitalia in terms of the generative force of the dead: the sex organs, metaphorically speaking, never die.

Sacrifice seems to form part of this complex of fertility, as it did also in ancient Mexico. Some Peruvian images show naked prisoners-of-war being sacrificed and dismembered, with prominent emphasis given to their genitals as if their life-force were being captured and used for the benefit of the capturing community. In one Mochica vase painting, a half-naked man is held by each hand by women who lead him in front of a seated priest. Dismembered arms, legs and head surround the man and it is likely that this represents the fate which is about to befall him. There are many similar representations in which the prisoners are shown with large erections.

According to this interpretation the pottery does not represent individual sexuality, and it represents individual sexual pleasure even less. The figures on the pottery, especially the women being penetrated from behind, tend to have a blank expression (though not always: on some pots both man and woman have a mischievous grin). Rather, these sexual acts represent a cosmic duty that must be performed if life is to continue in the face of death. In general, the prominent genitals and exhibitionistic postures of many of the figures make it clear that the emphasis of this cult of sexuality was on life force rather than on personal pleasure. As in other cultures that existed at this time, sexual images may have had talismanic properties. Some of the figures are surrounded by representations of types of seed, which to this day are used for magical protection against evil forces. On some pottery, a woman being penetrated, whether vaginally or anally, is shown with her baby next to her, or even suckling, suggesting perhaps that this may also be an act of ritual protection for the baby. In particular, these ritual sex acts often seem to have been the prerogative or duty of a ruling class since many of the figures show an implicit status difference between, for example, a male figure seated on a platform and a female figure kneeling at his feet on a lower level performing fellatio on him. There is an image from the nearby Santa culture of sexual intercourse taking place under a canopy which was held up at the four corners by four women in what is clearly a ceremonial setting. The sexuality of deities is also portrayed. A god called the Creator, who is part man, part jaguar, is sometimes portrayed with his penis erect or copulating with a woman. Here he is surrounded by his attendants, a dog, a lizard and a cormorant who throws some liquid over his genitals. In other portrayals, a tree is sprouting from the vulva of the jaguar's partner, its branches laden with oval fruits which themselves resemble vulvas. Although they are less clear, some scenes may also provide evidence for a female deity of the earth or sea, since they show a large woman leading or dragging a smaller man who wears the haircut of a prisoner. These may be representations of a goddess receiving a sacrificial victim.

Spanish Condemnation

Spanish chronicles from the 16th century provide little insight into the erotic world of the pre-Conquest peoples. Although they write of actual events that they witnessed, their accounts are often tainted with racial prejudice and a narrow outlook on sexual matters. Male homosexuality seems to have been widespread in the Spanish period, and chroniclers record that native shrines contained transvestite male priests who also spoke like women, and who were sodomized by local rulers at festivals as a form of religious worship.

The conquering Spaniards despised sodomy, and used its existence to justify their domination and destruction of Native Americans. It was ranked as a major crime alongside incest and cannibalism, which were also imputed to the local population. The rapid extinction of indigenous populations from diseases introduced by the Europeans was claimed as a sign of God's displeasure at these practices. In fact, although the Inca ruler traditionally practiced incest as a sign of his divine descent, any commoner found guilty of it would be put to death. There is also evidence that the Incas had anticipated the Spanish use of sodomy as a justification for persecuting others while building their own empire. A convicted sodomite would be burned with all his clothes, and in some villages conquered by the Incas there would be only one man left for every 15 women by the time all the accused sodomites had been purged.

The Incas were actually preoccupied with regulating heterosexual relationships. Once a year the ruler presided over a mass betrothal in Cuzco, while his representatives did the same in outlying regions. The betrothed were typically over the age of 18, and had usually been having sex with each other for at least several months. If her husband died, a woman was allowed to marry her brother-in-law or no one, a levirate custom that prompted several Spanish writers to describe the Incas as a lost tribe of Israel.

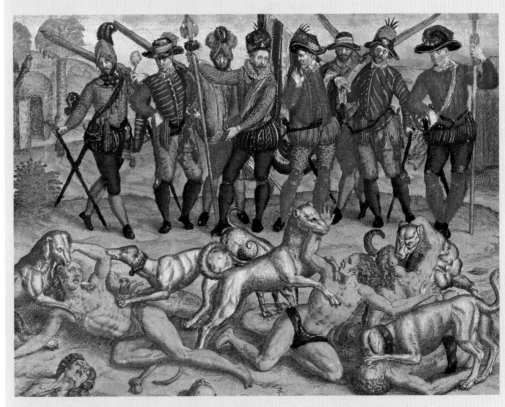

Theodor de Bry, *Spanish Explorer Balboa orders Indians Accused of Sodomy To Be Eaten Alive by Dogs*, 1594. Engraving, New York Public Library, Rare Book Room, De Bry Collection. In many parts of the New World, the Spanish were particularly disturbed by the obviously religious and spiritual connotations of sodomy. Early Spanish writers give numerous accounts, in shocked tones, of idols engaged in such acts. Indeed, the campaign to stamp out sodomy became a kind of new crusade. Numerous cross-dressing or transvestite priests of indigenous religions were burnt at the stake or thrown to the dogs to be torn apart. It is hard to know to what extent such behavior went underground in response to Spanish pressure.

Sex and Blood

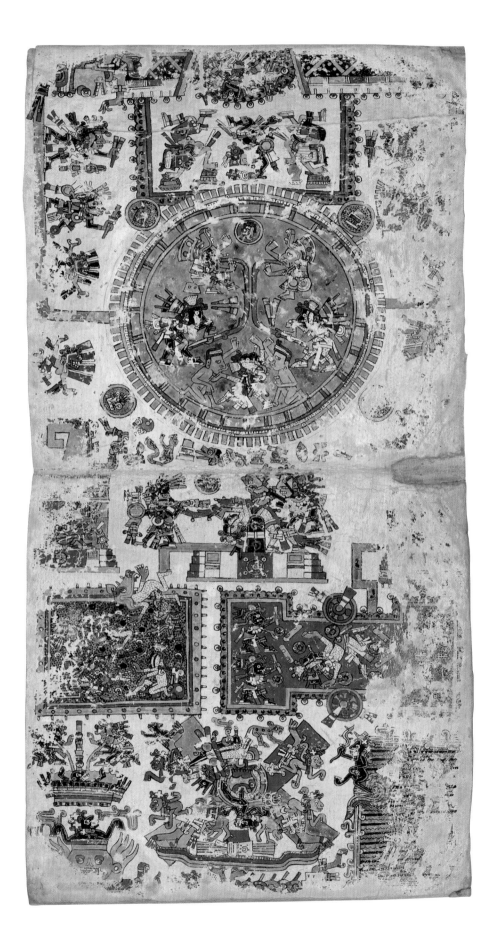

The ancient empires of Mexico placed great emphasis on the sacrifice of blood, which they thought the most precious and sacred substance that gave nourishment and sustenance to the world. This sacrifice often had sadistic and sexual components. For the Aztecs, the sun god Huitzilopochtli had to be nourished with a steady supply of human hearts in order to continue his regular daily journeys across the sky. Victims' hearts were ripped out of their chests, still beating, and their bodies flung down the steps of pyramids. The Maya of Yucatan Peninsula played a game with a rubber ball, in which the losers might be sacrificed. This game was associated with a myth in which a pair of ball-playing twins are sacrificed and come back to life. The key to these practices lies in the idea of the cyclical nature of life itself, and the repetitive movement of the heavenly bodies. It was thought that humans had been made by the gods to provide worship and keep them fed with blood. For the Maya, bloodletting from the human body was a sacred act which was performed on all important occasions such as the birth of children, the burial of the dead, the planting of crops or the dedication of buildings. Strips of paper made from the bark of a tree were typically used to soak up the blood. This paper was then burnt so that the blood would reach the gods in the form of smoke.

The bloodletting was focused on certain parts of the body: the ears, the tongue and the penis. Various implements were used, such as a cord set with cactus spines, or a lancet made of obsidian. In addition, in archaeological excavations, stingray spines are often found in graves near the pelvic area of the corpse, and model stingray spines were often carved out of precious stones. However, it seems likely that these were not actually used as lancets but as symbols of the power inherent in the lancet.

For the most important ceremonial occasions it seems from Maya carvings that both the king and his wife would perform an act of ritual

Two pages from the 15ᵗʰ-cent. Mexican manuscript
***Codex Borgia*, Biblioteca Apostolica Vaticana, Rome.**
In the circular "sun field" on top the Aztec god, Quetzacoatl, makes an offering of blood from his penis.

Carved Lintal from Temple 23, Yaxchilan, 726. Limestone, 120.5 x 80.6 x 10.1 cm, British Museum, London. King Shield Jaguar wearing the head of a sacrificial victim stands over his wife as she pulls a rope set with thorns through a wound in her tongue.

Figure of a noble letting blood, 600 – 800 A.D. Clay, 19 x 8.5 cm, American Museum of Natural History, New York. This figure is of a noble sacrificing blood from his penis.

bloodletting upon themselves. While the king would pass spines through his penis, his wife would perforate her own tongue. Persons of lesser status would also be sacrificed so that their blood would nourish the gods. Kings and lords were sometimes also portrayed with ropes around their necks, as if they were penitents or captives, in a way that confirms the analogy between the process of the king letting some of his own blood and the killing of the sacrificial victim.

There is a strong association in the iconography between blood, smoke and serpents. Early Spanish accounts speak of days of preparation involving fasting and steam baths and scholars have suggested that the loss of blood served to enhance a state of religious ecstasy in which visions of Quetzalcoatl, the serpent god, would appear to the worshippers, perhaps seeming to materialize from the blood itself.

Bloodletting also sustained agriculture. The gods had originally made humans out of maize, representing flesh, and water, representing blood. Maize continued to nourish humans, which was seen as an ongoing sacrifice by the maize god. In this philosophy, bloodletting was performed not only by humans but seems to also have been part of a cosmic circulation of blood in which the gods also lacerated themselves to release their own vital fluids. It seems that gods and humans nourished each other through the release of blood. Just as the gods created humans to worship them, the king created the gods through the act of bloodletting from his own penis. Some designs suggest that by giving them birth in this way, the king was seen as a "mother of the gods". The carvings, which show a king's rites of bloodletting, were often made to commemorate his accession and probably expressed his ability to make contact with the deities. Some show him receiving the perforator from his predecessor, making a clear link between the continuity of the dynasty and the continuity of human sustenance through the rite of bloodletting.

Modern Latin America and Machismo

Modern Latin America combines a rich heritage of indigenous Indian and post-Conquest Iberian cultural heritage. Among the survivors of the elaborate ancient civilizations of the Andes, a contrast can still be made between pre-Colombian complementary gender relations and the subordination of women introduced by the Spanish. Before the conquest, men and women had occupied separate male and female realms in the economy, but both husband and wife exercised appropriate authority in their own domain.

The combination of Spanish custom and the introduction of capitalism established and reinforced a male bias and the development of machismo, which is so characteristic of Latin America today. In Peru, for example, the development of the market and of a pattern of wage labor led large numbers of men to migrate to the coast, to sugar factories in the 19th century and later to a wider range of industries. Here, they were exposed to a much stronger Spanish influence than in the Quechua-speaking highlands, and they often stayed for years, even setting up a second family there. Meanwhile in the rural areas the establishment of haciendas superseded traditional peasant landholdings. Whereas previously inheritance had gone to men and women equally, this was now replaced by forms of rental arrangement between a feudal landlord and the male "head" of each household.

These developments left women more illiterate, trapped in economic activities that were poorly paid or valued. They have responded with various forms of resistance, drawn from both the modern and ancient worlds. For many rural Latin American women, their worldview allows room for both intense involvement in trade union activity and the use of love magic and sorcery, which are used in particular to assure a husband's fidelity and to eliminate competition from other women. The *curandero* (ritual specialist) who helps women with such magic is often a man, but this in itself is restrictive and open to abuse as he is likely to be reluctant to participate in any formal challenge to male authority.

Machismo is a concept that distinguishes men in terms of their greater or lesser honor. This notion of honor is bound up with the idea of manliness itself, as strength of body and spirit. The ultimate arbiter of this manliness is effectiveness and self-sufficiency in facing and solving the problems of life. A man who is not macho is *manso*, "effeminate".

For women the complementary notion of honor crystallizes around the idea of shame. A woman should be passive, gentle and patient. Machismo is concerned as much with relations between men as between men and women. A macho man must protect his family and dependents from other men's sexual aggression. But at the same time he is protecting his own social self, symbolized by the bodies and reputation of his womenfolk. Failure to do this leads to the man's dishonor, humiliation and ridicule. Inherent in this is an implicit double standard. A man may, or even should, pursue the sisters and wives of other men while at the same time not tolerating similar behavior on their part.

Machismo is thus a competitive concept: the assertion of one's own masculinity is linked to the denial of someone else's. This is connected to a wide range of imagery in which a macho man figuratively or even literally abuses other men sexually, thereby rendering the other not a "real" man. Thus, to be the one penetrating in homosexual activity does not necessarily undermine one's masculinity, since it symbolizes domination by the penetration. Being penetrated will definitely do so, since one is allowing oneself to be used and humiliated.

The logic of domination and penetration apply equally to a macho man's relationship with women. Any sign of initiative by the women, such as divorce or separation, is shameful because it implies the sexual inadequacy of the husband. The prostitute challenges all these assumptions by her independence in all senses, sexually, economically and emotionally. She is the woman who behaves like a man in terms of effectiveness and self-sufficiency. Yet although her strength threatens the macho male, like his it is based on a false display and is ultimately brittle. So the prostitute and her male customer

Christina Sanchez, the most successful of a small number of female bullfighters in the late 20th century. Bullfighters, who epitomize the macho spirit, habitually divide their time between Spain (from about April to October) and Latin America, especially Mexico. Despite her technical excellence, Sanchez felt compelled to retire when the public would not take her seriously, treating her on occasions as little more than a freak.

both understand each other's weaknesses because essentially they share them.

Since the ideal macho man is also strong in the political sense of not being "screwed" by patrons, bosses or landlords, many poor men are unable to keep up a convincing display of machismo. In a brothel studied in an Andean town, it was found that the night is divided into a cheap time in the early evening and an expensive time towards midnight. The men who come in the earlier part of the evening are those who cannot afford anything better and who are often in extreme doubt about their own machismo and their ability to control their own lives.

After 11 o'clock, the tone of the brothel moves decisively up market, with smarter clothes, better drinks, music and dancing. An important element of a man's behavior here is to show off to his male friends, in an attempt to portray himself as stronger and more macho than they are. This may include drinking, spending money and trying to violate or otherwise humiliate the women. Both men and women are vulnerable in these encounters, the woman vulnerable to abuse, the man vulnerable to her open taunting of his inadequacy and lack of prowess, which undermines the entire point of coming to the prostitute, which was in order to demonstrate his machismo.

In the multi-ethnic milieu of Latin America, sex has been related to race in complex ways. The entire continent has been subjected to the conquest of native peoples by Europeans. In terms of the ideals of machismo introduced by the conquerors, the weaker party to a political encounter is also seen as sexually weaker, or feminized. Thus as well as the dispossession of their territory, Indians were often subjected to various forms of sexual abuse.

In contrast to many rural areas, the cities of the 19th and 20th centuries have lost virtually all sense of a separate Indian population or identity. But their diverse waves of immigration introduced new associations between sex and race. In Rio de Janeiro, prostitution was separated into different districts according to a classification that was both class-based and racial. The district of Mangue, built on a reclaimed

Valentino, **still from the film by Ken Russell, 1977.** The tango evolved in the bordellos of 19th-century Buenos Aires. As shown in the film about the silent film star Rudolph Valentino it was originally danced by men, as a non-lethal way of displaying their speed, strength and physical grace – an alternative to knife fights.

The Tango

Even the Spanish-derived culture of the modern city has evolved its own distinctively Latin American forms and sensitivities. In the world of the Argentinean tango, women are not weak or subject to shame. The woman chooses for herself the man whom she will love. This romantic view of love constructs both male and female sexuality in a very different way from the model of machismo. The world of the tango and its lyrics portray a world of male and female archetypes. There is the independent woman, who steps out into the wider world of nightclubs and cafés and is lost forever. Among men there is the hero as the romantic lover, but there is also the rich older man who seduces the woman but in the end abandons her. On the way, the woman has abandoned the singer himself and the lyrics often portray the man looking back sadly on his lost happiness.

Tango lyrics show the dilemmas and uncertainties associated with romantic love and choice. The man loves passionately, but at the time of singing he is alone. The woman he has loved is an ideal, but not one associated with chastity and virginity as in the machismo model. Nor is the man looking for marriage and a conventional family life. The love and loyalty he seeks should be based purely on romantic passion. Significantly, the only woman's love that proves reliable to the singer turns out to be that of his own mother. In a twist that is not so far removed from the idea of machismo after all, maternal love is associated with sincerity, fidelity and self-sacrifice. It is the only love that is permanent. Significantly, the object of the singer's romantic love is never seen as a mother to any children, just as he is not a father. The entire world of tango romance is a childless one.

swamp, became the area of poor prostitutes, mostly Eastern European Jews and Brazilians of color who flocked to the city after the demise of slavery in 1888. Mangue was well away from the parts of town frequented by respectable people. Another district, Lapa, accommodated high-class European prostitutes (called, not always accurately, "French") as well as those of mixed race (*mulato*) who were quickly depicted as symbols of exotic sensuality on tourist posters.

Possessive Gods of the Caribbean

The black populations of the Caribbean and Brazil retain many legacies of their African origins. In Haitian Voodoo, the spirits called *loa* originate in West Africa, especially in Dahomey (today Benin), from where many of the slaves were taken to the Caribbean. There, the African spirit cults have merged in a complex way with Roman Catholicism, with most of the *loas* being identified with saints or other beings of the Christian iconography. One of the most important deities is the Voodoo goddess of love,

Erzulie, who is also identified with the Catholic Virgin Mary. Erzulie was originally a sea spirit but is now widely thought of as a light-skinned half-black goddess.

Voodoo deities possess their devotees, who must first enter into a state of trance. Erzulie's behavior (and therefore the behavior of those she inhabits) is almost a parody of femininity. When she possesses a worshipper she demands to be shown fine dresses, jewelry, ornaments, cosmetics and other attributes of beauty. Her

taste in foods is sweet and she requires champagne, cakes, and perfumed waters. As well as being attracted to pretty objects she speaks in a high-pitched, coquettish voice and responds with petulant tears if she does not receive everything she demands immediately. Erzulie is surrounded by an elaborate mythology, which includes numerous lovers among the other *loas*. One of these is the snake *loa* Damballah who inhabits the tops of trees and is also associated with water sources. Like many *loas*, Damballah's nature has been modified in the course of his migration from Africa, where he was originally the deity who moved the planets and stars around in the sky. When Damballah possesses a worshipper, they behave like snakes, climbing trees, writhing on the ground and hissing. He is also the guardian of underground treasure and it is believed that devotees who are specially favored will find such wealth. Another of Erzulie's lovers is the war god Ogeu whose adopted son, Nibo, is also infatuated with Erzulie but always rejected by her because of his extremely dark skin. When different *loas* possess worshippers on the same occasion they may act out dialogues among themselves through the mouths of their possessed worshippers.

The convulsions which are experienced by devotees possessed by a *loa* are sometimes clearly orgasmic. A *loa* is said to ride or mount a worshipper, and the loss of inhibition while under the influence of a *loa* includes the licence to say obscene and outrageous things which the worshipper would not be able to say while in a normal state of consciousness.

Similar possession cults occur throughout the Caribbean and also in much of South America – wherever there was a substantial trade in African slaves. In Brazil the main folk religion is called Candomblé, and the *orixas* (gods), originate among the Yoruba of Nigeria. Each cult member may have both male and female *orixas* and it is said that a person's repertoire of deities reflects the balance of masculine and feminine traits in their own personality. Relations with *orixas* are sexually charged but also full of paradox. When they possess a devotee, even male *orixas* tend to wear skirts, indicating

André Pierre, The Voodoo deities Dambala I'a Flambeau and Jean Dantor and the goddess Erzulie Dantor, c. 1965. Oil on cardboard, 91 x 76 cm, Kurt Bachmann Collection, New York. Although a goddess of love, Erzulie is unburdened by any responsibilities for fertility and childbirth.

A woman becomes possessed during the Haitian Ceremony of the Dead, rolling around in the mud. This event takes place every November. The gods are called in ceremonies that involve spraying – and drinking – large quantities of rum.

a close association between the realm of spirit and the domain of femaleness. On the other hand, any human who is possessed is relatively female, in the sense of sexually passive, compared to the spirit who in this context is "eating" them, that is, possessing them sexually. Members of each Candomblé *terreiro* (cult group) are considered to belong to one "family". They are initiated by the same "parent" and according to their generation are considered brothers and sisters or parents and children. They thus marry only people from other groups. This gives rise to sexual tensions and jealousies, as members of a single group may fall in love with each other, in what is seen as an incestuous passion. One solution is to have members of the same group initiated by different parental figures within the group.

The use of magical spells is widespread in many of these cults. In the Afro-Caribbean Santeria cult found in Cuba – whose gods are of Yoruba origin – spells are called *ebo*. As well

as *ebos* for good fortune or to win a lawsuit or a property dispute, love spells are particularly important. There are spells for every imaginable erotic need: to attract a man or woman, to control or dominate them, to arouse their flagging sexual energy, or to prevent them from being unfaithful or leaving town. They use a wide array of ingredients, some commonplace and some extremely hard, if not impossible, to find. These ingredients may include whale oil, aguardiente spirit, red ribbons, honey, turtle eggs, sulfur, poppy seeds, iron nails, cinnamon, holy water, mercury and hummingbird hearts. Common actions include calling out the loved one's name, or else writing it on paper and burying it or sending it out to sea. The procedure often involves turning the container in which the ingredients are mixed into a lamp, filling it with oil and secretly keeping it burning for a specified number of days.

Many of these spells are explicitly sexual and this is reflected in their key ingredients which

require the sexual fluids of the lover or loved one, their menstrual blood or semen or their pubic hairs. These may be easy to obtain if the object of the spell is already (or still) one's lover. But in other cases obtaining them may involve extreme difficulty or danger – anyone discovered collecting ingredients may be beaten or killed. The body effluences of either party may be used as the active ingredient in spells. A piece of cloth, soaked in the other person's sexual fluids, may be buried in order to ensure his or her undivided love; or the other person could be made to ingest their fluids and so become inescapably bound. One typical recipe requires the lover to dry seven earthworms and a pinch of his or her own excrement, pubic hair and semen or menstrual blood in the sun, then to grind them all to a fine powder and slip them into the loved one's food or drink. Another recipe instructs a woman to insert charmed honey into her vagina before making love to the man she wants to be joined with.

The Hidden World of the Amazon

The Amazon rain forest contains an enormous variety of diverse indigenous Indian cultures. Often the distinction between male and female reaches far into the cosmology and into myths about the origins of the world. Among the Tukanoan peoples of the Vaupes River, the world is conceived as an enormous six-faced rock crystal, which contains a concentration of male energy that acts upon a cosmic womb to fertilize it, thereby creating matter and the phenomena of the world around us. The same people also sometimes say that the Milky Way is a jet of semen which fertilizes the world; or that the world was created by the Sun Father, whose yellow rays are likened to male semen in contrast to the red that represents the principle of female menstrual blood.

The Piaroa of the Orinoco River have a myth explaining the origin of menstruation. Initially this was something that happened to men and the myth explains how the phenomenon of menstruation was transferred to women. A man called Buoka had an extremely long penis, which he kept wrapped around his shoulder. He could extend this penis an incredible distance to reach women and make love to them.

Kuyaparei, *Kapukwa*. Watercolor. Because of his desire for a Lizard Woman, a Mehinacu mythical character called Katsi grew a huge penis, named Kapukwa. It was eventually clubbed by other, jealous men until it shrank again.

Though he had no wife himself, he used this attribute to reach out and make love to all the wives of his brother. His brother then disguised himself as a woman and hid among his own wives. When Buoka's penis reached out and made contact with his own brother, it couldn't find an opening and so banged about hitting his brother's body in various places. The brother cut the penis down to what is today regarded as normal size. When Buoka saw the blood flowing from his severed penis he was very sad and built a separate house so he could live in isolation. There he lay in his hammock, still and silent. This is exactly how women are isolated in some cultures at the time of their first menstruation. Meanwhile his brother's wives missed their sport with Buoka and his long penis. They were very upset and went looking for him. They found him in his isolation hut and made love to him there. As soon as they did so the phenomenon of blood-flow was transferred to them and they began to menstruate. This is only one of many Amazonian myths that describe how attributes or powers that once belonged to one sex subsequently transferred to the other. Often such myths appear to reflect the insecurity of males about the rights and privileges they claim for themselves within their societies.

One Amazonian community whose sexual customs have been studied in detail are the Mehinacu. The Mehinacu have elaborate ideas about the complementarity of the sexes, but much of this also reflects a male uncertainty and self-doubt about their own masculinity. Every man needs a wife to form a viable household and those who remain bachelors are considered pitiful figures. However they regard the romantic love that they hear about in Portuguese over the radio as ridiculous. To be focused too intensely on one's spouse is considered undesirable and it is said that a person who acts like this will attract jaguars, snakes and dangerous spirits. So the nature of marriage is intimate rather than passionate, and its solidity is revealed in a number of ways, such as the shared meals between husband and wife and the way in which they pitch their hammocks

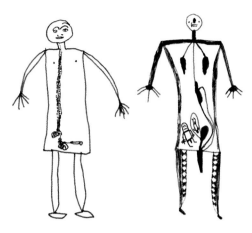

Shumoin, X-ray drawings. The drawing on the left shows how "feminine" foods (those which are grown rather than hunted) are turned into semen in the man. After repeated acts of sexual intercourse the baby grows. The substance of the child is semen as is shown in the drawing on the right.

very close to each other. If their hammocks are pitched far apart, this is taken as a sure sign that the marriage is heading for divorce.

At the same time there are extensive extramarital affairs. These are considered dangerous and exciting because husbands and wives are extremely jealous of their partners. In the Mehinacu idiom, they "prize each other's genitals". Men are more interested in sex than women and there appears to be no way of talking about female orgasm. Both male masturbation and male homosexuality are considered ridiculous: the Mehinacu say, "Why bother when there are so many women around?"

In the Mehinacu language eating and sex are closely equated. So the word for "to have sexual intercourse" means literally "to eat to the fullest extent". Both men and women may refer to their lovers as "food of my genitals". In particular, the female genitals are thought to resemble a human face with lips, mouths and noses. So sexual intercourse brings together two human faces in a literal act of mutual eating. Thus the clitoris is seen as the vagina's nose, which moves around "sniffing" for its food. The imagery that equates sex with eating is widespread throughout Mehinacu culture. The experience of sex is described with a range of vocabulary for strong and dull tastes. Perhaps inevitably, the taste of sex with one's own spouse is considered less exciting than sex in an illicit adulterous relationship.

In the same way, the fish traps that are laid in the river are interpreted in dreams as the vagina and the entry of a fish into the trap is the equivalent of sexual intercourse. Another reason why they symbolize male sexuality is that fish are caught and brought back to the village by men. A man returning to the village may secretly send the best fish from his catch to his lovers. So a sexually active woman in the house is also a good source of food since she will receive gifts from a number of men.

Among the Desana of the Vaupes, one word for hunting also means "making love to the animals". This emphasizes the analogy between the penetration of a woman by a man and the penetration of an animal by his arrow. But the analogy goes further than this: the prey must be courted and sexually excited. In this way the hunted animal is attracted to the hunter and gives itself to him willingly in a state of sexual excitement. Before seeking out his prey the hunter must make himself sexually attractive through a period of abstinence in which he keeps himself pure, adorns himself with special ornaments and surrounds himself with the power of special magic spells. Especially if the animal he kills is female, he will mourn it and express his sorrow at having killed such a "pretty creature".

The complementarity between the sexes often shades into a more antagonistic kind of opposition. Many Amazon peoples have versions of a myth in which it was men who originally carried out the most arduous domestic chores while the women did nothing but play music and dance. This was because the women owned the ritual flutes and trumpets. The women had originally found these by accident. While they were collecting firewood in the jungle they heard wonderful music coming out of a beautiful lake. They dropped their nets into the water and caught three fish. As they brought them onto land the fish turned into trumpets. From then onwards the women refused to do any housework and spent all their time playing music. But the men not only had to do all the

Ceremonies of Xingu Kuarup, Brazil. Men from the Kamiura tribe of the Xingu river. The flutes are said to transmit ancestral voices, and the headdresses are symbols of the sun, which is thought to give men their fertility.

domestic tasks, they also had to hunt because the trumpets contained the souls of ancestors and had to be given offerings of meat. So the men worked doubly hard both as hunters, which only men could and can do, and as housewives. The men were not even allowed to catch sight of the trumpets but had to hide indoors while the women were playing and dancing with them. The women would rape any man who accidentally caught sight of them. However, the men realized that because the trumpets required offerings of meat, they themselves had the power to withhold their hunting activity. Through this blackmail they persuaded, or in some versions forced, the women to hand over the trumpets. From then on the trumpets have been a men's mystery and it is the women who must hide indoors for fear of being raped when they are being played.

Among the Mundurucu, while the men play the trumpets in the village plaza, the women shut themselves away in their houses and lament the loss of the source of power in the battle of the sexes.

Among various peoples of the Amazon there is also a legend about a tribe of women who live without any men. The original women were abandoned by their husbands, who went on a fishing trip but turned into wild animals and so never returned. The women therefore abandoned their village. They dressed up in all the feathers and body paint that the men had previously used, then they sang and danced as the men had done before starting to move away from the village into the jungle, gathering up the women from all the other villages they passed through. This is known as "the story of the women who learned to live without their men".

Legend and Ritual in Native North America

The traditional attitudes of the Native North Americans towards fertility and nature as well as the relationship between the sexes, like those of many pre-industrial peoples, often have to be reconstructed from their surviving legends and the evidence provided by their arts and crafts. The Native Americans traditionally depended on agriculture and hunting, and broadly speaking it is possible to say that agricultural peoples such as the Mandan and other peoples of the Eastern Woodland tended to be matrilineal, with the extended family of a central woman living together in a longhouse, while hunting peoples tended to be patrilineal, with the domestic group focused around a central man.

In Native American culture, women are associated with creation in a range of ways. Among the Seneca Indians of New York State, it was said that there was no earth but merely water. Up above in the sky, people lived in a village through which grew a tree hung with white blossoms like stars. The first woman had a dream in which she was told to uproot the tree. She did so but the chief was angry and pushed her through the hole that had appeared. The woman fell down and down through space and below saw nothing but water. The birds swimming on the surface of the water saw her falling towards them and dived down to the bottom of the ocean to bring up some mud for her to land on. They piled the earth on a turtle's back and laid the woman upon it. It was here that she gave birth to all the humans who subsequently populated the world.

Among the peoples of the Southwest, the creation myth of the Hopi preserves a memory of gender-conflict that was healed with the help of a supernatural female being. The first Hopi lived in an unsatisfactory early world, where the men and women quarreled so bitterly that they decided to live on opposite banks of a river. As a result no babies were born and the Hopi were threatened with extinction. When finally this world began to fill up with floodwater, their chief enlisted the cooperation of Spider Woman – a widespread figure also known as Thought Woman, capable of making things out of thin air – to create a thread to a higher world into which the ancestors of the Hopi ascended. Such stories often center on an early gender ambiguity, which partly persists today with the institution of the berdache or ritual transvestite. In the creation myth of the neighboring Navajo the first man and the first woman were created simultaneously and implicitly have equal status. At first they lived in the first two of the five successive Navajo worlds, but these worlds were miserable and desolate so they moved on to the third. Here they began to engage in agriculture with the help of a pair of twins called White Shell Girl and Turquoise Boy, who were both berdaches. These twins invented the crafts that allow humanity to live well, molding clay into pottery, making bowls, tobacco pipes and other essential items, as well as weaving reeds into basketwork. The twins also worked out how to fashion stones into axes, grinders and other useful tools. Since Turquoise Boy could do all forms of women's work the first men decided they could do without women and moved across the river. The women later took over the role of grinding corn and the two sexes moved back together again.

Love Magic
The use of love magic was widespread and the Cree and the Ojibwa were specially famed for their skills. A young man could make a girl fall in love with him by making two little wooden figures, which he tied together with a strand from the girl's clothing or hair. Then after rubbing their mouths or hearts with magical ointment, he would place these figures in a little bag with some plants and, if these could be obtained, some clippings from the girl's fingernails.

Sioux moose effigy whistle, c. 1899. Wood, painted red and black, brass-tack eyes, 63.75 cm x 18.1 cm, Smithsonian Institution, National Museum of Natural History, Washington D.C. Whistles imitating the courting sounds of animals and birds were widely used by young men to attract girls. The Sioux and the Pawnee used flutes that imitated the mating cry of the male moose, which had an enviable power to attract female moose.

In the masculine world of the hunter, men are widely thought to receive their skills and powers through a sexual relationship with a spirit woman who is often the daughter of the owner of the wild animals. A hunter of the Thompson Indians was chasing two female wild goats that suddenly turned into human women. He married them and when it was time for him to return to his own people, his goat-wives assured him that he would be a great hunter but that he must always treat the bodies of goats he killed with respect, just as if they were humans. He should not kill female goats since they were all his wives, but he was allowed to kill the males who were his brothers-in-law. However, he was not to kill any kids in case they turned out to be his own children.

This kind of sexual relationship is associated with an enhanced perception of an alternative reality. A young hunter among the Mistasannee Cree was said to be stalking wild caribou, when suddenly he started to perceive the caribou around him as human beings like himself. The deer he was stalking became a beautiful girl surrounded by her father, mother and brothers. As the boy hovered midway between the world of human reality and caribou reality his bow fell from his confused fingers, and he could faintly hear the voices of his human father and brothers berating him for his indecisiveness. As he looked deeply into the huge brown eyes of the caribou girl, he fell in love with her. Now it was his human relatives who seemed strange alien creatures as they advanced, standing upright on two legs. He watched in horror as they killed one of his new caribou in-laws, then he fled along with his new bride and his human family never saw him again.

Whether to humans or supernatural beings, marriage was widely regarded as a lifelong commitment. At a traditional Hopi wedding, the family of the groom would present the bride with two wedding dresses made of white cotton. Only one of these would be worn at the wedding while the other would be kept for the rest of her life and used as her burial shroud. On the other hand, the Navajo for example, seem to have preferred a system of serial monogamy.

An Apache girl during her puberty ritual, marking the moment when she becomes a woman. Such rituals often reenact the coming of age of an ancestral being, in this case Changing Woman. The mud on her face represents growth upwards from the earth to the sky.

Cherokee, Ceremonial stone pipes with erotic scenes: copulating couple and fellatio, undated. Stone. Pipes were used in a variety of different rites among the Native North Americans. Each pipe was considered to be a microcosm, its various parts and decorative motifs all corresponding to some element of the universe at large. As such, the sacred pipes were intimately associated with concepts of life, death and reproduction. They might be involved in keeping souls near the family, and releasing them when it was a proper time for them to leave. In some groups, such as the Lakota, they also played a part in girls' puberty rituals.

A few groups, such as the Comanche and Pawnee, also allowed women to have several husbands simultaneously.

Among agricultural peoples, the woman was usually considered the origin of the maize on which they depend. Among the Natchez, when food was getting low Corn Woman would regularly enter her corn-house and emerge with a full supply of corn. One day her daughters found out that she made this corn by rubbing it off her own body and in disgust they ran away.

But Corn Woman explained that the time had come to kill her and burn her body. She would re-sprout each spring, nourishing them from the ashes of her own remains. For the Cherokee, the first woman was called Maize and gave birth to the plant by rubbing her stomach as well as creating the first beans from her breasts. The Pueblo peoples of the Southwest considered that the return of corn each spring was brought by twin Corn Sisters.

In such areas women controlled the rituals for agricultural plants. The Mandan considered that maize was linked to the migration of geese that were messengers between humanity and the female spirit of the corn who enabled it to regenerate each year. Members of the all-female Goose Woman Society controlled the planting and growing of maize.

Even where the economy was based on hunting, women sometimes had great power through such ritual societies. For the Blackfoot, the human race had originated with women who retained the power to make rituals succeed or fail. At the Sun Dance, where male warriors showed their prowess and endurance, the bundles of sacred objects which were needed by the men for the performance of the rite could be opened and handed to them only by women. Women also wore masks and acted out the stampeding of buffalo into a corral, in imitation of the men's hunt. A woman's menstrual period was widely regarded as a time of danger, both to herself and to men. During her first period, a girl would be isolated in a special menstrual hut or tent outside the camp. In particular she had to avoid allowing her blood to come into contact with ritual objects or hunting implements, as this would cause them to lose their power. Some peoples such as the Lakota believed that menstruation was a natural form of purification, so that women did not need to purify themselves in sweat lodges as men did.

Among the peoples of the northern plains the transfer of authority and magical powers between men was often effected through an act of ritual sexual intercourse with a woman who acted as intermediary between them. A younger man who wanted to acquire such powers among the Mandan and the Hidatsa would loan his wife to an older man who was willing to transfer these powers to him. A similar procedure was widely used in the Plains area when a young man wished to join one of the age-grade societies to which every adult male had to belong. The magical powers of men were equated with the magical procreative power of the bison. The woman and the older owner of the magical power were thus reenacting the sexual intercourse of the bison in order to transfer this prosperity and fertility to the married couple. In some cases the woman would act out gestures to draw the power from a bison medicine bundle into her own body. Among the matrilineal Hidatsa, a man's wife would have ceremonial intercourse only with men of his own father's clan, in doing so renewing and reinforcing the role of his father's clan in his own ceremonial lodge.

The combination of sexual and spiritual transfer of power is made clear by the Sun Dance among the Arapaho. The sponsor of a Sun Dance would send his wife out with a previous sponsor who was called the ceremonial "grandfather" of the new sponsor. In the middle of the night, the "grandfather" would pray to the spir-

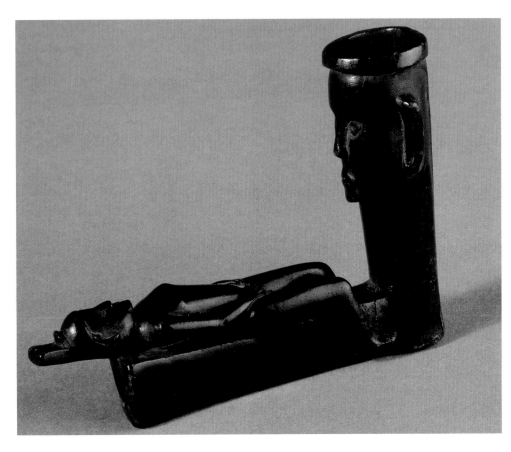

its and present the woman naked to them. He would then have ceremonial intercourse with her, at the same time transfering a root of a sacred plant from his mouth to hers. He would also offer a ceremonial pipe to the spirits, which was explicitly recognized as a phallic symbol. When the woman returned to the camp, she would give this root to her husband in the same way. Again, this act of intercourse also symbolized the mating of bison while the root that was transferred represented the potential of the people to grow and flourish. Among the Cheyenne the senior person, in this case the chief priest, would not actually have sexual contact with the sponsor's wife but the two of them would lie together under a bison robe surrounded by the smoke of burning sweetgrass. Similarly, among the Atsina, who were nomadic warriors, the transfer of power was combined with a test of a warrior's self-discipline. Here, despite the temptation of the woman's nudity, the "grandfather" was obliged to transfer the root from his mouth to hers without sexual consummation.

Pawnee, Man's head overlooking nude woman, bef. 1872. Blackstone, 8.75 cm x 11.25 cm, British Museum, London. A 19th-century Pawnee pipe showing a man's head overlooking a nude woman. As important ritual objects, pipes were often decorated with sexual imagery. Until the 19th century Pawnee ceremonial practice included the sacrifice of a captive adolescent girl to the morning star.

The Berdache – Native American Transvestites

The Native American berdache was a person who belonged anatomically to one sex but dressed as a member of the other. This cross-dressing was accompanied by a change of gender-specific behavior and occupation. However, the behavioral shift was not total and the berdache is better understood as occupying an intermediate status between male and female. The terms for *berdache* in Native American languages commonly reflected this intermediate status, usually translating into phrases such as "half-man, half-woman". The Navajo *nadle* (transformed person) could change sexual persona along with his or her clothes, and was addressed in masculine or feminine terms according to the costume he or she had adopted that day.

The berdache was widespread throughout Native North America but most commonly found in California, the Great Basin and the plains and prairies. The distribution of female berdaches was more limited and they were found especially in California and the Great Basin.

In California, berdaches carried out essential functions in death, burial and mourning rituals.

Theodor de Bry after Jacques Le Moyne de Morgues, Timucua berdaches working with women in carrying food (left) and transporting injured and deceased persons for burial (right), 1590. Engravings based on sketches, New York Public Library, Rare Book Room, de Bry Collection, New York. The Timucua were a tribe inhabiting Florida. The original expedition on which these engravings are based took place in 1564.

In many areas they were able to serve as go-betweens in disputes because of their ambiguous gender status. Among the Teton Dakota, they would give secret names to young children and be paid for this service in horses. Among the Cheyenne, berdaches would keep custody of scalps taken in war and heal the wounded, as well as organizing the dance upon the warriors' return to camp.

The male berdache would dress completely like a woman and adopt a female hairstyle. In tribes where women had a different speech, language or intonation they would adopt this too. In some areas, if a male berdache joined a war party he would change into male clothing during the expedition and change back again upon his return. The transformation was sometimes seen as a gradual or cumulative process: the last berdache among the Winnebago wore a mixture of man's and woman's dress because his brothers had threatened to kill him if he became a full berdache.

As well as cross-dressing, a berdache would adopt the work of the opposite sex. A common sign that a child was destined for this status was an exceptional interest in the tools, equipment and occupations of the other sex. A child might be surrounded by objects such as a bow and arrows and women's basket weaving equipment and watched closely to see which articles he or she chose to play with. It was often said that berdaches were even better at the work of their chosen gender than were those born into it. Female berdaches were said to be extremely skilled at hunting and men very skilled at deft finger-work such as sewing. Households based on marriage with a berdache, or containing an unmarried berdache as a member, were said to be exceptionally prosperous because of the full repertoire of skills available to them. Among the Kaska of the sub-Arctic, if a family had only daughters and no son to hunt big game, they might traditionally select their youngest daughter and start to train her in male behavior. While she was still a little girl they would tie the ovaries of a bear onto her

George Catlin, *Dance to the Berdache*, 1835–1837. Oil on canvas, 48.6 x 70 cm, National Museum of American Art, Smithsonian Institution, Washington D.C. This was drawn by George Catlin during a journey among the Sac and Fox Native American peoples in the 1830s. Most Native American peoples prized their berdaches, although the Apaches and Pinas were said to despise them.

Zuni berdache standing in the middle of a school group. In this group photograph taken in 1879 of the Zuni people, from west-central New Mexico, the women stand on the left and the men on the right, with a berdache called Whe-Wa in the middle, signifying his special position between the male and female world.

belt in the belief that this would later prevent her from menstruating or becoming pregnant but would instead give her great strength, power and skill in hunting. The neighboring Ingalik would even include such female berdaches in the male-only sweat baths. Here, participation was clearly based not on sexual morphology but on gender behavior. Such women could not have sexual relations with a man and instead obtained sexual satisfaction only with other women.

Elsewhere, the sexuality of berdaches was very varied. Some would engage in homosexual activity, even to the point of marrying a person of the same sex. Others were bisexual. Among the Hidatsa, a male berdache could be called the mother of a large family of adopted children. The berdache was poorly understood by Europeans and repeatedly condemned. As a result, the institution seems to have waned and has become hard to understand through the screen of disapproval found in early accounts. But it is clear that the berdache should not be confused with the hermaphrodite or the homosexual, though there may be some overlap at least with homosexuality. Indeed, it is not so much that a person of homosexual inclinations might become a berdache but that someone who becomes a berdache for other reasons will become either homosexual or at least bisexual. Some may even have been essentially asexual. As well as possible demonstrations of interest in male or female activities, berdaches were often selected by the spirits through dreams or visions. This usually occurred in adolescence or even later. Among many tribes, this vision came from the moon, which was considered by them to be a female spirit. In some languages the term for berdache means, "someone instructed by the moon". Among the Omaha, the moon would appear in a vision holding a bow and arrow in one hand and a woman's carrying strap in the other. Unlike the childhood test of a child's interest, here the male dreamer might reach out for the bow and arrow, only for the moon to withhold it and to force the carrying strap upon the dreamer. In one story from the Osage, a young man selected a battle-axe in his dream but when he returned to the village he found that it had turned to a digging hoe in his hands – a woman's implement.

The rediscovery and reassessment of the berdache tradition toward the end of the 20th century was significantly associated with the emergence of the Gay Rights Movement in North America, though this has sometimes involved playing down the many distinctions between the berdache tradition and modern homosexuality. The political development of the Gay Movement, the Black Movement and the Native American Movement have followed in close parallel, and the Gay Movement of Quebec in the late 1970s named their magazine *Le berdache*, pointing out that the berdache was integrated into Native American society in a way that the homosexual was not in white society. However, many modern Christianized Indians have particular difficulty in accepting homosexual tendencies within their own community precisely because they have turned their back on the traditional culture and religion within which such tendencies found an institutional framework and acceptance.

Eskimo

Living in harsh arctic conditions was a matter of life or death, which required close cooperation between men and women. The criteria for a good husband or wife among the Eskimo (or Inuit) were above all that they should be practical and competent. Historically, whenever there was a shortage of either sex, various forms of polygamy would be practiced. Such social realities are often mirrored in the stories with which people entertain and educate each other. In one Inuit tale, there was originally only one woman in the world, and even she was really a man who had turned his penis inside out to form a womb. One day a hunter who had been blown off course landed on the rocky shore of her island. He became her lover and stayed with her until one day his village headman came looking for him and saw the couple engaged in sex. The envious headman seized the woman and started to drag her out of the hut. A tug-of-war ensued and the woman was torn in two. The headman ran away with the woman's upper half, leaving the lower half behind with her lover. Each of them carved a replacement for the missing parts from walrus ivory, but when the headman got back to the village the woman's upper half again became an object of envy and as more and more men tugged at her she broke into smaller and smaller pieces. This was the origin of women, as each of the male hunters ended up with a very small part of her. In another story, the sky

fell upon the earth and destroyed everything, leaving only a mound from which two men emerged. One of these men then turned into woman by singing a powerful shamanic song and it was from the coupling of these two that the earth was repopulated.

Throughout Eskimo society today, an openness about gender roles remains. In particular, Eskimo personal names are not specific to male or female. Thus when a person dies and gives his name to a descendant (which is considered

Natar Ungalaq, *Sedna with a Hairbrush*, 1985. Gray stone, fur and bone, 18 x 21.5 x 20 cm, National Gallery of Canada, Ottawa. The sea mammals, metamorphosed from Sedna's fingers after her father chopped them off and cast her, and them, into the waves. The sins of humanity fall to the bottom of the sea and tangle in her hair which she cannot clean because she has no fingers.

Oviloo Tunnillie, *Seaman Seawoman and Fish*, 1981. Green stone, 12.5 x 50.3 x 6.3 cm, National Gallery of Canada, Ottawa. Much Eskimo art is concerned with the complex relationships between the sexes and the animals of the sea.

to be a partial form of reincarnation), this person may be either of the same sex or of the opposite sex, without any distinction being made. Indeed, a survey undertaken in 1986 in the central Canadian Arctic revealed that about 20 percent of children were not clothed and trained by their parents in the way that would be considered appropriate to their sex. Sons were raised as girls, and daughters as boys. However, this did not affect their sexual orientation. A girl raised as a boy was still likely to marry a man and raise children, but would typically leave housework to her female relatives and accompany her husband on hunting trips. Similarly, a feminized boy could kill a seal and marry (success in the hunt being a prerequisite for marriage).

Parents who raise their children in this way give several reasons for their decision. They may point out that a dead ancestor of the opposite sex willed his or her name to the infant, so raising the child in the same gender as the ancestor seemed appropriate. Others cite the Eskimo theory of Sila, a breath or force of knowledge that is said to enter the fetus at birth and provide it with some of the skills it will need in later life. The Sila, they say, changed the sex of their child when it was born, by providing it with the knowledge more appropriate to the other gender. In Greenland, the most common explanation is simply that the parents already have too many children of one sort – especially if they are girls.

Although it was the men who went out physically to hunt for whales in the sea, the women were considered to play an integral part in the process by imitating the whale. At the beginning of the spring hunting season, the men would carry their skin-boats out across the frozen surface of the sea and launch them at the edge of the sea ice. Meanwhile the captain's wife would lie down on the ice facing inland to the village. The whalers would set out to sea as if going on the hunt and then turn around as if returning. As they reached the place where the woman was lying the harpooner would lean overboard and touch her gently with the tip of his harpoon. Then without uttering a word or looking back, the woman would walk back to the

The Sun and The Moon

One of the most basic and widespread Eskimo myths tells how in the beginning, when there was no sun or moon, a brother and sister lived together in a house, both refusing to marry an outsider. The brother sneaked into his sister's bed nightly and, without revealing his identity, raped her. When his sister finally discovered the identity of her assailant, she took a sharp knife and sliced off her own breast. Mixing this in her chamber-pot with some of her own blood, urine and excrement, she put it in front of her brother, saying "If you desire me at night, you can eat me by day too," revealing the conceptual link, for the Inuit, between incest and cannibalism. Then the girl picked up a torch and slowly began to rise into the air. Her brother ran after her with a smaller torch of his own. As his sister rose her light burned brighter and brighter while that of the boy remained dull and feeble. She began to turn into the sun and he into the moon. From that day onward, the moon constantly chases the sun but never quite catches up with her. Just as he is rising above one horizon, she is usually already sinking below the other.

Mask representing the sun, from Nunivak Islands, Alaska, collected by the fifth Thule Expedition 1921–1924. Wood and feathers, 20.5 cm in diameter, National Museum of Denmark. Each month the moon wastes away from starvation until he is replenished from the dish containing the sun's breast and body fluids. Occasionally he gets close enough to grab at his sister and then people on earth see a lunar eclipse.

shore. In this way she represented the successful landing of the whale that was to be caught.

While the men were out on the real hunt, her every action was believed to have a direct effect on their fortune, safety and success. She was unable to do even the most basic tasks because these would involve processes like cutting with a knife or using thread. Any of these actions, the Eskimos believed might cause the harpoon line to snap or snag.

The Pacific – Signs of Adulthood

Early European travelers saw the Pacific as a sexual paradise. Though this impression was based largely on misunderstandings of the scantily-clothed women and the ease with which they appeared to approach strangers, in much of the Pacific attitudes to sexuality were indeed more liberal than in Europe at that time. The association of virginity with sexual purity made little sense since the indigenous cultures generally allowed sex play from a very early age. Throughout Polynesia heterosexual relations usually begin at or before puberty, and in many parts of the Pacific, such as in Tahiti, the Cook Islands, Easter Island and New Zealand, unmarried boys and girls traditionally had dormitories that provided a setting for sexual experimentation. In tribal regions where there are no dormitories, couples meet for assignations in a variety of places such as canoe sheds, the bush or the beach, or boys may visit girls secretly in their parents' homes while the rest of the household are asleep.

Bodily cleanliness is considered extremely important throughout the region. Much emphasis is also placed on the texture and color of the vulva. Among the Marquesans, baby girls are subjected soon after birth to treatment by special medicinal plants that shrink the mucous membranes of the vagina and tone the muscles of the interior, as well as diminishing the production of vaginal fluids, which are considered distasteful. In the same way, boys and men pay great attention to cleanliness around the foreskin and to keeping the foreskin flexible. Adolescent boys undergo a rite of supercision – the making of a slit in the foreskin while stretching it over a sliver of bamboo. Though it is not associated with any elaborate formal rites, this operation is considered a mark of sexual maturity. The bamboo must be kept afterwards, for if it is lost, stolen or damaged this may result in impotence. If the sliver is buried upright in the ground and a girl walks across it, then it is thought that the boy will experience a particularly forceful erection when he catches sight of her.

Supercision is practiced widely and is generally considered to be desirable for cleanliness. In Tahiti it is said that it allows the head of the penis to expand and give greater pleasure to women. It is also said that an unsupercised man has a quick and unsatisfying climax, called a "skin orgasm". Before this operation boys commonly masturbate but after the operation this is considered unnecessary as the boy is now ready to have sexual intercourse with girls. In the same way, it is widely said that female masturbation is unnecessary since there is a steady supply of boys. As in the Marquesas, the operation is not attended with any great ritual.

Pre-missionary attitudes to sex were highly sensual, as is shown by the emphasis placed on the tone of the vaginal muscles and in the frequent use of oral stimulation. Biting and scratching by girls was also common, especially in premarital or extramarital relations. A girl might bite or scratch her lover in order to leave him with an embarrassing scar if he was already married. However if he was single, such scars were great status symbols and would be shown and boasted about. Women expect and demand to be sexually satisfied and a man is expected to pay great attention to his partner's orgasm. Women also learn to contract their vaginal muscles to give greater pleasure to a man. Girls are encouraged to have sex soon after their first period because if they do not do so they may suffer from "filled-up sickness", in which the unreleased blood will cause a choking in the throat and may even cause death. The earliest sexual encounters between girls and boys are usually brief and furtive and it is only with greater maturity and experience that they learn to derive much pleasure and become suited for the long-term commitment of marriage.

Lintel from a Maori house, New Zealand, showing the creator god, Tane, separating his parents, Papa (the earth) and Rangi (the sky), c. 1850. Wood carved with stone tool, Auckland Institute und Museum, Auckland. In Maori cosmogony, this was the moment that sexual difference was introduced into the previously hermaphrodite universe. Tane went on to populate the earth by coupling with his own daughter, Hine-nui-te-po. However, as in the myths of many South Pacific peoples, it was also sex that introduced death into the world. When Hine found out that Tane was her father, she fled in horror to the underworld, leaving him to tend to their children while she waited to receive them in the land of the dead.

A pre-pubescent girl from the Southern Highlands of Papua New Guinea wearing a black bride's net-bag on her head as she enacts the role of bride of the spirits at a festival. Since she has not yet menstruated she does not pose a threat of pollution to the men as she sits in front of their cult house.

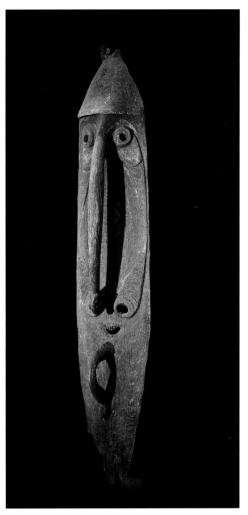

Carving from a men's meeting house representing an elongated face with long phallic nose, early 20th cent. Wood, Sepik River, Papua New Guinea. In much of New Guinea, the open display of sexual feeling across the sexes is largely forbidden. For example the Lelet are prudish in the discussion of sexual matters. What is shameful is not the commission of sexual acts, even forbidden ones like adultery, but their relevation. Within the men's house one of the most important lessons conveyed by the older men to the younger is discretion about their own sexual adventures, which should be shared "only with the lizard on the wall". So young men's banter and boasting about their adventures must be cautious. In particular they must not mention having sexual relations with the sister of any other man who is present, for fear that the man will fly into a murderous rage.

Adolescent boys and girls are both closely tied to groups of friends of their own age and sex. These groups often exert great pressure on them not to let sexual relations become too serious. When a relationship persists it is said to be because the two partners' bodies "fit" well. This is partly a matter of personality but also very much a matter of sexual compatibility that will enable a couple to survive many other problems in their personal relationship. The first pregnancy itself is not sufficient to cement

a relationship into a lasting marriage, because the wider kinship system means that the first one or two children are often given away to relatives for adoption. A marriage does not become stable and permanent until the couple starts to keep their own children. Thus marriage is highly experimental and allows many opportunities for testing and for escape.

In Tahiti, as in much of Polynesia, the contrast between the sexes is not sharply drawn. Men are not supposed to be significantly more

aggressive nor women more soft. Particularly in pre-Christian times there were many strong women chiefs. In Tahitian grammar there are no great differences between masculine and feminine, and even personal names, except for modern biblical names, can apply equally to men or women. The division of labor in domestic tasks is not strict, to such an extent that a father may even help his wife in cleaning up their young daughter at the time of her first menstrual period.

Among the many peoples of New Guinea, the contrast between the sexes is more clearly apparent, and certain themes recur again and again. First, there is a tendency to regard maleness or masculinity as a state that must be achieved with great difficulty through a process of maturation, rather than as something given at birth or during a boy's natural development. Initiating a youth is often referred to as "growing" a boy. Girls are already considered strongly female and their own initiation rites are relatively minor. Boys on the other hand are closely associated with their mothers and the world of women, and it requires a great deal of effort to make them into full men. In particular, during boyhood and early adolescence they are involved exclusively in homosexual activity and have no sexual contact whatsoever with girls. These activities are associated with ideas of female pollution and with secret male cults.

Men and women tend to live very separate lives. In some areas the men have a cult house which is used for ritual purposes rather than as a long-term men's dormitory, while in parts of the eastern highlands men spend almost all their time in male dormitories and very little time with their wives. Men dominate ritual and religion while generally spending little time in domestic partnership with women. Behind this lies the assumption that men and women are quite different in their physical make-up and their psychology, and in particular that female fluids and powers are dangerous for men. In particular, menstrual blood is considered to have immense power as well as to be enormously polluting to men.

It would not be an exaggeration to say that, in ritual, men appropriate women's functions and symbols. Among some groups such as the Sambia in the highlands, even male semen is considered to be equivalent to breast milk. The older men feed this semen to young boys undergoing initiation. In the creation of a baby, the Sambia believe that the father's semen

Nude figure from Rarotonga, Cook Islands. Wood, 16 cm high, British Museum, London. Many missionaries collected such figures, whilst condemning them.

forms the bones of the fetus. One single act of intercourse is not thought sufficient for the creation of a child. Rather, the fetus must be continually nourished by a fresh supply of semen until a late stage in the pregnancy. The baby's blood is supplied by the mother and will become part of the blood that both boys and girls contain. However, while both men and women contain circulatory blood, it is only women who have menstrual blood. Since blood is believed to be cold while semen is hot, and evil spirits are attracted to heat, men are considered more susceptible to illness than women. This is the explanation often given for why women live longer than men. Men also believe that women extract a man's strength by absorbing his semen. However, this belief applies only to marriageable women, and men can be close to their sisters and mothers. It is significant that wives often come from enemy villages and, in an atmosphere of endemic inter-village warfare, they represent a constant threat. For the Sambia, female identity is seen as natural, vigorous and fast growing, and as given by nature. Male identity, on the other hand, depends on acquiring semen. It is believed that the male body does not produce semen but can only store it. Semen must therefore be ingested from older men through fellatio during a boy's initiation. The older men themselves must drink the white sap of a tree in order to recharge their own stores of semen, which they expend either through being fellated by boys, or through sexual intercourse with their own wives. The effects of drinking a large amount of semen can be seen in those men who have alert eyes and a muscular physique. Manliness also requires dominant behavior in which men maintain a strong degree of self-control and competitiveness. This level of competitiveness is maintained by a shortage of women since powerful older men are able to marry several wives, leaving weaker, younger men as bachelors.

When boys are about to be initiated, they are taken away from their mothers, sometimes forcibly. The women lament while the men shout that the boys are being taken away to be "killed", in other words, to die as boys and be reborn again as men. An unripe immature boy is gradually turned into a full man through a step-by-step revelation of esoteric knowledge. An important part of their acquisition of knowledge comes through participation in events which strengthen their ability to withstand pain. Their noses are made to bleed and they are beaten with stinging nettles, in order to "stretch" and "cleanse" the skin. As new grass sporrans are fastened onto the boys' waists the men start to engage in highly suggestive sexual joking. It is clear that older men develop what may be called a fetishism regarding boys' mouths, which are seen as highly erotic and sexually exciting.

A central feature of the rite is the entrance of the secret flutes, which are made from bamboo and are carried in pairs, and help teach the boys about the act of fellatio which they will soon engage in. The boys are told that all the adult male warriors around them have become strong because they sucked the penis when it was their turn for initiation. They are told that this custom was instituted by the sun itself and that if they do not drink the semen of the initiating warriors they will not be able to blow the flutes properly, or to climb trees to the very top to hunt possum or gather nuts. The semen will strengthen their bones and will give them masculine qualities. They are also told that if they reveal its secrets to the women or the uninitiated boys they will be killed with stone clubs and axes. The flutes have a profound religious meaning to the Sambia. They are used to frighten and mystify women and children, who supposedly fear them and are obliged to hide from the sight of them.

Tattooing

Throughout much of the Pacific, tattooing has an explicit sexual significance. The Marquesan god of war, Tu, was upset because his wife was no longer sexually interested in him but was promiscuous with other men. So another god drew tattoos on Tu's body in order to make him attractive to his wife again. So powerful was this art that Tu became irresistible not only to his own wife but to every other woman as well. In pre-missionary times, tattooing was performed before puberty for Marquesan girls and shortly afterwards for boys. The acquisition of tattoos was associated with the beginning of an active sex life. Tattooing was strongly associated with fertility and was performed after the main harvest. The marks were made with a small piece of bone with a serrated edge which was dipped in dye made from plants and was then hammered or pounded into the skin. A boy would be tattooed almost all over his body, including the eyelids and the tongue, and sometimes also the penis. Occasionally the area covered was increased in several stages. Girls were tattooed in fewer places, with a stronger focus on their legs and genitalia as well as on some parts of their face.

Christian missionaries and French government officials disapproved of the association between tattooing and sexuality and banned it repeatedly during the 19th century. The adoption of Western-style clothing removed some of the rationale for tattooing although it probably survived for a while as a secret code underneath the clothes.

Anonymous, Naked Marquesan Warrior, 1813. Hand-colored copperplate engraving, Galerie Buchholz, Cologne. This sketch was made during the Krusenstern expedition of 1803. Each Marquesan design had its own individual name, which sometimes carried sexually explicit overtones.

Aboriginal Australia

Australian aborigines have been famous among outsiders for the claim that they did not traditionally understand the connection between sexual intercourse and pregnancy. However, this is probably based on a misunderstanding. When questioned by anthropologists, aboriginal informants would indeed say that a pregnancy was not the direct result of sexual intercourse. But by this they meant that a pregnancy requires more than a mere act of sex, since in order to create a human being, a spirit child must leap up from the land and enter the woman's body, a process which happens not through the vagina but usually through the woman's loins, navel or her mouth. This spirit child is generally found by the husband or dreamed of by the wife, and includes a process in which the child is guided into the womb by ancestors. Thus human procreation has a dual aspect: the sexual and the spiritual. Sexual intercourse may act as a stimulus to human reproduction but the creation of the fetus comes ultimately from the world of the spirits.

The landscape similarly serves as the means to understand the balance between the sexes. In southwestern Australia, the landscape is said to have been created by a hermaphrodite ancestral water snake. On a site near the modern city of Perth, the snake settled to lay his or her eggs, and pregnant women would traditionally come to give birth at this sacred spot in order to place their children under the protection of the water snake spirit, of whom their babies would be not merely descendants but also reincarnations.

Snake spirits are among the most fundamental in aboriginal cosmology and are believed to inhabit every river and water hole in the dry landscape. The most common form of the snake is as a rainbow-serpent, a form clearly associated with rain. On the Cape York Peninsula in the far north of Australia, a snake spirit called Taipan controlled rain, thunder and lightning. One day, Taipan's beloved son fell in love with a water snake and eloped with her, stealing her from her husband, the blue-tongued lizard. But the lizard caught up with them and killed the young man. The grieving Taipan smeared his son's blood on his sisters and sent them up into the sky where they added this red to the other colors of the rainbow, linking it to the regenerative power of menstruation. The rainbow serpent is generally conceived as male, with a counterpart in an earth spirit widely known as Kunapipi. In one story from Arnhem Land, Kunapipi's two young daughters emerged from the sea and camped by a watercourse. Since the younger sister was pregnant, the older sister went out hunting. But every time she caught an animal it would jump back into the water and come back to life. This was because the water belonged to the male rainbow serpent who was sleeping beneath its surface. When the elder sister accidentally spilt some of her own menstrual blood into the water, the snake awoke. Enraged by this pollution he reared up out of the water and swallowed up both sisters. However, his action unleashed the monsoon rains. The rainbow serpent was forced both by the monsoon and by the pressure of the other snakes around to vomit back the young women. Thus the fertile women are brought back to life in a myth that emphasizes that neither the male nor the female principle can dominate over the other, but both must be balanced in harmony for the continuation of life.

Throughout aboriginal Australia, initiation rites are an important aspect of culture. Among tribes such as the Arunta, the boy's initiation takes place in four stages. Before puberty, he is ceremonially tossed in the air and painted with designs said to promote his maturation. He starts to wear a nose-bone and is referred to by a word meaning "boy" rather than just "child".

Next, he is circumcised. He is snatched away from his mother and aunts by male relatives and told that he will be taught secrets which must never be revealed to women or to uninitiated boys. The several days of ceremony that follow are intended to separate him decisively from the world of women. While the women and children hide in the communal camp, the air is filled with the sound of bullroarers which represent the voices of spirits who will inhabit the boy's body during the operation. His foreskin is pulled out and cut off with a stone knife. Then bullroarers are pressed against the wound and the boy is told for the first time that it is these instruments that make the mysterious sound he has heard.

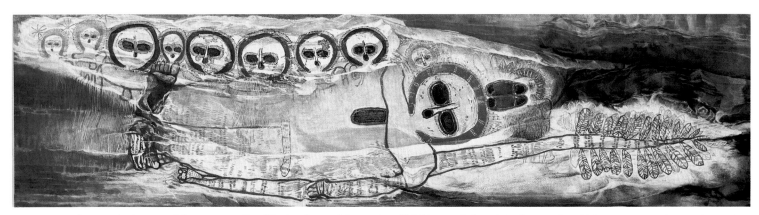

Rock painting from Kimberley. Staatliches Museum für Völkerkunde, Munich. A series of "child germs", the spiritual means by which women conceive, peering out from behind an ancestral figure. In much of Australia, a woman's pregnancy initiates an investigation to find out exactly where she conceived and which ancestral spirit was involved.

Rock painting showing the All-mother, Arnhem Land. The All-mother, or Old Woman, emerged from the sea in the form of a serpent and gave birth to all the ancestral beings. According to the Gunwinggu people, the Old Woman came to Australia from a place called Macassar, somewhere in the northeast.

Shortly afterwards, the boy is subincised. Again, without being told what will happen, he is seized by initiated men who use a stone knife to cut an opening at the base of the urethra next to the scrotum. In the final stage of initiation, the young men are made to lie down on a steaming, smoking fire in a trial by heat. Subincision is widely practiced among the tribes of central and western Australia. One possible interpretation is that the incision and the bleeding represent a symbolic imitation of female menstruation. Among one tribe, an ancestor who had two wives threw a boomerang which, when it returned, circumcised the ancestor himself and cut the vulvas of his two wives, so that they all began to bleed together. At a youth's subincision ceremony other older, initiated men may also offer themselves for

How Men Obtained the Ritual Secrets of Women

A myth from the islands off the Arnhem Land coast closely echoes stories from nearby New Guinea about how women were originally the custodians of sacred objects that were later stolen from them by men. According to this myth, there once lived a man and his two sisters who were also his wives, since in those days there were no rules against incest. All of them had enormous genitals that dragged along the ground, leaving trails that can still be seen to this day. It is even said that circumcision was introduced in order to bring the size of these genital organs under control. The brother, sisters and their descendants produced a stream of children who began to populate the Australian continent. But one day while the sisters were collecting shells, some of their own male descendants crept up and stole the bags which contained their sacred ritual objects. Both the magic and the songs became the property of men.

In a story from Victoria, the secret of fire also belonged to seven female elders who kept it at the glowing ends of the sticks that they used to dig for roots and insects. An ancestor called Crow-man realized that they possessed some great and important secret and cunningly decided to keep their company and help them with their women's work. In this way he found out that the women were fond of eating termites but afraid of snakes. So he invited the women to break open a termites' nest in which he had previously concealed some snakes. When the snakes emerged from the nest the women were thrown into a panic and allowed glowing embers to fall from the tips of their digging sticks. Crow-man gathered up these embers and rushed off with them. But in an ensuing scuffle with other men he dropped one of these embers and set fire to the vegetation around him. With the bush fire that resulted, the secret of fire was out. But Crow-man himself was so scorched and singed by the fire that he has remained black ever since.

repeated subincision or reopening of the wound. This is also done at moments of great danger such as after burying a dead body or going on an expedition to kill an enemy. The implication seems to be that the body has accumulated something unclean, which must be released through the flow of blood. This may be another argument for the parallel with menstruation, since menstrual blood is also regarded throughout aboriginal Australia as unclean, dangerous and polluting, and menstruation is regarded as the cleansing of a threatening force from within the body.

Whereas a boy must learn many bush skills such as tracking game and use of the boomerang, girls are generally ready to assume adult responsibilities much earlier. For example, in northwestern Australia a girl's first menstrual period was marked by the main rituals of initiation into adult life. Just before puberty, a girl would be taken away by the older women and smeared with black charcoal to the accompaniment of songs asking for the growth of her breasts and pubic hair. Later she would be painted with red ocher and a series of cuts would be made around her vagina by older women, said to be in order to facilitate childbirth. Women are segregated during their menstruation and it is striking that in this area men and women use a completely different word to mean menstruation. After this, the girl can take part in women's secret rites and learn the songs and mysteries that must never be divulged to men. When she becomes an old woman she will herself be in charge of such ceremonies.

In addition to being a polluting substance, menstrual blood is believed to have powerful sexual and magical properties. In one area of northwestern Australia, women would traditionally go to a sacred rock where ancestresses

Five boys prepare for an initiation ceremony, Nangalala, Arnhem Land. As Aborigines pass through life they experience a number of initiations, each of which invests them with spiritual power until, by the time they reach old age, they are thought to resemble the ancestors.

Aboriginal bark painting depicting a copulating couple and a snake, 20th cent. Eucalyptus bark, Art Gallery of New South Wales, Sydney. In aboriginal myth, the further one goes back in time the less difference there is between different animals, between humans and animals, or even between humans and objects. The ancestral spirits continue on earth through their participation in the process of human reproduction.

Phallic Stones

In the eastern MacDonnell ranges there is a large phallic stone. Local shamans would say that they can see an infinite supply of unborn people contained within the stone. The story of its existence was that an ancestor was once wandering around these hills when he caught sight of two women and tried to seduce them. But the women's spiritual guardian attacked him with a boomerang. The boomerang sliced off his penis, which fell upright on the ground, forming the rock. In ceremonies associated with this stone, the lead dancer wears a two-foot-high phallic headdress composed of a bundle of grass wrapped around the sacred bullroarer. In other parts of the country, similar ancestral penises have likewise turned to stone and become the focus of rituals. For example, one ancestor in the Northern Territory carried his enormous penis draped over his shoulder until he sank to earth, exhausted by its weight, and turned to stone.

had menstruated. There they would rub some blood on their hair and then wash it out before returning to their husbands with enhanced sexual attractiveness. Women could also take revenge on men by walking across their camp or touching their sacred objects while menstruating, thereby causing the men to fall sick. The secret women's rites involve putting mag-ical power into body paint and the genitals, as a preparation or a precipitator of courtship. The exercising or activating of such magical power is through song, and the old storytellers would talk of a girl "singing up" her own genitals as well as a lover's penis to make it grow long and to make the boy cry out for the woman. In the stories, if a girl sings well her lover's penis will grow so long that it will tumble to the ground like an umbilical cord. Women also have a range of secret songs that they are able to sing in order to keep their husbands faithful. For example, when a man is away on a long trip in the bush, the singing of these songs will make him sleep alone and wake in the morning missing his wife.

The Heartland of Genital Piercing

The use of penis pins has been known about for millennia. A bronze dog from Southeast Asia wearing a penis pin has been dated to the 4th century A.D. The practice probably originated in India – the *Kamasutra*, dating from the third to 5th centuries A.D., contains numerous references to penis pins – and it is possible that inserts continued to be used there until the 17th century. However, in recent centuries their use has been largely restricted to countries of Southeast Asia. The object inserted can be extremely varied. In Burma and Thailand inserts were traditionally in the form of bells that could be quite large and, as a ringing element, might contain a pebble or even a dried snake's tongue. One queen of Siam (modern-day Thailand) is reputed to have ordered that at birth all boys should be fitted with a golden bell which would go through their foreskin and glans, supposedly in order to prevent sodomy. According to this story, when the boy grew up and became ready for sexual intercourse, he was given a sleeping sedative and the bell was surgically removed. Many boys wore several bells at the same time that tinkled as they walked. A bell was closely identified with its wearer and a king might remove one of his own penis-bells and present it to a courtier as a sign of great favor. Elsewhere, penis inserts take the form of solid balls, irregularly-shaped objects or pins. Irregular forms can be inserted under the skin; these are used mostly in Sumatra. They are often made of a special kind of local stone but may also be made of gold, silver or ivory. Among the Batak of Sumatra, prism-shaped stones are inserted under the skin of the penis, and one man is on record as having had ten of them inserted. This was apparently done in order to please women. The inserts in question were made from a white translucent stone, said to have medicinal purposes, and found in the local lake. In the southern Philippines, a *sacra* – a star-shaped ring, held in place by another ring that passes through the penis itself – often surrounds the member.

The wearing of pins passing through the middle of the penis is today practiced mostly in Borneo, and in some communities almost all

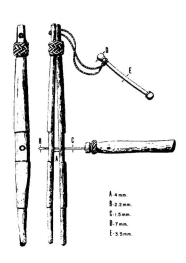

***Katiputan* (penis piercing device).** The penis is usually desensitized with cold water before being pierced. The boards shown here apply pressure, driving blood from the point where piercing occurs.

adult males wear them. The pins are usually placed piercing the glans horizontally above the urethra. During the piercing the penis is clamped with wood to desensitize it and reduce bleeding. The operation is usually performed around puberty, although it may also indicate some special status such as having successfully taken part in a headhunting raid. Having a pin is a point of pride and among the Iban a man may even sport tattoos, resembling the protrusion at the end of the penis pin, to indicate that he is wearing one.

Just as in other parts of Southeast Asia, a widely quoted explanation is that the pins are inserted to give pleasure to women. Many reports say that women will laugh at men who do not wear penis pins. One Bornean woman has been quoted as saying that a penis pin is to sex as salt is to rice, and a woman may place a cigarette of a given length in her man's rice bowl as a subtle hint that he should install a penis pin of the same length. One interpretation of the popularity of the penis insert is that the pin makes it difficult to withdraw the penis quickly after intercourse, thereby prolonging pleasure. However, while this explanation has been gathered most frequently from Borneo men, the evidence from local women is more ambiguous. They point out that many of the pins are

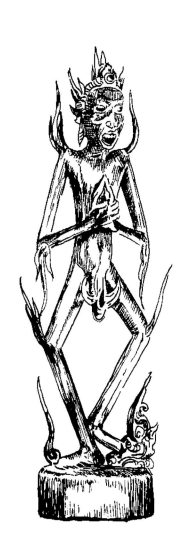

Tintiya. Tintiya, a Balinese deity, has elaborately pierced genitalia. The origin of penis inserts is sometimes explained in mythical terms, as in the Kayam story which tells how a woman mocked her lover because he was no more satisfying than a rolled up banana leaf, which goaded him into inventing the penis pin.

sharp and dangerous, and modern understanding of female anatomy suggests that they are unlikely to have any direct physiological effect on the woman's pleasure. In this light it is possible that the practice is linked more closely with male pride and fortitude, and in this sense it is significant that it is especially associated with men of special rank, prestige or achievement. The idea of the pins pleasing women can be seen then as something of a male fantasy.

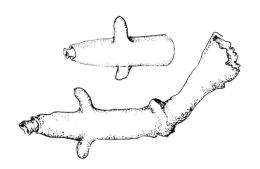

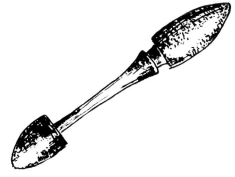

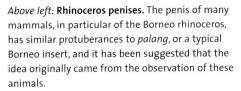

Above left: **Rhinoceros penises.** The penis of many mammals, in particular of the Borneo rhinoceros, has similar protuberances to *palang*, or a typical Borneo insert, and it has been suggested that the idea originally came from the observation of these animals.

Above right: **Talede.** The *talede*, a typical shape of penis pin from Sulawesi, as drawn in 1913.

The Spirit World in Southeast Asia

For the many forest-dwelling peoples of Southeast Asia, sex is intimately associated with the dangerous spirits of nature. Among the Temiar of Malaysia, spirits are particularly sensitive to breaches of the taboo against having sexual intercourse anywhere out-of-doors, or even indoors during daylight. Adults and even children are restrained from playing jumping games in case the spirit of Thunder should think that they are engaging in sex during the daytime. If Thunder is particularly displeased it may flood villages, destroy houses and drown people, or even send threads down from the sky which will strangle humans or cause them to trip and fall into the fire. A troubling sexuality may be credited to various forest animals. Among the Iban of Borneo, many illnesses were traditionally attributed to an incubus – an animal that assumes human form in order to charm its victim (usually a married woman) with passionate love songs, before abducting her soul.

The Barong and Kris Dance in Indonesia, Bali, Batubulan. In its origins, the Barong dance is essentially an exorcism ritual to drive away the evil, pendulous-breasted, long-tongued witch known as the *rangda*.

Sex Tourism in Southeast Asia

The sex industry in Southeast Asia grew at an astonishing rate in the 19th and 20th centuries. Every time there is a change in economic circumstances, usually brought about by war or a colonial incursion, it seems to act as the catalyst for an increase in prostitution. Since the 1960s, in parts of the region at least, the invading forces have been made up of tourists rather than soldiers, but in the past even patterns of tourism have been intimately linked to warfare and political turmoil. In Thailand, for example, the government began to promote its country as a major tourist venue during the Vietnam War. Bangkok had long been notorious as a refuge for Western and Chinese men interested in experiencing the world of prostitutes and cabaret stars, but achieved its wider international fame when thousands of American servicemen began to arrive there on leave from the Vietnam conflict.

By 1969 official reports stated that there were 50,689 prostitutes in Thailand, working out of nearly 2500 brothels, but unofficially the Thai Ministry of Public Health estimated that this was only about a third of the real total, and that the number of prostitutes had increased by 20 percent in the year from 1968–1969 (from 150,000 to 180,000). However, even this may have been an underestimate – the World Bank put the true number of Thai sex workers at up to 300,000. There was no attempt to stop the growth in prostitution. Indeed, General Prapas Charusathiarana, a hugely powerful minister of the interior during the 1960s, pressed for a larger sex industry because he was sure it would attract more tourists and help boost the economy.

The steady – and seemingly endless – supply of women to the urban red-light districts of Southeast Asia is not just a result of local poverty, but the way in which rural societies

Workers in the sex industry outside strip show bars in Pat Pong, Bangkok. This is a remarkably restrained example of self promotion by the existing standards of the Bangkok sex industry. It is much more common for passers-by to be pursued by touts, loudly describing the attractions on offer inside their establishments.

Bride School

Even in countries that are not noted for their sex industry, and where attitudes to foreigners are often ambivalent or even tinged with suspicion, the presence of an outside military force provides a focus for cross-cultural sexual relations. Many South Koreans are resentful of the US troops based in their country, yet this does not prevent some 1500 Korean women from marrying American soldiers every year. The USO, the charitable organization that looks after the interests of American soldiers abroad, even runs an American Bride School in Seoul, where Korean women can learn about such mysteries as greeting in-laws and how to cook a Thanksgiving dinner. The school was established in 1971, and by the end of the century some 5000 Korean women had graduated. Nevertheless, more than eight out of ten American-Korean marriages end in divorce.

have traditionally coped with their economic difficulties. When a family becomes impoverished, it is common to dispatch a daughter to the nearest town or city, with instructions to send money home. (A daughter's labor is more easily spared than that of a son, and daughters are thought to be more dutiful, and more likely to remit their earnings.) Many of these single migrant females find their way into the sex industry, although they are likely to hide this fact from their relatives. Even when a sex worker's parents are aware of their daughter's career, they will usually feign ignorance of it for the sake of a steady income.

By 1976 the Americans had closed their bases in Thailand, but the sexual services industry continued to grow, fueled by tourism and encouraged by the government. When deputy premier Boonchu Rojanasathien urged provincial governors to publicize and promote sex tourism in 1980, a local magazine used police figures to estimate that there were 400,000 female prostitutes in Thailand, in addition to untold numbers of male prostitutes. The cynical attitude of the Thai authorities was not unique. In some parts of Southeast Asia, the use of sex as a major local attraction was even more blatant.

Gogo bar in Bangkok, Thailand. Just as in sex clubs all over the world, a large part of the woman's job is to persuade men to buy her exorbitantly-priced drinks. If the man takes away a woman for sex, the fee he pays to the establishment is known as the "bar fine".

When President Ferdinand Marcos of the Philippines declared martial law in 1972, he desperately needed to generate foreign currency and decided that attracting foreign visitors was easier than attracting foreign investment. In the mid-1970s, the Tourism Ministry, under Marcos-appointed Jose Aspiras, began producing posters showing Filipina beauty queens with the slogan: "There's more where she comes from." Sure enough, the number of foreign visitors increased sevenfold during the decade, topping one million in 1980, with more than 70 percent of them male. After the overthrow of Marcos in 1986, the Aquino government made the abolition of prostitution one of its four main policies, and organized police purges of the red-light districts, chiefly as photo opportunities for the local and inter-

national press. However, there were and still are too many vested interests in the sex trade – including local politicians, military figures, police, hoteliers, gangsters and foreign investors – for it to be successfully obliterated. Although the Tourism Ministry claims that sex is no longer a selling point, it tacitly acknowledges that the possibility of sexual encounters is still a major attraction for Western, Chinese and Japanese visitors considering a trip to the Philippines. The Ministry has a target of five million visitors a year by 2010, a landmark already achieved by 1980 in Thailand.

Naturally, not all visitors to Southeast Asia are there for sex. By the same token, not all patrons of the sex industry are foreign tourists. It is thought that Westerners represent only a small percentage of the total market for sex workers

Lokalisasi

Since the 1960s in Indonesia, there has been a concerted program of clearing prostitutes from the streets and rounding them up in official prostitution complexes, called *lokalisasi*. The object of the exercise is ostensibly to rehabilitate them, but in practice the *lokalisasi* are profitable moneymaking ventures for the local government officials who manage them. Each prostitute is allowed to continue working in the complex – effectively using it as a brothel – for a maximum of five years, during which time she is medically supervised and, supposedly, taught how to get out of the sex trade. In practice, many continue working outside the *lokalisasi*, and when their five years is up they change their names and move to another district.

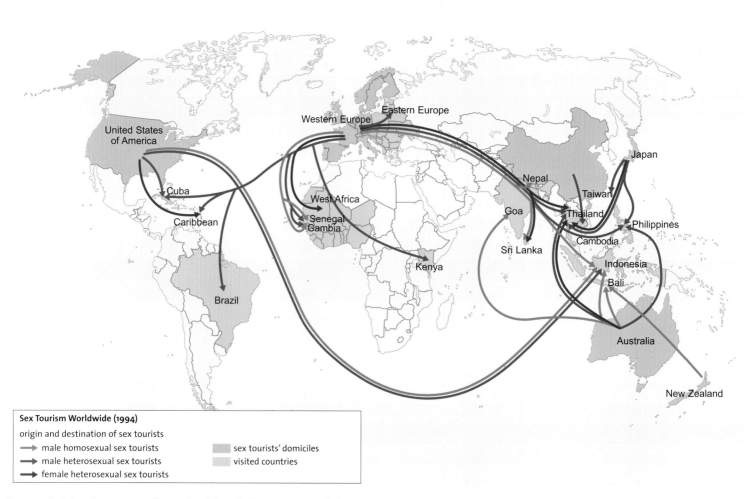

Sex Tourism Worldwide (1994)

origin and destination of sex tourists

→ male homosexual sex tourists
→ male heterosexual sex tourists
→ female heterosexual sex tourists

▨ sex tourists' domiciles
▨ visited countries

It seems that American men are the sex tourists with the greatest wanderlust – even passing up opportunities on their own continent, in countries such as Brazil, to trek all the way to Asia in pursuit of satisfaction.

Dancers on stage in a gogo bar, Bangkok, Thailand. Many clubs have a fairly mild, Western-style floor show – which often does not even involve full nudity – and a smaller one upstairs or a back room where much more hardcore novelty acts are on display.

Phi Manille Bars, Philippines. The Philippines is still less popular as a destination for sex tourism than Thailand. Competition for clients in the bars of Manila can often become intense, and can lead to violence among sex-workers.

in Thailand. In Indonesia, a great deal of the sex industry is concentrated around petrol stations, cafés and other stops on the nation's many long-distance trucking routes. An estimated two-thirds of Indonesia's truck drivers frequent prostitutes regularly at these venues. One of the greatest problems caused by all this casual, itinerant sex is the spread of venereal disease, and one of the common ways to say "prostitute" in Thai is *ying sanchon rok*, or "sexually diseased woman". Historically, in Southeast Asia, attempts to control prostitution have not been aimed at eradicating the sex industry as such, but at limiting the spread of disease. Nevertheless the transmission rate of sexually transmitted diseases in Asia, especially since the advent of AIDS, is alarming. The Ministry of Public Health monitored the Chiang Rai Province in the Northern Region of Thailand in the late 1980s. In August 1987, no sex workers were infected by HIV. In October 1988, the figure was close to one percent. In November 1989 it was 13 percent and in June 1990, 54 percent of sex workers were HIV-positive. Competition means that sex workers find it difficult to negotiate for the use of condoms, even if they are aware of the need to use them. Often, only the most highly-priced and desirable prostitutes are able to insist on safe sex. A survey in Bali in 1993 revealed that the lowest-priced prostitutes (male and female) only used condoms about 19 percent of the time, while those who charged the most used condoms with 90 percent of their clients (the mean across all price-ranges was 38 percent). On average, male prostitutes used condoms 48 percent of the time when acting as the receptive partner during anal sex, and 55 percent of the time when active. However, there are signs that things are changing, and by the mid-1990s, more than 90 percent of Bali's tourists were packing condoms for their visit (and about 75 percent were actually using them, both for vaginal and anal sex).

Import, Export

Although it is now almost a truism that the prostitutes of Southeast Asia are impoverished local people, while many of those who use their services are foreigners, this was not always the case. In the colonial past, many clients preferred women from their own race, and prostitutes were often imported to meet the demands of homesick officials and administrators. In the late 19th century, Singapore was one of the main clearing houses for the traffic of Japanese and Chinese prostitutes throughout Southeast Asia, with somewhere between 500 and 1000 women each year entering brothels or leaving them en route to other areas. At the turn of that century, official figures indicate that there were 3000 prostitutes in Singapore, of whom 75 percent were *ah-ku* (Chinese prostitutes), with most of the rest being *karayuki-san* (Japanese). There were also some Europeans who serviced the men of the British royal and merchant navies. Other estimates, taking the numbers of private, unregulated brothels into account, put the true figures at 4000 *ah-ku* and 1000 *karayuki-san* (more than half the entire Japanese population of Singapore at that time).

Half a million Filipinos receive foreign work permits every year, and approximately the same number also travel abroad as tourists before vanishing into the black economy in the countries of their destination. More than a third of these are women, many of whom end up as prostitutes. Even those who travel expecting legitimate work as maids or cooks are often extorted – under the threat of unemployment and subsequent deportation – into providing sexual favors. The most infamous example of overseas workers is that of the *japayuki* – women who are recruited in rural areas, trained by pimps in Karaoke bars and then exported to Japan to work in the sex trade.

Appendix

Sexual Luminaries

William Acton
British physician and author, 1813–1875

Living in the England of the 19th century, during which a growing middle class created Victorianism as a response to the immorality of both the lower and the upper classes, William Acton published the influential book *The Functions and Disorders of the Reproductive Organs in Youth, in Adult Age, and in Advanced Life* in 1875 and became an authority on venereal diseases, prostitution, chastity and, especially, masturbation. Acton believed sexual activity produced a loss of vital energy, and that women were indifferent to sex by nature in order to prevent men's vital energy from being expended. As a result, procreation was dangerous, but masturbation enhanced the risks and was considered even worse.

Karl Ernst von Baer
Embryologist, 1792–1876

Between 1810 and 1814 von Baer studied medicine in Tartu, Estonia, Vienna, Austria, and Wuerzburg, Germany. In 1819 he became prosector (pathological anatomist) in anatomy at the University of Königsberg, Prussia, and finally professor in 1822. There he made the famous discovery of the mammalian egg, which he described in *Epistola de ovi mammalium et hominis genesi* (On the Origin of the Egg of Mammals and Humans) in 1827. An even greater achievement was *Entwicklungsgeschichte der Thiere* (Developmental

History of Animals), 1828–1837 in which Karl Ernst von Baer developed the germ-layer theory. He set forth that early vertebrate embryos form four layers, which eventually differentiate into specific organs. In the same work, he explained that embryos of all animals begin as similar structures before growing into heterogeneous forms. In 1834 von Baer accepted a position as librarian of the Academy of Science in St. Petersburg. After moving to Russia he abandoned embryology, turning to anthropology and craniology.

Iwan Bloch
Dermatologist, sexologist, author, 1872–1922

Despite being a physician, Bloch wanted to study not only the biological and medical aspects of human sexuality, but also its role in history and anthropology. His monumental study *Sexual Life in our Time* (1907) is considered the theoretical foundation of modern sexology as a science. In 1913 Bloch, Hirschfeld and other physicians founded the Medical Society for Sexology and Eugenics, the first sexological society, and published its official organ *Zeitschrift für Sexualwissenschaft* (Journal of Sexology) in 1914. Of his project *Comprehensive Handbook of Sexology in Monographs* only the first and the third volume, entitled *Prostitution,* were published (1912 and 1925) because of the First World War and Bloch's early death in 1922.

Ernest Borneman
Sex researcher, psychotherapist, writer and musicologist, 1915–1995

Ernest Borneman enrolled at university in Berlin in 1931, but left for Cambridge (England) after two years, where he continued his studies in psychoanalysis, sexology, music and archaeology. He then worked as a jazz musician, author, and cameraman in

England, Canada and the United States before he moved to Austria in the early 1960s. At the age of 60, Bornemann earned his Ph.D. at the Universities of Salzburg, Austria and Bremen, Germany, specializing in child sexuality. *Phases of Maturity in Childhood* describes each phase of the psychosexual development of children from conception to age eight. He published *Lexikon der Liebe* (Lexicon of Love), 1968, *Sex im Volksmund* (Sex in Common Parlance), 1971, and *Enzyklopaedie der Sexualitaet* (Encyclopedia of Sexuality), 1990, but gradually retired from lecturing. Borneman committed suicide at the age of 80.

Andreas Capellanus/Andrew the Chaplain
Troubador, lived late 12th century.

The life of Andreas Capellanus remains mainly unknown. He most likely was a chaplain in the court of Count Henry of Troyes (France) and his wife the Countess Marie. Sometime between 1170 and 1186 Andreas wrote *De arte honeste amandi* (Treatise on Love), which was intended to describe the Courts of Love held by Eleanor of Aquitaine between 1170 and 1174 and set the rules of courtly love, which defined the experience of lovers for the later Middle Ages. Whether Andreas was writing a satire or more serious entertainment for the ladies of the Court of Countess Marie is still in question.

Alex Comfort
Physician, gerontologist, author, 1920–2000

After receiving his medical education at the Universities of Cambridge, England (B.A. 1943; M.A. 1945) and London (Ph.D. 1949), Alex Comfort devoted himself to the lifelong study and treatment of the mental and physical problems of growing old. He lectured and researched at the latter university (1945–1964) and then at the Universities of Stanford (1965–1983) and California (Irvine 1976–1979, Los Angeles 1979–1983). But Comfort is probably best known as the author of the best seller *Joy of Sex*, 1972 and its sequel *More Joy*, 1974, a celebration of the psychological and sociological aspects of a free sexual life. He also wrote many other works that include theories of sexuality as they relate to sociology and politics, e.g. *Come Out to Play* (1961) and *Tetrarch* (1980).

Helene Deutsch
Psychoanalyst, 1884–1982

Deutsch's will to achieve was revealed as a young girl, when she often threatened to run away from home unless her father would guarantee her a university education. For her medical studies, in protest at its refusal to admit women to law school, she chose Vienna University, where she went to Sigmund Freud for training. After graduating in 1918, Deutsch worked at the Wagner-Jauregg Clinic as a psychiatrist, when in 1923 Freud nominated her as the director of the Vienna Psychoanalytic Institute. Under the menace of Nazi occupation, Deutsch emigrated with her husband to the United States in 1935 and worked as clinician, teacher, and writer. Her most famous, though highly controversial study is the two-volume *The Psychology of Women*, 1945. Feminists heavily criticized her theory, which named passivity, narcissism and masochism as the ruling characteristics of the female personality. On the other hand she emphasized the important role of the clitoris in female sexuality, in direct contrast to Freud, who claimed that women who had only clitoral orgasms were frigid.

Henry Havelock Ellis
Physician and writer, 1859–1939

After growing up in Australia and England in the Victorian Era, Henry Havelock Ellis became a doctor and directed his energies toward a clinical study of human sexuality during a time when such topics were taboo, even among academics. While his first work *The New Spirit* (1890) rejected ingrained sexual naiveté, in his second work *Man and Woman* (1894) Ellis began to develop his opinion on the naturalness of homosexuality. During that time, he began a romantic relationship with the feminist Olive Schreiner, but eventually married the lesbian writer Edith Lees. Following this, E. started his most famous work, the seven-volume series *Studies in the Psychology of Sex*. Its first volume *Sexual Inversion* was published in 1897 – considered as the first scientific work to treat homosexuality neither as a crime nor a disease. The other six volumes of the *Studies in the Psychology of Sex* were published in the United States and until 1935 legally available only to the medical profession. Ellis also published numerous essays and books on masturbation, the physiology of sexual behavior, eugenics, birth control, and family.

Gabrielo Fallopia
Anatomist, 1523–1562

After becoming a canon of the cathedral of Modena and later studying medicine, Fallopia became professor of anatomy in Ferrara, Pisa (1548–1551) and Padua (1551–1562). As a student and the successor of the anatomist Andreas Vesalius, he studied the organs of generation in both sexes, discovering the tubes connecting the ovaries to the uterus (now known as fallopian tubes), and several major nerves of the head. He also named the vagina, placenta, and clitoris, as well as the palate and cochlea. In 1561 he described his findings in *Observationes anatomicae*.

Michel Foucault
Philosopher and historian, 1926–1984

In 1946 Michel Focault was admitted to the prominent École Normale Supérieure in Paris, from where he graduated with philosophy and psychology degrees in 1952. During the following years he worked for the universities in Lille, Uppsala, Warsaw (1958), Hamburg, Clermont-Ferrand, Sao Paulo, Tunis (1960–1968) and Paris (1968–1970). Foucault received his doctorate in 1961 for his thesis *Madness and Civilization*. In 1970 he was elected chairman of history of systems of thought at the Collège de France, where he scandalized

the university by appointing his male lover to a position in the department. F. turned to the topic of sexuality in the 1970s and published the first of a proposed six volumes: *History of Sexuality*, 1976, which pioneered the Queer Theory, contradicting the common thesis that sexuality has always been repressed in Western society, claiming that it is Western society's fixation with sexuality that has created sexual minorities. Volume two, *The Use of Pleasure*, 1984, and three, *The Care of Self*, 1984, examined the relationship between sexuality and morality of the ancient Greeks and the Christian influence on the Roman culture of marriage. Foucault's death of AIDS in 1984 prevented the completion of further volumes.

Sigmund Freud
Psychoanalyst, psychologist, physician, 1856–1939

Having proved to be an excellent student, Freud entered the University of Vienna at age 17, where he earned his M.D. after seven years. His Jewish background being a disadvantage in academic medicine, he became a resident physician at Vienna general hospital in 1882. After learning about the neurological causes for hysteria in Paris, Freud set up his own private practice for neurology in Vienna in 1886. He treated hysterical patients with hypnosis and published *Studies in Hysteria* in 1895, using the term "psychoanalysis" for the first time. Freud then began a self-analysis, which lead to *The Interpretation of Dreams*, 1900. Subsequent to replacing hypnosis with free association, he looked at the influence of unconscious mental processes on slips of the tongue (*The Psychopathology of Everyday Life*, 1901), humor (*Jokes and Their Relation to the Unconscious*, 1905) and cultural institutions (*Totem and Taboo*, 1912). Indeed, Freud is best known as a pioneer in the serious study of sexuality and the pansexualist understanding of the mind, identifying sexual desires of early infancy as the main unconscious force causing neuroses, as in *Three Essays on the Theory of Sexuality*, 1905. Freud described three phases of childhood: the oral stage, the anal stage, and the phallic stage. One of his most famous theories is that of the Oedipus complex, which states that essentially every male child has a desire to sleep with his mother, and was inspired by his analysis of his own reaction to his father's death. In 1916 he published his *General Introduction to Psychoanalysis* and presented an abstract framework for the structure of the mind in *The Ego and the Id* in 1923. Freud characterized civilization as compromise between wishes and repression in his best-known work *Civilization and Its Discontents*, 1930. Permitted to leave Nazi-occupied Austria in 1938, he died of cancer in exile a year later.

Magnus Hirschfeld
Physician, 1868–1935

Magnus Hirschfeld studied medicine in Munich and Berlin, where he settled in the fashionable Charlottenburg quarter and published *Sappho and Sokrates* in 1896, promoting homosexuality as integral part of human sexuality. In 1897 Hirschfeld founded the world's first homosexual rights organization *Wissenschaftlich-Humanitäres Komitee* (Scientific Humanitarian Committee). Its central objective was the decriminalization of homosexuality through scien-

tific studies and public education. Hirschfeld edited the Committee's periodical *Jahrbuch für sexuelle Zwischenstufen* (Yearbook for Sexual Intermediates), which was published between 1899 and 1923 and examined all aspects of homosexual behavior. The monumental study *Die Homosexualität des Mannes und des Weibes* (Male and Female Homosexuality), 1914, was unsurpassed until the end of the 20th century as a collection of current knowledge about homosexuality. In 1919 Hirschfeld founded the Institute for Sexual Sciences, the first of its kind in the world. Having limited success in turning public opinion in favor of homosexuals – especially during the Depression – Hirschfeld decided not to return to Germany from a world lecturing tour after the Nazis' rise in 1933.

Shere Hite
Sex researcher, b. 1942

After gaining a B.A. (1964) and an M.A. in History from the Universtity of Florida, Shere Hite went on to further graduate studies at Columbia University (New York City). She joined the National Organization of Women (NOW) and in 1971 developed a questionnaire on female sexuality. She was appointed director of the Feminist Sexuality Project (1972–1978). Hite then became instructor in female sexuality at New York University and director of Hite Research International (1977). She lectured at the universities of Harvard, Columbia, Cambridge (England) and the Sorbonne in Paris (1977–1983). Hite's studies *The Hite Report: A Nationwide Study of Female Sexuality*, 1976, *The Hite Report on Male Sexuality*, 1982, *Women and Love*, 1987, and *The Hite Report on the Family: Growing up under Patriarchy*, 1995 were praised for showing the average citizen's perspective, but also criticized for their inadequate methodology.

Carl Gustav Jung
Psychologist, psychiatrist, physician, 1875–1961

Jung, whose greatest achievement would be the construction of "a psychology for human beings who reach out toward … the spiritual" (*Time*), earned his M.D. degree in 1900 at the University of Basel, Switzerland and his Ph.D. in 1902 at the University of Zurich, Switzerland. During his time as a staff member at a psychiatric hospital (1900–1909), Jung developed his theory of complexes. In 1906 he began a professional collaboration with Sigmund Freud, which ended in 1912 when Jung established his own theory in *The Psychology of the Unconscious*. Jung then resigned as a lecturer in psychiatry and worked only in his private practice (founded in 1909). In 1916 and 1917 he published *Two Essays on Analytical Psychology* and in 1921 *Psychological Types*, in which he introduced his idea of the polarities of the personality. Later he returned to teaching psychology at the University of Zurich (1933–1941) and Basel (1943–1944) and spent his last years as a consultant and lecturer at the C.G. Jung Institute (1948–1961).

Alfred Charles Kinsey
Zoologist and author, 1894–1956

Being ill during much of his childhood and sheltered by his religious family, Alfred Kinsey avoided female companionship in High School rather than upset his parents. After receiving his doctorate from Harvard University in 1920, he became a professor of zoology at Indiana University in 1929, where he studied gall wasps. While teaching marriage courses for students in 1938, he saw the need for an objective study of human sexuality. He collected data through face-to-face interviews with 18,500 men and women, which led to the publication of his discoveries in *Sexual Behavior in the Human Male* (1948) and *Sexual Behavior in the Human Female* (1953). Because of the controversial findings of the widespread existence of masturbation, heterosexual petting and homosexual experiences, the Rockefeller Foundation withdrew its grants from the Institute of Sex Research, which Kinsey had founded in 1942.

Richard Freiherr von Krafft-Ebing
Psychiatrist, 1840–1902

Krafft-Ebing's interest in medical forensics, which was probably developed while living with his lawyer-grandfather when he attended the University of Heidelberg, led to professorships of psychiatry in Strasbourg (1872), Graz (1873), and Vienna

(1889). In addition to teaching and research, Krafft-Ebing worked as a forensic psychiatric consultant. He is primarily remembered today for his case study of sexual abnormalities *Psychopathia Sexualis* (1886). With this work, he helped initiate scientific discussion and study of sexual abnormality. More than anyone else in that period, Krafft-Ebing made sex-research respectable. By contrast, his view of masturbation as harmful and leading to homosexuality reinforced superstitions and moral judgments even up into the 20th century. *Psychopathia Sexualis* also found great popularity as an underground handbook for masochists, transvestites and others.

Antonie van Leuwenhoek
Biologist and microscopist, 1632–1723

Although a draper by profession, Leuwenhoek's hobby of improving lenses (originally to examine cloth) was nurtured by his insatiable curiosity. He attracted the attention of the scientific community after 1673, when he started to describe his observations of red blood cells in his correspondence  with the Royal Society in London. In 1674 Leuwenhoek gave the first description of the common green alga Spirogyra, and was the first to see living sperm cells in animals when he detected living spermatozoa in fresh semen in 1677. In 1683 he illustrated five different kinds of bacteria present in his mouth. He was elected a member of the Royal Society in 1680. In total he studied samples of about 200 biological species and built almost 500 microscopes.

Kaspar Bronislaw Malinowski
Anthropologist, 1884–1942

Having earned a doctoral degree in physics and mathematics in Krakow in 1908, Malinowski studied anthropology in Leipzig, Germany and at the London School of Economics, where he started lecturing in 1913, received his D.Sc. in 1916 and was appointed reader in 1924. In 1927 Malinowski occupied the university's first chair in anthropology. Among other field studies he published *Sex and Repression in Savage Society*, 1927, studying sex customs, family and social life within primitive tribal communities, and *The Sexual Life of Savages in North-Western Melanesia*, 1929. From 1939 Malinowski lectured at Yale University.

He is widely recognized as father of the functional school of anthropology, which emphasizes the significance of scientific method over abstract theory.

William Howell Masters
Psychologist, obstetrician, gynecologist, b.1915
Virginia Johnson
Sociologist, sex therapist, b.1925

Masters received his M.D. from the University of Rochester in 1943, then worked in obstetrics and gynecology in St. Louis and there in 1947 joined the faculty at the Washington University School of Medicine, where he advanced from instructor to professor (1969). Two years into his research on the physiology of sex, he hired Johnson as an assistant in 1956, forming what proved to be one of the most pioneering teams ever in the field of human sexuality, both in the domains of research and therapy. At that time Johnson was enrolled in sociology at Washington University after some music studies at the University of Missouri (1944–1947), different jobs and three marriages. Over the following eleven years Masters and Johnson analyzed the sexuality of almost 700 men and women under laboratory conditions. In 1966 they published their results in *Human Sexual Response*, which describes four phases of the human sexual response cycle common to men and women: 1. excitement, 2. plateau, 3. orgasm, 4. resolution. Despite its dry and scientific language, it became a best seller. Their counseling work on sexual problems (since 1959) led to their second book *Human Sexual Inadequacy* (1970), which was concerned with issues such as impotency, premature ejaculation and frigidity. They had been married for two years when they became co-directors of the Masters and Johnson Institute in 1973. Their theory of a possible change of the sexual orientation of homosexuals, set forth in *Homosexuality in Perspective* (1979), was heavily criticized by the gay community. Even more controversial was their speculation about an epidemic of AIDS among heterosexuals in *Crisis: Heterosexual Behavior in the Age of AIDS* (1988). After their divorce in 1992, Johnson continued working independently.

Margaret Mead
Anthropologist, 1901–1978

"The cool anthropologist, rational grandmother, symbol of common sense to millions of Americans" (*Life Magazine*) graduated from Barnard College (New York City) in 1923 and set off alone for her doctoral study in anthropology in Samoa in 1925. Her record *Coming of Age in Samoa*, 1928 stated that

anxieties of adolescence were not to be found among Samoan girls, and thus are a product of Western societies, which shrouds sexuality in secrecy. In 1926 she was appointed curator of ethnology at the American Museum of Natural History. In 1935, Mead published a study of sex roles in the cultures of the Arapesh, Mudugumar and Tchambuli of New Guinea, entitled *Sex and Temperament in Three Primitive Societies*. From the beginning, she made the lessons of all her field work relevant to public policy by also questioning Western gender roles and traditions. Between 1961 and 1978 she had a deep impact on society as columnist in Redbook magazine, promoting the ideal of a world in which women's and men's unique skills would be valued equally.

Wilhelm Reich
Psychoanalyst, 1897–1957

After his graduation as M.D. from University of Vienna, Reich became the first clinical assistant at Sigmund Freud's Psychoanalytic Polyclinic in 1922 and its vice-director in 1928. He entered the Socialist Party in 1924 and switched to the Communist Party in 1928, but was excluded in 1933 for his promotion of sexual politics. In 1927 he published *The*

Function of the Orgasm, exploring Freud's libido theory, which links sexual activity and neuroses, and criticizes his later digression from it. The International Psychoanalytic Association later expelled him because of his communist ties. From 1930, Reich lived in Berlin, but fled the Nazis to Norway in 1933 and then to the United States in 1939. He established the Orgone Institute Research Laboratories in Oregon in 1940. Reich came into conflict with the Food and Drug Administration, which considered his so-called "orgone accumulator" a fraudulent cancer cure. The authorities destroyed most of his books in the United States and he was sentenced to two years in prison, where he died in 1957.

Bertrand Russell, third Earl Russell
Mathematician and philosopher, 1872–1970

"Thou shalt not follow a multitude to do evil," his puritanical grandmother's motto, could also have been Bertrand Russell's, who grew up in her home after his parents' early death. In 1894 he graduated from Cambridge University. Because of his pacifist ideals and opposition to the British government during the First World War, Russell was dismissed as lecturer at Cambridge University in 1916. Russell could already claim worldwide impact and recognition for his research and work in mathematics, politics, philosophy, history, and education, when he published *Marriage and Morals* in 1929, in which he advocated limited sexual permissiveness in marriage. Because of his international acknowledgment as scientist and philosopher, Russell's approach to marital ethics caused a stir. A teaching appointment at the College of the City of New York was revoked when his beliefs were heavily criticized in the American Press by clergymen and city officials. In 1950 he was granted the Nobel Prize for Literature in recognition of his varied and significant writings, in which he championed humanitarian ideals and freedom of thought.

Marquis Donatien-Alphonse-Françoise de Sade
Author, 1740–1814

Seeing the promiscuous lifestyle of both his father and his uncle and being of violent and arrogant character, de Sade embarked early on a sexually-charged lifestyle himself. In 1754 he started a military career, which ended before he got married in 1763. De Sade soon began several affairs, and got arrested in 1768 for violent sexual abuse. After his release in 1772 he resumed his old habits and escaped to Italy from his death sentence for sexual offenses. When the conviction was overturned in 1776, he returned to his castle in La Coste where he lived in continuous scandal. De Sade was imprisoned again in 1777 and after his wife filed for divorce he began writing the sexually graphic novels *Dialogue Between a Priest and a Dying Man*, 1782, *One Hundred and Twenty Days of Sodom*, 1784, and *Crimes of Passion*, 1788. Upon his release in 1790 the Comédie Française produced some of his plays and in 1791 de Sade wrote his most famous work *Justine, or The Misfortunes of Virtue*. After 1792 he held some posts in the Revolutionary Government through which he was able to save his father- and mother-in-law from the guillotine, even though they had been responsible for his various imprisonments. Afterwards, he lived in poverty until he was imprisoned again in 1801 and was transferred to the mental asylum in Charenton in 1803 where he finally died in 1814.

Marie Stopes
Birthcontrol advocate, paleobotanist, 1880–1958

Marie Stopes received her B.Sc. from London University in Botany (1902), her Ph.D. from the University of Munich (1904), and – as the youngest person ever – her D.Sc. from University of London (1905). She then became the first female lecturer in the science faculty of Manchester University. Through her experience of being married to an impotent man, Stopes increasingly directed her energies on the topics of love, marriage and sex. Her first and most famous book *Married Love* (1918) was the first sex

handbook written for women, which promoted the then radical idea that people should seek joy in their sexual relationships. The same year *Wise Parenthood* provided easy-to-read information on birth control as a response to the huge number of inquiries she received about contraception following the publication of her first book. Other books on these subjects followed throughout the 1920s and early 1930s. In 1921 Stopes opened Britain's first birth-control clinic and founded the Society for Constructive Birth Control.

Andreas Vesalius
Anatomist, 1514–1564

Andreas Vesalius studied medicine at the Universities of Louvain (1529–1533 and 1536), Paris (1533–1536) and Padua (1537), where he finally became professor of anatomy. He insisted on doing dissections himself and gradually overthrew the anatomy of the Ancient Greek Galen, which had been passed down for centuries. In 1543 Vesalius published his revolutionary seven volume work *De humani corporis fabrica* (On the Structure of the Human Body), whose extensive and accurate

description of the human body gave anatomy a whole new language. He became a regular physician of the Holy Roman Emperor Charles V in Brussels, and in 1559 was appointed physician in the Madrid court of Philip II. He died returning from a pilgrimage to Jerusalem in 1564.

Human Sexual Attitudes and Behavior – a Chronology

c. 3000 B.C.	Sumer: texts describe what may be sacred prostitution.
c.2000 B.C.	Sumer: fragments of a legal codex dating back to the Sumerians (around 1750 B.C.) about marriage and slavery.
1825 B.C.	Egypt: the Kahun Papyrus – the earliest still extant Egyptian medical text – recommends a plug of crocodile dung to be inserted into the vagina to prevent pregnancy.
c.1500 B.C.	Egypt: the Ebers Papyrus recommends a piece of lint soaked in acacia tips and honey to be maneuvered over the opening to the uterus to create an environment hostile to sperm.
6th cent. B.C.	Greece: Sappho writes her love poems, giving a powerful picture of her emotions, pain and ecstacy. The lawgiver Solon establishes the first Athenian brothel.
third cent. B.C.	Greece: the sterilization of women is mentioned by Hippocrates for the first time. West Africa: male circumcision practiced.
second cent. B.C.	China: the emperor Shih Huang Ti chronicles sexual practices, sex techniques for curing backache, and further cures for infertility, impotence, hemorrhoids, deafness, and indigestion, as well as to aid conception.
first cent. A.D.	Europe: the church begins to identify sodomy as a homosexual sin.
	China: Ban Zhao writes the handbook *Nüjie* (Women's Precepts), a guide on how to raise a female child. Nile Valley and Arabia: female circumcision practiced.
c.100	Hindu World: the first systematized book of Hindu ritual laws *The Laws of Manu* appears which includes numerous rules about sexual conduct.
second cent.	China: Daoist monasteries are established, where sexual techniques are taught and put into practice during orgies.
third cent.	India: Vatsyana writes the *Kamasutra*, linking sexual pleasure to physical and spiritual well-being.
701	Japan: a law decrees that doctors should study illustrated sex manuals as part of their training.
9th cent.	Islamic World: the physician Rhazes names 17 substances for women to use as contraceptives, including animal ear wax, cabbage, and whitewash.
855	Vatican: a woman becomes Pope Joan/John.
11th cent.	Europe: polygamy among Ashkenazi Jews is prohibited. Rome: Pope Benedict VIII opens the biggest brothel in Rome. India: the Rajarajeshvara temple in Tajore employs 400 prostitutes.
12th cent.	Europe: the church declares marriage to be a sacrament and establishes the principle of clerical celibacy. Beginning of love-mysticism in the writings of the Church. Beginning of Troubadour Poetry. Constantinople: castrati appear for the first time in the service of Christian sacred music.
13th cent.	Europe: Saint Thomas Aquinas declares that the destruction of Sodom and Gomorrah could be blamed on homosexuality and decides that sodomies are damned for all eternity. Cambodia: Obligatory ceremonial defloration of girls before marriage takes place, known as Tchin-chan.
14th cent.	Europe: exaggerated codpieces emphasize the male genitalia.
1368–1644	China: erotic novels develop as a new literary genre during the Ming period.
1371	Italy: Boccaccio's *Decamerone* appears in form of an autobiographical manuscript.
15th cent.	India: Kalyana Malla writes *Ananga Ranga* (Stage of the Bodiless One), which later becomes one of the most important guides of all medieval sex manuals.

1454	Persia: Muhammad II builds the first seraglio.
1483	Persia: Jami writes *Yusuf and Zulaykha*, a Persian mystical love poem, based on the biblical story of Joseph (Genesis 37ff.). In his poetry, acclaimed worldwide, Jami elaborates on the idea that true love of God is always strongly connected to true love among human beings.
1487	Germany: *Malleus Malleficarum* is written by the Dominican friars Jakob Sprenger and Heinrich Kramer, and becomes the textbook for the witch-hunts.
16th cent.	Germany: the Reformation attacks the idea of clerical celibacy and monastic vows of continence. Tunisia: Sheikh Nefzawi writes the erotic manual *The Perfumed Garden.*
1564	Italy: the first real condom is invented by physician Gabrielo Falloppia. As a protection against sexually transmitted diseases he recommends a moistened linen sheath.
1588	Pope Sixtus V declares that all abortions are an act of murder.
17th cent.	Europe: persecution of witches begins to decline.
1629	Japan: female performers are banned from the stage of the Kabuki theater, because they also work as prostitutes.
1630	Spain: Tirso de Molina writes *El burlador de Sevilla*, the first work introducing the character of the womanizer to literature.
1642	England: the Puritans regard the public theaters as dens of iniquity and therefore force their closure.
1644 (–1911)	China: erotic books and pictures are banned during the Qing Dynasty.
1657	Japan: a district of pleasure is established in Edo, which is later known as Tokyo.
1800s	Europe: the first artificial breasts appear for sale. Russia: obscene poetry appears as a form of subculture.
1776	Switzerland: Simon André Tissot writes the influential anti-masturbation tract, *Diseases Produced by Onanism.*
1791	France: repeal of the ban on homosexuality.
1819	Italy: the Duke of Calabria, Francis I, suggests locking all erotic art in a single room at the Museum of Naples. This room is called "Cabinet of Obscene Objects".
1830	First experiments on male sterilization, which is also called "vasectomy".
1840s	Shortly after the vulcanization of rubber, which is invented in 1843 by Charles Goodyear, rubber condoms appear.
mid-19th cent.	Germany: the female ova are identified by the embryologist Karl Ernst von Baer. Ignaz Semmelweis, the "mother rescuer", promotes hand-washing because of the high death rate of women suffering infections after childbirth.
1852	USA: Brigham Young, leader of the Mormons, proclaims the duty of polygamy.
1854	Vatican: Pius IX decrees in a papal bull the "Immaculate Conception of Mary" which is declared an official doctrine.
1857	USA: the government prohibits polygamy for Mormons. English law is changed to allow married women the right to possess their own property.
1860s	Austria: Gregor Johann Mendel describes the process of genetic inheritance.
1861	UK: the death penalty for male homosexual acts is dropped and replaced by life imprisonment. New Orleans, USA: the first striptease takes place.

1863	Germany: the lawyer Karl Heinrich Ulrich speaks at a legal conference in Munich and declares himself to be homosexual. He is the first person in modern times to out himself.
1880	France: Émile Zola's novel *Nana* is published, depicting the life of a courtesan.
1880s	Europe, America: introduction of the diaphragm and the cap for contraception.
1883	UK: Richard Burton translates the *Kamasutra*.
1885	UK: The English pharmacist Walter Rendell develops the first commercial vaginal suppository as a contraceptive, using cocoa butter and quinine sulphate.
1886	Germany: Richard Freiherr von Krafft-Ebing, the author of *Psychopathia Sexualis*, claims that masturbation leads to insanity and that homosexuality is a form of disease.
1890s	Europe: the first commercially produced sanitary towels for use in menstruation go on sale.
1895	Austria: Sigmund Freud, the founder of psychoanalysis, writes *Studies in Hysteria*.
1897–1910	UK: Henry Havelock Ellis, the author of *Sexual Inversion* and *Studies in the Psychology of Sex* (10 vols.), states that homosexuality is not a disease and that women might enjoy sex. He is an advocate for sex education.
1899	UK: First prosecution of an "immoral film".
early 20th cent.	Russia: Ivan Petrovich Pavlov advocates the reconditioning of sexual tastes through the therapy of aversion. Germany introduces the two-piece bathing suit for women.
1900s	Europe, USA: female condoms are introduced. Female cicumcision used as a cure for epilepsy, hysteria, nymphomania, and masturbation. Make circumcision recommended to stop masturbation.
1904	Germany: Countess Gertrud Bülow von Dennewitz publishes her pamphlet *Das Recht zur Beseitigung des keimenden Lebens* (The Right to Remove Budding Life) and begins to campaign for the legalization of abortion.
1908	Germany: Introduction of film censorship.
1909	Germany: The physician R. Richter develops the first specifically designed IUD, a ring of silkworm gut.
1910	India: The sacrament of marriage of the Sikhs, which acknowledges and respects the rights of a woman, is accepted by state governments.
1911	Sweden: Introduction of film censorship. China: Polygamy is banned.
1913	UK: The "British Board of Film Censorship" bans nudity in films for the first time.
1914	Germany: Magnus Hirschfeld publishes *Die Homosexualität des Mannes und des Weibes* (Male and Female Homosexuality). In 1919 he founds the first institute of sexology in Berlin. *Sexual Anomalies and Perversions* appears in 1936. He campaigns for homosexual and lesbian rights throughout his career.
1917	USSR: After the October Revolution prostitution is prohibited. Women are granted the same rights as men. Marriage in church is abolished, abortion is legalized.
1918	UK: Marie Stopes causes a furore by campaigning for sexual and reproductive rights for women. Her books *Married Love* and *Wise Parenthood* are best sellers worldwide.
1918/19	China: Schools and kindergartens which allow girls as well as boys are established. Germany: After the proclamation of the Republic film censorship is temporarily abandoned and sex-education films are made.

1921	UK: Marie Stopes opens UK's first birth control clinic. China: the "Women's Union" demands equal rights for inheritance, franchise, education, work, and self-determination with regard to marriage.
1925	USA: Margaret Sanger, author of the book *The Woman Rebel and Family Limitation* and campaigner for "Women's rights to contraception and sexual pleasure", opens America's first birth control clinic. First international birth control conference.
1927	Austria, UK: Wilhelm Reich publishes *The Function of the Orgasm* and emphasizes the orgasm as the goal of sex therapy. USA: some states of the US start to compete for ever-quicker divorces. Hollywood opts for a form of self-censorship by agreeing to the Hays Code.
1933	Europe, USA: tampons are introduced. USSR: recriminalization of homosexuality.
1934	The Roman Catholic Church promotes the calendar method for family planning. Sweden: first involuntary sterilization law.
1935	USSR: ban on pornography.
1936	USSR: ban on abortion.
1940s	The temperature method is used for family planning.
1945	France: closure of brothels.
1947	UK, USA: penicillin is used to cure sexually transmitted diseases. USA: Alfred C. Kinsey founds the "Institute for Sex Research" at the University of Indiana (later known as "The Kinsey Institute"). India: in the state of Madras, girls are prevented from becoming temple prostitutes.
1948	India: the *International Journal of Sexology* is published for the first time.
1949	France: Simone de Beauvoir's book *The Second Sex* is published. A passionate plea for the abolition of what she calls the myth of the "eternal feminine", for many women it later becomes the bible of the New Women's Movement.
1950	USA: the gynecologist Ernst Gräfenberg describes female ejaculation and the G-spot.
1950s	Eastern Europe: in the socialist states, such as Russia and East Germany, abortion is legalized.
1951	Denmark: first sex-change surgery from male to female. USA: foundation of the homosexual liberation organization "The Mattachine Society".
1953	USA: the Kinsey Report, which surveys 12,000 people investigating premarital and extramarital intercourse, women's sexual capacities and the extent of homosexual behavior, is harshly attacked by conservative religious and political leaders.
1955	Publisher Hugh Hefner starts *Playboy*, a men's magazine, which combines sex with serious upmarket journalism. India: the Hindu Marriage Act attempts to emulate English customs and outlaws polygamy and child-marriage.
1956	First clinical tests for an oral contraceptive pill based on acombination of hormons. Vatican: Simone de Beauvoir's book *The Second Sex* is put on the index of banned books.
1959	Democratic Republic of Congo: possibly the first incidence of HIV, later detected in blood specimen of adult Bantu man.
1960	Hormonal birth control invented, known as "the pill". USA: opening of the striptease university in Los Angeles.

1960s	USA: implantation of silicone gel cushions for breast enlargement performed. Germany: sex-education films are produced again.
1960s–1970s	Western countries: the women's liberation movement enables women to challenge traditional policies. The legalization of abortion is secured.
1961	UK: approval of the contraceptive pill containing the substance estrogen.
1963	Tests with injectable drugs to be used as a short term contraceptive.
1964	Introduction of the Billings or ovulation method for family planning.
1965	USA: the Kinsey Institute publishes *Sex Offenders: An Analysis of Types*. UK: first publication of *Penthouse*.
1966	USA: William H. Masters and Virginia Johnson publish *Human Sexual Response*, which reports on the importance of the clitoris for sexual satisfaction, and which proves that women can have multiple orgasms.
1968	One year earlier than in West Germany, East Germany decriminalizes homosexuality.
1969	USA: homosexuals openly challenge police officers in Greenwich Village, NY (Christopher Street Day).
1969	Progestogen-only pills, which as their name suggests, contain no estrogen, are introduced.
1970	USA: Masters and Johnson publish *Human Sexual Inadequacy*, which becomes the basis for a new behavioral sex therapy.
1970s	China: two-child policy introduced to prevent overpopulation.
1973	USA: the "American Psychiatric Association" states that homosexuality is not an illness. Australia: the first "gay marriage" takes place. Germany: prostitution is no longer prohibited. USA: Nancy Friday writes *My Secret Garden: Women's Sexual Fantasies*.
1974	France: the first "World Congress of Sexology" is held in Paris. UK: Alex Comfort publishes the sex manual *Joy of Sex*.
1975	France: first "International Whore Congress" takes place in Paris. In Lyon, prostitutes go on strike. First publication of the international magazine *Playgirl*.
1976	USA: Shere Hite publishes *The Hite Report: A Nationwide Study of Female Sexuality*. It examines the sexual preferences and practices of thousands of women. France: Michel Foucault, philosopher and historian, de-medicalizes sex with the publication of *The History of Sexuality*.
1977	UK: Charlotte Wolff publishes *Bisexuality: A Study*.
1978	UK: first test-tube baby is born. Foundation of "World Association for Sexology". UK: Emily L. Sisley and Bertha Harris publish *The Joy of Lesbian Sex*.
1980s	China: one-child policy is established.
1981	USA: first Western cases of HIV/AIDS recognized.
1982	France: first court case on female circumcision, after the death of a baby.
1984	Extension of the license of injectable drugs as long-term contraceptive.
1985	Germany: the Gay Museum is founded in Berlin.
1986	France: in Paris the researcher Luc Montagnier identifies the AIDS virus (HIV).
1989	Denmark: the first country which legally recognizes homosexual partnerships.

1990	France: a court rules that a husband can be convicted for indecently assaulting and raping his wife.
1990s	Surrogate mothers help infertile couples to have children.
1991	India: first "International Conference on Orgasm".
1992	USA: silicone implantation for breast enlargement is prohibited. Canada: a court allows the victims of sex crimes to sue the publishers and distributors of pornography. Germany: opening of the Erotic Art Museum in Hamburg. Denmark: opening of the Copenhagen Erotic Museum.
1993	USSR: decriminalization of homosexuality. China: opening of a sex shop in Beijing.
1994	Germany: the Robert Koch Institute in Berlin opens an archive for sexology.
1996	UK: a man is jailed for downloading pornography from the internet. Germany: 1.5 million Catholics sign petition opposing the Pope's views on celibate priesthood and sexual morality.
1997	A frameless IUD is introduced, which is made of small copper beads threaded on nylon. India: first National Convention of Sex Workers. Spain: "World Congress of Sexology" issuing the declaration of sexual rights. USA: pedophile sex offenders are named on the internet.
1998	Korea: a human embryo is cloned. USA: Viagra, a drug to treat impotence, is launched. Israel: the forces describe sexual harassment as a crime for the first time. Russia: the first sex shop is opened in Moscow.
Since 1999	Sweden: prostitution is no longer a crime. The john, who wants to avail himself of the prostitute's services, is criminalized instead.
2000	The symptothermal method, combining all indicators of fertility, is widely used for family planning.
2001	Private and publicly funded organizations race to complete the first ever map of the human genome. Medical research begins to investigate seriously the "urban myth" that circumcision may help prevent transmission of HIV, based on the realization that the foreskin is lacking in a protective layer known as keratin, and is therefore more prone to infection. By the third millennium more than 23 million people in Sub-Saharan Africa are infected with HIV. Under intense political pressure and prompted by the high cost of Western medicines, which his country cannot afford, Thabo Mbeki, the President of South Africa, assembles a panel of dissident scientists to assert that HIV is not the cause of AIDS. They claim that Western AIDS and African AIDS are two different diseases, and that Africa must find its own solution to its AIDS problem.

Iceland

Norway Sweden Estonia
Denmark Latvia
United King- Lithuania
dom Belarus
Ireland
Netherlands Germany Poland
Belgium Czech Ukr
Republic Slovakia
Austria Hungary Moldova
Switzerland
France Slovenia Romania
Italy Bosnia & Herze- Serbia Bulgaria
Croatia govina
Portugal Spain
Albania Greece

Canada

United States of Ame-
rica

Tunisia
Morocco Algeria
Libya

Bermuda

Bahamas Mauritania Mali Niger Chad
Cuba Senegal
Mexico Haiti Dominican Republic Gambia
Belize Guinea-Bissau Burkina Nigeria
Guatemala Guinea Faso
Honduras Sierra Leone Benin
El Salvador Ivory Ghana Cameroon
Nicaragua Liberia Coast Togo
Costa Rica Equatorial Congo
Venezuela Guinea (Brazzaville)
Panama Surinam Gabon
Guyana French Guiana
Colombia

Ecuador

Peru Brazil Angola

Bolivia

Paraguay

Argentina South

Uruguay

Chile

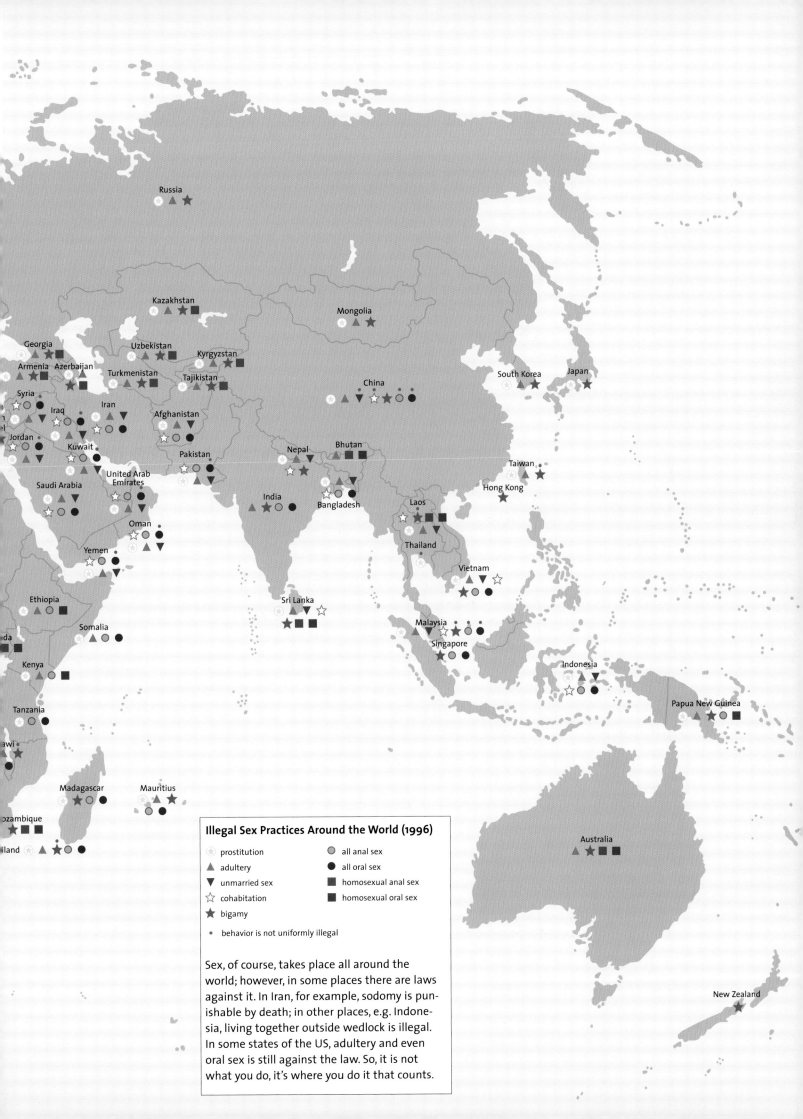

Illegal Sex Practices Around the World (1996)

- ⊛ prostitution
- ▲ adultery
- ▼ unmarried sex
- ☆ cohabitation
- ★ bigamy

- ⬤ all anal sex
- ● all oral sex
- ■ homosexual anal sex
- ■ homosexual oral sex

- • behavior is not uniformly illegal

Sex, of course, takes place all around the world; however, in some places there are laws against it. In Iran, for example, sodomy is punishable by death; in other places, e.g. Indonesia, living together outside wedlock is illegal. In some states of the US, adultery and even oral sex is still against the law. So, it is not what you do, it's where you do it that counts.

Bibliographie – A Selection

General Works

Andreae, Simon. *Anatomy of Desire: The Science and Psychology of Sex, Love, and Marriage*. London: Little Brown and Company, 1998.

Bishop, Clifford. *Sex and Spirit*. London: Macmillan, 1996.

Francoeur, Robert T. (Ed.). *The Complete Dictionary of Sexology*. New York: Continuum, 1995.

Gregersen, Edgar. *The World of Human Sexuality: Behaviors, Customs, and Beliefs*. New York: Irvington Publishers, 1994.

Hirschfeld, Magnus. *Geschlechtskunde*. 5 Vol. Berlin, 1925–30.

Onians, R. B. *The Origins of European Thought about the Mind, the Body etc*. New York: Arno Press, 1973.

Parrinder, G. *Sex in the World's Religions*. London: Sheldon Press, 1980.

Tannahill, Reay. *Sex in History*. London: Hamish Hamilton, 1980.

Taylor, G. Rattray. *Sex in History*. London: Thames and Hudson, 1953.

Mind and Body

Anderson, Bonnie, and Judith Zinsser. *A History of Their Own: Women in Europe From Prehistory to the Present*. London: Penguin, 1988.

Bradford, Nikki. *Men's Health Matters*. London: Vermillion Books, 1995.

Green, Shirley. *The Curious History of Contraception*. London: Ebury Press, 1971.

Kitzinger, Sheila. *New Pregnancy and Childbirth*. London: Penguin, 1997.

McPherson, Ann Dr., and Nancy Durham. *Woman's Hour Book of Health*. London: BBC Books, 1998.

Rathus, Spencer, Jeffrey Nevid, and Lois Fichner-Rathus. *Human Sexuality in a World of Diversity*. Boston: Allyn and Bacon, 1997[3].

Seager, Joni. *The State of Women in the World Atlas*. London: Penguin Reference, 1997[2].

Whitfield, Philip and Susan Greenfield. *How We Work*. Marshall Publishing, 1997.

Williams, Walter L. *The Spirit and the Flesh: Sexual Diversity in American Indian Culture*. Boston: Beacon, 1992.

Making Love

British Medical Association. *Complete Family Health Encyclopedia*. London: Dorling Kindersley, 1996.

Carter, Yvonne, Catti Moss, and Anne Weyman (Eds.). *RCGP Handbook of Sexual Health in Primary Care*. London: Royal College of General Practitioners, 1998.

Day, Trevor. *Teach Yourself Guide to Sex*. London: Hodder & Stoughton, 1997.

Matrimony and Partnership

Gilbert, Harriet, and Jonathan Cape (Eds.). *The Sexual Imagination from Acker to Zola: A Feminist Companion*. London: Cape, 1993.

Grant, Michael. *The Annals of Imperial Rome*. Harmondsworth: Penguin Classics, 1956.

Kenyon, Olga. *800 Years of Women's Letters*. Stroud: Alan Sutton, c. 1992.

Krishnanada, Swami Ram. *Classical Hindu Erotology*. Paris: Olympia Press, 1958.

Licht, Hans. *Sexual Life in Ancient Greece*. London: Routledge & Kegan Paul Ltd., 1952.

Lilar, Suzanne. *Aspects of Love in Western Society*. London: Thames & Hudson, 1965.

Loth, David. *The Erotic in Literature: A Historical Survey of Pornography as delightful as it is indiscreet*. New York: Messner, 1961.

Miles, Margaret R. *Carnal Knowing: Female Nakedness and Religious Meaning in the Christian West*. New York: Vintage Books, 1991.

Person, Ethel Specter. *Dreams of Love and Fateful Encounters: The Power of Romantic Passion*. New York et. al.: Penguin Books, 1989.

Pliny, the Elder. *Natural History: In Ten Volumes*. London: Heinemann, 1950.

Rawson, Philip. *Oriental Erotic Art*. Ware: Omega, 1984.

Husain, Shahrukh. *The Goddess*. Time-Life Books: Alexandria, VA, 1997.

Stone, Lawrence. *The Family, Sex and Marriage in England: 1500–1800*. London: Weidenfeld and Nicolson, 1977.

Stone, Lawrence. *The Road to Divorce: England 1530–1987*. Oxford et. al.: Oxford University Press, 1990.

Watkins, Oscar Daniel. *Holy Matrimony*. London: Faith Press, 1895.

West, Donald James. *Homosexuality*. London: Duckworth, 1968.

Westermarck, E. *History of Human Marriage*. London, 1891.

Westheimer, Dr. Ruth. *The Art of Arousal*. New York et. al.: Abbeville Press, 1993[1].

Origins – The Evolution of Sexual Culture

Beckwith, Carol. *Geerewol, the Art of Seduction*. In: *Fragments for a History of the Human Body*. Ed. Michael Feher. MIT Press, 1989.

Beckwith, Carol, and Angela Fischer. *African Ceremonies*. New York: Abrams, 1999.

Boyce, Mary (Ed.). *Textual Sources for the Study of Zoroastrianism*. Manchester: University Press, 1984.

Cole, W.G. *Sex and Love in the Bible*. London: Hodder & Stoughton, 1960.

Goodland, R. *A Bibliography of Sex Rites and Customs*. London: G. Routledge & Sons, 1931.

Griaule, Marcel. *Conversations with Ogotemmeli: An Introduction to Dogon Religious Ideas*. Oxford University Press, 1970.

Hart, George. *Egyptian Myths*. London: British Museum Publ., 1991.

James, Thomas G.H. An *Introduction to Ancient Egypt*. London: British Museum Publ., 1986.

McQuitty, William. *The Island of Isis: Philae Temple of the Nile*. MacDonalds and Janes Ltd., 1976.

Murdock, George Peter. *Africa: Its Peoples and their Cultural History*. New York: McGraw-Hill, 1959.

Nefzawi, 'Umar ibn Muhammad. *The Perfumed Garden: Man's Heart to Gladden*. London: N. Spearman, c.1963. Fortune Press, 1934.

Rachewiltz, Boris de. *Black Eros: Sexual Customs of Africa from Pre-History in the Present Day*. London: Allen & Unwin, 1964.

Robinson, Francis. *Atlas of the Islamic World since 1500*. London: Phaidon, 1982.

Rundle, R.T. *Myth and Symbol in Ancient Egypt*. London: Thames and Hudson 1978.

Symons, D. *The Evolution of Human Sexuality*. New York: OUP, 1979.

Taylor, T. *The Prehistory of Sex*. London: Fourth Estate, 1996.

The Classical World

Boardman, J., and E. La Rocca, *Eros in Greece*. London: J. Murray, 1978.

Dover, K. J. *Greek Homosexuality*. London: Duckworth, 1978.

Halperin, D. M., J. J. Winkler, and F.I. Zeitlin, (Eds.). *Before Sexuality: The Construction of Erotic Experience in the Ancient Greek World*. Princeton: P.U.P., 1990.

Johns, Catherine. *Sex or Symbol: Erotic Images of Greece and Rome.* London: British Museum Publications, c. 1982.

Keuls, E.C. *The Reign of the Phallus: Sexual Politics in Ancient Athens.* Berkeley: University of California Press, 1993.

Licht, H. *Sexual Life in Ancient Greece.* London:

Routledge, 1931.
Pomeroy, S.B. *Goddesses, Whores, Wives, and Slaves: Women in Classical Antiquity.* New York: Schocken, 1975.

Richlin, A. *The Garden of Priapus: Sexuality and Aggression in Roman Humor.* New York / Oxford: Oxford University Press, 1992.

Winkler, J. J. *The Constraints of Desire: The Anthropology of Sex and Gender in Ancient Greece.* New York / London: Routledge, 1990.

When Desire Turns to Sin

Andersen, J. *The Witch on the Wall.* London: Allen & Unwin, 1977.

Bailey, D. S. *Homosexuality and the Western Christian Tradition.* London: Allen & Unwin, 1955.

Blaicklock, E.M. (Ed.). *The Confessions of St. Augustine.* London: Hodder & Stoughton, 1983.

Borneman, Ernest. *Lexikon der Liebe.* München: List, 1968.

Brown, P. *The Body and Society: Men, Women and Sexual Renunciation in Early Christianity.* New York: Columbia University Press, 1988.

Cawthorne, N. *The Sex Lives of the Popes.* London: Prion, 1990.

Clifton, C. S. *The Encyclopedia of Heresies and Heretics.* Oxford: ABC-CLIO, 1992.

Eliade, M. (Ed.). *The Encyclopedia of Religion.* London: MacMillan, 1981.

Eskapa, D. Roy. *Bizarre Sex.* London: Quartet Books, 1987.

Foucault, Michel. *The History of Sexuality: An Introduction.* Harmondsworth: Penguin, 1992.

Friday, Nancy. *My Secret Garden: Women's Sexual Fantasies.* New York: Trident Press, 1973.

Friday, Nancy. *Men in Love: Men's Sexual Fantasies: The Triumph of Love over Rage.* New York: Delacorte Press, 1980.

George, L. *The Encyclopedia of Heresies and Heretics.* London: Robson, 1995.

Grant, Linda. *Sexing the Millenium: A Political History of the Sexual Revolution.* London: Harper Collins, 1993.

Hepworth, B. *Confession: Studies in Deviance and Religion.* London: Routledge & Kegan, 1982.

Institut für Sexualforschung Wien. *Bilder-Lexikon: Kulturgeschichte, Literatur und Kunst, Sexualwissenschaft.* Hamburg: Verlag für Kulturforschung, 1961.

Jung, C. G. *The Collected Works of C. G. Jung.* London: Routledge & Kegan, 1953–1978.

Kind, Alfred. *Die Weiberherrschaft in der Geschichte der Menschheit.* Wien/Leipzig: Verlag f. Kulturforschung, 1931.

King, F. *Sexuality, Magic and Perversion.* London: Neville Spearman, 1971.

Kinsey, C. Alfred. *Sexual Behavior in the Human Male.* Philadelphia: W. B. Saunders, 1948.

McDannell, C., and B. Lang. *Heaven: A History.* Yale: Yale University Press, 1988.

Mergen, Armand (Ed.). *Sexualforschung.* Hamburg: Verlag für Kulturforschung, 1963.

Muncy, R. L. *Sex and Marriage in Utopian Communities.* Bloomington: Indiana University Press, 1973.

Russell, Bertrand. *A History of Western Philosophy.* London: George Allen & Unwin, 1946.

Sacher-Masoch, Leopold von, and Wanda von Sacher-Masoch. *The first Masochist: A Biography of Leopold von Sacher-Masoch (1836–1895).* London: Blond, 1967.

Schiebinger, L. *Nature's Body: Sexual Politics and the Making of Modern Science.* London: Harper Collins, 1993.

Scott, Gini Graham. *Erotic Power: An Exploration of Dominance and Submission.* New York: Carol Publ. Group, 1997.

Simons, G. L. *Sex and Superstition.* New York: Barnes and Noble, 1973.

Summers, M. *The History of Witchcraft and Demonology.* London: Kegan Paul, 1926.

Tang, I. *Pornography: The Secret History of Civilization.* London: Channel 4 Books, 1999.

Ullerstam, Lars. *The Erotic Minorities.* New York: Grove Press, 1966.

Warner, M. *Alone of All Her Sex.* London: Picador, 1985.

Warner, M. *From the Beast to the Blonde.* London: Chatto & Windus, 1994.

Wehr, G. *The Mystical Marriage: Symbol and Meaning of the Human Experience.* London: The Aquarian Press, 1988.

Prostitution in the Western World

B., Elisabeth. *Das ist ja zum Peepen.* Frankfurt am Main: Eichborn, 1983.

Bauer, Fritz, Hans Bürger-Prinz, Hans Giese, and Herbert Jäger (Eds.). *Sexualität und Verbrechen.* Frankfurt am Main: Fischer, 1963.

Biermann, Pieke. *Wir sind Frauen wie andere auch: Prostituierte und ihre Kämpfe.* Reinbek bei Hamburg: Rowohlt, 1980.

Hoigard, Cecile. *Backstreets: Prostitution, Money, and Love.* Cambridge: Polity Press, 1992.

Kimball, Nell. *Her Life as an American Madame.* New York: Macmillan, 1970.

Lacroix, Paul. *Weltgeschichte der Prostitution von den Anfängen bis zum Beginn des 20. Jahrhunderts.* Frankfurt am Main: Eichborn, 1995.

Prostituierten-Projekt Hydra. *Freier: Das heimliche Treiben der Männer.* Hamburg: Galgenberg, 1991.

The Erotic Muse – Art and Artifice

Ariès, Philippe, André Béjin, and Michel Foucault (Eds.) *Die Masken des Begehrens und die Metamorphosen der Sinnlichkeit: Zur Geschichte der Sexualität im Abendland.* Frankfurt am Main: Fischer, 1984[3].

Barthes, Roland, Richard Howard, and Matthew Ward. *The Fashion System.* Berkeley, CA: University of California Press, 1990.

Cooper, Wendy. *Hair: Sex, Society, Symbolism.* London: Aldus, 1971.

Hollander, Anne. *Anzug und Eros: Eine Geschichte der modernen Kleidung.* München: Dt. Taschenbuch-Verlag, 1997.

Junker, Almut, and Eva Stille. *Zur Geschichte der Unterwäsche: 1700–1960, eine Ausstellung des Historischen Museums.* Frankfurt am Main: 1988.

Lucie-Smith, E. *Sexuality in Western Art.* London: Thames & Hudson, 1991.

Martin, Richard, and Harold Koda. *Jocks and Nerds: Men's Style in the Twentieth Century.* New York: Rizzoli, 1989.

Martischnig, Michael. *Tätowierung ostasiatischer Art.* Wien: Verlag der Österreichischen Akademie der Wissenschaften, 1993.

Rimmel, Eugene. *The Book of Perfumes.* London: Chapman and Hall, 1865[3].

Steele, Valerie. *Fetisch: Mode, Sex und Macht.* Reinbek bei Hamburg: Rowohlt, 1998.

A Culture Steeped in Sex – Europe and the USA

Ariès, Philippe, and André Bejin (Eds.). *Western Sexuality: Practice and Precept in Past and Present Times*. Oxford: Blackwell, 1985.

Belfield, Toni. *Handbuch der Sexuellen Aufklärung*. Ed. Ruth Midgley. Frankfurt am Main/Berlin: Ullstein, 1988.

Comfort, Alex. *The Joy of Sex*. London: Mitchell Beazley, 1996.

Comfort, Alex. *More Joy of Sex*. London: Quartet Books, 1977.

Costlow, Jane T., Stephanie Sandler, and Judith Vowels (Eds.). *Sexuality and the Body in Russian Culture*. Stanford, CA: Stanford University Press, 1993.

Deschner, Karlheinz. *Das Kreuz mit der Kirche: Eine Sexualgeschichte des Christentums*. München: Heyne, 1989.

Ellis, Havelock. *My Life: The Autobiography of Havelock Ellis*. London/Toronto: William Heineman Ltd., 1940.

Engelstein, Laura. *The Keys to Happiness: Sex and the Search for Modernity in Fin-de-Siecle Russia*. Ithaca, N.Y.: Cornell University Press, 1992.

Erotika v russkoi literature: Ot Barkova do nashikh dnei: Texty i kommenatrii. Literaturnoe obozrenie: Spetsialnyi vypusk. Moscow 1992.

Flegon, A. *Eroticism in Russian Art*. London: Flegon Press, 1976.

Freud, Sigmund. *Studienausgabe. 10 Vol*. Eds. Alexander Mitscherlich, Angela Richards, James Strachey. Frankfurt am Main: S. Fischer Verlag, 1989.

Frischauer, Paul. *Knaurs Sittengeschichte der Welt*. Vol. 1–3. München: Droemer Knaur, 1974.

Fuchs, Eduard. *Illustrierte Sittengeschichte der Sexualität in sechs Bänden*. Frankfurt am Main: Fischer Taschenbuch-Verlag, 1985.

Grant, Linda. *Sexing the Millenium: A Political History of the Sexual Revolution*. London: Harper Collins, 1993.

Grimme, Matthias J. *Käufliche Träume: Erfahrungen mit Pornographie*. Reinbek bei Hamburg: Rowohlt, 1986

Hesse, Peter G., and Georg Harig, Friedrich Karl Kaul, and Armin-Gerd Kuckhoff (Eds.). *Sexuologie: Geschlecht, Mensch, Gesellschaft*. Leipzig: Hirzel, 1979.

Hite, Shere. *The Hite Report: A Nationwide Study on Female Sexuality*. New York: Double Day, 1987[3].

Hite, Shere. *The Hite Report on Male Sexuality*. London: Optima, 1990, c. 1981.

Kokken, Sha. *A Happier Sex Life: A Guide to Married Life*. London: Souvenir Press, 1967.

Kon, Igor Semenovich. *The Sexual Revolution in Russia: From the Age of the Czars to Today*. New York: The Free Press, 1995.

Kon, Igor Semenvich. *Seksualnaya kultura v Rossii: klubnichka na beriozke*. Moscow: O.G.I., 1997.

Kon, Igor Semenovich. *Sexuality and Politics in Russia (1700–2000)*. Eds. Franz X. Eder, Lesley Hall, and Gert Hekma. Manchester: University Press, 1999.

Lautmann, Rüdiger, and Michael Schetsche. *Das pornographierte Begehren*. Frankfurt am Main: Campus Verlag, 1990.

Levin, Eve. *Sex and Society in the World of the Orthodox Slavs, 900–1700*. Ithaca, N.Y.: Cornell University Press, 1989.

Levitt, M., and A. Toporkov (Eds.). *Eros and Pornography in Russian Culture*. Moscow: Ladomir, 1998.

Lischke, Gottfried, and Angelika Tramitz. *Weltgeschichte der Erotik: Von Marilyn bis Madonna, Band IV*. München: Droemer Knaur, 1995.

Lovelace, Linda, and Mike McGrady. *Out of Bondage*. Secaucus, N.J.: L. Stuart, 1986.

Masters, William Howell, and Virginia E. Johnson. *Human Sexual Response*. New York: Bantam Books, 1980.

Pushkaryova, N. L. *Nevesta, zhena, liubovnitsa (chastnaya zhizn' zhenshchiny v doindustrialnoi Rossii X–nachala XIX vv.)*. Moscow: Ladomir, 1997.

Reich, Wilhelm. *The Function of the Orgasm: Sex-Economic Problems of Biological Energy*. London: Souvenir, 1983.

Schelsky, Helmut. *Soziologie der Sexualität*. Reinbek bei Hamburg: Rowohlt, 1955.

Toporkov, A. A. (Ed.). *Seks i erotika v russkoi traditsionnoj kulture*. Moscow: Ladomir, 1999.

Zilbergeld, Bernie. *The New Male Sexuality*. New York/London: Bantam Books, 1992.

The Art and Science of Sex – India and the Himalayas

Bhattacharya Mahodaya, S. C. V. *Principles of Tantra: the Tantratattva of Sriyukta Siva Candra Vidyarnava Bhattacarya Mahodaya*. Ed. Arthur Avalon. Madras: Ganesh & Co, 1916.

Briffault, R. *The Mothers*. London: Allen & Unwin, 1931.

David-Neal, Alexandra. *Initiations and Initiates in Tibet*. London: Rider & Co, 1931.

Douglas, N., and P. Slinger. *Sexual Secrets: The Alchemy of Ecstasy*. London: Hutchinson, 1979.

Dowman, K. *The Sacred Life of Tibet*. London: Thorsons, 1997.

Edwardes, M. *Indian Temples and Palaces*. London: Hamlyn, 1969.

Goldberg, B. Z. *The Sacred Fire: The Story of Sex in Religion*. New York: Black Cat /Grove Press, 1958.

Gregersen, E. *The World of Human Sexuality: Behaviours, Customs and Beliefs*. New York: Irvington Publishers, 1994.

Jha, A. *Sexual Designs in Indian Culture*. New Jersey: Humanities Publishers, 1979.

Kalayana, Malla. *Ananga Ranga: Stage of the Bodiless One: The Hindu Art of Love*. New York, Medical Press, 1964.

Kapadia, K. M. *Marriage and Family in India*. Bombay: Oxford University Press, 1966.

Marglin, F. A. *Wives of the God-King*. Oxford: Oxford University Press, 1985.

Maybury-Lewis, D. *Millennium: Tribal Wisdom and the Modern World*. Harmondsworth: Penguin, 1992.

Meyer, J. J. *Sexual Life in Ancient India*. London: G. Routledge & Sons, 1930.

Nanda, S. *Neither Man nor Woman: The Hijras of India*. Belmont: Wadsworth, 1990.

Rawson, P. S. *The Art of Tantra*. London: Thames and Hudson, 1973.

Rawson, P. S. *Erotic Art of the East*. London: Weidenfeld & Nicolson, 1973.

Sur, A. K. *Sex and Marriage in India: An Ethno-Historical Survey*. Bombay: Allied Publishers, 1973.

Thomas, P. *Kama Kalpa or the Hindu Ritual of Love*. Bombay: D. B. Taraporevala Sons, 1960.

Vatsyayana. *The Kama Sutra of Vatsyayana*. New York: Putnam's Sons, 1966[8].

Forbidden Zones – China and Japan

Anonym. *Dschu-Lin Yä-schi: Ein historisch-erotischer Roman aus der Ming-Zeit*. Hamburg: Die Waage, 1971.

Baschet, Eric. *From the Warlords to World War: China 1890–1938: A History in Documentary Photographs*. Zug: Swan, 1989.

Becker, Susanne. *Lyrik Chinesischer Dichterinnen: Von den Anfängen (11. Jh. v. Chr.) bis zum 10. Jh. n. Chr.* Frankfurt am Main: Lang, 1999.

Beurdeley, Michel et. al. *Chinese Erotic Art*. Secaucus: Chartwell Books, 1969.

Calza, Gian Carlo. *Hokusai: Il Vecchio Pazzo Per La Pittura. Catalogue of an Exhibition at the Palazzo Reale*. Milan: Electa, 1999–2000.

Chang, Jolan. *The Tao of Love and Sex: The Ancient Chinese Way to Ecstasy.* London: Panther, 1979.

Chubanshe, Falü. *Ehegesetz der Volksrepublik China.* 10. Nachdruck. Beijing: Gesetzestextverlag, 1996.

Chubanshe, Falü. *Erziehungsgesetz der Volksrepublik China.* 4. Nachdruck. Beijing: Gesetzestextverlag, 1995.

Döbler, Hannsferdinand. *Kultur- und Sittengeschichte der Welt: Eros, Sexus, Sitte.* München/Gütersloh/Wien: Bertelsmann-Kunst Verlag, 1971.

Dunn, Michael. *Los Shunga: El "Ars Amandi" Japonés.* In: *El Paseante*, Vol. 6. Madrid: Ediciones Sirueka, 1987.

Eberhard, Wolfram. *Guilt and Sin in Traditional China.* Berkeley, CA: University of California Press, 1967.

Egerton, Clement. *The Golden Lotus.* London: Routledge, 1939.

Evans, Tom, and Mary Anne Evans. *Shunga: The Art of Love in Japan.* New York/London: Paddington Press.

Hayashi, Yoshikazu, and Richard Lane et.al. *The Complete Ukiyo-e Shunga. 24 Vol.* Tokyo, 1996–1999.

Gernet, Jacques. *A History of Chinese Civilization.* Cambridge: Cambridge University Press, 1996.

Goodrich, Luther Carrington, and Nigel Cameron. *The Face of China: As seen by photographers and travelers 1860–1912.* London: Gordon Fraser, c. 1978.

Gulik, Robert Hans van. *Sexual Life in Ancient China.* Leiden: Brill, 1974.

Gulik, Robert Hans van. *Erotic Colour Prints: with an Essay on Chinese Sex Life from the Han to the Ch'ing Dynasty, B.C. 206-A.D. 1644.* 3 Vol. Tokyo: [Gulik], 1951.

Herbert, Franke (Ed.). *Djin Ping Meh: Ein Sittenroman aus der Ming-Zeit mit 200 Holzschnitten.* Berlin: Ullstein Verlag, 1987.

Hertzer, Dominique. *Das Mawangdui-Yijing.* München: Diederichs, c. 1996.

Hsia, Adrian. *Deutsche Denker über China.* Frankfurt am Main: Insel Verlag, 1985.

Huc, Régis-Evariste. *Das chinesische Reich.* Ed. Wolfgang Rieland. Basel: Stroemfeld/Roter Stern, 1987.

Ishihara, Akira, and Howard Seymour Levy. *The Tao of Sex: An annotated Translation of the Essence of Medical Presciptions Ishimpo.* New York: Harper & Row, 1970.

Krause, Brigitte, and Stefanie Ritter. *Fremde Schwester Liu: Frauenbilder aus der VR China.* Hamburg: Selbst Verlag Krause/Ritter, 1979.

Lane, Richard. *Images from the Floating World.* New York: Putnam, c. 1978.

Levy, Howard Seymour. *Chinese Footbinding: The History of a Curious Erotic Custom.* New York: W. Rawls, 1966.

Levy, Howard Seymour. *Chinese Jokes in Traditional Times.* Taipei: Chinese Association for Folklore, 1974.

Linck, Gudula. *Zur Sozialgeschichte der chinesischen Familie im 13. Jahrhundert: Untersuchungen am "Ming-gong shu-pan qing-ming ji".* Stuttgart: Franz Steiner, 1986.

Mengchu, Ling. *Chinesischer Liebesgarten.* Herren-alb/Schwarzwald : Erdmann, 1964.

Müller, Ernst Wilhelm (Ed.). *Geschlechtsreife und Legitimation zur Zeugung.* Freiburg/München: Alber Verlag, 1985.

O'Hara, Albert Richard. *The Position of Women in Early Modern China: According to the Lieh Nü Chuan, "the biographies of Eminent Chinese Women".* Taipei: Mei Ya Publications, 1971.

Polo, Marco. *The Travels of Marco Polo: The complete Yule-Cordier Edition.* New York: Dover Publications/London: Constable, 1993.

Robinet, Isabelle. *Taoism: Growth of a Religion.* Stanford, CA: Stanford University Press, c. 1997.

Rudelsberger, Hans. *Altchinesische Liebeskomödien.* Zürich: Manesse Verlag, 1988.

Ru Zhen, Li. *Flowers in the Mirror.* London: Arena, 1985, c. 1965.

Schliemann, Heinrich. *Reise durch China und Japan im Jahre 1865.* Konstanz: Rosgarten-Verlag, 1984.

Schon, Jenny. *Frauen in China : Eine Studie über die gesellschaftliche Stellung der chinesischen Frau vor 1949.* Bochum: Studienverlag Brockmayer, 1982.

Schumann, Hans Wolfgang. *Buddhism: An Outline of its Teachings and Schoolings.* London: Rider, 1973.

Schwarz, Ernst. *Chrysanthemen im Spiegel.* Berlin: Rütten & Loening, 1988.

Unschuld, Paul Ulrich. *Medicine in China: A History of Ideas.* Berkeley/London: University of California Press, c. 1985.

Wandel, Elke. *Frauenleben im Reich der Mitte.* Reinbek bei Hamburg: Rowohlt, 1987.

Xueqin, Cao. *The Story of the Stone: A Chinese Novel.* Harmondsworth: Penguin, 1977.

Yimen. *Frühlingsträume: Erotische Kunst aus China – Die Sammlung Bertholet.* Amsterdam, 1997.

Yu, Li. *The Before Midnight Scholar.* London: Corgi, 1974.

Yu, Li. *Chinese Women Through Chinese Eyes.* London: M.E. Sharpe, 1992.

Yuan, Qu. *The songs of the South: An Ancient Chinese Anthology of Poems.* Harmondsworth: Penguin Classics, 1985.

Sexual Crucibles

Balderston, D., and D. J. Guy, (Eds.). *Sex and Sexuality in Latin America.* New York: New York University Press, c. 1997.

Boddy, J. *Wombs and Alien Spirits: Women, Men and the Zar Cult in Northern Sudan.* Madison, Wis.: University of Wisconsin Press, c. 1989.

Brown, D. E., J. W. Edwards, and R.P. Moore. *The Penis Inserts of Southeast Asia.* Berkeley, CA: Center for South and Southeast Asia Studies, University of California at Berkeley, 1988.

Evans-Pritchard, E. E. (Ed.). *Man and Woman Among the Azande.* London: Faber, 1974.

Gregor, T. *Anxious Pleasures: The Sexual Lives of an Amazonian People.* Chicago/London: University of Chicago Press, 1985.

Herdt, G. H. *Intimate Communications: Erotics and the Study of Culture.* New York: Columbia University Press, 1990.

Herdt, G. H. (Ed.). *Ritualized Homosexuality in Melanesia.* Berkeley: University of California Press, 1984.

Hoyle, R. L. *Checan: Essay on Erotic Elements in Peruvian Art.* Geneva: Nagel, 1965.

Kaberry, P. M. *Aboriginal Women: Sacred and Profane.* London: George Routledge & Sons Ltd., 1939.

La Fontaine, J. S. *Initiation: Ritual Drama and Secret Knowledge Across the World.* Harmondsworth: Penguin, 1985.

Montagu, A. *Coming into Being Among the Australian Aborigines: The Procreative Beliefs of the Australian Aborigines.* London/Boston: Routledge & Kegan Paul, 1974[2].

Nunez, L. M. *Santeria: A Practical Guide to Afro-Caribbean Magic.* Dallas, Texas: Spring Publications Inc., 1992.

Radcliffe-Brown, A. R., and Forde, D. (Eds.). *African Systems of Kinship and Marriage.* London: KPI, 1987.

Richards, AI. *Chisungu: A Girl's Initiation Ceremony Among the Bemba of Northern Rhodesia.* London: Faber & Faber Ltd., 1956.

Shostak, M. *Nisa: The Life and Words of a Lkung Woman.* London: Earthscan Publications Ltd., 1990.

Suggs, R.C. *Marquesan Sexual Behaviour.* London: Constable, 1966.

Wiliams, W. L. *The Spirit and the Flesh: Sexual Diversity in American Indian Culture.* Boston: Beacon Press, c. 1992.

Contributors

The Editors

Clifford Bishop is a writer, journalist, and editor. He has traveled extensively in Africa and Asia, and spent two years as a development worker in Zimbabwe. Living as a guest among local people, he studied the ways in which their everyday preoccupations and traditional beliefs are fused in their figurative art, dance, and rituals. Clifford Bishop is the author of *Sex and Spirit* (1996), associate author of *Animal Spirits* (1995), coauthor of *The Goddess* (1996), and consultant on *Bertelsmann's Medica Series of Encyclopedias* (2000).

In addition to the chapter The Art and Science of Sex – India and the Himalayas and major parts of When Desire Turns to Sin and Sexual Crucibles, Clifford Bishop is the author of all the sections not listed below.

Xenia Osthelder has translated numerous works on sexology. She has a degree in English and French and also studied German literature and Art History. She worked as an interpreter for some years on a free-lance basis and has been a literary translator and editor since 1991, also having taught for many years in Britain and Germany.

The Authors

Sabine Hesemann specialized in Chinese art while still a student of Sinology, Art History, and Romance languages in Frankfurt. In 1989 and 1991 she studied at the University of Nanjing, People's Republic of China. She gave seminars and guided tours of Chinese art and culture, as well as organizing educational activities in museums in the context of special exhibitions. She also worked as a free-lance translator. She is currently writing her doctoral dissertation at the University of Frankfurt, dealing with the complex art of Chinese gardens.

For *Sexualia* she wrote the spreads China – Secrets and Misconceptions; Sex and Tradition; Harems and Courtesans; Ming Erotic Novels; Books of the Bedchamber; Erotic Art; Decadence and Barbarism of the Manchus; From the Start of the Republic to the Present.

Jane Hobden is a health writer and editor. She has worked widely on books, encyclopedias and magazines for both public and professional audiences. Before embarking on her free-lance career she developed and managed publications at the UK Family Planning Association, and has written especially widely on subjects relating to women's health. She is coauthor of *The Back Book* (Apple Press, 1999) and the forthcoming book *Getting the Best Out of the NHS* (Women's Press, 2001) – both published in England. She is also a member of the Guild of Health Writers in England, a professional organization for those writing about health.

Her contributions to *Sexualia* are the spreads Differences between Men and Women; Changing Sex; Homosexuality; Puberty – The Journey to Adulthood; Erogenous Zones; A Woman's Sex Organs; Menstruation; A Man's Sex Organs; Genital Mutilation; Sexually Transmitted Diseases; Aids; Contraception; Conception and Pregnancy; The Birth of a Child; Abortion; Arousal; Foreplay; Oral Sex; Intercourse and Orgasm; Sexual Difficulties.

Shahrukh Husain is a writer, psychotherapist and folklorist. Apart from writing books and screenplays, she has lectured extensively and worked as a consultant on documentaries and in an advisory role to Members of Parliament on cultural matters ranging from marriage and race to religion, language and censorship. She also acts regularly as a consultant for publishers on books about Islam. Her latest publications include *The Goddess* (Duncan Baird Publishing) and *Temptresses, the Virago Book of Evil Women* (Virago Press).

For *Sexualia* she contributed the spreads Choice of Partner; Exchange of Goods; Breaking the Maidenhead; Lovesickness; Famous Lovers; Fairy-tale Weddings; and jointly with Clifford Bishop: A History of the Bed; Jealousy; Guarding the Woman; Infidelity; Womanizers; La Femme Fatale; La Vie en Rose; Untying the Knot; Sexuality in Egyptian Myth; Men and Women in the Time of the Pharaohs; Passion in Ancient and Medieval Persia; Teachings of Islam, Women in the Modern Islamic World.

Professor Igor S. Kon was born in 1928, and is Chief Researcher at the Institute of Ethnology and Anthropology, Russian Academy of Sciences, and a well-known Russian sociologist and leading expert on sexuality. He has authored more than 40 books and 400 articles, including *Sexual Revolution in Russia* (Free Press, 1995), *Sexual Culture in Russia* (Moscow, 1997, rus.), *Tasting the Forbidden Fruit* (Moscow, 1997, rus.), *Moonlight at Dawn: Faces and Masks of Same Sex Love* (Moscow, 1998, rus.), and *Introduction to Sexology* (Moscow, 1999, rus).

His contribution to *Sexualia* is Russia – "We Have No Sex".

Cristina Moles Kaupp studied German Literature, Political Science and Journalism. Working as a journalist she concentrates on cultural-historic and cultural-sociological themes. For twelve years she has been working as a writer and editor, including for the Berlin city magazine *Tip*, the *Tagesspiegel* newspaper, *Spiegel-Online* and the Deutscher Taschenbuch Verlag.

For *Sexualia* she wrote the spreads The Significance of Clothing; Accentuating the Body; Sculpting the Body; Bathing Fashion; and jointly with Clifford Bishop: The Erotic Language of Hair; Depilation; Skin Signs; Piercing; The Changing Shape of the 20th-century Ideal Woman; The Beauty Business; Scent and Sensuality.

Angelika Tramitz was born in 1959 in Bremen, and studied Sociology, Psychology and Journalism in Berlin. She still lives there as a free-lance writer on culture-historical matters, largely in the sphere of sexuality. Together with Gottfried Lischke, in 1995 she published *Weltgeschichte der Erotik. (Band IV) Von Marilyn bis Madonna* (World History of the Erotic. (Vol. 4) From Marilyn to Madonna).

Her contributions to *Sexualia* are Monogamy; Last of the Summer Wine; New Forms of Cohabitation; The Ordained; Marquis de Sade; Double Standards in Victorian England; Transgression and Carnival; Privacy and the Law; Sex Murderers; War and Eros; Sex Education and Upbringing; Freud and his Successors; From Preference to Fetish; Masochism; A Job like Any Other; From Streetwalking to Luxury Bordello; Courtesans; Pimps and Madams; The Gray Zone – Casual Prostitution; Alternative Brothels; Johns; Men for Sale; Women of Easy Virtue; The Oldest Profession; Brothels in the Wild West; Mary Magdalen; The Pleasure Taboo; The Wild West; Sexual Utopias; The Sexologists; The Sexual Revolution; Feminism; Sexual Correctness; The Language of Sex; Telephone- and Cybersex; Out of the Bedroom; Exhibitions of Lust; Pinups; Striptease; Peep Shows; Pornography and Erotica; Erotic Film in Europe; Sex in Hollywood; Scandinavia, a Sexual Wonderland?

Dr. Piers Vitebsky is Head of Social Sciences and Russian Studies at the Scott Polar Research Institute in the University of Cambridge. He studied ancient languages at Cambridge and Social Anthropology in Oxford, London and Delhi. He has conducted fieldwork in many areas of the world, particularly among the aboriginal peoples of India and Siberia, specializing in religion and culture. His publications include *The Shaman*, London: Macmillan, 1995 (translated into 12 languages), *Sacred Architecture* (with Caroline Humphrey), Boston: Little Brown, 1996, and *Dialogues with the Dead: The discussion of mortality among the Sora of eastern India*, Cambridge: Cambridge University Press and Delhi: Foundation Books, 1993. His television documentaries include *Siberia – After the Shaman*, London: Channel 4, 1992, which won first prize at the film festival of the European Foundation for the Environment in Paris.

For *Sexualia* he wrote the spreads Sexuality in Mesopotamian Myth; Inanna and the "Sacred Marriage"; Eroticism in Judaic Scriptures; Old Testament Sins; Sex and Marriage in Judaism; Marriage in Africa; The Sex Life of an African Chief; Initiation Ceremonies; Written on the Skin; Peacock Males; Ways of the Warriors; Earth, Fire, Sex, and Fertility; Symbolic Architecture; Changing Sexual Attitudes in Sub-Saharan Africa; Systems of Dominance; Divine Sexuality; Greek Marriage and the State; Prostitutes, Concubines, and Courtesans; Lesbian Love and Female Autoeroticism; Male Homosexuality; Platonic Love; Hermaphroditus; Roman Marriage; The Vestal Virgins; The Roman Emperors; Love Poetry; Erotic Items and Jewelery; Pre-conquest Peru; Sex and Blood; Modern Latin America and Machismo; Possessive Gods of the Caribbean; The Hidden World of the Amazon; Legend and Ritual in Native North America; The Berdache – Native American Transvestites; Eskimo; The Pacific – Signs of Adulthood; Aboriginal Australia; The Heartland of Genital Piercing.

Ken Watanabe is a free-lance writer-photographer who focuses on recording old and new aspects of Japan.

His contributions for *Sexualia* are Japan – The Cultural Climate; Shunga – The Japanese Art of Love; The Floating World and Pleasure Districts; The Influence of the West; Modern Japan.

Index of Personal Names

Index of Subjects

A

abdomen 34
abortion 52, 221, 280, 381, 409, 410, 467
abortion tools 52
abstinence 373
abuse, sexual 468
Adamites 243
adultery 155, 158, 220, 371, 378
Adventists 375
Agapetae 242
AIDS 44, 186, 411
Albert, Prince 357
Albigensians 250
alchemy 256
alcoholism 300
amazon 191
amniotic sac 48
amor cortois 110
amour passion 318
Ananga Ranga 431
anima 286
animal 231
animus 286
apathy, erotic 289
aphrodisiac 62f., 147, 450, 469
apsaras 423
Arapaho 507
arena games 231f.
art 135, 316, 352, 355
art, erotic 228, 328, 398, 408, 410, 411, 436, 462, 474f.
art, feminist 35
Arunta 516
ascetic 248
asceticism 422
Atharvaveda 414
Atsina 507
Avesta 156
Awyu 24
Ayurvedic medicine 423
Aztecs 496

B

Bacchic cult 214
Bacchic Mysteries 225
Bala 25
Bantu 172
bathing fashion 346
beard 132, 348
beauty 24
beauty aids 361
beauty business 360
beauty spot 361
bed 104, 388
Bemba 167, 170, 182
berdache 508f.
betaera 202
bigamy 199
Billings method 46
Billy Boy 68
birth 50, 132
birth control 221, 369, 467
Blackfoot 506
blastocyst 48
blockage, sexual 286
blondness 350
body 334, 361

body hair 132, 352
body language 60
body modification 24
body shapes 12
body silhouette 344
body-fat level 131
Bollywood 442f.
bordel ambulant 388
brain 14, 133
branding 357
breast enlargement 363
breast licking 56
breast reduction 363
Bride School 523
bride-price 90, 167, 440
bride-service 167
brothel 321, 322f., 456, 457
brother-sister-marriage 117
Buddhism 414f., 421, 446, 454

C

calendar method 46
call girl 302
Candomblé 500f.
cannibalism 69
carnival 272
carvings 436
caste system 440
castrati 338f.
castration 41, 456
Cathars 243, 250
celibacy 244, 369, 374, 414, 423
censorship 330ff., 398, 401, 408
charivari 120
chastity 91, 109, 218, 222, 256, 415, 459
chastity belt 109
chastity commission 371
Cherokee 506
Cheyenne 507, 508
child-marriage 440
Chippendale dancers 395
chlamydia trachomatis 42
chocolate 68
choice of partner 56
Christianity 187, 214, 242ff., 355, 465, 214
Christianizing 407
Christopher Street Day 275
Church 277, 296, 331, 334, 339, 355
Church marriage 409
Church, Catholic 381
Church, English 369
cinema 442
circumcision 40, 173, 187, 451
circumcision, female (clitoridectomy) 41
cleanliness 512
clitoris 34, 60, 285
clothing 26, 135, 340ff., 358
clothing regulations 320
code, sexual 383
codes, Islamic 164
codpiece 343
cohabitation 122
coitus 56, 74
colonialism 490
Communism 409, 451
Communists 466
conception 48

concubine 202, 204
condom 46
Confucianism 452, 464, 466
contemplation 422
contraception 46, 373, 221
contraceptive 46, 147, 467
corona 38
corpus luteum 36
correctness, sexual 382
corset 344
corybantes 224
cosmetics industry 362
Counter Reformation 332
court minstrel 110
court protocol 104
courtesan 202, 204, 302, 478
cowboys 323
Cowper's gland 38
cowrie shell 169
crime 313
criminal 288
Crow Indians 72
cult of Cybele 224
cunnilingus 72, 428
curandero 498
cybersex 386

D

Dahomeans 41
Dahomey 82
dakini 446
Daoism 450, 452, 453f.
Daoists 465
date rape 383
datura 432
Davidians 375
death penalty 18
dependence, sexual 288
depilation 352
depilation, genital 353
Depo-Provera 47
devadisi 425
dharma 426
diaphragm 46
Digambara sect 415
dildo 207
Dionysian cult 214
Dionysian festival 212
divorce 82, 126, 147, 158f., 199, 244, 369, 441, 466
divorce rate 87
divorce therapy 127
Djibouti 40
Dogon 184
domina 292
domination 498
dopamines 68
dowry 90, 166, 169
drawers 344
dreams, wet 30
dress code 342
droit de seigneur 94
drug 212, 215, 300
drug addiction 304
duty, marital 310
Dyak 354
dysmenorrhea 37

Picture Credits

Authors and publisher made intensive efforts to locate all owners of rights to illustrations and text. Any persons who may not have been reached and who assert rights to illustrations or text used in this publicaton are asked to contact the publisher immediately.
(T = top, B = bottom, L = left, C = center, R = right)

2 © Lo Duca, Paris.
4 © The Bridgeman Art Library, London.
5 © ribu Film und Video Vertriebs GmbH, Hamburg.
6T © RMN, Paris (Ph.: R.G. Ojeda). C © Man Ray Trust, Paris / VG Bild-Kunst, Bonn 2000. B © AKG, Berlin.
7T © AKG, Berlin / Werner Forman Archive. C © Scala, Florence. B © Oronoz, Madrid.
8T © Staatliche Kunstsammlungen Dresden, Gemäldegalerie Alter Meister (Ph.: Klut). C © Staatliche Antikensammlung und Glyptothek, Munich. B © Studio X, Limours / Gamma.
9T © Sipa Press, Paris. C © *Dreams of Spring* (German: *Frühlingsträume*, French: *Rêves du Printemps*) – *Erotic Art in China*, The Pepin Press, Amsterdam 1998. B © Vatican Library, Rome.
10 © RMN, Paris (Ph.: R.G. Ojeda).
12 © Devendra Singh / Courtesy of the author and American Psychological Association, Washington, D.C.
13T © Ullstein Bilderdienst, Berlin.
14L © Focus, Hamburg / Science Photo Library, London/ P. M. Motta & S. Makabe. TR/BR © Focus, Hamburg (Phs.: Dr. J.–M. Levaillant, J. Grison / Rapho).
15 © The Ronald Grant Archive, London.
16 © PWE Verlag, Kinoarchiv, Hamburg.
17TL © Hulton Getty Picture Collection, London (Ph.: Wesley). TR © The Ronald Grant Archive, London. B © Sipa Press, Paris (Ph.: Dossier).
18T © Bildarchiv Preussischer Kulturbesitz, Berlin. B © dpa, Frankfurt/M.
19B © Schwules Museum, Berlin.
20L © Könemann Verlagsgesellschaft mbH, Cologne (Ph.: Bernd Obermann). R © AKG, Berlin (Ph.: Erich Lessing).
21B © AKG, Berlin.
22L © Focus, Hamburg / Memory Shop NY. R © Focus, Hamburg / Magnum (Ph.: Philipe Halsmann). Symmetrical lines: Karl Grammer, Ludwig Boltzmann Institut für Stadtethologie, Vienna.
23T © Karl Grammer, Ludwig Boltzmann Institut für Stadtethologie, Vienna. B © 2000 KFS Inc. / Fleischer Studios Inc.
24T © Studio X, Limours/Gamma Liaison (Ph.: Magubane). B © Studio X, Limours/Gamma (Ph.: Frédéric Rauch).
25L © dpa, Frankfurt/M. R © Robert Estall Photo Agency, Sudbury (Ph.: Carol Beckwith/Angela Fisher).
26 © dpa, Frankfurt/M.
27 © AKG, Berlin.
28L © AKG, Berlin / The Marvin and Janet Fishman Collection.
29B © dpa, Frankfurt/M.
30 © The Munch Museum / The Munch Ellingsen Group / VG Bild-Kunst, Bonn 2000 (Ph.: J. Lathion / Nasjonalgalleriet, Oslo).
31T © Musée Provincial Félicien Rops, Namur (Ph.: P. Altman). B from: E. J. Haeberle, *Die Sexualität des Menschen*, De Gruyter, Berlin/New York 1985, p. 177.
32T © Baaske Cartoon, Munich. B © Das Fotoarchiv,

Essen (Ph.: Wolfgang Eichler).
33 © Lucien Clergue, Arles.
34L/R © Markus Voll, Fuerstenfeldbruck.
35T Through the Flower Archives, Belen, NM. © Judy Chicago 1979 (Ph.: Donald Woodman). B from: Lo Duca, *Die Geschichte der Erotik*, Verlag Fourier und Fertig, Wiesbaden 1977, p. 271.
36T © Markus Voll, Fuerstenfeldbruck. B © Kimberly-Clark GmbH, Mühlheim-Kärlich.
37 © The Bridgeman Art Library, London / Whitford Fine Art, London UK.
38 TL/R © Marlen Raabe, Munich. B © Markus Voll, Fuerstenfeldbruck.
39T © 1999 WARA, Centro Camuno die Studi Preistorici, 25044 Capo di Ponte, Italy. B © DAI Athens (Ph.: Pierre Couteau).
40T © Suermondt-Ludwig-Museum, Aachen (Ph.: Anne Gold). BL/C/R © Markus Voll, Fuerstenfeldbruck.
41B © laif, Cologne (Ph.: M. Dorigny/REA).
42T © Manfred Kage, Institut für Wissenschaftliche Fotografie, Weissenstein.
43T © Bildarchiv Preussischer Kulturbesitz, Berlin (Ph.: Jörg P. Anders). B © Manfred Kage, Institut für Wissenschaftliche Fotografie, Weissenstein.
44 © Das Fotoarchiv, Essen (Ph.: Dennis Brack).
45C © Focus, Hamburg / NIBSC / Science Photo Library, London.
46L © Das Fotoarchiv, Essen (Ph.: Dirk Eisermann). R © Deutsches Medizinhistorisches Museum, Ingolstadt.
47C/B © Markus Voll, Fürstenfeldbruck.
48 © Science Photo Library, London (Ph.: Dr. Yorgos Nikas).
49T © Science Photo Library, London (Ph.: Petit Format, Nestle). B © Markus Voll, Fuerstenfeldbruck.
50 © University of Pennsylvania Museum, Philadelphia / neg. # S 8 – 8605.
51L © Austrian State Library, Vienna. R © Markus Voll, Fuerstenfeldbruck.
52T from: Heinrich Zille, *Klassiker der Karikatur*, ed. by Matthias Flügge, Eulenspiegel Verlag, Berlin, p. 17. B © Polizeihistorische Sammlung, Berlin.
53B © Hulton Getty Picture Collection, London.
54 © Man Ray Trust, Paris / VG Bild-Kunst, Bonn 2000.
56/57B © H.B. Wilson-DMK Co. s.r.o., Nuremberg.
57T © H.B. Wilson-DMK Co. s.r.o., Nuremberg.
58 © VG Bild-Kunst, Bonn 2000 (Ph.: Duisburg Agentur).
59T © H.B. Wilson-DMK Co. s.r.o., Nuremberg.
60 © The Bridgeman Art Library, London.
61 © Raymond Boy, Cologne.
62T © Soprintendenza archeologica delle Province di Napoli e Caserta, Naples. B © Wildlife, Hamburg (Ph.: B. Casals).
63T © Museum of Fine Arts, Leipzig (Ph.: MdbK, Gerstenberger). B © Austrian State Library, Vienna.
64 © The Ronald Grant Archive, London.
65 © Focus, Hamburg.
66 © Hulton Getty Picture Collection, London.
67 © Mary Evans Picture Library, London.
68L © PWE Verlag, Kinoarchiv, Hamburg. R © Action Press, Hamburg / Zenpress.
69TL © PWE Verlag, Kinoarchiv, Hamburg. TR © Stockfood, Munich (Photo: Walter Cimbal). B © 1994 Warner Bros / The Ronald Grant Archive, London.
70 © The Bridgeman Art Library, London.

71T © Scala, Florence. B © Institute for Sex Research, Bloomington (Ph.: Dellenback).
72 © Picture Press, Hamburg (Ph.: Wartenberg).
73T © Staatliche Kunsthalle, Karlsruhe. B © H.B. Wilson-DMK Co. s.r.o., Nuremberg.
74T © Descharnes & Descharnes, Paris.
75L © AKG, Berlin. R © BMJ, London (Ph.: Willibrord C.M. Weijmar Schultz).
76 from: M. Hirschfeld and R. Linsert, *Liebesmittel*, Mann Verlag, Berlin 1930, p. after p. 20.
77T © Baaske Cartoon, Munich. B © Studio X, Limours / Gamma (Ph.: Jean-Pierre Amar).
78 © Studio X, Limours / Gamma.
79 © The Bridgeman Art Library, London.
80 © AKG, Berlin.
82 © The National Gallery, London.
83 © Michael Friedel.
84T © Sipa Press, Paris (Ph.: Frilet). B © Das Fotoarchiv, Essen (Ph.: Klaus Reisinger).
85B © Das Fotoarchiv, Essen (Ph.: Henning Christoph).
86T © AKG, Berlin. B © Rijksmuseum, Amsterdam.
87 © The Bridgeman Art Library, London.
88 © Scala, Florence.
89 © Transpacific Marriage Agency, Tokyo and Berkeley/California.
90 © Bildarchiv Preussischer Kulturbesitz, Berlin.
91T © The Bridgeman Art Library, London. B © AKG, Berlin.
92/93 © The National Gallery, London.
94T from: *Bilder-Lexikon Kulturgeschichte*, vol 2., Verlag für Kulturgeschichte, Hamburg 1961, p. after p. 505. B © Historisches Museum, Basel (Ph.: M. Babey).
95 © RMN, Paris (Ph.: Arnaudet).
96 © Artothek, Peissenberg (Ph.: Blauel / Gnamm).
97T © Goethe-Museum, Düsseldorf (Ph.: Walter Klein). B © AKG, Berlin.
98T © The Ronald Grant Archive, London. B © Camera Press, London (Ph.: Cecil Beaton).
99 © Cinetext, Frankfurt/M.
100 © Lauros-Giraudon, Paris.
101 © The Bridgeman Art Library, London / Visual Arts Library, London UK ; Samuel and Mary R. Bancroft Memorial.
102T © Artothek, Peissenberg (Ph.: Peter Willi). B © Germanisches Nationalmuseum, Nuremberg.
103 © No. 217, 581D, Colour Library International / CLI House New Malden, England.
104 © Philippe R. Doumic, Paris.
105T © Musée Christofle, Paris. B © The Board of Trustees of the Victoria & Albert Museum, London.
106 © Kunstsammlung zu Weimar (Ph.: Roland Dreßler, Weimar).
107T © The Bridgeman Art Library, London. B © Artothek, Peissenberg / Christie's Images, London.
108 © Bildarchiv Preussischer Kulturbesitz, Berlin.
109T © Bibliothèque Nationale, Paris. B © Oronoz, Madrid.
110 © Musée des Arts décoratifs, Paris (Ph.: Laurent-Sully Jaulmes).
111 © The Bridgeman Art Library, London.
112T © The Bridgeman Art Library, London. BL © The Bridgeman Art Library, London / Christie's Images, London. BC © The Bridgeman Art Library, London. BR © The Bridgeman Art Library, London / Christie's Images, London.

113T © AKG Berlin. BL © The Bridgeman Art Library, London / The Illustrated London News Picture Library. 114T © Artothek, Peissenberg (Ph.: Bayer & Mitko). B © dpa, Frankfurt/M.
115L © Hessisches Landesmuseum, Darmstadt (Ph.: Sina Althöfer). R © Archiv Claus Hansmann, Munich.
116 © The Art Archive, London.
117T © AKG, Berlin. B © Bayerische Staatsbibliothek, Munich.
118L © Fine Arts Museum of San Francisco, Achenbach Foundation for Graphic Arts, Bruno and Sadie Adriani Collection, 1956. R © dpa, Frankfurt/M.
119 © Werner Neumeister, Munich.
120 © Germanisches Nationalmuseum, Nuremberg.
121L © Gemäldegalerie der Akademie der Bildenden Künste, Vienna (Ph.: Fotostudio Otto). R from: E. J. Haeberle, Die Sexualität des Menschen, De Gruyter, Berlin/New York 1985, p. 193.
122 © Will McBride, Frankfurt/M.
123T © dpa, Frankfurt/M. B © The Ronald Grant Archive, London.
124T © Special Collections, University of Maryland Libraries, College Park, Maryland. B © The Bridgeman Art Library, London.
125T © VG Bild-Kunst, Bonn 2000 (Ph.: Erich Lessing / AKG, Berlin). B © Picture Press, Hamburg / CORBIS / Bettmann.
126 © The Bridgeman Art Library, London.
127B © The Ronald Grant Archive, London.
128 © AKG, Berlin / Werner Forman Archive.
130 © Steve Bloom Images, Kent.
131 © Steve Bloom Images, Kent.
132 © Steve Bloom Images, Kent.
134 © Archiv Claus Hansmann, Munich.
135 © Steve Bloom Images, Kent.
136L © Antropos Institute, Moravské Zemské Muzeum, Brno, Czech Republic. B © LASCAUX II / cliché Semitour Périgord / J. Grelet, Périgueux Cedex.
137 © Archaeological Museum Varna, Bulgaria.
138 © C. M. Dixon, Kingston, Canterbury.
139T © C. M. Dixon, Kingston, Canterbury. B © RMN, Paris (Ph.: Hervé Lewandowski).
140L © Archiv Claus Hansmann, Munich. R © AKG, Berlin (Ph.: Erich Lessing).
141 © Archiv Claus Hansmann, Munich.
142L © Ashmolean Museum, Oxford. R © Lotos Film, Kaufbeuren.
143 © The British Museum, London.
144T © AKG, Berlin. B © Andrea Jemolo, Rome.
145 © AKG, Berlin.
146T © Ancient Art & Architecture Collection, Pinner (Ph.: Mary Jelliffe). B © AKG, Berlin / Werner Forman Archive.
147 © AKG, Berlin / Werner Forman Archive.
148T © Jürgen Liepe, Berlin. B © The Bridgeman Art Library, London
149L © Vatican Museums, Rome. R © Jürgen Liepe, Berlin.
150 © Niedersächsische Staats- und Universitätsbibliothek, Göttingen.
151 © The Art Archive, London.
152 © Bridgeman Art Library, London / Giraudon.
153L © Bridgeman Art Library, London / Giraudon. R © Artothek, Peissenberg.
154T © Joods Historisch Museum, Amsterdam. B © Bridgeman Art Library, London.

155T © Staats- und Universitätsbibliothek Carl von Ossietzky, Hamburg. B © Focus, Hamburg (Ph.: Erich Spiegelhalter).
156 © Reproduced by kind permission of the Chester Beatty Library, Dublin.
157T © RMN, Paris (Ph.: Hervé Lewandowski). B © Courtesy of the Freer Gallery of Art, Smithsonian Institution, Washington D.C.
158L © With kind permission of Edinburgh University Library. R © Henri Stierlin, Geneva.
159 © Courtesy of the Freer Gallery of Art, Smithsonian Institution, Washington D.C.
160 © Artothek, Peissenberg (Ph.: Peter Willi).
161T © Bridgeman Art Library, London / Giraudon. B © Bildarchiv Preussischer Kulturbesitz, Berlin.
162 © Sipa Press, Paris (Ph.: Minamikawa).
163L © The Bridgeman Art Library, London. R © Sipa Press, Paris (Ph.: Minamikawa).
164T © Hulton Getty Picture Library, London. B © Stern, Hamburg (Ph.: Bollinger).
165 © laif, Cologne (Ph.: G. Huber).
166L © Das Fotoarchiv, Essen. B © Robert Estall Photo Library, Sudbury (Ph.: Carol Beckwith, Angela Fisher).
167 © Robert Estall Photo Library, Sudbury (Ph.: Carol Beckwith, Angela Fisher).
168 © Robert Estall Photo Library, Sudbury (Ph.: Angela Fisher, Carol Beckwith).
169T © Robert Estall Photo Library, Sudbury (Ph.: Angela Fisher. C © Robert Estall Photo Library, Sudbury (Ph.: Carol Beckwith/Angela Fisher).
170L © Robert Estall Photo Library, Sudbury (Ph.: Angela Fisher, Carol Beckwith). R © Robert Estall Library, Sudbury (Ph.: Angela Fisher, Carol Beckwith).
171T © Das Fotoarchiv, Essen (Ph.: Henning Christoph). B © Museum Rietberg, Zurich (Ph.: Heini Schneebeli).
172 © Robert Estall Photo Library, Sudbury (Ph.: Angela Fisher, Carol Beckwith).
173 © Robert Estall Photo Library, Sudbury, (Ph.: Carol Beckwith, Angela Fisher).
174L © Robert Estall Photo Library, Sudbury (Ph.: Angela Fisher). R © Africa Museum, Tervuren, Belgium.
175 © Robert Estall Photo Library, Sudbury (Ph.: Carol Beckwith, Angela Fisher).
176 © Robert Estall Photo Library, Sudbury (Ph.: Angela Fisher).
177 L © Robert Estall Photo Library, Sudbury (Ph.: Angela Fisher). R © Robert Estall Photo Library, Sudbury (Ph.: Fabby Nielsen).
178 © Robert Estall Photo Library, Sudbury (Ph.: Carol Beckwith, Angela Fisher).
179T Robert Estall Photo Library, Sudbury (Ph.: Angela Fisher). BL © Bildagentur Schuster, Oberursel (Ph.: Hoffmann-Burchardi). BR © Robert Estall Photo Library, (Ph.: Carol Beckwith, Angela Fisher).
180 © Robert Estall Photo Library, Sudbury (Ph.: Carol Beckwith, Angela Fisher).
181 © Robert Estall Photo Library, Sudbury (Ph.: Carol Beckwith, Angela Fisher).
182T © AKG Berlin / Werner Forman Archive. B © Das Fotoarchiv, Essen.
183T © Museum Rietberg, Zurich (Ph.: Heini Schneebeli). C © Das Fotoarchiv, Essen (Ph.: Henning Christoph).
184 © Robert Estall Photo Library, Sudbury (Ph.: Angela Fisher).

185TL © Das Fotoarchiv, Essen (Ph.: Henning Christoph). TR from: G. Chesi, Die letzten Afrikaner, Perlinger Verlag, Itter 1990, p. 111. BL © Das Fotoarchiv, Essen (Ph.: Henning Christoph). BR © Robert Estall Photo Library, Sudbury (Ph.: Angela Fisher).
186T © Sipa Press, Paris (Ph.: Moctar). C © Hutchison Picture Library, London.
187L/R © Robert Estall Photo Library, Sudbury (Ph.: Fabby Nielsen).
188 © Scala, Florence.
190 © Scala, Florence.
191T © AKG, Berlin. B © DAI, Athens.
192 © Copyright The British Museum, London.
193 © Copyright The British Museum, London.
194 © Scala, Florence.
195 © Oronoz, Madrid.
196 © The National Gallery of Scotland, Edinburg / Duke of Sutherland Collection.
197 © The Bridgeman Art Library, London / State Hermitage Museum, St. Petersburg.
198 © The British Museum, London.
199 © RMN, Paris (Ph.: Hervé Lewandowski).
200T/B © DAI, Athens (Ph.: Jutta Stroszeck).
201 © AKG, Berlin.
202L © The British Museum, London. R © Soprintendenza Archeologica per la Toscana, Florence.
203 © Staatliche Antikensammlung und Glyptothek, Munich.
204 © Bildarchiv Preussischer Kulturbesitz, Berlin (Ph.: Ingrid Geske-Heiden).
205 © Soprintendenza Archeologica delle province di Napoli e Caserta, Naples.
206T © AKG, Berlin (Ph.: Erich Lessing). B © Rheinisches Landesmuseum, Trier (Ph.: H. Thörnig).
207T © Soprintendenza Archeologica delle province di Napoli e Caserta, Naples. B © The British Museum, London.
208 © Bibliothèque Nationale, Paris.
209T © Ashmolean Museum, Oxford. B © C. M. Dixon, Kingston, Canterbury.
210T/B © AKG, Berlin (Ph.: Erich Lessing).
211 © The Bridgeman Art Library, London.
212T © Staatliche Antikensammlungen und Glyptothek, Munich. B © Scala, Florence.
213 © The National Gallery, London.
214 © Scala, Florence.
215 © The Art Archive, London (Ph.: Dagli Orti).
216 © DAI, Rome.
217T © AKG, Berlin (Ph.: Erich Lessing). B © The Bridgeman Art Library, London.
218 © Archivio Fotografico dei Musei Capitolini, Rome.
219 © The Bridgeman Art Library, London.
220T © laif, Cologne (Ph.: Fulvio Zanettini). B © Artothek, Peissenberg (Ph.: Peter Willi).
221 © The Bridgeman Art Library, London.
222T © Bildarchiv Preussischer Kulturbesitz, Berlin. L © Archiv Claus Hansmann, Munich.
223 © AKG, Berlin / Werner Forman Archive.
224T © Soprintendenza Archeologica delle province di Napoli e Caserta / Archeological Museum, Naples. B © C. M. Dixon, Kingston, Canterbury.
225 © Scala, Florence.
226T © The British Museum, London. C © Soprintendenza Archeologica delle province di Napoli e Caserta / Archeological Museum, Naples.

B © Soprintendenza Archeologica delle province di Napoli e Caserta / Archeological Museum, Naples.
227 © Bildarchiv Steffens, Mainz (Ph.: Leonard von Matt).
228L © Soprintendenza Archeologica delle province di Napoli e Caserta / Archeological Museum, Naples. R © AKG, Berlin.
229T © Soprintendenza Archeologica delle province di Napoli e Caserta / Archeological Museum, Naples. B © AKG, Berlin / Werner Forman Archive.
230 © The Bridgeman Art Library, London (Ph.: Ali Meyer).
231 © Soprintendenza Archeologica delle province di Napoli e Caserta / Archeological Museum, Naples.
232T © Archiv Claus Hansmann, Munich. B © C. M. Dixon, Kingston, Canterbury.
233 © Archivio Fotografico dei Musei Capitolini, Rome.
234 © AKG, Berlin.
235T © The Bridgeman Art Library, London. B © Bibliothèque Nationale, Paris.
236 © AKG, Berlin.
237T © Scala, Florence. B © Kunsthistorisches Museum, Vienna.
238T/BL/BR © The British Museum, London.
239L/R © Soprintendenza Archeologica delle province di Napoli e Caserta / Archeological Museum, Naples.
240 © Oronoz, Madrid.
242 © Bildarchiv Foto, Marburg.
243T © Scala, Florence. B © Archiv Claus Hansmann, Munich.
244 © Scala, Florence.
245T © Art Resource N.Y. / The Pierpont Morgan Library B © Bildarchiv Preussischer Kulturbesitz, Berlin.
246 © Universitätsbibliothek Salzburg.
247 © Scala, Florence.
248 © The Bridgeman Art Library, London.
249 © Scala, Florence.
250 © Bodleian Library, Oxford.
251 © Oronoz, Madrid.
252T © Scala, Florence. B © Oronoz, Madrid.
253 © Bildarchiv Preussischer Kulturbesitz, Berlin.
254 © Art Resource, N.Y. / The Pierpont Morgan Library
255 © The British Library London, Roy 2BVII.
256T © Scala, Florence. B © Universiteitsbibliotheek Leiden.
257 © The Bridgeman Art Library, London.
258 © RMN, Paris (Ph.: Gérard Blot).
259 © AKG, Berlin.
260 © The Bridgeman Art Library, London.
261 © AKG, Berlin.
262L © Hulton Getty Picture Library, London. R © Oronoz, Madrid.
263 © Mary Evans Picture Library, London.
264 from: Bilder-Lexikon Kulturgeschichte, vol 2, Verlag für Kulturgeschichte, Hamburg 1961, p. 497.
265L © Artothek, Peissenberg (Ph.: Ursula Edelmann). R © Bildarchiv Claus Hansmann, Munich.
266 © H.B. Wilson-DMK Co. s.r.o., Nuremberg.
267T from : E. Fuchs, Die Weiberherrschaft, supplementary volume, Verlag Albert Langen, Munich 1914, pp. after p. 48. B © Christie's Images, London.
268T © Cinetext, Frankfurt/M. B © AKG, Berlin.
269T © Bibliothèque Nationale, Paris. B © Cinetext Frankfurt/M.
270T © AKG, Berlin (Ph.: Erich Lessing). B © The Bridgeman Art Library, London / The Stapleton Collection.

271T © Hulton Getty Picture Collection, London. B © Mary Evans Picture Library, London.
272 © The Bridgeman Art Library, London.
273L © dpa, Frankfurt/M (Ph.: Olivier C. Houchana). R from: Jean Rodolphe, Mit den fünf Sinnen, Verlag Karl Schustek, Hanau/M 1968, p. 459.
274 © Studio X, Limours (Ph.: Marcello Horn – FDB).
275 © Sipa Press, Paris (Ph.: Viviane Rivière).
276 © Peter Seidel, Frankfurt/M.
278T © Präsens Film, Zurich (Ph.: Deutsches Filmmuseum Frankfurt/M). BL © Hulton Getty Picture Collection, London. BR © dpa, Frankfurt/M.
279 © VG-Bild-Kunst, Bonn 2000 (Ph.: AKG, Berlin).
280T from: Heinrich Zille, Für Alle – Ernstes und Heiteres, Neuer Deutscher Verlag, Berlin 1929.
281 © Oronoz, Madrid.
282 © AKG, Berlin.
283T © AKG, Berlin. B © dpa, Frankfurt/M.
284 © AKG, Berlin.
285 © The Ronald Grant Archive, London.
286 © Hulton Getty Picture Library, London.
287 © AKG, Berlin.
288TL © Ullstein Bilderdienst, Berlin. TR: from: M. Hirschfeld, Geschlechtskunde, vol. 4. Julius Püttmann Verlagsbuchhandlung, Stuttgart 1930, p. 746. B © Hulton Getty Picture Collection, London.
289 © Bavaria Bildagentur, Munich / VCL.
290T from: M. Hirschfeld, Geschlechtskunde, vol. 4. Julius Püttmann Verlagsbuchhandlung, Stuttgart 1930, p. 738. B © The Kinsey Institute for Research in Sex, Gender, and Reproduction, Inc., Bloomington.
291 © Brown & Bigelow, St. Paul, MN.
292L from: Bilder-Lexikon Sexualwissenschaft, vol. 6, Verlag für Kulturforschung, Hamburg 1961, supplement LVI. R from: Paul Frischauer, Die Liebessitten der Völker, vol. 3, Bertelsmann, Gütersloh, p. 249.
293 © Studio X, Limours / Gamma (Ph.: Stéphane).
294 © Staatliche Kunstsammlungen Dresden, Gemäldegalerie Alte Meister (Ph.: Klut).
296 © Staatliche Kunsthalle Karlsruhe.
297T © Scala, Florence. B © The Bridgeman Art Library, London (Ph.: Peter Willi).
298L © Cinetext, Frankfurt/M. R © dpa, Frankfurt/M.
299T © Sipa Press, Paris (Ph.: Yobard). B © Focus, Hamburg (Ph.: Sacha Hartgers).
300 © dpa, Frankfurt/M.
301 © dpa, Frankfurt/M.
302 © Artothek, Peissenberg (Ph.: Joachim Blauel).
303T © Sipa Press, Paris (Ph.: Mooney). B © dpa, Frankfurt/M.
304 © Musée provincial Félicien Rops, Namur (Ph.: Salammbo).
305L © VG Bild-Kunst, Bonn 2000 (Ph.: Galerie der Stadt Stuttgart). R © Musée Royal de Mariemont, Morlanwelz, Belgium.
306 from: M. Hirschfeld, Geschlechtskunde, vol. 4. Julius Püttmann Verlagsbuchhandlung, Stuttgart 1930, p. 801.
307T © Mary Evans Picture Library, London. B © Bildarchiv Preussischer Kulturbesitz, Berlin.
308T © Bildarchiv Preussischer Kulturbesitz, Berlin. B © Bilderberg, Hamburg (Ph.: Hans-Jürgen Burkard).
309 © The Bridgeman Art Library, London.
310 © The Hulton Getty Picture Collection, London.
311 © Das Fotoarchiv, Essen (Ph.: Wolfgang Eichler).
312T © Roswitha Hecke, Hamburg. B © Allen Jones, London.

313T © Das Fotoarchiv, Essen (Ph.: Peter Hollenbach). B © Bodleian Library, Oxford.
314T from: Bilder-Lexikon der Sexualwissenschaft, vol. 5, Verlag für Kulturforschung, Hamburg 1961, p. 25. B from: Bilder-Lexikon Kulturgeschichte, vol. 7, Verlag für Kulturforschung, Hamburg 1961, p. 245.
315T © Cinetext, Frankfurt/M. B © Studio X, Limours / Gamma (Ph.: Gerez-Pueyo).
316 © RMN, Paris (Ph.: Hervé Lewandoski).
317 © Kunsthalle Bremen.
318L © from Opera, ed. by András Batta, Könemann Verlagsgesellschaft mbH, Cologne 1999, p. 453. R © Artothek, Peissenberg.
319 © dpa, Frankfurt/M.
320T © Heinz Finke, Constance. B from: Bilder-Lexikon Kulturgeschichte, vol. 1, Verlag für Kulturforschung, Hamburg 1961, supplement 31a.
321T © AKG, Berlin. B © from: Bilder-Lexikon Kulturgeschichte, vol. 2, Verlag für Kulturforschung, Hamburg 1961, p. 790.
322 © Mary Evans Picture Library, London.
323T/B © New York Public Library.
324T © Scala, Florence. B © Susan Haskins 2000.
325 © Musée des Beaux-Arts, Marseilles (Ph.: Jean Bernard).
326 © Staatliche Antikensammlung und Glyptothek, Munich.
328L © The Bridgeman Art Library, London. R © Artothek, Peissenberg.
329T © Artothek, Preissenberg. B © Charles Gatewood, San Francisco.
330R © Soprintendenza Archeologica delle province di Napoli e Caserta / Archeological Museum, Naples. B © The Uwe Scheid Collection, Überherrn, Germany.
331 © Préfecture de la Police, Paris (Ph.: British Library).
332T © British Library, London. B © Hulton Getty Picture Collection, London.
333L/R © Scala, Florence.
334 © Artothek, Peissenberg (Ph.: Joachim Blauel).
335L © Andrea Jemolo, Rome. R © Giraudon, Paris.
336L © Scala, Florence. R © RMN, Paris (Ph.: R.G.: Ojeda).
337 © The Bridgeman Art Library, London / James Goodman Gallery, NY .
338 © AKG, Berlin.
339L from: Hubert Ortkemper, Engel wider Willen, Henschel Verlag, Berlin 1993, p. 20. R © Cameraphoto, Venice.
340 © Artothek, Peissenberg (Ph.: Hans Hinz).
341T © The Ronald Grant Archive, London. B © Könemann Verlagsgesellschaft mbH, Cologne (Ph.: Rupert Tension).
342T © AKG, Berlin (Ph.: S. Dominigie). B © Bally Schuhmuseum, Schönenwerd, Switzerland.
343T from: Bilder-Lexikon Kulturgeschichte, vol. 1, Verlag für Kulturforschung, Hamburg 1961, p. 200. B © AKG Berlin (Ph.: Erich Lessing).
344T from: M. Platen, Die Neue Heilmethode, Deutsches Verlagshaus, Berlin 1905, p. 195. B © Mary Evans Picture Library, London.
345T © Wolfgang Pulfer, Munich. BL © Hulton Getty Picture Collection, London. BR © Studio X, Limours / Gamma (Ph.: Alexis Duclos).
346TL © Mary Evans Picture Library, London. TR © Mary Evans Picture Library, London. B © Hulton Getty Picture Collection, London.

347TL © The Robert Opie Collection, Gloucester.
TR © dpa, Frankfurt/M. BL © dpa, Frankfurt/M. BC ©
Das Fotoarchiv, Essen (Ph.: Claus Meyer).
348T © RMN, Paris (Ph.: Gérard Blot). B © dpa,
Frankfurt/M.
349 from: Bilder-Lexikon der Sexualwissenschaft, vol.
5, Verlag für Kulturforschung, Hamburg 1961, p. 363.
350 © The Uwe Scheid Collection, Überherrn,
Germany.
351T © AKG, Berlin / S. Domingie. B © VG Bild-Kunst,
Bonn 2000 / © The Munch Museum / The Munch
ELLINGSEN GROUP / Ph.: AKG, Berlin.
352 T © Bildarchiv Preussischer Kulturbesitz, Berlin.
B from : E. Fuchs, Die Weiberherrschaft, supplementary volume, Verlag Albert Langen, Munich 1914, p.
after p. 264.
353T © Picture Press, Hamburg / Camera Press (Ph.:
Henry Aeden). B © Museum of Advertising, Gloucester.
354T © The Ronald Grant Archive, London. BL © dpa,
Frankfurt/M. BC © Cinetext, Frankfurt/M.
355 from: M. Widmann, Anziehungskräfte, Carl
Hanser Verlag, Munich 1986, p. 546.
356T © Sipa Press, Paris (Ph.: Marc Bruwier).
B © Robert Estall Photo Library, Sudbury (Ph.: Fabby
Nielson).
357L © Das Fotoarchiv, Essen (Ph.: Lisa Quinones).
R unknown.
358T © The Hulton Getty Picture Collection, London.
C © Hulton Getty Picture Collection, London. B © Sipa
Press, Paris.
359T © Hulton Getty Picture Collection, London.
BL © dpa, Frankfurt/M. BR © dpa, Frankfurt/M.
360T © Archiv Claus Hansmann, Munich. B © Hulton
Getty Picture Collection, London.
361L © Wella Museum, Darmstadt. R © Roger-Viollet,
Paris.
362B © Sipa Press, Paris (Ph.: Witt).
363 © Dr. Panfilov, Nofretete Privatklinik für
plastische Chirurgie, Bonn.
364 © AKG, Berlin.
365T © drom fragrances international, Paris –
Munich – New York . B © AKG, Berlin.
366 © Studio X, Limours / Gamma.
368/69 © The Bridgeman Art Library, London.
370T © The Bridgeman Art Library, London. B © AKG,
Berlin.
371 © Archiv Claus Hansmann, Munich.
372 © Denver Public Library, Colorado / Western
History Collection (Ph.: J. Byers) neg. # X84.
373 © Hulton Getty Picture Collection, London.
374 © Bildarchiv Preussischer Kulturbesitz, Berlin.
375TL/R from: E. J. Haeberle, Die Sexualität des Menschen, De Gruyter, Berlin/New York 1985, p. 453.
B © Studio X, Limours / Gamma (Ph.: Agostini /
Liaison).
376 © Reproduced by permission of The Kinsey Institute for Research in Sex, Gender and Reprodcution,
Inc., Bloomington, IN (Ph.: Tripp-Dellenback).
377T © Associated Press, New York. B © Picture Press,
Hamburg / Corbis (Ph.: Douglas Kirkland).
378 © Hulton Getty Picture Collection, London.
379T © dpa, Frankfurt/M. B © Cinetext, Frankfurt/M.
380T © Bavaria Bildagentur, Düsseldorf / TCL.
B © AKG, Berlin.
381T © Hulton Getty Picture Collection, London.
B © Picture Press, Hamburg.

382 © dpa, Frankfurt/M.
383T © dpa, Frankfurt/M. B © Bavaria Bildagentur,
Düsseldorf / TCL.
384/385 © Archiv Claus Hansmann, Munich.
386 © Artspace Company K&Y / Mayumi Kubota
Uptight Co., ltd.
387 © Mike Masoni, Munich.
388T © Das Fotoarchiv, Essen (Ph.: Wolfgang Eichler).
B from: Bilder-Lexikon Sexualwissenschaft, vol. 5,
Verlag für Kulturforschung, Hamburg 1961, p. 25
389T © Studio X, Limours / Gamma (Ph: Adolfo).
B © dpa, Frankfurt/M.
390 © Erotisches Museum, Berlin (Ph.: Patrick Piel).
391 © Museum Erotica, Copenhagen.
392L © Sipa Press, Paris (Ph.: Zabci). R © Rapho, Paris
(Ph.: Robert Doisneau).
393 © Actionpress, Hamburg.
394T from: Jean Rodolphe, Mit den fünf Sinnen, Verlag Karl Schustek, Hanau/M 1968, p. 191. B © Hulton
Getty Picture Collection, London.
395 © Studio X, Limours (Ph.: Andrea Blanch).
396 from: Bilder-Lexikon Kulturgeschichte, vol. 8., Verlag für Kulturforschung, Hamburg 1961, p. 825.
397 © Isolde Ohlbaum, Munich.
398 © Sipa Press, Paris.
399 © Hulton Getty Picture Collection, London.
400T © Ronald Grant Archive, London. B © Cinetext,
Frankfurt/M.
401TL © Cinetext, Frankfurt/M. TR © Ronald Grant
Archive, London. B © Cinetext, Frankfurt/M.
402 © Ronald Grant Archive, London.
403T © Cinetext, Frankfurt/M. B © Cinetext,
Frankfurt/M.
404 © Interfoto, Munich.
405T © dpa, Frankfurt/M. B © Penismuseum
Reykjavik, Iceland.
406 © Verlag AURORA, St. Petersburg.
407T from: Frédéric Lacroix, Les Mystères de la Russie,
Pagnerre, Paris 1845, p. 153. B © Sergej Jurewitsch
Skuratow, Wladimir.
408T from: A. Flegon, Eroticism in Russian Art, Flegon
Press, London 1976, p. 41. B from: A. Flegon, Eroticism
in Russian Art, Flegon Press, London 1976, p. 168.
409 © The Nishny Novgorod State Museum of Art,
2000.
410T © VG Bild-Kunst, Bonn 2000 (Ph.: The Bridgeman Art Library, London). B © Sipa Press, Paris (Ph.:
East News).
411 © gay.ru, Moscow.
412 © Sipa Press, Paris.
414 © Angelo Hornak Library, London.
415 © Bilderberg, Hamburg (Ph.: Christophe
Boisvieux).
416 © AKG, Berlin (Ph.: Jean-Louis Nou).
417T © Robert Harding Picture Library, London / JHC
Wilson. B © Dirk R. Frans / Hutchison Picture Library,
London.
418 © The Bridgeman Art Library, London.
419T © Archiv Claus Hansmann, Munich. B © Hutchison Picture Library, London (Ph.: Goycoolea).
420 © Sipa Press, Paris.
421 © Ann & Bury Peerless, Birchington-on-Sea.
422 © Museum Rietberg, Zurich (Ph.: Wettstein & Kauf).
423T © Sipa Press, Paris (Ph.: Dieter Ludwig). B © Foto
Features, Jaipur (Ph.: N.S. Olaniya).
424T © The Bridgeman Art Library, London / Dinodia

Picture Agency, Bombay, India. B © Foto Features,
Jaipur (Ph.: N.S. Olaniya).
425 © Studio X, Limours / Gamma (Ph.: Sarah Caron).
426 © The Bridgeman Art Library, London.
427 © Sipa Press, Paris.
428/429 © Sipa Press, Paris.
430 L © Foto Features, Jaipur (Ph.: J.S. Olaniya).
R © The Bridgeman Art Library, London.
431 © Sipa Press, Paris.
432 © The Bridgeman Art Library, London.
433 © Foto Features, Jaipur (Ph.: Jitendra S. Olaniya).
434 © Images / Charles Walker Collection, London.
435T © Rex Features, London. B © Foto Features, Jaipur
(Ph.: Jitendra S. Olaniya).
436 © The Bridgeman Art Library, London.
437T © Hutchison Picture Library, London (Ph.: Dirk R.
Frans). BL © AKG, Berlin / Werner Forman Archive.
BR © Foto Features, Jaipur (Ph.: N.S. Olaniya).
438 © The Bridgeman Art Library, London.
439 © The Bridgeman Art Library, London.
440 © Xavier Zimbardo, Sarcelles, France.
441 © Sipa Press, Paris (Ph.: Cindy Andrew).
442 L © Hulton Getty Picture Collection, London.
R © Studio X, Limours / Gamma (Ph.: Batholomew /
Liason).
443 © Focus, Hamburg (Ph.: Dayanita Singh /
Network).
444 © Elke Hessel, Düsseldorf.
445 © Elke Hessel, Düsseldorf.
446 © AKG, Berlin / Werner Forman Archive.
447T © The Bridgeman Art Library, London. B © Robert
Harding Picture Library, London (Ph.: Alison Wright).
448 © Dreams of Spring (German: Frühlingsträume,
French: Rêves du Printemps) – Erotic Art in China, The
Pepin Press, Amsterdam 1998.
450 from: L. Carrington Goodrich and Nigel
Cameron, China in Fotografien und Reiseberichten
1860–1912, Könemann Verlagsgesellschaft mbH,
Cologne 1999, p. 60.
451T © Cultural Relics Publishing House (Ph.: from:
Ostasiatische Kunst, vol I, ed. by Gabriele Fahr-Becker,
Könemann Verlagsgesellschaft mbH Cologne 1998,
p. 21.) B © AKG, Berlin / Werner Forman Archive.
452 © The State Hermitage Museum, St. Petersburg,
Russia.
453 © The Art Archive, London (Ph.: Eileen Tweedy).
454 © Palace Museum, Beijing.
455T © The British Museum, London. B © The British
Museum, London.
456 © AKG, Berlin / Werner Forman Archive.
457 © Dreams of Spring (German: Frühlingsträume,
French: Rêves du Printemps) – Erotic Art in China, The
Pepin Press, Amsterdam 1998.
458L © Dreams of Spring (German: Frühlingsträume,
French: Rêves du Printemps) – Erotic Art in China, The
Pepin Press, Amsterdam 1998. R © Staatliche Kunstsammlungen Dresden (Ph.: Herbert Boswank).
459 © Palace Museum, Beijing.
460 © The Art Archive, London.
461 © Dreams of Spring (German: Frühlingsträume,
French: Rêves du Printemps) – Erotic Art in China, The
Pepin Press, Amsterdam 1998.
462 © Dreams of Spring (German: Frühlingsträume,
French: Rêves du Printemps) – Erotic Art in China, The
Pepin Press, Amsterdam 1998.
463T © Stiftung für Kunst und Kultur e.V., Bonn (Ph.:

Norbert Faehling). B © Sabine Hesemann, Egelsbach, Germany.
464 © Collection of the National Palace Museum. Taiwan, Republic of China.
465T © Bildarchiv Preussischer Kulturbesitz, Berlin (Ph.: Knut Petersen). B © *Dreams of Spring* (German: *Frühlingsträume*, French: *Rêves du Printemps*) – *Erotic Art in China*, The Pepin Press, Amsterdam 1998.
466 © Hulton Getty Picture Collection, London.
467 © Richard and Sally Greenhill, London.
468 © dpa, Frankfurt/M.
469T from: *Freies China*, Nov/Dec 1991, p. 31. B © dpa, Frankfurt/M.
470 © The Bridgeman Art Library, London.
471T/C/B © The Bridgeman Art Library, London.
472L Archiv Claus Hansmann, Munich. TR/R from: Friedrich S. Krauss, *Das Geschlechtsleben des japanischen Volkes*, Verlag Karl Schustek, Hanau/M. 1965, pp. 59/64.
473 © Kazumi Saito, Tokyo.
474 © Mita Arts Gallery Ltd., Tokyo.
475T © Mita Arts Gallery Ltd., Tokyo. B © Archiv Claus Hansmann, Munich.
476/477 © Courtesy of Museum of Fine Arts, Boston.
478 © Theaterwissenschaftliche Sammlung Universität zu Köln.
479T © Mita Arts Gallery Ltd., Tokyo. B © Archiv Claus Hansmann, Munich.
480 © Hulton Getty Picture Collection, London.
481T © Axiom, London (Ph.: Paul Quayle). B © Sipa Press, Paris (Ph.: Ozawa).
482/483 © Hulton Getty Picture Collection, London.
483 © The Bridgeman Art Library, London.
484 © Nobuyoshi Araki (Ph.: Axel Schneider / Museum für Moderne Kunst, Frankfurt/M.).
485 © Studio X, Limours / Gamma (Ph.: Hosaka).
486 © Studio X, Limours / Gamma (Ph.: Dieter Blum).
487 © Studio X, Limours / Gamma (Ph.: Dieter Blum).
488 © Vatican Library, Rome.
490 © The Bridgeman Art Library, London.
491 © Artothek, Peissenberg (Ph.: Hans Hinz).
492 © AKG, Berlin / Werner Forman Archive.
493 © Museo Arqueologico Rafael Larco Herrera, Lima.
494T © Museo Arqueologico Rafael Larco Herrera, Lima. B © AKG, Berlin / Werner Forman Archive, London.
495 © New York Public Library / De Bry Collection.
496 © Vatican Library, Rome.
497L © The Bridgeman Art Library, London. R © Trans. No. # 276 Courtesy Department of Library Services, American Museum of Natural History, New York.
498 © dpa, Frankfurt/M.
499 © The Ronald Grant Archive, London.
500 © Archiv Claus Hansmann, Munich.
501 © Picture Press, Hamburg / Sygma.
502 from: Thomas Gregor, Anxious Pleasures: The Sexual Lives of an Amazonian People, The University of Chicago Press, Chicago/London 1985, pp. 87/89/134.
503 © Robert Harding Picture Library, London.
504 © Smithsonian Institution, Washington D.C., National Museum of Natural History neg.# 78-15882.
505 © Stephen Trimble, Salt Lake City, UT.
506 T/B © AKG, Berlin / Werner Forman Archive.
507 © The British Museum, London.
508TL/TR © New York Public Library, De Bry Collection. B © Art Resource, New York.

509 © Courtesy of the Southwest Museum, Los Angeles (Ph.: J.K. Hillers # N.29488).
510T © National Gallery of Canada, Ottawa; purchased 1989. B © National Gallery of Canada, Ottawa; gift of Dorothy M. Stillwell, M. D. 1986.
511 © The National Museum of Denmark, Department of Ethnography (Ph.: Anne Vibke Leth).
512 © AKG, Berlin / Werner Forman Archive.
513L © Malcolm S. Kirk, New York. R © AKG, Berlin / Werner Forman Archive.
514 © The Bridgeman Art Library, London.
515 © Galerie Buchholz, Cologne.
516 © Staatliches Museum für Völkerkunde, Munich.
517 © 1999 WARA, Centro Camuno di Studi Preistorici, 25044 Capo di Ponte, Italy.
518 © Panos Pictures, London.
519 © AKG, Berlin / Werner Forman Archive.
520/521TL/R from: Donald E. Brown, The Penis Inserts of Southeast Asia, University of California, Berkeley 1988, pp. 24, 25, 28.
521B © Robert Harding Picture Library (Ph.: Philip Craven).
522 © Axiom, London (Ph.: Jim Holmes).
523 © Axiom, London (Ph.: John McDermott).
525T © Axiom, London (Ph.: John McDermott). B © Studio X, Limours / Gamma (Ph.: Vogel).
526 from: A. Flegon, *Eroticism in Russian Art*, Flegon Press, London 1976, p. 284.
528L © AKG, Berlin. R © dpa, Frankfurt/M.
529BL © Corbis, London. R © AKG, Berlin.
530 © AKG, Berlin.
531TL © dpa, Frankfurt/M. TR © Hulton Getty Picture Collection, London. BL © dpa, Frankfurt/M. BR © AKG, Berlin.

Maps
13B © Könemann Verlagsgesellschaft mbH, Cologne / Map: Rolli Arts, Essen, after: E. Gregersen, *The World of Human Sexuality*, Irvington Publishers, New York 1994.
19T © Könemann Verlagsgesellschaft mbH, Cologne / Map: Rolli Arts, Essen, after: E. Gregersen, *The World of Human Sexuality*, Irvington Publishers, New York 1994.
21T © Könemann Verlagsgesellschaft mbH, Cologne / Map: Rolli Arts, Essen, after: Joni Seager, *The State of Women in the World Atlas*, Myriad Editions Limited, Brighton 1997.
28/29T © Könemann Verlagsgesellschaft mbH, Cologne / Figure: Rolli Arts, Essen, after: unknown.
41T © Könemann Verlagsgesellschaft mbH, Cologne / Map: Rolli Arts, Essen, after: WHO Publications, Female Genital Mutilation: An Overview, Geneva 1998.
42B © Könemann Verlagsgesellschaft mbH, Cologne / Map: Rolli Arts, Essen, after: WHO Reviews, Global Epidemiology of Sexually Transmitted Diseases, vol. 351, Supplement 3, 20 June 1998.
45T © Könemann Verlagsgesellschaft mbH, Cologne / Map: Rolli Arts, Essen, after: UNAIDS Aids Epidemic Update: December 2000.
47T © Könemann Verlagsgesellschaft mbH, Cologne / Map: Rolli Arts, Essen, after: United Nations World Contraceptive Use 1998 and United Nations World Abortion Policies 1999.
53T © Könemann Verlagsgesellschaft mbH, Cologne / Map: Rolli Arts, Essen, after: United Nations World Abortion Policies 1999.

59B © Könemann Verlagsgesellschaft mbH, Cologne / Chart: Rolli Arts, Essen, after: unknown.
74B from Nevid Rathus and Fichner-Rathus, *Human Sexuality in a World of Diversity*, p. 147. © 2000 Allyn & Bacon. Reprinted/adapted by permission.
85T © Könemann Verlagsgesellschaft mbH, Cologne / Map: Rolli Arts, Essen, after: C. Bishop, *Sex and Spirit*, Duncan Baird Publishers, London 1996, p. 163.
127T/C © Könemann Verlagsgesellschaft mbH, Cologne / Chart: Rolli Arts, Essen, after: Eurostat Bevölkerungsstatistik Daten 1960–1990.
130L © Könemann Verlagsgesellschaft mbH, Cologne / Figure: Rolli Arts, Essen, after: T. Taylor, *Sexualität der Vorzeit*, Pichler Verlag, Vienna 1997.
133 © Könemann Verlagsgesellschaft mbH, Cologne / Map: Rolli Arts, Essen, after: Roger Lewin, *Human Evolution: An illustrated introduction*, Oxford: Blackwell Publishers.
277 © Könemann Verlagsgesellschaft mbH, Cologne / Map: Rolli Arts, Essen, after: Nigel Holmes.
280B © Könemann Verlagsgesellschaft, Cologne / Map: Rolli Arts, Essen, after: Joni Seager, *The State of Women in the World Atlas*, Myriad Editions Ltd, Brighton 1997.
362T © Könemann Verlagsgesellschaft mbH, Cologne / Chart: Rolli Arts, Essen, after: 1998 Top 5 Cosmetic Procedures, American Society of Plastic and Reconstructive Surgeons.
362 BL © Könemann Verlagsgesellschaft mbH, Cologne / Chart: Rolli Arts, Essen, after: 1998 Top 5 Male Cosmetic Surgery Procedures, American Society of Plastic and Reconstructive Surgeons.
362 BR © Könemann Verlagsgesellschaft mbH, Cologne / Chart: Rolli Arts, Essen, after: 1998 Top 5 Female Cosmetic Surgery Procedures, American Society of Plastic and Reconstructive Surgeons.
524 © Könemann Verlagsgesellschaft mbH, Cologne / Map: Rolli Arts, Essen, after: Judith Mackay, *The Penguin Atlas of Human Sexual Behavior*, Myriad Editions Ltd, Brighton 2000.
538/539 © Könemann Verlagsgesellschaft, Cologne / Map: Rolli Arts, Essen, after: The Face Magazine, April 1996, Wagadon Ltd.

Acknowledgments

The editors wish to thank Alexander Osthelder for the spread on castrati and Gudrun Kloes for her help with the Iceland text.
Xenia Osthelder would like to thank especially Rita Hortmann for all her help.
Clifford Bishop would like to thank Claire Galliphant and Peter Mansell.

The publishers wish to thank all those who have contributed to the realization of the present volume.
For the contribution of pictures we thank Mita Arts Gallery Ltd., Tokyo, the Archaeological Museum Varna, Antropos Institue Moravské Zemské Muzeum, Brno, Pepin Press, Amsterdam, the Transpacific Marriage Agency, Semitour Périgord, Timothy Taylor, and Astrid Juette as well as Silke Schoppe and Uschi Baetz for picture editing.
We also thank Uwe Doeringer for research and writing the short biographies in the appendix, Tony McManus for contributing to the textbox on sexshops, Rob Taylor for proof corrections, Kirsten Skacel for her work on the extensive index, Thomas Colby for his assistance with translations, Jason Kassab-Bachi and Sally McVay for their limitless support with layout, typography, and corrections, Tamara Girke, Zeineb Kadi, Sylvia Mayer, and Fenja Wittneven for support in picture research and acquisition.

© 2001 Könemann Verlagsgesellschaft mbH, Bonner Str. 126, 50968 Cologne, Germany

Publishing and art direction: Peter Feierabend

Project management: Kirsten E. Lehmann (resp.), Claudia Hammer, Tanja Krombach
Assistance: Astrid Barth, Annette Ocker, Stefanie Rödiger
Layout and typography: Bauer + Möhring Grafikdesign, Berlin, Meike Lorenz

Picture research: Monika Bergmann, Stephanie Rebel, Markus Weh
Translation into English: Maia Costa (When Desire Turns to Sin), Dr. Bernd Rullkötter (Prostitution in the Western World, A Culture Steeped in Sex, China and Japan), Gabriele Westphal (The Erotic Muse – Art and Artifice)
Copy editing: Lilian G. Bernhardt, Michael Scuffil
Cartography: Rolli Arts, Essen

Production: Stefan Bramsiepe
Reproductions: Typografik, Cologne
Printing and binding: MOHN Media - Mohndruck GmbH, Gütersloh

Printed in Germany

ISBN 3-8290-2729-X

10 9 8 7 6 5 4 3 2 1